PERSONALITY DEVELOPMENT AND PSYCHOTHERAPY IN OUR DIVERSE SOCIETY

PERSONALITY DEVELOPMENT AND PSYCHOTHERAPY IN OUR DIVERSE SOCIETY

A SOURCE BOOK

Edited by
Rafael Art. Javier, Ph.D.
and
William G. Herron, Ph.D.

JASON ARONSON INC.
Northvale, New Jersey
London

This book was set in 11 pt. Adobe Caslon by CompuDesign of Rego Park, New York and printed and bound by Book-mart Press, Inc. of North Bergen, NJ.

Library of Congress Cataloging-in-Publication Data

Personality development and psychotherapy in our diverse society :
    a sourcebook / edited by Rafael Art. Javier and William G. Herron.
        p.   cm.
    Includes bibliographical references and index.
    ISBN 0-7657-0167-7 (hardcover : alk. paper)
        1. Mental health—Social aspects. 2. Mental illness—Social aspects.
    3. Personality development—Social aspects. 4. Multiculturalism.
    I. Javier, Rafael Art. II. Herron, William G.
    RA790.5.M44   1998
    616.89—DC21   98-5659

Printed in the United States of America on acid-free paper. Jason Aronson offers books and cassettes. For information and catalog write to Jason Aronson Inc., 230 Livingston Street, Northvale, NJ 07647-1726. Or visit our website: http://www.aronson.com

To my mother
for helping me appreciate the power of the cultural and ethnic values
which define who I am today.
"Gracias, Mama por su apoyo!"

R.A.J.

To my children
who are so much a part of the diverse society.

W.G.H.

Contents

PART II: SPECIFIC SYMPTOMATOLOGIES

PART IV: EVALUATION, TREATMENT, AND SUPERVISORY ISSUES

PART V: CONCLUSION

Acknowledgments

It is impossible to enter into the kind of journey required to prepare a book of this magnitude without the intellectual collaboration and support of a number of important individuals. My co-author, Dr. William Herron, has been such a person, a tremendous influence in my life over the years. I am fortunate indeed to have him as a friend and colleague. I am also very appreciative of the invaluable assistance provided by Phil Yanos, who was instrumental in organizing and editing many of the chapters. The assistance of Angela Martinez, Rachel Winer, Mayling Gutierrez, Fatimah El-Jamil, and Alicia Benedetto facilitated the completion of this volume. Edwidge Ulysse and Veronica Negron were wonderful, pitching in at the final stage of preparation. Margaret Cashin and Florence Sisenwein's assistance cannot be emphasized enough, as well as the support provided by Dr. Willard Gingerich, Dr. Louis Primavera, and Father David O'Connell who were there for me as my friends when the work was most difficult. I also extend heartfelt thanks to Johanna Lynch, whose organizational skills and meticulous attention to detail expedited the completion of this project. She took on the arduous task of ensuring that everything was in place and provided invaluable editorial assistance. The support of Carolyn DeCesare, Clare Douglas, Lorraine Baisley, and Alejandro

(Alex) Alvarez was also of great value. My students at St. John's have my deep appreciation for being a source of so much inspiration.

Finally, thanks to two important people in my life: my son Joshua for his understanding and for giving me the room to complete this work, and my mother to whom this book is dedicated. She should be celebrated because it was she who instilled in me the importance of education and academic pursuit.

R.A.J.

This is the second book that Rafael and I have edited, and it represents a significant part of the results of our collaboration over the past ten years. It has been a mutual learning experience that continues to grow, and I am very appreciative of his ongoing presence. Many of my students have been of assistance, and I give special thanks for their input to Lydia Warner, Sonja Ramirez, and Paul Bulman. The same has been true for my colleagues, and I am grateful to Lou Primavera for being there at crucial times and to my wife, Mary Jane, for always being there. This book is dedicated to all my children who in their various developmental stages are so much a part of the diverse society.

W.G.H.

Contributors

Miriam Azaunce, Ed.D., is senior psychologist, department of psychiatry, at Kings County Hospital Center, Brooklyn, NY and clinical instructor at SUNY/HSCAB department of psychiatry/College of Medicine, Brooklyn. She has held teaching appointments at Teachers College, Columbia University, and New York University. Her research interests are in the areas of psychological assessment and treatment of individuals from culturally diverse backgrounds. She is in private practice.

Frank Biafora, Ph.D., is an assistant professor of sociology in the department of sociology/anthropology at St. John's University, Jamaica, NY. Since receiving his doctoral degree in medical sociology in 1991, Dr. Biafora has researched and published widely in the areas of mental health and substance use. His most recent research explores the impact of culture on patterns of substance use experimentation and delinquency among young adolescents.

Maria Biafora, M.A., M.L.S., received a double masters in political science and library and information sciences at St. John's University in 1995. She is currently a doctoral candidate in the higher education program at New York University School of Education.

William Bracero, Ph.D., is currently senior psychologist, instructor and supervisor in the multicultural psychology internship program at Sunset Park Mental Health Center of the Lutheran Medical Center, Brooklyn, NY, and faculty at Ferkauf Graduate School of Psychology of Yeshiva University, School Psychology Program, NY. Research and publication interests include narrative metaphors in the treatment of culturally diverse peoples, intersubjectivity and modifications of psychoanalytic control mastery theory with Asian clients, and spirituality and indigenous healing systems with Latino client populations.

Lisa Bowleg, Ph.D., is a social psychologist and adjunct assistant professor of women's studies at Georgetown University.

Lydia P. Buki, Ph.D., received her doctorate in counseling psychology at Arizona State University. She has worked extensively with Latino populations in research in clinical settings. Dr. Buki has coauthored "Intergenerational Perspectives of English and Spanish Speaking Mexican American Grandparents," an article published in *International Journal of Aging and Human Development*. A major area of interest is in the cross-cultural equivalence of family assessment measures. She has a private practice in Washington, DC.

Giuseppe Costantino, Ph.D., is the clinical director of the Sunset Park Mental Health Center of the Lutheran Medical Center, adjunct professor of Psychology at St. John's University, and senior research associate with the Hispanic Research Center, Fordham University, Bronx, NY. Dr. Costantino is the author and developer of TEMAS, a multicultural thematic apperception test, and of the Cuento and Hero/Heroine Modeling Therapies for Hispanic children and adolescents. He has published more than fifty articles and several book chapters on culturally sensitive treatment and assessment of minority individuals. He is consulting editor of *Journal of Personality Assessment, Hispanic Journal of Behavioral Science,* and *Revista Iberoamericana de Psicologia.*

Cora L. Díaz de Chumaceiro, Ph.D., is a clinical psychologist in Caracas, Venezuela, an international affiliate and member of Division 39 of the American Psychological Association, and an editorial board member of *The Arts in Psychotherapy* and *Journal of Poetry Therapy.*

Juris G. Draguns, Ph.D., completed his primary schooling in Latvia and Germany and obtained his university degrees in the United States. Dr.

Draguns is professor emeritus of psychology at Pennsylvania State University. He has published widely in psychological, psychiatric, and interdisciplinary journals on the relationship of abnormal behavior and culture. He has co-edited *Counseling Across Cultures,* now in its fourth edition. He is past editor of the *Journal of Cross-Cultural Psychology,* and is currently involved in editing several books on such topics as personality in culture, cultural aspects of psychotherapy, and defense mechanisms in laboratory settings and in the social world.

Fatimah El-Jamil is a doctoral fellow in the clinical psychology program at St. John's University. Her research interests lie in the area of expression and treatment of anger across cultures. She is focusing on the shame response as a precursor to anger and aggression.

Rachel Goodman, M.A., doctoral student in the clinical psychology program at St. John's University, is studying the effects of psychoeducational support groups on caregiver stress in caregivers of Alzheimer's disease and related disorders patients.

Sharon-ann Gopaul-McNicol, Ph.D., is an associate professor of psychology at Howard University and a licensed clinical and school psychologist in Washington DC and New York. She is also the executive director of multicultural educational and psychological services, a mental health practice devoted exclusively to culturally sensitive assessment and treatment. Dr. Gopaul-McNicol is the author of *A Multi-CMS Approach to the Treatment of Immigrant Families.* She has also co-authored *Cross-Cultural Practice: Assessment, Treatment, and Training, A Bio-cultural Approach to Intellectual Assessment,* and *Working with Linguistically and Culturally Different Children: Innovative Clinical and Educational Approaches.*

William G. Herron, Ph.D., is a professor in the department of psychology, St. John's University, and in private practice in New Jersey. He is a faculty member, senior supervisor, and training analyst at the Contemporary Center for Advanced Psychoanalytic Studies, Livingston NJ, a fellow of the American Psychological Association, and a diplomate of the American Board of Professional Psychology. Dr. Herron is the co-author of *Narcissism and the Psychotherapist* and *Money Matters: The Fee in Psychotherapy and Psychoanalysis,* and coeditor of *Domestic Violence: Assessment and Treatment.*

Rafael Art. Javier, Ph.D., is a clinical professor of psychology in the St. John's University doctoral program and director of the Center for Psychological

Services and Clinical Studies at St. John's. He is also on the faculty of the Object Relations Institute in New York City and is a diplomate of the American Board of Professional Psychology. Dr. Javier conducts research in the areas of language, memory, and bilingualism, and is currently writing a book on thinking, feeling, and speaking in two languages. He is coeditor of *Reaching Across Boundaries of Culture and Class* and *Domestic Violence: Assessment and Treatment*.

Larry G. Knauss, M.A., is a doctoral student in the clinical psychology program at St. John's University. He is working with Dr. Louis Primavera on the development of a social distance scale to measure people's willingness to discriminate against those who are diagnosed as mentally ill.

Jeffrey I. Lewis, Ph.D., has a full-time practice of clinical psychology in New York City. He was formerly the director of psychology at South Beach Psychiatric Center. He is also an adjunct associate clinical professor in the doctoral program at St. John's University and has been invited as an instructor at the Eötvos Lorand University in Budapest, Hungary. Areas of writing interest include countertransference analysis, evolutionary psychology, and the work of Sandor Ferenczi.

Robert G. Malgady, Ph.D., is professor of quantitative studies at New York University and senior research associate at the Hispanic Research Center, Fordham University. He is the author of four books on Hispanic mental health research and more than sixty book chapters and journal articles on minority mental health, statistical and measurement techniques, and human cognition. He was a collaborator in the development of TEMAS, a culturally sensitive test. He is a fellow of the American Psychological Association and serves as a reviewer of research grants for the National Institute of Mental Health. Professor Malgady currently serves on the editorial board of *Psychological Assessment*.

Luis R. Marcos, M.D., is president of the New York City Health and Hospitals Corporation and professor of psychiatry at New York University School of Medicine. Former commissioner of mental health services of New York City, Dr. Marcos has contributed extensively to the study of the effects of language and culture barriers in the psychiatric evaluation and treatment of immigrant patients.

Angela M. Martinez is a doctoral fellow in the clinical psychology program at St. John's University. Her current research focuses on the effect of ethnic matching and its relation to therapy outcome.

Sonia Pardoe Matthews, M.A., is currently studying for her Ph.D. in multi-lingual multicultural studies at New York University, where she works as a teaching fellow. She has traveled to more than fifty countries and has worked as a language teacher in Canada, Japan, Singapore, and New York at the United Nations International School. Her interests include cross-cultural communication, sociolinguistics, and second language acquisition.

Arthur G. Mones, Ph.D., is a diplomate in clinical psychology, A.B.P.P., and approved supervisor of the American Association for Marital and Family Therapy. He is coordinator of the specialization in family and marital psychology within the doctoral program in Clinical Psychology at St. John's University. He has published several articles and has lectured extensively on child-focused family therapy, a systems approach to oppositional children, and an integrative model of couples therapy. Dr. Mones is in private clinical practice in Hewlett, NY.

Dolores O. Morris, Ph.D., A.B.P.P., is a supervisor at the New York University postdoctoral program in psychotherapy and psychoanalysis, the clinical psychology program of the City University of New York and the New Hope Guild for Emotionally Disturbed Children, East New York. She is a member of the New York State Board for Psychology. Her special interest and publications are in the area of cultural-ethnic differences as they impact on training, supervision, and the analytic process. She has a private practice in New York City.

Michael Moskowitz, Ph.D., is in private practice in New York City, and is publisher at The Other Press. He is also an adjunct associate professor in the City University of New York doctoral program in clinical psychology and a member of the Institute for Psychoanalytic Training and Research.

B. Runi Mukherji, Ph.D., is currently associate professor of psychology at SUNY, Old Westbury, NY. Her research interests are in the area of cognitive and cross-cultural factors in learning and memory, and psychopathology. She has authored numerous articles in this field and is co-editor of a book which examines healing practices across cultures, *Spirit versus Scalpel: Traditional Healing and Modern Psychotherapy*, which also includes her chapter on healing practices in India.

Kendra L. Mulvey, M.A., is a graduate of the general/experimental masters program at St. John's University. She is currently a psychotherapist at Mountain

Crest Hospital at Fort Collins, Colorado, where she also teaches psychoeducation classes to the community.

Jeffrey S. Nevid, Ph.D., is professor of psychology at St. John's University where he also directs the doctoral program in clinical psychology. He holds a diplomate in clinical psychology (A.B.P.P.) and has been active in research in such areas as health psychology, behavior therapy, and smoking cessation. He has authored and coauthored several books including the text, *Abnormal Psychology in a Changing World*.

Louis H. Primavera, Ph.D., is associate dean of the Graduate School of Arts and Sciences and professor of psychology at St. John's University. He teaches courses in advanced statistics, multivariate statistics, and psychometric theory. He has published extensively and has practiced as a clinical psychologist for more than twenty-four years with a specialty in rational emotive behavior therapy. Dr. Primavera has developed an extensive research program in stigma and discrimination against those who are diagnosed as mentally ill.

Sonja M. Ramirez, M.A., is a doctoral candidate in clinical psychology at St. John's University. She is an adjunct professor at the College of New Rochelle, NY, and is currently conducting research on the quality and specificity of forensic reports. She has most recently co-authored an article entitled "Cultural Attunement and Personality Assessment" in the *Journal of Social Distress and the Homeless*.

Mario Rendon, M.D., is director of the department of psychiatry at Lincoln Medical and Mental Health Center and professor of clinical psychiatry at New York Medical College. He is also a training and supervising analyst with the American Institute of Psychoanalysis and in private practice. He is currently investigating the relationship between depression and culture.

Susan (Shanee) Stepakoff, M.A., is a doctoral candidate in clinical psychology at St. John's University. Her current research focuses on the role of infant gender in mother–infant nonverbal communication. She received the 1997 Student Research Award from the American Psychological Association's clinical psychology division for an empirical study of the relationship between sexual victimization and suicidal behavior.

Edward C. Stewart, Ph.D., has taught in several universities throughout the United States and in Japan and Europe. Now retired, he devotes his time to research and writing in his specialty of the biological roots of organized violence and cultural memories of war.

Tania N. Thomas-Presswood, Ph.D., is a certified school psychologist in Texas and New York and a licensed clinical psychologist in New York. She has worked for ten years with culturally and linguistically diverse children and families through direct services in New York public schools. Dr. Thomas-Presswood has published articles and books in the areas of acculturation, assessment, cultural differences, and second language acquisition. In her most recent publication, she is the co-author of *Working with Linguistically and Culturally Different Children: Innovative Clinical and Educational Approaches.*

Ellen C. Tsui, Ph.D., is a staff psychologist at the Sunset Terrace Family Health Center of the Lutheran Medical Center in Brooklyn, NY. She also has a private practice in New York City. She works with Asian patients of all ages and socioeconomic backgrounds, from new immigrants to American-born Chinese, with a culturally sensitive focus on the acculturation process.

Carmen I. Vazquez, Ph.D., is clinical associate professor at New York University School of Medicine and director of NYU-Bellevue clinical internship. Her publication interests center on cross-cultural and training issues. Dr. Vazquez has a private practice in New York City.

Lydia K. Warner, Ph.D., received her doctorate at St. John's University. The topic of her dissertation was: "A Comparison of Dose Response Curves in Psychodynamic and Cognitive/Behavioral Psychotherapies." She is currently working as a psychologist for the New York City Police Department.

Wayne J. Warren, Ph.D., received his doctorate from Hofstra University, Hempstead, NY. He is a graduate of the post-doctoral program in psychoanalysis and psychotherapy at the Derner Institute at Adelphi University, Garden City, NY. He is also president of Psychologic Management Consulting, P. C. Dr. Warren is in private practice in New York City and Long Island, NY, specializing in executive development, workplace concerns, and workplace violence.

Philip T. Yanos, M.A., is a doctoral candidate at St. John's University. He is presently conducting research on the process of recovery from serious mental illness. Mr. Yanos has co-authored an article in the *Bulletin of the Menninger*

Clinic entitled "Methodological Problems Encountered in Research with Psychiatric Inpatients: A Case Example."

Marcela B. Yussef is a doctoral candidate in clinical psychology at St. John's University. The topic of her dissertation is psychological culture, anger scripts, experience, and expression among a group of Colombian immigrants, non-immigrant Colombians, and Americans. Other areas of interest are the psychological impact of immigration and psychotherapeutic integration.

Personality Development and Psychotherapy in Our Diverse Society : An Introduction

RAFAEL ART. JAVIER AND WILLIAM G. HERRON

There has been a great deal of controversy among behavioral scientists and mental health providers with regard to the best way to assess mental illness and personality structure (Culbertson 1997, McCrae and Costa 1997). Part of the reason for this controversy has to do with the problem of defining mental illness and normal development in a society whose population has become more and more diverse (Javier and Herron 1992, U.S. Census 1990). Although attempts have been made to identify the universal elements of personality and human functioning (McCrae and Costa 1997), the fact is that the perception of abnormality of a specific behavior is a function of factors not always within the participants' conscious repertoire. All that is immediately known is that the assessor finds the specific behavior difficult to incorporate within the parameters of his/her repertoire of normality (Dana 1993).

We are reminded of the case of an African-American adolescent with a stocking on his head coming to a mental health center to see a foreign psychiatrist in a predominantly African-American community. He had been brought in by his parents for consultation because of his poor conduct at school and at home. He was described as belligerent and verbally abusive. His generally defiant demeanor during his visit indicated he was coming to the consultation against his will. The diagnosis emphasized a psychopathic tendency. When the psychiatrist was describing his mental status, the stocking was used as an example of "bizarre" behavior. Although many aspects of this case are worthy of discussion, we will focus our attention only on the question of perception or predetermined assumption about this patient's assumed level of pathology. African-American and other minority groups are more likely to be diagnosed as sicker in comparison to the white population and they have been found to be overrepresented in mental health institutions (Louden 1995, Marcos et al.1973, Neighbors et al. 1989). Was this professional's mind influenced by a true manifestation of psychopathology or by a set of behaviors that could not easily be subsumed as typical adolescent behavior in this professional's personal cultural experience? If the latter was more prominent in his/her decision making, then it is likely that this professional would have difficulty recognizing that the stocking on the head could be part of an adolescent fad to keep the braided hair in place. Similarly, it is also likely that he/she will be more inclined to pathologize some of the adolescent's behavior, although some of these behaviors may be considered normal defiance in adolescence. But to the extent to which they cannot be explained from his/her point of cultural reference, they are likely to be considered abnormal.

A similar level of misunderstanding was described by Ghali (1982) with regard to a condition called *ataque*, or the Puerto Rican syndrome. It refers to a culturally expected reaction that can best be described as hyperkinetic seizure or epileptic-like attack at a time of acute tension and anxiety. This type of reaction, observed in many recent Puerto Rican immigrants and other Latino immigrants in response to the tremendous stress associated with immigration (Godoy 1995), frequently resulted in hospitalization with a diagnosis of schizophrenia. When the same behavior is exhibited in a culturally syntonic setting, members of the cultural group are more likely to intervene by holding the individual down to ensure that he/she does not get injured and to offer some comfort. At the height of *ataque* the individual acquires a supernatural strength, wails, and tends to lose consciousness. After awhile, it is not unusual for the individual to gain composure and resume whatever interaction was taking place prior to the *ataque*. These symptoms are more likely to be exhibited by females, especially at the time of death of a close family member.

What we are suggesting is that the personal perceptions (projections) of the clinician and researcher will determine the extent to which a specific behavior is considered pathological. Since personal perceptions are developed in the context of the individual's relationship with important others and his/her sociopolitical, socioeconomic, ecological, and historical reality, it is not surprising that one's perception can be so powerfully influenced by these forces. The conception of self and others, good or bad, health and illness, normal and abnormal is established in this manner (Javier and Rendon 1995), and once established, these perceptions are used as reference points to understand the reality around us. To the extent to which others' reality and personal experiences are different from our own, the likelihood for misunderstanding increases. A problem develops when psychopathological connotation is applied to these differences. As Moskowitz amply develops in Chapter 17, "Ethnicity and race are fantasies that we use to deny our badness and displace it onto others."

This is the main theme of Dana's excellent contribution (1993). It is further expanded in Chapters 5,15,18, 30, and other contributions included in this book. It leaves us with the poignant question of how to define and assess mental health and illness and how to design appropriate treatment interventions in a multicultural society where the possibility for distortion is so great. There are serious research, educational, legal, and moral consequences when the scientific community and mental health professionals are unable to meet the challenges associated with these demands. Aware of the urgent nature of these challenges as well as the complexity associated with the issue, we have gathered a number of distinguished experts in the field to assist us in getting some answers to our questions, or at least to guide our thinking. We wanted to provide readers with a variety of analyses about the role of culture and ethnicity, with regard not only to mental illness, but to the variety of forces impacting on personality development and the human condition in general. These contributions advance the idea that different cultural norms result in very different perceptions about the nature of human reality and condition, the view of health and personality development, and pathology and treatment. They become influential elements in the development of what is described in this book as "ethnic unconscious" by Herron, Herron and associates, Javier and Rendon, Moskowitz, Javier and Yussef, and Chumaceiro in Chapters 14–20. These elements dictate the code of conduct that influences the individual's response to events in his/her life and the quality of the individual's personality and ethnic identity.

We have included contributions that are rather critical of a cultural perspective (Lewis in Chapter 7), that are inclined to endorse a more universal approach to human condition (Appiah 1997), in order to offer a balanced view of the issue. Such a view found support in a recent study by McCrae and Costa (1997) that found the structure of individual differences in personality to be uniform across several cultures and perhaps universal. Their study investigating the relevance of the five-factor model of personality traits (neuroticism, extroversion, openness, agreeableness, and conscientiousness) found the traits to be present in five different linguistic and ethnic groups in some way. But the authors agreed that there are culturally unique factors of personality not included in this model and hence put into question the cultural generalizability of these findings.

This is a comprehensive book specifically organized to address a number of essential questions that individuals interested in exploring the issue of culture, ethnicity, and language have raised over the years. It includes not only theoretical formulations (six chapters), but also a discussion of specific symptomatologies (six chapters) and treatment implications (eleven chapters). In addition, there is a section dealing specifically with the role of ethnicity and culture on the nature of the unconscious and personality development (seven chapters). Mental health policy recommendations are included as well.

VIEWS OF MENTAL HEALTH AND ILLNESS

The view of mental illness with regard to its cause and course is cast in these analyses as a function of multiple factors and social forces that are culture-specific and that color the nature of the individual's identity and view of the world. This point is made repeatedly from different vantage points and theoretical formulations by the various contributors. It is also one of the main points made in the rich and provocative chapters by Draguns and Stewart. These examples of the kinds of analyses readers will find throughout the book are important and comprehensive contributions. They require careful reading in order to capture the multiple layers of analyses advanced by the authors. Their analyses are psychological, sociological, anthropological, and philosophical in nature; the implication for mental health is also clear throughout.

For instance, Draguns in Chapter 2 discusses the two basic contrasting orientations in organizing cultural data gathering and conceptualization (i.e., emic and etic), while rejecting both the universalist and the relativist positions in the extreme forms due to little empirical support. The emic view refers to the primacy of cultural uniqueness and encourages factual and sensitive description of a phenomenon within its cultural context. The etic view, on the other hand, proceeds from the premise of worldwide reality of a phenomenon or category of abnormal experience. To the extent to which the etic view is perverted, stereotyping and misconception are possible. In terms of clinical implications, the concept of self is discussed as the key element in explaining both the constancy and the variation of experience across cultures. A strategy for understanding the relationships between culture and psychotherapy is proposed based upon Holstede's four dimensions of individualism-collectivism, power-distance, uncertainty-reduction, and masculinity-femininity. It is his view that of these four dimensions, individualism-collectivism has apparently proven to be the most heuristically useful and has the potential to serve as a unifying principle of cross-cultural research and conceptualization. According to Draguns, our greatest challenge is for us to be able to combine clinical sensitivity with cultural sophistication while avoiding stereotyping. This can occur only if we can look at a culture and cultural factors in terms of their multiple layers of meanings and influences while allowing universal factors that explain the human condition to be an essential part of the explanatory paradigm.

This point is emphasized again in Chapter 4 by Stewart who attempts to delineate factors that contribute to the development of individual identity, the cultural configuration bearing upon that, and a description of what he calls the *cultural trilogy*, which is basically a description of a paradigm to explain cultural differences. This trilogy includes analysis from a psychological perspective, through which an individual's analysis of behavior is presented; a sociological perspective, through which the influences on an individual's cultural identity of "time-factored activities" in social environments are discussed; and an anthropological perspective, through which an analysis of the primordial sentiments in the social organization of a culture is made. In the context of the psychological analysis, issues such as surface culture (whose content is observable behavior), deep culture (whose content is cognition, values, systems of knowledge, emotions, etc.), and procedural culture (whose content is performance and communication) are included. The individual's psychology derived from a surface culture is one based upon external perception, contextualized in time, place, and conditions of experience. The individual's psychology derived from a deep culture is one characterized by internal perception in the absolute and universal time and space of the body, while procedural cultural analysis provides a synthesis of surface and deep culture contents.

In the context of the sociological analysis, influences deriving from factors such as interpersonal culture, economic-technical culture, and political-social culture are included in the discussion. But the anthropological analysis is what ultimately brings the point home most clearly to the reader. In this context the analysis of the powerful influences of language, tradition and customs, ethnicity, region, religion, and race are amply discussed.

We can now appreciate the tremendous impact of these factors on an individual's cultural identity and the complexity of the multiple factors bearing on his/her actions and view of the self. The development of the ethnic unconscious is also influenced by these qualities, as described in Chapters 14–20 in Part III. To emphasize his points further, Stewart presents a fascinating analysis of a research finding on the view of pain and anger cross-culturally, with emphasis on the Old American, Italian, Jewish, and Irish styles of dealing with these emotions. The subjects were all male. For the Old Americans and the Jews, pain was viewed as a signal that triggers purposeful, rational behavior directed toward the rational management of pain. The Italians, on the other hand, became preoccupied with the immediate pain experience. The Irish have a "resigned and defeated attitude" about pain experience and were the most depressed of the group, expressing worry and pessimism about the effect of their illness upon their body and masculinity. According to this author, these findings provide a striking demonstration of the power of procedural culture to encode human experience into a culture-specific mode. The view of mental health and the reaction to mental illness are subject to the same impact, triggered by procedural culture.

With regard to the American culture specifically, the view of the human condition and of mental illness is influenced by the American "cultural" identity that, Stewart believes, has gone through a transformation in thought and emotion from an emphasis on "practical, problem-solving style of decision making to a mode of thought based on the cognitive structure of anger." According to him, this emotion is one of the driving motivational forces in social and interpersonal activities that is responsible for the increase in violence, anger, and distrust and the deepening of social divisions.

In Chapter 5, Javier and associates focus on a slightly different analysis than the one offered by Draguns and Stewart, although the implications are the same. That is, multiple factors enter into the development of an individual identity. As it was for Stewart, Javier and associates strongly endorse the view that cultural, ethnic, and socio-economic factors should be seriously considered as influential in personality development. Although they focus their analysis on the reality of the minority individuals in the United States, particularly Latinos and blacks, their interest is also on the larger picture of the multiple influences in the development of the human condition in general. They review the traditional theoretical formulations of Freud, Sullivan, and the object relations tradition to demonstrate their basic thesis in this regard. According to these authors, failure to include cultural and ethnic factors in the conceptualization of personality formations has resulted in a detrimental assessment of mental health or illness in these populations. More pathology is thus expected in these individuals with less possibility to benefit from treatment. The consequences of this basic philosophy with regard to treatment delivery are fully discussed in Part IV.

The deleterious impact of this basic philosophy was recently demonstrated by Louden (1995) in an epidemiological analysis of the prevalence of schizophrenia among Caribbean individuals in Great Britain. He concludes from his extensive analysis of multiple studies bearing on the subject that Afro-Caribbean people in England are overrepresented in the diagnosis of schizophrenia. It is his belief that the social condition (which includes unemployment, social disadvantaged status, social adversity, racism in the health and criminal justice system, and misdiagnosis) contributes to a perception of these individuals' condition that is not conducive to an objective appraisal of the true prevalence of schizophrenia and other pathological conditions in this group. Rather, these factors contribute to the high rates of schizophrenia found in this population. He cautions researchers to find careful ways to control for possible intervening variables (such as age, social background, sex, educational status, and regional differences) to ensure objectivity in the assessment of the etiology of schizophrenia in this population. This issue is more fully developed by Nevid and Goodman (Chapter 3), who provide an excellent and comprehensive review of the literature with regard to mental illness in general. They found that there is no evidence that members of ethnic minority groups are predisposed to more severe mental illness and alcohol and drug abuse disorders, that the most detrimental factors are related to the failure to account for differences in socioeconomic status (SES) and the tendency toward racial/ethnic stereotyping. This point is further emphasized by Yanos and his colleagues (Chapter 13) in their comprehensive presentation. According to Primavera and his colleagues (Chapter 6), once the individual is diagnosed as mentally ill, he or she has to contend with additional discrimination and stigma. In the case of culturally diverse patients, it leads to multiple levels of discrimination.

MULTICULTURAL PERSPECTIVE ON SPECIFIC PSYCHOPATHOLOGICAL MANIFESTATIONS

We have argued up to now about the importance of looking at cultural and ethnic factors in the conceptualization of mental illness and personality formation in general. Looking at the influence of these factors is particularly important with regard to assessment and treatment; hence our decision to dedicate several chapters to address specific symptomatologies. Readers will be treated to an array of different perspectives on schizophrenia (Azaunce and Yanos and his colleagues in Chapters 12 and 13, respectively), depression (Rendon, Mukherji, and Biafora and Biafora in Chapters 8, 9, and 10, respectively), and oppositional behavior in children (Mones in Chapter 11). These authors provide comprehensive analyses, including discussions of serious methodological issues in the assessment of these symptomatologies. Mukherji's chapter, for instance, starts from the premise delineated above of the importance of cultural factors in the human condition. Using the phenomenon of depression as a point of reference, she ventures into a discussion of the issues of cultural relativism and commensurability of diagnosis and evaluation of outcomes across cultures. She believes that cultural factors do influence biopsychological processes with regard to the etiology, symptom manifestation and report, diagnosis, course, and appropriateness of intervention modalities in illness. It directs the assessment of success of the outcomes of treatment. As an example of that, she discusses how somatic symptomatology is experienced by various cultural groups and its role in illness and health.

According to Biafora and Biafora (Chapter 10), we cannot assume that one factor can provide a full explanation of causality of psychopathology, particularly depression. Their findings indicate that an independent race effect was present when the data were controlled for income, but not when they were controlled for occupational status, education, or a composite of SES, as also suggested by Nevid and Goodman in Chapter 3 with regard to mental illness in general. They conclude that the conceptualization and operationalization of SES will determine the results one obtains in the investigation of race, SES, and depressive symptomatology. As they state, "Poverty is hazardous to one's psychological well-being and . . . race, by itself, is merely a proxy for socioeconomic status."

Following the importance of cultural influences on the view of pathology, Azaunce challenges us in her chapter with a poignant question on how to assess the nature and functionality of a culture-specific condition. In her contribution entitled "Is It Schizophrenia, Spirit Possession, or Both?" the role of religious beliefs on the personal identity becomes the central focus of her analysis and she posits the possibility of spirit possession to explain the psychiatric condition of some of the patients whose cultural background predisposes them to such a belief. It is her contention that "cultural, religious, and spiritual practices and belief systems can significantly influence the way in which illnesses and diseases are defined and ultimately treated." From the perspective of the theory of spirit possession, whose phenomenological manifestations bear uncanny similarities to schizophrenic manifestations with regard to delusions and hallucinations, possession occurs in the context of cultural customs supporting the phenomenon, beliefs, or traditions with supernatural premises, and highly stressful situations for the individual. From this cultural dimension, the concept of the self "is not discrete, bounded, fully separated or unique." It is conceptualized as "a receptacle of immaterial forces that is created and re-created in social interactions, contexts, and relationships and can consist of persons and forces over which the individual has little control." This definition of self emphasizes a less individualistic view and provides the dynamic structure for the phenomenon of spirit position to occur. While her view may appear controversial with regard to the traditional view of schizophrenia, it leaves one with the question, What is curative in the treatment of this condition when cultural factors are involved?

TREATMENT AND INTERVENTION

The implications for assessment and treatment derived from the theoretical formulations presented in this volume can be comprehensive only when the individual's unique characteristics are essential elements of the treatment and intervention decision. It is with that in mind that we have made Part IV the most extensive one, so as to include discussions not only on the essential factors to be considered but on how these factors tend to appear in a variety of settings. Discussions of the impact of race, immigration, language, gender, and so forth in service delivery are included in general (Herron and his associates in Chapter 21) and with regard to specific ethnic groups such as African-American and Caribbean blacks (Gopaul-McNicol, Thomas-Presswood, and Morris in Chapters 22, 23, and 29, respectively), Hispanic and Latino individuals (Costantino and Malgady, Malgady and Costantino, and Vazquez and Buki in Chapters 24, 25, and 26, respectively), and Asian individuals (Bracero and Tsui in Chapter 28). Chapters dealing with the assessment of violence in the workplace (Warren and his associates in Chapter 30), the issues surrounding the use of interpreters (Javier and associates in Chapter 27), the treatment of Hispanic elderly (Vazquez and Buki in Chapter 26), and gender (Stepakoff and Bowleg in Chapter 31) were also included as these are issues frequently confronted by professionals dealing with diverse populations.

We hope to leave the reader with the kinds of questions and curiosity that guided the preparation of this volume. We hope that the information included herein can serve as reference points for further exploration. Indeed, the impressive group of scholars we gathered left us with a great deal of material to think about. We invite your comments about any aspect of these chapters and urge you to become part of our journey. We hope that you enjoy the book as much as we enjoyed preparing it!

REFERENCES

Appiah, K. A. (1997). The multiculturalist misunderstanding. *The New York Review*, October, pp. 30–36.

Culbertson, F. M. (1997). Depression and gender: an international review. *American Psychologist*, 52 (1): 25–31.

Dana, R. H. (1993). *Multicultural Assessment Perspectives for Professional Psychology*. Boston: Allyn & Bacon.

Ghali, S. B. (1982). Understanding Puerto Rican traditions. *Social Work* (January): 98–102.

Godoy, I. (1995). *El rol de los objectos transcionales en el proceso de la separacion de la tierra madre: un estudio realizado con mujeres Latinas imigrantes*. Tesis doctoral, Pontificia Universidad Catolica del Ecuador, Quito, Ecuador.

Javier, R. A., and Herron, W. G. (1992). Introduction to the special issue on social distress and family in crisis: a multicultural perspective. *Journal of Social Distress and the Homeless*, 1(3/4): 199–202.

Javier, R. A., and Rendon, M. (1995). The ethnic unconscious and its role in transference, resistance and countertransference: an introduction. *Psychoanalytic Psychology* 12 (4): 213–220.

Kessler, R. C., and Neighbors, H. W. (1986). A new perspective on the relationships among race, social class, and psychological distress. *Journal of Health and Social Behavior*, 27: 107–115.

Louden, D. M. (1995). The epidemiology of schizophrenia among Caribbean-born and first and second generation migrants in Britain. *Journal of Social Distress and the Homeless*, 4 (3): 237–253.

Marcos, L. R., Urcuyo, L., Kesselman, M., and Alpert, M. (1973). The language barriers in evaluating Spanish-American patients. *Achives of General Psychiatry* 29: 655–659.

McCrae, R. P. and Costa, P. T. (1997). Personality structure as a human universal. *American Psychologist* 52 (5): 509–516.

Neighbors, H. W., Jackson, J. S., Campbell, L. S., and Williams, D. (1989). The inference of racial factors on psychiatric diagnosis: a review and suggestions for research. *Community Mental Health Journal* 25: 301–311.

U.S. Bureau of Census (1990). *Census of population and housing summary* (Tape file IC, CD-ROM), Washington, DC: Government Printing Office.

Part I

General Conceptual Issues

Cultural Influences on Psychopathology

JURIS G. DRAGUNS

INTRODUCTION

The Nature and Extent of Cultural Influence on Abnormal Behavior

There is generally consensus that maladaptive patterns of behavior are in some manner and to some degree affected by the social milieus within which persons have been socialized and by the host of culturally mediated experiences to which they have been exposed from birth. The question, however, is wide open as to the extent, nature, and direction of this influence. In reference to the culture's importance in shaping psychopathology, estimates vary from superficial to pervasive and from trivial to fundamental. As far as the specifics of cultural influence are concerned, there is an urgent and as yet unmet need not only to acknowledge but to pinpoint and explicate the role of cultural factors in shaping psychopathology. All of these considerations are germane to the clinical tasks of intervention in and reversal of mental disorder.

In reference to the weight of cultural factors in abnormal behavior, the polar relativist and universalist positions have been articulately expressed.

Universalists maintain that the basic symptoms and syndromes of psychopathology are essentially alike regardless of the site and context of their occurrence. Even these proponents cannot deny that psychological disturbance acquires a different guise depending on the cultural milieu and experience of the persons affected. They assert, however, that these features represent only the external trappings of psychopathology, even though in some cases they may be obtrusive and conspicuous. To paraphrase Berne (1959), schizophrenics in France speak schizophrenic with a French accent, and schizophrenics in Thailand with a Thai accent. Once these outside features are peeled off, the manifestations of the disorder appear in their undisguised and true state.

The advocates of cultural relativism (e.g., Benedict 1934) are equally articulate in emphasizing on an a priori basis the complete cultural plasticity of abnormal manifestations, expressions, and experiences. According to this view, one society's psychiatric patients could function in another society as its leaders and sages. Thus some of the paranoids and psychopaths in our midst could rise to positions of prominence and prestige in another culture. Conversely, members of other cultures would recognize or impute psychopathological motives and traits to some persons of powerful and influential status within our society. The relativist view implies that psychopathology in two or more cultures is utterly incomparable and that the only avenue of research is to study its expressions and forms on its own terms, that is, physically, in the milieu in which this behavior is expressed and, conceptually, on the basis of terms and notions that are current within that cultural context.

In their pure or extreme version, these two positions have received little empirical support. In fact, it is easy to refute either or both by recourse to the accumulated evidence. The importance of these outspoken formulations, however, is that they serve as markers or reference points for reviewing the research-based knowledge on the interplay of culture and psychopathology. Once this task is completed, the questions posed at the beginning of this chapter will be addressed: What is the relative impact of culture on psychopathology and what are the discernible strands of influence that connect cultural features and individual expressions of maladaptation? The conclusions from this survey will be brought to bear upon the practical challenges of providing clinically effective and culturally sensitive services for the contemporary, ethnically diverse, American clientele of mental health and human services.

The Two Meanings of Culture

Culture impinges upon psychopathology in two contexts. On the one hand, culture is equated with the socially shared and intergenerationally transmitted way of life of nation states. It is in this sense that we speak of Chinese, Finnish, Mexican, and Ethiopian culture. The term and concept of culture, however, is also employed to refer to the shared heritage and social distinctiveness of the multiplicity of the ethnic components within the American mosaic. Thus we refer to African Americans, Puerto Ricans, American Indians or Native Americans, Irish Americans, Italian Canadians, and many other ethnic groups. It is this multicultural diversity that challenges North American mental health professionals in their clinical contexts.

Even though the concept of culture is appropriately used both across nations and across ethnicities, two additional problems must be faced before cross-cultural comparisons and programs derived from them are applied to the multicultural diversity of many United States communities. The first of these factors is the history and experience of inequality, often shading off into discrimination and oppression, that many ethnic groups have endured. In light of the continuing impact of these experiences, how can the various ethnic groups be fairly and realistically compared? At the very least, great care must be taken lest the cumulative effects of deprivation and inequality be mistaken for the intrinsic and fundamental characteristics of the group in question. If this precaution is not exercised, there is the risk of obtaining a slanted and distorted view of the phenomena investigated. In the worst case, the result would be to once more blame the victims. In view of this danger, spokespersons and advocates of minority groups are understandably cautious about any proposals to involve their members in cross-ethnic research. It can be pointed out, however, that, over the last thirty years or so, organized cross-cultural psychology, in this country and elsewhere, has succeeded in comparing persons across culture lines without opprobrium and without any explicit or implicit assumption or expectation of superiority or inferiority of any cultural groups investigated (Berry et al. 1992, Brislin 1992, Moghaddam et al. 1993, Segall et al. 1990, Triandis 1994).

The second point is less often recognized. It pertains to the interlocking and overlapping aspects of identity so frequently encountered in a multicultural society. Thus a person is not only a Greek American, but a member of the national American culture in which he or she participates and with which he or she identifies. Yet, for exposition purposes, it is easy to succumb to the temptation of describing the several ethnic components within the American macrocosm as though they were living in self-containment and isolation. Instead, researchers should proceed from the reality of two or more identities coexisting within persons of various ethnic backgrounds. The interrelationship of these identities may be one of dominance, submersion, conflict, integration, or blending, to mention but a few of the possibilities. In any case, the study of the effects and ramifications of ethnic culture on psychopathology is greatly complicated by the supraordinate American identity with its associated tenets and values.

Moreover, as Berry (1990) has demonstrated in his research on the acculturative process, there are several ways of coming to grips with the duality of majority and minority cultures. Within the mental health field, these considerations should put professionals on guard against two dangers. One of them is stereotyping all members of an ethnic group by obliterating the perception of differences among its members. The other one involves a misguided, if well meaning, disregard of ethnic or cultural features and characteristics as though the recognition of these factors were irrelevant to, or even harmful for, the various kinds of treatment services. Instead, the challenge is to combine clinical sensitivity with cultural sophistication while avoiding stereotyping.

RESEARCH ON CULTURE AND PSYCHOPATHOLOGY: THE INCOMPLETE STATE OF CURRENT KNOWLEDGE

Methodological and Conceptual Considerations

Given the great variety of available research approaches, it may be useful to begin with a taxonomy of methods for the cross-cultural investigation of disturbed behavior, which is provided in Table 2–1.

The two contrasting orientations of cultural data gathering and conceptualization are emic and etic. The emic view is based on the primacy of cultural uniqueness. This orientation aspires to a factual and sensitive description of a phenomenon within its cultural context. Examples of emic research approaches, as listed in Table 2–1, include the recording of expressions of distress and helplessness among the Alaskan Inuit (J. M. Murphy 1976), the investigation of indigenous explanations of trance or possession states (Pfeiffer 1994, Prince 1980), the observation and description of the healing techniques and rituals in a traditional Salish Indian culture (Jilek 1988), and the study of a characteristic pattern of psychological disturbance within China in relation to its antecedents, concomitants, and consequences (Kleinman 1982). A major topic of emic investigation has been the description of culturally unique patterns of disturbance or culture-bound syndromes, as exemplified by *Taijin-Kyofushu*, or morbid shyness and social anxiety in Japan (Tanaka-Matsumi 1979) and *koro* or *suo-yang*, a catastrophic reaction to the perceived prospect of genital retraction or shrinkage that sometimes reaches epidemic proportion

TABLE 2–1. CULTURAL RESEARCH IN
PSYCHOPATHOLOGY: CONTRASTING OPTIONS

Approaches:	EMIC (culturally indigenous)	ETIC (universal, cross-culturally comparable)
Related to:	Idiographic	Nomothetic

Objective:	Sensitivity to Cultural
	    Uniqueness
		Objectivity, comparability
		    of dimensions across cultures

Examples:	Anthropological Descriptions
	    Indigenous Concepts &
	    Explanations
		Epidemiological Studies (WHO)
		Multicultural Comparisons

	Culture-Bound Syndromes Native Healers	Bicultural Comparisons Traditional Transcultural Psychiatry
	Within-Culture Relationships "New Transcultural Psychiatry"	

Product:	Abnormal Behavior and
	    Experience in a Unique
	    Social-Historical
	    Context
		Worldwide Panorama of
		    Abnormal Behavior Across
		    Cultures

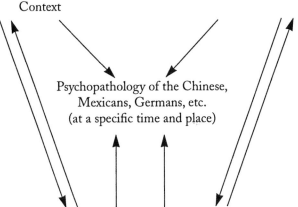

Psychopathology of the Chinese,
Mexicans, Germans, etc.
(at a specific time and place)

Principles Linking Culture, Normal Adaptation
and Psychopathology

in Southeastern Asia, from Guandong to Singapore (Edwards 1985, Tseng et al. 1988, 1992). Collectively, these efforts have yielded a rich picture of the experience of disorder at a specific geographic site and social context.

Contrast these approaches with the application of the etic perspective in psychopathology. It proceeds from the premise of a worldwide reality of a phenomenon or category of abnormal experience. The multicultural programs of investigation of the culturally constant or immutable symptoms of schizophrenia, sponsored by the World Health Organization (1973, 1979; Sartorius et al. 1986) exemplify the etic approach. On a less ambitious scale, another example is provided by the comparisons of psychiatric inpatients or outpatients of several ethnicities and cultures (Marsella et al. 1973, Radford 1989). Such comparisons assume the reality or existence across cultures of such categories as schizophrenia or depression. Numerous studies of this type have been pursued within the framework of traditional transcultural psychiatry (H. B. M. Murphy 1982). This framework is sometimes juxtaposed to the more emically oriented new transcultural psychiatry (Kleinman 1977), which seeks primarily to advance the understanding of a psychopathological manifestation within its own sociocultural environment and to shift the focus of observation from social category to personal experience.

The results of both emic and etic strands of research are pooled and integrated with the objective of formulating generalizations about the characteristic manifestations of psychopathology in specific cultures, such as Germany, Mexico, Japan, or Australia. Systematic information has, for example, accumulated about psychological disorders and therapeutic interventions in China (Draguns 1996a, Lin et al. 1995); information concerning psychopathology in other major cultures and regions is ripe for review and integration. The ultimate and ambitious goal of the cross-cultural research enterprise is the discovery of general principles that would link culture and psychopathology in all contexts and locations.

Cross-cultural research faces a great many conceptual and methodological challenges, which must be met if comparable data across geographic and social barriers are to be obtained. Over the last few decades considerable progress has been registered toward this goal (Brislin et al. 1973, Draguns 1996b). Problems and proposed solutions for this type of research are presented in schematic form in Table 2–2.

The major concern of cross-cultural methodologists is with the equivalence of measures and stimuli, which translates into appropriateness and fairness of the units of comparison. It just would not do to compare, for example, psychiatric patients in China and in the United States by means of an American paper-and-pencil anxiety scale even if this instrument was competently

TABLE 2–2. CONCEPTUAL AND METHODOLOGICAL PROBLEMS RELEVANT TO CROSS-CULTURAL ASSESSMENT OF ABNORMAL BEHAVIOR

Equivalence of stimuli and instruments:
1 physical
2 conceptual
3 contextual

Problem: Comparing equivalent stimuli that are not physically identical and physically identical stimuli which are not equivalent.
Solution: Limit comparisons to stimuli meeting criteria of 1, 2, and 3.
Cost: Restriction of range of the stimuli compared.

Comparability of samples and populations:
1 in distress and disability (DSM-IV definition of mental disorder)
2 in diagnosis
3 in demographic and social characteristics
4 in (premorbid) personality characteristics
5 in nonpersonality variables, e.g., intelligence
6 in the manner of recruiting

Problem: Comparing samples/groups widely divergent in relevant characteristics.
Solution: Concentrate on (reasonably) comparable sample, use appropriate statistics (e.g., partial correlation, analysis of covariance, multivariate methods), record and note remaining discrepancies.
Caution: Avoid artificial matching.
Cost: Restriction of the scope of comparisons, limitations of generalizations.

Comparability (or identity) of concepts:
1 diagnostic, e.g., schizophrenia, agoraphobia
2 affective-motivational, e.g., anxiety, depression

Problem: Making sure that identical words carry constant meanings.
Solution: Obtain systematic empirical data on the equivalence of concepts, use explicit rules of diagnosis and group assignment, use objective measures if valid and appropriate; employ a multimethod approach and conduct a series of studies.
Cost: Incomplete understanding of the meaning, context, and social consequences of the concepts employed.

Special Problems:
1 Translation of verbal materials:
  a back-translation
  b decentering
2 Constancy of demand characteristics and contextual variables:
  a verbal questionnaires
  b brass instrument experimentation
  c personal interview (intrusion)
3 Observer's/tester's demand characteristics:
  a in behavior
  b in subjects'/testees' perception

translated. Test stimuli must be equivalent not only in their physical properties or verbal content, but also in their meaning, functional characteristics, and
metric values. This standard is exceedingly difficult to achieve, and all the
more so as geographic distance and cultural dissimilarity are increased. In the
multicultural milieu of the United States, however, these issues usually do not
have to be faced in stark and absolute terms. The subtler aspects of nonequiv-
alence may result in revision and elimination of questionable or inappropriate
stimuli and the addition of items that could be realistically compared across
two or more cultural groups. The use of local experts and consultants and
extensive pilot work are realistic expedients to that end. A more radical solution is often recommended, though rarely implemented. It involves starting
with the construction of the instrument at both or several sites of its intended
application. For example, a new thematic or verbal test of social anxiety would
sample scenes and/or statements relevant to the several milieus in which the
proposed measure is to be applied. To this end, it needs to be pretested with
all of its target groups. Very likely, several of the items would not survive this
scrutiny. Moreover, this procedure would restrict the range and variety of the
stimuli employed and would eliminate some of the verbal, pictorial, or other
items that may be rich in local color, but are less meaningful outside the group
for which they were designed. Thus the concern with equivalence tips the scale
in the etic direction, at the expense of emic sensitivity.

   Equally important is the concern with the comparability of samples and
populations in the relevant dimensions of appraisal, which typically include
degree of disturbance or distress, distribution of diagnostic categories, premorbid personality characteristics, selected cognitive variables, and the manner in which the samples have been drawn from within the population.
Accomplishing all of these objectives is a tall order, however, not only for the
obvious practical reasons, but also because of the possible confounding of various artifactual disparities between the samples with the genuine differences
between cultures. Cross-cultural methodologists (Brislin et al. 1973, Draguns
1982, Guthrie and Lonner 1985) warn against the dangers of artificial over-
matching in the misguided pursuit of seeking in another culture an exact
counterpart for each subject in the original sample. Inevitably, such a procedure increases the likelihood of Type II errors—that of rejecting true differences between samples. Moreover, it is impossible to generalize from these
kinds of artificial samples to the population in the "real world." It is preferable
to tolerate a certain degree of messiness that reflects the incomparabilities and
disparities across ethnic and/or cultural lines. Two responses are recommended
to address the imperfect comparability of research groups. First, a complete
record of the pertinent characteristics would be an important help in replicating

findings with future samples and in applying them in various practical situations (Brislin and Baumgardner 1971). Second, increasing the availability of flexible and sophisticated research designs and statistical procedures would permit more conclusive comparisons of less than perfectly matched samples.

It is well known that diagnostic categories have been applied differently across cultural and national lines. In a comparison of British and American diagnostic practices (Cooper et al. 1972), dramatic differences in the numbers of schizophrenic and depressed patients in the psychiatric institutions of the two countries were traced to the operations and concepts of the diagnosticians. The advent of the American Psychiatric Association's symptom-based rules of diagnostic assignment, from *DSM-III* to the new *DSM-IV* (1994), has resulted in improvements so that the findings reported by Cooper and colleagues may no longer reflect the current situation (Good 1993). Still, in reference to the diagnostic categories less intensively investigated across cultures and nations, such as agoraphobia, there is the residual question of whether the current diagnostic practices are adequate. Specifically, can they detect and prevent any cultural hypersensitivities and/or "blind spots" in diagnostic application? It is safer to pretest the diagnostic operations than to assume their cross-cultural constancy.

Finally, cultural variations in the valence or demand characteristics of procedures and instruments should be considered. Interviews, self-report questionnaires, projective tests, and experimental methods of psychophysiological recording are potentially subject to these distortions. Variables such as the culturally accepted limits of personal intrusion, topics that are taboo within a specific culture, rules of verbal decorum and etiquette, and conventions of self-report and of imaginative self-expression all come into play. Exploration and pretesting may be necessary to avoid inapplicable or misleading methods and procedures. Artifactual and extraneous affective arousal may be so strong as to override the anticipated specific effects of the stimuli.

What Do We Know: A Brief Review of Findings

Studies of psychopathology and culture are of three kinds: clinical, epidemiological, and cross-cultural. Clinical research ranges from case studies to large-scale investigations. Their focus is on the characteristics of a disorder, which may include some culturally distinguishing features. In epidemiological research, a psychiatric census or "head count" is conducted of psychiatrically identified or diagnosed persons within a catchment area or on a representative or random sample of persons from within that site. In a cross-cultural comparative study, data are obtained on psychopathological variables of several population groups, such as hospitalized American, Taiwanese, and Japanese psychiatric patients (Rin et al. 1973) or on the depressive responses of students of Caucasian, Chinese, and Japanese descent in Hawaii (Marsella et al. 1973).

What have these studies yielded? About the general nature and scope of the relationship between culture and psychopathology, tentative answers can be provided:

1. No disorder has been found to be entirely immune to cultural shaping.
2. None of the disorders so far investigated is traceable in its entirety to cultural or social characteristics, nor do disorders vary over their entire range in response to cultural differences.
3. Schizophrenia and other disorders of comparable severity are influenced in their manifestations to a lesser degree by culture than are less disabling, ambulatory disorders.
4. Major depression is more susceptible to cultural shaping than are the schizophrenic disorders.
5. Symptoms of psychological disorders appear to be significantly and meaningfully related to social, technological, religious, and other features of their societies.
6. Regardless of the diagnostic category, cultural differences are more marked on the plane of symptom than syndrome.
7. Both major depression and schizophrenia are characterized by a few culturally immutable symptoms.
8. The cultural plasticity of the patient characteristics has been overestimated by many, while the cultural plasticity of the other, nonpsychopathological participants in the transactions involving the patient has been very widely, or perhaps even universally, underestimated (Draguns 1980).
9. Cultural variation in symptoms is accompanied by the variations in diagnosticians' perceptions as well as in treatment milieu and community responses; all of these influences coalesce to produce a culturally distinctive experience of psychological disorder.

In reference to more specific findings, represented in Table 2–3, the following conclusions are offered:

1. The World Health Organization's (1973, 1979; Sartorius et al. 1986) international studies of schizophrenia have identified several symptoms that were presented in all of the nine participating countries

TABLE 2–3. OVERVIEW OF FINDINGS ON CROSS-CULTURAL PSYCHOLOGY OF ABNORMAL BEHAVIOR

1. Core symptoms of schizophrenia: (WHO 1973)
   Restricted affect
   Poor insight
   Thinking aloud
   Poor rapport
   Incoherent speech
   Unrealistic information
   Bizarre/nihilistic delusions

2. Core symptoms of major depression: (WHO 1983)
   Sad affect
   Less enjoyment
   Inability to concentrate
   Ideas of insufficiency
   Ideas of inadequacy
   Ideas of worthlessness

3. Other research on depression: less guilt in non-Western countries (Asia, Africa)

4. More benign course of schizophrenia in developing countries (WHO 1979—tentative)

5. Negative correlation between course of schizophrenia and educational level (WHO 1979—very tentative)

6. Somatization as a prominent avenue for expression of depression (Kleinman 1982: the relationship between culture, somatic distress, and depressive experience is complex and subtle).

7. Psychopathology represents the exaggeration of modal adaptive pattern (Draguns 1989: suggestive support from a variety of studies

8. Suicide—a result of social disintegration (Paris 1991).

9. Cultural influences on psychopathology are major in scope (refutes Berne 1956).

10. The concept of mental disorder is not culturally relative in its entirety; one culture's madmen are not another culture's prophets or leaders (refutes Benedict 1934).

(Colombia, Czechoslovakia, Denmark, Great Britain, India, Nigeria, Russia, Taiwan, and the United States). As listed in Table 2–3, these symptoms reflect withdrawal, confusion, and reality distortion. They may approximate the acultural worldwide common denominator of this disorder in the form of direct, minimally elaborated symptomatology of withdrawal and disorientation.

2. Similar findings were obtained in hospitalized depressed patients at research sites in Canada, Iran, Japan, and Switzerland (Marsella et al. 1985, World Health Organization 1983). Again, one is struck by the predominance of organismic and affective manifestations of depression.

3. A variety of qualitative and quantitative findings confirm the underemphasis on guilt-related symptoms in depression in East Asia (e.g., Kimura 1965, 1967, Yap 1965) and in Africa (Diop 1967, German 1972).

4. A more benign course for schizophrenia was reported for the two developing countries, India and Nigeria, in the World Health Organization (1979) project on schizophrenia. Similar reports have come from a variety of other non-Western, and not necessarily developing, locations (e.g., Lo and Lo 1977, Waxler 1974). However, some Western studies, for example, from Germany (Huber et al. 1980) and Switzerland (Bleuler 1972), have also reported surprisingly high remission rates. Clearly there is an urgent need to replicate and extend the World Health Organization outcome studies through a series of sequential, standardized, and thorough cross-cultural investigations to determine the scope and stability of its findings.

5. Another provocative result that emerged from the World Health Organization (1979) research provided an exception to the well-established positive relationship between remission from schizophrenia and socioeducational attainment, based on data from developed countries (Dohrenwend and Dohrenwend 1974). Results in India and Nigeria suggested a negative correlation between education and prognosis (World Health Organization 1979), but the generality and stability of these findings remain to be established.

6. Somatization has emerged as a prominent avenue of experiencing psychic distress in China (Kleinman 1982) and elsewhere (Kirmayer 1984).

7. Suggestive evidence points toward the prominence of inappropriate exaggeration of modal adaptive patterns (Draguns 1990a). Tseng and colleagues (1990) conducted a comparison of anxiety-related symptoms at four Asian sites: Japan, Mainland China, Taiwan, and Bali (Indonesia). They concluded that "neurotic manifestation is a magnification of a baseline mental symptom observed among the normal

group, while the baseline among the normal group varies according to the sociocultural and ethnic difference" (p. 259). These interpretations, however, have been advanced post hoc. Tests of predictions based on normal characteristics and applied to pathological samples, as well as vice versa, are urgently needed.

8. Suicide has been solidly associated with social disintegration (Paris 1991) thereby confirming one of the oldest hypotheses extant, that of Durkheim (1951) and his formulation of anomic suicide. Of course, the complex phenomenon of suicide defies being reduced to a unitary cause.

9. To echo conclusions already anticipated earlier in this chapter, the composite of the available results is difficult to reconcile with the notion that the effects of sociocultural factors are trivial, superficial, minor, or inconsequential. As pointed out, no disorder is free of cultural shaping.

10. At the same time, there is no support for the notion that psychopathology is shaped de novo in every culture in which it appears. The opposite seems to be the case, and the major, intensively investigated syndromes, such as schizophrenia and depression, tend toward worldwide representation. Al-Issa (1995) has gone even further and has proposed that "major mental health problems and concerns all over the world seem to be quite similar: schizophrenia, depression, suicide, alcoholism, culture-specific syndromes, mental illness among ethnic minorities and immigrants, and so on" (p. 32). Conceding the general validity of this statement, it remains for investigation to pinpoint the limits of this similarity and to identify any exceptions to this principle. Moreover, even if symptoms and syndromes may approach constancy across cultures, the antecedents, concomitants, consequences, meanings, and contexts of their occurrence are culturally divergent and variable (Draguns 1973).

Unanswered Questions in Cross-Cultural Psychology of Abnormal Behavior

Let us now take note of several open and unresolved questions in this active but as yet young field. Schematically, these issues are presented in the following list.

1. Worldwide variations in incidence of specific disorders and their relationship to culture.
2. The pathway of cultural influence on psychological disturbance.

3. Interaction of biological factors (predispositions) with cultural factors.
4. The specific cultural influences that shape psychopathology.
5. The cultural factors that promote resilience and resistance to psychopathology.
6. Is the influence of culture pathoplastic and not pathogenic?
7. What is the diagnostic status of culture-bound syndromes, such as *Amok, Latah, Pibloctoq*, and others?
8. Are some widespread current disorders the culture-bound syndromes of our time and place (e.g., anorexia nervosa, agoraphobia, and borderline personality disorder)?
9. What cultural influences promote or counteract alcohol and substance abuse?

Comparisons of epidemiological data across culture lines have barely begun. The remote antecedents of this endeavor go back to the classical Midtown (Manhattan) Study (Srole et al. 1962), which attempted to identify the strands of cultural and ethnic, as well as socioeconomic, influence in the diverse midcentury American urban environment. Actual collection of epidemiological psychiatric symptom data at geographically removed sites was initiated only recently. This approach is exemplified by the retrospective comparison of diagnostic and symptom information collected by means of identical instruments in Taiwan and in Maryland (e.g., Compton et al. 1991). It deserves to be emulated and extended, which has not, as yet, been done.

How is cultural influence crystallized into a symptom? This progression has not yet been explored, even though Kleinman's (1980, 1982) and Ware and Kleinman's (1992) observations are beginning to shed light on some aspects of this process. Specifically, Kleinman (1988) has spelled out the following four components of this transformation: the conventional meaning of symptoms within the context of a socially constructed idiom of distress; the social significance of culturally salient disorders, including any social stigma associated with them; the significance of chronic illness in the person's network of relationships, interactions, and experiences; the explicit interpretations of the disorder by family members, community leaders, and health practitioners. These four aspects remain to be operationalized and investigated in relation to their antecedents and consequences.

Biology and culture are sometimes misleadingly presented as opposite and mutually exclusive factors in psychopathology. This is definitely not so. However, little information exists on how bodily processes interact with cultural influences to produce psychological symptoms. The continued investigation of somatization, centered on the body but shaped by culture, may provide the common ground for such exploration. Another promising lead to explore is the demonstrated Chinese "flushing response" to ethyl alcohol (Wolff 1972) and its possible role in shaping cultural patterns of alcohol consumption and "drunken comportment" (McAndrew and Edgerton 1969).

Similarly, the field lacks information on the cultural factors that enhance resilience and hardiness in the face of stress and prevent and/or counteract psychopathology. Lee (1981, 1985) has contributed detailed descriptions of coping mechanisms that permitted Chinese in Hong Kong to reduce and mitigate the stress caused by extreme residential crowding.

The bulk of accumulated information pertains to how culture helps shape psychopathology. We know very little about whether cultures contribute to psychopathology's causes and, if so, how (Jilek 1982) they promote it, before shaping its expression and direction. H. B. M. Murphy (1982) ventured upon this new ground by providing a stimulating if speculative account of the possibly crucial differentiating features of cultures that are characterized by unusually low or high incidence rates of schizophrenia.

The controversy concerning the diagnostic status of various exotic and culture-bound syndromes, such as *amok*, *latah*, *koro*, and others, remains unresolved, although articulate positions have been presented. On the one hand, the expectation continues to be maintained that these "exotic" patterns of behavior are but the emic manifestations of the etic, worldwide entities of mental disorder (DSM-IV 1994, Yap 1974). On the other hand, Tseng and colleagues (1988, 1992) have contributed solid epidemiological and psychometric data on the *koro* victims of Southern China, which point to their greater similarity to normal individuals in their milieu rather than to the local residents presenting the symptoms of anxiety disorder. Voices (e.g., Bartholomew 1994) that urge the observers of the field to view culture-based syndromes as phenomena of social psychology of their respective place and time rather than as a local variety of universally encountered mental disorder continue to be heard. Empirical resolution of this issue can proceed only piecemeal and is difficult.

The provocative notion that a number of prevalent conditions, such as anorexia nervosa, agoraphobia, and borderline personality disorder, constitute the culture-bound disorders of modern North America (and, possibly, Western Europe) has been advanced (Paris 1991). The demonstration of this proposition would involve the collection of epidemiological data on these disorders across cultures, a task that has barely begun.

Similarly, there are a great many leads and post hoc explanations on the links between cultural factors in alcohol and substance abuse, but as yet there is little systematic knowledge on these topics, especially as it may pertain to the role of ethnic and cultural variables (Heath 1982, McAndrew and Edgerton 1969).

CLINICAL IMPLICATIONS

The Self as a Unifying Concept

Potentially, the findings recapitulated—even in their current "unfinished" state—have bearing on program development and service delivery for the multicultural mental health clientele. These implications remain to be pinpointed on the plane of macroscopic development of culturally fitting programs of intervention and within the personal counseling and therapy relationships.

A pivotal concept that links the two domains of cross-cultural research and psychotherapeutic intervention is the self. A number of influential formulations by Markus and Kitayama (1991), Gaines (1982), Landrine (1992), and Roland (1988) have highlighted the subtle contrast between the self-experience in the Euro-American mainstream culture and in various settings in Asia, Africa, and elsewhere. This contrast, moreover, reverberates in the multicultural environment of North America's cities, suburbs, towns, and villages. The distinction is between what Landrine called "the separated, encapsulated self of the Western culture [which] is conceptualized as a god, in the sense that it is presumed to be the originator, creator and controller of behavior" (p. 402). Landrine further stated: "The self is presumed to be an entity: a bounded, unique, singular, encapsulated, noncorporeal, ghostlike, and godly entity. . . . The self is presumed to be a cognitive and emotional universe, the center of awareness, emotion, judgment and action" (p. 403). This kind of self is described as referential. It stands in contrast to the indexical self (Gaines 1982), which "has no enduring, trans-situational characteristics, no traits or desires or needs of its own from its relationships and contexts. . . . The indexical self is not a separate entity that can be referred to or reflected upon in isolation" (Landrine 1992, p. 406). Such a self "includes other people and portions of the natural and supernatural world" (p. 407). To articulate the contrast between the two kinds of self-conception, the referential self is experienced as an autonomous unit, complete with its traits and attributes that tend toward constancy across situations and time. By contrast, the indexical self is principally manifested as a pattern of social roles; its unity is more illusory than real.

The sophistication and articulateness of the conceptual formulations has so far outstripped the development and application of empirical measures based on these provocative distinctions. However, hypotheses have been posited that self-experience in sociocentric environments is qualitatively different from the individual-centered environments, as epitomized by the mainstream North American culture. On the basis of her review and interpretation of relevant writings, Landrine (1992) concluded that "the referential conception of the self is unknown among most Asians and Asian Americans; among most black Americans, Mediterranean Americans, Hindu Americans and indeed, among most white American women, as well as among the vast majority of the world's peoples" (p. 405).

This conclusion is almost certainly a marked overstatement. It overlooks the fact that a great many minority group members are socialized by and within the North American mainstream culture, and it confounds quantitative and qualitative distinctions and lumps tentative impressions with more solidly established and clinical, empirically founded formulations. Nonetheless, the message at its core is sound: self-experience is deeply embedded in a person's culturally determined socialization process. As such, it has far-reaching implications for the experience and expression of psychopathology and for the implementation of culturally fitting and clinically effective treatment services.

Confounding Disturbance and Deviance

On the practical plane, the implications of culturally oriented conceptions and data are above all general and attitudinal. It is imperative for the mental health professional who practices in a multicultural environment to be flexible in both outlook and technique and to be prepared for revision and modification of his or her views, convictions, and service. The most insidious error to be counteracted is the tendency to equate deviance with disturbance. It is all too easy for a clinician steeped in the classificatory grid of *DSM-IV* to find a slot within this system for a person whose actions are both confused and confusing and whose social reactions just do not make sense or violate the prevailing standards of propriety or convention. In the case of the culturally different individual who presents these patterns of behavior, it is imperative for the clinician to consider alternative hypotheses based on cultural difference. Horror stories occasionally appear in the professional literature (e.g., Sue 1996) and in the general media of persons psychiatrically institutionalized, sometimes for decades, on the basis of culturally based misreading of the person's behavior. On a subtler level, however, the tendency to equate deviance with disturbance may operate to bias the clinician toward the diagnosis of more conspicuous and extreme disorders across a wide cultural gulf.

This trend translates into overdiagnosis of schizophrenia in culturally different individuals and underrepresentation of depressive diagnosis among culturally deviant persons. For example, within the Amish communities in
Southeastern Pennsylvania, local psychiatrists—none of whom were Amish—
tended for a long time to diagnose acutely disturbed Amish patients as schizophrenic. Upon the systematic application of objective, rule-based diagnostic
procedures, these diagnoses were found to be faulty in 78 percent of the cases
(Egeland et al. 1983); instead, manic depressive disorder was diagnosed.
Egeland and colleagues (1983) concluded:

> By self-definition the Amish are a "peculiar people" in dress, hairstyle,
> speech, behaviors, and mechanisms. When this unique personal coloration is
> enhanced further by delusional or other pathological signs, it may increase
> the likelihood that the physician will use a singular diagnostic focus. An area
> psychiatrist is alleged to have said: "I know the diagnosis immediately, all our
> Amish patients are schizophrenic!" [p. 68]

Similar diagnostic insensitivities have been documented in the case of
African Americans, Hispanic Americans, and other culturally distinct groups
(Abedimpe, 1981, 1984, DeHoyos and DeHoyos 1965, López, 1989,
Mukherjee et al. 1983).

Stereotyping versus Empathy

It is tempting to attribute these diagnostic errors to racism and prejudice. On
the basis of my unsystematic and unscientific observations, however, virulent
antiminority attitudes are rare among American mental health professionals,
while misattributions are widespread. As Ridley (1989) put it, "Prejudiced
people stereotype, but people who stereotype are not necessarily prejudiced"
(p. 59). In a searching analysis of the attributions of clinicians, López (1989)
concluded that these errors are traceable to information processing rather than
to an active rejection of minority groups. This recognition implies, however,
that clinicians who are free of ethnic, religious, or racial prejudice may still be
at risk for systematic errors in the diagnostic process. López suggested that
emphasis in training be shifted from changing attitudes and values to promoting more effective and realistic modes of processing information.

An overlooked antidote to these cognitive distortions is empathy. In relation to the present problem, the literature provides suggestions of an inverse
relationship between empathy and social distance (cf. Draguns 1990b, 1996b,
Tanaka-Matsumi 1992). The latter variable is closely linked with familiarity,

which, of course, is greatly reduced as cultural barriers are crossed. Going beyond cross-cultural data, it may not be accidental that depression has historically been overlooked or underestimated in populations dissimilar to the typical professional interviewers and observers, that is, the young (including children), the old, the poor, and the culturally different. The challenge is to train and equip clinicians with skills that would permit them the full exercise of empathic sensitivity with clients who are different in appearance, behavior, background, and outlook. This challenge has been taken up by Ridley and Lingle (1996), who have recognized the difficulties of experiencing and communicating empathy across cultural lines and have proposed a model for enhancing empathic skills on the perceptual, cognitive, affective, and communicative planes.

From Therapy Planning to Culture Accommodation at Social and Individual Levels

Increasingly, planning mental health services is regarded as a worldwide challenge. Desjarlais and colleagues (1995) have taken a searching look at the panorama of statistics pertaining to the mental health problems in the Third World. They then proceeded to identify unmet needs and to provide recommendations for designing services for various problem areas, such as violence and substance abuse, as well as for chronic and/or disabling mental disorders, such as depression, toxic psychosis, and schizophrenia. Desjarlais and colleagues also focused their attention on the underserved and overstressed segments of the population in many developing countries, namely women and children. Their effort culminated in formulating a set of recommendations for public policy and action. Desjarlais and colleagues also articulated several research priorities, among them focused ethnographic studies, community-based interventions, and interdisciplinary collaborations. Above all, they advocated the creation of a culturally informed database. It would include basic sociodemographic characteristics, psychiatric diagnoses, local manifestations of distress, behavioral and social pathologies, disability and physical health status, and care-seeking and coping responses.

Higginbotham and colleagues (1988) went even further in introducing culture accommodation as an inclusive term for fitting mental health services to the needs and expectations of a culturally different clientele. Culture accommodation can be practiced on an individual as well as a group scale. In exporting and adapting mental health services, it may entail formal data collection and complex negotiations with persons of influence and power. On an individual level, culture accommodation boils down to the clinician's readiness to adjust his or her accustomed modus operandi to the cognitive framework and subjective affective state of clients whose sociocultural experience has been different from the modal one. In both cases, culture accommodation includes four aspects: culture-specific definitions of disturbance, accepted norms of behavior, expectations of social influence techniques, and approved change agents. Input is solicited from the client(s), local mental health experts, and persons in positions of authority. A process of negotiation is involved, and its goal is the delivery of clinically indicated service or intervention in a maximally meaningful and relevant manner. Knowledgeable and experienced persons from within the culture or the community may be enlisted as informants or culture brokers or mediators.

In the model proposed by Higginbotham and colleagues, culture accommodation is implemented on the plane of a community, region, or state. On the individual level, three innovative psychotherapists have exemplified it in their operations. Nathan (1994), a Parisian psychoanalyst with an extensive African clientele, described extensive modifications in rationale, format, and technique in his attempts to make psychodynamically oriented intervention both effective and meaningful to his clients. Verbal communication was complemented but never supplanted by the presentation and manipulation of culturally meaningful objects and artifacts. Interpretations were grounded in the client's culturally mediated beliefs and practices. The strictly dyadic format of psychoanalysis was loosened to include simultaneous or separate contact with family members, friends, and other informants from within the client's culture. Recognition was accorded to the more interpersonal and less intrapsychic problems, a pattern that was predominant within Nathan's African clientele. Finally, the traumatic experience of being wrenched from one's accustomed reference group and exposed to the baffling and imperative pressures of a metropolitan Western culture was given due recognition in both conceptualizing and implementing therapy.

Similarly, Peltzer (1995), a German clinical psychologist, has pioneered interventions in several African countries. He was able to effectively apply several techniques of psychodynamic, behavioral, and cognitive inspiration. This objective was accomplished by embedding these interventions in a culturally distinctive relationship between the therapist and the client. The sociocentric expectations rooted in the traditional African culture were incorporated into therapy planning and intervention. The subtly different apprehension of reality, in relation to one's body, time, and authority and peer relations, was also taken into account in anticipating and implementing therapy experiences.

These modifications are consonant with the conclusions by Fish (1996), an American psychotherapist who adapted both his practice and orientation to Brazilian conditions and expectations. In particular, he helps dispel the implicitly ethnocentric conviction of many therapists that intervention in other cultures is inherently more superficial and less effective than it is on home grounds. "In interpersonal terms, Brazilians, as opposed to Americans, are warmer, better conversationalists, more interpersonally skilled, and more skilled at interpersonal manipulation. (Naturally this is a broad generalization with many exceptions.) As a result, they are natural therapists" (p. 208).

The common ground of the three innovators' experience is that they advocate focused, direct, problem-centered, and time-limited intervention, with a minimum of open-ended exploration and a maximum of concentration on the relief of distress and/or solution of the concrete dilemma or difficulty.

Techniques and Avenues of Intervention

What is the value and what are the limitations of the clinician's armamentarium of techniques that are available for use in a culturally different situation or setting? There are probably no major interventions that could be applied only to the members of a specific cultural group. Therapeutic intervention rests on a set of universally or widely applicable attitudinal and/or relationship variables that are transformed into specific techniques depending on the sociocultural context. Ministrations of native healers and those of modern professional psychotherapists have been persuasively broken down to the same active ingredients or crucial components of psychotherapy (Torrey 1972).

Still, there are potentially demonstrable differences among cultures and groups in preferences for, and aversions to, various styles and patterns of intervention. Thus it is probably true that "the culturally appropriate treatment of minorities includes treatment of the socially defined family, kin, community, or network. This view has been echoed by clinicians who specialize in treating Native Americans, Asian Americans, African Americans, and Latino Americans. Treating the minority client in isolation is perhaps the most frequent cross-cultural, psychotherapeutic error" (Landrine 1992, p. 409).

A recurrent theme in writing on cross-culturally appropriate interventions is the alleged preference by a variety of groups, from Asian international students (Alexander et al. 1976) to Hispanic clients from the barrio (Abad et al. 1974, Rivera Ramos 1984), for directive and authoritative interventions as opposed to the spontaneous, open process associated with conventional psychotherapy. Results obtained in an analogue study by Folensbee and colleagues (1986), however, reveal no clear-cut pattern of preference for directive interventions on the part of Puerto Rican and African-American clients. Perhaps such a preference, if it exists at all, can be attributed to situational factors. A preliminary formulation of this issue posits the wish for direction and guidance as a result of the imperative need for relief in the presence of intense suffering and the absence of a relationship between the helper and the helpee. Under such circumstances, the client's communication is reduced to a cry for help—to be answered by quick, decisive, and direct intervention (Draguns 1996c). Where crisis or posttraumatic intervention is required, premium is placed on goal-oriented intervention—which should be informed as much as possible by culture knowledge and cultural sensitivity.

INDIVIDUALISM-COLLECTIVISM AND OTHER CULTURAL CHARACTERISTICS AND CULTURALLY SENSITIVE INTERVENTIONS: A SPECULATIVE ANALYSIS

Let me end this chapter by going beyond the available findings and propose a bold and speculative scheme of culture and psychotherapy relationships. The point of departure for this undertaking is Hofstede's (1980) well-known analysis of work-related attitudes around the world. Hofstede's analysis was gigantic in scope. In his original study a total of 116,000 respondents in forty countries participated. Later, his research was extended to ten more nations (Hofstede 1983). The objective of this worldwide undertaking was focused on the identification and subsequent comparison of responses to thirty-two questions that pertained to values relevant to the working situation. On the basis of multivariate analysis of this mass of data, four universal cross-culturally useful dimensions were identified and labeled: individualism-collectivism, power-distance, uncertainty-avoidance, and masculinity-femininity. Individualism-collectivism pertains to the degree of a person's integration into supraordinate social institutions: the family, the community, the nation. At the individualistic extreme, persons are socialized and encouraged to strive for realization of their potential and attainment of their goals. The paramount concern of collectivistic cultures is with the lifelong integration of the person within the family and other permanent and self-perpetuating social groupings (Triandis 1990). Power-distance describes the gulf between the leaders of a society and their followers. It refers to the acceptance of status inequality and limitations of interaction between the power-holders and their subordinates. Uncertainty-avoidance refers to the extent to which anxiety is experienced in unstructured, ambiguous, or unforeseen situations. Rules, regulations, and traditions are emphasized in high uncertainty-avoidance settings. Low uncertainty-avoidance fosters spontaneity, improvisation, and innovation; it thrives on unplanned, open-ended change. Finally, in feminine cultures there is extensive overlap in roles between genders; in masculine cultures such overlap is much reduced. Masculine cultures prize performance; feminine cultures value caring. Of these four dimensions, individualism-collectivism has apparently proved to be the most heuristically useful and has the potential of serving as a unifying principle of cross-cultural research and conceptualization in a number of areas beyond the work environment.

Hofstede (1986) has extended all four of these dimensions to the educational setting and to the interaction of students and teachers. More recently (1991) he has explored the relevance of his four factors to a variety of domains of conceptual and practical interest, from self-experience to political behavior. His effort has also served as a model for exploring the relevance of all four of Hofstede's dimensions in accounting for the cultural preferences and expectations in psychotherapeutic and counseling interventions (Draguns 1990a,b). These preferences and expectations refer to the goals of psychotherapy, its modalities and techniques, the styles of therapy interaction, the nature of the therapy relationship, and the social and legal context within which psychotherapeutic services are rendered. At this point all of these characteristics are hypothetical. They were formulated on the basis of Hofstede's (1980) extensive description of the cultural characteristics associated with these four dimensions. These descriptions were "transposed" to the therapy situation and were transformed into therapy characteristics. Some of these characteristics are subtle and others obvious. In principle, all of the posited contrasts are empirically testable, although a mosaic of discrete cross-cultural comparisons will probably be required rather than one encompassing worldwide investigation. On a tentative basis, practicing psychotherapists with a multicultural clientele may venture to explore the relevance of these predictions on a case basis. The specific features of the proposed scheme are presented in Table 2–4.

In reference to individualism-collectivism, it is predicted that the objective of psychotherapy will be focused on the self and on relationships, respectively. The specific contrasts are derived from this principle: insight is promoted in individualistic milieus and harmony is fostered in collectivistic settings. Power-distance is directly pertinent to the therapy relationship. The role of the therapist as an expert and an authority figure is contrasted with the conception of the therapist as a facilitator. In settings where power-distance is high, therapists are sought and admired for their expertise and status, which experience and seniority help to bestow. The social and affective gulf between the therapist and client is expected to be wide. In low power-distance cultures, personal qualities, egalitarianism, and informality are valued in a therapist, and therapist and client roles are subordinated to genuineness of human interaction. Uncertainty avoidance is expected to be reflected in the emphasis on

TABLE 2–4. HOFSTEDE'S DIMENSIONS IN COUNSELING AND PSYCHOTHERAPY

Individualism	*Collectivism*
Insight, self-understanding	Alleviation of suffering
Guilt, alienation, loneliness	Relationship problems, shame
Therapist as father figure	Therapist as nurturant mother
Development of individuality	Social integration
Development of responsibility	Acceptance of controls
Conflict and resolution	Harmonious relationships

High Power Distance	*Low Power Distance*
Directive psychotherapy	Person-centered psychotherapy
Therapist as expert	Therapist as sensitive person
Therapist as change-agent	Therapist as catalyst
Conformity and social effectiveness	Self-discovery and actualization
Differentiation of therapist and client roles	Dedifferentiation of therapist and client roles
Emphasis on professional credentials	Promotion of self improvement
	Patient movements

High Uncertainty Avoidance	*Low Uncertainty Avoidance*
Biological explanations	Psychological explanations
Behavioral techniques	Experiential psychotherapy
Medical orientation	Multiprofessional orientation
Few schools of therapy	Many schools of therapy
Tightly regulated therapy practice	Loosely regulated therapy practice

Masculinity	*Femininity*
Pro-society orientation	Pro-person orientation
Responsibility, conformity, adjustment	Expressiveness, creativity, empathy
Guilt	Anxiety
Enabling	Caring

factual and scientific status of intervention. Multiplicity of therapists' orientations would be decried; the ideal of one optimal mode of psychotherapy would be maintained. Legal and administrative control of psychotherapeutic services and their providers would be rigorous and comprehensive. In general, biological explanations would be preferred over psychological ones and among psychological theories, preference would be accorded to behavioral explanations over psychodynamic or humanistic ones. The effect of masculinity-femininity would be felt in the implicit conceptions of psychotherapy. In masculine cultures, psychotherapy may be conceived of as an avenue leading toward restoration of the person to his or her role as a producer. In feminine cultures, the focus would be on relieving suffering and attaining well-being. More recently, Hofstede (1991) has added a fifth construct, Confucian dynamism, to the four dimensions discovered in his worldwide factorial investigation. The identification and investigation of this new variable have proceeded along a radically different path compared with the research on Hofstede's original four factors. As yet, the implications of confucian dynamism for psychotherapeutic intervention remain to be specified; Leung and Lee (1996) have suggested that striving for moderation in emotional expression and for harmony in interpersonal relations is consistent with Confucian maxims. The current Western emphasis on assertiveness, however, apparently clashes with the acceptance of things as they are and with the imperative of accommodating to external circumstances.) Whether, in fact, these hypothesized relationships are confirmed depends on the realization of ambitious and difficult research projects. Pending the attainment of these objectives, the ideas proposed here may guide and direct both systematic empirical data gathering and naturalistic clinical observation in the therapy context.

CONCLUDING COMMENT

A rapid survey has been taken of the methods and findings of cross-cultural psychopathology and these results have been brought to bear on the challenges faced by psychotherapists with a multicultural clientele. The impact of culture on abnormal behavior is considerable and the potential for increasing cultural sensitivity on the basis of this knowledge is great. At the same time, dangers and risks of insensitivity must be avoided. As empathy is increased, stereotypes are expected to recede. The prospect exists for developing a generic, culturally sensitive psychotherapy and for accommodating to the needs, expectations, and practices of a wide range of cultural groups whose members seek relief from distress and freedom from disability.

REFERENCES

Abad, V., Ramos, J., and Boyce, E. (1974). A model for delivery of mental health services to Spanish-speaking minorities. *American Journal of Orthopsychiatry* 44:584–595.

Abedimpe, V. R. (1981). Overview: white norms and psychiatric diagnosis of black patients. *American Journal of Psychiatry* 138:279–285.

——— (1984). American blacks and psychiatry. *Transcultural Psychiatric Research Review* 21:81–111.

Alexander, A. A., Workneh, F., Klein, M. H., and Miller, M. H. (1976). Psychotherapy and the foreign student. In *Counseling Across Cultures*, ed. P. B. Pedersen, W. J. Lonner, and R. J. Draguns, pp. 82–97. Honolulu: University Press of Hawaii.

Al-Issa, I., ed. (1995). *Handbook of Culture and Mental Illness: An International Perspective*. Madison, CT: International Universities Press.

Bartholomew, R. T. (1994). The social psychology of "epidemic" koro. *International Journal of Social Psychiatry* 40:46–60.

Benedict, R. (1934). Culture and the abnormal. *Journal of General Psychology* 10:59–82.

Berne, E. (1959). Difficulties of comparative psychiatry. *American Journal of Psychiatry* 113:193–200.

Berry, J. W. (1990). Psychology of acculturation. In *Nebraska Symposium on Motivation 1989*, ed. J. J. Berman, pp. 201–234. Lincoln: University of Nebraska Press.

Berry, J. W., Poortinga, Y. H., Segall, M. H., and Dasen, P. R. (1992). *Cross-Cultural Psychology*. New York: Cambridge University Press.

Bleuler, M. (1972). *Die schizophrenen Geistesstörungen im Lichte langjähriger Kranken-und Familiengeschichten*. Stuttgart: Thieme.

Brislin, R. W. (1992). *Understanding Culture's Influence on Behavior*. Fort Worth, TX: Harcourt Brace Jovanovitch.

Brislin, R. W., and Baumgardner, S. R. (1971). Non-random sampling of individuals in cross-cultural research. *Journal of Cross-Cultural Psychology* 2:397–400.

Brislin, R. W., Lonner, W. J., and Thorndike, R. M. (1973). *Cross-Cultural Research Methods*. New York: Wiley.

Cooper, J. E., Kendell, R. E., Gurland, B. J., et al. (1972). *Psychiatric Diagnosis in New York and London*. London: Oxford University Press.

Compton, W. M., Helzer, J. E., Hwu, H. G., et al. (1991). New methods in cross-cultural psychiatry in Taiwan and the United States. *American Journal of Psychiatry* 148:1697–1704.

Desjarlais, R., Eisenberg, C., Good, B., and Kleinman, A. (1995). *World Mental Health: Problems and Priorities in Low Income Countries*. New York: Oxford University Press.

DeHoyos, A., and DeHoyos, G. (1965). Symptomatology differentials between Negro and white schizophrenics. *International Journal of Social Psychiatry* 11:245–255.

Diagnostic and Statistical Manual of Mental Disorders (1994). 4th ed. Washington, DC: American Psychiatric Association.

Diop, M. (1967). La Dépression chez le noir Africain. *Psychopathologie Africaine* 3:183–195.

Dohrenwend, B. P., and Dohrenwend, B. S. (1974). Social and cultural influences upon psychopathology. *Annual Review of Psychology* 25:419–452.

Draguns, J. G. (1973). Comparisons of psychopathology across cultures: issues, findings, directions. *Journal of Cross-Cultural Psychology* 4:9–47.

—— (1980). Disorder of clinical severity. In *Handbook of Cross-Cultural Psychology. Psychopathology, vol. 6,* ed. H. C. Triandis and J. G. Draguns, pp. 99–174. Boston: Allyn & Bacon.

—— (1982). Methodology in cross-cultural psychopathology. In *Culture and Psychopathology,* ed. I. Al-Issa, pp. 33–70. Baltimore: University Park Press.

—— (1990a). Culture and psychopathology: toward specifying the nature of the relationship. In *Cross-Cultural Perspectives: Nebraska Symposium on Motivation 1989,* ed. J. Berman, pp. 235–277. Lincoln: University of Nebraska Press.

—— (1990b). Applications of cross-cultural psychology in the field of mental health. In *Applied Cross-Cultural Psychology,* ed. R. W. Brislin, pp. 302–324. Newbury Park, CA: Sage.

—— (1996a). Abnormal behavior in Chinese societies: clinical, epidemiological, and comparative studies. In *Handbook of Chinese Psychology,* ed. M. H. Bond, pp. 395–411. Hong Kong: Oxford University Press.

—— (1996b). Multicultural and cross-cultural assessment of psychological disorder: dilemmas and decisions. In *Multicultural Assessment in Counseling and Psychology (Buros-Nebraska Symposium on Measurement and Testing Volume 9),* ed. J. Impara and G. R. Sodowsky, pp. 37–84. Lincoln, NE: Buros Institute of Mental Measurements.

—— (1996c). Ethnocultural considerations in the treatment of post-traumatic stress disorder: therapy and service delivery. In *Ethnocultural Aspects of Post-Traumatic Disorder: Issues, Research, and Clinical Applications,* ed. A. J. Marsella, E. T. Friedman, E. T. Gerrity, and R. M. Scurfield, pp. 459–482. Washington, DC: American Psychological Association.

Durkheim, E. (1951). *Suicide,* trans. J. A. Spaulding and G. Simpson. Glencoe, IL: Free Press, 1897.

Edwards, J. W. (1985). Indigenous *koro,* a genital retraction syndrome of insular Southeast Asia: a critical review. In: *The Culture-Bound Syndromes: Folk Illnesses of Psychiatric and Anthropological Interest,* ed. R. C. Simon and C. C. Hughes, pp. 169–192. Dordrecht, Netherlands: Reidel.

Egeland, J. A., Hofstetter, A. M., and Eshleman, S. K. (1983). Amish study III: the impact of cultural factors on diagnosis of bipolar illness. *American Journal of Psychiatry* 140:67–71.

Fish, J. (1996). *Culture and Therapy: An Integrative Approach.* Northvale, NJ: Jason Aronson, Inc.

Folensbee, R. W., Draguns, J. G., and Danish, S. T. (1986). Impact of two types of counselor intervention on black American clients. *Journal of Counseling Psychology* 331:446–453.

Gaines, A. (1982). Cultural definitions, behavior, and the person in American psychiatry. In *Cultural Conceptions of Mental Health and Therapy*, ed. A. J. Marsella and A. White, pp. 167–192. Dordrecht, Netherlands: Reidel.

German, G. A. (1972). Aspects of clinical psychiatry in Sub-Saharan Africa. *British Journal of Psychiatry* 121:461–479.

Good, B. J. (1993). Culture, diagnosis, and comorbidity. *Culture, Diagnosis, and Psychiatry* 16:427–446.

Guthrie, G. M., and Lonner, W. J. (1985). Assessment of personality and psychopathology. In *Field Methods in Cross-Cultural Research*, ed. W. J. Lonner and J. W. Berry, pp. 231–264. Beverly Hills, CA: Sage.

Heath, D. B. (1982). Sociocultural variants in alcoholism. In *Encyclopedic Handbook of Alcoholism*, ed. E. M. Pattison and E. Kaufman, pp. 426–440. New York: Gardner.

Higginbotham, H. N., West, S., and Forsyth, D. (1988). *Psychotherapy and Behavior Change: Social, Cultural and Methodological Perspectives*. New York: Pergamon.

Hofstede, G. (1980). *Culture's Consequences: International Differences in Work Related Values*. Beverly Hills, CA: Sage.

—— (1983). Dimensions of national cultures in fifty cultures and three regions. In *Expiscations in Cross-Cultural Psychology*, ed. J. B. Deregowski, S. Dziurawiec, and R. C. Annis, pp. 335–355. Lisse, Netherlands: Swets & Zeitlinger.

—— (1986). Cultural differences in teaching and learning. *International Journal of Intercultural Relations* 10:301–320.

—— (1991). *Cultures and Organizations: Software of the Mind*. London: McGraw-Hill.

Huber, G., Gross, G., and Schüttler, R. (1980). Langzeitentwicklung schizophrener Erkrankungen. In *Psychiatrische Verlaufsforschung: Methoden und Ergebnisse*, ed. G. W. Schimmelpfennig, pp. 110–143. Berne: Huber.

Jilek, W. G. (1982). Culture—"pathoplastic" or "pathogenic"? A key question of comparative psychiatry. *Curare* 5:57–68.

—— (1988). *Indian Healing: Shamanistic Ceremonialism in the Pacific Northwest*. Vancouver, BC: Hancock House.

Kimura, B. (1965). Vergleichende Untersuchungen über depressive Erkrankungen in Japan und Deutschland. *Fortschritte der Psychiatrie und Neurologie*, 33:202–215.

—— (1967). Phänomenologie des Schulderlebnisses in einer vergleichenden psychiatrischen Sicht. *Aktuelle Fragen der Psychiatrie und Neurologie*, 6:54–65.

Kirmayer, L. (1984). Culture, affect, and somatization: Parts 1 and 2. *Transcultural Psychiatric Research Review* 21:159–188, 237–262.

Kleinman, A. (1977). Depression, somatization, and the new cross-cultural psychiatry. *Social Science and Medicine* 11:3–10.

—— (1980). *Patients and Healers in the Context of Culture*. Berkeley: University of California Press.

—— (1982). Neurasthenia and depression: a study of somatization and culture in China. *Culture, Medicine, and Psychiatry* 6:117–190.

—— (1986). *Social Origins in Distress and Disease*. New Haven, CT: Yale University Press.

———— (1988). *Rethinking Psychiatry: From Cultural Category to Personal Experience.* New York: Free Press.

Landrine, H. (1992). Clinical implications of cultural differences: the referential versus the indexical self. *Clinical Psychology Review* 12:401–415.

Lee, R. P. L. (1981). Sex roles, social status, and psychiatric symptoms in urban Hong Kong. In *Normal and Abnormal Behavior in Chinese Culture*, ed. A. Kleinman and T. Y. Lin, pp. 273–289. Dordrecht, Netherlands: Reidel.

———— (1985). Social stress and coping behavior in Hong Kong. In *Chinese Culture and Mental Health*, ed. W. S. Tseng and D. Y. H. Wu, pp. 193–214. Orlando, FL: Academic Press.

Leung, P. W. L., and Lee, P. W. H. (1996). Psychotherapy with the Chinese. In *The Handbook of Chinese Psychology*, ed. M. H. Bond, pp. 441–456. Hong Kong: Oxford University Press.

Lin, T.-Y., Tseng, W.-S., and Yeh, E.-K. (1995). *Chinese Societies and Mental Health.* Hong Kong: Oxford University Press.

Lo, W. H., and Lo, T. (1977). A ten-year follow-up study of Chinese schizophrenics in Hong Kong. *British Journal of Psychiatry* 131:63–66.

López, S. R. (1989). Patient variable biases in clinical judgment: conceptual overview and methodological considerations. *Psychological Bulletin* 106:184–203.

Markus, H. R., and Kitayama, S. (1991). Culture and the self: Implications for cognition, emotion, and motivation. *Psychological Review* 98:224–253.

Marsella, A. J., Kinzie, D., and Gordon, P. (1973). Ethnic variations in the expression of depression. *Journal of Cross-Cultural Psychology* 4:435–458.

Marsella, A. J., Sartorius, N., Jablensky, A., and Fenton, F. R. (1985). Cross-Cultural Studies of Depressive Disorders. In *Culture and Depression*, ed. A. Kleinman and B. Good, pp. 299–324. Berkeley: University of California Press.

McAndrew, C., and Edgerton, R. B. (1969). *Drunken Comportment: A Social Explanation.* Chicago: Aldine.

Moghaddam, F. M., Taylor, D. M., and Wright, S. C. (1993). *Social Psychology in Cross-Cultural Perspective.* New York: Freeman.

Mukherjee, S., Shukla, S., Woodle, J., et al. (1983). Misdiagnosis of schizophrenia in bipolar patients: a multiethnic comparison. *American Journal of Psychiatry* 140:1571–1574.

Murphy, H. B. M. (1982). *Comparative Psychiatry.* Berlin: Springer-Verlag.

Murphy, J. M. (1976). Psychiatric labeling in cross-cultural perspective. *Science* 191:1019–1028.

Nathan, T. (1994). *L'influence qui guérit.* Paris: Odile Jacob.

Paris, J. (1991). Personality disorders, parasuicide, and culture. *Transcultural Psychiatric Research Review* 28:25–39.

Peltzer, K. (1995). *Psychology and Health in African Cultures: Examples of Ethnopsychotherapeutic Practice.* Frankfurt/Main: IKO-Verlag für interkulturelle Kommunikation.

Pfeiffer, W. M. (1994). *Transkulturelle Psychiatrie* 2nd ed. Stuttgart: Thieme.

Prince, R. H. (1980). Variations in psychotherapeutic experience. In *Handbook of Cross-Cultural Psychology. Psychopathology*, vol. 6, ed. H. C. Triandis and J. G. Draguns, pp. 291–349. Boston: Allyn & Bacon.

Radford, M. H. B. (1989). *Culture, depression, and decision making behaviour: a study with Japanese and Australian clinical and non-clinical populations.* Unpublished doctoral dissertation, Flinders University of South Australia.

Ridley, C. R. (1989). Racism in counseling as an adversive behavioral process. In *Counseling across Cultures*, ed. P. B. Pedersen, J. G. Draguns, W. J. Lonner, and J. E. Trimble, 3rd ed., pp. 55–78. Honolulu: University of Hawaii Press.

Ridley, C. R., and Lingle, D. W. (1996). Cultural empathy in multicultural counseling: a multidimensional process model. In *Counseling across Cultures*, ed. P. B. Pedersen, J. G. Draguns, W. J. Lonner, and J. E. Trimble, 4th ed., pp. 21–46. Thousand Oaks, CA: Sage.

Rin, H., Schooler, C., and Caudill, W. (1973). Symptomatology and hospitalization: culture, social structure and psychopathology in Taiwan and Japan. *Journal of Nervous and Mental Disease* 157:296–312.

Rivera Ramos, A. N. (1984). *Hacía una psicoterapia para el puertoriqueño.* San Juan, PR: Centro para el Estudio & Desarollo de la Personalidad Puertoriqueña.

Roland, A. (1988). *In Search of Self in India and Japan.* Princeton, NJ: Princeton University Press.

Sartorius, N., Jablensky, A., Korten, A., and Ernberg, G. (1986). Early manifestation and first contact evidence of schizophrenia. *Psychological Medicine* 16:909–928.

Segall, M. H., Dasen, P. R., Berry, J. W., and Poortinga, Y. H. (1990). *Human behavior in Global Perspective: An Introduction to Cross-Cultural Psychology.* New York: Pergamon.

Srole, L., Langner, T. S., Michael, S. T., et al. (1962). *Mental health in the Metropolis: The Midtown Study.* Vol. 1. New York: McGraw-Hill.

Sue, S. (1996). Multicultural assessment in counseling and clinical psychology. In *Multicultural Assessment in Counseling and Clinical Psychology*, ed. G. R. Sodowsky and J. C. Impara, pp. 37–84. Lincoln, NE: Buros Institute of Mental Measurements.

Tanaka-Matsumi, J. (1979). Taijin-Kyofusho: diagnostic and cultural issues in Japanese psychiatry. *Culture, Medicine, and Psychiatry* 3:231–245.

———— (1992). *Cultural and social factors in depression.* Unpublished paper.

Torrey, E. F. (1972). *The Mind Game: Witchdoctors and Psychiatrists.* New York: Emerson Hall.

Triandis, H. C. (1990). Cross-cultural studies of individualism and collectivism. In *Nebraska Symposium on Motivation 1989: Cross-Cultural Perspectives*, ed. J. J. Berman, pp. 41–135. Lincoln: University of Nebraska Press.

———— (1994). *Culture and Social Behavior.* New York: McGraw-Hill.

Tseng, W. S., Asai, M., Jieqiu, L., et al. (1990). Multi-cultural study of minor psychiatric disorders in Asia: symptom manifestations. *International Journal of Social Psychiatry* 36:252–264.

Tseng, W. S., Mo, K. M., Hsu, J., et al. (1988). A sociocultural study of koro epidemics in Guangdong, China. *American Journal of Psychiatry* 145:1538–1543.

Tseng, W. S., Mo, K. W., Li, L. S., et al. (1992). Koro epidemics in Guangdong, China: a questionnaire survey. *Journal of Nervous and Mental Disease* 180:117–123.

Ware, N. C., and Kleinman, A. (1992). Culture and somatic experience: the social course of illness in neurasthenia and chronic fatigue syndrome. *Psychosomatic Medicine* 54:546–560.

Waxler, N. E. (1974). Culture and mental illness: a social labeling perspective. *Journal of Nervous and Mental Disease* 159:379–395.

Wolff, P. H. (1972). Ethnic differences in alcohol sensitivity. *Science* 175:149–150.

World Health Organization (1973). *Report of the International Pilot Study of Schizophrenia*. Geneva: World Health Organization.

——— (1979). *Schizophrenia: An International Follow-up Study*. New York: Wiley.

——— (1983). *Depressive Disorders in Different Cultures: Report on the WHO Collaborative Study on Standardized Assessment of Depressive Disorders*. Geneva: World Health Organization.

Yap, P. M. (1965). Phenomenology of affective disorders in Chinese and other cultures. In *Transcultural Psychiatry*, ed. A. De Reuck and R. Porter, pp. 84–114. Boston: Little, Brown.

——— (1974). *Comparative Psychiatry: A Theoretical Framework*. Toronto: University of Toronto Press.

Race, Ethnicity, and Mental Illness

JEFFREY S. NEVID AND RACHEL GOODMAN

Race is arguably the most divisive issue facing American society today. American history is replete with oppression and persecution of racial minorities, from the institution of slavery to attempts to eradicate native cultures. Though much progress has been made toward racial equality in the latter half of the twentieth century, we remain a society deeply divided by race and culture. Some observers of the American scene perceive our society as a balkanized assemblage of disparate ethnicities that identify more strongly with their own ethnic identities than with a common identity as Americans. The hyphenization of ethnic identities in the United States (African-American, Hispanic-American, Asian-American, Euro-American, etc.) may serve only to reinforce the concept that American identities are inherently divided.

The word *ethnicity* is derived from the Greek word *ethnikos*, meaning people. Ethnicity is associated with race, but not defined by it. Hispanics, for example, represent different racial groups who share a common ethnicity reflecting their descent from Spanish-speaking peoples of Latin America (Javier 1997). Ethnic groupings can in turn be subdivided into ethnic subgroups and subcultures. Each Spanish-speaking nation in Latin America, for example, has its own distinctive cultural traditions as well as subcultures. Identification with countries or peoples of origin may be an even stronger source of ethnic identity than the larger ethnic designations. People of Hispanic background in the United States often identify themselves first as Chicanos, Puerto Ricans, or Dominicans, rather than as Hispanics or Latinos.

The ethnic composition of the United States is changing in the direction of increasing representation of ethnic minorities. In fact, the term *minority* has become something of a misnomer, as whites of European background are now a minority in many American communities and cities. If present trends continue, (non-Hispanic) whites will become a minority in our most populous state, California, by about the year 2000. For the nation overall, non-whites are expected to become the majority sometime around the middle of the twenty-first century.

African Americans currently represent the largest nonwhite population group, constituting about 12 percent of the population, followed by Hispanic-Americans, at nearly 10 percent. Hispanic Americans are the fastest growing ethnic group in the U.S., with their numbers rising about 40 percent during the 1980s as a result of increased immigration and a burgeoning birth rate. Hispanics are expected to overtake African Americans as the nation's largest ethnic minority group during the early part of the next century. The three largest Hispanic subgroups, according to the 1990 census, were Mexican Americans (10+ million), Puerto Ricans (2.5 million), and Cuban Americans (1+ million) (De La Cancela and Guzman 1991, Gonzalez 1992). These figures, based on census bureau data, are believed to underestimate the population of Americans of Hispanic origin to an unknown extent due to a large number of undocumented immigrants; in addition, the population of Puerto Rico is not usually counted in computing the numbers of Hispanic Americans (Rogler et al. 1991). Asian Americans, constituting about 3 percent of the population at present, are also a fast-growing ethnic group. Like other white and nonwhite groups, Asian Americans represent a wide background of cultures and ancestries, originating from such diverse areas as China, Japan, Korea, Indochina, Thailand, the Philippines, India, and Pakistan.

Given the highly charged issue of race in our culture, it is worth considering the benefits we might derive from an examination of relationships between ethnicity and mental illness. Perhaps the most important potential benefit is that knowledge gained about differences in prevalences of specific types of mental disorders in relation to ethnicity could be used to inform policy decisions regarding the allocation of limited mental health resources. Thus intervention and prevention programs could be targeted toward groups showing the greatest need. Moreover, findings of differential prevalences across racial/ethnic groups could lead to the discovery of specific vulnerability factors that might explain causal pathways for these disorders in particular population groups and lead to preventive efforts that focus on reducing these risk factors. Knowledge could also prove useful in debunking common ethnic stereotypes that link minority group status with certain diagnostic statuses, such as antisocial personality disorder, schizophrenia, and alcohol and drug use disorders.

FACTORS CONFOUNDING THE RELATIONSHIP BETWEEN ETHNICITY AND MENTAL ILLNESS

Any attempt to account for relationships between ethnicity and mental illness must take into account factors that tend to covary with ethnic group status, such as socioeconomic level and language differences. Moreover, investigators should attempt to account for subgroup differences in the relative risk of particular disorders and for such factors as cultural expectations and acculturation. For example, evidence discussed later shows differences in depression among Hispanic subgroups in relation to acculturation and country of origin.

Socioeconomic Status and Mental Illness

Relationships between socioeconomic status and mental illness are well established, dating back at least as far as the classic New Haven study by Hollingshead and Redlich (1958) which showed an inverse relationship between prevalences of schizophrenia and socioeconomic class. This inverse relationship between schizophrenia and low socioeconomic status (SES) has been repeatedly demonstrated in other studies, including the two largest epidemiologic surveys, the Epidemiologic Catchment Area (ECA) survey and the National Comorbidity Survey (NCS). In the ECA study, for example, schizophrenia was found to be five times more common among people at the lowest rung of the socioeconomic ladder than at the highest (Keith et al. 1991).

Two major theories have been advanced to account for the inverse relationship between SES and mental illness: the social causation model and the social selection (drift) model. According to the social selection model, people with schizophrenia tend to drift downward in social status, eventually winding up in impoverished statuses because of a lack of social and cognitive abilities needed to function effectively at higher levels. Consistent with the prevailing diathesis-stress model, the social causation model posits that stress associated with poverty increases the potential for schizophrenia in genetically vulnerable people, which might account for the greater frequency of the disorder among people in the lower socioeconomic statuses. By this reasoning, the development of schizophrenia in some genetically predisposed individuals might possibly be averted if environmental stressors remained relatively benign. Though there is supportive evidence for both theoretical models, it is conceivable that both views are at least partially correct. People who develop schizophrenia may drift downward occupationally in relation to their parents and peers, while others may have been reared in families suffering from high levels of economic stress.

Socioeconomic factors have also been implicated in explaining the higher observed rate of depression in the African nation of Lesotho in relation to the United States. Researchers suspect that depression may be a response to the harsh living conditions in this impoverished African country, ranked among the poorest nations in the world. Supporting this belief is the finding of a linear relationship between the severity of depression and the frequency and intensity of adverse life experiences (Hollifield et al. 1990).

Our purpose here is not to examine underlying factors accounting for the relationship between socioeconomic status and mental health, but rather to point out the potential confounding role of SES in cases in which rates of mental illness are found to vary in relation to ethnicity. Since ethnic minorities in our society tend to be overrepresented among the lower socioeconomic classes, findings of higher rates of psychiatric disorders among ethnic minorities may be a function of socioeconomic status rather than ethnicity. Researchers increasingly have recognized the need to take socioeconomic status into account in their statistical analyses, usually by identifying control variables like education and income level that are entered along with race/ethnicity within a multivariate analysis.

Cultural Factors in Diagnosis and Assessment

In addition to SES, an examination of relationships between ethnicity and mental illness must also take into account cultural factors, as ethnicity and culture are intertwined. Behavior considered normal in one culture (or by one people) may be deemed abnormal in another. The latest edition of the *DSM*, the *DSM-IV* (1994), places greater emphasis than its predecessors on taking cultural factors into account in reaching a diagnostic impression. According to the *DSM*, a diagnosis of a mental disorder can be made only when the behavior in question falls outside the range of culturally expectable and sanctioned responses to particular events, even when the behavior appears odd in the light of the examiner's own cultural standards. For example, the *DSM-IV* recognizes that fears of magic or spirits are common among members of some cultures and should not be taken as signs of phobic disorder unless they are excessive in light of the cultural context in which they occur and are associated with significant emotional distress or impaired functioning (*DSM-IV* 1994). The *DSM* also warns clinicians not to label as schizotypal certain behavior patterns reflecting culturally determined beliefs or religious rituals, such as beliefs in voodoo and other magical beliefs (*DSM-IV* 1994).

Let us consider hallucinations as another example. Though hallucinations are taken as a hallmark feature of the Western concept of psychosis, cross-cultural evidence shows that hallucinations are commonly experienced—indeed socially valued—within some developing countries and are not in themselves signs of mental illness (Bentall 1990). For example, hallucinations are known to be a common experience in some cultural groups, such as among Australian aborigines (Spencer 1983). Aborigines also hold certain beliefs which in Western society might be viewed as delusional, such as beliefs that they can communicate with the spirits of their ancestors and that dreams are shared among people, especially close relatives. Failure to account for these cultural variations can lead to misdiagnosis and result in spurious differences in diagnostic rates for a given disorder across ethnicities. Some diagnoses may also have little or no ecological validity for some cultural groups. However, as we shall see, most Western diagnostic concepts hold up rather well when applied in other cultures.

Clinicians also need to weigh sociopolitical and sociocultural factors carefully in making diagnostic judgments. Immigrants, ethnic minority group members, political refugees, and people from foreign cultures may be guarded or defensive in their presentation upon interview. Their interview behavior may reflect unfamiliarity with the language, customs, or rules and regulations of the majority culture, or represent an appropriate level of cultural mistrust arising from a history of neglect or oppression of the majority culture against the individual's cultural or ethnic group. In either case, the behavior should not be taken as evidence of a disturbance in personality, such as might be found in paranoid personality disorder (*DSM-IV* 1994).

Mental disorders may also be expressed differently in different cultures. Anxiety disorders and depression, for example, may involve more somatic features in some societies, especially in Eastern cultures (Bebbington 1993). Though in Western cultures anxiety may be experienced in terms of worrisome concerns about paying the mortgage or losing a job, among some non-Western peoples, it may take the form of concerns about witchcraft or fears of sorcery or beliefs that one is in mortal danger from evil spirits (Kleinman

1987, Spencer 1983). In Eastern cultures depression is often manifested by complaints about such physical symptoms as headaches, fatigue, or weakness, rather than by the feelings of guilt and sadness common in Western cultures (*DSM-IV* 1994).

Cultural differences in the expression of psychological disturbance does not imply that the diagnostic categories used in Western countries to classify abnormal patterns of behavior cannot be applied in other cultures. However, recognizing that behavior must be interpreted within a sociocultural context places a burden on mental health professionals to show that the diagnostic concepts and instruments used to arrive at diagnostic formulations are valid when "taken on the road" (Bebbington 1993, Kleinman 1987). The reverse also bears mentioning. The concept of "soul loss" that characterizes states of psychological distress in some non-Western societies (Shweder 1985) may have no diagnostic equivalent in the *DSM* system. It may or may not have any relevance to the experiences of middle-class, contemporary Americans. The argument here is that when diagnostic concepts are not derived from indigenous experiences, they must be validated locally to have any value in judging whether behavior deviates from expectable norms.

There is a growing body of evidence pointing to the cross-cultural relevance of at least some Western concepts of mental illness. Multinational studies conducted by the World Health Organization (WHO) in the 1960s and 1970s showed striking similarities in the behavioral patterns characterized as schizophrenia by Western psychiatry in such far-flung countries as Colombia, India, China, Denmark, Nigeria, and the former Soviet Union, among others (Jablensky et al. 1992). Prevalences of schizophrenia as well as the general features associated with the disorder were quite similar among the countries studied. Investigators report that for both developing and developed countries the negative features of schizophrenia, characterized by deficit behaviors such as neglect of usual activities and social withdrawal, were the earliest occurring signs of schizophrenia rather than the more flagrant positive features such as hallucinations and delusions.

Paranoid schizophrenia was the most frequently encountered subtype in the WHO study population. However, some differences among sites were reported, especially between developed and developing countries. Visual hallucinations were reported more frequently in developing countries while affective symptoms, especially depression, occurred more frequently in developed countries. Differences in symptom expression, though, were insignificant in light of the similarities found with respect to other presenting symptoms.

In addition, catatonic schizophrenia was more prevalent in developing countries, accounting for 10 percent of diagnosed cases, but was found in very few of the developed countries. In contrast, the hebephrenic type was found in 13 percent of patients in developed countries as compared to only 4 percent of patients in developing countries. The major cross-cultural differences, however, involved patterns of onset, with a tendency for acute onset to predominate in developing countries while a more gradual or insidious onset was more typical in developed countries. Moreover, there were tendencies for a more favorable course and outcome for individuals with schizophrenia living in developing countries.

In another cross-cultural study, *DSM* diagnosable mood and anxiety disorders were common among medical patients in some fourteen countries in the research sample, including Germany, the Netherlands, India, Turkey, Nigeria, Japan, China, and Brazil, although prevalence rates did vary across countries (Ormel et al. 1994).

Cultural Labeling of Psychiatric Disorders

Different societies may come to different understandings of disturbed behavior. Even in the same society, differences may emerge across periods of history in the models and concepts used to explain aberrant behavior. In contemporary Western society, the dominant explanations involve medical, psychological, and sociocultural explanations (Nevid et al. 1997). In European societies of the Middle Ages, psychological disturbance was widely attributed to supernatural causes, such as states of possession. Supernatural explanation is found even today among many preliterate societies and in some subcultures in developed or developing countries (Lefley 1990).

Related to cultural conceptions of psychological disturbance are the labels applied by particular cultures to people exhibiting disturbed behavior. The role of cultural labeling of abnormal behavior has been largely overlooked in the empirical literature. In one of few published examples, Jenkins and Karno (1992, Jenkins 1988) focused on the use of the label *nervios* ("nerves") among Mexican-Americans, a cultural designation attached to a wide range of disturbed behaviors ranging from anxiety to depression and even schizophrenia. *Nervios* carries less stigma and a more hopeful expectation than the label of schizophrenia and may have the effect of *destigmatizing* people with schizophrenia (Jenkins and Karno 1992):

> Since severe cases of *nervios* are not considered blameworthy or under an individual's control, the person who suffers its effects is deserving of sympathy, support, and special treatment. Moreover, severe cases of *nervios* are potentially curable. It is interesting to note that Mexican-descent relatives

do not adopt another possible cultural label for craziness, *loco*. As a *loco*, the individual would be much more severely stigmatized and considered to be out of control with little chance for recovery. . . .

Defining the problem as *nervios*, a common condition that in its milder forms afflicts nearly everyone, provides them a way of identifying with and minimizing the problem by claiming that the ill relative is "just like me, only more so." [pp. 17–18]

A person with schizophrenia may be treated differently within the family if family members attribute the person's behavior to a temporary or curable condition over which the person has some control than if they attribute it to a permanent, uncontrollable brain abnormality. The degree to which family members perceive people with schizophrenia as having some degree of control over their behavior may affect how they respond to schizophrenic family members, which in turn may hold prognostic significance in determining the risk of relapse. There is a good deal of evidence showing that negative family interactions, especially expressed emotion, increase the risk of recurrent episodes in family members with schizophrenia (Bellack and Mueser 1993, Miklowitz 1994). Perhaps a more favorable prognosis may be found in families that adopt a balanced view of their affected relative's condition, believing on the one hand that people with schizophrenia can maintain some degree of control over their behavior, while holding that some of their odd or disruptive behavior stems from underlying pathology (Weisman et al. 1993). It remains an open question whether the ways in which family members conceptualize schizophrenia and label people with the disorder are associated with differential outcomes.

MAJOR EPIDEMIOLOGICAL SURVEYS

The major sources of evidence relating ethnicity and mental health come from the results of two large-scale epidemiological surveys, the Epidemiologic Catchment Area (ECA) survey and the National Comorbidity Survey (NCS). Both used trained interviewers who administered structured psychiatric interviews to ascertain rates of psychiatric diagnoses in community samples. Rates of diagnosis were then analyzed in relation to such factors as ethnicity and gender.

The ECA survey was based on interviews of nearly 20,000 residents in five United States communities (New Haven, CT; Baltimore, MD; St. Louis, MO; Durham, NC; and Los Angeles, CA) (Robins and Regier 1991). The

ECA represents the largest community survey based on the use of standard-ized psychiatric interviewing techniques conducted to date. It represents a major advance over earlier efforts to examine relationships between ethnicity and mental health because of its size, its geographical diversity, its use of structured interview methods, and, perhaps most important, its control of socioeconomic level and other potentially confounding factors such as age, gender, and marital status. However, neither the sites selected for data collec-tion nor the respondents polled within these sites were randomly selected, so the extent to which data can be generalized to the United States population at large, or even to the local communities in which the respondents were sam-pled, remains unknown. Moreover, samples of African-Americans in the ECA study contained an overrepresentation of poor, elderly, and female respondents. Differences between ethnicities may relate to these sampling characteristics rather than to race or ethnicity.

The NCS, by contrast, was based on a representative national sample of more than 8,000 people from various parts of the mainland United States, providing the most precise estimates we have available of the prevalences of particular psychiatric disorders extant in the general population (Kessler 1994, Kessler et al. 1993, 1994). It remains the most representative psychiatric epi-demiological survey of the U.S. population yet conducted. Like the ECA, the NCS also examined ethnic differences in psychiatric diagnoses while control-ling for SES. However, direct comparisons between the two surveys are lim-ited not only by differences in sampling methodology, but also in how specific diagnostic questions were phrased.

An overview of the NCS results shows that nearly half (48 percent) of the people interviewed had experienced diagnosable psychological disorders at some point in their lives. Nearly a third (30 percent) had diagnosed disor-ders during the year preceding the interview and more than half of the peo-ple who had ever experienced a psychological disorder had two or more disorders. The prevalences of psychiatric disorders varied in relation to factors such as age, gender, region, social class, and ethnicity. People in the 25- to 32-year-old age range were at the greatest risk of psychiatric disorders, with rel-ative risk declining with advancing age. Women were more prone to depression and anxiety disorders than men, while men were more likely to have experienced alcohol and substance abuse disorders. Past year and lifetime prevalences of psychiatric disorders were no greater among urban residents than among rural residents, but were more common among people from lower socioeconomic levels. People from the South had the lowest prevalences of psychiatric disorders, while Easterners were most likely to have experienced three or more disorders.

Racial/Ethnic Differences in Prevalences of Mental Disorders

Though some ethnic differences in the NCS survey did emerge—Hispanic Americans, for example, were more likely than (non-Hispanic) white Americans to have a current mood disorder—perhaps most revealing was what was not found. The NCS failed to reveal any disorder that occurred significantly more frequently among African Americans than (non-Hispanic) white Americans when controlling for SES as measured by income level and education (Kessler et al. 1994). This evidence flies in the face of the common perception that African Americans have higher rates of psychiatric disturbance, especially more severe forms of psychiatric disturbance such as schizophrenia. Moreover, NCS researchers reported significantly lower prevalences of affective disorders and substance use disorders among African Americans as compared to whites.

We next focus on racial/ethnic differences for some major categories of psychiatric disturbance, based on the ECA and NCS findings as well as other sources. We should note, however, that despite attempts to include ethnic minority participation in large-scale surveys such as the ECA and NCS, some ethnic groups remain underrepresented in the research literature. We still lack any national survey of the prevalence of psychological disorders among Asian Americans and Native Americans. Recent reviews of the available evidence indicate that prevalences of mental disorders are not significantly lower among Asian Americans than other ethnic groups, which contrasts with the popular stereotype that Asian Americans are relatively free of mental health problems (Sue et al. 1994, Zane and Sue 1991).

Schizophrenia

The results of the two large-scale studies, the NCS and ECA, showed African Americans were no more likely than (non-Hispanic) whites to have developed nonaffective psychoses[1] (NCS) and schizophrenia (ECA) (Keith et al. 1991, Kessler et al. 1994). The ECA report did find a low rate of schizophrenia among Hispanics in particular, but the NCS failed to find any disorder in which Hispanics presented with a significantly lower prevalence rate than (non-Hispanic) whites.

---

1. Nonaffective psychosis is a category that includes schizophrenia, schizophreniform disorder, schizoaffective disorder, delusional disorder, and atypical psychosis.

Affective Disorders

Increasing evidence points to differences in prevalences of diagnosable depression across racial and ethnic groups in the United States. The ECA survey found blacks to be less likely to present with a history of major depression than either (non-Hispanic) whites or Hispanics (Weissman et al. 1991). Similarly, the NCS survey showed blacks to have lower estimated lifetime prevalences of affective disorders overall and major depression in particular than either (non-Hispanic) whites or Hispanics, at least for most age groups (Blazer et al. 1994, Kessler et al. 1994). Black males were by far the least likely racial or ethnic group to have experienced a major depressive disorder. Consistent with earlier findings of a gender gap in depression, women interviewed in the NCS study were about twice as likely to present with major depression as men, with greater gender differences occurring among blacks and Hispanics than whites. As compared to blacks, Hispanics in the NCS were twice as likely to have experienced a depressive disorder during their lifetimes (Blazer et al. 1994).

Differences between Hispanics and (non-Hispanic) whites remain somewhat clouded. Despite the NCS findings of similar lifetime prevalences of major depressive episodes between the two groups, higher prevalences of current mood disorders were found among Hispanics. This is inconsistent, however, with ECA findings of similar prevalences among racial/ethnic groups in rates of current disorders. In other research, investigators reported no differences in rates of major depression between a sample of Mexican Americans and (non-Hispanic) whites (Golding and Lipton 1990).

Differences in diagnostic prevalences between blacks and (non-Hispanic) whites are not mirrored in reports of depressive complaints. Blacks in the ECA study reported more depressive complaints than did whites, even though they were less likely to have experienced a major depressive disorder. Investigators suspect the greater life stress resulting from economic hardship and racism that blacks are likely to experience may take its toll on their emotional well-being (Somervell et al. 1989). However, depression may be less likely to progress to the level of severity associated with a diagnosable disorder than is the case with (non-Hispanic) whites.

Cross-cultural studies show that affective disorders occur in many cultures and tend to take a similar form. One recent study found a high degree of homogeneity in the categories of affective disorders found among samples of mostly native-born Canadians as compared to Southeast Asian refugees (Beiser et al. 1994). Though culture-specific expressions of depression may occur, such evidence argues against the stereotype that Asians do not express emotional distress in psychological terms (Beiser et al. 1994).

Depression also appears to be on the rise in many cultures. The Cross-National Collaborative Group study (1992) used similar methods and applied similar criteria for diagnosing depression in nine countries in North America (United States and Canada), the Caribbean basin (Puerto Rico), western Europe (Italy, France, Germany), the Middle East (Lebanon), and Asia and the Pacific Rim (Taiwan and New Zealand). First a random sample of adult household members from designated population areas in each country was obtained. Structured psychiatric interviews were then conducted based on the Diagnostic Interview Schedule (DIS) to arrive at *DSM-III* diagnoses. On the basis of an age-cohort analysis, investigators showed that depression had increased among successive generations in all of the sampled countries, although the rate of increase varied from country to country. For some countries, younger cohorts born after 1955 were about three times more likely to have experienced major depression than were older cohorts at the same age (Goleman 1992). The greatest increases were found in Florence, Italy; the smallest in Christchurch, New Zealand.

The factor or factors accounting for increased rates of depression worldwide remain unclear. However, suspicions have focused on social and environmental changes, such as increased urbanization and fragmentation of families, greater exposure to wars and violent crime, and possible influences of environmental toxins or infectious agents (Cross-National Collaborative Group 1992). Consider Beirut, Lebanon, as an example. In Beirut, rates of depression fell sharply during the period 1960 to 1970, a time of relative prosperity and stability, but increased sharply during the 1970s, which was a period of internecine warfare and massive social upheaval.

Rates of depression in the U.S. have also been on the rise, with the sharpest rise occurring between the baby-boomer generation of people born after the end of World War II and the preceding generation (Klerman and Weissman 1989). The increased susceptibility of "boomers" to depression may be a function of such factors as unfulfilled economic expectations, family relocations dissolving social support networks, and pressures resulting from changing gender role expectations.

Substance Abuse Disorders

There is a relatively large body of research examining ethnic differences in alcohol and drug use and abuse. Despite extensive media attention to problems of drug use in minority communities, evidence from the NCS study shows that (non-Hispanic) whites are significantly more likely to have used drugs at some point in their lives than nonwhites (Warner et al. 1995). Moreover, evidence from the NCS (Anthony et al. 1994) and other sources (e.g., Grant et al. 1994) show African Americans to be less likely than (non-Hispanic) white Americans to have alcohol or drug abuse/dependence disorders. Nonetheless, blacks are nearly twice as likely as (non-Hispanic) white Americans to develop alcohol-related cirrhosis of the liver and more likely to incur alcohol-related coronary heart disease and oral and throat cancers (Rogan 1986). These differences in alcohol-related morbidity may reflect the fact that blacks tend to have poorer access to medical services and may present at later stages of disease progression resulting from alcohol abuse than whites. Blacks may also be subject to more life stress resulting from prolonged unemployment and financial hardship, which may compound damage caused by heavy alcohol consumption.

Rates of alcohol consumption and alcohol abuse and related physical problems among Hispanic-American men tend to parallel those among (non-Hispanic) white men (Caetano 1987, Kessler et al. 1994). Hispanic-American women, however, are much less likely than their (non-Hispanic) white counterparts to use alcohol and to develop alcohol use disorders. This difference may be accounted for by traditional cultural expectations that place more severe restrictions on alcohol use by Hispanic women, especially patterns of heavy consumption. However, greater similarity in alcohol use and abuse patterns to those of Euro-American women appear to be developing among more acculturated Hispanic women.

Neither the ECA nor NCS studies examined alcohol or drug use patterns among Native Americans. However, other evidence shows Native Americans to be at greater risk of alcohol and drug abuse problems than (non-Hispanic) white Americans (e.g. Westermeyer and Neider 1994). Native Americans represent the American ethnic group most severely affected by alcohol-related physical problems. Their death rate from alcohol-related cirrhosis of the liver is more than four times the national average (Beauvais and LaBoueff 1985). Native Americans are also at the highest risk of alcohol-related diabetes, fetal abnormalities, and automobile and other accident fatalities (Moncher et al. 1990). Native American women are thirty-seven times more likely to die from alcohol-related cirrhosis of the liver than (non-Hispanic) white women. (Moss et al. 1985). Native American women are also more than three times as likely to give birth to children with fetal alcohol syndrome.

Alcohol use disorders among Native Americans reflect a broader range of mental health problems, including other substance abuse problems, depression, and suicide. Kahn (1982), among other writers, attributes the greater incidence of psychopathology among Native Americans to the disruption of their traditional cultures brought about by Euro-American society's attempt to eradicate tribal language and cultural traditions, together with a failure to integrate native peoples within the mainstream society. The resulting cultural disruption has led to social disorganization and a pervasive sense of hopelessness in Native American communities that can set the stage for alcoholism, drug abuse, and depression, and contribute to problems reflecting social decay, including child abuse and neglect, and criminal behavior. Child abuse and neglect, in turn, may give rise to feelings of hopelessness and depression among adolescents, which in turn may lead youths to turn to alcohol and other drugs to mollify negative feelings (Berlin 1987). Other factors, especially poverty, are additional stressors that can exacerbate problems of alcohol and drug abuse.

Mental health problems of Native Americans are not confined to the American mainland. Like other Native American groups, native Hawaiians are economically disadvantaged as compared to Euro-Americans and suffer from a disproportionate share of physical and mental illness. The life expectancy of native Hawaiians is five to ten years lower than that of other Hawaiian residents (Hammond 1988) and the death rate among native Hawaiians is one third higher than that of the general U.S. population, largely because of increased rates of life-threatening diseases such as cancer and heart disease (Mokuau 1990). Native Hawaiians also have higher than average rates of mental health problems including suicide (among males), alcoholism and drug abuse, and antisocial disorders (Mokuau 1990). Depression and associated feelings of despair, hopelessness and self-doubt, are also more commonly reported among native Hawaiians than their white counterparts.

The psychological distress experienced by many native Hawaiians may partly reflect the alienation and disenfranchisement from the land and a way of life that resulted from European colonization. Native peoples themselves often attribute their mental health and drug and alcohol problems to the collapse of their traditional cultures resulting from colonization by European cultures (Timpson et al. 1988). Depression may be the emotional consequence of losing the traditional relationship that native peoples had with the land that was based on a concept of maintaining a state of harmony with nature (Timpson et al. 1988). Consider, for example, how a native Canadian elder in northwestern Ontario explains depression in his people (Timpson et al. 1988):

> Before the White Man came into our world we had our own way of worshiping the Creator. We had our own church and rituals. When hunting was good, people would gather together to give gratitude. This gave us close contact with the Creator. There were many different rituals depending on

the tribe. People would dance in the hills and play drums to give recognition to the Great Spirit. It was like talking to the Creator and living daily with its spirit. Now people have lost this. They can't use these methods and have lost conscious contact with this high power. The more distant we are from the Creator the more complex things are because we have no sense of direction. We don't recognize where life is from. [p. 6]

Alcohol and drug use disorders are less common among Asian Americans than other ethnic groups (e.g., Warner et al. 1995). Alcohol use is also lower among Asian Americans than the general population, perhaps because of greater cultural constraints on excessive drinking, but perhaps too because of a greater flushing response to alcohol consumption. Supporting this argument is evidence that Asians from groups that tend to show a more marked flushing response (Koreans, Taiwanese, Japanese Americans, and Hawaiian Asians) consume less alcohol on the average than other Asian groups who typically show less flushing (Nakawatase et al. 1993, Park et al. 1984).

Anxiety Disorders

Evidence relating ethnicity to anxiety disorders remains mixed. The NCS failed to confirm the earlier ECA finding (Robins et al. 1984) of a greater prevalence of anxiety disorders overall among blacks than (non-Hispanic) whites (Eaton et al. 1994). The NCS also failed to confirm the ECA findings that African Americans were more likely to have developed simple phobias and agoraphobia (Eaton et al. 1991, Kessler et al. 1994). The NCS failed to find any differences in anxiety disorders between blacks and whites. Neither the NCS nor the ECA found significant differences in panic disorder between African Americans and (non-Hispanic) white Americans. Other researchers report highly similar lifetime prevalences of panic disorder for African Americans (1.2 percent) and (non-Hispanic) whites (1.4 percent) as well as nonsignificant differences in age of onset and years of duration of panic disorder (Horwath et al. 1993).

Other differences in the results of the two major surveys, the ECA and NCS, emerged in the analysis of panic disorder among Hispanic Americans, with the ECA showing lower lifetime prevalences among Hispanics than (non-Hispanic) white Americans, while the NCS reported no significant differences between these groups (Eaton et al. 1991, Kessler et al. 1994).

Though race was not significantly associated with prevalences of posttraumatic stress disorder (PTSD) in the NCS data, there was a trend for African Americans and "other" (mainly Asian) minorities to be more likely to develop PTSD in response to a trauma than Hispanics or (non-Hispanic) whites (Kessler et al. 1995). Moreover, prevalence rates for obsessive-compulsive disorder and generalized anxiety disorder appear similar between African Americans and (non-Hispanic) white Americans (Friedman et al. 1993).

Overall, it appears that similarities in the rates of anxiety disorders overall and in specific disorders in particular among American racial/ethnic groups outweigh the differences. Nor are anxiety disorders unique to Western cultures. Panic disorder is known to occur in many cultures, perhaps even universally (Amering and Katschnig 1990). A cross-national study showed remarkably consistent rates of obsessive-compulsive disorder across seven national sites, with rates ranging from 1.1 percent in Korea and New Zealand to 1.8 percent in Puerto Rico. The one exception was Taiwan (0.4 percent), which showed low rates of psychiatric disorders overall (Weissman et al. 1994). Other researchers find higher rates of panic disorder and generalized anxiety disorder in Lesotho, Africa, than in the United States (Hollifield et al. 1990).

The *DSM* construct of posttraumatic stress disorder first emerged to account for the prolonged effects of exposure to battlefield trauma, or what was formerly labeled "battlefield neuroses." It has since been extended to apply to people suffering traumatic stress reactions to other types of stressors, including rape and other forms of violence. Though not much is known about the prevalence of PTSD in other cultures, a recent study of Cambodian Khmer refugees indicates that it may be very common indeed among people subjected to wartime barbarities. This study of civilian survivors of the 1975–1979 Pol Pot War in Cambodia showed incidences of PTSD of about 50 percent in the mothers, 33 percent in the fathers, and 20 percent in adolescent children (Sack et al. 1994).

Cultural factors may help to account for the particular ways in which people manage and cope with traumatic stressors, as well as for their vulnerability to traumatic stress reactions and the specific form these disorders may take (de Silva 1993). Even so, evidence exists of cross-cultural similarities in symptom expression of PTSD between Cambodian war refugees and U.S. trauma survivors (Carlson and Rosser-Hogan 1994).

Eating Disorders

While there have been few epidemiological studies of eating disorders, the available evidence supports the commonly held view that eating disorders are relatively infrequent, even rare, in non-Western cultures and among ethnic minority group members in Western cultures, including U.S. culture, which place a great cultural emphasis on slimness and dieting (Chun et al. 1992, Davis and Yager 1992, Gibbs 1991, Leon et al. 1995, Lucero et al. 1992, Mumford 1993, Stice 1994). It is well to point out some exceptions, however, as noted by Mumford (1993): a sharply rising incidence of anorexia nervosa in Japan and a greater than expected rate of eating disorders among South Asian schoolgirls in Bradford, England. Even in Western countries, eating disorders are generally more prevalent in the United States than in less weight-obsessed countries such as Greece or Spain (Stice 1994). Though eating disorders are less common among African-American adolescents in the United States than their white peers, recent evidence suggests that disordered eating behaviors that may give rise to eating disorders occur more often among young African-American women identifying more strongly with the dominant white culture (Abrams et al. 1993). Anorexia nervosa among African Americans may also be rising, perhaps because of increasing assimilation within the majority culture (Pate et al. 1992). There is also evidence that disturbed eating behaviors among Native American adolescents may be more common than is generally believed (Smith and Krejci 1991). With the increasing influence and internationalization of Western culture spread through popular media, it would not be surprising to find rising prevalences of eating disorders among Third World nations.

Personality Disorders

Little is known about ethnic differences in personality disorders. The ECA study reported no ethnic differences in the rates of antisocial personality disorder (Robins et al. 1991). A prison-based study comparing African Americans and (non-Hispanic) white Americans with antisocial personality disorder showed that the measures used to classify the disorder were generalizable across groups (Kosson et al. 1990). The disorder was also more common among inmates from lower SES levels in both groups. However, the degree to which psychiatric labeling of inmates of lower socioeconomic status as antisocial personalities reflects a cultural stereotype remains unclear, even though the *DSM-IV* (1994) specifically warns clinicians not to apply the diagnosis to people living in impoverished conditions who may become involved in antisocial behavior as a type of defense strategy in order to survive.

Others have argued that conceptualizations of personality disorders may fail to account for social inequalities in society and differences in power between men and women or between the dominant and minority cultures that may give rise to the types of problem behaviors that fall under the diagnostic rubric of personality disorders. Citing the high prevalence of childhood physical and sexual abuse in the backgrounds of women diagnosed with personality disorders, Brown (1992) and Walker (1988) have argued that personality disorders have come to be used as labels to stigmatize victims of abuse. Ways of coping with abuse come to be seen as a flaw in the person's character, rather than viewed in the larger social context of factors underlying abusive relationships and the limited options available to people who suffer abuse.

Failure to take into account cultural differences may lead to an overdiagnosis of personality disorders by clinicians unfamiliar with a patient's cultural background. For example, displays of exuberance and highly dramatic behavior among Hispanic men may be culturally appropriate but taken as evidence of emotional instability, inappropriate anger, and impulsivity consistent with a diagnosis of borderline personality disorder by clinicians lacking an understanding of the cultural context of the behavior (Casteneda and Franco 1985).

We currently lack any reliable evidence of the prevalences of personality disorders in other cultures. This may change as the result of a recent initiative undertaken jointly by the World Health Organization and the federal Alcohol, Drug Abuse, and Mental Health Administration (ADAMHA). The program seeks to develop and standardize diagnostic instruments that could be used to determine prevalences of psychiatric diagnoses worldwide. One recent result of the program was the development of the International Personality Disorder Examination (IPDE), a semistructured interview protocol used for diagnosing personality disorders (Loranger et al. 1994). The IPDE has been pilot-tested in eleven different countries (India, Switzerland, the Netherlands, Great Britain, Luxembourg, Germany, Kenya, Norway, Japan, Austria, and the United States) and has shown reasonably good reliability among the countries included in the sampling despite linguistic and cultural differences. Though evidence of prevalence rates is sketchy, investigators report that borderline and avoidant personality disorders were the most frequently diagnosed types of personality disorders. Perhaps the characteristics that underlie these disorders reflect some commonly identifiable dimensions of personality disturbance existing throughout the world.

Cognitive Impairment

ECA researchers report a higher prevalence of severe cognitive impairment among older blacks than whites (Robins et al. 1991). The finding that cognitive impairment was affected by race/ethnicity even when controlling for education may indicate that the quality of the educational experiences may not be comparable across racial or ethnic groups. Many ECA respondents had been of school age at a time in which the educational system was more sharply segregated along racial lines than is the case today, but even today the educational experiences of white and nonwhite students remain largely separate and unequal.

FACTORS RELATING TO MISDIAGNOSIS OF SCHIZOPHRENIA IN BLACKS

Though data from the ECA and NCS studies show no significant differences in rates of schizophrenia between blacks and (non-Hispanic) whites, a different picture emerges when one looks at diagnoses in ordinary clinical practice. Researchers find schizophrenia is often overdiagnosed among blacks and other traditionally disadvantaged minority groups (Coleman and Baker 1994, Loring and Powell 1988, Pavkov et al. 1989, Strakowski et al. 1995).

Several factors may account for the overdiagnosis of schizophrenia in minority group members, especially African Americans. Failure to take into account ethnic or cultural differences in symptom expression, language, and mannerisms, as well as racial biases and stereotyping, can lead to misdiagnoses (Garretson 1993, Marquez et al. 1985, Solomon 1992). Clinicians may be operating under the myth that blacks rarely suffer from affective illness, which may explain tendencies of clinicians to mislabel psychotic features of affective disorders as signs of schizophrenia (Strakowski et al. 1993). The underdiagnosis of affective disorders in blacks has also been observed in other countries, including South Africa, where it was attributed to linguistic differences impairing communication of symptoms and the possible use of metaphorical and somatic terms to express feelings of depression by black patients (Elk et al. 1986). In some cultures grief may be expressed in ways that might be described as psychotic in Western countries, even taking the form of hallucinations, as Kleinman notes (1987):

> Ten psychiatrists trained in the same assessment technique and diagnostic criteria who are asked to examine 100 American Indians shortly after the latter have experienced the death of a spouse, a parent or a child may determine with close to 100% consistency that those individuals report hearing, in the first month of grieving, the voice of the dead person calling to them as the spirit ascends to the afterworld. [While such judgments may be consistent across observers] the determination of whether such reports are a sign of an abnormal mental state is an interpretation based on knowledge of this group's behavioural norms and range of normal experiences of bereavement. [p. 453]

Members of nondominant cultural groups who lack fluency in English may have difficulty making themselves understood or may misunderstand questions posed to them, which may lead examiners to misinterpret their symptom complaints. Failure to appreciate idiomatic expressions or linguistic subtleties may also lead to misdiagnosis. For example, patients from nondominant cultural groups may not recognize the distinction between "hearing voices" (as in hallucinations) and "hearing voices" (as in people speaking to them or hearing voices on the radio or TV) and may nod affirmatively when questioned whether they ever hear voices of people who are not physically present.

Racial biases in the diagnosis and assessment of mental illness may play a significant role in the overdiagnosis of schizophrenia in blacks. Tendencies to stereotype members of minority groups and other nondominant cultural groups as dangerous or bizarre may lead to hospital diagnoses of more severe pathology than is the case with members of the dominant white majority. Lending support to the belief that hospital diagnoses may reflect racial biases, Simon and colleagues (1973) found no differences in the rates of schizophrenia and depression when hospital diagnoses were reevaluated in terms of Research Diagnostic Criteria (RDC) criteria. With the tightening of diagnostic criteria with the *DSM-III* and *DSM-IV*, we might anticipate a lessening, though perhaps not an elimination, of misdiagnosis in comparison to earlier years. Failure to account for social class differences may also give rise to putative racial differences in diagnostic rates, especially since SES tends to vary inversely with rates of severe mental illness.

Some observers have argued that the manifestation of paranoid behaviors among blacks may represent a coping response to interacting with an oppressive white majority (Pavkov et al. 1989). The sensitivity of many African Americans to the potential for maltreatment and exploitation has been a survival tool that may take the form of a heightened level of suspiciousness or reserve (Greene 1986). The appearance of culturally laden paranoia or suspiciousness may be misinterpreted as signs of schizophrenia, leading to an overdiagnosis of the disorder by clinicians who are unaware of the cultural relevance of the behavior. Clearly, clinicians need to be sensitive to the values, languages, and cultural beliefs of members of minority groups they are called upon to examine or treat (Comas-Diaz and Griffith 1988, Lee and Richardson 1991).

Cultural variations may also lead to diagnostic confusion and misdiagnoses. Rogler (1993) describes a hierarchical framework that predicts that maximum potential of diagnostic error arises from situations involving pronounced cultural distance in which the so-called "category fallacy" occurs— "the reification of a nosological category developed for a particular cultural population and the application of that category to members of another culture without establishing its validity to that culture" (Good and Good 1986, p. 10).

Studies that base prevalence rates on data only from public institutions may also give rise to misleading results, as blacks and other minority group members tend to be overrepresented in state and county mental hospitals while whites tend to be overrepresented in private facilities (Garretson 1993, Wade 1993). Clinicians in public institutions may be less disposed to find alternate, less stigmatizing diagnoses than schizophrenia than their counterparts in private facilities. Blacks are also more likely than whites to be hospitalized after visits to psychiatric emergency rooms, even after accounting for sociodemographic and clinical differences (Snowden and Holschuh, 1992).

Though research on diagnostic biases for disorders other than schizophrenia is limited, there is evidence that among patients receiving a nonpsychotic disorder, blacks are more likely to receive a diagnosis of an alcohol or drug use disorder, while whites are more likely to be diagnosed with personality disorders, especially borderline personality disorder and personality disorder not otherwise specified (NOS) (Chung et al. 1995). Though such differences point to possible biases in diagnoses, investigations that account for any actual differences in the rates of these disorders in the study samples are needed.

Experimental Studies of Racial Bias

There are few experimental investigations of racial biases in diagnosis. In one case, Loring and Powell (1988) studied the effects of psychiatrists' and patients' gender and race on *DSM-III* diagnoses. Two hundred ninety psychiatrists were presented with case studies in which information about patient gender and race was altered. Regardless of psychiatrist gender and race, agreement on diagnosis was greater when information on patient gender and race was missing than when this information was given.

In another study, Jenkins-Hall and Sacco (1991) found white therapists rated Black depressed subjects more negatively than white depressed subjects. This appears to support earlier research (e.g., Gaertner and Dovidio 1977) showing that white therapists are strongly influenced to discriminate against blacks where situational cues—in the Jenkins-Hall and Sacco case, a diagnosis of depression—provide a justification for viewing blacks more negatively. Jenkins-Hall and Sacco also found that white therapists rated black nondepressed subjects as more depressed than their white counterparts, which gives further credence to the view that white therapists are predisposed to find pathology in blacks.

ACCULTURATION AND MENTAL HEALTH

Acculturation, the process by which immigrant groups adapt to the host culture, may moderate the relationship between ethnicity and psychological adjustment of immigrant peoples. Similarly, identification with the mainstream culture may moderate psychological adjustment of members of traditionally oppressed minority groups.

Two conflicting theories have emerged to account for relationships between acculturation status and mental health. The "melting pot" theory holds that acculturation facilitates psychological adjustment, while the bicultural theory posits that mental health is fostered by a dual identification with the traditional and host cultures (Griffith 1983). Much of the evidence examining relationships between acculturation and mental health status has focused on Hispanic Americans. Studies with Mexican Americans show an association between depression and anxiety with low acculturation status (Neff and Hoppe 1993, Salgado de Snyder 1987, Warheit et al. 1985, Zamanian et al. 1992). Complicating the relationship between acculturation and mental health is the fact that low acculturation status is often a marker for low socioeconomic status. More acculturated immigrant groups are by and large better able to compete economically in the host culture, so findings of greater depression and anxiety among more poorly acculturated groups may merely reflect the effects of economic hardship and resulting stress. More poorly acculturated groups also tend to have lower language proficiency in the primary language of the host country, which can further impede their ability to adjust to the host country and succeed economically. The importance of accounting for economic and social stress when examining relationships between acculturation and mental health is supported by findings based on a national study of more than a thousand Puerto Rican, Mexican-American, and Cuban-American adults that showed the lowest levels of depression among married and employed individuals and the highest levels among the unmarried and unemployed (Guarnaccia et al. 1991). Clearly, investigators need to control for economic differences when examining cultural components of acculturation. Still, we should recognize the prognostic value of low acculturation status in predicting psychological distress.

It remains an arguable question whether a bicultural identification is associated with better outcomes than a more acculturated status. In a recent study of Mexican-American elders, researchers found that poorly acculturated subjects showed higher levels of depression than did those who were either acculturated or bicultural (Zamanian et al. 1992). The acculturated and bicultural groups did not differ from each other in levels of depression. Quoting from the research report, "The strong relationship between low acculturation and high depression scores indicates that retention of aspects of Mexican culture without concomitant attempts to incorporate aspects of the dominant culture results in the most vulnerable position to depression" (p. 109).

Support for the bicultural theory comes in part from studies of Asian-Americans that show less withdrawal and separation among individuals who maintain an ethnic identity while also making attempts to reach out to the larger society (Huang 1994, Phinney et al. 1990). Among Asian-American adolescents, achieving an ethnic identity is also associated with better psychological adjustment and higher self-esteem (Huang 1994, Phinney 1989).

Acculturation can be a double-edged sword, however. A nationwide probability sample of Hispanic Americans showed that heavy alcohol consumption was nine times more common among highly acculturated Hispanic-American women than among relatively unacculturated women (Caetano 1987). Traditional Latin-American cultures have strict gender-based cultural prohibitions against female drinking that constrain excessive alcohol use among women. These constraints appear to have loosened among Hispanic-American women who identify more strongly with mainstream American attitudes and values, which are less sharply drawn along gender lines. Other evidence shows a higher risk of delinquency among third-generation Mexican-American male adolescents as compared to first- or second-generation Mexican Americans (Buriel et al. 1982) and eating attitudes more closely linked to anorexia nervosa among higher acculturated Hispanic-American high school girls than among their less acculturated peers (Pumariega 1986). Reflective of acculturative stress, there is also evidence of greater levels of depression, drug and alcohol abuse, phobias, and suicidal thinking among acculturated, United States-born Mexican Americans than among Mexican-born nationals (Burnam et al. 1987, Sorenson and Golding 1988).

Depending on gender expectations, acculturative stress may place greater burdens on one gender or the other. In a study with Hispanic immigrants, higher levels of depression were found in women, suggestive of the greater acculturative burden that women may bear in adapting to the different gender roles found in the mainstream American culture (Salgado de Snyder et al. 1990). Because they were reared in cultures in which a woman's role was largely defined in terms of homemaking and child rearing, immigrant Hispanic women may encounter more family conflict and stress when they enter the work force in their new country, regardless of whether they seek to work from economic necessity or personal choice. Javier (1997) comments on the stress faced by the husband when traditional gender roles in Hispanic cultures conflict with the financial realities of life in the United States:

I have seen in my own work in treating Hispanic couples in therapy that marriages are under increasing strain from the conflict between traditional and modern expectations about marital roles. Hispanic American women have been entering the work force in increasing numbers, usually in domestic or child-care positions, but they are still expected to assume responsibility for tending their own children, keeping the house, and serving their husbands' needs when they return home. In many cases, a reversal of traditional roles occurs in which the wife works and supports the family, while the husband remains at home because he is unable to find or maintain employment.

It is often the Hispanic American husband who has the greater difficulty accepting a more flexible distribution of roles within the marriage and giving up a rigid set of expectations tied to traditional machismo/ marianismo gender expectations. Although some couples manage to reshape their expectations and marital roles in the face of changing conditions, many relationships buckle under the strain and are terminated in divorce. While I do not expect either the machismo or marianismo stereotype to disappear entirely, I would not be surprised to find a greater flexibility in gender role expectations as a product of continued acculturation. [pp. 166–167]

We should caution that methodological limitations, especially differences in the indices used to measure mental health outcomes, restrict the ability to generalize results on acculturation and mental health of immigrant groups and may account for some inconsistencies found in the literature. We should also note that acculturative stress depends on many factors, such as economic opportunity, language proficiency, and the availability of a supportive network of acculturated individuals of similar cultural background.

DIFFERENCES IN EXPRESSION OF MENTAL DISORDERS

States of psychological distress may be experienced differently in different cultures. Western diagnostic categories such as depression and schizophrenia may appear with a different constellation of symptoms in other cultures. In other cases, disorders may be distinctive of a particular culture that may have no direct parallel in other cultures. The *DSM* recognizes the existence of locally identified syndromes, called *culture-bound syndromes*, which are found in certain cultures but only infrequently if at all in others. These syndromes are believed to reflect folk beliefs and common superstitions in the particular culture, though sometimes in an exaggerated form.

One example is *taijin-kyofu-sho* or TKS, which is common in Japan but rare elsewhere. This is characterized by an excessive fear that one's behavior will embarrass or offend others (McNally et al. 1990). Unlike the *DSM* concept of social phobia, which involves an excessive concern that one will be rejected by others or become embarrassed in front of others, TKS involves the fear of embarrassing other people, a cultural-laden concept that appears to be related to the emphasis in Japanese culture placed on not embarrassing others as well as deep concerns about issues of shame (McNally et al. 1990, Spitzer et al. 1994). The syndrome primarily affects young Japanese men and is diagnosed in 7 percent to 36 percent of people treated by psychiatrists in Japan (McNally et al. 1990, Spitzer et al. 1994). Table 3–1 lists several other culturally bound syndromes described in the *DSM-IV*.

Some culture-bound syndromes have features similar to DSM diagnoses. For example, researchers in Puerto Rico have identified a culture-bound syndrome labeled *ataque de nervios* ("attack of nerves") that is similar in some respects but different in others to *DSM*-defined panic attacks (Guarnaccia 1993, Guarnaccia et al. 1989). Like panic attacks, *ataques de nervios* are characterized by symptoms such as dizziness and fears of going crazy, losing control, or dying. Yet other features are distinctive, such as screaming, hitting oneself or others, breaking things, and becoming hysterical (Liebowitz et al. 1994). Also, unlike panic attacks, *ataques* do not seem to come out of the blue but rather tend to follow stressful events, such as the death of a loved one, natural disasters, or arguments with family members (Guarnaccia 1993).

Examples of differences in the behavioral expression of psychiatric disorders are found across cultures and between ethnic subgroups within particular cultures. Though the syndrome we recognize as schizophrenia may well exist universally, the particular cluster of symptoms that characterize the disorder may vary from culture to culture. Visual hallucinations, for example, may be more common behavioral manifestations in some non-Western cultures than in Western societies (Ndetei and Singh 1983, Ndetei and Vadher 1984). Researchers in Kenya, for instance, report that people with schizophrenia who were of African, Asian, or Jamaican background were about twice as likely to experience visual hallucinations as those of European background (Ndetei and Vadher 1984). In the U.S., Hispanic patients with affective disorders more often present with evidence of delusions and hallucinations than do (non-Hispanic) white patients (Lefley 1990). Though not much has been reported about ethnic differences in symptomatic expression of schizophrenia in the U.S., the available evidence indicates that African Americans with the disorder seem to exhibit fewer negative symptoms of schizophrenia than their (non-Hispanic) white counterparts (Fabrega et al. 1988).

DIFFERENCES IN RELATION TO RELIGIOUS BACKGROUND

Research examining differences in prevalences of mental disorders in relation to religious background is scant. In one of the few reported studies, data from the Epidemiologic Catchment Area (ECA) showed no significant differences between Jews and non-Jews in lifetime prevalences of psychiatric disorders overall (Yeung and Greenwald 1992). However, differences in some specific types of psychiatric disorders did emerge. Jews were more likely than Catholics and Protestants to have experienced major depression and dysthymia, but were less likely to have developed alcohol abuse. These differences remained even when factors such as gender, age, race, and SES were taken into account. The earlier New Haven study (Roberts and Myers 1954) showed Jews to have higher rates of neuroses than non-Jews, but lower rates of schizophrenia and alcoholism. The lower reported incidence of alcohol abuse among Jews may reflect strong cultural restraints on excessive and underage drinking as well as the exposure of children to the ritual use of wine within a religious context. Strong cultural restraints may also help account for low rates of alcohol abuse among Asian Americans.

SUMMARY AND CONCLUSIONS

This review has focused on racial/ethnic differences in psychiatric disorders in the U.S. and emerging evidence of cross-cultural patterns in psychopathology. Perhaps the most compelling finding is the lack of support for racial/ethnic stereotypes that members of ethnic minority groups are predisposed to more severe mental illness and alcohol and drug abuse disorders. In our view, perceptions of ethnic minorities as more psychologically disturbed reflect a number of factors, especially failure to account for differences in SES and tendencies toward racial/ethnic stereotyping of nonwhites within the general population as well as the mental health system. The ECA and NCS surveys have gone a long way toward correcting misperceptions relating ethnic groups status to mental illness. Still, it is important to recognize that economic hardship and other stressors faced by many members of ethnic minority and immigrant groups in the United States can increase the risk of psychological disorders ranging from depression to schizophrenia among vulnerable individuals. Addressing these problems may involve broader societal changes resulting in wider opportunities and improved economic conditions for traditionally disadvantaged groups.

TABLE 3–1. EXAMPLE OF *DSM-IV* CULTURE-BOUND SYNDROMES

Culture-Bound Syndrome	Description
amok	A disorder principally occurring in men in southeastern Asian and Pacific island cultures, as well as in traditional Puerto Rican and Navajo cultures in the West, it describes a type of dissociative episode (a sudden change in consciousness or self-identity) marked by a violent or aggressive outburst following a period of brooding. These episodes are usually precipitated by a perceived slight or insult. During the episode the person may experience amnesia or have a sense of acting automatically, as if robotic. Violence may be directed at people or objects and is often accompanied by perceptions of persecution. A return to the person's usual state of functioning follows the episode. In the West, we use the expression "running amuck" to refer to an episode of losing oneself and running around in a violent frenzy. The word *amuck* is derived from the Malaysian word *amoq*, meaning "engaging furiously in battle."
ataque de nervios ("attack of nerves")	A way of describing states of emotional distress among Latin American and Latin Mediterranean groups, it most commonly involves features such as shouting uncontrollably, fits of crying, trembling, feelings of warmth or heat rising from the chest to the head, and aggressive verbal or physical behavior. These episodes are usually precipitated by a stressful event affecting the family (e.g., receiving news of the death of a family member) and are accompanied by feelings of being out of control. After the attack, the person returns quickly to his or her usual level of functioning, although there may be amnesia for events that occurred during the episode.
bouffée délirante	A French term used to describe a syndrome occurring in West Africa and Haiti that is characterized by a sudden change in behavior, in which the person becomes highly agitated or aggressive, confused, and experiences a speeding up of body movements. Auditory or visual hallucinations and paranoid thinking may be present.
dhat	A disorder affecting males found principally in India that involves intense fear or anxiety over the loss of semen

TABLE 3–1. *(continued)*

through nocturnal emissions, ejaculations, or through excretion with urine (despite the folk belief, semen doesn't actually mix with urine). In Indian culture, there is a popular belief that loss of semen depletes the man of his vital natural energy.

falling out or *blacking out* Occurring principally among southern United States and Caribbean groups, the disorder involves an episode of sudden collapsing or fainting. The attack may occur without warning or be preceded by dizziness or feelings of "swimming" in the head. Although the eyes remain open, the individual reports an inability to see. The person can hear what others are saying and understands what is occurring but feels powerless to move.

ghost sickness A disorder occurring among American Indian groups, it involves a preoccupation with death and with the "spirits" of the deceased. Symptoms associated with the condition include bad dreams, feelings of weakness, loss of appetite, fear, anxiety, and a sense of foreboding. Hallucinations, loss of consciousness, and states of confusion may also be present, among other symptoms.

koro Found primarily in China and some other South and East Asian countries, the syndrome refers to an episode of acute anxiety involving the fear that one's genitals (the penis in men and the vulva and nipples in women) are shrinking and retracting into the body and that death may result.

zar A term used in a number of countries in North Africa and the Middle East to describe the experience of spirit possession. Possession by spirits is often used in these cultures to explain dissociative episodes (sudden changes in consciousness or identity) that may be characterized by periods of shouting, banging of the head against the wall, laughing, singing, or crying. Affected people may seem apathetic or withdrawn or refuse to eat or carry out their usual responsibilities.

Source: Nevid, J. S., Rathus, S. A., and Greene, B. (1997). *Abnormal Psychology in a Changing World* 3rd ed. pp. 82–83. Upper Saddle River, NJ: Prentice-Hall. Used by permission of the publisher.

This overview of ethnicity and psychiatric disorders is limited to an examination of several major types of disorders, including schizophrenia, affective disorders, substance abuse disorders, and anxiety disorders. It is possible that ethnic and cultural variations may exist for other disorders. Dissociative identity disorder (formerly multiple personality disorder) is a case in point. Controversy continues over whether dissociative identity disorder is a Western culture-bound disorder. Though some investigators report cross-cultural evidence of dissociative identity disorder (e.g., Coons et al. 1991), others fail to find evidence of the disorder in other cultures such as Japan (Takahashi 1990). Even in Western cultures, the disorder appears to be largely restricted to North America with very few cases reported in other Western countries such as Great Britain and France (Spanos 1994). In Switzerland, researchers found that 90 percent of psychiatrists polled had never seen a case of the disorder (Modestin 1992, Spanos 1994). Then too, relatively few clinicians in North America have reported treating cases of multiple personality.

Finally, we should recognize that the misdiagnosis of members of ethnic minority groups within the mental health system underscores the need for more culturally appropriate services for minorities, especially in the larger urban areas (Pavkov et al. 1989) as well as continued educational efforts aimed at overcoming biases among mental health professionals. Evidence shows that ethnic matching of clients and therapists may obviate cultural biases. For example, Flaskerud and Akutsu (1993) report that Asian patients interviewed by Asian therapists in ethnic-specific programs received milder diagnoses than did Asians at mainstream clinics. The investigators surmised that Asian therapists may have gathered more information by speaking in the client's own language or dialect and were more likely to use their cultural understanding of the client's presenting complaints in formulating a more accurate diagnosis.

REFERENCES

Abrams, K. K., Allen, L., and Gray, J. J. (1993). Disordered eating attitudes and behaviors, psychological adjustment and ethnic identity: a comparison of Black and White female college students. *International Journal of Eating Disorders* 14:49–57.

Amering, M., and Katschnig, H. (1990). Panic attacks and panic disorder in cross-cultural perspective. *Psychiatric Annals* 20:511–516.

Anthony, J. C., Warner, L. A., and Kessler, R.C. (1994). Comparative epidemiology of dependence on tobacco, alcohol, controlled substances, and inhalants: basic findings from the National Comorbidity Survey. *Experimental and Clinical Psychopharmacology* 2:244–268.

Beauvais, F., and LaBoueff, S. (1985). Drug and alcohol abuse intervention in American Indian communities. Special Issue: Intervening with special populations. *International Journal of the Addictions* 20:139–171.

Bebbington, P. (1993). Transcultural aspects of affective disorders. *International Review of Psychiatry* 5:145–156.

Beiser, M., Cargo, M., and Woodbury, M. A. (1994). A comparison of psychiatric disorder in different cultures: depressive typologies in Southeast Asian refugees and resident Canadians. *International Journal of Methods in Psychiatric Research* 4:157–172.

Bellack, A. S., and Mueser, K. T. (1993). Psychosocial treatment for schizophrenia. *Schizophrenia Bulletin* 19:317–336.

Bentall, R. P. (1990). The illusion of reality: a review and integration of psychological research on hallucinations. *Psychological Bulletin* 107:82–95.

Berlin, I. N. (1987). Effects of changing Native American cultures on child development. *Journal of Community Psychology* 15:299–306.

Blazer, D. G., Kessler, R. C., McGonagle, K. A., and Swartz, M. S. (1994). The prevalence and distribution of major depression in a National Comorbidity Survey. *American Journal of Psychiatry* 151:979–986.

Brown, L. S. (1992) A feminist critique of the personality disorders. In *Personality and Psychopathology: Feminist Reappraisals*, ed. L. Brown and M. Balou, pp. 206–228. New York: Guilford.

Buriel, R., Calzada, S., and Vazquez, R. (1982). The relationship of traditional Mexican American culture to adjustment and delinquency among three generations of Mexican American male adolescents. *Hispanic Journal of Behavioral Sciences* 4:41–55.

Burnam, M. A., Hough, R. L., Karno, M., et al. (1987). Acculturation and lifetime prevalence of psychiatric disorders among Mexican Americans in Los Angeles. *Journal of Health and Social Behavior* 28:89–102.

Caetano, R. (1987). Acculturation and drinking patterns among U.S. Hispanics. *British Journal of Addiction* 82:789–799.

Carlson, E. B., and Rosser-Hogan, R. (1994). Cross-cultural response to trauma: a study of traumatic experiences and posttraumatic symptoms in Cambodian refugees. *Journal of Traumatic Stress* 7:43–58.

Castaneda, R., and Franco, H. (1985). Sex and ethnic distribution of borderline personality disorder in an inpatient sample. *American Journal of Psychiatry* 142:1202–1203.

Chun, Z. F., Mitchell, J. E., Li, K., et al. (1992). The prevalence of anorexia nervosa and bulimia nervosa among freshman medical college students in China. *International Journal of Eating Disorders* 12:209–214.

Chung, H., Mahler, J. C., and Kakuma, T. (1995). Racial differences in treatment of psychiatric inpatients. *Psychiatric Services* 46:586–591.

Coleman, D., and Baker, F. M. (1994). Misdiagnosis of schizophrenia in older, Black veterans. *Journal of Nervous and Mental Disease* 182:527–528.

Comas-Diaz, L., and Griffith, E. (1988). Introduction: on culture and psychotherapeutic care. *Clinical Guidelines in Cross-Cultural Mental Health*. New York: Wiley.

Coons, P. M., Bowman, E. S., Kluft, R. P., and Milstein, V. (1991). The cross-cultural occurrence of MPD: additional cases from a recent survey. *Dissociation* IV (3):124–128.

Cross-National Collaborative Group (1992). The changing rate of major depression: cross-national comparisons. *Journal of the American Medical Association* 268:3098–3105.

Davis, C., and Yager, J. (1992). Transcultural aspects of eating disorders: a critical literature review. *Culture, Medicine, and Psychiatry* 16:377–394.

De La Cancela, V., and Guzman, L. P. (1991). Latino mental health service needs: implications for training psychologists. In *Ethnic Minority Perspectives on Clinical Training and Services in Psychology* ed. H. F. Myers, P. Wohlford, L. P. Guzman, and R. J. Echemendia, pp. 59–64. Washington, DC: American Psychological Association.

de Silva, P. (1993). Post-traumatic stress disorder: cross-cultural aspects. *International Review of Psychiatry* 5:217–229.

DSM-IV: Diagnostic and Statistical Manual of Mental Disorders (1994). 4th ed. Washington, DC: American Psychiatric Association.

Eaton, W. W., Dryman, A., and Weissman, M. M. (1991). Panic and phobia. In *Psychiatric disorders in America: The Epidemiologic Catchment Area Study* ed. L. N. Robins and D. A. Regier, pp. 155–179. New York: Free Press.

Eaton, W. W., Kessler, R. C., Wittchen, H. U., and Magee, W. J. (1994). Panic and panic disorder in the United States. *American Journal of Psychiatry* 151:413–420.

Elk, R., Dickman, B. J., and Teggin, A. F. (1986). Depression in schizophrenia: a study of prevalence and treatment. *British Journal of Psychiatry* 149:228–229.

Fabrega, H., Jr., Mezzich, J., and Ulrich, R. F. (1988). Black–white differences in psychopathology in an urban psychiatric population. *Comprehensive Psychiatry* 29:285–297.

Flaskerud, J. H., and Akutsu, P. D. (1993). Significant influence of participation in ethnic-specific programs on clinical diagnosis for Asian Americans. *Psychological Reports* 72:1228–1230.

Friedman, S., Hatch, M., Paradis, C. M., et al. (1993). Obsessive compulsive disorder in two black ethnic groups: incidence in an urban dermatology clinic. *Journal of Anxiety Disorders* 7:343–348.

Gaertner, S. L., and Dovidio, J. F. (1977). The subtlety of white racism, arousal, and helping behavior. *Journal of Personality and Social Psychology* 35:695–707.

Garretson, D. J. (1993). Psychological misdiagnosis of African Americans. *Journal of Multicultural Counseling and Development* 21:119–126.

Gibbs, N. (1991). When is it rape? *Time Magazine*, June 3, pp. 48–54.

Golding, J. M., and Lipton, R. I. (1990). Depressed mood and major depressive disorder in two ethnic groups. *Journal of Psychiatric Research* 24:65–82.

Goleman, D. (1992). A rising cost of modernity: depression. *The New York Times,* December 8, pp. C1, C13.

Gonzalez, D. (1992). What's the problem with "Hispanic"? Just ask a "Latino." *The New York Times,* November 15, Section 4, p. 6.

Good, B. J., and Good, M. D. (1986). The cultural context of diagnosis and therapy: a view from medical anthropology. In *Mental Health Research and Practice in Minority Communities: Development of Culturally Sensitive Training Programs,* ed. M. R. Miranda and H. H. L. Kitano, Rockville, MD: National Institute of Mental Health.

Grant, B. F., Harford, T. C., Dawson, D. A., et al. (1994). Prevalence of *DSM-IV* alcohol abuse and dependence: United States, 1992. *Alcohol Health & Research World* 18:243–248.

Greene, B. A. (1986). When the therapist is white and the patient is black: considerations for psychotherapy in the feminist heterosexual and lesbian communities. *Women & Therapy* 5:41–65.

Griffith, J. (1983). Relationship between acculturation and psychological impairment in adult Mexican-Americans. *Hispanic Journal of Behavioral Sciences* 5:431–459.

Guarnaccia, P. J. (1993). *Ataques de nervios* in Puerto Rico: Culture-bound syndrome or popular illness? *Medical Anthropology* 15:157–170.

Guarnaccia, P. J., Angel, R., and Worobey, J. L. (1991). The impact of marital status and employment status on depressive affect for Hispanic Americans. *Journal of Community Psychology* 19:136–149.

Guarnaccia, P. J., Rubio-Stipec, M., and Canino, G. (1989). *Ataques de Nervios* in the Puerto Rican diagnostic interview schedule: the impact of cultural categories on psychiatric epidemiology. *Culture, Medicine and Psychiatry* 13:275–295.

Hammond, O. (1988). Needs assessment and policy development: native Hawaiians as Native Americans. *American Psychologist* 43:383–387.

Hollifield, M., Katon, W., Spain, D., and Pule, L. (1990). Anxiety and depression in a village in Lesotho, Africa: a comparison with the United States. *British Journal of Psychiatry* 156:343–350.

Hollingshead, A. B., and Redlich, F. C. (1958). *Social Class and Mental Illness: A Community Study.* New York: Wiley.

Horwath, E., Johnson, J., and Hornig, C. D. (1993). Epidemiology of panic disorder in African-Americans. *American Journal of Psychiatry* 150:465–469.

Huang, L. H. (1994). An integrative approach to clinical assessment and intervention with Asian-American adolescents. *Journal of Clinical Child Psychology* 23:21–31.

Jablensky, A., Sartorius, N., Ernberg, G., et al. (1992). Schizophrenia: manifestations, incidence and course in different cultures: a World Health Organization ten-country study. *Psychological Medicine* 20 (Monograph Suppl.):1–97.

Javier, R. (1997). Machismo-marianismo stereotypes and Hispanic culture. In *Human Sexuality in a World of Diversity,* ed. S. A. Rathus, J. S. Nevid, and L. Fichner-Rathus, pp.166–167. Boston: Allyn & Bacon.

Jenkins, J. H. (1988). Ethnopsychiatric interpretations of schizophrenic illness: the problem of *nervios* within Mexican-American families. *Culture, Medicine, and Psychiatry* 12:301–329.

Jenkins, J. H., and Karno, M. (1992). The meaning of expressed emotion: theoretical issues raised by cross-cultural research. *American Journal of Psychiatry* 149:9–21.

Jenkins-Hall, K., and Sacco, W. P. (1991). Effect of client race and depression on evaluations by white therapists. *Journal of Social and Clinical Psychology* 10:322–333.

Kahn, M. W. (1982). Cultural clash and psychopathology in three aboriginal cultures. *Academic Psychology Bulletin* 4:553–561.

Keith, S. J., Regier, D. A., and Rae, D. S. (1991). Schizophrenic disorders. In *Psychiatric Disorders in America: The Epidemiologic Catchment Area Study* ed. L. N. Robins and D. A. Regier, pp. 33–52. New York: Free Press.

Kessler, R. C. (1994). The National Comorbidity Survey: preliminary results and future directions. *International Journal of Methods in Psychiatric Research* 4:114.1–114.13.

Kessler, R. C., McGonagle, K. A., Nelson, C. B., et al. (1993). Sex and depression in the National Comorbidity Survey I: lifetime prevalence, chronicity and recurrence. *Journal of Affective Disorders* 29:85–96.

Kessler, R. C., McGonagle, K. A., Zhao, S., et al. (1994). Lifetime and 12–month prevalence of *DSM-III-R* psychiatric disorders in the United States: results from the National Comorbidity Survey. *Archives of General Psychiatry* 51:8–19.

Kessler, R. C., Sonnega, A., Bromet, E., et al. (1995). Posttraumatic stress disorder in the National Comorbidity Survey. *Archives of General Psychiatry* 52:1048–1060.

Kleinman, A. (1987). Anthropology and psychiatry: the role of culture in cross-cultural research on illness. *British Journal of Psychiatry* 151:447–454.

Klerman, G. L., and Weissman, M. M. (1989). Increasing rates of depression. *Journal of the American Medical Association* 261:2229–2235.

Kosson, D. S., Smith, S. S., and Newman, J. P. (1990). Evaluating the construct validity of psychopathy in black and white male inmates: three preliminary studies. *Journal of Abnormal Psychology* 99:250–259.

Lee, C. C., and Richardson, B. L. (1991). *Multicultural Issues in Counseling: New Approaches to Diversity*. Alexandria, VA: American Association for Counseling and Development.

Lefley, H. P. (1990). Culture and chronic mental illness. *Hospital and Community Psychiatry* 41:277–286.

Leon, G. R., Fulkerson, J. A., Perry, C. L., and Early-Zald, M. B. (1995). Prospective analysis of personality and behavioral vulnerabilities and gender influences in the later development of disordered eating. *Journal of Abnormal Psychology* 104:140–149.

Liebowitz, M. R., Salmán, E., Jusino, C. M., et al. (1994). *Ataque de nervios* and panic disorder. *American Journal of Psychiatry* 151:871–875.

Loranger, A. W., Sartorius, N., Andreoli, A., et al. (1994). The international personality disorder examination: the World Health Organization/Alcohol, Drug, Abuse and Mental Health Administration international pilot study of personality disorders. *Archives of General Psychiatry* 51:215–224.

Loring, M., and Powell, B. (1988). Gender, race, and *DSM-III*: a study of the objectivity of psychiatric diagnostic behavior. *Journal of Health and Social Behavior* 29:1–22.

Lucero, K., Hicks, R. A., Bramlette, J., et al. (1992). Frequency of eating problems among Asian and Caucasian college women. *Psychological Reports* 71:255–258.

Marquez, C., Taintor, Z., and Schwartz, M. A. (1985). Diagnosis of manic depressive illness in blacks. *Comprehensive Psychiatry* 26:337–341.

McNally, R. J., Cassiday, K. L., and Calamari, J. E. (1990). *Taijin-kyofu-sho* in a black American woman: behavioral treatment of a "culture-bound" anxiety disorder. *Journal of Anxiety Disorders* 4:83–87.

Miklowitz, D. J. (1994). Family risk indicators in schizophrenia. *Schizophrenia Bulletin* 20:137–149.

Modestin, J. (1992). Multiple personality disorder in Switzerland. *American Journal of Psychiatry* 149:88–92.

Mokuau, N. (1990). The impoverishment of native Hawaiians and the social work challenge. *Health and Social Work* 15:235–242.

Moncher, M. S., Holden, G. W., and Trimble, J. E. (1990). Substance abuse among Native-American youth. *Journal of Consulting and Clinical Psychology* 58:408–415.

Moss, F., et al. (1985). Sobriety and American Indian problem drinkers. *Alcoholism Treatment Quarterly* 2:81–96.

Mumford, D. B. (1993). Eating disorders in different cultures. *International Review of Psychiatry* 5:109–113.

Nakawatase, T. V., Yamamoto, J., and Saaso, T. (1993). Association between fast-flushing response and alcohol use among Japanese Americans. *Prevention Pipeline*, July/August, p. 72 (Abstract).

Ndetei, D. M., and Singh, A. (1983). Hallucinations in Kenyan schizophrenic patients. *Acta Psychiatrica Scandinavica* 67:144–147.

Ndetei, D. M., and Vadher, A. (1984). A comparative cross-cultural study of the frequencies of hallucination in schizophrenia. *Acta Psychiatrica Scandinavica* 70:545–549.

Neff, J. A., and Hoppe, S. K. (1993). Race/ethnicity, acculturation, and psychological distress: fatalism and religiosity as cultural resources. *Journal of Community Psychology* 21:3–20.

Nevid, J. S., Rathus, S. A., and Greene, B. (1997). *Abnormal Psychology in a Changing World* 3rd ed. Upper Saddle River, NJ: Prentice-Hall.

Ormel, J. VonKorff, M., Ustun, T. B., et al. (1994). Common mental disorders and disability across cultures. *Journal of the American Medical Association* 272:1741–1748.

Park, J. Y., Huang, Y. H., Nagoshi, C. T., et al. (1984). The flushing response to alcohol use among Koreans and Taiwanese. *Journal of Studies on Alcohol* 45:481–485.

Pate, J. E., Pumariega, A. J., Hester, C., and Garner, D. M. (1992). Cross-cultural patterns in eating disorders: a review. *Journal of the American Academy of Child and Adolescent Psychiatry* 31:802–808.

Pavkov, T. W., Lewis, D. A., and Lyons, J. S. (1989). Psychiatric diagnoses and racial bias: an empirical investigation. *Professional Psychology: Research and Practice* 20:364–368.

Phinney, J. (1989). Stages of ethnic identity in minority group adolescents. *Journal of Early Adolescence* 9:34–49.

Phinney, J., Lochner, B., and Murphy, R. (1990). Ethnic identity development and psychological adjustment in adolescence. In *Ethnic Issues in Adolescent Mental Health*, ed. A. Stiffman and L. Davis, pp. 53–72. Newbury Park. CA: Sage.

Pumariega, A. J. (1986). Acculturation and eating attitudes in adolescent girls: a comparative correlational study. *Journal of the American Academy of Child Psychiatry* 25:276–279.

Roberts, B. H., and Myers, J. K. (1954). Religion, national origin, immigration, and mental illness. *American Journal of Psychiatry* 10:759–764.

Robins, L. N., and Regier, D. A. (1991). *Psychiatric Disorders in America: The Epidemiologic Catchment Area Study*. New York: Free Press.

Robins, L. N., Helzer, J. E., Weissman, M. M., et al. (1984). Lifetime prevalence of specific psychiatric disorders in three sites. *Archives of General Psychiatry* 41:949–958.

Robins, L. N., Tipp, J., and Przybeck, T. (1991). Antisocial personality. In *Psychiatric Disorders in America: The Epidemiologic Catchment Area Study,* ed. L. N. Robins and D. A. Regier, pp. 258–290. New York: Free Press.

Rogan, A. (1986). Recovery from alcoholism: issues for black and Native American alcoholics. *Alcohol Health and Research World* (Fall) 10:42–44.

Rogler, L. H. (1993). Culturally sensitizing psychiatric diagnosis: a framework for research. *Journal of Nervous and Mental Disease* 181:401–408.

Rogler, L. H., Cortes, D. E., and Malgady, R. G. (1991). Acculturation and mental health status among Hispanics: convergence and new directions for research. *American Psychologist* 46:584–597.

Sack, W. H., McSharry, S., Clarke, G. N., et al. (1994). The Khmer Adolescent Project: I. Epidemiological findings in two generations of Cambodian refugees. *Journal of Nervous and Mental Disease* 182:387–395.

Salgado de Snyder, V. N. (1987). Factors associated with acculturative stress and depressive symptomatology among married Mexican immigrant women. *Psychology of Women Quarterly* 11:475–488.

Salgado de Snyder, V. N., Cervantes, R. C., and Padilla, A. M. (1990). Gender and ethnic differences in psychosocial stress and generalized distress among Hispanics. *Sex Roles* 22:441–453.

Shweder, R. (1985). Cross-cultural study of emotions. In *Culture and Depression*, ed. A. Kleinman and B. Good. Berkeley: University of California Press.

Simon, R. J., Fleiss, J. L., Gurland, B. J., et al. (1973). Depression and schizophrenia in hospitalized black and white mental patients. *Archives of General Psychiatry* 28:509–512.

Smith, J. E., and Krejci, J. (1991). Minorities join the majority: eating disturbances among Hispanic and Native American youth. *International Journal of Eating Disorders* 10:179–186.

Snowden, L. R., and Holschuh, J. (1992). Ethnic differences in emergency psychiatric care and hospitalization in a program for the severely mentally ill. *Community Mental Health Journal* 28:281–291.

Solomon, A. (1992). Clinical diagnosis among diverse populations: a multicultural perspective. *Families in Society* 73:371–377.

Somervell, P. D., Leaf, P. J., Weissman, M. M., et al. (1989). The prevalence of major depression in black and white adults in five United States communities. *American Journal of Epidemiology* 130:725–735.

Sorenson, S. B., and Golding, J. M. (1988). Suicide ideation and attempts in Hispanics and non-Hispanic whites: demographic and psychiatric disorder issues. *Suicide and Life-Threatening Behavior* 18:205–218.

Spanos, N. P. (1994). Multiple identity enactments and multiple personality disorder: a sociocognitive perspective. *Psychological Bulletin* 116:143–165.

Spencer, D. J. (1983). Psychiatric dilemmas in Australian aborigines. *International Journal of Social Psychiatry* 29:208–214.

Spitzer, R. L., Gibbon, M., Skodol, A. E., et al. (1994). *DSM-IV Case Book: A Learning Companion to the Diagnostic and Statistical Manual of Mental Disorders*, 4th ed. Washington, DC: American Psychiatric Press.

Stice, E. (1994). Review of the evidence for a sociocultural model of bulimia nervosa and an exploration of the mechanisms of action. *Clinical Psychology Review* 14:633–661.

Strakowski, S. M., Lonczak, H. S., Sax, K. W., et al. (1995). The effects of race on diagnosis and disposition from a psychiatric emergency service. *Journal of Clinical Psychiatry* 56:101–107.

Strakowski, S. M., Shelton, R. C., and Kolbrener, M. L. (1993). The effects of race and comorbidity on clinical diagnosis in patients with psychosis. *Journal of Clinical Psychiatry* 54:96–102.

Sue, S., Nakamura, C. Y., Chung, R. C. Y., and Yee-Bradbury, C. (1994). Mental health research on Asian Americans: Special issue: Asian-American mental health. *Journal of Community Psychology* 22:61–67.

Takahashi, Y. (1990). Is multiple personality disorder really rare in Japan? *Dissociation* III:57–59.

Timpson, J., McKay, S., Kakegamic, S., et al. (1988). Depression in a native Canadian in northwestern Ontario: sadness, grief or spiritual illness? *Canada's Mental Health* 36:5–8.

Wade, J. C. (1993). Institutional racism: an analysis of the mental health system. *American Journal of Orthopsychiatry* 63:536–544.

Walker, L. E. (1988). The battered woman syndrome. In *Family Abuse and Its Consequences: New Directions in Research*, ed. G. T. Hotaling, D. Finkelhor, J. T. Kirkpatrick, and M. A. Straus, pp. 139–148. Newbury Park, CA: Sage.

Warheit, G. J., Vega, W. A., Auth, J., and Meinhardt, K. (1985). Psychiatric symptoms and dysfunctions among Anglos and Mexican Americans: an epidemiological study. In *Research in Community and Mental Health*, ed. J. R. Greenley, pp. 3–32. London: JAI.

Warner, L. A., Kessler, R. C., Hughes, M., et al. (1995). Prevalence and correlates of drug use and dependence in the United States. Results from the National Comorbidity Survey. *Archives of General Psychiatry* 52:219–229.

Weisman, A., Lopez, S. R., Karno, M., and Jenkins, J. (1993). An attributional analysis of expressed emotion in Mexican-American families with schizophrenia. *Journal of Abnormal Psychology* 102:601–606.

Weissman, M. M., Bland, R. C., Canino, G. J., et al. (1994). The cross national epidemiology of obsessive compulsive disorder. *Journal of Clinical Psychiatry* 55 (Suppl 3):5–10.

Weissman, M. M., Livingston Bruce, M., Leaf, P. J., et al. (1991). Affective disorders. In *Psychiatric disorders in America: The Epidemiologic Catchment Area Study*, ed. L. N. Robins and D. A. Regier, pp. 53–80. New York: Free Press.

Westermeyer, J., and Neider, J. (1994). Substance disorder among 100 American Indian versus 200 other patients. *Alcoholism: Clinical and Experimental Research* 18:692–694.

Yeung, P. P., and Greenwald, S. (1992). Jewish Americans and mental health: results of the NIMH Epidemiologic Catchment Area Study. *Social Psychiatry and Psychiatric Epidemiology* 27:292–297.

Zamanian, K., Thackrey, M., Starrett, R. A., et al. (1992). Acculturation and depression in Mexican-American elderly. Special issue: Hispanic aged mental health. *Gerontologist* 11:109–121.

Zane, N., and Sue, S. (1991). Culturally responsive mental health services for Asian Americans: treatment and training issues. In *Ethnic Minority Perspectives on Clinical Training and Services in Psychology*, ed. H. F. Myers, P. Wohlford, L. P. Guzman, and R. J. Echemendia, pp. 49–58. Washington, DC: American Psychological Association.

The Feeling Edge of Culture in the American Sensitivity Shift

EDWARD C. STEWART

INTRODUCTION

This chapter offers a multicultural perspective of mental illness that concentrates on the cultural changes in American society from the 1960s to the present. From a psychological perspective, changes in ideas and feelings about civil rights, empowerment, and individual choice, combined with an erosion of ethics and moral sentiments, have loosened civil ties and replaced them with cultural bonds. Traditional American individual feelings of self based on civility have changed and become more firmly attached to primordial sentiments toward race and ethnicity, bringing about a cultural shift.

The diversity of the minority groups that were formed in the United States is a mild example of social and political changes, driven by a cultural shift, that have taken place in many parts of the world. The American Way in the social organization of culture succeeded in containing primordial cultural discontent over race and ethnicity, framing it as a malaise. In Canada, primordial discontent over language generated a political movement for the separation of Quebec. In the Balkans, the collapse of the communist political order spawned primordial conflict over religion, tradition, and region. Although the effects in the United States are quite different from those in Canada and in the Balkans, the character of the cultural forces at the vortex of change are the same throughout the world. What is different is the intensity of the cultural forces, their patterning over the six primordial sentiments, and the capacity of the society to absorb and to temper the primordial rage and the violence incited by a people's perception of the nation's power groups suppressing civil rights and oppressing cultural identity.

The ebbing of "civic" identity and belonging in America has revealed a "cultural" identity that many social scientists believed had disappeared from American society. The graded shift from "civic" to "primordial" identity, driven by the causal force of emotions—particularly anger—is linked to the cultural shift in American thought and emotion from a practical, problem-solving style of decision making to a mode of thought based on the cognitive structure of anger. The cultural change increased violence, anger, and distrust and, simultaneously, exposed American political and cultural fault lines, deepening social divisions. The social and political effects changed the norms and concepts of social adjustment and mental illness, reducing the influence and power to control of American institutions. The malaise created poses a threat to the mental health of Americans.

My analysis of the cultural malaise begins with a brief description of American society as a cultural configuration, touching upon issues in American cultural change and malaise, particularly those concerning identity, emotions, and cognitive meaning. The next subject in my analysis is a paradigm of cultural differences, the cultural trilogy, which will be used to organize the analysis, focusing first on pain and anger and their roles in changing American culture and second on the influences of psychological, social, political, and cultural processes in mental health. The objective of this chapter is to describe the need to improve and to develop strategies in therapy, counseling, education, and cross-cultural training to alleviate the cultural malaise.

AMERICAN INDIVIDUALISM AS CULTURAL CONFIGURATION

In the early generations of American colonial society, cruel conditions for survival left a permanent mark on the American character. Conquering the wilderness bred self-reliance in colonists who developed a distinctive American "way of life" and a view of human nature grounded in individual actions and not on the accomplishments and wealth of the collectivity. Perhaps more so than any other people, Americans aggressively pursue their own interests, guided by their own purposes, making their own decisions, according to their own values. Each one is the architect of his or her own fate, master of his or her own decisions, and inventor of his or her own choices (Stewart and Bennett 1991). Since everyone is self-reliant and free, it is the "individual"—not the environment or society—who is presumed to be the locus of causation. If there is a "law" that Americans accept to govern their behavior, it is motivation, ultimately based on the biology of the individual, with behavioral patterns entrained on universal physiological needs, that provides a common base for human nature.

In Maslow's classical formulation of the motivational ladder (Maslow 1954), the lowest rung is physiological needs, the next rung up is security, followed by affiliation, esteem, and finally self-actualization; but emotion can be interpreted in the hierarchy of needs. For instance, it is possible to imagine someone climbing the motivational ladder and, on the rung under "affiliation," to interpret the need to be laden with the emotions of "love." Even so, Maslow's ladder is primarily a "cognitive," not an "affective," system. The top rung leads to the self in the form of self-actualization; it does not lead to society, to a social role offering some balance of rights and responsibilities, of privileges and duties.

But the deep American cultural configuration of "rugged individualism," as one Japanese writer has called it, leads Americans to neglect the social side of life. With a tone of slight surprise in his voice, Tsuru writes: "The idea that a society might evolve in accordance with laws to which individuals may unknowingly be subject completely escapes the comprehension of representative Americans." (Tsuru 1956, p. 525).

The cultural orientation leads to an existence unhampered by customs, traditions, or "powers" in the community. The individual is seen as the basic unit of the society and the quantum of the culture. Individualism is the hub of American culture and social emotions are the black hole. Both the changes in American culture and the malaise can be understood to center around the two poles of psychology of individualism and sociology of the primordial sentiments toward cultural belonging. Their "way of life," pursuing their own interests, Americans define as *culture*, with the implication that it is universal.

Individualism is a cultural configuration with deep roots in unconscious patterns of values and procedures coupled to social norms controlling the actions of members of the culture (Voget 1973). *Configuration* was introduced by Benedict (1934) to connote a temperament of a type of personality, but usage has veered toward a cognitive interpretation replacing the ongoing emotional meaning. When Bateson adopted Benedict's "configuration," he insisted that its meaning should be divided into emotion (*ethos*) and cognition (*eidos*) (Bateson

1958). In explaining his position, Bateson asserts that "emotional emphases" and the "cognitive processes" are based on the same principles that individuals use in tailoring their behavior to prevailing cultural norms in society.

The first step in the psychological analysis of cultural meaning is to start with the details of behavior and search them for the elements of cognition and for their logical structure. The movement of the analysis from the details to the general structure is based on external perception and is inductive. On the other hand, when attending to emotions, the process is more complex.

Emotions are expressed by facial expressions, body movements, and other behaviors, but the inductive value of emotions is limited. Some researchers have identified basic emotions, each with its differentiated physiology and the same universal facial expressions (Ekman et al. 1972). Although the code for expressing emotions in facial expressions and body movements is "impressive" and conveys a "feeling," nevertheless, the language of the body is scarcely articulate and conveys little information. The expression of emotions is contextualized and personalized. Communication through emotions improves in face-to-face interactions taking place in familiar events and situations. Under these circumstances the structure of the context and of the relation among the "communicators" can be used to interpret and to articulate the information or the meaning of the expression of emotion. For these reasons the analysis of emotion should begin with the emotional figures in the cultural configuration as a whole and proceed to identify specific needs and desires. The movement from the general to the specific is deductive (Bateson 1958). The implication of Bateson's thought is that emotions originate in the body. They are somatic, function deductively, and drive behavior. In comparison, cognition is structural and functions inductively to guide behavior.

Cultural differences range from the details of behavior and belief to abstractions and generalizations. Differences are greatest in the details and in the generalities, while maximum similarity tends to exist in the middle domain. Mental illness makes the point. The experience of depression, paranoia, aggressiveness, or psychosomatic symptoms occurs in all societies, and there is an intuitive agreement about the physical and emotional conditions surrounding their expression from culture to culture. But at the "general" level with psychosomatic symptoms, for instance, the Japanese accept them as a normal part of emotional disposition while Americans consider them to be a malfunction. The attitudes toward and the treatment of psychosomatic symptoms vary in the two societies.

Since culture influences thought, feelings, and behavior, an accurate diagnosis of deviant behavior is difficult to make without knowledge of the relevant sociocultural premises in the society. The problem occurs in the United

States with some behavior patterns of Latinos. Are they normal or deviant or are they mental illness?

The personal lifestyle of Latino men is characterized by *machismo*, which translates as "assertive masculinity." The macho man takes full advantage of sexual opportunities and should be able to sustain his desire and capacity beyond those of his partner. Physical courage is stressed, and the macho man does not weep when injured. Honor must remain inviolate. If affronted by another man, the macho man interprets the insult as a challenge for him to restitute his honor, often through retaliation. It is not difficult to see how American psychiatrists may perceive altercations with police officers or exploitation and domination of women by Latino men as deviant or pathological when it is normative behavior (Padilla and Ruiz 1973). Another source that can bungle diagnosis is emotion. When compared with American men, Latino men appear "more 'open' in their expression of emotion and seem to demonstrate extremes of joy and anger more freely. Furthermore, affection toward other males is expressed casually, routinely, and without embarrassment by handshaking, an embrace upon meeting (*el abrazo*), and frequent touching during conversation." (Padilla and Ruiz 1973, p. 50).

The example from the sociocultural psychology of Latinos leads to the conclusion that the Latino concept of the nature of masculinity and the behavioral details of its expression differ from the Anglo patterns.

Americans peering through the cultural lens of their own values of individualism typically believe that, deep down, people from any other culture are just like themselves. These beliefs represent the middle domain of understanding that everyone is a biological specimen and in that realm unique, that in some way each person must be treated as an individual, and, finally, that each one has basic needs rooted in biology. Either more detailed or more general than that, analysis enters the domain of cultural differences.

CULTURE

An explanation of the changes in American life requires a concerted analysis of individual psychology and the social environment in American society. The duality of the change points to culture as the concept with the structural resources required for an explanation. At a simple level, culture is a creative tension between psychology, with roots in biology, and sociology. Webs of symbols are constructed in the interaction between the two in the form of "contrasting simultaneous determination," creating language and systems of knowledge (Stewart 1995). The symbols of culture culminate in a cultural configuration, filled with meaning, that is used to reduce the uncertainty of perception, to derive cognitive applications for survival, and to bolster belonging in the communal group (Stewart 1995). Beyond culture stretches the desert of the mind in the form of universal principles of individual psychology and communal group sociology. To articulate the American configuration of culture, it is necessary to establish the cultural base separately from psychology and sociology.

The reality that both the details and the generalities differ, while similarity holds the middle ground, explains the selection of a paradigm of cultural differences, the cultural trilogy, as the cognitive instrument used to analyze a cultural configuration and compare it with other cultural configurations. The cultural trilogy is presented schematically in Figure 4–1.

The twelve basic parameters of the trilogy are selected as mid-domain concepts that necessarily exist in all cultural configurations, but in different modes, values, and intensity. The parameters of the cultural trilogy are listed in Table 4–1.

The relationships among the parameters depicted in the figure and detailed in the table serve as a map of cultural differences. Terms such as *surface culture*, parameter 1 in the psychological triad, and *political culture*, parameter 5 in the sociological triad, are properties found in all cultures, but with variable organization, content, and prominence. The cultural trilogy will be used as a map to guide the analysis of cultural differences, beginning with perception.

Perception

Perception has been compared to the Roman deity Janus, with two faces looking in opposite directions: one into the past and the other into the future. Janus served as the god of gates and doors and received the prayers of Romans at the beginning and end of courses of action, especially war. The Janus-like duality featured in perception qualifies it as the central process in psychology. One face looking outward is riveted to sensory stimuli that impinge on and enter the sensory organs, such as eyes, ears, nose, and skin. The receptors convert the energy of stimuli into electric impulses that stream to the brain where tens of thousands of neurons fire off electric impulses. Simultaneously, impulses from the body itself arrive in the brain as somatic sensations and feelings of the organs, muscles, bones, and other body tissues. The two patterns of neuronal firing integrate into a pattern of firing that is interpreted as a primordial schema of the external order.

Somatic sensations, the second face of perception, register the physiological state inside the body. The inward face, composed of the sensations of

Figure 4–1

CULTURAL TRILOGY: A PARADIGM OF CULTURAL DIFFERENCES

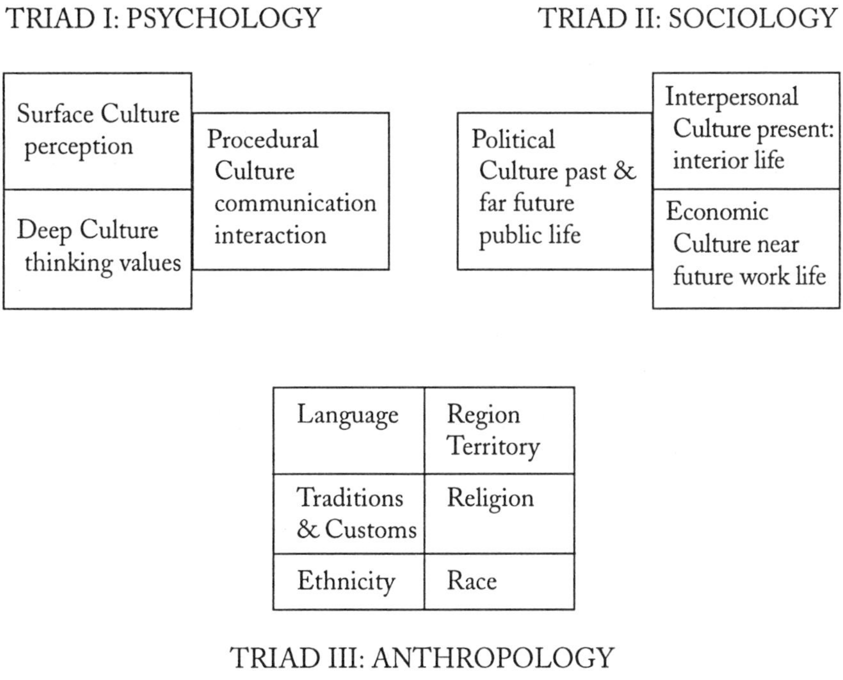

TRIAD I: PSYCHOLOGY   TRIAD II: SOCIOLOGY

Surface Culture perception	Procedural Culture communication interaction
Deep Culture thinking values	

Political Culture past & far future public life	Interpersonal Culture present: interior life
	Economic Culture near future work life

Language	Region Territory
Traditions & Customs	Religion
Ethnicity	Race

TRIAD III: ANTHROPOLOGY

---

the body image, impressions, feelings, and emotions, embodies and absorbs the sensory stimulation of external perception. The fundamental principle that emerges is that the emotions in somatic sensations have not only intensity but also cognitive structure.

Pain

Pain is an integrated and unitary perceptual modality like vision, hearing, and touch (Geldard 1953, Zborowski 1969), but a quixotic one different from the other modalities (McConnell 1986). It is a subjective and powerful human experience with a perceptible and distinctive range of negative somatic sensations that are difficult to understand. The figurative experience of pain has no

TABLE 4–1. THE TWELVE PARAMETERS
OF THE CULTURAL TRILOGY

Triad I. Individual Analysis of Behavior

1. *Surface Culture*: Content is observable behavior (speech, facial expressions, hand gestures, actions, etc.), artifacts (foods, dress, architecture, farmland, etc.); psychology is external perception, contextualized in time, place, and conditions of experience.
2. *Deep Culture*: Content is cognition, emotions (thinking, values, systems of knowledge, etc.); psychology is internal perception in the absolute and universal time and space of the body.
3. *Procedural Culture*: Content is performance and communication; agent in interaction in pursuit of goals in context (pattern of managing self/others, decision making, counseling, conflict resolution, modes of production, etc.); psychology is synthesis of surface and deep culture.

Triad II. Time-Factored Activities in Social Environments

4. *Interpersonal Culture:* Activities of interior life pursued with family and others known face to face to satisfy *physiological*, *security*, and *belonging* needs; time factored in cyclic present.
5. *Economic–Technical Culture*: Activities of work life pursued with others as experts to satisfy *achievement* need; time factored in near future in linear form of time.
6. *Political–Social Culture*: Activities of public life pursued to satisfy *power* need; competition between civil and cultural time-factored identity formed in time-factored episodic past.

Triad III (Double). Primordial Sentiments in Social
Organization of Culture

7. *Language*: Cultural belonging and identity through interpersonal and mass communication.
8. *Traditions & Customs*: Traditions develop belonging in social side of procedural culture; customs as social manners; in U.S., called "habits of the heart" by Tocqueville.
9. *Ethnicity*: Extended family-community.
10. *Region* (Territory): Attachment to style of life (economic) and locus of homeland.
11. *Religion*: Ideal form of human relations and governing moral sentiment.
12. *Race*: Attachment and identity based on physical differences.

clear contrast. Pleasure or hedonic tone, with which pain is usually contrasted, is not a sensation but a pleasant and ambiguous feeling reported in generalizations about the quality of life, health, and experience. The singularity of pain begins in neurophysiology: there is no center in the brain for pain as for the other senses. Parts of the brain that act as pain receptors

> receive inputs from virtually all of the body, can modify information transmission at almost every synaptic level of the somatosensory projection system. These ascending and descending interactions present a picture of dynamic modifiable processes in which inputs impinge on a continually active nervous system that is already the repository of the individual's past history, expectations and value systems. This concept has important implications: it means that the input patterns evoked by injury can be modulated by other sensory inputs or by descending influences, which may thereby determine the quality and intensity of the eventual experience. [Melzack and Wall 1982, p. 145]

The consequence of pain physiology is that the primary quality of the experience is aversion and privacy. The more the individual suffers from pain, the greater is the sufferer's sense of being alone. Pain constructs no objects and has no cognitive forms, only feelings of intensity of the sensory qualities described as temporal, spatial, pressure, thermal, and other properties (Melzack and Wall 1988). In contrast, the response constructed in vision has a cognitive form of an object in the external world as, for instance, "the red Chinese vase sitting on the ledge," and, in hearing, someone speaking. In both cases the object is externalized in contrast to the sentient experience of pain that takes place in the interior of the body. The objectless quality and the privacy of pain, when intense, can drive out of mind all conscious thought and feeling and grant to the imagination free rein to invent instruments that explain the causes of pain (see Scarry 1985, pp. 161–180).

The singular qualities of pain make its experience similar to that of the emotions, the second major content of the somatic sensations. Anger, with an accessible and strong form, will be described and used to illustrate the cognitive structures, which is self-evident in all emotions.

Emotion

The folk mind in American culture separates "feeling" and "emotion" (D'Andrade 1987). *Feeling* refers to the tone of the mind and body: pleasant, unpleasant, excited, dull, or heavy as the tone may be. The experience of a feeling is generalized and lacks focus or meaning. A complex organism has "feelings" of both bodily sensations such as pain and of emotions such as anxiety, and they are an independent means of guiding behavior. They prepare the organism, not for specific innate response, but for a general course of action appropriate to the situation. They do not require complex inferential processes. Indeed, they are an evolutionarily older method of control and their effects can be rapid and effective (Johnson-Laird 1988).

Feelings precipitated by external percepts—such as touch, kinesthesis, and pain—with their symbolic structure often uncertain, are intuitively grasped as a body schema and understood as a body image. When a feeling acquires symbolic structure, with reference to the outside world, it acquires meaning and becomes what the folk mind understands as emotion.

As a subdivision of feelings, emotions are created and terminated by cognitive evaluations of situations. They have psychological causes, which led Johnson-Laird (1988) to assume that emotions originated during evolution in the form of a control mechanism for interaction with other members of the species.

Using a behavioral criterion of universal facial expression, Ekmann and colleagues (1972) have identified six basic emotions: happiness, sadness, anger, fear, disgust, and surprise. Each has a distinctive physiological pattern that is universal and the same among all peoples. As an example, the physiological effects of anger are rise in body temperature, increase in blood pressure and muscular pressure, body agitation, and interference in the perception of the external world. The receptor organs for warmth, pressure, movement, and so on convert the sensory stimulation into electric impulses that stream to the brain, where neuronal firing is organized into one pattern. Anger is perceived as a "mass," as an "object" under pressure, as the heat of a fluid inside the body serving as its container. Anger has a cognitive structure and, in the American folk mind, also a narrative: as pressure builds up and the heat increases, there is danger that the container will boil over, or explode (Lakoff 1987).

Memory as Procedure

But the construction of a final product of perception, an image or a concept, is not yet complete when emotions and other somatic sensations integrate into a pattern of neuronal firing. The schema under construction gains a distinctive form only after it is partially disembodied from the perceiver's somatic sensations. The integrity of the schema is constructed when the image in formation is compared with a past event that in some way has been associated with the primordial schema. Through its function, memory is recognized as a procedure inseparable from perception, using past events to identify and impart meaning to a neuronal firing pattern. Finally, the time-factored face of Janus, the one peering into the past, enters into the process of perception. In perception, the present appears vividly as sensory stimulation and the past is recognized in memory as procedure. As for the Janus look into the future, its provenance in the past and continuing into the present and then moving onward requires the concept of linear time. In many cultures people do not see time in this form, nor do they use the principle of chronology leading to the future. Indeed, belief in the past does not necessarily imply a belief in a history that will deliver the future. For some, it is dreams that portend what is to come. The origin of the future sketched in perception is simpler.

The distinctive feature of the present is duration and flow of time conveyed by sensory stimulation. But before the moment of the present is stopped, its crest slips away into the past and is gone. The simplest way to form a stable present is to orient perception to anticipate the forward edge of the present. The perceptual set of anticipation also makes sense in the development of the body image—that structure of cognition that regulates perception. The young child learns how to move the arms to block a flying object or to soften the shock of falling down. In social interaction and in listening to language the same time orientation prevails. The listener in a conversation has to listen to the end of the sentence to learn what happens to the subject or to the end of the message before preparing the proper response. Although it is a speculation, it seems reasonable to conclude that if there is a natural orientation to time, it is in anticipation. Experience with time elaborates the silver moment in anticipation into a concept of the future through the emotions of pleasure-hope or displeasure-fear over prospects of an event (Ortony et al. 1988).

In conclusion, the perception of external order is formed in a fusion of external sensory stimulation, internal somatic sensations, and reconstructed past events yielding images and concepts. The brain begins the task of integrating the products into cognitive structures called patterns of thinking, values, and systems of knowledge. The perception of the external order turns out to be the construction of a reality in the brain, containing a "system" of the external order that can monitor survival of the human being. The external world is a mystery that never enters the recesses of inner reality and remains accessible only to Janus and other creatures of the imagination. Verbal concepts and the creativity of language play critical parts in developing the mind of deep culture.

Considered as a current in the process of perception, sensory stimulation has been weak in American culture in comparison to its prominence in Japanese and to a lesser degree in German culture. In the period since 1960, external perception has declined even more in American culture, in part precipitating a "great sensitivity shift," which will be discussed later on.

CULTURAL ANALYSIS

Surface Culture and Perception of the External Order

External perception overlaps considerably with the content of surface culture defined as culture exhibiting human crafting or decoration. These include preferences in food, dress, and other necessities and amenities; nonverbal signs, facial expressions, and sounds of speech; and, finally, good manners. The common denominator in all these items is that they are observable either as behavior—nonverbal communication—or as artifacts—cheeseburger, kimono.

External perception refers to the weight placed on sensory stimulation in comparison to the weight of somatic sensations and past events. Human beings are so accustomed to seeing objects that it is extraordinary to realize how much objects are creatures of the imagination and how their existence is largely unknown to the senses. "We sense them as fleeting visual shades, occasional knocks against the hand, sniffs of smells—sometimes stabs of pain leaving a bruise—record of a too-close encounter. The extraordinary thing is how much we rely on properties of objects which we seldom or never test by sensory experience" (Gregory 1970, p. 11).

On rare occasions when the sensory experience is available, as in an experiment when subjects are tested for their color vision with patches of colors, cultural differences have been measured, but they are few and relatively insignificant (Cole and Scribner 1974). Culture intrudes into perception through the internal perception and reconstruction of past events, not through sensory stimulation.

Pain

Pathological pain is a sense with four functions that register somatic impressions and feelings elaborated by both emotion and cognition (Zborowski 1969). The first function of pain is to warn the biological organism against dangers threatening its integrity. The *reaction* to the alarm is automatic and acts to mobilize cognitive activities directed toward the protection of the body from harm and destruction. The *response* to pain can be triggered by the mere presence of objects associated with pain—burning flame, gun, machete—or even their symbolic representation in social situations or words. More than any other sensation, pain is associated with the fear of death.

The reaction to alarm triggers a cognitive interpretation of pain and its threat, which arouses anxiety. Without a cognitive elaboration of the significance of the pain sensation, anxiety does not invade the feelings and emotions of the individual (Zborowski 1969). The sources of anxiety are cognitive and emotional, not biological. Anxiety refers to a diffuse emotion, low in cognition; to a general feeling of apprehension and uneasiness; to a disturbance of spirits and to agitation of body. Once anxiety loses its generality by focusing on another person as an "agent" threatening mental and perhaps physical security as well, anxiety acquires cognitive content, symbolic structure and meaning.

At this juncture the door is opened for the influence of culture on the experience of pain. With pain and anxiety universally disliked by all normal people, no culture has refrained in some way from exploiting its dread. The second function of pain is in the social/cultural symbolization of its physical experience:

> The most obvious sociocultural bearing of pain is implied in the word itself, which has derived from the Latin word *poena* ("punishment"), which can be traced to the Sanskrit root *pu*, meaning purification. . . . Infliction of pain is one of the oldest, although certainly not universal, forms of punishment. In the process of teaching children correct behavior, and in forcing adults to comply with group norms, the unpleasant quality of pain sensation and the biological fear of it have fulfilled an important social function. In many societies parental and national authorities were, and still are, based on infliction of pain. Pain in German (*Schmerz*), Russian (*bol*), Polish (*bol*), or Hebrew (*K'eyv*) does not have a punitive implication at all. However, in all these languages it is used as in English or French to denote mental anguish and anxiety. [Zborowski 1969, pp. 38–39]

The original Latin word for pain, *dolor*, is the main word used in French and Spanish and *dor* in Portuguese. The word *mal*, meaning *evil* and *wickedness*, is used alongside *dolor*. In summary, pain is inflicted as punishment to coerce obedience, conformity, and allegiance. Its meaning centers around "punishment" and "redemption" (Zborowski 1969, p. 38).

Although all cultures expect pain as a natural experience in life, the acceptance of pain is specific to a culture. American women, for instance, expect childbirth pain, but do not tolerate it to the same degree as the English. Another area where there are cultural differences in the acceptance of pain symbols is in the mass media used for entertainment. Violence, blood, and death in movies, music, and other forms of the mass media attract many people who seem to enjoy the vicarious experience of the pain and destruction of others, but the boundaries of toleration are very much influenced by the norms of the society (Zborowski 1969).

In the attitudes and behavior toward pain, the cultural component is constrained by the sensory nature of the pain experience. Pain is located in the body, unlike a visual experience located in the visual object outside; the sensation is native and the feeling triggers dread of harm and destruction of the integrity of the body. The anxiety associated with feelings about life and death may become specifically conditioned to objects, canalizing anxiety into the emotion of fear. Defensive responses to anxiety in some individuals may precipitate a panic syndrome with characteristic physiological, emotional, and behavioral reactions. In a second line of defense, panic can be overcome with anger.

Anxiety links the cognitive and emotional experiences of pain to an array of individual and cultural responses. The range of responses increases when anxiety is uncoupled from sensory pain. Judgments made about health and illness, normal and abnormal, then rely even more on cultural and social norms of the society.

Deep Culture and Perception of the Internal Order

In Western cultures, cognition consisting of patterns of thinking, values, and systems of knowledge are elaborated into patterns of thought, constellations of values, and systems of knowledge. Their structure is largely based on the cognitive structure of the language spoken in the society. The essential and distinguishing feature of Western cognitive systems is that they are "theoretical," existing in abstract time and space, purified of all contingencies, circumstances, and variations. Although the state of absolute truth is never attained, it remains the ideal inherited from the Enlightenment.

In contrast, cognition in cultures such as Chinese, and even more so Japanese, is based on the principles of perception and emotion. In comparison to Western European concepts, Japanese patterns of thinking, constellations of values, and systems of knowledge are concrete, like the prototypes, images, and emotions of perception. The famous logic of the Western world, built on mutually exclusive dichotomies of language, has no parallel in Japanese culture, where reason rests on the impressions of social perception. In the Western sense, Japanese deep cultures are not so deep. In a practical sense, Japanese concepts are much more concrete, specific, and impressionistic than Western ones. The insistence in the cultural trilogy that perception of surface culture gradually merges with the cognition of deep culture accommodates the difference between Western and Japanese cultures and all deep cultural differences in between, including the American great sensitivity shift in thinking of the last forty years.

Cognitive Forms of American Culture

The traditional American pattern of thinking is an inductive process that begins with facts and moves upward in abstraction to the formation of concepts. The chief feature of American facts is that they are measurable and, unlike German facts, do not require a history to possess the privilege of objectivity. American induction begins with the facts in a given case, which are arranged according to a single dimension from the point of view of some purpose. Facts are rational, not emotional, and they should be accepted as self-evident.

The attachment of Americans to monodimensions and monocauses is reinforced by language. The English lexicon more naturally forms dichotomies than do many other languages, including Portuguese and certainly Japanese. Adjective pairs such as far-near, good-bad, and light-heavy convey a greater separation than conceptually equivalent adjectives in Japanese and Portuguese (Stewart and Bennett 1991). English language dichotomies often are less balanced than in some other European languages. Typically, one end is given a positive and the other end a negative marking. The cognitive structure of English one would presume would support the American tendency to use dichotomies and polarities in their thinking.

Performance is often reduced to a single "issue." "Adaptation" to an environment or a situation is one example. "Happiness" becomes a measure of overall adjustment, and the margin of "profit" indicates the business success of a company. The *monodimensional* formulation is often matched by the idea of *monocausation*. Americans are deeply interested in finding out "who made the decision," "who did it," or "what caused it." The concentration on a single cause can be seen in the field of industrial safety.

American safety programs typically follow the pattern of "mono" dimension and cause. Safety specialists trace the sequence of events leading up to an accident and examine the actions taken in each event to determine the specific act that deflected the sequence away from safety and toward the accident. Safety programs will be designed to intervene at the point of deviation to prevent a future accident. The analysis is based on the concept of a cause–effect sequence in linear time. Japanese specialists in a similar situation, not sharing American cultural assumptions, would be more likely to identify a lack of "concentrated consciousness of perception," *kokoro gake*, as an explanation of what happened to bring about the accident.

The Emotion of Anger

The fleshing out of anger in the analysis relies on Lakoff (1987). The form and content of the thought in anger is extracted from words by the linguistic analysis of the metaphors and mental images used by the imagination in perception to convert angry experience into concepts and images and eventually into words (Lakoff 1987). The fixed expressions of English, reported in parentheses, are adaptations taken from Lakoff and used in the text to elaborate the conceptual metaphors.

In the folk mind, anger is understood as a negative emotion that produces undesirable physiological reactions and is considered dangerous to others and inhibiting of normal functioning (Lakoff 1987). From the point of view of psychology, anger motivates the angry one to respond aggressively, in contrast to fear, which motivates flight, withdrawal, or avoidance of the source of fear.

The emotion of anger noticeably increases body heat, internal blood pressure, and muscular pressure. More subtle is physical agitation ("she was shaking with anger") and interference with accurate perception ("I was so mad, I couldn't see straight"). The emotion is understood to be inside the body, which is viewed as a container ("she was brimming with rage" and "she could not contain herself"). An explosion may be prevented by the application of sufficient force and energy to contain anger inside, but when anger increases past a certain limit, the pressure explodes and the person loses control ("he blew his stack"); what was inside comes out ("smoke poured out of his ears") (Lakoff 1987, p. 381). The "smoke" of the example reminds us that "fire" is a concept used in instances of heat applied to solids ("your insincere apology just added fuel to the fire") (p. 382).

Recognizing the danger inherent in anger, the angry person views it as an opponent in a struggle ("she fought back her anger"). When anger focuses on danger to others, there is a widespread metaphor in Western culture that passions are beasts inside a person.

> . . . there is a part of each person that is a wild animal. Civilized people are supposed to keep that part of them private, that is, they are supposed to keep the animal inside them. In the metaphor, loss of control is equivalent to the animal getting loose. And the behavior of a person who has lost control is various passions—desire, anger, etc. In the case of anger, the beast presents a danger to other people. [Lakoff 1987, p. 492]

The folk mind imagines that the animal is "sleeping and is dangerous to awaken" ("he has a monstrous temper"). The dangerous animal's aggressiveness is angry behavior ("he unleashed his anger" and "his anger is insatiable") (Lakoff 1987, pp. 392–394). At the heart of anger, the "insatiable appetite" of the dangerous animal drives behavior, and it can be linked to a corresponding idea, "demands," found in the "opponent" metaphor. Both concepts suggest that the cause of anger is a physical annoyance ("he's a pain in the neck") (pp. 394–395). This form of annoyance involves both an offender and a victim. Since the offender is at fault, in English, the strong polarity of American dichotomies makes out the victim to be a person who is innocent and who has the right to get angry. The clear separation between victim and offender does not seem to be so strong in Japanese culture. The difference probably reflects an American cultural theme (see Stewart and Bennett 1991). The concept of victim and offender will be the major metaphor to be extracted from anger and applied to American culture.

In the folk mind, for someone to go wild, flail arms, and foam at the mouth is a sign of anger, but the agitation is also a sign of insanity ("he got so angry he went out of his mind"). The overlap of signs provides a basis for the metaphor that anger is insanity. The cognitive structure of anger is expanded and articulated around the metaphor that anger is lust and rape. A lustful person is a dangerous animal ("he's a wolf"; "she's a tigress in bed"), and lust is connected to the animal's insatiable appetite in the form of lust as hunger and the object of hunger as food ("he is sex-starved"; "she had him drooling"). As with anger, heat is also a concept for lust ("I'm burning with desire"; "she's an old flame"), and so is insanity ("I'm crazy about her"; "she got me delirious") (Lakoff 1987, p. 409). Finally, anger has a direct metaphor in "lust is war" ("he's known for his conquests"; "that's quite a weapon you've got there"; "I'd better put on my warpaint"; "she surrendered to him"). Sexuality is a physical force, and lust is a reaction to that embodied force ("she's devastating"; "she's dressed to kill"; "what a bombshell") (pp. 410–411).

The scenario for producing anger—as well as violence and many wars— begins with an offending event that constitutes an injustice. The scale of justice can be balanced only by some act of retribution by the victim, who has the right to anger. The wrongdoer is the target of the retribution. Since anger is insatiable, responses to anger often take on the shape of reparations and revenge. The work of anger is to inflict harm and destruction on the other. The outcome is pain of the body and suffering of the mind.

Among the conceptual metaphors elaborated, "danger" and "struggle" offer the elements for the narrative of anger in human conflict. In anger as in danger, an impression forms of anger, the self out of control, standing in a struggle in an attempt at an act of retribution. The ontology of anger must include a self, divided from anger, body, and mind like a window opening upon the psychologies of projection onto others, introjection into the self, images of others, myths of the enemy, stereotypes and scapegoats. Anger is separate from the self and it can explode out of control. The self cannot then be held responsible for its acts, because the self is acting under coercion (Lakoff 1987).

The narrative for seeking retribution is not the only one. Someone who turns away from anger, responding kindly, is morally raised. A second narrative is of someone who manages to control anger and is praised for it. A third narrative is of someone who cannot control anger and is considered emotionally "unbalanced." The norm in the culture, however, is that someone with intense anger is forced to attempt an act of retribution (Lakoff 1987). The cultural expectation is that a "real man" has the force of character and the strength to respond energetically to a painful injustice inflicted on him.

The analysis of the cognitive structure and narrative of anger moves its role out of deep and into procedural culture, filling the empty narrative with protagonists engaged in struggles in specified contexts. Emotions will be treated as issuing from cognitive interpretations imposed on external reality, rather than directly from reality itself (Ortony et al. 1988). The reality of procedural culture comes from concepts in the social psychology of procedural culture in the form of functional cognitive systems, conceived as "flexible and variable organizations of cognitive processes directed toward some fixed end." Procedural culture is the core of culture and cultural differences; it is central to the cultural trilogy, offering "the possibility of an eventual integration of theory and fact" (Cole and Scribner 1974, pp. 192–194).

Procedural Culture and the Pursuit of Goals

Procedural culture is a synthesis of surface and deep culture. In a generalized form it preserves the context of surface culture and a direction in behavior that can be interpreted as purpose, intention, or goal orientation. The perceiver of surface becomes the self in deep and an "agent" or "role-player" in the pursuit of goals in procedural culture. Causation includes aspects of the social environment, probable conditions, and, to a degree, agencies beyond logic that might be called "circumstantial" and "systemic." In many cases their origins are in culture, as in the case study of pain reported below, patterns of managing the body.

Patterns of Managing Pain, the Body, and Others

In many societies the ability to control the expression of the physical anguish, the dread, and fear of pain and to suppress fight-or-flight reactions becomes a test of strength of character and masculinity. Mastery of the experience of pain is also used in many societies to test whether someone is qualified for membership in privileged groups, many of which require inflicting pain in the education, training, or rites of passage for admission (Zborowski 1969). This is the third function of pain.

The fourth function of pain is communication. The response, whether a cry, a lamentation, an exultation, or silent suppression, tells the community about the individual's courage, strength, devotion, or grief (Zborowski 1969). The pain experience is an expression of a need for help, and its communication is a request for help. When the request is frustrated, the persistence of the pain becomes a symbol of rejection. The repeated complaint of pain is also a disguised form of aggression in the guise of retribution against frustrating, rejecting authorities such as a physician or family. Unyielding symptoms of pain can be upsetting to the physician. The symptom's structure bears some important similarities to that of the paranoid delusion of persecution (Szasz 1957).

The two functions of pain discussed above offer a useful background for analyzing findings of a research study on the different reactions to the experience of pain of four ethnic groups of war veterans in a veteran's hospital (Zborowski 1969). The objective of the research study was to test the hypothesis that the cultural background of a sick individual is a major factor in shaping the patient's attitudes and behavior in pain and illness. Four ethnic groups were selected for the study: Jewish, Italian, Irish, and Old American patients. The last ethnicity, Anglo-Saxon, Protestant, was selected to represent the attitudes and behavior patterns of the cultural majority in the United States.

The veterans selected for the study were divided into two groups. In one group all patients suffered from a herniated disc. The origin of the experience of pathological pain was the same from patient to patient. Any differences in reporting pain could be attributed to individual differences in the patient, including the four different ethnic identities. In the second group the patients were selected randomly from veterans with different diagnoses. If similarity of responses clustered according to ethnic identities rather than medical diagnosis, the results would be powerful evidence for the role of ethnicity in determining pain experience.

The characteristic behavior patterns of the Old American were described as responses to pain as a warning signal that triggers purposeful, rational behavior directed toward the rational management of pain. The Old Americans were "good" patients who cooperated with the staff and complained about their pain with restraint. The patients' attitudes were generally optimistic and at times sprinkled with humor. Old American patients tended to conceal their pain and to withdraw from other people. Pain was seen as a source of information that should not necessarily be shared with members of the family but should be discussed with specialists (doctor and nurses) whose attitude is technical and rational. The Old American patients were similar to the Jewish patients in treating their pain experience as a sign of the future, and both differed from the Italian patients, who were preoccupied with their immediate pain experience and gave little thought to the future course of their disease.

The Jewish patients, along with the Italians, were more dissatisfied, critical, and demanding than the Old Americans or the Irish patients. The characteristic attitude toward pain of the Jewish patient was emotional expressiveness. They were inclined to emphasize the perception and feeling of pain and, more so than any other group, showed anxiety about their illnesses and had forebodings about the outcome. They believed that pain was an experience that had to be understood to dispel the uncertainty that their pain and illness held in store for them in the future. These feelings led the Jewish patients to consult a physician earlier than patients in other groups. In the final analysis, however, the Jewish patient believed that the patient knows best and not the doctor. This motivated the patients to consult more than one physician and weigh their opinions against one another.

That the Irish seemed to be the most cooperative patients could be evidence of the "resigned and defeated attitude that they seemed to adopt after a prolonged period of pain and illness" (Zborowski 1969, p. 242). They were the most depressed of the four groups, expressing worry and pessimism about the effect of their illness upon their body and masculinity. They spoke of their illness as suffering that must be endured alone. Their descriptions of the sensations of pain were confused and vague. The Irish used comparative illustrations and metaphors to describe their pain experiences, while the Old American and Jewish patients were precise in describing theirs. The Irish displayed little of the optimism and forethought of the Old American, experienced little of the family support of the Jewish patients, and did not share the Italians' preoccupation with the present. The Irish, along with the Old Americans, were more likely than the other two groups to describe the quality of their pain as sharp and stabbing rather than aching and dull. The Italians described their pain as constant and present all the time. The Irish, Old Americans, and Jewish patients described it as intermittent, which is probably more clinically accurate (Zborowski 1969).

The Italian patients resembled the Jewish in emotional expressiveness but differed in the preoccupation with relief from pain and disregard for the illness. The Italians wanted relief because pain interfered with pleasure. Concentration on the delights of everyday life led Italian patients to respond to pain expressively and dramatically, in vague and confusing terms, creating an impression among the hospital staff that they were "unstable, overemotional or hypochondriac" patients (Zborowski, 1969, p. 163). An Old American patient observed that an "Italian needs to be psychoanalyzed" (p. 55). The Italian time orientation to the present impelled the patients to concentrate on their pain and lost pleasures rather than on their illnesses, as if their only purpose was to gain relief for the pleasures of bodily integrity, sex, personal relations, and good Italian food home-cooked by mother. In keeping with their time orientation to the present, the Italians, unlike the Jews, were mostly concerned with the immediate experience of pain rather than the future effect or the significance of the symptoms. As they endured pain, the sensation seemed unrelieved, constant, and intolerable. More frequently than the Jewish patients, the Italians claimed that they could not tolerate pain (Zborowski, 1969). Their behavior raised doubts in the minds of doctors and nurses, and in Old Americans about their emotional stability.

During the hospital treatment of the war veterans, cultural values toward health, illness, and pain pervaded the attitudes of both medical staff and patients. The cultural differences in values and behavior of the four ethnic groups of patients offer a striking demonstration of procedural culture's power to encode the human experience of pain. With the cultural differences in details of the experience of pain demonstrated, we shall look at sociocultural premises of emotion from the point of view of society. The analysis will follow the parameters of the second triad of the trilogy.

TIME-FACTORED ACTIVITIES

Daily activities of life flow in three currents marked by time orientations of present, future, and past. Interior life, conducted among family members and close associates, is present factored to satisfy urgent physiological, security, and belonging needs. The second activity current, work life, is time factored in the near future and satisfies the achievement need, while the third current, activities of public life, in social-political culture, is time factored in the past and far future to satisfy the need for power. The patterns of activities, with their motives and styles of life, form the structure of the social order.

The cognitive structure of time orientation used to construct the model of society spontaneously generates diffuse emotional forces that permeate interior, work, and public life. In American society the feeling edge is weak but the field of mental health offers a good example. For a long time psychiatrists and clinical psychologists have observed that anxiety is more a feeling of dread about the future than about the present. One clinical psychologist, Rappaport, has elaborated time experience as a central concept in the symptoms of clinical patients. He describes a young woman, diagnosed with schizophrenia, who declined to talk about her life before hospitalization and would not consider the question of life beyond the hospital. She seemed totally immersed in a "narrow-slice of present-centered time" (Rappaport 1990, p. 16). Another patient with a manic disposition conceived the present as a series of disconnected images that seemed to run one into another (Rappaport 1990). About time beyond, Rappaport writes that "when the future ceases to be part of experience, the result is a sense of hopelessness that we call depression" (Rappaport 1990, p. 18).

The depressed person reviews the disappointments in the past, one dismal memory leads to another, and depression sets in. The three time perspectives of past, present, and future are out of balance. The goal of therapy is to create temporal balance by working through the time elements of succession and duration of events.

Rappaport's system of therapy is consistent with both his explanation of depression and American time assumptions. Outside Old American culture, however, the theory may falter. In therapy, the client's time orientation must shift from the cyclic present to future linear order. Simultaneously, the client has to shift from the motive of affiliation to achievement and from an emotional tone of "being" to one of "happiness," or at least "optimism." Depression is caught in the jaws of the past, and the client has to be shaken loose in order to assume an open view of the future. He or she must glance beyond the boundaries of the extended present and enter the future. In so doing, the client is involved in deep and procedural cultural differences that may work against the therapeutic process.

The second source of emotion in American society originates directly in the cultural bonds of belonging of interpersonal culture. From the societal point of view the emotions are the six primordial sentiments of the third triad of the cultural trilogy, forming the social organization of the culture. American primordial sentiments evoked by the social actualities of language, region, tradition, customs, and ethnicity have been relatively weak and have never threatened the political integration of the nation. Race, however, is a different matter. Its prejudice provoked a bloody civil war and its effects linger on. Since race is central to the great sensitivity shift, we shall return to the subject.

The third source of emotion in the society, originating in the interpersonal procedures of "belonging," has been consigned to a historical reserve of meaning. In the eighteenth century, Americans expressed their emotions in ways no longer admired. The change that took effect in the cultural ethos was driven by the economic-technical culture. Emotions such as anger, fear, happiness, and sadness are not readily accessible in social life, forming the black hole in American culture today. They have been drained of their meaning in social life during the development of American values and methods in work life. Economic-technical culture has been dominant in American life for at least one hundred and fifty years, and in that period of time has reshaped the values and procedures of both interior and public life as well as those of work life.

Since anger is a major force in the great sensitivity shift in American culture, it is important to gain a perspective on how the status and role of anger in American life was created in economic-technical culture. The few comments below about the history of anger present an example of top-down causation—work life changes individual values and behavior—and an example of lateral diffusion—work values infiltrate interior life and public life, changing their values and procedures.

Economic-Technical Culture and Anger

American preference for individualism, practicality, and rationality over "passion" in human relations appeared already in the eighteenth century, competing with and eventually banishing emotions into benign neglect. The practical attitude of "technicism" conquered the wilderness and showed its mettle once again at the closing of the eighteenth century, in 1799, when Eli Whitney and Simon North invented the mass-assembly line. As American business developed throughout the new century, technicism invaded work environments and gave shape to American industry. By the end of the nineteenth century, American managers had started the effort to establish rational thought and efficient operations in the workplace—creating what Max Weber called the "iron cage of rationality."

There was no room within the cage for passion in human work relations. During the nineteenth century the competition between the emotions—particularly anger—and rationality was settled by a concerted effort to replace emotions with practical problem-solving procedures. Technicism became a dominant force in American life and a major support for the ethic of good works. A rational peak of sorts was reached in 1911 with the publication of Frederick W. Taylor's *The Principles of Scientific Management*. Impersonal efficiency, time control of activities, and the management of anger replaced social discipline imposed by authority.

By the 1920s industrial morality had infiltrated private life alongside the pocket watch, electricity, and the internal combustion engine. The American home was rationalized as had been the workplace. Family life became drier and less emotional, but more efficient. In the new climate, anger was incompatible with love and affiliation. In the 1940s American social psychologists once more turned their attention to human relations. By the 1960s achievement scores had declined, and the motive for power had been dismissed as a tool for interpreting human relations. The important cultural evolutions were around racial and ethnic relations. At that time rebellion against rational and efficient home, school, and workplace environments became common, and training programs conducted to sensitize people to the feelings of each other and to help them improve their human relations came into vogue (Stearns and Stearns 1986). In the late 1960s and early 1970s Americans debated the role of anger in interpersonal relations. Although some constraints were lifted against its expression (Stearns and Stearns 1986), American culture retained its dislike of anger.

In the second half of the twentieth century, anger returned in the form of social rage. Today the presence of anger and rage is one of the major ingredients in the malaise in American society. The top-down effect of events since World War II ended have wrought a shift from the ethic of good works to an ethic of sensitivity. Since the events that brought about the change occurred in the social side of culture, we shall turn to interpersonal culture to gain a better grasp of the interpersonal dynamics of social life in American society.

Interpersonal Culture

Interpersonal culture is the riverbed for all cultural systems. The web of cultural forms constructed from the satisfaction of the basic need *belonging* functions as the "infrastructure" or the "infraculture" in the society. Interpersonal culture is changed and adapted to the special requirements of economic-technical and sociopolitical activities, but the core values and procedures of adaptations remain in interpersonal culture. In the United States, life in interpersonal culture can be equated with "private" life and with "personal and informal" culture among intimates. But these are limited and misleading terms in the cross-cultural field because cultures with a strong sense of a social order have radically different ideas of what is personal and private and, among some cultures—Chinese, for example—there is no idea conceptually equivalent to "private" life. All cultures, however, can be described as having an *interior life*.

Belonging

The social psychology of belonging revolves around the two principles of "inclusion" and "exclusion." When a group forms, some people are included but others are excluded. The relative emphasis placed on inclusion or exclusion in establishing group norms and solidarity is a major source of cultural differences. American individuals traditionally join a group to pursue common interests, in the process emphasizing the principle of inclusion.

Traditional American habits of the heart ascribe neutrality or perhaps indifference, but certainly not hostility, to the other, the outsider. This is the only culture in the world in which "Hello, stranger" is received as a friendly greeting. Americans typically remain in groups because they choose to do so. It is the inclusion principle that establishes social cohesion, the desire of group members to remain together. Americans since the beginning of the nation have held the value of equality in high regard, disliked status, and preferred achievement. Their individualistic and informal values in interpersonal culture parallel their democratic procedures in public life. Americans developed a comprehensive interpersonal culture called the American Creed. The Swedish sociologist and economist, Myrdal, writing in 1944, described it as "'the *most explicitly expressed* system of general ideals' of any country in the West: the ideals of the essential dignity and equality of all human beings, of inalienable rights to freedom, justice, and opportunity" (Schlesinger 1992, p. 27).

These ideals were taught in the schools, preached in the churches, and accepted as standards in the courts. The American Creed was saturated with procedural culture, in such expressions as Benjamin Franklin's "There are no Gains without Pains," or as Poor Richard observed, "One to-day is worth two to-morrows" (Foerster 1947, p. 137). The expressions were general in value and procedural in spirit, connecting the individual with the social-political culture. The creed served as a guide for American pragmatism of self-government. A problem-solving approach was applied to community issues in which citizens had a voice. Pragmatism required sensitivity to the facts rather than sensitivity to theories or traditions. Much of the weight of the courses of action accepted was judged by the anticipated consequences to the actions. Furthermore, the American style of thinking was case-particular. Conclusions reached in one locality did not generalize to another situation, where participants had to decide anew on their course of action. In this pragmatic climate it was essential that participants be able to discuss the issues and reach a political consensus.

From the early days of the country, the basic need for physical security was based on individualism. The right to bear arms still lingers as an issue in the society today. Psychological security also has its roots in individualism and in keeping busy: "Idle hands are the devil's workshop." The core of individualism in interpersonal culture eventually supports the fundamental moral sentiment Americans inherited, the Puritan ethic of good works. A man was to be judged not by his status or his position but by the consequences of his efforts. Ethics becomes associated with the achievement motive and with the performance of the individual.

These observations about American interpersonal culture suggest that Americans believe in an objective, concrete reality out there. The assumption is rooted in the action and performance mode of procedural culture. The commitment to an external physical reality, the reality of nature (Diaz-Guerrero 1967), leads Americans to introduce the technicism of procedural culture into their interior lives. The "American method" is strong and famous throughout the world. Introduced into American interpersonal culture, technicism conveys a pragmatic feeling of convenience but also an appearance that is mechanical and impersonal. The objective reality of American interior life is ultimately rooted in individualism that reduces the emotional need for belonging.

In contrast to American technical interior life, Latino minority groups in the United States have an interpersonal culture that provides security and belonging on a social, not individual, basis. Writing about Mexicans, Diaz-Guerrero (1967) describes "the reality created by the interactions between two or more people in a social or communicative relationship—their attitudes toward each other, their expectations of each other, the many intangibles, conscious and unconscious, of their mental feelings" (p. 17).

Mexican "interpersonal reality" is an internal state of mind and emotion rooted in interior life. The rubbing of the two realities, Mexican and American, against each other in the United States creates difficult problems in those situations where the dominant Anglo culture delivers social and psychological services to Latino minorities that require intrusions by Anglo culture into Latino interpersonal culture. The major cross-cultural obstacle is found in the tension between American procedural culture and Latino interpersonal culture.

In the field of mental health, for instance, Latinos do not have a concept equivalent to the procedural concept of Americans: *salud mental* does not exist (Padilla and Ruiz 1973). The technical focus on purely "psychological" qualities of the "individual," and getting something done in treatment, are not separated by Latinos from the total well-being of the "person." The Latino conceives of his condition of well-being and expresses it in terms that include both physical and psychological components (Padilla and Ruiz 1973). The total view of the person is based on interpersonal reality in distinction to American external and objective reality (Diaz-Guerrero 1975). The differences in the two cultural views of reality create difficulties for the delivery of mental health services.

Specialized mental health clinics staffed by professionals usually do not attract many Latino clients, who perceive the professional staff as alien and hostile. The use of a punctual fifty-minute therapy session once a week on schedule has proven ineffective. Better results in therapy have been obtained in centers that combine, in some form, (1) community consultation as a preventive measure, (2) crisis intervention as a matter of course, and (3) "backup" treatment with individual, group, family, or drug therapies. In these cases delivery of health services is based on the broad perspectives of the continual flow of time and the social background of family and community. Clinics are more effective when they function like community centers, providing facilities for sports and for social and educational activities.

At the abstract level of epistemology, Latinos act as if an out-of-awareness social order exists that imposes social controls and imperatives on their behavior. The social order is differentiated into strata, roles, manners, and values that create a sense of identity and belonging within their interpersonal reality. The social side of culture influences behavior to a degree not found with Americans. The principle of exclusion in forming groups, mostly ignored in Anglocentric cultures, becomes more important with Latinos. Outsiders and strangers are more likely to be seen as dangerous and threatening. Group solidarity derives much of its strength from fear. Some groups develop categorical enemies, if real ones do not exist, and myths of the enemy that exaggerate threats from outsiders against members of the group, spurring them to hang together rather than separately—as Benjamin Franklin once said.

In many places—Eastern Europe for one—where group solidarity depends inordinately on exclusiveness, the need for categorical enemies to bolster group morale naturally influences the explanation of negative events as conspiracies plotted by outsiders. Under these social conditions, reports of conspiracies blamed on outsiders raise the question of whether such beliefs are abnormal or are standard operating procedures. It is clear that groups formed primarily on the principle of exclusion function in an emotional climate that would be considered paranoid in the United States, leading to the conclusion that the diagnosis of paranoia, and generally of emotional states of all kinds, must take into account the norms and procedures of an individual's reference culture.

In the United States the realism of racial prejudice creates social conditions for blacks to be suspicious of outsiders and consider them as potential enemies. Black novelists writing in the midst of the civil rights movement described the damage done to blacks by the condition of their lives. The effect prevented any black from entering into American competition and incapacitated him as a social being. James Baldwin, writing in 1961, insisted that the quality of black life was tragic. As for the primitive virtues of the black community, Baldwin writes of the "gates of paranoia," in reference to the black intellectual living among those who have no solutions (Berman 1968, pp. 73–74).

The plight of African Americans in the United States has qualities similar to paranoia. In some cases paranoid individuals develop elaborate systems of delusion and persecution. Paranoid feelings and cognition create an enemy and require evidence to confirm the reality of persecution. The search for persecutors produces symptoms of paranoia. Feeling powerless, the paranoid localizes control and power in the external society. Personal failures and undesirable qualities are projected onto others, but ideal qualities are introjected. The narrative of a good but vulnerable self persecuted by a wily enemy dramatizes the plight and struggles of a victim who lives in an oppressive social world. Although the paranoid views of self and others contrast sharply with traditional American social behavior, the cognitive structure and narrative of paranoia resembles in many respects the cognitive structure and narrative of African Americans in their civil rights movement.

The changes wrought in the society to include African Americans within the American Creed can be described as a shift from a civil to a cultural organization of society. The feeling of identity and belonging, once almost entirely a civil phenomenon of American citizenship, has changed to emotional identification with the social actualities of ethnicity and race and, to a lesser degree, of language, tradition, religion, and region. Although the shift is limited and does not threaten the country's political integrity, many Americans are perceptibly disturbed by the changes, among them the historian Schlesinger (1992). He writes that, with the ending of the cold war, ideological conflicts subsided and humanity reentered "a possibly more dangerous era of ethnic and racial animosity" (Schlesinger 1992, pp. 9–10).

The malaise in American life will be described and analyzed in the following section. The disturbance of spirits, according to the analysis, was caused by changes in the identity of Americans, which in turn involved a fundamental shift in thinking and in ethics.

SOCIAL-POLITICAL CULTURE

Social-political culture refers to the recognition of a people's saying, "I am American," "I am German," or "I am Japanese." The reference is to "passport" identity and national culture. The three nationalities stand for three separate prototypes of identity.

"American" suggests someone who is a citizen of the United States and whose self-image is civic. Pressed a bit further, the American is likely to reveal a North European origin, perhaps Anglocentric. The Old American veteran in the case study of pain fits the category. Although each veteran in the study had several identities—"veteran" was one, "patient" was another—all the self-images integrated into one summit identity composed of two centers. The first is civic identity and, in the case of the Old American, the status of veteran and of patient in a government veteran's hospital are civic factors. The second, the cultural identity, is interpreted as the particular way taken by each veteran to express his experience of pain. It was composed of behavior and relations in interactions with each other and with the medical staff and feelings of belonging with other Old Americans made prominent by contrast with the different and distinctive way the Italians responded to pain. The Italian patients' way of responding to pain diverged from the dominant culture of the hospital and set them aside as a minority in the sense that their culture was different from the dominant Anglocentric culture. While the Old Americans seemed to respond to pain and to the medical staff in a way appropriate to the role of patients recovering from illness, the Italian did not adapt to the sociocultural expectations in the situation, earning the reputation of not being a good patient. The general conclusion about Old American veterans holds for American citizens. Their summit identity is well anchored in civic matters in the way that the Old American patient is businesslike about being a patient. The cultural component in the American citizen is centered on civic factors, not cultural.

German citizens, somewhat like the Italian veteran in the hospital study, have self-images in which the duality between civic and cultural forces is evident. The civic identity may be negative: many Germans have strong and mixed feelings toward their country. Whether positive or negative, they establish a civic identity grounded in German ideology and politics. On the cultural side of the self-image, Germans will show attachments to language, traditions, and region and probably display attitudes toward race and ethnicity. The integrated summit identity will be dual, divided between civic and cultural factors.

The Japanese, like the Old American, will display little duality in their summit identities rooted in all six primordial sentiments. Japanese culture is a seamless web that begins in the individual and ends in the entire people, with the Emperor and his family as symbols standing at the head of the Japanese nation and culture. American as civic, German as dual, and Japanese as cultural provide three prototypes of the possible summit identities of social-political culture.

The process of identification, ending in summit identity, parallels the process of perception and its construction of the self-concept. In forming summit identity, pain and emotion play central roles, particularly fear and anger for minority groups. As for suffering, the ethic of sensitivity has refreshed the desire of Americans to abolish pain from interpersonal life. The effort at suppression raises the question of what is the meaning of tragedy in life and its role in American culture.

Tragic Vision of Life

Pain is a physiological signal that warns the body about threats to its integrity and mentally lays down the challenge for the mind to defeat grief and misery. The experience of pain functions as a reality check on the range and the limits of potential human responses to the facts of life. Historically, pain has accelerated human progress and provoked cultural advances that stimulated human elation. Pain has also spurred advances in the sciences, particularly in applications to medicine and health care. Turning to the long Western traditions in the humanities, epic tragedies attempt to relieve pain by giving deep meaning to suffering, and, parallel to it, comedy celebrates joy and happiness by suppressing pain with laughter.

Societal reactions in the past treated pain as experiences that should be slighted and even ignored, but, at the same time, the lost experiences should be shaped and retained as natural parts of life. Religious observances in days past were full of awe at suffering exacted from the experiences of pain (Sykes 1992). Teachers were demanding of discipline and performance at the cost of punishment rather than the pleasure of reward. Secret societies, privileged groups, and even the society at large collected a toll in pain for admission to their orders.

The reserves of discipline, awe, invention, and mystery entrenched in the pain of the body have often been exploited for the power and wealth of societies. All modern nations have adopted the ethic of heroic sacrifice that commits the lives of its youth to the defense and the ventures of the state. In primordial wars such as the one in progress in the Balkans, where the contest is in culture more than in politics, the uses of pain are exploited not only in frames of combat but also in the frames of torture, rape, and genocide.

Pain is a central part of life and, lifted to the higher plane of human suffering, dedicates the tragic vision of life. Each human being becomes a creature in the hands of fate whose suffering yields unbounded insights about life. In the tragic view, pain is a reality and part of the inevitable suffering shared by all human beings. The bleak view of life can be illuminated by the humanities, arts, and religion, making the duration of the present more enjoyable. Humanism can also function to reduce the risks of materialism embodied in economics. But the most important implications of the tragic vision in the world today are in politics and ideology. The psychology of culture yields several views of human nature held in various societies. The Japanese, who have never been strangers to either natural or human disasters, accept the source of victimhood to be fate and the worldly conditions of life rather than the social order. Since everyone is a victim, the Japanese grasp the fate of a victim as ontology rather than sociology. The moral sentiment that emerges is endurance, the perception of ruling power as benevolence, and the goals of societal life as peace and harmony.

In other societies, as in Serbia, victims are created in the past. But remembering the past is episodic: each reconstruction of a past event is only a window opening upon past events selected for a view that reflects the emotions and intentions in the present. Chronology is not part of the process of remembering the past. In the Balkans, where history moves in circles, Serbs, Croats and Bosnians, Austrians, Hungarians, and Turks alike have had their periods as conquerors and as victims. But the Serbs feel that the defeats and oppression dealt by the fortunes of history have stigmatized them as victims at the hands of other Balkan peoples. The moral sentiment appearing in Serbian consciousness is based on pain:

> As a moral ideal, nationalism is an ethic of heroic sacrifice, justifying the use of violence in the defense of one's nation against enemies, internal or external. These claims—political, moral, and cultural—underwrite each other. The moral claim that nations are entitled to be defended by force or violence depends on the cultural claim that the needs they satisfy for security and belonging are uniquely important. The political idea that all peoples should struggle for nationhood depends on the cultural claim that only nations can satisfy these needs. The cultural idea in turn underwrites the political claim that these needs cannot be satisfied without self-determination. [Ignatieff 1993, p. 5]

Consecrated to the primordial struggle, the Serbs aim to gain hegemony in regions they consider homeland, to cleanse the region of non-Serbs, and to exact retribution through military power. There seems to be no vision of the future emerging other than creation of cultural integrity for a "master race." Both in reconstructing the past and in planning for the future, economic and political realities are twisted and often ignored to fit into the cultural narrative of victims driven by the ethic of heroic sacrifice.

Finally, it is possible to identify groups of people with self-images of victims, living in societies where perpetrators of victimization are part of the political power structure. This is the American situation, but its activities have veered away sharply from the tragic vision. "Although victimism can trace its lineage to liberalism, it is not itself liberalism. Nor is it updated Christianity.

It militates against ideas of equity, fairness, and process. Its natural tone is one of assertion of prerogatives, a demand for reparations" (Sykes 1992, p. 20).

The American formulation of victims conveys a strong impression of ideology and political goals driven by the cognitive structure of anger. It does not have the redeeming feature of the tragic view of life that incorporates pain as a natural part of life and then transcends it to a higher plane of meaning in human existence. In the United States the attack on pain has been unrelenting. Religious observances have neutralized the suffering and awe of their teachings with the injection of therapeutic ideas and feelings from popular psychology and human relations training. Teachers devote an inordinate amount of time and effort to coping with problems of human relations and discipline. The societal attack on pain makes it dangerous for the teacher to risk measures of punishment, discipline, correction, teaching to content, or objective grading of failing performances. Public language has been purged of words, phrases, and sayings that might in any way embarrass, insult, or irritate students.

Harsh as they may sound, these statements by Grudin, quoted in Sykes (1992), convey the impression that the assault on pain launched upon society has taken refuge in a maudlin morality based on the belief that it is possible to banish both pain and insensitivity from human relations. When people are insensitive, say and do "hurtful" things, the cause is prejudice. Society is goaded to believe that happiness and sensitivity are natural in human nature and infringements are violations of human rights that should be treated with litigation supported by authority. But the logic of sensitivity is asymmetrical: victims are not responsible for their own social attitudes and prejudices, which are the bitter fruits of their own suffering from oppression. Victims occupy the moral high ground and are granted a "culture of infinite entitlement" (Sykes 1992, p. 19).

The change raises several questions. First, what were the events that brought about the change? Second, what was the nature of the change? Third, what mechanism operated to replace the ethic of good works with the ethic of sensitivity? Fourth, what are the prospects for the future?

AMERICAN CULTURAL CHANGES: GREAT SENSITIVITY SHIFT

Events That Brought About the Change

The chain of events that brought about the great sensitivity shift was initiated by the civil rights movement. In the 1940s, following the end of World War

II, American blacks were emboldened by the American Creed to organize for equal opportunities in employment and to oppose segregation in the armed forces. How could Americans sustain a policy of white supremacy when they had fought and defeated Hitler and his doctrine of the master race? Such thoughts and feelings sparked the movement for civil rights of minorities.

A second chain of events formed the social-political background for the civil rights movement. The generation that fought in World War II ushered in a new age of modernism in its interior life. Under the G.I. Bill of Rights, veterans stormed the citadels of higher learning in unparalleled numbers and social diversity. As they moved into their careers and started families, in the role of parents they indulged their children and egged on a youth culture that was in full swing and in revolt by the 1960s. "They had, in effect, created a new world for their children by dismantling the repressive structures of the past. They had challenged obsolete notions of character and rejected outmoded ideas of morality. And they had raised the banner of human happiness at the very center of the dour bourgeois power structure" (Sykes 1992, p. 65).

The new generation adopted an adversarial posture and acquired a subversive intent to revise the culture that had produced it, attempting to act out the values of their parents that, sometimes, they had only talked about. The counterculture movement of the '50s, permeated by cultural anxiety, adopted an existential vocabulary centered on terms like *human*, *warmth*, and *compassion* and avoided a direct treatment of power. The liberals and writers of the decade were more interested in moral protest than political analysis. Substitution of the term *human* for *political* was the crucial event in constructing a narrative for the perception of reality that sinks into resentful subjectivity while minimizing sensory evidence from external perception (Berman 1968). The counterculture created dwelt upon a psychological state of "permanent aggrievement" seeking targets for indignation. In the 1960s they found what they were looking for in the civil rights movement. They saw in it a riveting moral drama in the appeal to basic human rights. For many the movement resonated a social ethic about community (Sykes 1992).

In the beginning of his leadership, Martin Luther King Jr. rejected victimization as the defining experience of the American black. He insisted upon "respect for our lives" and opposed violence. King created a momentum of nonviolence and passive resistance with an emphasis on moral restraint and forgiveness. But with the passage of time, the tone changed as King spoke about "psychological and spiritual genocide and compensatory treatments" from white society (Sykes 1992, pp. 71–72).

In the 1950s the civil rights movement began with demonstrations for individual rights—the right to sit on any seat on a public bus or to eat at a white lunch counter. These actions were white-led or at least white-supported and were conspicuously middle class. Much resentment was aroused "by the brutalities suffered by Northern students, ministers, housewives" (Berman 1968, p. 79). But the demonstrations dwindled, shrinking down to public failures or fragmenting into isolated gestures. The first stage of the movement was over as demonstrations were replaced by riots in the cities. In Harlem and Watts the uprisings were spontaneous and gave the impression of a more genuine reflection of black feelings than the demonstrations. The idea of individual rights gave way to collective struggle and the legalism of the demonstrations was replaced by direct action. The movement was radicalized, changing from class to race as black activists replaced white moderates and black radicals replaced white radicals (Berman 1968).

The next step taken in the movement was revolutionary. While most blacks sought only to enjoy the fruits of American society as they were, their quest could not be objectively "satisfied within the framework of existing political and economic relations." (Berman 1968, p. 81). The quest for equality moved beyond the legalism of civil rights and race relations and entered the domains of economics and education in modern society. It became clear that movement toward equality had outstripped private, voluntary efforts and required government action with special consideration granted to blacks as a group (Berman 1968). The idea of communal consideration was seen as a desecration of the principle of individual rights and effectively fragmented the liberal support of the movement (Berman 1968). In 1974 Congress passed the Ethnic Heritage Studies Program, which applied the ethnic ideology to all Americans, compromising their historic right to decide their ethnic identities for themselves. "The ethnic upsurge . . . began as a gesture of protest against Anglocentric culture. It became a cult, and today it threatens to become a counter-revolution against the original theory of America as 'one people,' a common culture, a single nation" (Schlesinger 1992, p. 43).

Americans have lived through a shift in their political culture as the civil ties of the citizen have declined in importance and the cultural bonds among people have increased in value. The feeling of identity and of belonging among African Americans, Hispanics, and other ethnic groups in the United States is rather different from that of traditional Old Americans.

When a group searches for its identity and belonging, it reveals an issue with its own social and cultural cohesion, which may be compared with emotional turbulence of depressed individuals. From the cultural perspective the searcher leaps from one historical episode to another. Episodic memory is selective and is influenced by the prevailing conditions of the group seeking its origins. In the case of American blacks, very quickly cultural identity encounters the realities of slavery, oppression, and suppression. It is a long history of suffering and degradation of human potential. But there are distortions, gaps, and myths connected with all reconstructions of a people's identity and belonging based on a search of origins. The same judgment applies to the reconstructed identity of groups judged, with reason or not, to be dominant or oppressors. The question is not whether one or the other is more accurate, but whether the notion of cultural identity and belonging offers a good and attainable vision of the future.

Changes in American culture have succeeded in cooling the heat of primordial rage. The nature of the change involved some profound aspects of perception, thinking, values, and procedures. The cultural shift has helped to defuse the American potential for primordial conflict.

The Nature of the Change

The changes in American culture ramify throughout surface, deep, and procedural culture. Beginning with perception, the external component, perception of the world, has weakened. Dominating the "new-see" is the impulse to strip external perception of its symbolism and meaning, reducing it to material surfaces of single dimensions that, like pain, are available for almost any interpretation that feelings of anger or pity may require. In a typical study, designed to prove racial prejudice, a frontal photograph of a bearded white male's face is darkened until it is perceived to be a black male. The black and white versions are shown to different groups of subjects to whom each is described in the same way as the perpetrator of a vicious crime in the neighborhood. The subjects in the experiment are then asked to report their fears for their personal safety. The typical result is that the white subjects shown the "black" version of the photograph report significantly more anxiety than those who looked at the "white" version. Since the only difference between the two versions is darkness interpreted as skin color, the conclusion is drawn that the anxiety reported is caused solely by skin color, and it represents racial prejudice. Apparently spared of any doubt, the photographic experiment is generalized to real life. The conclusion seems to be that blacks and whites and presumably everyone else are exactly alike except for skin color. The function of memory as a procedure in forming perception is ignored as well as the symbolism and gestalt of perception. External perception is treated as a sign that can be assigned any meaning. Perception is identified with internal perception with an emphasis placed on opinion or value of perceiver, dismissing sensory stimulation as merely a cover that can be removed mechanically. In other words, the strategy is to dismiss external perception as a mere category that does not influence "perception" itself.

The shift away from external perception results in the growth of "insensitivity to evidence." The reality is that people register differences in physical features among people—and African Americans are particularly perceptive of details of physical appearance and dress—that are interpreted as "racial differences." The evidence seems to sustain the theory that racial and ethnic prejudice is not necessarily a product of the natural attachment to intimates and the invariant perception of difference in others that forms the basis of both ethnicity and race. The source of prejudice is found in human experience that is passed on from one to another, or from generation to generation (Schermerhorn 1978). Racial prejudice is learned in experience or acquired as a "tradition," but it is not inherent in the perception of skin color.

The growing insensitivity to evidence in society seems to be largely unnoticed by Americans, but more noticeable to outsiders. The Australian art critic Hughes has commented upon it. In his treatment of American culture, Hughes stresses the subjectivism that has overtaken American ways of thinking, illuminating his impressions by quoting Auden to the effect that reason has been replaced by insight, knowledge has degenerated into subjective vision, idealism has been supplanted by materialism, and justice by pity (Hughes 1993). These general observations lead beyond perception and into patterns of thinking of deep culture.

Deductive Thought Replaces Inductive Thought

Deductive thought moves from general ideas and feelings toward detailed facts. Inductive thought moves in a reverse direction, beginning with facts and proceeding toward conclusions and general ideas. The weakening of external perception in American society could be expected to lead to an increased reliance on deduction and its emphasis on general ideas and feelings, and that is what has happened in public life. Impelled by their developing social consciousness and driven by anger, American structure of thought and values have been substantially changed.

Following the paradigm of anger, the social order is seen through the eyes of victims in the form of a dichotomy. Victims stand on one side of the field of struggle and oppressors on the opposite side. Victimhood articulates identity and power within the frame of weakness, deficiencies and perceived history of victimization. The complexity of social relationships is reduced to a single issue: all is blamed on oppressors motivated by racism. But victims occupy the moral high ground (Sykes 1992). For example, allegations of white racism by blacks tend to be accepted at face value, but allegations of black racism by whites, if voiced at all, are typically regarded as white racial oppression. In conflict resolution involving victims and oppressors, irrespective of the facts, any judgments reached should be weighed in favor of victims. These feelings and customs guiding communication have acquired values of a morality in the form of an *ethic of sensitivity*, which ordains empathy and compassion for victims. In the field of culture, the ethic applies with particular strength to two groups: members of other cultures from Third World societies and members of minority groups in a field of cultural diversity.

In the ethic, judgments that acts are right or wrong, good or evil, are partly suspended. Acts are judged primarily on whether they are sensitive to or performed by victims. The primary virtues of victim morality are awareness and understanding of victims and the expression of compassion for them. Racial slurs are serious offenses. Allegations by women about sex harassment are more or less treated as facts or as a sign of the frequency of harassment. Furthermore, when victims participate or appear in the content of communication, it is necessary to use correct political language and to confer expected privileges. Performance and achievement are less important than sensitivity. The motive of power in the form of empowerment diminishes the motive of achievement. In education and training, empowerment is sometimes used in place of learning.

The sharp and hostile division between victims and oppressors, and the cohesiveness of the figure of racial prejudice, discourages efforts to relieve discontent and to resolve conflict through persuasion and negotiation. Instead, the tendency is to resort to intimidation and litigation, interjecting into human relations an element of trust and confidence vested primarily in those who wield power. At this point the divide between culture and ideology has been crossed.

The culture of victimhood offers few procedures for coping with tragedy in life. Experiences of life's hard passages are interpreted as the lot of victims. There is little recognition of suffering in life apart from victimization. The victim's distance from tragedy and from a sense of emotional responsibility turns the moral sentiment into a maudlin morality. It is in this context that Americans have learned to plead the innocence of victims as a strategy in persuasion and the mass media to highlight the suffering of victims to stimulate the compassion of consumers as strategies in operations and sales. The cultivation of victimism has taken its toll of compassion and sense of guilt by way of becoming an integrated element in the politics of victimization (Sykes 1992). In the field of business, victim stories in newspapers and on television exhibit several general themes from the ethic of sensitivity. Its driving force based on personal emotions is exploited in fight and struggle stories using anger metaphors.

The range of application for the ethic of sensitivity has changed in three ways. One, the ethic has been extended beyond the tolerance of victim anger to include expression of compassion toward victims and sensitivity to their fear, pride, and esteem. Two, the category of social groups of victims has extended selectively to include Hispanics, women, homosexuals, and others. Asian minorities technically qualify, but their victimhood is often ignored. Three, the identity of victims as individuals threatens to include everyone.

The ethic is dismembered from external perception and from the motor side. Implementation of the ethic runs against American common sense (Howard 1994), violates the American Creed, and disarms American pragmatism. The acute awareness of the ethic of sensitivity is likely to contribute to the sensitivity of the individual, but also to the anxiety. For this reason it has been called "malaise." To succeed in containing primordial conflict, the victim–oppressors dichotomy in some way must conjugate moral and social sentiments in behavior in a way that victims' morality prevails over both the hate and the rationality of perceived oppressors. There is always the danger that an ideology of victimism, together with the abuses and opportunism it generates, will backfire in white anger and in formation of a counterculture that may already be taking place.

In keeping with the ethic of sensitivity, the American view of society has changed. One, in a society reduced to a polarity between victim and oppressors, victims remain individuals connected to society by means of their rights and entitlement, but unencumbered by responsibilities or social obligations uncoupled from their victimhood. Two, victims with different patterns of identity and belonging are likely to see each other not as allies but as competitors. Oppressors, on the other hand, are seen as statistical distributions of being-alike people with differences concealed underneath their cloaks of oppression.

CONCLUSIONS AND PROSPECTS

In this chapter the analysis of the sensitivity shift in American society is based on the duality of the cultural concept. American cultural change is treated as a product of the physiology and social psychology of culture interacting with the sociology of communities. The results obtained from the analysis yield two substantial changes in American society. First, the cognitive structure and content of the American Creed has changed into an ethic of sensitivity. The change is in the *eidos* of the society and consists of a distortion of external perception into a single surface effect, decline of the inductive style in thought, overcasting of achievement motivation by power, classification of the individual as victim or oppressor, and the spoiling of the ethic of good works.

Second, the change simultaneously created a disturbance of spirits, an angry mood described as malaise. Schlesinger (1992) speaks of a "disunited" political nation; Hughes (1993), of a "culture of complaining"; Sykes (1992) analyzes the creation of a "nation of victims"; and Howard (1994) is concerned with the "death of common sense." The change is in the *ethos* and consists of the suppression and repression of pain, release of anger, and the commodification of compassion. The cognitive and emotional changes were inducted by many factors. In this chapter the sources of the sensitivity change have been restricted largely to the agencies of pain and anger in responding to racism. Initial efforts in the civil rights movement to integrate the races and to establish common grounds in education, government, and economics were deflected toward building a power base in sociopolitical life. Although the causes for the shift are many and complex, the acceptance of rage as an agency in the movement naturally explains most changes, if the cognitive structure of anger is included in the analysis as a major factor in the formation of the malaise.

Many questions arise about the depth and the permanence of the ethic of sensitivity. Do the changes contain substantial and permanent redirections of American culture? Answers to the question rely on three factors: cognitive changes summarized as relations between the American Creed and the ethic of sensitivity, values of deep culture and emotional changes summarized as pain, and anger in procedural culture.

The change from the American Creed to the ethic of sensitivity relies on the redistribution and redeployment of social values of equality, justice, and the dignity of all human beings. Derived from the American Creed, these values are rooted in civil, not cultural, rights. They originated in the Enlightenment as ideas of freedom of masterless man, living in a society with political institutions that were separate from the seats of religious, military, and cultural power. The values of the civil rights movement came from Anglo culture and not from African, American Indian, Islamic, or Asian cultures. Democracy's failure in American society has not been induced by the primordial sentiments toward race and ethnicity that have blocked value distribution and deployment to minority populations. The Anglo origin of values gives every reason to believe that the effects of the changes of redistribution and redeployment will endure.

Much of the change, however, has been in value emphasis-deemphasis (special privileges to minority groups) and in the technical areas of value standardization (busing of school children to preserve integration of schools) and retargeting value implementation (affirmative action). In these areas of value change the nature of the change may often represent an oscillation of effort that, in time, will swing back once more toward the practicality of the American Creed.

The most controversial change may well be the self-styling of many Americans as victims. The change strikes at the heart of beliefs of the American Creed such as individualism, self-reliance, achievement, and pragmatism of decision making. The idea of victim evokes passionate defense in some and guarded revulsion in others. The narrative of the mass media as well as of compassionate persons and causes in American society has become so deeply committed to victimhood as an emotional commodity that the subject may well be a leading issue in the years ahead.

The challenge to education, to psychology and psychiatry, is to devise constructive responses, redressing the malaise by incorporating in its vision a tragic view of life in which culture is separated from ideology, commodification is divided from compassion, and cultural analysis is used to determine the real commitment that people have to their programs and symbols. The school system and political-social cultures have been profoundly influenced by the malaise, and only time will tell whether the political wisdom of the American people and their politicians will succeed in restoring the civil principle to government and integrate cultural diversity into a single system and halt the careening of society under the weight of its commitment to the ethic of sensitivity.

REFERENCES

Bateson, G. (1958). *Naven.* 2nd ed. Stanford, CA: Stanford University Press.

Benedict, R. (1934). *Patterns of Culture.* Boston: Houghton Mifflin.

Berman, R. (1968). *America in the Sixties.* New York: Harper & Row.

Cole, M., and Scribner, S. (1974). *Culture and Thought.* New York: Wiley.

D'Andrade, R. (1987). A folk model of the mind. In *Cultural Models in Language and Thought*, ed. D. Holland and N. Quinn, pp.112–150. Cambridge, UK: Cambridge University Press.

Diaz-Guerrero, R. (1967). *Psychology of the Mexican.* Austin, TX: The University of Texas Press.

Ekman, P., Friesen, W. V., and Ellsworth, P. (1972). *Emotion in the Human Face.* New York: Pergamon.

Foerster, N., ed. (1947). *American Poetry and Prose.* 3rd ed. New York: Houghton Mifflin.

Geldard, F. A. (1953). *The Human Senses*. New York: Wiley.

Gregory, R. L. (1970). *The Intelligent Eye*. New York: McGraw-Hill.

Howard, P. K.(1994). *The Death of Common Sense*. New York: Random House.

Hughes, R. (1993). *Culture of Complaint*. New York: Oxford University Press.

Ignatieff, M. (1993). *Blood and Belonging*. New York: Farrar, Straus and Giroux.

Johnson-Laird, P. N. (1988). *The Computer and the Mind*. Cambridge, MA: Harvard University Press.

Lakoff, G. (1987). *Women, Fire, and Dangerous Things*. Chicago: University of Chicago Press.

Maslow, A. (1954). *Motivation and Personality*. New York: Harper & Row.

McConnell, J. V. (1986). *Understanding Human Behavior*. New York: Holt, Rinehart and Winston.

Melzack, R., and Wall, P. D. (1988). *The Challenge of Pain*. London: Penguin.

Ortony, A., Clore, G. L., and Collins, A. (1988). *The Cognitive Structure of Emotions*. Cambridge, UK: Cambridge University Press.

Padilla, A. M., and Ruiz, R. A. (1973). *Latino Mental Health*. Rockville, MD: National Institute of Mental Health.

Rappaport, H. (1990). *Marking Time*. New York: Simon & Schuster.

Scarry, E. (1985). *The Body in Pain*. Oxford: Oxford University Press.

Schermerhorn, R. A. (1978). *Comparative Ethnic Relations: A Framework for Theory and Research*. Chicago: University of Chicago Press.

Schlesinger, A. M., Jr. (1992). *The Disuniting of America*. New York: Norton.

Stearns, C. Z., and Stearns, P. N. (1986). *Anger: The Struggle for Emotional Control in American History*. Chicago: University of Chicago Press.

Stewart, E. C. (1995). The cultural trilogy. *Newsletter: Intercultural Communication*. Kanda University of International Studies, Chiba, Japan, March.

Stewart, E. C., and Bennett, M. J. (1991). *American Cultural Patterns*. Yarmouth, ME: Intercultural Press.

Sykes, C. J. (1992). *A Nation of Victims*. New York: St. Martin's.

Szasz, T. S. (1957). *Pain and Pleasure*. London: Tavistock.

Tsuru, S. (1956). Japanese images of America. In *Paths of American Thought*, ed. A. M. Schlesinger Jr. and Morton White, pp. 515–530. Boston: Houghton Mifflin.

Voget, F. W. (1973). The history of cultural anthropology. In *Handbook of Social and Cultural Anthropology* ed. J. J. Honigmann, pp. 1–88. Chicago: Rand McNally.

Zborowski, M. (1969). *People in Pain*. San Francisco: Jossey-Bass.

Urban Poverty, Ethnicity, and Personality Development

RAFAEL ART. JAVIER, WILLIAM G. HERRON, AND PHILIP T. YANOS

INTRODUCTION

It is not an easy task to discuss the multiple factors that contribute to the final product in human development, a *person* (Sullivan 1953). All the major disciplines—from philosophy and theology to physics, medicine, and the behavioral and social sciences—have attempted to define the intrinsic characteristics that make a person a unique entity. One can define the human condition from the perspective of its physiological, biochemical, and neurological characteristics, or from the perspective of the unique motivational structures that lend meaning to its activities and behaviors (Freud 1923, 1937, Kohlberg 1969, Sullivan 1953). It can be said, however, that what makes all these factors uniquely human is the extent to which they are organized and guided by principles, the nature of which cannot be explained through tangibles alone. It is the capacity to think, feel, and transform, to love and hate, to conquer and to live, to influence and be influenced, to do and be done to. It is the capacity to believe, to want, and to dream. And it is the capacity for "recall and foresight, of functional history and adaptation to a foreseen goal, which is commonly meant by anticipation" (Sullivan 1953, p. 110). It is the combination of these factors that makes one human.

The accumulation of these experiences into "a relatively enduring pattern" (Sullivan 1953, p. 110) is what is referred to as *personality*, which is assumed to develop in the context of the vicissitudes of different developmental demands. For Freud, these demands have an instinctual and unconscious quality, while for Sullivan and the object relation theorists, such as Fairbairn and Winnicott, these demands are more connected to the interpersonal field. For Ellis (1973) and other cognitive psychologists, these demands are fueled by well-established and irrational beliefs that become part of the organizing principles of behavior. Pathological formations are established when irrational beliefs prevail in the person's cognitive organization in spite of what reality dictates. Self and other representations are developed in the context of the dynamic interplay of these different demands, which ultimately determine the nature and quality of one's relationship with others.

While the importance of the descriptions of the determining factors in personality formation provided by Freud, Sullivan, Winnicott, Ellis, and others is indisputable, what is missing from these theoretical formulations is a concerted discussion of the impact of factors such as race, ethnicity, and poverty in personality development. While the role of these factors is certainly implied in some of these theories, as discussed in Javier and Herron (1992) and Javier and Yussef (1995), the fact remains that poverty, race, and ethnicity are not essential parts of them. This makes it difficult to understand the true nature of individuals whose socioeconomic, sociopolitical, cultural, and ethnic characteristics differ from the white, middle-class background that is usually presupposed by these theoretical formulations.

It is our contention that poverty, race, and ethnicity do affect personality development in very concrete and real ways that traditional psychodynamic and cognitive theories do not account for (Dana 1993). The fact that not much attention has been given to the impact of these factors in personality development is difficult to understand in light of the reality around the world and in many metropolitan cities in the United States (U.S. Census 1992). Indeed, the war in Bosnia and racial tension in many cities in the United States and abroad (Javier and Rendon 1995) have forced many to become painfully aware of the powerful role ethnicity, race, and poverty can have in human interactions. This is particularly the case for African-American and Latino individuals in the United States.

Thus we will focus our attention in this chapter on a discussion of the impact of poverty, and of ethnic and cultural factors in reference to the personality development of black and Latino individuals, since members of these groups are more likely to be represented in many educational and mental health facilities in the United States. As these groups have been found to be most vulnerable to biases and misdiagnoses (Marcos et al. 1973, Neighbors et al. 1989), a discussion of specific aspects of these groups will be used only as a point of discussion for the larger issue of concern, namely, the extent to which poverty, culture, and ethnicity may affect personality formation.

POVERTY AND PERSONALITY DEVELOPMENT: MYTHS AND FACTS

Poverty refers to a condition in which an individual experiences socioeconomic and sociopolitical alienation from the society at large (Lewis 1964, 1966), does not have access to adequate means to take care of the basic necessities of life (such as food, housing, and education), and is forced to live a life of socioeconomic and sociopolitical deprivation. The impact of poverty on the human condition remains an area of great concern for social and behavioral scientists. It is frequently the subject of political debate without any clear goal to eradicate its cause. Socioeconomic and sociopolitical policies are often proposed with the intention of improving the lives of the poor; however, the end result is frequently that conditions remain fundamentally unchanged or worsened. This is particularly the case for the minority population in this country, of whom more and more individuals still live below the poverty line (U.S. Census 1992) at a time when the government is threatening deep cuts in many of the social programs.

The mental health needs of the poor have historically been given disproportionate inattention. In a 1978 review of research on mental health interventions with this population, Lorion commented on previously existing pessimism about the ability of low socioeconomic status (LSES) groups to use mental health resources. However, he was optimistic about new interest in this area. Unfortunately, an updated review in 1986 (Lorion and Felner) dashed these hopes and suggested that the situation is deteriorating, with even less interest being shown in the mental health needs of the disadvantaged. Although it is clear that poverty and psychopathology are highly correlated (Bird et al. 1988, Koegel et al. 1988), there is limited concern for the particulars of the relationship. Instead, stereotypes prevail, preventing the development of solutions.

We have noted elsewhere (Javier and Herron 1992) the desire for disaffiliation from the disadvantaged on the part of psychotherapies, motivated by a mix of factors that allow this patient population to be neglected both in theoretical development and corresponding preventive and treatment efforts. For example, despite the comprehensive nature of psychoanalytic explanation, middle-class psychodynamics remain as relatively universal offerings and become LSES-inappropriate. The issue is complicated by the fact that a disproportionate percentage of the LSES urban group in the United States is Hispanic and African-American, bringing in additional stereotyping. Our belief is that the situation can be improved by developing more appropriate formulations that can in turn lead to the effective use of psychological principles for prevention and treatment of psychopathology in LSES patients. We have previously given some examples of how, for instance, psychoanalytic therapy could be successfully used with poor and Hispanic patients (Javier 1990, Javier and Herron 1992). It should be acknowledged, however, that there are indeed serious obstacles that need to be overcome to allow factors related to the impact of poverty and ethnicity to become more centrally and meaningfully included in psychological formulations regarding personality development and treatment interventions.

Generalization of the Culture of Poverty

The first obstacle is the overshadowing application of the "culture of poverty," a concept that Marcus (1974) notes as being derived from Engels's description of the working classes in Manchester, England, at the time of the Industrial Revolution. The main ingredients of this hypothesized culture were all based on some form of impulsiveness, and included drunkenness, promiscuity, lack of discipline and planning, instability, and general maladaptation. The concept of the culture of poverty is perpetually reappearing, as in the work of Lewis (1959), though the subjects this time were Hispanic. It has become relatively common to assign these observed characteristics to the black underclass and other minority groups and as a consequence to write them off as hopelessly pathological.

Wilson (1987) makes note of the misuses of the culture-of-poverty concept, and particularly the belief that once the cultural traits appear to be in place, they tend to be self-perpetuating regardless of changes that occur in environmental, intrapsychic, or intersubjective conditions. Actually, changes in the latter two would be suspect as possibilities anyway, because this type of cultural habituation is seen as mitigating and deflecting efforts such as psychotherapy, as well as reinforcing a pessimistic view of psychopathology in the poor. This is particularly unfortunate because the African-American urban underclass in the United States, and to a lesser extent the Latino poor, does have severe social problems, namely high unemployment, high school dropout rate, poverty, welfare dependency, and a large number of female-headed households (Wilson 1987), which could have serious psychological consequences. However, it is misleading to conclude that ghetto-specific culture creates an intractable group, as suggested in findings reported by DeParle (1991). According to these findings, in 1970 about 30 percent of black students between ages 16 and 24 had not completed high school. In 1980, however, the percentage of noncompletion had dropped to about 14.

Equalizing and Stereotyping of the Minority Population

Another misconception is that African-Americans and Hispanic individuals are homogeneous groups. This is a belief that tends to be in place about all LSES people (Lorion and Parron 1985), and in turn often about minority groups. While the diversity of countries of origin of Hispanics has made this view easy to refute (Javier and Yussef 1995), it has stuck with blacks to a greater extent, despite ample evidence of heterogeneity in African-American families and lifestyles (Willie 1974). The danger in "equalizing" the minority and poor population in this way is that it does not allow for a more sophisticated discussion of the unique issues affecting each group separately and in combination. (We will return to a further discussion of this issue later in this chapter.)

While it is true that life for the black urban underclass is difficult in many ways, that does not mean universal failure or total lack of positive interpersonal experiences or the absence of enjoyment. Thus all poor people are not replete with psychopathology (Nisbett 1993), despite the high level of stress in their environment. Nevertheless, there has been a tendency to emphasize two personality traits, unreliability and impulsivity, as the essence of the underclass, without regard to the contexts in which they may be observed. Zuckerman (1990) has made the point that while there are racial differences in crime rates in the United States, there is no evidence to support a greater prevalence of antisocial personalities in blacks as compared to whites. Furthermore, there is variability within the LSES population in thresholds for emotional and interpersonal concerns as well as in degrees of insight and abilities to change (Lorion and Felner 1986).

Still, what has remained primarily undisturbed is the stereotyping of urban poor African Americans and Latinos as hopelessly pathological, with personality structures that defy change and would be particularly unsuitable for interventions that require an ability for delay gratification and high-level thought processes. Psychoanalytic psychotherapies, with their relatively lengthy duration, emphasis on insight, and relatively clear boundaries, were thus concluded to be inappropriate for these groups. As an example of the attitude too frequently encountered, a series of interviews with ten relatively experienced psychotherapists regarding their fee practices was conducted. One response was particularly revealing: "One therapist sees himself as having no ethical responsibility to the poor, as he experiences poor people, because of the prepotency of basic survival needs, poor candidates for depth psychotherapy" (Citron-Bagget and Kempler 1991, p. 57).

In summary, although poverty and the impact of race and ethnicity are expected to have clear consequences on the individual's psychological condition, these consequences are differentially experienced by each individual. Thus, to apply the psychological consequences delineated under the "culture of poverty" to all poor and minority individuals is to negate the complexity of the differential impact of this phenomenon on these individuals and to perpetuate a biased view of this population. Not all poor and minority individuals develop an antisocial personality structure or a personality dynamic characterized by an inability to delay gratification, nor do they exhibit thinking processes that are exclusively primary or concrete in nature, act out sexual escapades, suffer from alcoholism, or a sense of helplessness and hopelessness about the future. What can be said is that the demands associated with poverty and racial and ethnic condition represent a number of important challenges to the psychic structure of the poor in ways not experienced by more privileged individuals. How these challenges are ultimately met and resolved determines the nature, quality, and flavor of the personality structure of these individuals.

ETHNIC AND CULTURAL INFLUENCES ON PERSONALITY DEVELOPMENT

One can see that attempts at defining the psychological characteristics of the poor and African-American and Hispanic individuals are fraught with a great deal of complexity and difficulty. As indicated earlier, the traditional theories of human development espoused by Freud, Skinner, and even the object relations theorists have fallen short in explaining the numerous variables normally associated with these individuals. Thus the view that human motivation can be explained in terms of the vicissitudes, neutralization, and transformation of instinctual drives (Freud 1923, 1937) or the extent to which a happy medium is found regarding the internalization of good-bad objects (Winnicott 1965), or the extent to which a functional self-system is developed in the context of which a healthy interaction with the world is possible (Sullivan 1953) may have a limited explanatory power for these individuals unless motivational forces such as the ones that derive from the ethnic, cultural, and linguistic dimensions are also included. The effect brought about by the presence of poverty also needs to be included since this dimension characterizes the minority reality in our society (Cuciti and James 1990).

But what elements specific to African-American and Hispanic poverty are likely to impact on personality development? We will now focus our attention on a more detailed discussion of some of the issues likely to affect the psychological dimension of these individuals in various ways.

Name Definition

Up to now, many of the attempts toward a definition of "Hispanicness," "Latinos," "black," and "African American" have resulted in simplistic and politically motivated conceptualizations. The so-called Hispanic culture, for instance, is a complex mixture of individuals with different and yet similar histories, of individuals who belong to different countries with ecological similarities, whose poetry and literature is diverse, rich, and greatly influenced by each group's unique reality, yet portraying universal themes. For instance, we can all resonate with many of the themes portrayed in Garcia Marquez's *One Hundred Years of Solitude* (1967), but there are unique themes that more accurately define the Colombian tradition, and hence are uniquely Colombian.

With regard to the Hispanic groups in the United States, the immigration histories are also very different, resulting in very different perspectives about themselves regarding the host country. Attempts to communicate the differences among the Hispanic groups have resulted in different descriptions or definitions, such as Hispanic, Latino, Spanish-speaking, Chicano, Boricua, Dominican, Colombian, and so on, to categorize individuals from different Spanish-speaking countries. Although we can find a common denominator in that Hispanics as a group are stubbornly affected by the socioeconomic and sociopolitical deprivation normally ailing the minority population (Cuciti and James 1990, Rogler et al. 1989), it is important to recognize the unique ways in which each group tends to deal with the same reality. In this context, the reasons for immigration, whether politically or economically motivated, will determine how and the extent to which the individual's self-definition will be affected. Additionally, legal status will also influence self-definition along with the nature of psychological, socioeconomic, and sociopolitical function and the professional status the individuals enjoyed prior to immigration (Godoy 1995).

Thus Puerto Ricans, Dominicans, Salvadorians, Mexicans, and Colombians will experience themselves very differently in comparison to each other and to other minority populations. For instance, a high level of suspicion of government agencies is likely to characterize the behavior of Latinos with illegal alien status. Their belief systems and their ego and superego structures may thus be affected in the service of their realities.

For African Americans, a similar situation may be pointed out relative to development of the self in a political environment that has historically been hostile to the African-American cause (West 1993). The name changes from Negro to black to African American have been fueled by attempts to find a self-definition with a more positive historical base than the one allowed by traditional Anglo-Saxon views (Dana 1993, Thompson 1995). The self-definition by opposition that may result in reaction to this hostile environment may leave an individual with a feeling of tremendous vulnerability and the need to develop self-protective devices in the context of his or her personal realities. A distortion of basic personality operations may result. Individuals who can withstand the pressure on their psychic reality generated from these forces possess a personality strength that protects them against pathological transformations. The same is the case for an individual who is able to relate with his/her environment in a functional manner in spite of a cumulative experience of prejudice and other abuses.

Other cultural characteristics are assumed to impact on the personality development of individuals from minority groups. Conceptions of time and space, views of authority, the role of religious beliefs and practices, and views of the supernatural are considered essential elements in the development of morality for the Latino and black communities (Dana 1993, Javier and Yussef 1995). With regard to the Latino community, the code of *respeto* and *honra* (Ghali 1982, Lauria 1964) and the gender-specific codes of conduct that result in the *machismo* and *hembrismo/marianismo* modes of behavior are also critical in the development of socially acceptable personality characteristics for these individuals. Ego and superego functions, the nature of introjects, and the development of self-concepts and belief systems about self and others are all influenced by these cultural ingredients in various ways. How these ingredients are ultimately incorporated in personality requires further exploration.

Family Influence

The role of the family and important members of the family in personality formation has been of critical importance in many psychological formulations

(Sullivan 1953, Winnicott 1965). However, a view of family from a middle-class perspective has prevailed in these formulations. Psychoanalysis, for instance, has generally spun its theories about the importance of object relations around middle-class white family structures, as though the type of physical, psychological, and social environment available to children could be relatively constant, with parents getting the blame for inconsistencies and aberrations. Yet race and socioeconomic status influence the environment in significant ways that are not given due emphasis in dynamic hypothesizing. Black families in the United States are devalued relative to white (West 1993), as are Latinos relative to white and poor relative to middle class. Many black and Latino families live in urban areas and are relatively poor, though within these populations there has been a growing division between the middle class and the underclass, and it is the latter that primarily claims our attention based on their dual issues of poverty and race.

The first point to be noted is that blacks and Latinos make considerable use of the extended family. This is a useful adaptive mechanism in view of the large number of female-headed families and adolescent mothers. Thus the concept of intact family needs to be reassessed in these communities, because the extended family provides caregiving functions that in customary psychological schema were the province of the traditional mother–father dyad. (Even that pattern is due for an overhaul because most families in the United States no longer fit the model of father as the worker outside the home, mother as homemaker and child caregiver).

There is also the issue of personal identity that develops within the family, perhaps always stays there in different ways, yet definitely moves on to the world of others. In the social devaluation of blacks and Latinos, it has been assumed that children from these groups automatically internalize the devaluation and develop poor self-esteem. However, there is an important difference between racial identity and racial evaluation (Norton 1983). Becoming aware of one's racial identity occurs roughly between the ages of 3 and 4; this process is independent, however, from the evaluation placed on that identity by the society at large. If the sense of self is developed positively by the immediate environment, then a positive identity may not be so destructively limited by societal devaluations of the racial group (Thompson 1995).

Norton states: "Racism in the economic, political, and social structure exists but, in spite of it, black families not only have survived but have interacted with their children in ways that foster the development of a positive sense of self . . . positive self-esteem is found in black children at all socioeconomic levels" (1983, p. 188). Furthermore, Powell (1983) notes that, while most theorizing about African Americans (and other minority individuals) is based on a deficit model, there is little evidence to support widespread devastation of self-esteem. She reiterates, for instance, that the socialization and self-conceptualization of black children do not have to be destroyed by racism, and stresses the utility of social networks in urban ghetto areas. These networks include kin-based households and extended kin related through children, marriage, and friendship that can provide holding environments. A similar characteristic was observed in the case of the Latino family structure. As described by Javier and Yussef (1995) with regard to the role of extended family in the moral development of the Latino individual, "It includes grandparents, aunts and uncles, cousins, in-laws, and so-called second-aunts and second-uncles. The 'compadres' (co-parents) and 'vecinos' (neighbors) subsystems, as well as all the major institutions, such as school and church, are also part of this large system of moral influence that functions as an extension of the parental influence" (p. 85).

A case in point is the one provided by a 15-year-old black male who at intake had a family constellation of a working mother, three younger siblings—one of whom had a child at age 13—and an absent father. His sister, now 14, lived with her child in the family's apartment and also had daytime child-care responsibility for one of her brothers, age 4, while the other brother, age 7, was in school. The patient had an awareness of who his father was, and even where he was, through his father's sister who was friendly with his mother, though the patient had not seen or talked to his father since he was 6. Also, his father's sister had a boyfriend who lived with her most of the time, and who spent a considerable amount of time with the patient and his siblings.

The family structure described is not usual, nor would it tend to be judged as normal, much less ideal, by the larger society. Yet to understand the patient, the family network needs to be viewed in terms of the opportunities it can provide rather than emphasizing its actual and potential difficulties. Certainly there are inconsistencies in it, and others are possible that have not yet occurred, but it provides the basis for developmental lines. As Tyson and Tyson (1990) point out in their integration of psychoanalytic theories of personality development: "The developmental process, . . . takes place through the differentiation, organization, transformation, and reorganization of networking, branching, and interrelated systems" (p. 32).

The extended family network is an example of the developmental framework that can be available to poor black and Latino urban children. It needs to be discovered, unearthed, and then appreciated in terms of its functional relationship with personal identity, and self and object representations, as opposed to the assumption of a personality deficit derived from an assumed family deficit.

Basic Psychological Operations

It is clear that the basic psychological functions traditionally described in theoretical formulations of personality development are in need of reevaluation in view of the cultural and ethnic influences discussed in this chapter. We are referring to ego and superego functions, introjection, self-definition, coping mechanisms, and other operations. The functions of the ego are of particular interest because they are involved in the adaptation process, which has often been depicted as one of the failings of the underclass (Herron and Javier 1996). Although ego functions are interrelated, and ultimately to be understood in such a context, for illustrative purposes we will consider only two of them, language skills and coping strategies, which of course are themselves interrelated.

Difficulties in school, along with high dropout rates from school and high unemployment, are often combined to lead to the assumption that minority children have cognitive deficits. Language is a major area of concern because it is conceptualized as being based on environmental models. The point to be noted is that minority ghetto children do not lack language models, but these models differ from the models for middle-class children. Norton (1983) summarized a number of studies of ghetto language and concluded that a definite, consistent language is present. The children are able to communicate with peers and families within that environment and learn the rules of that language. However, it does differ from Standard English, and so the children do not do well on standardized academic tests and are believed to have a language deficit. In contrast to this belief, what usually occurs are language differences.

This means that members of the underclass may come into structured situations, such as schools or mental health clinics, with a language system that differs from what is usually spoken in those situations. Powell (1983) has made the point in this regard that strengths of African Americans are frequently ignored or misinterpreted in these situations. In the case of language in black children, for instance, it is important to understand its development from the perspective of the individual within the black family. This can provide an awareness of the state of knowledge and learning style that opens an avenue to translation, because the latter is also necessary for the underclass to function effectively within the larger society.

Our second concern is coping abilities. Clearly, it is necessary to have coping methods that can be employed in the larger society or developmental options are sharply reduced, and language is certainly a crucial variable in having such options. Also, in considering a developmental schema for cognition, the onset of speech is a milestone as it makes apparent the capacity to symbolize. It is essential to consider the "various languages" that are involved, as well as the ongoing interplay of primary and secondary processes. The sequential nature of language development means that respect for what is in place must accompany new learning, and in essence there is a need for mastery of movement in diverse language and symbolic environments.

Adaptation as originally conceptualized emphasized the average expectable environment (Hartmann 1958). The expectable environment that the ego psychologist had in mind, however, is not the environment of the black and other minority urban poor. The inner city is a high-stress environment, probably from conception on, considering the relationship between LSES and prematurity, birth defects, and infant mortality, described by Myers and King (1983) as the basal stress level preceding birth. Birth and growth continue the external stress pattern, with accompanying intrapsychic conflicts. These stresses include inadequate living conditions, poor nutrition and limited health care, including mental health, lack of employment and limited educational possibilities, racism, and socioeconomic discrimination. The fact is that the social order has not been designed to favor the development of urban poor minorities, who are most likely to be subject to accumulating patterns of disrupting life events along with everyday life struggles. Thus, although it is true that the idea of uniformly low levels of self-esteem is in question for this population, there are social and interpersonal processes that foster sensitivity and uncertainty with regard to self-competency in mastering the world as experienced. The environment offers significant reasons for the persistence of paranoid-schizoid views that can limit coping abilities, yet it is erroneous to consider these operations as self-generated deficits.

Myers and King (1983) describe the developmental demands faced by poor urban black children, starting with being born into a "stress-primed" reality, then having to develop ego strengths within contexts that often are severely restricted, including the availability of models for coping, particularly with reality outside the immediate environment. For all children there is an intermingling of self and social influences resulting in an ego structure that processes reality and works with the results. However, the relative effects of the societal ego and superego are increased because for poor urban blacks it is incorrect to assume that there is a predominantly constructive social structure. King (1978) has indicated that, historically, African Americans in the United States attain a position of marginal status, and that, despite legislation and good intentions, full participation is still not the norm. Thus the average expectable urban poor black environment, as well as the environment of other poor minority individuals, appears to be a fertile breeding ground for paranoid-schizoid mechanisms, uncertainty, insecurity, and the extremes of ambivalence. However, the extent to which these qualities are present in various degrees in the personality structure of the minority individuals has to be assessed on an individual basis.

A question of particular importance is how the effects of this high external stress can be treated. In essence, what is the degree of transactional competency, which at present can be realistically described as closer to survival than mastery, and how can that be improved? A major step toward improvement is the understanding of personality development within the context of ethnicity and poverty.

It can be expected that, in the process of development, the influences of both racism and poverty will be recognized by the individual; in turn, reactive defenses and character styles will be put into place as adaptations, both to the immediate and the larger environment, and will usually have to vary in keeping with the different structures involved. The basic motivation is to control the impact of the environment, but confusion can be created for others because of the apparent dynamic that underlies the observed behavior.

For example, in dealing with a therapist, a patient is likely to limit anxiety by avoiding unpleasant or difficult material to an extent that makes it look and sound as though that patient lacks the ability to recall and be introspective. Or a patient may appear resistive and limited in the recounting of affectively charged events, even relatively indifferent to psychic trauma. Attempts may be made by patients to restructure therapists' designs of the therapeutic environment. Distrust of therapists and the psychoanalytic process may be apparent, causing therapists to feel at a loss as to how to make therapeutic contact with these patients (Thompson 1995).

An unfortunate and inaccurate conclusion is then often drawn by therapists that such patients lack ego capacities to the extent that they are inappropriate candidates for introspective psychotherapy. It is as though a paranoid-schizoid pathological position is locked into place, with an absence of caring and responsible object relations and with a world dominated by suspicion and the potential for violence. Although in developmental theory the normal paranoid-schizoid position precedes the normal depressive position by several months, and these positions coexist throughout life, this type of patient is seen as though no depressive position, which is morally reparative, was ever really in place, or is at best poorly developed.

The flaw in such a view is that the probability that the patient's reality dictates his or her approach to any therapist is overlooked. Preceding the therapeutic encounter, appraisals have been made by patients of the environment and the people in it, and coping capacities have been developed that may well include selective withdrawal, careful scrutiny, and delay of gratification. There is little or no reason to treat the therapy situation as different from many other unpleasant encounters with authority figures. If therapy even starts, it may be looked on as something to dispense with, unless the therapist understands that ego capacities indeed exist, and learns to engage the patient through that person's reality.

CONCLUSION: IN SEARCH OF A PARADIGM

For a psychological theory and therapy to be useful with the population we have been describing, the effects of poverty and ethnicity must be addressed rather than merely acknowledged. In the latter situation, which tends to prevail at the moment, there is a predominance of models of either basic pathology, or vulnerability, as though there were a relative catholicity of average expectable environments that went beyond mother–child interactions. Take, for instance, the psychoanalytic formulation which, in the majority of its emphases, has stayed with the psychology of the individual, whether cast in drive or relational terms. When it becomes sociopolitical, it in one sense continues to take an individualized position, such as replacing drive-generated conflicts with the primacy of relationships, which in turn stresses the role of the self. Then there is a great expectation about revising the roles of mother and father, and understanding the forces that generated the original conceptions. These are certainly important issues, and they have broad implications, but the social focus tends to be narrow relative to the issues raised in this paper.

As suggested by Myers and King (1983),

> the analysis of mental health in a class-caste society ... cannot ... be made simple on the basis of the presence or absence of illness symptoms ... it must necessarily include the analysis of the transactional processes between individuals and social classes, ... and the social structures ... that create the conditions of differential mental health vulnerability as a function of social class and race ... the concept of mental health in an oppressive reality must also include the active commitment to personal and social transformation. [p. 297]

This transformation could be jolting. As Wilson (1987) states with regard to the Black reality: "Any significant reduction of the problems of black joblessness, and the related problems of crime, out-of-wedlock births, single-parent homes, and welfare dependency will call for a far more comprehensive program of economic and social reform than what Americans have usually regarded as appropriate or desirable" (p. 139).

A similar comment may be aimed at psychoanalysis, yet the possibilities for significant change are available because psychoanalysis was designed to be a comprehensive theory of human behavior. However, it was also designed from clinical experience, and in that regard may often have been limited by the content of its processes, as well as the values of its processors, both of which in essence were class-conscious. But the expansion of theory to understand both the psychological forces that contribute to poverty and racism and the psychological impact of poverty and racism is a major task not only for analytic theory but for other theories as well.

An example of such expansion is suggested by Alford (1989), namely, considering a psychoanalytic social theory that uses the connection between the intrapsychic and the intersubjective. He cites projective identification as an example of this, indicating its prevalence as a dynamic in groups. In a further elaboration, he describes a Kleinian social theory that considers humanity as the maker of the environment, with split-off and projected affects setting the tone of the environment. It is certainly time for psychologists to use their understanding, whatever their theoretical orientations, to constructively foster societies in which poverty and racism will exist only as bad memories. What is inescapable is the fact that poverty, racism, and cultural and ethnic factors affect personality structure in various ways. The degree and nature of this influence on personality formation are to be determined by the individual characteristics and the strength and stubbornness of these factors in the individual's life.

REFERENCES

Alford, C. F. (1989). *Melanie Klein and Critical Social Theory: An Account of Politics, Art, and Reason Based on her Psychoanalytic Theory.* New Haven, CT: Yale University Press.

Bird, H. R., Canino, G., Rubio-Stipec, M., et al. (1988). Estimates of the prevalence of childhood maladjustment in a community survey in Puerto Rico. *Archives of General Psychiatry* 45:1120–1126.

Citron-Bagget, S., and Kempler, B. (1991). Fee setting: dynamic issues for therapists in independent practice. *Psychotherapy in Private Practice* 9:45–60.

Cuciti, P. and James, F. (1990). A comparison of Black and Hispanic poverty in large cities of the Southeast. *Hispanic Journal of Behavioral Sciences* 12 (1):50–75.

Dana, R. H. (1993). *Multicultural Assessment Perspectives for Professional Psychology.* Boston: Allyn & Bacon.

DeParle, J. (1991). Without fanfare, blacks march to greater high school success. *The New York Times*, June 9, pp. 1, 26.

Ellis, A. (1973). *Humanistic Psychotherapy: The Rational-Emotive Approach.* New York: Julian.

Freud, S. (1923). The ego and the id. *Standard Edition* 19:1–66.

———— (1937). Analysis terminable and interminable. *Standard Edition* 23:209–253.

Garcia Marquez, G. (1967). *Cien anos de soledad.* (One Hundred Years of Solitude) Buenos Aires: Editorial Sudamericana, S.A.

Ghali, S. B. (1982). Understanding Puerto Rican tradition. *Social Work* January, 98–102.

Godoy, I. (1995). *El role de los objetos transicionales en el proceso de separacion de la tierra madre: un estudio realizado con mujeres latinas inmigrantes.* Tesis doctoral, Pontificia Universidad Catolica del Ecuador, Quito, Ecuador.

Hartmann, H. (1958). *Ego Psychology and the Problem of Adaptation.* New York: International Universities Press.

Herron, W. G., and Javier, R. A. (1996). The psychogenesis of poverty: some psychoanalytic conceptions. *Psychoanalytic Review* 83:611–620.

Javier, R. A. (1990). On the suitability of insight-oriented therapy for the Hispanic poor. *American Journal of Psychoanalysis* 50:305–318.

Javier, R. A., and Herron, W. G. (1992). Psychoanalysis, the Hispanic poor, and the disadvantaged: application and conceptualization. *Journal of the American Academy of Psychoanalysis* 20:455–476.

Javier, R. A., and Rendon, M. (1995). The ethnic unconscious and its role in transference, resistance and countertransference: an introduction. *Psychoanalytic Psychology* 12:513–520.

Javier, R. A., and Yussef, M. B. (1995). A Latino perspective on the role of ethnicity in the development of moral values: implications for psychoanalytic theory and practice. *Journal of the American Academy of Psychoanalysis* 23:79–97.

King, L. M. (1978). Social and cultural influences on psychopathology. *Annual Review of Psychology* 29:405–433.

Koegel, P., Burnam, A., and Farr, R. K. (1988). The prevalence of specific psychiatric disorders among homeless individuals in the inner city of Los Angeles. *Archives of General Psychiatry* 45:1085–1092.

Kohlberg, L. (1969). Stages and sequence: the cognitive-developmental approach to socialization. In *Handbook of Socialization Theory and Research*, ed. D. A. Goslin, pp. 347–480. Chicago: Rand McNally.

Lauria, A. (1964). "Respeto," "relajo" and interpersonal relations in Puerto Rico. *Anthropological Quarterly* 38:53–66.

Lewis, O. (1959). *Five Families: Mexican Case Studies in the Culture of Poverty.* New York: Basic Books.

———— (1964). The culture of poverty. In *Explosive Forces in Latin America*, ed. J. J. Tepaske and S. N. Fisher, pp. 149–174. Columbus: Ohio State University Press.

———— (1966). *La Vida: A Puerto Rican Family in the Culture of Poverty–San Juan and New York.* New York: Random House.

Lorion, R. P. (1978). Research on psychopathology and behavior change with the disadvantaged. In *Handbook of Psychotherapy and Behavior Change*, 2nd ed., ed. S. L. Garfield and A. E. Bergin, pp. 903–908. New York: Wiley.

Lorion, R. P., and Felner, R. D. (1986). Research on mental health interventions with the disadvantaged. In *Handbook of Psychotherapy and Behavior Change*, 3rd ed., ed. S. L. Garfield and A. E. Bergin, pp. 739–775. New York: Wiley.

Lorion, R. P., and Parron, D. L. (1985). Countering the countertransference: a strategy for treating the untreatable. In *Handbook on Cross-Cultural Counseling and Therapy*, ed. P. Pederson, pp. 79–86. New York: Greenwood.

Marcos, L. R., Alpert, M., Urcuyo, L., and Kesselman, M. (1973). The effect of interview language on the evaluation of psychopathology in Spanish-American schizophrenic patients. *American Journal of Psychiatry* 130:540–553.

Marcus, S. (1974). *Engels, Manchester and the Working Class*. New York: Random House.

Myers, H. F., and King, L. M. (1983). Mental health issues in the development of the black American child. In *The Psychosocial Development of Minority Group Children*, ed. G. J. Powell, pp. 275–306. New York: Brunner/Mazel.

Neighbors, H. W., Jackson, J. S. , Campbell, L., and Williams, D. (1989). The influence of racial factors on psychiatric diagnosis: a review and suggestions for research. *Community Mental Health Journal* 25:301–311.

Nisbett, R. (1993). Violence in the U.S. regional culture. *American Psychologist* 48:441–449.

Norton, D. G. (1983). Black family life patterns, the development of self and cognitive development of black children. In *The Psychosocial Development of Minority Group Children*, ed. G. J. Powell, pp. 181–193. New York: Brunner/Mazel.

Powell, G. J. (1983). Coping with adversity: the psychosocial development of Afro-American children. In *The Psychosocial Development of Minority Group Children*, ed. G. J. Powell, New York: Brunner/Mazel.

Rogler, L. H., Malgady, R. G., and Rodriguez, O. (1989). *Hispanics and Mental Health: A Framework for Research*. Malabar, FL: Robert E. Krieger.

Sullivan, H. S. (1953). *The Interpersonal Theory of Psychiatry*, New York: Norton.

Thompson, C. (1995). Self-definition by opposition: a consequence of minority status. *Psychoanalytic Psychology* 12:533–545.

Tyson, P., and Tyson, R. L. (1990). *Psychoanalytic Theories of Development: An Integration*. New Haven, CT: Yale University Press.

U.S. Bureau of Census. (1992). Washington, DC: U.S. Department of Commerce, Economics and Statistics, Administration Bureau of Census.

West, C. (1993). *Race Matters*. Boston: Beacon.

Willie, C. V. (1974). *A New Look at Black Families*. Englewood Cliffs, NJ: Prentice-Hall.

Wilson, W. J. (1987). *The Truly Disadvantaged. The Inner City, the Underclass, and Public Policy*. Chicago: University of Chicago Press.

Winnicott, D. W. (1965). *The Maturational Process and the Facilitating Environment* New York: International Universities Press.

Zuckerman, M. (1990). Some dubious premises in research and theory on racial differences: scientific, social, and ethical issues. *American Psychologist* 45:1297–1303.

6

Stigma and Discrimination against Persons Diagnosed with Mental Illness

LOUIS H. PRIMAVERA, LARRY G. KNAUSS,
KENDRA L. MULVEY, LYDIA K. WARNER,
AND WILLIAM G. HERRON

INTRODUCTION

Stigma involves ascribing negative attributes to *all* members of a category or group, which in turn can discredit and disgrace everyone in that group when the attributes pertain only to *some* of the members (Goffman 1963). Stigma is often accompanied by *discrimination*, which is the act of treating people unfairly based on some characteristic.

Stigmatizing ideas and beliefs often have some truth to them, but distortion occurs when what is true about a few individuals in a group is generalized to every individual in that group. This can result more often in the formation of incorrect rather than correct beliefs and ideas about persons within a group. Acting on these beliefs and ideas can result in treating people inappropriately and, at times, unfairly. For example, if society holds the belief that *all* persons diagnosed as mentally ill are unable to do complex and demanding tasks, the likely result is a rehabilitation program that is structured inappropriately for many patients. This contradicts the idea that rehabilitation and growth require challenge. Rehabilitation programs that lack challenge are counterproductive because they reinforce the notion that the person is weak and incapable, yet such programs persist. For example, a patient with a Ph.D. in sociology who was hospitalized for a psychotic break once said to one of the authors that making ashtrays and filing papers reinforced his own negative feelings about his emotional problems. He said that when he informed his therapist that his goal was to resume his academic life and publish papers, he was told that he had delusions of grandeur. This person now leads a major patient advocacy group and has a schedule that would exhaust even the most energetic individual.

Stigma and discrimination against those who have been diagnosed as mentally ill are much more common and pervasive than many people think (e.g., Rabkin 1974). Too many people hold stigmatizing views of individuals who have been diagnosed as mentally ill. These views are frequently based on societally reinforced fears of the unknown as well as personal ignorance. A large body of literature, some of which is summarized below, supports this assertion. A number of studies have shown that the general public holds negative views toward individuals who are diagnosed as mentally ill (e.g., Nunnally 1961, Rabkin 1972). These negative views include many undesirable traits, especially those indicating dangerousness, unpredictability, and incapability. Several studies have also demonstrated that mental health professionals and students in training for mental health careers have negative views of individuals who are diagnosed as mentally ill (e.g., Calicchia 1981, Khandelwal and Workneh 1986). All of these research results support the idea that negative attitudes toward people who are diagnosed as mentally ill are pervasive and in need of substantial restructuring.

IDENTIFYING STIGMATIZING VIEWS

The ongoing issue of stigma highlights the importance of becoming aware of the meaning of the words people use. At a public presentation, Thomas Szasz referred to a concept called *operational semantics* which is defined as follows: the meaning of a word is understood in terms of the consequences or associations it elicits. If two words elicit similar consequences (emotional and/or behavioral), they share a meaning even though they may have different dictionary definitions.

Consider an exercise that has been used in an introductory psychology course to make students aware of their own stigma attached to those diagnosed as mentally ill. A student is chosen at random from the class and the professor asks the class to imagine that this person has been found to be *evil*. The professor then asks the class to consider their answers to the following questions, given that this person is evil:

Would you like this person to live next door to you?
Would you like this person to marry someone in your family?
Would you like this person to be your friend?
Would you hire this person to work for you?
Would you work for this person?
Would you allow this person to drive a car?
Would you like this person to have access to personal information about you?
Would you like this person to be in any responsible position in society?

After the students have considered their answers to these questions, a second student is chosen at random and the class is asked to imagine that this person is diagnosed as *mentally ill*. The professor then asks the class to consider the same questions that were posed to them about the person who was evil. The professor asks the class to consider what it means if their answers to these questions are the same for both people. The professor then suggests to members of the class that if the answers to the questions were the same for both persons, then the two terms, *evil* and *mentally ill*, must have a common meaning. This exercise can be repeated using any other negative attribute in place of evil, such as *incompetent, destructive, unreliable, unpredictable, dangerous,* or *undesirable.* It is very likely that the results will be the same. In our experience, this type of exercise makes clear the point that many people hold rather negative views about people labeled *mentally ill.* Consider how you would respond.

Another exercise involves asking the students to consider how they would react if someone approached them at a party and enthusiastically told them that he had just recovered completely from cancer. The students are asked to consider how they would feel, what they would be thinking, and what they might do. They are then to consider how they would react if someone else at the party approached them and enthusiastically told them that he had just completely recovered from schizophrenia. The students are again asked to consider how they would feel, what they might be thinking, and what they might do. It is not hard to imagine that many people would have

very different reactions toward these two people and the most skeptical and
negative reactions would be toward the person who claimed to have recovered
from schizophrenia. It is our impression that most people would be skeptical
of the person who claimed to be completely recovered from schizophrenia
even though the recovery rate for those diagnosed with schizophrenia might
be equal to or higher than that for some types of cancer. Consider again how
you would respond.

HISTORY AND RESEARCH

The study of stigma and discrimination toward people diagnosed with a mental illness has appeared in the literature for many years. The seminal studies
used attitude measures (Cumming and Cumming 1957, Nunnally 1961). The
findings were unequivocal: people who were seen as mentally ill were viewed
very negatively. In an early literature review Rabkin (1972) reported that
stigma toward the mentally ill exists in all groups, including the general community and mental health workers. Primavera (1993) notes that, although
many of these studies date back a number of years, no real attitude changes
have taken place. A brief history of the empirical research on stigma against
those who are diagnosed with a mental illness will be presented in two sec-
tions: public opinion and attitudes of mental health professionals and students
in training for mental health careers.

PUBLIC OPINION

Of the first systematic studies about the attitudes toward the mentally ill,
Nunnally's (1961) was the most comprehensive. The study spanned a six-year
period in the 1950s and was designed to learn what the public *knows and thinks*
about mental illness. The 250 respondents lived in central Illinois, and at the
time were judged to be a representative sample of the country as a whole in
terms of a number of demographic variables, such as education, sex ratio,
income, religious affiliation, and age. Nunnally constructed a questionnaire that
measured the respondent's knowledge and attitudes about mental health and
those diagnosed as mentally ill. He used a semantic differential format (Osgood
and Tannenbaum 1957) to measure attitudes and constructed a 240-item scale
to measure "the causes, symptoms, prognosis, treatment, incident, and social significance of mental health problems" (p. 14). He chose the 240 items from a

larger list of 3,000 items that had been taken from members of the public, experts, and mass media. The questionnaires were mailed to the participants. The findings clearly indicated that the respondents saw those diagnosed as mentally ill as "bad" (p. 51). "Old people and young people, highly educated people and people with little formal schooling all tend to regard the mentally ill as relatively dangerous, dirty, unpredictable, and worthless" (p. 51).

Nunnally also reported that members of the general public had very little information about the mentally ill, especially about their daily lives. Because the public lacked information, Nunnally concluded they could be educated and thereby have their negative opinions changed. He provided some strategies for this educational process. Education of the general public became a major focus of mental health advocates in the 1970s.

Research during the 1970s produced mixed results compared to that done in the 1960s. In 1976 Olmsted and Durham did a study similar to Nunnally's 1961 study. They found no change in the public's attitude and subjects in their study had a uniformly negative view of those diagnosed as mentally ill. Other studies found that the public had become better educated and more sympathetic (Rabkin 1974, Spiro et al. 1973). These authors attribute this change to the media and antistigma campaigns.

One way to account for these discrepant findings is to make the inference that antistigma campaigns were making the public more aware of their negative views toward those diagnosed as mentally ill. As the societal norm changed toward being more sympathetic toward those who were diagnosed as mentally ill and other minority groups, a response bias may have been created and thus reflected in the measured attitudes. This change may not have been a real change in attitude but may have occurred because it was viewed as being *politically incorrect* to view those diagnosed as mentally ill as they did in the 1950s and 1960s.

It can be inferred that, with increased media attention, it was no longer acceptable to report any personal negative attitudes. However, it is likely that negative stereotypes continued and behavior toward those diagnosed as mentally ill changed very little (Gove and Fain 1973). Because it was no longer socially acceptable to view those diagnosed as mentally ill in a negative manner, ascertaining exactly what people thought and how they truly felt became more difficult. It might be hypothesized that the public's stigma placed on those diagnosed as mentally ill is displayed indirectly through the reluctance of community acceptance as is evidenced by the opposition encountered to the opening of group homes in residential communities.

In the 1980s Weinstein (1982) reported that stigma and discrimination were generalized from low-functioning, highly symptomatic individuals to those patients who are high functioning with a low occurrence of symptoms. In fact, the latter recipients of mental health services are apprehensive about others learning of their psychiatric history. These individuals harbor a constant fear of rejection from others because of the general attitude of the community toward mental health recipients. In a later study Mansouri and Dowell (1989) confirmed that psychological distress was conjoined by perceived stigma from the public. By using a social distance measure, they were able to test the magnitude of perceived stigma against those who were diagnosed as mentally ill. They found a high degree of stigma and concluded that mental health recipients rate the reduction of stigma in the community as an important factor in improving their quality of life.

An additional problem that occurs for stigmatized people is that they may identify with what is being said and/or written about them and thereby stigmatize themselves. This self stigma (Herman 1993) can have devastating consequences in that it greatly affects a person's expectations and goals and thereby impedes progress and rehabilitation. It creates a self-fulfilling prophecy.

Penn and colleagues (1994) examined the types of information that reduce stigmatization of schizophrenia. Three hundred and twenty-nine undergraduates read one of six varying vignettes about a person who was described as having recovered from a mental disorder. The six vignettes varied in the type of information that was provided about the former patient. One of the vignettes described a person who had been hospitalized for depression; a second described a person only with the label of *schizophrenia*. A third vignette provided the label of schizophrenia and a description of the individual's symptoms at the time of hospitalization. A fourth vignette provided the label of schizophrenia with a description of the aftercare setting, in which the individual was consulting a case manager at a community mental health center. A fifth vignette included information about the label and symptoms associated with schizophrenia, and a description of the aftercare setting. A sixth vignette provided information only about the symptoms associated with schizophrenia.

Five dependent measures were used to measure attitudes about the former patients: a social distance measure and a dangerousness scale, a measure of the target individual's characteristics and skills, and a measure of affective reaction to the target individual. The subjects who completed the measures were also asked if they knew someone who was mentally ill. Those individuals who had had no previous contact with those diagnosed as being mentally ill perceived them as dangerous and indicated that they would maintain a greater social distance. In general, if a subject was given knowledge of the symptoms associated with the acute phase of schizophrenia, this created more stigma than the label of schizophrenia alone. However, if the knowledge about the target individual's posttreatment living arrangements were known, the negative judgments were reduced.

In summary, it appears that the general public has a long-standing negative attitude toward those who are diagnosed as mentally ill. Although public education may have had some impact on changing this attitude, it appears that this change may be reflected primarily in unwillingness to express this negativity.

Attitudes of Mental Health Professionals and Students in Training for Mental Health Careers

In addition to the general public's holding negative views of mental health recipients, research has demonstrated that professionals and students in the mental health field also hold negative beliefs about those diagnosed as mentally ill. Primavera (1993) suggested that the primary source of stigma and discrimination toward mental health recipients comes from the mental health system itself. His suggestion is based on testimony given by recipients and former recipients at town meetings held by the Stigma and Discrimination Task Force of the New York State Commissioner of Mental Health's Planning Advisory Committee.

Calicchia (1981) was one of the first to explore the attitudes of psychiatrists, psychologists, and social workers toward individuals who were hospitalized for psychiatric care. A semantic differential scale and a social distance questionnaire were distributed to all three professional groups. Calicchia evaluated the responses on five dimensions reflecting characteristics of individuals diagnosed with mental illness, including worthy/worthless, safe/dangerous, effective/ineffective, understandable/mysterious, and acceptance/rejection level. Although there were significant group differences among the three professional groups, it was reported that, overall, all three groups projected negative opinions toward the *ex-patient* on all five of the above dimensions.

Unfortunately, students in the mental and medical health fields have also been found to hold negative beliefs. While these students are being educated about psychological issues, concepts, and methods, there is little opportunity to gain insight about their own beliefs and opinions concerning those with whom they aspire to work. Without this awareness it is likely that their attitudes and beliefs will affect their work.

In a study by Khandelwal and Workneh (1986), students were given a series of vignettes that represented specific mental disorders, such as mania, depressive psychosis, process schizophrenia, acute psychosis, mental retardation, and epilepsy. They were asked a series of questions including the prediction of social consequences for each disorder. Khandelwal and Workneh found that individuals with schizophrenia and acute psychosis were predicted to have unsuccessful outcomes in the areas of marriage, family relations, and work. Although the individuals with more acceptable illnesses, such as mental retardation and epilepsy, were also thought to have serious disorders, their social consequences were seen as more favorable. The importance of adequate student training to reduce the stigma imposed on their future clients was stressed.

Roskin and colleagues (1986) assessed the attitudes of students before and after a psychiatric clerkship that focused on more biological etiologies of mental disorders. It was found that after the clerkship, students' attitudes toward mental health recipients became more accepting and positive. The authors reported a positive increase in the attitude toward the person diagnosed with schizophrenia and a less positive attitude toward the diabetic and healthy person. The authors claimed that psychiatric residents develop a more positive attitude toward persons who are diagnosed as schizophrenic because of their increased contact, seeing the medications work, dispelling of the fear of dangerousness, and learning more about the psychopathology.

Roskin and colleagues (1986) concluded that classroom instruction was not enough to reduce negative attitudes and beliefs toward those who are diagnosed as mentally ill. They also concluded that contact with people diagnosed as mentally ill by itself was not enough to reduce negative attitudes. Increased contact needed to be coupled with the increased education that an internship provided.

Conclusion

It seems apparent that more education and training is necessary for both the public and professionals in mental health to decrease the problem of stigma. As suggested in the study by Roskin and colleagues (1986), education about mental illness utilizing a more biological approach seems to accomplish this task with psychiatric students. This further suggests that effective educational programs aimed at changing attitudes toward those diagnosed as mentally ill need to use appropriate models and concepts tailored to the group that is being educated.

More research into the etiology of the negative attitude and beliefs about those diagnosed as mentally ill is clearly indicated. Also, research is needed to help decide what types of educational and other interventional programs will be most effective with different groups in reducing their negative attitudes and beliefs.

LABELING THEORY

The negative connotations associated with the label *mental patient* raise the possibility that it would be preferable to use other terms, such as *recipient, former recipient,* or *individuals who are diagnosed as mentally ill.* Some use the term *consumer* in place of *patient*; however, the use of this term connotes a voluntary use of services that does not always apply, and all labels can be considered to have some inaccuracy. The question that arises is what role the label *mental patient* or *mentally ill* plays in stigma and discrimination.

There are a number of different views about the role. One of the most extreme views has been called *labeling theory* (Scheff 1974, 1986). Socall and Holtgraves (1992) state that, according to labeling theory, negative stereotypes of those diagnosed as mentally ill play an important role in the etiology of mental disorders. Scheff suggested that people who are labeled mentally ill internalize the negative societal conceptions of mental illness and their identity crystallizes around the label. In other words, the label causes the disorder.

Socall and Holtgraves (1992) support a variation of labeling theory: even if the label does not cause mental illness, it increases negative evaluation by others and self-devaluation, increasing vulnerability to the chronicity and severity of mental disorders. Labeling theory posits that negative societal conceptions of mental illness exist prior to, and are independent of, a labeled person's actual behavior.

Walter Gove has been the leading critic of Scheff and labeling theory (Cockerham 1981). Gove and Fain (1973) state that labeling theory does not explain how the label is gotten to begin with. They admit that the public stereotype of the person diagnosed as mentally ill is negative and has the possibility of serious discrimination. However, they make the claim that a psychiatric hospital stay will not necessarily lead to a negative label or to negative outcomes. To illustrate this point, Gove and Fain evaluated 429 persons who had been treated in a state mental hospital one year after their hospitalization. The results indicate that these people showed marked improvement in their relationships with their co-inhabitants and modest improvements in their instrumental performance and community activities. In general, patients evaluated their hospital experience positively and reported that their situation and their ability to deal with problems had improved. Only a small minority appeared to see the stigma of hospitalization as having posed a serious problem. Although Gove and Fain's results are positive and encouraging, they contradict all of the studies reported here and elsewhere that show a strong negative impact of stigma on all aspects of everyday life and functioning.

Cockerham (1981) attempted to account for the atypical results of the study by pointing out that the treatment program was a progressive one that included an extraordinary degree of attention and support. This program is not at all representative of the treatment programs in the typical mental health hospital.

In a laboratory study of stigma, Piner and Kahle (1984) found that once persons were labeled as mentally ill, they were stigmatized regardless of their behavior. Confederates labeled as mentally ill, or not labeled at all, behaved identically. Subjects perceived the labeled, but not the unlabeled, confederates as unusual. Piner and Kahle inferred that preconceived notions exist about what individuals diagnosed as mentally ill are like. This inference is based on the differential perception of individuals who behaved the same, but were labeled differently.

In a landmark study Rosenhan (1973) showed that once people were labeled mentally ill, their actions were perceived by others in a distorted manner to fit the label. He and seven colleagues gained secret admission to twelve psychiatric hospitals on the east and west coasts of the United States, presenting themselves with complaints of hearing voices. When asked about the voices, they said the voices were unclear, but seemed to be "empty," "hollow," and "thud." The voices were unfamiliar and the same sex as the pseudopatient. Once admitted to the psychiatric unit, the pseudopatient ended the feigning of any aberrant behaviors. Despite the pseudopatients' appearance of sanity, they were never detected by the staff as being impostors, although thirty-five of the 118 fellow patients with whom they came in contact voiced their suspicions. The length of hospitalization ranged from seven to fifty-two days, with an average of nineteen days. Upon discharge, seven of the eight pseudopatients were diagnosed with schizophrenia *in remission*, while the eighth case was diagnosed with schizophrenia.

This study brings the full impact of labels into light. Once the pseudopatient was labeled as schizophrenic, no amount of normal behavior could change the fact that the person was seen as schizophrenic. This fact painfully illustrates the extreme difference between a physical and mental diagnosis. If someone were to break a leg, it would heal and be forgotten. The label of a psychiatric disorder endures and often will outlast the symptoms.

DIAGNOSIS AND STIGMA

There continues to be great controversy among professionals about the validity and usefulness of diagnosis in mental health. Particular criticism has been directed toward diagnosis as presented in the *Diagnostic and Statistical Manual of Mental Disorders* (*DSM-IV* 1994).

Primavera (1993) pointed out that mental health researchers have emphasized the necessity of diagnosis so that they can discover which treatments work most effectively for which particular problems. He also states that some clinicians see diagnosis as helpful in understanding and conceptualizing treatment planning. These clinicians also hold the belief that diagnosis provides a useful shorthand for talking to other professionals about their clients. Insurance companies insist on a diagnosis in order to provide reimbursement for clinical services. It is clear that diagnosis is seen as an important function in mental health research and service providing.

Primavera (1993) asserted that, although diagnosis may have its place in clinical science and practice, it has a number of potentially negative side effects. Each diagnosis has a list of characteristics and behaviors that are referred to as symptoms of some process. These symptoms are used to decide which diagnosis applies to any individual. The problem that can ensue is that a clinician may assume that the symptoms associated with a diagnosis apply totally to each individual given that diagnosis. The possibility exists that we will expect all individuals diagnosed as schizophrenic to have aberrant thought patterns, delusions, hallucinations, and other symptoms all of the time and possibly for their entire life.

This idea may be easy to acquire because clinicians who work in hospitals and/or in private practice see people only when they are going through their worst times. Clinicians who work in state hospitals have a lot of experience with those diagnosed as schizophrenic. The majority of their contact involves times when the individuals are exhibiting many of the symptoms that clinicians have learned to associate with this diagnosis. When the symptoms are not present, the patients are discharged, and the clinicians see them again only if the symptoms return. Given this experience, it is not surprising that so many clinicians have such a negative attitude and low expectations for recovery toward those with this diagnosis. Cohen and Struening (1962) referred to this negative attitude as the *clinician's error* (see also Cohen and Cohen 1984).

According to Primavera (1993), another problem with diagnosis is that clinicians tend to think of the person as the diagnosis. Those diagnosed as mentally ill are often referred to as *schizophrenics, paranoids, psychotics,* and so on. When people are referred to by a diagnostic category, it implies that everything to be known about this individual is captured and summarized in the diagnosis. This fails to acknowledge each person's individuality and the large variations of behaviors that can be exhibited by persons who are diagnosed similarly. Professionals recognize this problem when they are confronted with it, but many seem to lose this recognition when they engage in discussions with other professionals and nonprofessionals about a person diagnosed as mentally ill.

It should be pointed out that those diagnosed with a physical problem are not usually referred to in the same way as those diagnosed as mentally ill. If a person has cancer or hypertension, we would not assume that knowing the diagnosis has provided us with a complete description of that person and what can be expected from him or her. We say that a person *has* cancer and that another person *is* schizophrenic. The most recent version of the American Psychological Association publication manual (1994) has a section on the use of language in which this point is elaborated in detail and specific guidelines against this use of language are outlined.

Diagnosis is not likely to be discontinued and we are not suggesting that it should be. We are suggesting that, in using diagnosis, it is vital to be aware of its potentially negative side effects.

CONCLUSIONS AND IMPLICATIONS

The research with both the general public and mental health professionals has demonstrated long-term negative attitudes and beliefs about those diagnosed as mentally ill. Research has also demonstrated that these attitudes and beliefs can have negative consequences on the lives of those diagnosed as mentally ill. The exact role of the label is in question, but not its generally negative impact.

If the general public continues to hold negative and unfounded beliefs about those who are diagnosed as mentally ill, how will those so diagnosed ever be able to get the opportunity to maximize their lives? If people continue to believe that *all* people so diagnosed are bad, dangerous, dirty, unpredictable, and worthless they will limit their interaction with those people and never give them a chance to be known as individuals with individual personalities, strengths, and weaknesses.

Given the pervasive stigma attached to those diagnosed as mentally ill, the amount of discrimination against this group is not surprising. At the same time, discrimination is difficult to prove because it is hard to establish that a person's diagnosis is the major cause for exclusion or denial of services or opportunities. Discrimination is likely to be much more prevalent than would be implied by the number of lawsuits concerning it. Given the pervasiveness of negative attitudes and beliefs, will judges and lawyers believe that accusations of discrimination are true?

The negative attitude is not always directly expressed. As pointed out above, this change in the expression of stigma toward those who are diagnosed as mentally ill happened in the early 1970s. People rarely express their negative attitudes and beliefs publicly, but often express them indirectly, usually by what they do or don't do. Politically correct attitudes are more difficult to counteract than a manifest negative view since they are harder to identify. People are unlikely to be affected by an educational program aimed at dispelling negative and unfounded beliefs if they don't recognize themselves as holding such beliefs.

What is needed is an intensive, thorough educational program to help people get in touch with their beliefs and attitudes and provide them with the tools to change these attitudes. These programs need to include interaction with persons who are diagnosed as mentally ill and who are in recovery. Research reviewed above (Roskin et al. 1986) has indicated that an educational program coupled with contact with those who are stigmatized is the most effective way to reduce stigma. More research is needed to determine which types of educational interventions would be most effective for different groups of people as well as the best ways to deliver this educational material.

An examination of the media shows that negative views of those diagnosed as mentally ill are as ingrained in the images portrayed on film and television as were those of African Americans before there was awareness of these negative stereotypes. Those of us in the field of mental health need to voice our objection to these stereotypes and insist that a more representative and informed picture be presented to the public.

Educational and awareness programs are needed for mental health professionals as well as for students in training for mental health careers. These programs must include interaction with persons who are diagnosed as mentally ill and those who are in recovery (Anthony 1993) to help counteract the clinician's error (Cohen and Struening 1962) and help professionals and students understand that some of those diagnosed have a good prognosis for a good quality of life.

Educational programs must attack the disability model that permeates mental health and replace it with an ability or capacity model. The approach must be to deemphasize the limitations of those diagnosed and emphasize the capabilities and individual talents each person has. This approach does not ignore the severity of the symptoms and problems that some persons have some or a great deal of the time. Rather, it emphasizes the importance of dealing with each person as an individual who needs a rehabilitation program that maximizes his or her chances for the highest degree of recovery possible.

152

GENERAL CONCEPTUAL ISSUES

REFERENCES

Anthony, W. A. (1993). Recovery from mental illness: the guiding vision of the mental health service system in the 1990s. *Psychosocial Rehabilitation Journal* 16:11–23.

Calicchia, J. P. (1981). Differential perceptions of psychiatrists, psychologists, and social workers toward the ex-patient. *Journal of Community Psychology* 9:361–366.

Cockerham, W. C. (1981). *Sociology of Mental Disorder*. Englewood Cliffs, NJ: Prentice-Hall.

Cohen, P., and Cohen, J. (1984). The clinician's illusion. *Archives of General Psychiatry* 41:1178–1182.

Cohen, J., and Struening, E. L. (1962). Opinions about mental illness in the personnel of two large mental hospitals. *Journal of Abnormal Social Psychology* 64:349–360.

Cumming, E., and Cumming, J. (1957). *Closed Ranks: An Experiment in Mental Health Education*. Cambridge, MA: Harvard University Press.

Diagnostic and Statistical Manual of Mental Disorders (1994). 4th ed. Washington, DC: American Psychiatric Association.

Goffman, E. (1963). *Stigma: Notes on the Management of Spoiled Identity*. Englewood Cliffs, NJ: Prentice-Hall.

Gove, W. R., and Fain, T. (1973). The stigma of mental hospitalization: an attempt to evaluate its consequences. *Archives of General Psychiatry* 28:494–500.

Herman, N. J. (1993). Return to sender: reintegrative stigma-management strategies of ex-psychiatric patients. *Journal of Contemporary Ethnography* 22:295–330.

Khandelwal, S. K., and Workneh, F. (1986). Perception of mental illness by medical students. *Indian Journal of Psychological Medicine* 9:26–32.

Mansouri, L., and Dowell, D. A. (1989). Perceptions of stigma among the long-term mentally-ill. *Psychosocial Rehabilitation Journal* 13:79–91.

Nunnally, J. C. (1961). *Popular Conceptions of Mental Health: Their Development and Change*. New York: Holt.

Olmsted, D. W., and Durham, K. (1976). Stability of mental health attitudes: a semantic differential study. *Journal of Health and Social Behavior* 17:35–44.

Osgood, C. E., and Tannenbaum, P. (1957). *The Measurement of Meaning*. Urbana, IL: University of Illinois Press.

Penn, D. L., Guynan, K., Daily, T., et al. (1994). Dispelling the stigma of schizophrenia: What sort of information is best? *Schizophrenia Bulletin* 20:567–578.

Piner, K. E., and Kahle, L. R. (1984). Adapting to the stigmatizing label of mental illness: foregone but not forgotten. *Journal of Personality and Social Psychology* 47:805–811.

Primavera, L. H. (1993). Fighting stigma and discrimination in the mental health system. *Empowerment* 4(2).

Publication Manual of the American Psychological Association (1994) 4th ed. Washington, DC: American Psychological Association.

Rabkin, J. (1972). Opinions about mental illness: a review of the literature. *Psychological Bulletin* 77:153–170.

———— (1974). Public attitudes toward mental illness: a review of the literature. *Schizophrenia Bulletin* 10:9–33.

Rosenhan, D. L. (1973). On being sane in insane places. *Science* 179:250–258.

Roskin, G., Carsen, M. L., Rabiner, C. J., and Lenon, P. A. (1986). Attitudes towards patients. *Journal of Psychiatric Education* 10:40–49.

Scheff, T. (1974). The labeling theory of mental illness. *American Sociological Review* 39:444–452.

———— (1986). *Being Mentally Ill: A Sociological Theory.* 2nd ed. Chicago: Aldine.

Socall, D. W., and Holtgraves, T. (1992). Attitudes toward the mentally ill: the effects of labels and beliefs. *Sociological Quarterly* 33:435–445.

Spiro, H. R., Siassi, I., and Crocetti, G. (1973). Ability of the public to recognize mental illness: an issue of substance and an issue of meaning. *Social Psychiatry* 8:32–36.

Weinstein, R. M. (1982). Stigma and mental illness: theory versus reality. *Ortho-molecular Psychiatry* 11:87–99.

7

Answering the Contemporary Trend toward Cultural Particularism in Psychotherapy

JEFFREY I. LEWIS

INTRODUCTION

There is a debate dominating the concerns of the social sciences today, a debate as timeless and ancient as the ongoing nature-versus-nurture controversy, as timely and in vogue as the wave of "political correctness" that has swept through society and the universities. Though the debate has occurred mainly among cognitive anthropologists, ethnologists, sociologists, and academic social psychologists, there are far-reaching implications resulting from the "romantic rebellion" (Shweder 1984) and these implications have stirred a questioning, at times severely emotionally driven, about the validity of the practice and theory of certain widely used types of psychoanalysis and psychotherapy.

The issue is whether culture, defined as "a shared organization of ideas that includes the intellectual, moral, and aesthetic standards prevalent in a community and the meanings of communicative actions" (LeVine 1984, p. 67), is so unique a determinant of human actions and comprehension as to render all cultures incomparable and beyond the pale of judgment, or whether cultural influences have a more generic-universal function in transforming the young members of a group from mammals into human beings so that the apparent diversity observed in cultures is best regarded as the exterior variations of a more deeply common structure that makes us all equally human. Stated another way, the debate is whether culture is essentially relativistic, comprising such arbitrariness as to make it illogical and nonrational, thus falling outside the determination of evidence or scientific evaluation. Or, as the other side sees it, that there are universal cultural similarities that, when combined with transcultural biological drives interacting with the common aspects of social intercourse, result in a generic human mind that operates the same everywhere it is found (much the same way that a heart or lung exists in all peoples).

According to Melford Spiro (1984), the trend in anthropology and other allied social sciences is characterized by views reflecting "particularistic cultural determination" that tends to depict each culture as a monad, expressing a set of arbitrary ideas encoded within a set of arbitrary symbols. In this conceptualization the diversity of cultures resembles a "Babel" wherein they are virtually incomprehensible to each other and not given to scientific evaluation or explanation. As such, he laments that, given this incommensurability, "we can't have a cross-cultural theory of incest-taboos, because "incest" has different meanings in different cultures, we can't have a cross-cultural theory of religion, because "religion" means different things in different cultures" (p. 345). The consequences within his own field of anthropology are such that field researchers and cultural theorists are faced with a trend that constricts their activities in the following ways: anthropologists are cautioned not to describe or explain any culture other than the one to which they natively belong; it is believed that only researchers who have been socialized into a given cultural group can satisfactorily investigate and understand that culture; finally, it is believed that the native language of the culture must be utilized to report on its ideas and institutions since the conceptual system of such a group cannot be treated adequately by using the linguistic concepts of another.

For quite some time now a similar trend has entered into the debates that occur regarding the relevancy and saliency of the psychotherapies. The result has been that it is now argued by some that only individuals who have been enculturated within a particular group, employing the dominant language of that group, are suited and appropriate psychotherapists for patients who may be drawn from that group. If the argument does not quite go this far, it may at least require that out-group psychotherapists be culturally sensitized to the cultural patterns and nuances of the particular reference group before entering into treatment with one of its members, and even having done so, the therapist is thought to be at a marked disadvantage since only another cultural affiliate can ever truly understand.

Naturally, given the title of this chapter, my primary purpose is to discuss this current intellectual trend, also alternately referred to as *poststructuralism* or *postmodernism*, as it has impacted upon the practice of psychotherapy and not more generally as a means of interpreting history, art, or science. In order to do so, there must be a description of how the concept of psychotherapy is specifically intended in this work since there has been such an inundation of analytic styles since Glover's (1940) initial survey, all reflecting the different emphases, educations, and cultural predilections of the various theorists and practitioners. Psychotherapy is used herein to refer to that process that allows personal growth and the liberation of the personality by viewing psychological problems and crises as opportunities for patients to discover deeper levels of human experience and the unexpressed possibilities in their personality and behavior (Lewis 1996). The concept is not meant in the narrow sense of suggesting a routinized psychological treatment aimed at a homogeneous goal of adjustment and symptom amelioration, but rather a process that respects the wholeness of the psyche and proceeds in regard to the uniqueness and individuality of each patient or analysand.

This interpretation of the project of psychotherapy has important roots in the workings of many significant schools of thought, actually tracing back to Freud's (1912) early writings in which the analyst is advised to proceed with an open mind free from any presuppositions and without any purpose in view so as to be potentially taken by surprise in how the course of treatment progresses. As described by Haynal (1989), years later, in the 1920's and '30's, as controversy swirled in the inner circles of psychoanalysis over the search for rules to provide an authorized frame of reference that constituted "correct" Freudian technique, theorists such as Theodor Reik (1933) emphasized the importance of surprise that followed the analyst's elimination of preconceived views about patients taken into therapy, and Fenichel (1941) advised that analysts always be prepared to be led by their patients into areas quite different from what they might have expected.

Furthering this intention of being guided by the patient's uniqueness are the theoretical conceptions of Carl Jung (1935), which describe patients as individuals to begin with and suggest that therapy's only true aim is to help the patient become what he or she is and always was. Naturally, the humanistic tradition in psychotherapy complements this position in orienting the therapist never to assume that he or she is more expert or knowledgeable than the patient about the patient's own experience; even in the practice of self psychology described by Kohut (1971), the therapist serves primarily as a catalyst for the release of a largely unknown quantum of potentials and latent skills in the process of a patient becoming him- or herself. Always within the rationale of these variants of psychoanalysis and psychotherapy is the idea that therapy consists of a process that allows the unfolding of something contained essentially within the person that cannot be foreseen at the outset of treatment and, as Michael Balint (1932) illustrated, is concerned primarily with apprehending everything that makes the patient a unique individual, reaching beyond the mere analysis of symptoms and complexes. Though more will be said later in the chapter about what constitutes the therapeutic attitude underlying the technique or process, it is this particular interpretation of psychotherapy that is being used in the discussion of culture theory and cultural determinism that is the subject before us.

THE CASE FOR THE "PSYCHIC UNITY OF MANKIND"

In his 1939 lectures and at other times during the course of his illustrious career, the psychoanalyst Harry Stack Sullivan (1940), who devised the principles of interpersonal psychiatry, advocated for a viewpoint that highlighted the continuity between even the most extreme psychiatric disturbances and the common facets of life for each human:

> . . . it will finally have demonstrated that there is nothing unique in the phenomena of the gravest functional illness. The most peculiar behavior of the acutely schizophrenic patient, I hope to demonstrate, is made up of interpersonal processes with which each of us is or historically has been familiar. For the greater part of the performances, the interpersonal processes of the psychotic patient are exactly of a piece with processes which we manifest some time every twenty-four hours. Some of the psychotic performances seem very peculiar indeed, and, as I surmised in 1924, for the explanation and familiarization of these performances, we have to look to the interpersonal relations of the infant, to the first eighteen months or so of life after birth. In most general terms, we are all much more simply human than otherwise, be we happy and successful, contented and detached, miserable and mentally disordered, or whatever. [pp. 15–16]

This emphasis upon the continuity and commonality among all humanity is the issue dividing the two previously cited schools of thought. Referred to variously as the debate between enlightenment thinking and romanticist thinking, reductionist ideas and cultural phenomenology, and universalist conceptions and relativism, the issue is whether there is a single generic human mind that is evolutionarily determined and subject to contextual variations on a theme, or whether the context determines the mind in such a way that there can be no normative comparisons since human culture is unique wherever it is found. What Shweder (1984) refers to as the enlightenment school consists of figures such as Wittgenstein, Chomsky, Levi-Strauss, Piaget, and Freud, where the unifying concept is that our minds work essentially in the same way and that beyond the surface variations in behavior or thought lie deep structures. In addition, there is the supposition of progress or a developmental point of view that construes the life cycle as consisting of universally valid steps, from Kohlberg's (1981) description of moral progress, which asserts that an objective morality comparable to Kant's categorical imperative is discoverable through logic and reasoning, to Piaget's steps, which trace the path to formal operational thought.

In opposition to this perspective of modernity–enlightenment thought is the position of the postmodernist, or romanticist school. As an example of the contrast in views, consider the approach of Michel Foucault to Freud's efforts to refine theory and provide a method for discovering the true workings of the psyche's nature. Foucault contended that the psyche was not some discoverable reality that could be revealed by more and more refined theories, but rather that the psyche itself was a subjective notion constituted by the theories describing it and that there is no mind independent of the practices that shaped it, including the ways that have been fashioned to "examine it." Thus Freud's very technique was itself shaping the mind externally, and psychoanalytic theory, with its supposition of essence or deep structure (manifest versus latent content), was regarded with distrust and replaced by representations emphasizing discontinuity, surface specificity, and textuality (Sarup 1966).

This trend continues into cultural studies in theories that propose to elevate the significance of the local context and of surface content through asserting that cultural practices are arbitrary, symbolic, expressive, and not normative, that is, there are no standards worthy of universal respect dictating what to think or how to act (Levi-Bruhl 1910). Likewise, post-Marxist critics such as Laclau and Mouffe (1985) point out that modern societies have no real center, cannot be characterized by any organizing principle or universal truth claims, and are instead a "proliferation of particularisms." Like Foucault, they stress their opposition to master narratives that, through the tyranny of reason and certainty and the suppression of ambivalence, attempt to devise singular theories and history with only one valid meaning rather than rejecting general meta-theories in favor of particular answers to particular questions.

This opposing view arose partly in protest to the logical bottom line implied (and often stated) in universalistic or developmental theories that, in the spectrum of human cultures, some idea systems and practices were considered to be more superstitious, primitive, erroneous, and immoral than others. Their point was that primitive and modern cultures were coequal, that the "mind," which could be derived by observing life among primitive peoples, was not the result of the deficient or inadequate application of the rules of science and rationality, that it is not necessarily the case that the overall history of the practices of humanity is a record of progressively better adaptations to the demands of the environment, and that the history of ideas is more a reflection of entrenched fashions than something that must be and must have been. Translated into the vernacular of our present societal trends, this perspective more closely meets the requirements of being "politically correct" by avoiding possible bias in describing another culture as inferior or judging cultural frames as being either "better" or "worse." Naturally, this relativistic position poses some of the most painful difficulties for scientists studying the vicissitudes of cultural variation who must suspend judgment and hierarchical comparison in considering cultures that institutionally degrade and dehumanize women or employ practices such as female genital mutilation that serve as a means of subjugating one gender to the absolute authority of the other.

Additionally, relativism or pure particularism as an explanation is doomed to failure since it paradoxically leads to its own destruction. Sarup (1996) shows how pluralism must have limits; otherwise, if particularity is taken as the only valid principle, it would result in having to defend the rights of each diverse social and national minority, including those whose reactionary purposes would aim to wrench from others their rights. In other words, there must be an appeal to more general principles. Likewise, in asserting social indeterminacy and the absence of common standards, the relativist position confers an overarching unity upon the question of social evolution. Yet it is just this kind of coherence, the "mega-narrative" or big story, that is claimed to have been abolished for being invalid. The self-contradiction embedded in all purely relative positions is that the assertion that values are incommensurable across cultures is itself an absolute truth claim, the very something that is held to be impossible by proponents of this point of view.

One of the compelling aspects for advocating a theory that suggests that there is an intricate web of human commonality that binds all of us despite the cacophony of thematic variations is that both formal investigation and casual observation reveal the recurring patterns so consistently as to make the conclusion just plain obvious. When Darwin's friend, Thomas Henry Huxley, cited in Wright (1994), grasped the simplicity and obviousness of Darwin's theory of natural selection he exclaimed, "How extremely stupid not to have thought of that" (p. 23). The place to begin is with the unavoidable fact that all of us share a virtually indistinguishable physiology consisting of organs and systems that have survived into the present due to their having adapted their designs and mechanisms in such a way as to optimize the survival fitness of our ancestors. As Wright put it, "every page of *Gray's Anatomy* applies to all people in the world" (p. 26).

Of considerable importance within this universally given biological system is the presence of a brain structure consisting of the "recently" evolved equipment, the two massive cerebral hemispheres, sitting atop the older parts of the brain that still nonetheless have retained their full functional integrity. During the evolution of human brain structure, the newer additions did not invalidate or replace the more ancient parts of the brain, but rather came to coexist by deriving some approximation of dynamic equilibrium.

In a rough characterization earlier in this century by James Olds (1956), the older brain structure was called the "hot brain" in that its domain included impulses, appetites, instinctive drive states, and all that has become associated with the Freudian id, governed by the incautious pleasure principle. The neo-cortex was given the name "cold brain" in that its functions are amenable to social conditioning and that a major part of its evolutionary purpose was to mediate or dampen the fire of the hot brain causing the organism to respond more efficiently to the restraints of environmental necessity. In this sense this more recent structure could be likened to the functioning of the Freudian reality principle. The fact that each member of our species has the same operational equipment for experiencing, processing, and responding to the need requirements of their own bodies and the predictable vagaries of global stimuli sets the stage for rectifying the neglect of the phylogenetic aspects of development that have been ignored or neglected in the behavorial-cultural deterministic formulations of human development.

The more sharply focused the look that is taken of diverse human activity on this planet, the clearer is the coalescence of recurring themes and familiar patterns across even the most dissimilar cultures. Though groups inevitably vary by virtue of geographical peculiarities and local customs, the field study results reassuringly expose constant, typically human patterns of existence easily recognized whether one is among the inhabitants of the North Pole or the denizens of the Kalahari desert. This is so because the human organism, from the larger phylogenetic perspective, proceeds through a predetermined series of sequences as the stages of the life cycle unfold. Stevens and Price (1996) make the point that development for the species involves a systemic readiness at each stage of the life cycle to process information, have certain experiences, and manifest certain types of species-typical behaviors associated with a particular stage, such as maternal bonding or attachment, speech acquisition, peer play, mating rituals, and so forth. They contend that this phylogenetic blueprint, the basis for all of the ontogenetic or particularized individual life experience for any given person, has been detoured by the tabula rasa assumption that underlies formulations by behaviorists and learning-theory advocates.

Essentially, behaviorism and particularistic cultural determinism are variants of each other and as such jointly overplay the "nurturance" card in the ongoing nature-versus-nurture controversy. In this sense the cultural relativists, who suggest that cultural groups are unique unto themselves, seem to be making the behaviorist claim that what determines the individual is a result of shaping, conditioning, reinforcements, stimulus–response (S–R) connections upon an ultimately malleable blank slate; hence the claim of arbitrariness . . . in short, that human development can be understood by knowing the conditioning circumstances to which the individual has been exposed during his or her lifetime. But even if one attends mainly to environmental factors and minimizes the a priori evolutionary constants, still, cultural influences can be taken only as one (though an important one) aspect of the dynamic factors that contribute to the individual's shaping. If an individual has had educational exposure and thus acquired a rich personal resource for understanding and explaining all of the chaos of life, politics, and how people behave; or if a person was raised within a family of ten children as opposed to someone who had only one sibling and thus only one competitor, these individual factors must be taken into account along with culture as weighted and competing influences. It must also be kept in mind that the socializing constructions of ethnicity, religion, and culture, dynamically influential as they might be, do not in total determine an individual's identity due to the possibility of the exercise of free will. One's option to employ choice in the interpretation and even the selection of which social institutions to stress or diminish makes for some extent of limit setting and adapting external determinants rather than being passively formed by them.

The constancy and regularity of human patterns suggest that the cultures found throughout the world are more likely the end result of a generic, species-specific human mind (human nature) responding to varying circumstances. Thus the theorists who propose the importance of universal themes note that in every culture one finds the formation of families, a concern with social status and the quest for social approval, the capacity to experience guilt and shame in certain circumstances that are fundamentally the same, and certain patterns of difference between males and females that seem to be biologically established. Regarding this last point, a study was conducted by David Buss (1989) in which thirty-seven diverse cultures across the world were sampled to determine a wide view of patterns of selecting a mate. His results indicated that in every one of the thirty-seven cultures, the females placed prime importance on the potential mate's current resources and financial prospects and thus tended to prefer males who were older than themselves, whereas males uniformly tended to minimize or disregard the financial status of the potential mate and preferred females who were younger, theoretically because of the built-in appeal for females whose fertility has not yet begun to decline. The overarching principle in all mating preference and subsequent courtship rituals is that human females biologically have only limited opportunities to produce offspring; thus the decision to assume the burden of reproduction usually follows a selection procedure resulting in the aim to couple with the male who is most apt to yield the fittest children and who is judged to have resources or resource potential that will further enhance the survival chances of the offspring. For males, again regardless of culture, it is of great benefit in the competition for access to fertile females to be reputed as having personal attributes that contribute to fitness and the materialistic means to fortify the survival of possible offspring, or at least to present oneself in this light even if this is accomplished through exaggeration and out and out deceit. The point is that courtship and mating practices, no matter how exotic, raw, and esoteric, no matter how sublimated, civilized, and sophisticated, are all constituents of the same dance, and can be recognized and understood in whichever culture is under consideration.

Another transcultural human phenomenon that has received extensive consideration, and that is relevant to this debate from the perspective of clinical know-how, is the acquisition of a moral sense and the occurrence of moral behavior in society. Though different cultural groups may judge rather varied norms to be in the best interests of their particular community, beyond these particulars it is widely understood that groups commonly have such moral codes as a matter of innate disposition, given the universal high sensitivity that humans have to public opinion. In *The Moral Animal* previously cited, Wright (1994) eloquently makes this point by stating, "A breach of norms can cause a man 'agony,' and the violation of some trivial bit of etiquette, when recalled even years after, can bring back a 'burning sense of shame'"(p. 184). The basis for the positive or negative appraisal of public opinion is rooted in culturally specific ground rules that are codified into societal values and beliefs and formulated into customs, laws, practices, and standards. The continuity and orderly regularity of each society is dependent upon the transmission of these important vessels of information to each new member of the group;

most often this responsibility falls to the parents who pass the torch to their children. Each child does not simply memorize the code, but, much more profoundly, incorporates a personalized interpretation of the rules into his or her own psychic organization, where it forms the basis of a mental moral agency most usually described as the conscience or Freudian superego. This process of integration is distinctively psychological and culturally transcendent in that it describes a capacity that, through eons of human adaptation, has been built into the standard equipment. The persistence of this capacity for self-regulation and the experience of self-generated punishment in the form of guilt feelings for transgressions of the standards is best appreciated by acknowledging how it enhances the survival possibilities for the individual since survival, after castigation, devaluation, or excommunication from the group, is not likely. Clinicians work with the suffering and damage associated with the exaggerated deviations of guilt, shame, and feelings of rejection and unworthiness every single day, and these clinically recurring issues most assuredly detract from the lives of peoples in all cultures and are due to quite similar and comparable processes.

THE SELF AND CULTURAL PERSONALITIES

In a criticism of universalism, Alan Roland (1996) cites research by Catherine Ewing on Pakistanis and their extent of differentiation between internal representations of self and object. Roland's point is that she failed to acknowledge the degree to which Pakistanis may have a sense of "we–self," consisting of introjects of family and community as part of the self, much more so than the typically more individualistic "I–self" assumed to predominate in American self-conceptions. Thus, if one posits the universal observation that separation of self and object representation is necessary developmentally to avoid serious pathology of the self, they have failed, through omission, to appreciate the culturally different selves that emerged in these environments.

Yet recent social psychological research on theories of self have articulated the likelihood that differing levels of self-definition may be present simultaneously within a given person though assuming varying salience depending upon immediate dynamic influences such as needs or upon normative expectations based upon enculturation. This research has studied the degree to which shifts may occur within individuals between the individuated self-concept, consisting of the unique identity that is separated from others, and the social self-concept, made up of aspects of self derived from relationships with others and membership within significant social groups. In fact, in a study by Trafimow and colleagues (1991), the finding that retrieval cues intended to "activate" "private" self-representations yielded very different self-ideations than when collective self-representations activated by other cues led to the speculation that the individualized and social aspects of self may actually be stored in separate areas of the memory capacity.

Taking these findings further, a study was made to investigate the symbolic shift in point of self-reference from "I" to "we" (Brewer and Gardner 1996). The experimenters set out to activate the more inclusive "social self," characterized by the importance of relations and similarities to others, by priming subjects with the pronouns "we" or "us." This was operationally accomplished by having the subjects read a brief story paragraph with directions to circle all pronouns as part of a proofreading and word-search test. The independent variable was the manipulation of pronouns in either "we–us," "they–them" or "it" conditions. In one experiment it was demonstrated that the priming of the social representations of the self caused respondents to be more likely to interpret ambiguous attitude statements as similar to their own position since the threshold for assimilation and perceived similarity between self and other had been lowered. In another variation of the procedure subjects who had again been primed for collective self-identity activation showed a higher proportion of spontaneous social self-descriptions on the Twenty Statement Test than responses oriented toward personal self-descriptions ("I am a psychologist" rather than "I am very perceptive" types of statements). These findings give rise to the notion of a dynamic self-concept that reflects the oppositional tension between internal and external factors that either push in the direction of increased differentiation from others or alternately push in the direction of assimilation and group identification. A homeostatic process may be involved by means of which increased inclusiveness or increased distinctiveness result as a function of changes in the distance between self and others; at times, circumstances may promote the motivation to emphasize intimacy or collective self-categorizations; just as readily, other circumstances may enhance the need for separated and distinctive self-conceptualizations. It is hypothesized therefore that psychotherapies that generally prompt individuated self-representations simply shift the dynamic equilibrium over to the "I" or "ego" irrespective of any preconceived ideas regarding culturally given inclinations to experience or describe the self collectively. The research seems to indicate that our self-concept is dynamic, not statically fixed as in any particular cultural manifestation; thus we need not be so intent upon defining the characteristic selves that might predominate in a specific subgroup.

Another pertinent aspect of identity formation (or building self-representations) related to this discussion is the contemporary view of identity not as a set point, but rather as a work in progress consisting of the active inclusion of some events and socializing factors and the subordination of others. In the construction of self rendered through the assimilation of certain attributes of models, an identity is formulated that consists of shifting subjectivities not easily and unitarily explained by highlighting any single social dynamic as in the appeal to the primacy of cultural factors.

It may also be troublesome to be too quick in believing that a given culture may naturally yield individuals with a distinctive personality type or a recognizable means of experiencing the self, processing information, and so on. If one goes back to the classic study by Adorno and colleagues (1950), the limitations of such thinking become apparent. The Adorno study, *The Authoritarian Personality*, was inspired by the atrocity that had recently ended in Europe whereby the Jewish population was nearly exterminated by the purposeful leadership of Germany, a country regarded as progressive, civilized, and culturally rich. The magnitude of the Holocaust could not easily be understood, taking place as it did in modern history within a sophisticated populace, and so questions emerged about the nature of the German people and what about them could have allowed such an impossible horror to occur.

Adorno's work attempted to answer this question by proposing that certain personality types might be more inclined to harbor deep prejudices toward minority out-groups and that certain cultures, for example pre-1945 Germany and Austria, may contain within their practices, values, and other enculturation elements, the greater likelihood of producing these personality types. However, this thesis did not get very far before its American authors realized that within the American culture, an apparently very different culturally layered society from Germany, there was profound evidence of prejudice including overt anti-Semitic and anti-black sentiments. This observation resulted in a shifting of the work away from trying to illuminate the workings of a prejudiced society to attempting to describe the dynamics of a prejudiced personality. The study itself finally revealed that a cluster of factors, including poor education, low IQ, and low socioeconomic status, were present in individuals who were most likely to develop authoritarian personalities and thus the inclination to be prejudiced against out-group members. In a highly egalitarian way, the research warrants the conclusion that prejudice can be found in any culture if the researcher identifies individuals high on the Potentiality for Fascism Scale.

In a timely appearance of thoughts similar to those conceived in the early Adorno hypothesis, Daniel Goldhagen (1996) attempted to explain the Holocaust by looking closely at the German culture of the 1930s and concluding that such a thing could have occurred only in Germany because of the way the German people were, that is, the German culture was dominated by a belief structure that held a set of deep anti-Semitic ideas, including the belief that the Jews needed to be eliminated. Therefore, when the time was opportune, the people were motivated to support the program of annihilation. Goldhagen has been broadly criticized for indicting a whole culture and for doing so with a monocausal theory (Joffe 1997), but perhaps most of all for not giving enough weight to the idea that the "ordinary people" who became perpetrators were not operating in a normal setting—that perhaps factors such as indoctrination, peer pressure, and mob dynamics, and establishing locales for the atrocities far from the morally constraining settings of their ordinary lives, allowed the unthinkable behavior to take place, not some culturally determined tendency toward genocide. Even the critics of the Adorno study (Cherry and Byrne 1976) were able to demonstrate that the situation or context that a person is in is a more reliable predictor of whether prejudice will be expressed than the attainment of high scores on the Potentiality for Fascism Scale.

Thus generalizations about distinctive and widely occurring traits, types, and inclinations thought to typify or characterize members of a cultural group may be more apparent than actual. Not only is the identity of a given individual hard to pin down by the person's belonging to a cultural group, but the very idea of particularistic culturalism proves to be itself a variation of the universalistic notions it purports to oppose. It is just that its totalizing statements are applied to a slightly more restricted universe. The solution, it is believed, lies in a psychotherapeutic method wherein the intent of the recognition of sameness, humanness, is to provide the possibility for the exploration of uniqueness and individuality. A critic of postmodern theory, Terry Eagleton (1990), has written that universalizing concepts are not set in opposition to unique particularities but rather assure the right that each individual's difference will be allowed and respected since these universal concepts provide the basis through which all can participate in the common process whereby the fulfillment of individuality can be achieved. Dialectically, the inseparability and interrelatedness of sameness and difference is captured in the notion that one can never know what one is without knowing what one is not, that identity is conceivable only in recognition of the other; the "not–me" is necessary in defining any "me."

What was thought to be a straightforward and relatively uncluttered project was undertaken several years ago at a hospital in which I worked as part of the administrative operations. A meeting had been called for department heads to design a cultural-sensitivity module that would prepare the clinicians at the outpatient sites for the recent influx of Asian immigrants into the hospital's geographic catchment areas. The idea was to construct an educational workshop and manual that would familiarize the therapists with Asian culture, Asian ways of doing things, and how the "mind" and expectations of an Asian immigrant in need of mental health services differed from other patient groups and needed to be understood and fittingly accommodated. The meeting had just gotten under way when one of my colleagues from China saw the necessity to caution the work group that there was no monolithic "Asian culture"; the Chinese differed vastly from the Japanese, who differed from the Koreans, and so forth. Well, the assembled group took appreciative note of this remark and proceeded about their task, which now was not quite so simple since it had become diversified to account for the various countries constituting the Eastern world. Though the training would now have to proceed through the diverse national jigsaw puzzle of Asia, it still seemed a manageable project until someone pointed out that within the various nation states there existed very different ethnic subgroups and religious divergences such that one could not easily speak of the Chinese people per se. This discouraging matter of fact began to seriously erode the illusory idea that a single training exposure would be able to accomplish anything remotely approaching a primer on "Asian culture" and in fact had the effect of opening the sluice gates and yielding a torrent of further considerations not yet imagined. What about those who were here after having been political prisoners or dissidents? What about the Vietnamese immigrants who had been fathered by American infantrymen during the war or who had been left devastated by the incendiary destruction of the war? What about communist versus noncommunist?

What was occurring within this attempt to separate people of Asian culture from the psychological understanding of all other people was that ever more complex elaboration within the sample was brought into the project, since no one wanted to offend any group or subgroup by inadvertently failing to be sensitive to their distinctness and difference from the larger, though variegated, sample. In the manner of an infinite regression, a hierarchical pyramid was forming with further branches and subdivisions from the original concept at the top. It occurred to me that in order to be fair to everyone and not offend anyone's sensibilities, it would be best to turn the pyramid on its head so that the top, which had been the base, would now consist of unique individuals, none of whom could be best understood by studying a primer of their cultural heritage. This perspective, the exploration of unique individuals, is the professed domain of many variations of psychotherapy anyway—a lot of effort to get back to the beginning.

IS EMPATHY POSSIBLE?

The question remains whether it is possible, or desirable, for a member of one cultural grouping to ever really understand the personality and inner experiences of another cultural group. Since culture is in the public domain in the sense that it consists of collective representations often presented as symbols, it should be possible for persons who are not natives to learn any culture if they so wish. However, even though a foreigner may master the culture such that the meanings within a culture are captured and grasped to the same extent as they are for a native, it remains the case that without having been socialized into the group, the foreigner misses the surplus meanings that have become invested by virtue of the native having undergone the primary social experiences. As explained by Spiro (1984), "To learn a culture is to acquire its propositions; to become enculturated is, in addition, to internalize them as personal beliefs, as propositions that are thought to be true, proper, or right" (p. 326).

This raises the question of whether there is actual benefit in urging clinicians to become knowledgeable about a patient's cultural background as part of the preparation for therapy as opposed to allowing this knowledge to unfold during the process of analysis or therapy. Moskowitz (1996) makes a strong point in claiming that in the clinical setting empathy alone is not sufficient to learn about and become sensitive to the patient's cultural heritage. He cites Gedo and Gehrie (1993), cautioning that empathy and other intimate aspects of the communication exchange depend upon shared cultural meanings; without such a context the possibility for errors and serious misunderstandings is vast. But how is the situation made any better by the specific undertaking of trying to learn the culture under the limitations previously discussed? It might be far more advisable to elevate the awareness of clinicians in general to the importance of cultural influences upon behavior and personality so that their curiosity about their patients would include eliciting the experiential phenomenology of being a member of a particular cultural group in the patient's own words, through their eyes. If clinicians in training were oriented more successfully to the idea of psychotherapy as a social fact, that is, as both a technique and a relationship between two people in which the attitude of the therapist counts as much as the technical interventions made, then the currently perceived need to culturally sensitize clinicians would lose its urgency. Therapy practitioners who see their role as being able to listen empathically to the revealing of an individual's entire personality, free from the demands of the environment (and of the therapist as well) so that the patient/analysand can find his or her own way and not be provided with some prescribed "right" way, have minimal need for special cultural training since their mindset is already one of respect for the patient as a person.

Besides the fact that I could no more really "know" anything about Spanish culture that would be clinically advantageous after having read or studied anything *about* the culture than I could about what it's like to be a woman after having taken a course on women's issues, the idea in both instances is that the learned concepts are so far from the immediate experience as to be only of pedantic value. The psychoanalyst Heinz Kohut (1971) spoke of this in describing the distinction between experience-near versus experience-distant concepts, a distinction between a way of expressing what one sees, feels, or thinks—effortlessly and immediately apparent to others (or to us if used by others)—and concepts primarily used by scientists or specialists to explain or advance their aims. This division of experience is further clarified by the ethnologist Clifford Geertz (1984) in suggesting that "love" is an experience-near concept, whereas "object-cathexis" is experience distant; fear is experience near, whereas phobia is experience distant, and ego-dystonic symptom is farther distant still. The raw data of a psychoanalytic exchange consist of the immediacies of experience-near communications; the reality of the transference, the feasibility of the "corrective emotional experience," depend upon this immediacy or the treatment becomes too built upon rationalization and intellectualization. The study of another's culture may give the purveyor a requisite knowledge of the propositions, representations, and symbolizations of the alien culture, but this knowing is probably too experience distant to be of much utility in helping assure an empathic understanding of the patient.

The trick with real empathy lies in being able to achieve a shift in perspective that allows the perceiver to "see" the world temporarily the way that the subject sees it. This capacity to shift perspective, and presumably demonstrate the rudiments of an empathic potential, has been looked at by researchers in child development employing a Piagetian-type experimental schema. In it the participants may sit around a table upon which are arranged various toys or items in a given spatial configuration, and they are asked to demonstrate what the view of the objects might look like if they were sitting in the chair occupied by participant A, B, C, and D. Though the Piagetian task may have been devised to measure children's spatial abilities, it is a convenient metaphor for the aspect of empathy that involves seeing the others' experiences from their own point of view. It is not, however, merely being able to "stand inside someone else's shoes" as the saying goes, but to be able to do so as that person. In order to be able to lay aside conceptual frameworks, personal biases, and value judgments long enough to imagine the world as it appears to the patient, to hear the mythical construction of his or her own psychological reality, and to grasp for a moment what it must be like to be another requires an astute curiosity about what being human is all about and the personal security to be able to let go of one's own frame of reference in order to truly see the other's life.

CONCLUDING REMARKS

This essay has emphasized the universal aspects of the human experience that transcend and are superordinate to cultural influences, and that are but one of the multifactional vectors that shape the particular way in which human nature will become manifest. I have concentrated on the observation that the experience of being human on this earth is the same in vital respects for all of us, and it is this "humanness" that is the gist of many psychotherapeutic explorations. Regardless of the specific culture, life consists of a series of transitions and developmental acquisitions and milestones. In all cases, life begins as absolute dependency; families prevail; separation reliably creates anxiety; and painful experiences such as guilt, shame, and disappointment with the self constitute internal means of punishment in all human groupings. The difficulties that would qualify someone for the help available through analysis and psychotherapy consist uniformly of psychological pain and suffering, fear and anxiety; feelings of being unwanted, unworthy, or unloved; feelings of inadequacy, powerlessness, or uselessness; the sickness over love lost; the pain and doubt of failure. Depression, the most common condition encountered in clinical psychology and psychiatry, has a characteristic "face" wherever it is found in the world, and it results in human misery and debilitation in each and every case.

Perhaps the point of view that elevates particularistic cultural influences to the level that is challenged in this chapter is actually most compatible with the workings of the behavioral therapies and behavior modification. In behaviorist formulations the familiarity or even the proficient knowledge of specific cultural nuances is important in order to establish the antecedent–behavior–consequence sequence with accuracy. Behaviorists must know what contingencies are sustaining a particular behavior and what specific stimuli in the culture are considered to be rewarding (Goldfried and Davison 1976, Korchin 1976, Schaefer and Martin 1969). Such knowledge is necessary to alter maladaptive behavioral responses; it would be ineffective to choose a modifier that had strong positive valence in one social group while being negative or neutral in another. Yet, even within this allowance, a working behavioral plan would have to so individualize the reward to be sure that it had value as a reinforcer. On the other hand, the subject matter and intent of psychoanalytic psychotherapies are with the patient's deep structure, and beyond the surface variations and symptom complexes we are all made of the same stuff.

REFERENCES

Adorno, T. W., Frenkel-Brunswick, E., Levinson, D. J., and Sanford, R. N. (1950). *The Authoritarian Personality*, New York: Harper.

Balint, M. (1932). Character analysis and new beginning. In *Primary Love and Psycho-Analytic Technique* (2nd ed.), pp. 151–164. London: Tavistock. (American edition: New York: Liveright, 1965).

Brewer, M. B., and Gardner, W. (1996). Who is this "we"? Levels of collective identity and self representations. *Journal of Personality and Social Psychology* 71:83–93.

Buss, D. M. (1989). Mate preferences in 37 cultures. In *Psychology and Culture*, ed. W. J. Lonner and R. Malpass, pp. 197–201. Boston: Allyn & Bacon, 1994.

Cherry, F. and Byrne, D. (1976). Authoritarianism. In *Personality Variables in Social Behavior*, ed. T. Blass. Hillsdale, NJ: Lawrence Erlbaum.

Eagleton, T. (1990). *The Ideology of the Aesthetic.* Oxford: Basil Blackwell.

Fenichel, O. (1941). Problems of psychoanalytic technique. *Psychoanalytic Quarterly*, p. 48.

Freud, S. (1912). Recommendations to physicians practicing psycho-analysis. *Standard Edition* 12:111–120.

Gedo, J. E. and Gehrie, M. J., eds. (1993). *Impasse and Innovations in Psychoanalysis: Clinical Case Seminars.* Hillsdale, NJ: Analytic Press.

Geertz, C. (1984). "From the native's point of view": on the nature of anthropological understanding. In *Culture Theory: Essays on Mind, Self, and Emotion*, ed. R. A. Shweder and R. A. LeVine, pp. 123–136. New York: Cambridge University Press.

Glover, E. (1940). *The Technique of Psycho-Analysis.* New York: International Universities Press, 1955.

Goldfried, M. R. and Davison, G. C. (1976). *Clinical Behavior Therapy.* New York: Holt, Rinehart & Winston.

Goldhagen, D. (1996). *Hitler's Willing Executioners.* New York: Vintage.

Haynal, A. E. (1989). Controversies in Psychoanalytic Method: *From Freud and Ferenczi to Michael Balint*, trans. E. Holder. New York: New York University Press.

Joffe, J. (1997). Reply to Daniel Goldhagen's letter to editor. In *The New York Review of Books*, Vol. XLIV, Number 2, p. 40.

Jung, C. G. (1935). Principles of practical psychotherapy. In *The Collected Works of C. G. Jung*, vol. 16, pp. 3–20. Princeton, NJ: Princeton University Press, 1966.

Kohlberg, L. (1981). *The Philosophy of Moral Development*, vol. 1. New York: Harper & Row.

Kohut, H. (1971). *The Analysis of the Self.* New York: International Universities Press.

Korchin, S. J. (1976). *Modern Clinical Psychology: Principles of Intervention in the Clinic and Community.* New York: Basic Books.

Laclau, E., and Mouffe, C. (1985). *Hegemony and Socialist Strategy: Towards a Radical Democratic Politics.* London: Verso.

LeVine, R. (1984). Properties of culture: an ethnographic view. In *Culture Theory: Essays on Mind, Self and Emotion,* ed. R. A. Shweder and R. A. LeVine, pp. 67. New York: Cambridge University Press.

Levy-Bruhl, L. (1910). *Les Fonctions Mentales dans les Sociétés Inférieures.* Paris: Alcan.

Lewis, J. (1996). *Unexpected outcomes in psychotherapy: normalizing the "exception."* Paper presented at the 1st Congress of the World Council for Psychotherapy, Vienna, Austria, June 30–July 4.

Moskowitz, M. (1996). The end of analyzability. In *Reaching Across Boundaries of Culture and Class: Widening the Scope of Psychotherapy,* ed. R. Perez Foster, M. Moskowitz, and R. A. Javier, pp. 179–193. Northvale, NJ: Jason Aronson.

Olds, J. (1956). Pleasure centres in the brain. *Scientific American* 195 4:104.

Reik, T. (1933). New ways in psycho-analytic technique. *International Journal of Psycho-Analysis* 14:321–334.

Roland, A. (1996). How universal is the psychoanalytic self? In *Reaching Across Boundaries of Culture and Class: Widening the Scope of Psychotherapy* ed. R. Perez Foster, M. Moskowitz, and R. A. Javier, pp. 70–90. Northvale, NJ: Jason Aronson.

Sarup, M. (1996). *Identity, Culture, and the Postmodern World.* Athens: University of Georgia Press.

Schaefer, W. H., and Martin, P. L. (1969). *Behavior Therapy.* New York: McGraw-Hill.

Shweder, R. A. (1984). Anthropology's romantic rebellion against the enlightenment, or there's more to thinking than reason and evidence. In *Culture Theory: Essays on Mind, Self, and Emotion,* ed. R. A. Shweder and R. A. LeVine, pp. 27–66. New York: Cambridge University Press.

Spiro, M. (1984). Some reflections on cultural determinism and relativism with special reference to emotion and reason. In *Culture Theory: Essays on Mind, Self, and Emotion,* ed. R. A. Shweder and R. A. LeVine, pp. 323–346. New York: Cambridge University Press.

Stevens, A., and Price, J. (1996). *Evolutionary Psychiatry: A New Beginning.* London/New York: Routledge.

Sullivan, H. S. (1940). *Conceptions of Modern Psychiatry.* New York: Norton.

Trafimow, D., Triandis, H. C., and Goto, S. G. (1991). Some tests of the distinction between the private and the collective self. *Journal of Personality and Social Psychology* 60:649–655.

Wright, R. (1994). *The Moral Animal. Why We Are the Way We Are: The New Science of Evolutionary Psychology.* New York: Vintage.

Part II

Specific Symptomatologies

8

Cultural Issues in the Clinical Management of Depression

MARIO RENDON

The prevalence of depression is an undeniable fact in our society. Findings from the recent Epidemiologic Catchment Area (ECA) study testify to this fact. This study, which involved approximately 20,000 respondents between 1978 and 1986 at five study sites in the United States, reported rates of major depression at levels of 6.7 percent in New Haven, 5.5 percent in St. Louis, and 3.7 percent in Baltimore (Robins et al. 1984). This seems to be the most accurate reflection of the prevalence of major depression, at least in larger cities, to this date. However, to assume that these statistics provide a full picture of the actual rate of depression negates the fact that depression is a dynamic entity that affects certain groups more than others. These statistics hide a very complex phenomenon related to the hierarchy of social events that tends to affect a number of depressed individuals. These factors are discussed in the ensuing pages.

DEPRESSION AS A SOCIAL FACT: A PROBLEM WITH DEFINITION

Implied in the concept of the social dynamics of depression is a rather relative phenomenon. For instance, in the United States, some subgroups of the general population have rates of depression many times higher than the average numbers presented. Such is the case for women, the poor, and certain minority groups. Even taking the population at large, the picture of depression changes with time, with social evolution, and with changes in culture. For example, there is a reported increase in rates of depression in the United States in cohorts born after World War II. Between 1960 and 1975 the rate of depression was found to increase for all ages, but more among the young, with a decrease in the age of onset (Klerman and Weissman 1989). Additionally, a study of almost 40,000 subjects from nine epidemiological surveys and 4,000 relatives from three family studies in several countries found an increase in lifetime rates of major depression. Each younger birth cohort had an increase in almost every country although the magnitude of the increase varied (Cross-National Collaborative Group 1992). Although one may be inclined to conclude from these studies that the phenomenon of depression is on the rise around the world, one needs to caution against such a generalization because different cultures may use constructs other than depression to express their losses, grief, or distress.

The fact of the matter is that epidemiological studies have historically suffered form serious limitations that make findings discrepant and noncomparable. This is particularly the case with regard to different definitions of the boundaries of depression. During this century, for example, different terminologies have been used—such as neurotic, reactive, endogenous, minor—to refer to depression. These terms to some extent reflect society's position regarding etiology and classification. Today the term *bipolar disorder* is used to indicate a manic component along with the depression. In cases with depression alone the categories of unipolar or major depressive disorder and dysthymia are used, depending upon severity and duration. There is also a category for atypical depressions when the nature of the depressive phenomenon cannot be classifed as major or any other specific affective disorder. In spite of all these attempts at categorizing depressive phenomena, however, there is a great deal of etiological uncertainty. It is in recognition of this fact that the *DSM-IV* (1994) of the American Psychiatric Association takes a phenomenological approach to these syndromes. The boundaries of depression are thus defined by a consensus of experts based on observation and without etiological implication.

One must keep in mind, however, that the "experts" who define the boundaries of depression are mostly physicians who are primarily from the same culture. Thus it is not surprising that the way depression is viewed by the psychiatric profession is in terms of a disease. Today depression is compared with hypertension and diabetes, with reference, for example, to their similar prevalence rates and their deleterious effect on the national economy. Thus, when one refers to depression without a qualifier, it usually means illness. This emphasis on illness has been further encouraged by a shift in American psychiatry from a psychological to a biological view of depression. This shift has been ushered in by remarkable advances in psychopharmacology and in the understanding of neurotransmitters in the brain. These followed the serendipitous discovery that some chemicals used for the treatment of tuberculosis were effective in improving depressive symptoms while, on the other hand, some antihypertensives produced depression.

Another complication to the definition and assessment of depression has to do with the difficulty of separating depression from other comparable phenomena. For instance, the term *demoralization* was introduced to explain high symptom levels of depression in epidemiological studies (Link and Dohrenwend 1980). Demoralization refers to states of hopelessness and helplessness often explainable on the basis of adverse life events (Mollica 1989). But how are we to distinguish between this and other similar conditions and depression proper? These kinds of confusion may explain the fact that less than a third of depressed patients are properly diagnosed (Rush 1994). Other factors that have been found to affect diagnosis are level of awareness and method of payment for treatment. For instance, it was found that physicians' level of awareness of depression led to diagnosis in less than half the cases, and that patients receiving care financed by prepayment were less likely to have their depression detected (Wells et al. 1989).

The problems in the definition and assessment of the prevalence of depression are further magnified when it comes to determining the extent of the problem on a global level and across different societies. Cultures differ in the way they interpret social events, and even phenomena such as illnesses are often explained in a nonmedical fashion. Groups also differ accordingly in their utilization of language idioms to express distress. For this reason it is difficult to agree at face value with the statement that depression, as constructed by our culture, is a universal phenomenon. On the other hand, it is hard to imagine cultures where helplessness and demoralization with all their physical consequences are not present.

Conflicting Historical Views of Depression

Conflicting views of depression are certainly not just a contemporary problem, and have been the object of concern since the early history of humankind. Most of the early explanations of depression were philosophical and religious in nature, which later became part of the medical tradition.

These conceptualizations were derived from views of the human condition in general and of reality at large. According to one early view, the human is composed of four elements, two of which are different types of bile. Depression was viewed as an outcome of the predominance of black bile.

A religious influence could be seen in the views of Mesopotamians, Egyptians, Hebrews, and Persians on mental illness. They blamed the demons and invoked gods to explain insanity. This is what Freud (1921) referred to later as a psychological mechanism of projection. We can also see desperate attempts to understand depression in the biblical story of Saul, described in the first book of Samuel, which provides one of the earliest examples of depression and suicide. Saul first tried to convince his servant to kill him and upon failing in this endeavor proceeded to do it himself (Alexander and Selesnick 1966).

In spite of Hippocrates's introduction of the medical "notion" to understand the phenomenon of depression, later historical developments brought the explanation of depression back into the realm of the soul. This concept appears at the time of another pioneer physician, Galenus. See, for instance, a quote from Barcia-Goyanes (1987):

> Bodily organs are *instruments of the soul* and thus vary as souls differ. That animals differ in their souls is reflected in their ferocious or timid stand, in their wildness or domesticity, their sociability or solitariness. To those habits and faculties the body must submit. The horse being proud, fast and generous has strong hooves and beautiful mane; likewise the lion, brave and ferocious is provded with teeth and claws. In the same fashion, the bull and the wild boar are armed the first with horns and the latter with tusks, their natural weapons. In contrast, the shy deer and the rabbit are fast but harmless: This because—I am of the opinion—speed is in the best interest of the timorous while weapons best serve the fierce. [pp. 52–53].

Here we see the dialectic relationship of body and soul in what we could construct as a prelude to the Reichian character armor (Reich 1949). The soul enters into a causal relationship with the body. As has been best documented in posttraumatic stress disorders, it is perfectly possible to turn causality around and attribute neurotransmitter changes in the brain to helplessness. This is not currently the prevailing way of thinking, however.

Guilt, a singularly human emotion, comes into the picture and takes precedence in the sixteenth and seventeenth centuries' explanations of depression. *Hypochondriasis*, from *hyp*, the spleen, came then to represent some organ-focused forms of melancholia while other Latin terms such as *acedia* revealed a growing psychological awareness (Jackson 1985). *Acedia* was one of the capital sins, and was not quite differentiated from laziness and passivity. Therapeutic recommendations at the time emphasized work and activity. It was in fact considered a sin in itself to sit and allow the soul to get into such a deplorable state.

Thus, in the history of depression, body and soul, medicine and psychology have always competed as explanatory models. Even though it has been suggested that discoveries in medicine have brought about historical corrections in etiological explanations (such as in the case of tabes dorsalis, originally attributed to sexual indulgence), it is unlikely, in my opinion, that depression will ever become purely a medical problem such as a sexually transmitted disease of a blood dyscrasia.

From a psychological perspective, other competing theories have been advanced to explain depressive phenomena today. For instance, after observing a phenomenon now referred to as "learned helplessness" in laboratory animals, Seligman (1974) concluded that such a condition was basically what we refer to as depression. From this perspective depression was viewed as a belief in futility, or the learned conviction that responding is independent of reinforcement (Seligman 1974). This theory has been very influential in other disciplines. In anthropology, for instance, Brown and Harris (1978) rely heavily on this explanatory model in their study of the social origins of depression in London. Another contemporary model that has gained significant ground in the diagnosis and treatment of depression is the "cognitive" model, which sees depression as the result of a negative, "idiosyncratic" mind framework in the individual (Beck et al 1979). Here, "schemata" that filter other- and self-perception have a pessimistic component that can be therapeutically manipulated by helping the individual to alter the negatively framed cognitions. Negative cognitions may well be the result of learned helplessness, loss, stress, poor self-esteem, and the like.

Another important and influential model in understanding depression is the psychoanalytic model that prevailed relatively unquestioned in this country for the first half of the twentieth century and is still endorsed by many. It sees depression as a result of either low self-esteem, real or symbolic loss, conflict, ego helplessness in response to stress, passivity, aggression turned inward, self hate, or internalized relationships. Melanie Klein (1935) postulated a "depressive position" taking place sometime during the second year of life and reflecting a progressive integration of partial split objects in the infant. Klein's theory is provocative in that it correlates depression with development. From epidemiology and clinical practice we know that it is often in the most developed individuals or countries that depression and suicide occur most frequently. Klein's concept is also reminiscent of Freud's theory that group formation is based on the renunciation of individual narcissistic aggression for the sake of group identifications (Freud 1921).

Finally, another view of depression is the one derived from Horney's perspective. In the "culturalist" tradition, Karen Horney (1937) took a radical proculture position and replaced biological with social drives. Horney was the first to postulate a cultural causation for mental illness. Although she focused more on personality types, her descriptions of the resigned individual come the closest to depression. This particular type of culturally determined character typically retreats from both love and aggression into an illusive or neurotic form of "freedom," which is in fact fear of commitment or of interpersonal friction.

Cultural Perspectives on the Understanding of Depression

Perhaps no other human experience has the ambiguity and compelling interest that depression has. Although today experts present it as a medical illness with a certain prescribed phenomenology, a characteristic epidemiology, and a typical response to a number of chemical and verbal treatments, we are far from the hard confirmation that laboratory type of proof offers for other medical disorders. Furthermore, the concept of a depressive disorders spectrum such as conduct disorders, alcoholism and drug abuse, eating disorders, sociopathic personalities, and hysteria, for example, makes the picture even more complex. The same is the case with dual diagnosis such as the mentally ill chemical abusers (MICA). It makes one wonder whether depression may not be better construed as part of a profile, or as a quotient, rather than as a discrete entity. Anger attacks have been postulated recently to be possible variants of major depression as they respond favorably to antidepressants (Fava et al. 1990). Additionally, the relationship between anxiety and depression has not quite been clarified. In many studies, and particularly in the multicenter studies of the World Health Organization, anxiety is one of the most prevalent symptoms of depression. Thus we can see how some forms of anxiety respond best to antidepressant treatment.

But one of the greatest challenges to a universal view of depression is that, compared to most medical illnesses, the phenomenology of depression, as well as its management, is still highly variable in different cultures. An example of this variability is offered by a description of *Tamazai* among the Tuareg, nomads of Central and Western Sahara. For the natives, this is an illness of the heart and soul curable by music, jokes, and noise rather than by other approaches such as the reading of Koranic verses. The sufferers of Tamazai are described as listless, withdrawn, and avoidant, occasionally running wild. A loss, adversity, or disruption of the social routine is considered to be the cause (Leff 1994). This sounds remarkably similar to depressive states with agitation. But unlike the usual treatment approach, which may include medication, this particular culture introduces the importance of social supports and the hopeful enactment of opposite behaviors.

It is my contention that the fact that most of the abundant literature on depression today takes such a strong medical viewpoint is in itself influenced by cultural perspective. Cultures tend to legitimize their beliefs and to rationalize their actions by resorting to unquestionable givens such as biology or nature. The fact that the medical view of depression includes the role of biology and, hence, of nature implies a set of cultural beliefs and unquestionable givens regarding its etiology. Nature is unquestionable, and turning to nature in this manner confers legitimacy to scientific hypotheses.

The most remarkable outcome of the biological approach to this human ailment is that the patient's subjectivity disappears and becomes a number in a series of identical units in a group characterized only by responses to questionnaires, or to therapeutic trials. From this perpective we can easily understand an interesting view on suicide advanced in a 1994 article by Angier in *The New York Times* reporting some reputable scientists' theory. According to that theory, suicide is probably a genetic problem geared to the regulation of the population by means of Darwinian laws. This argument is supported by the "fairly high rate" of suicide reported among different cultures. For instance, Hungarians and Finns, who have about three times the rates of the United States and other European countries, allegedly carry their rates when they migrate. This is allegedly a strong argument for inherited predisposition.

Yet for the practicing clinician who has to face a depressed patient in the context of a therapeutic relationship, these statements are almost meaningless. Why a culture would present a painful subjective human experience such as depression or suicide in a fashion that strips it of its dramatic meaning is a puzzling question and in itself a reflection of how the culture operates. As with other cultures, this produces certain pathologies and then explains them in the most current "scientific" terms, which of course are relative to history and contingent on ideological and other social interests.

Cultural Variation in the Experience of Depression

The medical model compels the thought that depression must be ubiquitous since man's physiology and biochemistry are universal and uniform. Research, particularly when driven by biological assumptions, is therefore geared to prove such a hypothesis. Anthropologists warn, however, that we must be careful not simply to reify our construct, in the old fashion, and then apply it to other human groups. For example, anthropologists point out that some cultures do not even have a word that could be translated for depression. Cultures from countries such as Nigeria, China, Eskimo Canada, Japan, and Malaysia do not always recognize depression as an illness, and many lack much of the elaborate language to refer to depressive phenomena (Marsella 1979).

Specifically in the case reported by Schieffelin (1985) of the Kaluli of New Guinea, who do not have a word to denote our concept of depression, the syndrome is rarely, if at all, observable. This author—who postulates that affects are a behavioral system with a structure located in the social field— points out how this is perhaps due to the fact that this is a culture that places great emphasis on personal assertion around an ethos of reciprocity. Anger in this culture is expressed openly and in full range. Its opposite is described as an expression of appeal, the extreme of which is grief, always a reaction to an external loss. Kaluli ceremonies consequently emphasize a counterpoint between anger and grief. In contrast, the Hopi Native Americans, who experience their share of depression (by usual standards), also do not have a word for the disease.

A relationship between depression and anger has been postulated in psychoanalytic theory (Freud 1917). From anthropology there seems to be a similar proposition. Referring to this, for example, Fernando (1969) and Kendell (1970) have both concluded that depression is more likely to occur among cultural groups that strongly inhibit aggressive impulses. These observations lend some credibility to the psychoanalytic postulate of internalized anger (Freud 1921), or retreat from friction (Horney 1937), which is based on clinical observation. They are also isomorphic with Seligman's learned helplessness model, in that anger and aggression are great adaptational tools in the animal kingdom. In our own culture, although aggression is ever present in ideology and everyday transactions as well as displayed incessantly by the media, it is usually considered poor taste or even punishable to express aggression openly in interpersonal interactions. This attitude can perhaps be best summarized in the famous motto, "Speak softly but carry a big stick."

Somatization: Organ-Focused Depression?

A repeated observation in the cross-cultural study of depression is that it overlaps with what in today's psychiatric nomenclature is called somatization. Several authors have found somatization to be a form of expression of depression. It has been observed that somatization is more frequent in non-Western cultures, and particularly in Eastern cultures (Kleinman 1982). High rates of somatization in depressive disorder have been described in Saudi Arabia, Iraq, West Africa, India, Sudan, the Philippines, Taiwan, and Hong Kong. In matched studies somatization has been found to be more prevalent in Peru than in the United States, and more prevalent in East Africa than in London (Kleinman and Kleinman 1985). A comparison of depression in Indonesian and German patients found that the former presented with more somatic symptoms while the latter expressed more guilt and suicidal tendencies (Pfeiffer 1968). The same is true of a comparison between Nigerians and Londoners (Binitie 1975). Similarly, depressive symptomatology reviewed in thirty countries found similarities in expression across the four classic signs of depressed mood, diurnal variation, insomnia, and loss of interest in the environment in only twenty-one of those. In the remaining, largely "non-Western," countries, these signs were not found to be frequent. Instead, the primary symptoms included somatic disturbances like fatigue, anorexia, weight loss, and loss of libido (Murphy et al. 1964). A World Health Organization study that found similar cultural patterns of depression across countries still reported great variation regarding individual symptoms. For example, guilt was present in 68 percent of the Swiss but in only 32 percent of Iranians, suicidal ideas in 70 percent of Canadians but 40 percent of Japanese, and somatization was 57 percent for Iranians and 27 percent for Canadians (Sartorius et al. 1980).

Regarding the explanation for this phenomenon, besides the seemingly obvious one of "development," at least as far as East–West differences are concerned, one factor that may be invoked is a different philosophical outlook. Monism and dualism are opposite paradigms for these two civilizations (Varma 1994). If body and mind are culturally construed as not separate, as is the case in the East, it is to be expected that expressions of pain and reactions to loss and frustration are to be shared in the unitary body-mind. On the other hand, the Cartesian dualistic paradigm of the West makes for a differentiation of psychological and somatic symptoms. Here depression and somatization belong in different domains because subjective feelings are translated into different idioms and thus "psychologized."

Other dichotomies that are familiar, such as individual/society and cognition/affect, for example, are also less marked in other non-First World countries. While Eastern societies privilege human relationships and large social networks, the West is more oriented toward the individual and personal autonomy. Such a philosophical orientation is still integral to the constitution of our scientific outlook and cultural explanations.

In the United States it has been reported that as many as 50 percent of patients utilizing primary care clinics actually have psychosocial rather than biomedical precipitants (Katon et al. 1982). It has also been repeatedly demonstrated that people with emotional problems are seen and treated first in primary care settings. Around 80–97 percent of emotional problems seen by primary care physicians are depression and anxiety. The prevalence of mental illness within this patient group is estimated to be as high as 26.7 percent. Major depressive disorder alone constitutes 21.7 percent of the psychiatric diagnoses. Primary care physicians diagnose depression in about 0.5 to 4.5 percent of their cases; this seems close to the prevalence rate in the general population while rates in medical patients are definitely higher. More than half the patients presenting to primary care physicians have been found to have significant somatic symptoms as part of their depression. Physicians treat many of these problems symptomatically without attending to the possible underlying symbolism or idiom of expression of distress (Katon et al. 1982).

Other Social Aspects of Depression

It has been pointed out that in societies where Buddhism prevails, many of the characteristics of what could be considered depression are part of a normal outlook on life; some Buddhist beliefs, deeply ingrained in some cultures, are

> that hopelessness lies in the nature of the world, and salvation lies in understanding and overcoming that hopelessness . . . that life is suffering and sorrow . . . that the cause of sorrow is attachment or desire or craving . . . that there is a way (generally through meditation) of understanding and overcoming suffering and achieving the final goal of cessation from suffering, or *nirvana*. [Obeyesekere 1985, p. 134]

Dysphoria–sadness, grief, despair–is essential to the ethos of these groups (Good et al. 1985) and it is most often associated with personal depth. In some of these cultures the self is constituted first by an affective core, shared only in intimacy, that involves emotional expression. Superimposed is a public self that acts to protect the deep core. So in this regard the expression of sadness seems to be as important for some cultures as, for example, anger is for others. According to Horney (1937), this would definitely have a shaping impact on the character of the individuals. An interesting finding in this regard is the fact that depression in some immigrant groups to the United States decreases with the number of years after migration (Good et al. 1985). Such findings provide support to the cultural relativity hypothesis.

In this country data from the ECS survey examined for association between religious affiliation and major depression found that adults affiliated with Pentecostal churches had three times the rate of major depression as the general population. Although some hypotheses were generated to explain it, the mechanism of the association remains unclear (Meador et al. 1992).

Similarly, an epidemiological study of the Amish found an extremely high prevalence of affective disorders in active psychiatric cases. The most frequent diagnosis was unipolar depression, accounting for 37 percent of the cases, while bipolar disorders accounted for 34 percent. If one adds "minor depression," which accounted for 8 percent, the number comes up to 79 percent. Different from most other studies, here men and women had similar prevalence rates, and it was hypothesized that females may have even masked some of their depression with somatic symptoms (Egeland and Hostetter 1983). Even more interesting in this study is the fact that 79 percent of the bipolar patients had been previously misdiagnosed as schizophrenic (Egeland et al. 1983). This type of transcultural misunderstanding is similar to what took place in the middle of the century with Hispanics in New York. Patients with more benign conditions were diagnosed and treated as schizophrenics. The corresponding epidemiological data reflecting these abnormally high rates caused great concern (Rendon 1974) and ultimately led to corrective attempts through the implementation of bilingual programs (Trevino and Rendon 1994).

DEPRESSION AND GENDER

Current literature states that being a woman is probably the most significant risk factor for depression. In the United States the lifetime prevalence of depression for women has been found to be as much as three times higher than that for men (Boyd and Weissman 1994). The difference has involved all types of depression and women have predominated in every age group and also cross-culturally, especially in Western industrialized nations. Here explanations have ranged from hormonal to psychosocial or psychological

> and covering factors as diverse as genetics, hormones, brain biochemistry, innate behavioral tendencies, reproductive functioning, psychological reactions to anatomical differences, childhood socialization, family roles of mothers and fathers, cultural stereotypes, and the political-economic distribution of power in a male-dominated society. [Herman 1983, p. 493]

More and more authors describe additional evidence for possible socialization factors as accountable for this phenomenon (Block 1973, Gilligan 1994, Sherman 1971). It has been shown that married women are more depressed than married men and, conversely, unmarried men more than unmarried women (Radloff 1975). Estrogen levels, premenstrual syndromes, and postpartum depression are some of the hypotheses offered to give feminine depression a biological slant. On the other hand, Gilligan (1994) and others have called attention to the possible social roots of feminine change around puberty when women seem to surrender a significant part of their selfhood. In addition, the previously discussed study by Brown and Harris (1978), entitled *Social Origins of Depression*, found unemployment, three or more children under age 14 at home, lack of a confiding relationship, and childhood loss of a parent as risk factors in the high prevalence of depression in females.

It is important to note that the overwhelming majority of childhood disorders have a higher prevalence in males. However, during adolescence this trend in fact reverses itself and women take the lead, particularly with the diagnosis of depression (Rendon 1994). At the same time, males in adolescence are more represented in diagnoses such as oppositional, conduct, and antisocial disorders, which portray a different type of social deviance that involves activity and externalization rather than the female lot of passivity and internalization. This is another area in which the relationship between anger and depression seems to be in effect.

DEPRESSION IN THE LIFE CYCLE

So far, my discussion has been mostly concerned with adults. However, as mentioned earlier, there seems to be a tendency for depression to manifest itself earlier in more recent population cohorts. Depression in children is problematic since it is assumed that childhood depression must manifest itself with the same symptoms as in adults. This axiom does not correspond with developmental theories or to clinical practice. Prior to the present position, the prevailing opinion was that depression, if present in children, manifested itself differently because of different maturational and structural conditions. Thus one spoke about "depressive equivalents" or "masked depression," for example. Furthermore, somewhat in contradiction to the official stand, it is generally accepted that in adolescents depression often takes atypical forms (Dunner 1994). In younger children a sad face has been deemed to be a most important indicator of depression. One study compared children who were sad with normal counterparts and found thirteen times more overactivity and restlessness, ten times more refusal to go to school, seven times more somatic complaints and fighting, and six times more low self-esteem in the sad group (Kashani and Simonds 1979). Broken homes, loss of parents, frequent moves and unemployment, prior exposure to suicide, excessively harsh discipline, critical parents, and role reversals in the family have been associated with depression in children. These environments are often linked to socioeconomic status, as shown by the fact that the number one risk factor for both physical and sexual abuse is income under $15,000 (Cappelleri et al. 1993).

One important ramification of this is the question of what is the impact of multiple traumatic events in children on the development of helplessness and depression as well as of depressive spectrum disorders such as drug abuse. Some preliminary findings seem to indicate a positive correlation between past physical or sexual abuse and chemical dependency (Fullilove et al. 1993).

In old age, on the other hand, although the prevalence of depression is probably similar or even higher than that of adults (Blazer 1982), the syndrome is typically underdiagnosed. This seems to be the result of a prevailing bias that considers depression to be either part of senility or a relatively normal component of old age and therefore negligible. Depression in the elderly is quite often misdiagnosed as dementia. One study found 29 percent of depressed patients over 60 to present first with hypochondriacal symptoms; according to the author, somatic complaints typically preceded the appearance of depression in the elderly by two to three months (De Alarcon 1964).

DEPRESSION IN ETHNIC MINORITY GROUPS

At first it would appear that the prevalence of depression in the United States is simply up to 6 percent or so. However, these homogenized statistics hide great subcultural differences. One of the American cultural subgroups described as most affected by depression is the Native Americans. Manson and colleagues (1985) mention that depression is the most frequently diagnosed problem among Native American patients presenting for treatment at mental health facilities, accounting for as much as 40 percent of the daily patient caseloads in many clinics. In selected Indian communities the prevalence of depression is four to six times higher than in the general population. Yet there is no word among the Hopi that is equivalent to the English word depression. In one group it was reported that 50 percent of Native Americans had "double depression," a term used to denote the coexistence of major and less severe but chronic forms of depression. What seems to have been remarkable in these cases was the unusually high degree of adverse life events.

Another subculture with high rates of depression in the United States is the Hispanics. Here there is an interesting contrast between Hispanic subgroups. In a comparison of Mexican Americans, Cuban Americans, and Puerto Ricans, depression was found to be more than twice as prevalent among Puerto Ricans than among Mexican Americans and approximately three times more prevalent among Puerto Ricans than among Cubans (Mosciki et al 1987). Among all groups, rates for females were much higher than those for males. Rates were also higher for persons of lower educational achievement, those living below the poverty level, and the unemployed. Similarly, nonmarried persons were less protected against depression (Mosciki et al. 1987).

The case of depression in the Hispanic group in the United States is one that illustrates many of the contradictions of how the culture approaches the issue. Although psychiatric prevalence in general in Puerto Rico has been found to be similar to the United States (Canino et al. 1987), epidemiological studies since the '50s describe a high rate of mental illness for Puerto Ricans, particularly recent immigrants, on the mainland (Malzberg 1965). This phenomenon has been described specifically for depression by several authors (Dohrenwend and Dohrenwend 1969, Rodriguez 1987), and for chronic abdominal pain and depression in one study (Magni et al. 1992). In the Hispanic Health and Nutrition Examination Survey, point prevalence rates of abdominal pain were 4.6 percent for Mexican Americans, 5.8 percent for Cuban Americans, and 8.3 percent for Puerto Rican Americans; using the Center of Epidemiological Studies Depression Scale (CES-D), 18.7 percent of Mexican and Cuban Americans with abdominal pain were depressed to an extent likely to require intervention while the equivalent number for Puerto Ricans was 40.8 percent (Magni et al. 1992). Different reasons have been given for the high prevalence of depression among Puerto Ricans, such as the stress posed by migration, poverty, and discrimination. However, it has been reported that Puerto Ricans tend to answer positively questions about symptoms more often, because the desirability of expressing symptoms may be culturally different (Dohrenwend and Dohrenwend 1969) or because the symptom checklist may represent a great similarity with cultural idioms for distress such as "nervios" (Guarnaccia et al. 1989). Elsewhere (Trevino and Rendon 1994) I have suggested the possibility of another factor: the ecological difference in the migratory habitat. This is reflected, for example, in the possibility of a strong seasonal component in depression, which has been observed in clinical practice with immigrants to New York from Caribbean countries. In the literature this is known as seasonal affective disorder. According to this hypothesis, Puerto Ricans, in migrating predominantly to the New York area, are subject to a radical ecological change. In contrast, Cubans, who have migrated predominantly to Miami, and Mexicans, who linger in the Southwest, remain close to their ecological environments of origin. It has been estimated that the North of the United States receives about half the amount of sunlight received by the South. Both seasonal affective disorders and their milder variation, "winter blues," are directly related to latitude (Johnson and Somers 1994). This hypothesis remains to be empirically explored.

In a study of North and South American patients with major depression, the authors found an impressive similarity in symptoms of depression across cultures, supporting the idea of a universal core depressive syndrome; however, differences were still found in somatization indexes, psychomotor components, and levels of psychopathology; a physical symptom was frequently the major presenting concern in Colombians (Escobar et al. 1983).

Community studies of affective disorders and social class have found higher rates of depression among lower socioeconomic level blacks than among some white populations (Warheit et al. 1973). Culturally based misdiagnosis of affective disorders among black patients has been reported also (Bell and Mehta 1980). In a large sample of randomly selected adult residents in Kansas City and Washington County, Maryland, depressive symptoms were more prevalent among blacks with no differences between black males and females; the possibility of having symptoms was highest among persons who were young adults, unmarried, not employed outside the home, poorly paid, and not well educated (Comstock and Knud 1976).

Among Asian Americans, lower rates of admission and utilization of mental health services have been noted; it seems that, compared to other ethnic groups in the United States, this group delays seeking help the most; among those who seek services, more serious disturbances have been found as compared to other ethnic groups. Asians prefer to keep patients within their family networks rather than institutionalizing them. One study (Kuo 1984) found Koreans presenting with higher depression scores than other Asian groups. Also, among the Asian Americans at large, the prevalence of CES-D symptoms was at least as high as that of the white population.

Depression in migrant populations is a subject of interest from a worldwide perspective. In 1992 the number of refugees in the world reached 20 million. In one study, Hispanic refugees in Sweden were reported to have four times the risk of mental illness as matched Swedish controls (Sundquist 1993). This would seem to confirm migration-related stress as an etiological factor, as postulated in the case of Puerto Ricans.

DEPRESSION AND SOCIOECONOMIC STATUS

Depression is prevalent in lower social classes (Weissman et al. 1994). Using the Center for Epidemiological Studies Depression Scale in a clinic population of low socioeconomic status, 60 percent of a sample of subjects were diagnosed as clinically depressed. In individuals of low socioeconomic status, depression has been linked to high incidence of loss and limited coping skills in dealing with distress. It has been suggested also that in some individuals depression may be a trait condition resulting in lesser adaptation rather than the result of socioeconomic status (Warheit 1979). A study examined the relationship between the national suicide rate and economic fluctuations for almost four decades starting in 1920. During years of recession or depression, with high unemployment, suicide rates increased. On the other hand, a good economy and high employment decreased suicide rates (MacMahon et al. 1963).

One group that is a main source of concern in our society today is the homeless. Uniformly, reports on mental health of the homeless present high rates of mental illness in general and of depression in specific. One report described major depression as being twice as prevalent among homeless as compared to the general population. High rates of posttraumatic stress disorder and substance abuse were also found (Smith et al. 1993). Another study of 150 homeless persons found a probable clinical condition in 59 percent, with younger and less educated persons being more vulnerable to mental illness (la Gory et al. 1990). A strong association was found between depressive symptoms and beatings and sexual abuse in homeless women, as well as with injuries in homeless men (Padgett and Struening 1992). A study of homeless parent–child pairs found 28 percent of the parents to exhibit mild to severe depression (Fox et al. 1990) and in homeless children one author found 40 percent to have depressive scores that indicated need for further psychiatric intervention and 25 percent with frank depressive psychopathology (Wagner and Menke 1991). Another author found developmental delays, severe depression and anxiety, and learning difficulties to be common in homeless children, with 50 percent of those in need of psychiatric referral (Bassuk and Rubin 1987). Bassuk and Rubin, in what they call the "feminization of homelessness," describes the typical homeless family in Boston as being female headed, with children who are described as having chaotic developmental histories, severe developmental lags, and severe anxiety and depression interfering with their schooling. In adolescence, homelessness has been found to be a predictor of depression (Smart and Walsh 1993). In homeless postadolescents aged 18–21 a study found higher levels of drug abuse and depression, and 69 percent of the subjects had a *DSM-III* diagnosis (Warheit and Biafora 1991). Finally, one author reports one third of elderly homeless men to be chronically depressed (Cohen et al. 1988). Thus depression definitely seems to be a constant companion of the homeless throughout their life cycles; as in migrants, it seems clearly related to stress.

CONCLUSIONS

Several conclusions are possible based on the material covered in this chapter:

1. A feeling, symptom, syndrome, and illness, depression is a complex biopsychosocial phenomenon that seems to have been ever present in human history although in different forms. It also seems quite prevalent throughout the world today. However, societies have traditionally differed and still differ in their approach to representing distress, helplessness, hopelessness, and illness. The clinician must question how his or her culture's construction of depression may differ from the patient's. He or she must also seek the patient's partnership in constructing the dynamic explanation of depression along the shared frames of reference.

2. Although the human body seems to respond to biological as well as psychological stress in a biological fashion, as in Harlow's (1962) monkeys, in Spitz's (1946) nursery infants, in Seligman's (1975) animal experiments, or in posttraumatic stress disorder, bodily idioms are also metaphors to express psychological distress. Clinicians must be familiar with and attuned to the idioms of patients from different cultural groups. Even medical illnesses that are less ambiguous than depression are often understood and treated differently by various cultural groups; taking this into consideration in the treatment may solve issues such as dropouts and poor compliance to treatment interventions. The therapist is typically positioned in an ethnocentric context that tends to interpret interpersonal and social phenomena in his/her particular ways. Conscious of this fact, the therapist must be constantly open to look not only at the clinical phenomena, but also at the cultural context in which they occur. This may change the diagnostic picture, as well as the approach to the problem and prognosis. Even response to psychotropic medications is mediated by the genetic makeup of individuals, which is culturally determined.

3. Our society presents a contradiction in that depression constructed as a medical illness is typically not readily recognized by physicians. This may in part be the result of the ambiguity that depression presents, and of the limitation of the medical scope to "hard" facts and technological findings. Teamwork among primary care physicians and mental health workers is of paramount importance. Professional education must also emphasize cultural sensitivity and cultural competence.

4. Some cultures that express anger openly and unambiguously seem to be less likely to present high levels of depressed individuals. This insight, described at the individual level by Freud in the dynamics of mourning, may be of great clinical value when dealing with disadvantaged cultural subgroups. Techniques like assertiveness training and empowerment are useful in helping individual patients with issues such as these when they are transculturally relevant.

5. What may look like depression may be part of a deeply ingrained value system such as religion and alternative world views shared by cultural groups. In these situations, the clinician must carefully explore the clinical picture while respecting the value system associated with it.

6. Anthropologists have talked about depression as possibly being a culture-bound syndrome of the West. However, a review of the literature about depression in this country, for example, seems to indicate that depressive phenomena may differ etiologically according to social class. In the lower social groups depression may be the result of massive trauma such as migration, poverty, abuse, crowding, social discrimination, or homelessness. Here depression is more clearly linked to stress, distress, or experienced powerlessness and helplessness in dealing with social events. The clinician must be aware of concrete support services and referrals. Education may be important for this type of patient.

7. In developed countries, on the other hand, and in upper social classes, depression may be the result of very different circumstances. Here the concept of *anomie* may be helpful. Along with the narcissistic psychopathology described in these groups, depression may be a result of loss of social bonds and of an experience of futility. Concrete helplessness may not be as important here, although helplessness may be present at different levels of problem solving. Here it may be more related to alienation, solitude, or disenfranchisement. Contemporary narcissistic man is described as self-involved and in retreat from public life (Lasch 1979). Could that be the result of hopelessness in meaningfully affecting the course of society and even of one's life?

8. It is a commonplace that present approaches to psychiatric diagnosis largely neglect cultural and subcultural beliefs. This may not be construed, however, to mean that we are knowledgeable about how and why our own culture construes mental illness as it does. When we talk about transcultural or cross-cultural issues, the emphasis is on the other end, not ours. Although it is important to look at other cultures, it is even more crucial to understand the cultural parameters that we use in our definitions and approaches to deviant behavior and illness.

There is a role for the mental health clinician as a social critic of one's own culture's presuppositions.

9. The fast pace of cultural developments in our society and the growing inequality in the distribution of resources may be the source of a growing feeling of helplessness. This may explain, at least in part, the trend for the growing depressive rates and for the fact that the onset of depression has been found in early ages in the new population cohorts. As the social systems become more complex, the targets for appropriate action and even affective discharge may become less and less transparent. This process of mystification may lead to hopelessness and despair. The mental health professional may be helpful in discussing processes of mystification regarding social causation and other social issues.

10. It would also be difficult to think about the high incidence of depression among groups such as the American Indians, Latinos, or even women as exclusively biologically caused. Looking at depression only as a biological entity may serve to hide serious social problems that need to be addressed. One of those very important issues may be the social causation of the increasing rates of depression.

I will end my discussion on depression with a cultural vignette. At a professional panel presentation a colleague presented an experience that he learned from a Mexican-American *curandera*: a middle-aged Mexican woman went to consult with the *curandera* (folk healer) after she had seen two Anglo therapists who failed to resolve her predicament. She was depressed as a result of an ongoing extramarital affair. Their treatment, mostly supportive and dynamic in nature, was geared at decreasing what was considered excessive guilt perhaps based on oedipal problems. The *curandera's* reported success with this patient was based on her change of strategy. Her response to the patient was, "Yes, you should be ashamed of yourself." By enacting a culturally expected role, the healer was able to validate and thus make fully understandable to the patient what the traditional therapists had missed, namely the importance of using what is culturally syntonic before venturing into other therapeutic approaches.

REFERENCES

Alexander, F. G., and Selesnick, S. T. (1966). *The History of Psychiatry*. New York: American Library.

Barcia-Goyanes, J. J. (1987). La melancolia en los medicos arabes del medioevo. In *Psiquiatria Antropologia*, ed. D. Barcia, pp. 52–53. Murcia, Spain: Universidad de Murcia.

Bassuk, E. L., and Rubin, L. (1987). Homeless children: a neglected population. *American Journal of Orthopsychiatry* 57:279–286.

Beck, A. T., Rush, A. J., Shaw, B. F., and Emery, G. (1979). *Cognitive Therapy of Depression*. New York: Guilford.

Bell, C. C., and Mehta, H. (1980). The misdiagnosis of black patients with manic depressive illness. *Journal of the National Medical Association* 72:141–145.

Binitie, A. (1975). A factor analytical study of depression across cultures—African and European. *British Journal of Psychiatry* 127:559–563.

Blazer, D. (1982). Epidemiology of late life depression. *Journal of the American Geriatric Society* 30:587–592.

Block, J. H. (1973). Conceptions of sex role: some cross-cultural and longitudinal perspectives. *American Psychologist* 28:512–526.

Boyd, J. H., and Weissman, M. (1994). Epidemiology of major affective disorders. In *Psychiatry*, ed. R. Michaels, vol. III, pp. 1–16. Philadelphia: Lippincott.

Brown, G. W., and Harris, T. (1978). *Social Origins of Depression*. London: Tavistock.

Canino, G. J., Bird, H. R., Shrout, P. E., and Rubio-Stipec, M. (1987). The prevalence of specific psychiatric disorders in Puerto Rico. *Archives of General Psychiatry* 44:727–735.

Cappelleri, J., Eckenrode, J., and Powers, J. L. (1993). The epidemiology of child abuse: findings from the Second National Incidence and Prevalence Study of Child Abuse and Neglect. *American Journal of Public Health* 83:1622–1624.

Cohen, C. I., Teresi, J. A., and Holmes, D. (1988). The mental health of old homeless men. *Journal of the American Geriatric Society* 36:492–501.

Comstock, G. W., and Knud, J. H. (1976). Symptoms of depression in two communities. *Psychological Medicine* 6:551–563.

Cross-National Collaborative Group (1992). The changing rate of major depression: cross-national comparisons. *Journal of the American Medical Association* 268:3098–3105.

De Alarcon, R. (1964). Hypochondriasis and depression in the aged. *Gerontological Clinics* 6:266–277.

Diagnostic and Statistical Manual of Mental Disorders (1994). 4th ed. Washington, DC: American Psychiatric Association.

Dohrenwend, B. P., and Dohrenwend, B. S. (1969). *Social Status and Psychological Disorder: A Causal Inquiry*. New York: Wiley.

Dunner, D. L. (1994). Affective disorder: clinical features. In *Psychiatry*, ed. R. Michaels, vol. I. Philadelphia: Lippincott.

Egeland, J. A., and Hostetter, A. M. (1983). Amish study I: affective disorders among the Amish, 1976–1980. *American Journal of Psychiatry* 140:56–61.

Egeland, J. A., Hostetter, A. M., and Eshleman, S. K. (1983). Amish study III: the impact of cultural factors on diagnosis of bipolar illness. *American Journal of Psychiatry* 140:67–71.

Escobar, J. I., Gomez, J. S., and Tuason, V. B. (1983). Depressive phenomenology in North and South American patients. *American Journal of Psychiatry* 140:47–51.

Fava, M., Anderson, K., and Rosenbaum, J. F. (1990). "Anger attacks": possible variants of panic and major depressive disorder. *American Journal of Psychiatry* 147:867–870.

Fernando, S. (1969). Cultural differences in the hostility of depressed patients. *British Journal of Medical Psychology* 42:67–75.

Fox, S. J., Barnett, R. J., Davies, M., and Bird, H. R. (1990). Psychopathology and developmental delays in homeless children: a pilot study. *Journal of the American Academy of Child and Adolescent Psychiatry* 29:732–735.

Freud, S. (1917). Mourning and melancholia. *Standard Edition* 14:243–258.

——— (1921). Group psychology and the analysis of the ego. *Standard Edition* 18:67–145.

Fullilove, M., Fullilove, R., Smith, M., and Winkler, K. (1993). Violence, trauma and post-traumatic stress disorder among women drug users. *Journal of Traumatic Stress* 6:533–543.

Gilligan, C. (1994). Joining the resistance: Psychology, politics, girls and women. In *Women after Freud*, ed. M. Berger. New York: Brunner/Mazel.

Good, B. J., Good, M. D., and Morady, R. (1985). The interpretation of Iranian depressive illness and dysphoric affect. In *Culture and Depression*, ed. A. Kleinman and B. Good, pp. 369–428. Berkeley: University of California Press.

Harlow, H. F. (1962). The heterosexual affectional system in monkeys. *American Psychologist* 17:1–9.

Herman, M. F. (1983). Depression and women: theories and research. *Journal of the American Academy of Psychoanalysis* 11:493–512.

Horney, K. (1937). *The Neurotic Personality of Our Time*. New York: Norton.

Jackson, S. W. (1985). Acedia the sin and its relationship to sorrow and melancholia. In *Culture and Depression*, ed. A. Kleinman and B. Good. Berkeley: University of California Press.

Johnson, R., and Somers, S. (1994). NIMH, JAMA shed light on seasonal affective disorder. *Psychiatric Times*, February 19.

Kashani, J., and Simonds, J. F. (1979). The incidence of depression in children. *American Journal of Psychiatry* 136:1203–1205.

Katon, W., Kleinman, A., and Rosen, G. (1982). Depression and somatization: a review. *American Journal of Medicine* 72:127–135.

Kendell, R. (1970). Relationship between aggression and depression: epidemiological implications of a hypothesis. *Archives of General Psychiatry* 22:308–318.

Klein, M. (1935). A contribution to the psychogenesis of manic-depressive states. *Contributions to Psychoanalysis*. London: Hogarth.

Kleinman, A. (1982). Neurasthenia and depression: a study of socialization and culture in China. *Culture, Medicine, and Psychiatry* 6:117–190.

Kleinman, A., and Kleinman, J. (1985). Somatization: the interconnections in Chinese society among culture, depressive experiences and the meanings of pain. In

Culture and Depression, ed. A. Kleinman and B. Good, pp. 429–490. Berkeley: University of California Press.

Klerman, G. L., and Weissman, M. M. (1989). Increasing rates of depression. *Journal of the American Medical Association* 261:2229–2235.

Kuo, W. H. (1984). Prevalence of depression among Asian-Americans. *Journal of Nervous and Mental Disease* 172:449–457.

la Gory, M., Ritchey, F. J., and Mullis, J. (1990). Depression among the homeless. *Journal of Health and Social Behavior* 31:87–102.

Lasch, C. (1979). *The Culture of Narcissism*. New York: Norton.

Leff, J. (1994). Cultural influences on psychiatry. *Current Opinion in Psychiatry* 7:197–201.

Link, B., and Dohrenwend, B. P. (1980). Formulation of hypotheses about the true prevalence of demoralization in the United States. In *Mental Illness in the United States: Epidemiological Estimates*, ed. B. P. Dohrenwend, pp. 114–132. New York: Praeger.

MacMahon, B., Johnson, S., and Pugh, T. F. (1963). Relation of suicide rates to social conditions: evidence from U.S. vital statistics. *Public Health Reports* 78:285–293.

Magni, G., Rossi, M. R., Rigatti-Luchini, S., and Merskey, H. (1992). Chronic abdominal pain and depression: epidemiologic findings in the United States: Hispanic Health and Nutrition Examination Survey. *Pain* 49:77–85.

Malzberg, B. (1965). *Mental Disease among the Puerto Rican Population in New York State 1960–1961*. Albany, NY: Research Foundation for Mental Hygiene.

Manson, S. M., Shore, J. H., and Bloom, J. D. (1985). The depressive experience in American Indian communities: a challenge for psychiatric theory and diagnosis. In *Culture and Depression*, ed. A. Kleinman and B. Good, pp. 331–368. Berkeley: University of California Press.

Marsella, A. J. (1979). Depressive experience and disorder across cultures. In *Handbook of Cross-Cultural Psychology, Psychopathology*, ed. H. C. Triandis and J. G. Draguns, Boston: Allyn & Bacon.

Meador, K. G., Koenig, H. G., Hughes, D. C., and Blazer, D. G. (1992). Religious affiliation and major depression. *Hospital and Community Psychiatry* 43:1204–1208.

Mollica, R. F. (1989). Mood disorders: epidemiology. In *Comprehensive Textbook of Psychiatry*, vol. I, ed. H. I. Kaplan and B. J. Sadock, pp. 859–867. Baltimore: Williams & Wilkins.

Moscicki, E. K., Rae, D., Regier, D. A., and Locke, B. Z. (1987). The Hispanic Health and Nutrition Examination Survey: depression among Mexican Americans, Cuban Americans, Puerto Ricans. In *Health and Behavior: Research Agenda for Hispanics*, ed. M. Gaviria and J. D. Arana, pp. 145–159. Chicago: University of Illinois at Chicago.

Murphy, H., Wittkower, E., and Chance, N. (1964). Cross-cultural inquiry into the symptomatology of depression. *Transcultural Psychiatric Research Review* 1:5–21.

Obeyesekere, G. (1985). Depression, Buddhism, and the work of culture in Sri Lanka. In *Culture and Depression*, ed. A. Kleinman and B. Good. Berkeley: University of California Press.

Padgett, D. K., and Struening, E. L. (1992). Victimization and traumatic injuries among the homeless: association with alcohol, drug, and mental problems. *American Journal of Orthopsychiatry* 62:525–534.

Pfeiffer, W. (1968). The symptomatology of depression viewed trans-culturally. *Transcultural Psychiatric Research Review* 5:121–123.

Radloff, L. (1975). Sex differences in depression: the effects of occupation and marital status. *Sex Roles* 1:249–269.

Reich, W. (1949). *Character Analysis.* New York: Farrar, Straus & Giroux.

Rendon, M. (1974). Transcultural aspects of Puerto Rican mental illness in New York. *International Journal of Social Psychiatry* 20:18–24.

———— (1994). Discussion of the papers of Jean Baker Miller and Carol Gilligan. In *Women after Freud,* ed. M. M. Beyer, pp. 153–159. New York: Brunner/Mazel.

Robins, L. N., Helzer, J. E., Weissman, G. L., and Orvaschel, H. (1984). Lifetime prevalence of specific psychiatric disorders in three sites. *Archives of General Psychiatry* 41:949–958.

Rodriguez, O. (1987). *Hispanics and Human Services: Help Seeking in the Inner City.* New York: Fordham University.

Rush, J. A. (1994). Research and clinical practice: bridging the gap. *Current Opinion in Psychiatry* 7:3–4.

Sartorius, N., Jablensky, W., Gulbinat, W., and Ernberg, G. (1980). WHO collaborative study: assessment of depressive disorders. *Psychological Medicine* 10:743–749.

Schieffelin, E. L. (1985). The cultural analysis of depressive affect: an example from New Guinea. In *Culture and Depression,* ed. A. Kleinman and B. Good, pp. 101–133. Berkeley: University of California Press.

Seligman, M. E. (1974). Depression and learned helplessness. In *The Psychology of Depression,* ed. R. J. Friedman and M. M. Katz. Washington, DC: Winston.

———— (1975). *Helplessness. On Depression, Development and Death.* San Francisco: W. H. Freeman.

Sherman, J. A. (1971). *On the Psychology of Women.* Springfield, IL: Charles C Thomas.

Smart, R. G., and Walsh, G. W. (1993). Predictors of depression in street youth. *Adolescence* 28:41–53.

Smith, E. M., North, C. S., and Spitznagel, E. L. (1993). Alcohol, drugs and psychiatric comorbidity among homeless women: an epidemiologic study. *Journal of Clinical Psychiatry* 54:82–87.

Spitz, R. (1946). Anaclitic depression. *Psychoanalytic Study of the Child* 2:313–342.

Sundquist, J. (1993). Ethnicity as a risk factor for mental illness: a population-based study of 338 Latin American refugees and 996 age, sex and education matched Swedish controls. *Acta Psychiatrica Scandinavica* 87:208–212.

Trevino, F. M., and Rendon, M. I. (1994). Mental illness/mental health issues. In *Latino Health in the US: A Growing Challenge,* ed. C. W. Molina and M. Aguirre-Molina, pp. 447–495. Washington, DC: American Public Health Association.

Varma, V. K. (1994). Personal communication. Department of Psychiatry, Post

Graduate Institute of Medical Education and Research Chandigarh, India.

Wagner, J., and Menke, E. (1991). The depression of homeless children: a focus for nursing intervention. *Issues in Comprehensive Psychiatric Nursing* 14:17–29.

Warheit, G. J. (1979). Life events, coping, stress and depressive symptomatology. *American Journal of Psychiatry* 136:502–507.

Warheit, G. J., and Biafora, F. (1991). Mental health and substance abuse patterns among a sample of homeless post-adolescents. *International Journal of Adolescence and Youth* 3:9–27.

Warheit, G. J., Holzer, C. E., and Schwab, J. J. (1973). An analysis of social class and racial differences in depressive symptomatology: a community study. *Journal of Health and Social Behavior* 14:291–299.

Weissman, M. M., Merikangas, K. R., and Boyd, J. H. (1994). Epidemiology of affective disorders. In *Psychiatry*, ed. R. Michaels. Philadelphia, PA: Lippincott.

Wells, K. B., Hays, R. D., Burman, M. A., and Rogers, W. (1989). Detection of depressive disorders for patients receiving prepaid or fee-for-service care. *Journal of the American Medical Association* 262:3298–3302.

9

Cultural Factors in Diagnosis and Intervention in Depression: A Need for Rethinking Causality

B. RUNI MUKHERJI

CROSS-CULTURAL ISSUES IN ILLNESS AND WELLNESS: IMPLICATIONS FOR DEPRESSION

The last two decades have seen a remarkable growth of interest in the relationship between cultural variables and psychopathology. The proliferation of the terminology about the discipline alone is quite daunting: cross-cultural psychology, psychiatric anthropology, ethnic psychology, social psychiatry, transcultural psychology, just to name a few. Marsella (1993) has characterized the series of questions that have fueled this burgeoning field in the following way:

A. What is the role of sociocultural variables in the etiology of mental disorders? How do sociocultural variables interact with biological, psychological and environmental variables to influence psychopathology?

B. What are the sociocultural variations in standards of normality and abnormality?

C. What are the sociocultural variations in the classification and diagnosis of psychopathology?

D. What are the sociocultural variations in the rates and distribution of psychopathology according to both indigenous and Western categories of psychopathology?

E. What are the sociocultural variations in the experience, manifestation, course and outcome of psychopathology? [P. 101]

While this is a broad list of issues and well describes a large body of research, it neatly sidesteps a core concern that is at the very heart of the debate in the field, that is, is there in fact a definition of psychopathology that transcends cultural boundaries in such a way that meaningful comparisons of sociocultural variation can be made? As pointed out by Marsella (1993) and others (Bebbington 1993, Kleinman 1988, Mirowsky and Ross 1989, Skultans 1990), the "old" transcultural psychologists set about measuring abnormality of behavior against the yardstick of Western diagnostic categories. There was assumed to be a core set of behaviors, to which Western diagnosis could be applied; if other behaviors occurred that did not fit the category, it was claimed that this was the effect of cultural variations. In other words, this was the "Russian doll model," as Littlewood (1986) calls it, consisting of outer layers of behaviors that are culturally or idiosyncratically determined; when these are peeled back, some core of illness remains that is common to all people and that transcends culture. This approach was soundly castigated by the "new" cross-cultural psychologists as relying on ethnocentric (in this case, Western) assumptions, and they argued that disease categories must be examined and analyzed within the context of the values of the culture in which they are embedded. In a provocative article hailing the emergence of the "new" cross-cultural approach, Kleinman (1977) decries the "category fallacy" of the old transcultural psychologists, that is, the assumption that psychiatric categories themselves were culture free. They are not, he claimed, but are in fact culture-specific. They are, as he puts it, "explanatory models specific to the Western context; culture was less something which shaped an already existing natural phenomenon than the context in which any idea of illness was conceived" (p. 308).

The new breed of cross-cultural psychologists claims to conduct a contextual analysis of indigenous disease categories, and argues against the importation of Western categories and conceptual schemes. However, the central problem still remains: How exactly is the construction of indigenous illness categories and the behaviors to which they are related arrived at? Why is a certain group of feelings, behaviors or responses considered to be mental illness at all? As Littlewood (1990) and Skultans (1990) have pointed out,

Kleinman himself fell into the "category fallacy" trap in his study on Chinese depressives, reported in his 1977 paper. He says in his methodology section that he and his research assistants "assembled a group of 25 depressives with depressive syndrome" (p. 5). How were these patients identified as having depressive syndrome? Ten of the patients identified as depressives never admitted to depressive feelings, while twenty-two out of twenty-five of them presented somatic complaints. Somatization is, however, a common corollary of depression within the Western diagnostic scheme. Thus, even though he decries the use of Western diagnostic categories, it would appear that a very Western notion of "masked depression" manifesting as somatic symptoms crept into his diagnostic scheme.

Where does this leave us then? While the use of Western diagnostic categories of psychopathology leads to the pitfalls of ethnocentrism, cultural relativism has a minefield of its own. In order to see the minefield more clearly, let us examine the concept of relativism a little more closely. There are two conditions that relativism of any kind must satisfy. The first is very simple: relativism is a logical condition; something (the subject) is relative to something else (the background). Thus far there is no problem. The second condition is much more difficult: relativism entails a condition of incommensurability. In other words, a claim of relativism about anything is a claim that there is no common measure or standard of comparison. A relativist must claim that the standards of comparison about the subject matter are dependent on the background, and to the extent that relevant aspects of the background are not shared, comparisons are impossible. How then are translations about cultures possible? Moderate relativists would argue that while there are aspects of culture that are incommensurable, there are aspects that are shared and therefore some set of comparisons is possible. The question, therefore, with respect to cross-cultural comparisons of psychopathology, becomes: What are the aspects of pathology that are shared across cultures and what are not?

It is easy to understand and accept the idea that subject matter such as values, rituals, gods, and demons exist in relation to a background culture and need to be understood contextually. It is harder for most of us to appreciate this relativity when the subject matter is broken bones or arthritis. There is a "factness" about biology that makes biological universals easily acceptable. This difficulty has led many cross-cultural psychologists, tacitly and without examination, to accept the idea that the biological processes that underlie psychopathology cut across the boundaries of culture, and that it is the manifestation of these biological processes that is culturally determined, as culture-specific "idioms of distress." Even Kleinman himself, while publicly arguing *against* biologically based, culture-free universalist assumptions about psychiatric disorders, falls into the same "category fallacy" that he denounces in the old transcultural approach. In an article in the *International Review of Psychiatry*, Hinton and Kleinman (1993) restate the tenet that *DSM* and *International Classification of Diseases* (World Health Organization 1992) diagnostic categories do not map universal neurobiological domains of illness, but are culture-bound categories. They cite Carr and Vitalino (1985), who point out in a comparison of *amok* and major depression that these are both best viewed as culturally determined responses to conditions of life stress. Hinton and Kleinman go on to say: "As a system of specifically meaningful symbols, culture orients the subject not only to the outer world but also to the inner world. . . . Culture patterns the perception, evaluation, and experience of biopsychological processes" (p. 113). However, at the close of the article they say, "A *DSM-IV* diagnosis may be helpful in terms of prescribing medication, whereas a diagnosis of a particular idiom of distress may be more important in prescribing psychosocial treatment and interventions" (p. 123). This statement indicates an implicit acceptance of a universal biological core. In other words, since pharmacological intervention specifically addresses the biological processes that underlie the problem, for the *DSM* diagnostic categories to be appropriate in guiding the prescribing of medication, the biological core must necessarily be commensurable across cultural boundaries.

This differentiation between an "objective" biological core and the culture-specific manifestation of symptoms is parallel to Eisenberg's (1977) now famous distinction between disease and illness: "Illnesses are experiences of disvalued changes in states of being and social function; diseases, in the scientific paradigm of modern medicine, are abnormalities in the structure and function of bodily organs and systems" (p. 11). Notice that in this conceptualization the biological bases of disease are seen as factual entities existing in the patient, awaiting diagnosis. This view of disease ignores the fact that the concept of disease is itself a social construction (Mishler 1981). In the words of Conrad (1980, p. 114, cited in Kawanishi 1992):

> Illnesses are human judgments on conditions that exist in the natural world. They are essentially social constructions—hypothetical constructs of our own creation. The fact that there is high agreement on what constitutes an illness does not change this: The high degree of consensus on what "objectively" is disease is not independent from the social consensus that constructs these "facts." [p. 28]

In this context it is interesting to point out that *drapetomania*, the tendency of slaves to run away from their masters, and *masturbational insanity* were nosological categories of mental illness just a few short decades ago.

In addition to the issue of the social construction of disease, the idea that biological processes are themselves exempt from the effects of culture needs to be examined more closely. Many researchers have argued that the assumption of biology transcending cultural interactions is deeply rooted in a Western philosophical dualism of mind and body, and that the dominance within biological psychiatry of neurochemical explanations of psychopharmacological correlations is a simplistic reduction (see Gillett 1990, Rudnick 1990, and Wallace 1990 for comprehensive reviews). These arguments are much too lengthy to reproduce here, but, in simple terms, the argument made for the consideration of the influence of cultural interactions on biological processes is that while there are many "hard-wired" aspects of brain function and development, there is a vast and relatively undifferentiated network where patterns of transmission are laid down as a function of the person's learning history. Thus the ways in which information is transmitted through the brain, and the actual form of the networks themselves, are modified by learning, by the person's experiential history, and the different interchanges of the individual with persons, events, and situations outside himself. As Wallace (1990) says:

> There is no valid distinction between biology and culture . . . nor is there a boundary between culture and personality for they are abstractions, referring to *inextricably* mutual interactions. [p. 69]

> Sociocultural variables affect not only the disordered individual's illness experience, behaviors, attributions, and treatment adherence, but figure in pathogenesis, pathophysiology, pathoplasticity, course and outcome. . . . So unitary is the reality abstracted into the biological, the psychological, and the sociocultural, that limiting the influence of this last to pathoplasticity, as Kleinman does, is probably erroneous—for the etiology, pathophysiology, phenomenology, treatment, and response are all biopsychological. [pp. 68–69]

One area that makes reference to many of the issues raised above is the pervasive characterization of non-Western populations as being relatively more prone to somatization. Kirmayer and Robbins (1991) noted that somatization is the most common form of presentation of depression or anxiety disorders. Somatization means the presentation of bodily symptoms as explanations for one's psychological problems; even in the face of no physical evidence for the complaint, the patient continues to maintain somatic distress. Somatic symptoms may be the most universal expression of psychological distress all over the world, and psychological distress is almost always accompanied by physical discomfort. In fact, Silver (1987) has argued that subjective physical distress should be considered a part of the core depressive syndrome. However, there have been repeated reports that non-Westerners, particularly Asian groups, are significantly more likely to somatize their emotional distress than are their Western counterparts (Binitie 1975, 1983, Chang 1985, Crittenden et al. 1992, Derasari and Shah 1988, Gada 1982, Kleinman 1977, Marsella et al. 1973, West 1985, Yamamoto et al. 1985, and others). Explanations of this finding may be found at several levels of analysis:

1. *Linguistic or idiomatic differences in the expression of symptoms.* As Tanaka-Matsumi and Marsella (1976) have pointed out, the word *yuutsu* (depression) tends to be associated with external referents such as rain and clouds and somatic referents such as headache and fatigue for Japanese nationals, whereas depression is associated with internal mood state referents such as lonely or sad for Caucasian Americans. Yanping and colleagues (1986) have reported a similar finding with depressed and normal patients in China. They found that in Chinese expressions for feeling states, key emotional terms such as depressed, fearful, and anxious were expressed in somatic or neutral terms rather than psychological or deficit terms. However, their research indicates that the somatic factor score on the SCL-90 was not correlated with increased somatic expression. Mumford and his colleagues (Mumford 1989, Mumford et al. 1991) have provided a similar analysis for Urdu-speaking Pakistani depressed patients as compared to British samples. For example, they point out that the Urdu expression *dil ghatna* (literally, heart/spirit shrinking or falling), an idiomatic expression commonly used to indicate a sense of loss of motivation or depressed state, may often be translated as a problem with the heart. However, their research indicates that when this type of idiomatic expression is taken into account, there is no significant difference in symptom rates between Pakistani and British samples.

2. *Indigenous cultural concepts of illness and disease may affect the interpretation symptoms as well as their expression.* As Hinton and Kleinman (1993) has pointed out, "The organization and division of ICD and *DSM* into disorders of mood, anxiety, and soma reflect dualisms between mind and body, thought and emotion, which have strong roots in Western philosophical, medical and religious traditions" (p. 120). Other traditional systems of medicine such as Unani-Islamic and Ayurvedic have humoral concepts of illness in which emotions are thought to originate in organic systems such as the heart or liver so that the interpretation of emotional distress occurs in somatic

terms (see Mrinal et al. 1995 for a more detailed analysis of these systems of medicine). This holds true for Chinese traditional medicine as well. Chen (1995) points out that somatization in Chinese patients has its roots in traditional Chinese medicine, in which diseases are regarded as resulting from the imbalance of the two polar principles, yin and yang. Yin is the female, cold, and negative aspect of nature, whereas yang is the masculine, hot, and positive aspect, and both exist within the individual. Disease results when the two aspects are not proportionally balanced. Furthermore, internal organs such as the liver, heart, lung, kidney, and gallbladder are considered to be centers for both physiological and psychological function. According to Lin (1981, as cited in Chen 1995), *shen* (spirit or mind) is seen as residing in the heart, which is the center of psychological functions, whereas *ching* (essence or energy) arises from the kidney. The lung is vulnerable to sadness, while the liver and gallbladder are particularly predisposed to anger. The Chinese term for the study of mental functioning is *ching-shen ko*, which when translated literally would appear to refer to the study of the heart and kidney. Chen argues that the prevalence of somatization in symptom manifestation among the Chinese is not due to a lack of awareness of psychological states but rather reflects the tendency to associate emotional states to the related body organ.

3. *The influence of cultural sanctions or social desirability factors in the presentation of symptoms.* As Kawanishi (1992) and Chen (1995) pointed out, in many cultures, particularly East Asian, open display or expression of emotion may be socially inappropriate or unacceptable. Thus a legitimate entry into the sick role in these cultures may be by the communication of somatic or physical illness. As Chen remarks, "The substitution of psychological and emotional concerns in the form of a physical complaint is more culturally acceptable. It removes the blame from the family; at the same time it relieves the associated psychological burden of shame and guilt, and the fear of the stigma of a mental disorder" (p. 189).

Social class and perceived social desirability also play a role in symptom presentation. In a study of the prevalence of depression and suicide in men and women from different social classes in the United States, Opler and Mouchly (1968) found that women from a lower social class tend to somatize their difficulties, as compared to women from the middle or upper social class. Upper-class women are not only less likely to report somatic symptoms but are also significantly less likely than their lower-class counterparts to receive organic treatments. According to Opler and Mouchly, upper-class women regard organic therapy as inferior to psychological forms of therapy. It could be argued that the more psychological focus of symptom presentation on the part of the upper-class women was directed by their knowledge that this form of description would be more likely to elicit psychological intervention whereas a focus on somatic symptoms would tend to elicit organic intervention.

4. *Expectations of patients and practitioners may influence symptom presentation.* The belief that members of certain ethnic groups are less likely to be "emotional" or more likely to present somatic symptoms can lead the practitioner to inadvertently solicit more somatic symptoms. Stereotyping of members of ethnic minority groups, another form of cultural sanction, may also contribute to the perception of the prevalence of somatization among non-Western peoples. Kawanishi (1992), in his review of the literature finds that there is in fact conflicting data that do *not* support ubiquitous somatization on the part of non-Westerners. He suggests that the prevalence of this assumption is a form of racial stereotyping that enables many Western practitioners to deal with the "inscrutable Asian." Perris (1981) found that depressed patients from Northern Sweden gave higher self-ratings for weight loss, tachycardia, and agitation, whereas Southern Italian patients' self-ratings scored higher on indices of hopelessness, loss of interest, and dissatisfaction. In contrast, on doctors' ratings of these same patients, Italians scored higher on variables referring to psychomotor retardation and hypochondriasis, whereas the Swedish subjects scored higher on variables regarding inability to feel. The author concludes that these discrepancies might reflect cultural differences either in the way that patients in the two countries are able to verbally express their symptoms or in the way that doctors from the two countries rated, or gave weight to, the symptoms. It is worth pointing out that the doctors' ratings closely conform to the cultural stereotypes of the lazy Southern Italian and the emotionally constrained Swede!

Zola (1966) found that ethnicity plays a role in the way patients present their symptoms to doctors. He found that Italians were stylistically more emotional and voluble and tended to focus on a variety of somatic symptoms, whereas Irish patients were more constrained, appeared to be more specific in their terminology, and reported fewer symptoms. He also pointed out that, while the reported incidence of peptic ulcers in a British population is higher than among groups of rural Africans, and is interpreted as confirming effects of modern life stress in the etiology of ulcers, autopsy data on the African groups showed an equal incidence of scars of undetected peptic ulcers. Thus the presentation of symptoms in the doctor–patient dialogue in fact may be a socially conditioned selection process that is integrally determined by the expectations of the patient in the diagnostic situation and of the practitioner in terms of what symptoms he or she implicitly or explicitly solicits, and then gives weight to in the diagnosis.

There is a high degree of medical specialization and compartmentalization in the Western world, particularly in this country. In a psychiatric setting patients are expected to adopt a psychological idiom of distress regardless of the physical symptoms they may be experiencing. For patients who have not compartmentalized the medical setting in such a fashion, presentation of their physical symptoms is a culturally appropriate response. Thus the finding of somatization may be due to a mismatch between patient and practitioner expectations of the situation. In this context, findings from other ethnic samples may be relevant. Escobar and colleagues (1983), in a comparison between depressed patients in the U.S. and Bogota, Columbia, found a greater degree of somatization in the Columbian sample. A similar finding is reported by Mezzich and Raab (1980), who found higher complaints of somatic symptoms in a sample of Peruvian adult depressives as compared to a matched U.S. sample.

Thus far, the issue of cultural variables and their relationship to the presentation and diagnosis of psychopathology, particularly depression, has been examined. In the following section, some thoughts about the issue of cultural variations in the definitions of wellness and the conditions and outcomes of intervention will be discussed in the context of conceptualizations from modern physics, which provide the impetus for rethinking our concepts of causality.

MODERN PHYSICS, MODERN MEDICINE, AND UNDERSTANDING OF CAUSALITY

Cartesian dualism has had an enormous impact on the form and paradigms of modern medicine. According to Descartes, the universe is divided into two classes of entities that are essentially different: thinking things (*res cogitans*) and extended things (*res extensa*). Descartes also held that extended substance, or nature, can best be understood by the method of analysis, that is, by dividing substance into its smallest constituents.

This method of understanding by analysis into its smallest constituents forms the foundation of classical or Newtonian physics. In the classical scientific model, the universe is a totality of particles that obey causal laws, and, epistemologically, reality does not depend upon the observer. The observer of a system does not have any effect upon it; all changes that occur in the system can be accounted for in terms of the Newtonian model of cause and effect. The view that reality exists independent of the observer in combination with the dualistic view of existence led scientists to focus increasingly on extended material objects, not thinking material ones. Thus, the human body could be studied as an extended material object whose component parts can be understood by analysis. Mind, therefore, became an entity that was not studied by scientists, and certainly mind as a thinking entity that *constructs* reality was far outside the realm of classical science for many centuries.

This classical scientific model guided the development of science in many fields, but modern medicine as we know it today did not really adopt this paradigm until the germ theory of Pasteur. Soon after the discovery of microorganisms and development of the understanding of the role they play in the etiology of illness, medicine and its practitioners became firmly entrenched in the classical scientific model. The study of illness was a study of the extended substance, the body; the analysis of the constituent parts that functioned to produce symptoms; and the eradication of illness by eradicating the agents that caused disease. This model, by the early twentieth century, had almost completely replaced all other competing theories of illness, certainly in the Western world, and persists to this day. Increasingly, doctors became scientists and patients' supine bodies became the battlegrounds where physicians with magic bullets vanquished the fulminating hordes of germs that caused disease. Symptoms defined the enemy against which the external armaments of the physician waged war. Since disease was defined as "organic dysfunction," the idea of "patient" as thinking, active agency having some control over the course of illness lost meaning.

However, even as this dualistic and mechanistic model that is the legacy of classical physics became so entrenched in the field of medicine, the field of modern physics has called these issues into question. One of the most cherished assumptions of classical physics, the notion that reality is absolute, knowable, and independent of the observer, has been shown to be incorrect. Modern physics has challenged the Newtonian assumptions of determinacy and infinite knowability. Heisenberg's Uncertainty Principle is the most famous expression of an idea that is fundamental to modern or quantum physics: the idea that we cannot precisely measure the position and the momentum of a particle simultaneously. In other words, that in choosing to measure precisely the momentum or speed of a particle, the position of the particle is changed, or that in choosing to know precisely *where* a particle is located will change the velocity of the particle by an unpredictable amount. The implication of this principle is not simply that the methods we as scientists employ to study the phenomena of physics are intrusive, but that the aim of classical physics—to discover the precise nature of reality independent of the observer—is unattainable. This unknowability is not because of the clumsiness of the experimenter or the imprecision of the investigative apparatus, but because this unknowability is inherent and essential to the universe. Reality is not something absolute, awaiting discovery, but our understanding of it and the methods we use to investigate it essentially play an unavoidable role in determining the way in which nature will reveal itself to us. The observer and what is being observed are inextricably intertwined. (For a more complete discussion of Heisenberg's Principle and quantum physics principles in general, see Capra 1977, Dossey 1982, Zukav 1979.)

Niels Bohr's (1934) principle of complementarity demonstrates that the notion of the ultimate constituents of matter as particulate, distinct, and indivisible—another cherished classical conception—does not hold. Bohr's work demonstrates that, in order to understand the behavior of subatomic particles it is necessary to conceptualize them as both particles *and* waves. Bohr maintained that these concepts were complementary, that is, that they were both necessary to account completely for the behavior of the particle, even though they seem mutually exclusive. This principle is arguably one of the most revolutionary concepts of modern physics, and Cartesian dualism needs to be revisited in its context. Bohr's principle of complementarity indicates that two seemingly opposing aspects of existence are not contradictory, but in fact are illuminating and *complementary*, and need to be taken together for a complete understanding of the totality of the phenomenon.

A third important principle that modern physics brings us is that of interconnectedness. Einstein's famous equation, $E = mc^2$, is well known to most of us. The implication of this equation is that matter and energy are equivalent and interchangeable; actually, fundamental to modern physics is the idea that every "particle" is in fact a field of force, and that it is the interaction of these fields that makes up reality, and creates a system of interaction. Einstein and colleagues (1935, as cited in Pelletier and Herzing 1988) have shown that two electrons from a single atom spinning away from each other affect each other's behavior even where they are separated, indicating that the interrelationship of the parts of a system hold even when separated.

Thus, in modern physics, as Bronowski (1978) puts it, "Relativity is the understanding of the world not as events, but as relations" (p. 103). This view of relativity and interconnectedness requires a rethinking of the Newtonian sense of causality: there is no scientific justification of viewing the universe as a series of unconnected events. The particles of the universe are not themselves distinct and unconnected billiard ball-like structures, but rather extended and interacting fields of force with no specific boundaries between them. Therefore, the notion of causality as a linear sequence of events, ordered in time, cannot hold.

Many other implications from modern physics are relevant to the current context, and are dealt with extensively by other writers (Dossey 1988, Pelletier and Herzing 1988), but will not be elaborated here in the interests of space. However, it is critical here to point out that to take the implications from the conceptualizations from modern physics and apply them uncritically and in whole cloth to pillory modern medicine, is to be guilty of sloppy thinking and irresponsibility (see Dossey 1988 for a clear articulation of these issues). What is essential to recognize is that the paradigmatic shift that has taken place in modern science has yet to reach the field of medicine in general, and mental illness in particular. While the field of modern medicine could be termed as emphasizing "matter over mind," the field of psychology is usually in the position of treating "mind as matter," or asserting the primacy of "mind over matter." It is imperative that the theory and practice of psychology recognize the complementarity of the conceptions of *both* mind and matter as essential to the understanding of illness and wellness. Causality as a simple linear sequence of events, ordered in time and space, conceptualized as discrete unitary entities, is no longer a tenable hypothesis. Thus our hypotheses about the etiology and course of illness need to be reconceptualized. In this context, culture and cultural contexts are another form of investigative tool that shapes the form in which the nature of illness will reveal itself to us.

The interconnectivity principle has clear implications for the ways in which we need to conceptualize the various *levels* or *scales* of activity at which an individual can be affected: the physiological, personal, social, cultural, and geographic, to mention a few. The multiplicity of interactions of causality in both etiology and intervention need to be understood at each of these levels. Each of these levels are systems within themselves and components of the system interact within themselves at that level. Analysis at each of these levels gives us a partial picture of the factors that affect the system, and no one level of analysis can provide complete understanding of the forces that are at play.

COMPLEMENTARITY AND THE NEED FOR A NEW PARADIGM: A TENTATIVE FRAMEWORK FOR THE INTEGRATION OF MIND–BODY CONCEPTS IN HEALING

Rossi's (1986) state-dependent memory, learning, and behavior theory (SDMLB) provides a significant framework within which to conceptualize the connections between mind and body. While this model has largely been applied to explicate the mechanism of healing through hypnotic induction, it is in fact a much broader formulation of the ways in which the mind communicates to the body. The theory is based on the last four decades of research on memory and learning and on the behavioral effects of psychoactive drugs. The fundamental idea underlying the SDMLB model is that when, for example, drugs such as alcohol or barbiturates are administered, memories are *conditioned* or associated with the altered state. When the drug is metabolized out of the body, the state or the person is altered, and these memories appear to be lost. They are not really lost but are recoverable when the person is again in the state in which these memories were conditioned. This is the definition of state-dependent memory. The SDMLB model integrates the findings from two areas of research: state-dependent memory and the role of the limbic system in the modulation of learning and memory.

State-dependent memory is an example of the encoding specificity principle (Tulving 1983), which states that memory or recall of events is dependent on the congruence of the context of the learning of information and the context of the retrieval or recall of the information. Recall is better if the retrieval context is the same as the learning context. Research on mood congruence, for example, shows that depressed people are more likely than people who are not depressed to recall negative material (Blaney 1986, Bower 1987). Further, recall of information is dependent on the state of the individual. People are more likely to recall information when they are in the same mood or the same state as when they learned the information (Bower and Mayer 1989). This state-dependent learning and memory effect is strongest in adults and with information that pertains to real life rather than abstract concepts (Ucros 1989).

It is obvious that state-dependent memory has important clinical implications. Not only does it clarify why the cognitive content of depressed people is overwhelmingly negative in affect, but also the reason for the "cognitive distortions" of depressed people. These are the distortions that Beck (1967) described as characterizing the cognitive processing of depressed people, the "long, uninterrupted sequences of depressive associations, completely independent of the external situations . . . that are automatic, i.e., without any apparent antecedent reflection or reasoning" (pp. 231, 236). According to Beck, the cognitions of depressed individuals are "paralogical" or irrational in that they are arbitrary and selective, and maximize depressive content while minimizing positive content. However, the findings of cognitive psychology indicate that the cognitive processes of depressed people have the same characteristics as those of normals, in that the cognitive content and memory recall is mood-congruent. When people are depressed, they are more likely to have access to memories that are congruent with their mood states, and they are also more likely to encode information that is congruent with their negative mood state. Thus they are more likely to retrieve negative information while they are depressed, and more likely to encode available information that is congruent with their mood state, that is, negative information.

Research on the psychobiology of memory has shown that the limbic system, particularly the amygdala and the hippocampus, are important modulators of short- and long-term memory, learning, and the processes associated with motivation and emotion, which in turn modulate the hypothalamic regulation of the autonomic, endocrine, immune , and neuropeptide systems (see Crosson 1992 and McGaugh 1983 for extensive reviews). In particular, the neurotransmitters implicated in the modulation of learning and memory are the same neurotransmitters that are released during periods of prolonged stress and that modulate the functioning of the hypothalamic-pituitary-endocrine system, the system that has long been implicated in stress-related psychosomatic problems (Selye 1976). While it is beyond the scope of this discussion to detail the specifics of the SDMLB model, it is important to recognize here that the model indicates the way in which the limbic-hypothalamic system, which plays a major role in the body's internal regulation of autonomic, nervous, endocrine, immune, and neuropeptide systems, operates as a filter through which the cognitive and physiological systems operate (Rossi 1987).

Specifically, memories and cognitions, as well as *physiological processes* that are encoded during an earlier time when the body was in a particular physiological state of arousal, are selectively accessible when the body is in a similar physiological state at a later time. Once these memories and behaviors are accessed, they can be reframed or resolved through psychological intervention. The overt process of healing through psychological intervention, such as using hypnosis or other mind–body therapies, has long been known, but has largely been relegated to the domain of "placebo effects" and regarded as spurious artifacts. However, the SDMLB model articulates the specific way in which these interventions work, by linking psychological processes (memory, learning, and behavior) with the physiological substrate (the limbic-hypothalamic system).

Pert (1986) discusses the fact that neuropeptides and their receptor sites form an informational network inside the body, making it necessary to recognize mind and body as an integrated mind–body system. Indeed, there is an entire class of substances that includes not only the neuropeptides and their receptor sites but also the classical neurotransmitters, peptide hormones, and the proteins that encode, transcribe, and instruct genetic information and act as messengers facilitating the conveyance of information from one part of the body to another. As Rossi (1986) points out:

> The neurosecretory cells of the hypothalamus vividly illustrate the process whereby the neural impulses of the mind are transduced into the "hormonal messenger molecules" of the body. The actual existence of many such *neuroendocrinal information transducers* throughout the body is the basis for conceptualizing the new field of psychobiology as a branch of information theory. [p. 52, italics original]

In other words, there needs to be a paradigmatic shift that sees the mind and body as an integrated informational system and therefore examines the role of mind–body communications as an integral consideration in illness and wellness.

COMPLEMENTARITY AND MIND–BODY CONSIDERATIONS IN THE RETURN TO WELLNESS

While Eisenberg's (1977) distinction between illness and disease is persuasive in the context of Western or orthodox medicine, as has been pointed out at several junctures in the previous section, it is a distinction most traditional or nonorthodox systems of medicine do not make (see Adler and Mukherji 1995 for a review of several systems of traditional medicine that are widely practiced across four continents). Dysfunctions of bodily systems and organs and dysfunctions in states of being and social functions are not seen in etiological disjunction. All traditional healing systems see illness as both a dysfunction of bodily systems and a dislocation of one's sense of self and place within a social system. Traditional systems of healing recognize that illness fractures one's sense of self, both physically and socially. Thus, not only do traditional healing systems treat bodily dysfunction through herbs, diet, and other healing agents, but these interventions are embedded within important ritual practices that directly address the relationship of the individual to his or her family, community, ancestors, and spirits. The return to wellness is not simply the cessation of the symptoms, but, importantly, the restoration of the balance of the interrelationships of all of these factors and the individual. Wellness is seen as the return to the sense of security in knowing what one can expect of one's body and the experience of one's physical life.

> Disease is thus conceived in terms of a breakdown of human relationships, and the healing rituals . . . restore or attempt to restore, harmonious social life. In this sense, then, traditional healing is "holistic." It treats disease, not only by powerful medicines, but also with rituals that place the patient in the centre of a social drama in which emotions are not only highly charged but symbolically expressed. The afflicted person is not only made to feel important and the subject of social concern, but the ritual also relates what is happening to her wider cosmological and social concerns. . . . Thus, satisfactory healing involves, not merely the recovery from bodily symptoms, but the social psychological reintegration of the patient into his community. [Hammond-Tooke, 1989, p. 123, as cited in Louw and Pretorius 1995, p. 44]

This concept of illness and wellness stands in stark contrast to the view of orthodox Western medicine. While the concept of illness as the dislocation of one's sense of self and one's relationship to the larger community are acceptable to the diagnosis of *mental* illness and may direct the course of intervention toward the healing of fractures of *this* kind, this is certainly not a primary focus in the diagnosis and treating of bone fractures or other types of diseases in Western medicine.

In this context it is important to draw a distinction between healing and curing. *Curing* is the removal of the cause of the disease, and the cessation of physical symptoms. It is not a necessary condition for healing, but may be entailed by it. The word *healing* has its roots in Middle English *helens* and in the Anglo-Saxon *haelan*, to make whole, from the root *hal*, which means whole. In Western conceptualizations, a treatment is not considered effective if there is no abatement of physical symptoms. Conceptualizations of disease are based on the doctrine of specific etiology, which provides the basis for the differentiation of treatment of etiology versus the treatment of symptom. The dislocation of the patient's sense of self and connection to his or her community would not be seen as the genesis of physical disease, and the restoration of the sense of connection to his or her community would not typically be a focus of treatment of disease. Traditional systems of *healing* are "holistic" in that they see the individual as a part of a larger "whole," and the reintegration of the part to the larger system is intrinsic to the return to wellness and is the focus of the healing rituals.

All cultures have indigenous systems of healing within which concepts of the etiology of illness and return to wellness are embedded. The issues raised above with respect to incommensurability in diagnosis also apply to the comparisons of orthodox or Western medical and nonorthodox or traditional conceptions of wellness.

As Risjord (1993) points out, the concept of successful outcome is intrinsically related to the conceptions of health and illness, disease and disease etiology, goals and explanations of the medical system in question. Given the difference in the concepts of illness and wellness in traditional (nonorthodox) systems of healing and Western (orthodox) medicine, it is important to examine the cultural variations in the notion of "success" in the outcomes of intervention. Risjord contrasts the approach of orthodox (allopathic) medicine and homeopathy in the explanation of a successful outcome. In orthodox medicine a treatment substance or intervention is considered successful if it can be demonstrated to be better than the rate of spontaneous recovery. This is the logic of the controlled experiment, where the substance used is demonstrated to be the causal agent in recovery. The homeopath, on the other hand, does not draw that kind of distinction between spontaneous and nonspontaneous recovery. Within the homeopathic system, the substance given to the patient only aids and reinforces the body's own vital force. It does nothing on its own. In that sense all recoveries are spontaneous. Thus these two physicians will disagree on what is effective treatment because of their different conceptions of health and disease. Their judgments about success are incommensurable.

In his review of placebo effects Sullivan (1993) argues that the historical development of orthodox medicine as a profession can be viewed as the struggle for exclusive authority, first as the *most successful* medicine, and later as the *only valid* medicine. He goes on to assert that "increasing professional authority for orthodox medicine led to increasing epistemic control over what constituted legitimate and valid medical knowledge. Placebo controls are one device by which this epistemic control has been consolidated . . . placebo effects are not merely artifacts. They are *that form of healing against which contemporary scientific therapeutics is defined*" (p. 224, italics added). According to Sullivan, the double-blind, placebo-controlled clinical trials that are the touchstone of modern orthodox treatments serve to dissociate knowing from the process of healing. He argues that orthodox medicine has lost the conception of the power of the physician as healer; that today the physician has healing power only as the vehicle through whom medicines or surgery (which are seen as the healing agents) are dispensed. According to Sullivan, the healing power of the physician lies in his or her ability to provide explanations of events to the patient, restore a sense of control through knowing and understanding, and reconnect the patient to the world of the well. In this sense the physician manages not only medication for the patient, but also meaning. This conceptualization of the role of the physician is closer to the role of the healer in nonorthodox or traditional medicine.

The developments in the field of biological psychiatry and clinical pharmacology have served to hasten the erosion of this aspect of the power of the physician and clinician. The last three decades have seen the advent of an astonishing array of psychoactive medications: neuroleptics, antidepressants, anxiolytics, just to name a few. With them have also come a dazzling array of diagnostic categories. Medications have become the tools for the dissection of illness. Given the lack of *easier* alternatives to understand the biological underpinnings of mental disorder, it is not unreasonable for clinicians to have looked to the effects of drugs to understand the etiology of disease. Certainly, the biogenic amine theory of depression, based on the effectiveness of substances such as imipramine and iproniazid, is a potent example of this medication–response approach, as in the case of lithium and manic depression (see Lickey and Gordon 1991 for a comprehensive review). However, while the many types of antidepressants are remarkably effective with a wide variety of patients, there is still substantial uncertainty about why a particular drug works for some patients and not others. Biological psychiatry has provided us with a clear idea of the effects of drugs on particular neurotransmitters, but there still is only a low correlation between the locus of the effect of a given drug and the response of a particular patient.

The mere availability of medication and the predominance of medication-supported biological models strongly influences the way in which we frame both diagnosis and treatment. As Kramer (1993) points out, "Contemporary technology plays a dominant role in shaping ideology. What we look for in patients depends to a great deal on the available medication . . . the mere availability of a substance [that] colors our beliefs about deviance and how it is produced" (pp. 35–36). It is the belief of this author that the reliance of symptom abatement as the primary guide in the choice of treatment is another example of the erosion of the power of the clinician as healer. The physician becomes only the vehicle through whom healing agents are dispensed.

It has been only recently, with the burgeoning of the field of psychoneuroimmunology, that orthodox physicians are taking the effects of the patient's state of knowing seriously. In traditional healing systems the healer is the agent who translates the concept of disease as uncontrollable, unpredictable, and unavoidable into an interpretation that is meaningful for the patient and provides the rituals and procedures through which the patient can take an active role in his or her healing. Increasingly, orthodox medicine is moving in the same direction by supporting the active participation of the patient in the understanding of disease and the procedures of treatment, providing coping strategies, and eliciting the help of family and support groups to reconnect the patient to their communities. Taylor (1990) has reviewed the effects of cognitive factors in the process of healing in his review of the field of health psychology, and finds that the effectiveness of the coping strategies depends more upon the *match* between the coping strategies with the belief system of the person than the specific strategy per se.

There is good evidence that demonstrates that a combination of drugs and cognitive therapy is the most effective intervention for the most severely ill patients, while cognitive therapy alone is the treatment of choice for a wide variety of other patients. Given the discussion above, it can be argued that cognitive therapy-or, for that matter, any intervention that reconstructs the patient's illness in a way that is consonant with his or her belief systems, provides a procedure that is meaningful, and restores a sense of control and competence to the individual—would provide the start of the healing process. An examination of the recent changes in health care practice unfortunately shows a movement away from such conceptualizations and approaches to treatment and a greater reliance on a far more limited, medication-based approach.

It is unfortunate that, in the rare instances when traditional interventions (from other systems of medicine) are successfully applied, they are seen as anecdotal (and therefore unscientific); even more rarely, when a traditional approach can be shown to be effective using modern scientific testing methods, it is presented as modern science coming to the defense of folk medicine, or as scientific "confirmation" of the knowledge, skills, and utility of older therapies. There is little serious attempt toward integration. The modern wave-particle principle of complementarity, which is also a great lesson from Taoist and Buddhist philosophy, has yet to become the spirit of modern approaches to illness and wellness. It would be far wiser to see these events not as confirmation, or validations, or as defenses of traditional approaches, but rather as translations of useful knowledge from one system or language to another. In fact, it could be argued that illness and wellness are themselves complementary principles. While they appear to be mutually exclusive and irreconcilable opposites, they are both necessary for human life, and health and wellness would be unknowable without the knowledge or experience of nonhealth.

> Were we able to see all medical knowledge without the parochial vanity of modernism, we would also see the other medicines as potentially complementary and supplementary to other treatments in dealing with distressful

symptoms. We need not be confined to *either* scientific medicine *or* the unconventional therapies but are blessed with the opportunity to use *both* the relevant treatments of the ancients *and* the modern, *both* the East *and* the West, *both* rationalist *and* the empiricist, *both* the sophisticated *and* the primitive. [Grossman 1985, p. 50, italics original]

In summary, the findings of modern medicine *require* us to treat the mind and the body as an integrated informational system: A perspective that nonorthodox, traditional healing systems have consistently assumed. There needs to be a paradigmatic shift in our approaches to healing in the Western cultural context, which is, ironically, necessitated by the findings of modern science; it is a shift that requires us to see traditional and orthodox approaches as complementary systems, and to appreciate that the mind affects bodily processes at many levels, of which culture is the largest overarching rubric. Cultural factors influence the biopsychological processes in the etiology, symptom manifestation and report, diagnosis, course, and appropriateness of intervention modalities in illness, and, importantly, direct the evaluation of the "success" of the outcomes of treatment. To the degree to which we, as practitioners, remain alive to the powerful set of cultural forces that shape our experiences and the experiences of people with whom we come in contact, we will be able to develop new models of diagnosis and treatment that can combine traditional and non-orthodox methods of healing with mainstream orthodox practices.

REFERENCES

Adler, L. L., and Mukherji, B. R., eds. (1995). *Spirit vs Scalpel: Traditional Healing and Modern Psychotherapy.* Westport, CT: Bergin & Garvey.

Bebbington, P. (1993). Transcultural aspects of affective disorder. *International Review of Psychiatry* 5:145–156.

Beck, A. T. (1967). *Depression: Causes and Treatment.* Philadelphia: University of Philadelphia Press.

Binitie, A. (1975). A factor analytic study across cultures (African and European). *British Journal of Psychiatry* 127:559–563.

——— (1983). The depressed and anxious patient: care and treatment in Africa. *International Journal of Mental Health* 12(3):44–57.

Blaney, P. H. (1986). Affect and memory: a review. *Psychological Bulletin* 99:229–246.

Bohr, N. (1934). *Atomic Theory and the Description of Nature.* Cambridge, England: Cambridge University Press.

Bower, G. H. (1987). Commentary on mood and memory. *Behavior Research Therapy* 25:443–455.

Bower, G. H., and Mayer, J. D. (1989). In search of mood-dependent retrieval. *Journal of Social Behavior and Personality* 4:39–42.

Bronowski, J. (1978). *The Common Sense of Science.* Cambridge, MA: Harvard University Press.

Capra, F. (1977). *The Tao of Physics.* New York: Bantam.

Carr, J. E., and Vitalino, P. P. (1985). Theoretical implications of converging data on depression and culture-bound symptoms. In *Culture and Depression,* ed. A. Kleinman and B. Good, pp. 244–286. Berkeley, CA: University of California Press.

Chang, W. C. (1985). A cross-cultural study of depressive symptomatology. *Culture, Medicine and Psychiatry* 9(3):295–317.

Chen, D. (1995). Cultural and psychological influences on mental health issues for Chinese Americans. In *Spirit vs Scalpel: Traditional Healing and Modern Psychotherapy,* ed. L. L. Adler and B. R. Mukherji, pp. 185–196. Westport, CT: Bergin & Garvey.

Conrad, P. (1980). On the medicalization of deviance and social control. In *Critical Psychiatry—The Politics of Mental Health,* ed. D. Ingleby, pp. 102–119. New York: Pantheon.

Crittenden, K. S., Fugita, S. S., Bae, H., et al. (1992). A cross-cultural study of self-report depressive symptoms among college students. *Journal of Cross-Cultural Psychology* 23(2):163–178.

Crosson, B. (1992). *Subcortical Functions in Language and Memory.* New York: Guilford.

Derasari, S., and Shah, V. D. (1988). Comparison of symptomatology of depression between India and USA. *Indian Journal of Psychiatry* 30:129–134.

Dossey, L. (1982). *Space, Time, and Medicine.* Boston: New Science Library.

——— (1988). Mind, medicine, and the new physics: a time for reassessment. *Advances* 5 (1):57–69.

Einstein, A., Podolsky, B., and Rosen, N. (1935). Can quantum mechanical description of reality be complete? *Physics Review* 44:777.

Eisenberg, L. (1977). Disease and illness: distinctions between professional and popular ideas of sickness. *Culture, Medicine and Psychiatry* 1:9–23.

Escobar, J. I., Gomez, J., and Tuason, V. B. (1983). Depressive phenomenology in North and South American patients. *American Journal of Psychiatry* 140(1):47–51.

Gada, M. T. (1982). A cross cultural study of symptomatology of depression–Eastern versus Western patients. *International Journal of Social Psychiatry* 28(3):195–204.

Gillett, G. R. (1990). Neuropsychology and meaning in psychiatry. *Journal of Medicine and Philosophy* 15(1):21–40.

Grossman, R. (1985). *The Other Medicines: An Invitation to Understanding and Using Them for Health and Healing.* Garden City, NY: Doubleday.

Hammond-Tooke, D. (1989). *Rituals and Medicines: Indigenous Healing in South Africa.* Johannesburg: Donker.

Hinton, L., and Kleinman, A. (1993). Cultural issues and international psychiatric diagnosis. *International Review of Psychiatry* 1:111–129.

Kawanishi, Y. (1992). Somatization of Asians: An artifact of Western medicine? *Transcultural Psychiatric Research Review* 29:5–36.

Kirmayer, L. J., and Robbins, J. M. (1991). Three forms of somatization in primary care: prevalence, co-occurrence and demographic characteristics. *Journal of Nervous and Mental Disease* 179(11):647–655.

Kleinman, A. M. (1977). Depression, somatization and the "new cross-cultural psychiatry." *Social Science and Medicine* 11:3–10.

—— (1988). *Rethinking psychiatry: From Cultural Category to Personal Experience.* New York: Free Press.

Kramer, P. D. (1993). *Listening to Prozac.* New York: Viking.

Lickey, M. E., and Gordon, B. (1991). *Medicine and Mental Illness.* New York: Freeman.

Lin, K. M. (1981). Traditional Chinese medical beliefs and their relevance for mental illness and psychiatry. In *Normal and Abnormal Behavior in Chinese Culture*, ed. A. Kleinman and T. Y. Lin. Holland: D. Reidel.

Littlewood, R. (1986). Russian dolls and Chinese boxes: an anthropological approach to the implicit models of comparative psychiatry. In *Transcultural Psychiatry*, ed. J. L. Cox, pp. 308–327. London: Croon Helm.

—— (1990). From categories to Contexts: a decade of the "new cross-cultural psychiatry." *British Journal of Psychiatry* 156:308–327.

Louw, D. A., and Pretorius, E. (1995). The traditional healer in a multicultural society: the South African experience. In *Spirit vs Scalpel: Traditional Healing and Modern Psychotherapy*, ed. L. L. Adler and B. R. Mukherji, pp. 41–57. Westport, CT: Bergin & Garvey.

Marsella, A. J. (1993). Sociocultural foundations of psychopathology: a historical overview of concepts, events and pioneers prior to 1970. *Transcultural Psychiatric Research Review* 30:97–1142.

Marsella, A. J., Kinzie, D., and Gordon, P. (1973). Ethnic variations in the expression of depression. *Journal of Cross-Cultural Psychology* 4:435–448.

McGaugh, J. (1983). Preserving the presence of the past: hormonal influences on memory storage. *American Psychologist* 38(2):161–172.

Mezzich, J. E., and Raab, E. S. (1980). Depressive symptomatology across the Americas. *Archives of General Psychiatry* 37(7):818 – 823.

Mirowsky, J., and Ross, C. E. (1989). Psychiatric diagnosis as reified measurement. *Journal of Health and Social Behavior* 30:11–25.

Mishler, E. G. (1981). The social construction of medicine. In *Social Contexts of Health, Illness, and Patient Care*, pp. 141–168. New York: Cambridge University Press.

Mrinal, N. M., Mrinal, U. S., and Mukherji, B. R. (1995). Traditional healing in India. In *Spirit vs. Scalpel: Traditional Healing and Modern Psychotherapy*, ed. L. L.Adler and B. R.Mukherji, pp. 76–94. Westport, CT: Bergin & Garvey.

Mumford, D. B. (1989). Somatic sensations and psychological distress among students in Britain and Pakistan. *Social Psychiatry and Psychiatric Epidemiology* 24:321– 326.

Mumford, D. B., Bavington, J. T., Bhatnagar, K. S., et al. (1991). The Bradford Somatic Inventory: a multi-ethnic inventory of somatic symptoms reported by anxious and depressed patients in Britain and the Indo-Pakistan sub-continent. *British Journal of Psychiatry* 158:379–386.

Opler, M. K., and Mouchly, S. S. (1968). Cultural variables affecting somatic complaints and depression. *Psychosomatics* 9(5):261–266.

Pelletier, K. R., and Herzing, D. L. (1988). Psychoneuroimmunology: toward a mind-body model. *Advances* 5(1):27–56.

Perris, C. (1981). Transcultural aspects of depressive symptomatology. *Psychiatrica Clinica* 14(2):69–80.

Pert, C. B. (1986). The wisdom of the receptors. *Advances* 3(3):8–17.

Risjord, M. (1993). Relativism and the social scientific study of medicine. *The Journal of Medicine and Philosophy* 18:195–212.

Rossi, E. L. (1986). *The Psychology of Mind–Body Healing: New Concepts of Therapeutic Hypnosis.* New York: Norton.

——— (1987). From mind to molecule: a state-dependent memory, learning, and behavior theory of mind-body healing. *Advances* 4(2):46–60.

Rudnick, A. (1990). Toward a rationalization of biological psychiatry: a study in psychobiological epistemology. *Journal of Medicine and Philosophy* 15:75–96.

Selye, H. (1976). *The Stress of Life.* New York: McGraw-Hill.

Silver, H. (1987). Physical complaints are part of the core depressive syndrome: evidence from a cross-cultural study in Israel. *Journal of Clinical Psychiatry* 48(4):140–142.

Skultans, V. (1990). Anthropology and psychiatry: the uneasy alliance. *Transcultural Psychiatric Research Review* 28:5–24.

Sullivan, M. D. (1993). Placebo controls and epistemic control in orthodox medicine. *Journal of Medicine and Philosophy* 18:213–231.

Tanaka-Matsumi, J., and Marsella, A. J. (1976). Crosscultural variations in the phenomenological experience of depression: I. Word association studies. *Journal of Cross-Cultural Psychology* 7:379–396.

Taylor, S. E. (1990). Health psychology: the science and the field. *American Psychologist* 45:40–50.

Tulving, E. (1983). *Elements of Episodic Memory.* New York: Oxford University Press.

Ucros, C. G. (1989). Mood-dependent memory: a meta-analysis. *Cognition and Emotion* 3:139–167.

Wallace, E. R. (1990). Mind–body and the future of psychiatry. *Journal of Medicine and Psychiatry* 41–74.

West, J. (1985). Comparison of depressive symptomatology between Saudi and American psychiatric outpatients in an Eastern Province medical center, Saudi Arabia. *International Journal of Social Psychiatry* 31(3):230–234.

World Health Organization. (1992). *International Statistical Classification of Diseases and Related Health Problems,* 10th revision. Geneva, Switzerland: World Health Organization.

Yamamoto, J. (1985). Are American psychiatric outpatients more depressed than Chinese outpatients? *American Journal of Psychiatry* 142(11):1347–1351.

Yanping, Z., Leyi, X., and Qijie, S. (1986). Styles of verbal expression of emotional and physical experiences: a study of depressed patients and normal controls in China. *Culture, Medicine and Psychiatry* 10:231–243.

Zola, I. K. (1966). Culture and symptoms—an analysis of patients presenting complaints. *American Sociological Review* 31:615–630.

Zukav, G. (1979). *The Dancing Wu Li Masters.* New York: Morrow.

10

Differences in Depressive Symptomatology between Blacks and Whites

FRANK BIAFORA AND MARIA BIAFORA

OVERVIEW

Few topics in the social and psychological literatures have provided grounds for as much discussion and passionate discourse as those focused on the relationship between race and mental illness. Whether researcher or politician, scholar or practitioner, those who have considered the issues surrounding racial differences in mental condition over the past century have offered a wide array of competing hypotheses, conclusions, and interpretations. This lack of consensus can be traced in part to the varied methodologies used by researchers to obtain their data. For example, early mental health researchers, who relied mainly on census data and nonprobability samples of populations

This research was funded by a grant from the National Institute on Alcohol Abuse and Alcoholism (Grant # AA05793). The authors wish to acknowledge the support of the Principal Investigator, George J. Warheit, Ph.D.

in treatment, reported rates of depression and predisposition to melancholia as lower among blacks than whites in the United States (Bevis 1921, O'Malley 1914, Prudhomme 1938). Later estimates, based on hospital admissions data, showed blacks as having higher rates of depression than whites (Malzberg 1944).

A number of studies using nontreatment samples found whites to have higher rates of manic depression than blacks (Lemkau et al. 1942, Pasamanick 1959). But later research drawing on large random samples of the general population determined that blacks exhibit higher levels of depressive symptomatology than whites (Warheit et al. 1973, Weissman and Myers 1978).

Research methodology should not be blamed for all of this confusion, however. In fact, studies of race and mental illness and the corresponding interpretation of findings have often been skewed in favor of competing sociocultural dogmatism and political self-interest. Obvious examples of this can be found in published reports and commentary that first emerged during the middle of the nineteenth century, most of which attributed racial differences in mental illness rates to "race" itself. Alternative sociological and macro-level explanations for differences in depression and other psychological disorders were later offered and were (and still are) widely accepted among members of the mental health research community.

As described in more detail below, this shift in etiologic interpretation of racial differences was prompted partially by improvements in research design and multivariate statistical modeling. Statistically speaking, once epidemiologic data are simultaneously controlled for socioeconomic status (SES), that is, when comparisons are made between blacks and whites of comparable social status or class level, "race" ceases to be a significant predictor of depression.

Numerous researchers affirmed this finding during the 1970s and 1980s (Antunes et al. 1974, Mirowsky and Ross 1980, Warheit et al. 1973, Weissman and Myers 1978). Today this widely held explanation for racial differences is again being challenged (Kessler and Neighbors 1986, Ulbrich et al. 1989). In its place, nonsociological interpretations are once again surfacing.

What follows is an overview of some of the more important benchmarks in this pendulumlike history of research on race and mental illness in general, and on race and depression specifically. This is followed by a presentation of original findings from a large epidemiologic field survey of 2,098 adults residing in Gainesville, Florida. The specific aims of this study are to (1) determine and compare the rates of depressive symptomatology between blacks and whites in the general population; (2) determine and compare the rates of depressive symptomatology between blacks and whites of comparable socioeconomic standing; and (3) reexamine a recent controversial finding in the literature that suggests that lower status blacks are more depressed than lower status whites primarily because of differential vulnerability to stressful life events.

HISTORICAL BACKGROUND

Census and Treatment Studies

One of the first attempts to determine the rates of mental illness in the general population can be traced to the U.S. Census of 1840. In the midst of brewing tensions over slavery, this census provided the first look at the prevalence of "insanity and idiocy" among black and white Americans (Pettigrew 1964, Stanton 1960). Using census figures, Jarvis (1971) determined that blacks in the North were nearly ten times more likely to experience mental illness than blacks in the South. When comparisons across racial groups were made, Jarvis determined that blacks had poorer mental health than whites in the northern states, but in the South blacks had much better mental health. In the North the ratio of insanity and idiocy between blacks and whites was six to one. In the South it was three to five. Jarvis concluded from these findings that slavery must have a "wonderful influence upon the development of moral faculties and the intellectual powers" of blacks (p. 17). John Calhoun, a strict advocate of slavery, merged these findings into his political platform for the continuation of slavery, arguing that abolition would prove to be "a curse instead of a blessing for the Negro" (Stanton 1960, p. 65).

The Journal of American Medicine published a report by Powell (1896) that compared pre- and post-Civil War census figures on the rates of insanity and idiocy in Georgia. This report supported the prior warnings of Jarvis and Calhoun and others by confirming "rapid increases of insanity . . . every year since emancipation" (p. 1185). Powell determined that Georgia had only one insane black to every 10,584 one year prior to the start of the Civil War. This ratio changed to one in 4,225 in 1870; one in 1,764 in 1880; and one in 943 in 1890. Powell concluded from these findings: "Too much liberty and freedom, so far as the laws of health are concerned, is dangerous to the mental integrity of any people" (p. 1188). In addition, the author maintained that blacks were mentally healthier than whites prior to the war and that the present increase in mental illness among blacks would never have occurred since:

> . . . the slave owners made sure their Negroes ate one half to one pound of fat meat every day and lived in the open air. Freedom removed all hygienic

restraints and they were no longer obedient to the inexorable laws of health, plunging into all sorts of excess and vices, and having apparently little control over their appetites and passions. Since the war the colored race as a race is no longer a healthy and robust one; their vitality is in a condition of unstable equilibrium, liable from any undue strain to give way. [p. 1186]

Despite the severe inferential limitations of census data, the findings from these original mental health reports sparked an interest in the emerging field of psychiatric epidemiology. After 1900, the census stopped securing information on mental illness. For many years such data were secured mainly on persons who came to the attention of physicians or those who were being treated in public institutions. Findings from these early rates-under-treatment investigations were consistent in that blacks were typically found to have higher rates of psychotic disorders than whites (Bevis 1921, Frumkin 1954, Greene 1914, Malzberg 1935, O'Malley 1914). This was found in studies of treatment populations in the South and in the North. In addition, Malzberg (1935) noted that blacks in the State of New York had an annual rate of 150.6 per 100,000 for first admissions to all institutions for all mental disease. This exceeded the comparative rate among whites by a ratio of two to one. The rate for dementia praecox was 44.4 and 19.2 per 100,000 for blacks and whites, respectively. Schizophrenia, paresis, and alcoholic psychosis were also determined to be consistently higher among blacks than whites in state hospitals (Bevis 1921, Greene 1914, Malzberg 1944).

One research finding that puzzled early mental health investigators was that while blacks appeared to have higher rates of psychotic disorders than whites, blacks tended to manifest lower rates of depression than whites (Bevis 1921, Frumkin 1954, Greene 1914, O'Malley 1914). O'Malley (1914), for example, determined that among 800 patients treated in a public mental health hospital in Washington D.C., 3.0 percent of the whites had experienced melancholia or a depressed state as opposed to only 0.3 percent of the blacks. Similarly, Greene (1914) determined in his study of 5,410 admissions to the Georgia State Sanitarium that 2.2 percent of the whites had symptoms associated with depression as opposed to only .09 percent of the blacks.

As with earlier census interpretations, adequacy of methodology was not of central concern. Moreover, etiologic explanations for these findings were centered on racial factors. Greene (1914) argued that blacks were "happy-go-lucky" rather than philosophical, and that this did not allow them to accept the same levels of responsibility as the white race. As a result, one would rarely expect depression to be encountered by blacks even under circumstances in which a white person would be overwhelmed by it (Greene 1914). Along these same lines, another mental health physician/researcher suggested that blacks were "naturally" carefree, fond of excitement and motion, and that their mental unbalance would not lend itself to dwelling on sorrowful thoughts (Bevis 1921).

The general view that blacks had lower rates of depression than whites was widely held among the research community from the early 1900s until the mid-1940s. But in 1944 a follow-up study by Malzberg (1944) reported blacks in New York public hospitals were one and one-half times more likely to be admitted for depressive illness than whites. Malzberg suggested that this noticeable change in patterns of depression from prior studies may have been a result of the mass migration of blacks from the South to the industrial cities of the North after World War I. In particular, Malzberg (1944) speculated there was a selection factor to the migration process, in that those most likely to migrate were blacks from the South who lacked psychological stability.

In summary, there was a moderate consensus among mental health investigators by the middle of the twentieth century that blacks, particularly those living in the North, had higher rates of mental illness than whites. The research community found this to be especially evident when schizophrenia and other disorders of a psychotic nature became the mental health measures under scrutiny. With the exception of Malzberg's initial study of manic depression in New York hospitals, whites almost always were found to manifest higher rates of depression than blacks in rates-under-treatment studies. In terms of etiology, biological and psychological factors associated with race were commonly suggested to explain observed differences in mental illness.

Post-World War II: Epidemiologic Field Surveys

During the middle of this century, mental health researchers began to pay increasing attention to methodological issues associated with probability sampling and mental health measurement. One of the most significant factors leading researchers to reconsider their methodologies was the World War II experience. Results of psychiatric screening instruments used with draftees during the war indicated that the prevalence of mental health problems was far greater than expected. Forty-three percent of all disability discharges (980,000) from the Armed Forces were granted on psychiatric grounds, and 865,000 young men were rejected for psychiatric reasons in Selective Service System examinations (Star 1950, Weissman and Klerman 1977). In fact, psychiatric problems accounted for the largest proportion of military nonacceptance.

The findings of these military research units provided new theoretical insight into the race/mental illness relationship. Environmental stressors, rather than biogenetic constitution, became viewed as the underlying social psychological precipitants of mental illness. In addition, "stress" became the major focus of researchers in postwar studies of civilian populations. Indeed, one of the maturing concepts among sociologists and social psychologists since the close of the war has been that psychosocial stress rather than race, gender, and/or other biogenetic factors is a primary antecedent to many psychiatric illnesses, including depression. Poverty, urban anomie, racism, sexism, migration, and the experience of life events became some of the civilian stress equivalents of wartime stress (Weissman and Klerman 1977).

The experience gained from World War II prompted the passage of the Mental Health Systems Act in 1963 and it produced a concomitant distribution of federal funds for large-scale epidemiologic studies of the general population. Link and Dohrenwend (1989) described this new era of mental health studies as consisting of two generations. The first consisted of more than sixty field studies conducted after the war. (For a review, see Dohrenwend and Dohrenwend 1980.) The second generation, known as the Epidemiologic Catchment Area (ECA) projects, began in 1977 and the data from these projects are still being analyzed (Eaton and Kessler 1985, Regier et al. 1984, Robins et al. 1981). The ECA project was a five-site nationwide study funded by the National Institute of Mental Health (NIMH). It was designed to determine the prevalence of specific mental disorders in the United States as determined by the criteria of the third (revised) edition of the American Psychiatric Association's *Diagnostic and Statistical Manual* (1987). In addition, the ECA project was designed to discern the extent to which those afflicted with mental disorders were receiving mental health care.

The findings in the literature from postwar epidemiologic field research is so voluminous that a full description is beyond the scope of the present review. Suffice it to say that by the mid- to late 1960s several relationships regarding the social and demographic distribution of depressive illness in the community had generally been accepted. Depression usually occurred more frequently with increasing age, and more often among females than males. The association between socioeconomic status and mental illness was also consistent and eventually opened new avenues for exploration of the relationship between race and mental health and illness. Most epidemiologic field studies demonstrated an inverse correlation between socioeconomic status and prevalence rates for most forms of psychological disorder (Leighton et al. 1963, Lindenthal et al. 1970, Srole et al. 1962, Warheit et al. 1973, 1975). Whether socioeconomic status was directly responsible for mental illness or merely triggered or irritated a preexisting psychological condition remained an empirical question. Concepts associated with psychosocial stress provided fresh theoretical insights on this issue. (Dohrenwend 1973, Holmes and Rahe 1967, Lazarus and Folkman 1984, Paykel et al. 1971, Snider and Osgood 1969). Life events provided a conceptual bridge that later linked the constructs of socioeconomic status and psychological disorder.

What about race and depression? For many years following the war, field research left many questions regarding this relationship unresolved, and in some cases entirely unexamined. Were there racial differences in the rates of various types of psychological distress? And if so, what were the etiologic factors associated with these differences? These remained empirical questions to be addressed.

In the early 1970s, researchers in Florida provided the first empirical evidence that could adequately address these issues (Warheit et al. 1973, 1975). The Florida Health Study researchers determined from their statistical probability sample of 1,648 adults that when the data were analyzed without controls, blacks had significantly higher levels of depressive symptomatology than whites. But when the data were simultaneously controlled for SES using a multiple regression procedure, the variable "race" ceased to be a significant predictor. SES accounted for almost all of the difference in depressive symptom scores between the races. The researchers concluded from these findings that race by itself is not an important predictor of depression, and further, that SES is the most powerful explanatory factor of high mental health scores across racial groups (Warheit et al. 1973).

RACE AND DEPRESSION:
THE CURRENT ISSUES

Numerous reports throughout the 1970s and early 1980s by other investigators both corroborated and extended this finding (Antunes et al. 1974, Comstock and Helsing 1976, Mirowsky and Ross 1980, Neff and Husaini 1980, Weissman and Myers 1978). Based on this confluence of replicative findings, it became widely held among psychologists, sociologists, and social epidemiologists that there are no racial differences in depression levels once factors associated with SES are statistically controlled. Stated otherwise, race itself was no longer viewed as an independent predictor of depression.

More recent findings by Kessler and Neighbors (1986), however, have reopened the question of whether SES is a unique predictor of observed racial differences in depression. These researchers suggest instead that other factors associated with race, which are not socioeconomic in nature, may also contribute to racial differences in depression. These include the psychological impact of racism and discrimination that serves to compound the effects of lower socioeconomic status among blacks. Another group of psychosocial factors, including inadequate coping skills and/or weaker social supports and social networks, are also advanced as possible etiologic components by these researchers.

Kessler and Neighbors' (1986) argument emerged from their initial methodological criticism that prior researchers had incorrectly specified their analytic models by failing to control for the interaction effects of race and SES in their main effect regression models. By not including interactions, Kessler and Neighbors believed that the importance of race had been underestimated while at the same time the importance of SES had been overestimated.

To test their interaction hypothesis, Kessler and Neighbors performed a series of hierarchical regression models on pooled data from eight epidemiologic field surveys conducted by other researchers between the late 1950s and mid-1970s. The first part of their analyses tested for the effects of race on depression with no controls. This supported prior field research by indicating that blacks had significantly higher depression scores than whites. Results from their second model, which controlled simultaneously for gender, age, and SES, also replicated the findings from prior research in that racial variance was explained away by SES. However, when they tested for the interaction between race and SES in their final model, Kessler and Neighbors found a residual "black" effect on depression. As they had expected, lower-status blacks were found to have significantly higher depression scores than blacks or whites of higher status. However, the finding of most interest was that lower-status blacks were found to be significantly more depressed than whites of the same status. Kessler and Neighbors concluded from this provocative finding that race does indeed remain an important etiologic factor to be considered for mental health and illness even when SES is held constant.

Kessler and Neighbors issued a call for a renewed interest in studying the associations between race and depression. The first group of investigators to answer that call was Ulbrich and associates (1989), who reexamined this controversial issue using a similar methodological design on a sample of nearly 2,000 respondents in North Central Florida. The results of this study partially supported the findings of Kessler and Neighbors. In addition to their parallel conclusion that lower-status blacks had higher depression scores than either whites or blacks of higher status and whites of lower status when interactions between race and SES are considered, Ulbrich and her colleagues (1989) also offered interesting theoretical insight for this residual race difference. These researchers empirically tested two psychosocial stress hypotheses using a statistical mean decomposition strategy designed by Iams and Thornton (1975). The first hypothesis, known in the literature as the *differential exposure* hypothesis, emphasizes the importance of life conditions as determinants of emotional disorder. The essential idea of differential exposure is straightforward. The underlying argument is that some people in society, as a result of their lower social and economic position and their overall poorer opportunities for vertical mobility, have a greater chance of being exposed to socioenvironmental stressors than persons of higher status. This in turn acts as a precursor to higher rates of emotional problems. Persons of higher status on the other hand are hypothesized to manifest lower psychological problems because they have resources available to help shield them against undue stress exposure.

The second hypothesis, referred to as the *differential vulnerability* hypothesis, posits that differences among distress levels between different social status groups are a function of one group's being more emotionally responsive or psychologically vulnerable to stressful events than another. The process of differential vulnerability may occur in a number of ways. One of them may be determined by the subjective meanings with which some status groups or persons may interpret life experiences. This stems from one's perceived chances to adequately cope with life stress (Kessler 1979). In the case of race, one argument could be that omnipresent racial discrimination exacerbates blacks' perceived life chances, resulting in their being more emotionally vulnerable than whites to the impact of life events. As Kessler (1979) pointed out, life events are not inherently stressful, but must instead be interpreted through subjective filters. It is these interpretations that are partly dependent on the context of one's life, that is, one's socioeconomic status.

A second way in which the social environment can act as a source of differential vulnerability stems from the availability of social supports or other emotional/instrumental resources that can reduce or buffer the impact of life stressors. Specifically, some persons or status groups may have fewer social supports and support networks than others to fall back on when the stressors become too difficult to manage on one's own. The stress-buffering effect of social support systems have been widely discussed (Lin et al. 1986, Mirowsky and Ross 1989, Pearlin 1989). Together, the differential exposure and differential vulnerability hypotheses suggest that socially disadvantaged persons experience higher rates of psychological disorder because they are more highly exposed to and more highly influenced by stressful experiences than socially advantaged persons (Kessler 1979).

A vast literature supports the exposure hypothesis (Dohrenwend 1973, Dohrenwend and Dohrenwend 1969, Gove 1973, Hollingshead and Redlich

1958, Myers et al. 1974, Neff 1984). However, the research of Ulbrich and colleagues (1989) provides new support for the vulnerability hypothesis. These researchers determined that there were no significant differences in the total number of undesirable life events, health-related events, and economic problems experienced by the two groups within the past year. However, given comparable levels of exposure to these events, lower-status blacks responded more negatively in terms of depression than higher-status blacks or whites of similar status (Ulbrich et al. 1989).

REEXAMINATION OF CURRENT ISSUES

This historical review indicates that researchers who have focused on the rates and levels of depressive symptomatology between blacks and whites have arrived at diverse conclusions. Furthermore, the review reveals that the etiologic explanations for racial differences have varied considerably. Researchers in the late 1800s and earlier parts of this century attributed differences in mental illness rates to race itself (Bevis 1921, Greene 1914, O'Malley 1914). Then, social structural explanations were offered to explain racial differences in the rates of depression and other psychological disorders between blacks and whites (Warheit et al. 1973, 1975). At present, explanations of higher rates of these disorders among blacks are moving away from social-structure explanations to once again include dimensions attributed to racial vulnerability (Kessler and Neighbors 1986, Ulbrich et al. 1989).

A careful examination of the research methodologies employed by Kessler and Neighbors and Ulbrich and her research team reveal two key characteristics, either one of which could have resulted in their challenges to existing theory and findings. The first issue stems from the way these researchers conceptualized and operationalized depression, the second from their choice of socioeconomic status measures used to test for interactions with race.

Both teams of researchers artificially bifurcated their measures of depression into psychological distress scales that measured only symptoms of depressed mood. The physiological components of depression were systematically deleted from their analyses based on statistical reasoning, that is, factor analysis. Depressed mood is characterized by feeling sad, lonely, demoralized, hopeless, and worthless. Physiological symptoms of depression are more directly associated with body states such as loss of appetite, weight gains and losses, restlessness, chronic fatigue, dizziness, sleeping problems, headaches, and gastrointestinal distress. The bifurcation employed by Kessler and

Neighbors (1986) and Ulbrich and associates (1989) violates decades of clinical research that has clearly shown that depression is a multidimensional condition comprising (1) affective symptoms related to lowered mood such as sadness, loneliness, apathy; (2) a variety of somatic symptoms such as physical agitation and/or psychomotor retardation; (3) altered patterns of psychobiologic reactivity such as insomnia or hypersomnia every day or unusual decrease or increase in appetite in short periods of time; (4) negative self-evaluation involving lowered self-esteem, self-blame, suicidal ideation, and a sense of guilt; and (5) an existential dimension typified by continuous pessimism, despair, and a gloomy outlook on the future (Beck 1967, *DSM-III-R* 1987, Klerman 1987, Schwab et al. 1967a, b). Therefore, the deletion of physiological symptoms for purposes of determining the prevalence of depression is both scientifically and clinically unsound, and research that does not include these multiple dimensions could lead to erroneous results.

Findings might also be contaminated by these researchers' choice of socioeconomic status indicators. Specifically, the residual race differences in depression scores were found to be significant only for specific single-item measures of SES. Kessler and Neighbors (1986) employed household income and Ulbrich and colleagues (1989) used occupational status. No racial differences in symptomatology were found when education was introduced independently into the stress models presented by these investigators. Surprisingly, neither study examined a comprehensive measure of SES combining all three items customarily used in SES models: education, occupation, and income. Because socioeconomic status is a multidimensional phenomenon representing one's social and economic standing in a society as well as a general assessment of one's overall opportunities or life chances, a comprehensive measure of SES might have provided a more powerful construct than income, occupation, or education alone when assessing the relationships among race, SES, and mental health measures (Nam and Powers 1983). It is quite possible that the residual race differences in depression as determined by Kessler and Neighbors and Ulbrich and her colleagues may not have been found had this more comprehensive measure of SES been used in their analyses.

As a result of these two methodological shortcomings, it may be premature to conclude that blacks in the general population are more depressed than whites. Clearly, additional research into this particular area of social-psychiatric epidemiology is warranted. It is the purpose of the present research to further this investigation by carefully reexamining the data used by Ulbrich and colleagues (1989) in light of the methodological issues presented above.

DATA AND METHODOLOGY

Survey Design

The data used for the current research were obtained as part of a large-scale epidemiologic field survey of health and family life in Alachua County, Florida, a metropolitan statistical area (MSA) with approximately 190,000 people. This is the same data utilized by Ulbrich and associates (1989). A stratified sample of persons, including university students ages 18 and older, was selected using multistaged, statistical probability sampling procedures. Blacks and elderly persons were of primary concern in the study, and as a result were oversampled. The research team used two sampling procedures. In the first, random digit dialing techniques developed by the Rand Corporation (Lucas and Adams 1977) were used to make an initial contact with an adult in the household and to secure a list of all household members. A total of 15,840 numbers were called at least once. Of the total, 77 percent, or 12,197, were working numbers. Of these, 62 percent, or 7,562, included households with eligible respondents. Of the eligibles, 7 percent refused to provide any information over the telephone. Therefore, of the eligible respondents, 93 percent were successfully enumerated.

From this large pool of eligible households, a probability sample of respondents was chosen using procedures developed by Kish (1965). The Kish method was selected because it gives each adult in the household an equal probability of being selected. Once respondents were selected using these procedures, they were sent a self-addressed letter stating the nature of the study and requesting their cooperation.

Because earlier census reports and information from the phone company revealed that 11.7 percent of respondents, predominantly in black census tracts, did not have telephones, a second, supplemental, sampling procedure employing personal door-to-door canvassing was conducted in those areas. Here again, statistical probability procedures were used to enumerate and select respondents. The census tracts in predominantly black neighborhoods were divided into equal-size quartiles. In each quartile every other street was selected, and every other house on each side of the selected street was contacted. This latter sampling strategy resulted in 151 interviews, or 7.1 percent of the total sample.

Of the total number of households in which respondents provided initial consent during the enumeration process, 17.0 percent later refused to be interviewed. Another 12.2 percent could not be interviewed because of illness and/or various other reasons after initial cooperation was established. The majority of this group (7.3 percent) had moved from the area. The remainder of the nonrespondents were too ill to be interviewed (2.3 percent). All interviews were conducted face to face, usually in the respondent's home. Although the length of the interviews ranged from thirty-five minutes to four hours, the average was about one and one-half hours.

A total of 2,115 respondents participated in the Florida Health Study. Of these, 1,648 (78 percent) were white, 450 (22 percent) were black, and 17 (1 percent) were Hispanic. Because whites and blacks were of main interest in this study, the seventeen Hispanic respondents were excluded, providing a final sample size of 2,098. A chi-square analysis of the age and gender characteristics of the refusals and of the respondents who were successfully interviewed revealed no significant differences.

Operationalizations

Depression was conceptualized and measured as a scale designed to assess the signs, symptoms, and dysfunctions associated with depression. In this way depression is a continuum of depressive symptoms and related dysfunctions rather than a distinct diagnostic category. Throughout the analysis depression is referred to and is measured in terms of depression scale scores and depressive symptomatology. The higher the scale scores, the greater the magnitude of the depressive symptoms and dysfunctions. Depressive symptoms were assessed for the past year.

Depressive symptoms were measured by means of the eighteen-item Florida Health Study Depression Scale (FHS) (Schwab et al. 1979, Warheit et al. 1973, 1975). These items are found in Appendix A. The FHS depression scale was designed for use in general population surveys to measure the symptoms and dysfunctions associated with clinical depression. It was not designed, nor does it attempt, to make a *DSM* (1987) type diagnosis. Nevertheless, the items in the FHS were developed directly out of extensive treatment and research with client populations (Schwab et al. 1967a,b, Warheit et al. 1973, 1975). Several items in the Center for Epidemiologic Studies—Depression checklist (CES–D), the most widely used measure of depression in the research literature, are similar in content to the FHS depression measure (Aneshensel et al. 1983, Radloff 1977, Weissman et al. 1977). Responses to the FHS depression scale items were framed within the context of the past year.

Extensive field research employing the depression scale from the Florida Health Study has been reported in the literature. Data have been gathered on approximately 22,000 household residents by various researchers throughout the U.S. For a review of this literature see Warheit and associates (1985). The FHS depression scale has been tested for reliability and validity with considerable success in a large number of settings using a variety of methods (Warheit et al. 1985).

All respondents included in the present study were asked each of the eighteen FHS depression scale items. All items were scored by means of a Likert-type scale. Of the eighteen items, six were originally scored on a three-point basis as either never-sometimes-often or very few times-sometimes-most of the time. In addition, twelve of the original items were scored on a five-point basis. Scoring for these items included never-seldom-sometimes-often-all the time, bad-poor-fair-good-excellent, always-seldom-sometimes-often-all the time, and strongly disagree-disagree-undecided-agree-strongly agree. To maintain consistency for scoring, the FHS items were rescored as 0, 2, 4 or 0, 1, 2, 3, 4. Thus the possible scores for each respondent ranged from a low of 0 to a high of 72. A Cronbach's alpha (Cronbach 1951) was computed as a measure of internal consistency for the total FHS scale employed in this study. The eighteen items scaled very well, with an overall alpha coefficient of .821. The alpha for blacks was slightly higher than it was for whites, .829 compared to .817.

Depression scores tend to be highly skewed in the general population. As such, a variety of transformed FHS distributions were compared with the nontransformed one. Results of the K-S Z-test (Smirnov 1961) indicated that the raw data for the FHS provided more normally distributed functions than any of the respective transformed distributions. As such, the statistical analyses that follow were performed on nontransformed data.

Race is a categorical variable based on self-reports contrasting blacks (0) and whites (1). *Gender* is also a dummy variable contrasting females (0) and males (1). *Age* is an individual's self-reported age.

Socioeconomic Status (SES) is used as a proxy for social class and both terms will be used interchangeably. In the present study, SES is a composite measure based on a respondent's educational attainment, total household income, and occupational status. The choice to use such a measure is based on the general assessment that social status in the United States is most commonly referred to and expressed in terms of a combination of these. Furthermore, it was believed that such a multi-item measure would reveal more about the socioeconomic status of respondents than single items alone.

The coding of socioeconomic status follows the methodology used by Nam and Powers (1983). In addition to this composite SES measure, single measures of occupation, education, and income were also used to help facilitate a conceptual and methodological comparison with the recent work of Kessler and Neighbors (1986) and Ulbrich and colleagues (1989).

The three single item measures are presented first, followed by the details of the Nam and Powers (1983) operationalization procedures for the composite SES measure.

Education is based on a respondent's report of his or her last year of formal schooling completed. As a single item, education is examined as a continuous variable.

Household Income is based on a respondent's answer to the question, "Can you tell me your approximate total household income from all sources in the last year?" As a single item, household income is examined as a continuous variable.

Occupational status is measured as a multiple-item index based on a formula developed by Nam and Powers (1983) that combines two pieces of information: average education and average income for a particular occupation in a specified geographic location. This differs from occupational prestige, which refers more to the subjective evaluations people have of the social importance of an occupation. This procedure produces an occupational status score between the values of 0 and 100, which represents the approximate percentage of persons whose combined average levels of education and income fell below that of a specified occupation. For example, if the status score for a high school teacher was 70, it could be estimated that 70 percent of all persons in the civilian labor force had combined average education/income levels below those of a high school teacher.

Respondents were asked, "Which of the following most accurately describes your present status? Are you: retired, disabled, unemployed, employed full-time, employed part-time, housewife, or a student?" If respondents were not currently employed, their prior occupation or spouse's occupation was substituted, whichever was highest. Retired persons were assigned scores for their prior occupation. Sample scores for occupational status ranged from 1 to 99, with a mean status score of 63, a median of 69, and a standard deviation of 27.

Composite SES. For purposes of a combined index of SES, the procedures developed by Nam and Powers (1983) were again borrowed. A full description of the mathematical formulae used in this calculation are lengthy and beyond the scope of this chapter. Interested readers are encouraged to write the author or consult Nam and Powers (1983). Very briefly, the multi-item SES index was based on a cumulative range of scores from 0 to 100 that was generated by summing and averaging three separate scores that were themselves based on an averaging procedure: (1) an educational status score; (2) an occupational status score, and (3) a household income score. If only two scores were known (e.g., education and income), those two scores were summed and divided by two rather than three.

Scores for each of the three variables were first calculated and standardized relative to the distribution of that particular variable within the metropolitan statistical area. This provided a cumulative range of nonoverlapping percentile scores for which each respondent could be fitted on each variable. The average SES score for the sample was 58.72 with a standard deviation of 24.39.

Stressful life events. An additive measure of undesirable life events selected from the Paykel inventory were used (Paykel et al. 1971). Each event was scored 1 if it was experienced by an individual within the past year and 0 otherwise. This measure is an unweighted summated index of undesirable life events within the past year and is derived by summing twenty-one undesirable events. A list of these events is found in Appendix B.

FINDINGS

Table 10–1 illustrates some of the demographic characteristics of the sample. The sample consists of 1,648 (78.6 percent) whites and 450 (21.4 percent) blacks. Females constituted the majority of both racial groups. The respondents ranged in age from 18 to 96 with a mean age of 52.9. Due to the oversampling of elderly, plus the fact that the study was conducted in a university town, the age of respondents is bimodally distributed with more representation of the young and old. The largest proportion of respondents (34.4 percent) were full-time employees, followed by retirees (27.6 percent), housewives (11.7 percent), and students (10.1 percent). The present sample is also a highly educated one. The mean and median number of formal schooling years is 13.1. Nearly one of three respondents had completed at least four years of college. Finally, the average household income for the sample was $22,000, with a standard deviation of $20,000.

The findings on the relationship between race and depressive symptomatology can be found in Table 10–2. The mean FHS depression scale score for the entire sample was 14.97 (SD = 9.11); the median was 13, and the mode 10. A review of the frequency distribution for the entire sample showed that FHS scores were slightly skewed, with 14.7 percent of the respondents having scores of 24 or above, or, rather, 85.3 percent having scores below 24. This finding closely parallels the findings of other researchers who have used the FHS to determine the level of depressive symptomatology in the general population (Vega et al. 1984, Warheit et al. 1973, 1975, 1985).

TABLE 10–1. SOCIODEMOGRAPHIC
CHARACTERISTICS OF THE SAMPLE (N=2,098)

		N	%
RACE	White	1,648	78.6
	Black	450	21.4
GENDER	Male	887	42.3
	Female	1,211	57.7
RACE/GENDER	White Male	743	35.4
	Black Male	144	6.9
	White Female	905	43.1
	Black Female	306	14.6
AGE	18–29	410	19.5
	30–39	240	11.4
	40–49	197	9.4
	50–59	176	8.4
	60–69	582	27.7
	70 +	492	23.5
PRESENT	Retired	578	27.6
WORK	Disabled	181	8.6
STATUS	Unemployed	35	1.7
	Employed Part Time	125	6.0
	Employed Full Time	721	34.4
	Housewife/Homemaker	245	11.7
	Student	211	10.1
SES	Low 0–19	184	8.8
	20–39	312	14.9
	40–59	467	22.2
	60–79	626	29.8
	High 80–99	509	24.3
EDUCATION	Less than H.S.	367	24.7
	High School Grad	466	22.3
	Some College	223	22.8
	College Grad	251	12.0
	Graduate or Higher	378	18.2
HOUSEHOLD	Less than $5,000	227	11.6
INCOME	$5,000–$9,999	346	17.7
	$10,000–$14,999	289	14.8
	$15,000–$19,999	238	12.2
	$20,000–$29,999	307	15.7
	$30,000–$39,999	236	12.1
	$40,000–$49,999	127	6.5
	$50,000 or more	184	9.4

TABLE 10–2. t-TESTS FOR FHS DEPRESSION
SCALE SCORES BY RACE

	N	MEAN	SD	SE	t/df/Sig
FHS DEPRESSION SCALE SCORES (alpha = .82)					
TOTAL	2,098	14.98	9.11	.20	
WHITES	1,648	14.40	8.75	.23	t = 5.64 df = 2,096 p < .001
BLACKS	450	17.11	10.05	.47	

T-test procedures determined that blacks had significantly higher FHS depression scores than whites (t = 5.64; p < .001). The mean score for blacks was 17.11. For whites, the mean score was 14.40. The standard deviation on the FHS was 10.05 for blacks and 8.75 for whites.

Next, statistical controls for socioeconomic status were considered to determine whether the relationships between race and depression were altered. Using the same analytic strategies as Kessler and Neighbors (1986) and Ulbrich and associates (1989), a series of hierarchical regression analyses was conducted to explore this issue. FHS depression scores were first regressed on race by itself. This was followed by a main-effect model in which race and SES were introduced simultaneously. Because of their importance in the literature as predictors of depression, gender and age were also controlled. The final model in the hierarchy was similar to the main-effect model, except for the inclusion of interaction terms. Each pair of possible cross-product combinations from the original variables were force-entered, one at a time, following the main-effect variables. This provided an assessment of the added significance of each interaction, independently, in the overall regression model. All statistically significant interactions were then introduced simultaneously into a fourth and final model.

Table 10–3 presents the estimates from the hierarchical regression procedure. Results from the simple regression are presented at far left. This is followed by the results from the two main-effect models in the middle, and finally the interaction model at far right.

The simple regression reiterates what was found earlier with the t-test: blacks have significantly higher FHS depression scores than whites when the

TABLE 10–3. SUMMARY TABLE OF REGRESSION MODELS PREDICTING FHS DEPRESSION SCALE SCORES

MULTIPLE REGRESSIONS

	Model 1		Model 2		Model 3		Model 4	
	b	Beta	b	Beta	b	Beta	b	Beta
Race	-2.71	-.12**	-.85	-.04	1.03	.05	1.21	.05
SES			-.12	-.33**	-.13	-.34**	-.13	-.35**
Age					-.03	-.07*	-.06	-.13**
Sex					-1.38	-.08**	-5.06	-.27**
Sex X Age							.07	.22**
R²	.01		.10		.11		.12	
F, df	(31.80; 1, 2,096)		(117.04; 2, 2,095)		(64.64; 4, 2,093)		(54.66; 5, 2,092)	
Sig.	p < .001		p < .001		p < .001		p < .001	

* p < .01

** p < .001

241

data are not controlled (F = 31.80, p = .001). Still, it is important to note that not much explanatory power can be attributed to race in this equation. Only 1 percent of the overall variance in depression scores could be explained by race alone. As hypothesized, the introduction of a composite SES control variable in Model 2 eliminated the race differential. This finding suggests that the effect of race on depression is largely due to socioeconomic factors. Less than half of 1 percent of the variance was explained by race in this model. The overall regression equation was significant: the F was 64.64, with 4 and 2,093 degrees of freedom.

Adding controls for gender and age in Model 3 did not significantly alter this relationship. Gender was statistically significant (p < .001). Females had significantly higher FHS depression scores than males (beta = -.08, b = -1.38). Being young was also correlated with higher FHS depression scores (p <.01; beta = -.07, b = -.03). SES was still the most powerful variable in the equation (p < .001; beta = -.34, b = -.13). In other words, for every decrease of thirty-four standardized units in SES, there was, on average, an increase of one additional unit in the FHS depression scale.

The introduction of interaction terms into a full model did not alter the relationships among the variables. Of the multiple combinations of interaction terms tested, gender by age was the only interaction found to be statistically significant; young females in particular had significantly higher scores than any of their age/gender counterparts (p < .001; beta = .22, b = .07).

Single SES Indicators

In addition to the general objective of determining the relationships among race, SES, and depression, an additional objective of this research was to assess any change in this relationship when various single-item measures of SES were considered.

The findings from the analyses controlling for income are presented in Table 10–4a. When the data were controlled for income (Model 2), blacks continued to have significantly higher depression scores than whites (p < .001). The standardized regression coefficient for race in this multiple regression was -.07. The unstandardized coefficient was -.26. The introduction of income increased the amount of variance explained from .01 to .06.

Blacks continued to have significantly higher depression scores in a more developed model that included controls for gender and age (Model 3). The negative relationships between gender and depression scores indicates that females were also more likely than males to manifest higher levels of depressive symptomatology.

TABLE 10-4a. SUMMARY TABLE OF REGRESSION MODELS PREDICTING FHS DEPRESSION SCALE SCORES WITH INCOME

MULTIPLE REGRESSIONS

	Model 1		Model 2		Model 3		Model 4	
	b	Beta	b	Beta	b	Beta	b	Beta
Race	-2.71	-.12**	-.26	-.07**	-1.38	-.06*	-1.38	-.06*
Income			.00	-.21**	.00	-.20**	.00	-.20**
Age					.00	.00	.00	.00
Sex					-1.83	-.10**	-1.83	-.10**
R^2	.01		.06		.07		.07	
F, df	(31.80; 1, 2,096)		(65.80; 2, 2,095)		(38.53; 4, 2,093)		(38.53; 4, 2,093)	
Sig.	p < .001		p < .001		p < .001		p < .001	

243

When the data were controlled for occupational status (Table 10–4b), unlike income, the independent effect of race on depression was almost entirely eliminated. The unstandardized regression coefficient was reduced from -2.71 when depression was regressed on race alone to -.10 when occupational status was controlled. Occupational status accounted for all of the variance in Model 2. The inclusion of gender and age did not alter this relationship.

The findings from the hierarchical regression models controlling for years of formal education presented in Table 10–4c are similar to the findings from the occupational status models presented above. The inclusion of education in a model that regressed depression scores on race eliminated the significant relationship between being black and higher depression scores. As indicated in Model 2, there was a significant negative relationship between educational attainment and depression scores.

To summarize, three models controlling for the effects of different independent SES indicators on FHS depression scores were tested. In only one model, when depression scores were regressed on race controlling for income, did race emerge as an independent predictor of depression scores.

Differential Exposure versus Differential Vulnerability to Life Events

Ulbrich and her colleagues (1989) recently posited that differential vulnerability to life events may help to explain why lower-class blacks in their study exhibited significantly more psychological distress than whites of comparable status. In a replicative effort to examine the possibility that their findings may have been the result of their choice of SES measures, a series of post hoc analyses were conducted for the different measures. The first of these analyses was designed to test the exposure hypothesis. The remaining analyses were designed to test the vulnerability hypothesis.

Descriptive life-event data are presented in Appendix B. Chi-square comparisons found blacks significantly more exposed than whites on six of the twenty-one life events. The most common event was the death of a family member. Almost 25 percent of the sample had a member of their family die in the past year. Part of this can be explained by the oversampling of the elderly.

The mean number of life events (table not shown) experienced during the year prior to the interview for everyone in the sample was 1.47. On average, blacks experienced more life-crisis events than whites in the twelve months prior to the interview. The mean score for blacks was 1.64. For

TABLE 10–4b. SUMMARY TABLE OF REGRESSION MODELS PREDICTING FHS DEPRESSION SCALE SCORES WITH *OCCUPATIONAL STATUS*

MULTIPLE REGRESSIONS

	Model 1		Model 2		Model 3		Model 4	
	b	Beta	b	Beta	b	Beta	b	Beta
Race	-2.71	-.12**	-.10	.00	-.01	.00	1.08	.00
Occupational Status			-.08	-.24**	-.08**	-.24**	-.08	-.24**
Age					-.02	.00	-.04	-.08*
Sex					-1.76	-.10**	-4.59	-.25**
Sex X Age							.05	.17*
R^2	.01		.06		.07		.07	
F, df	(31.80; 1, 2,096)		(69.21; 2, 2,095)		(40.24; 4, 2,093)		(33.79; 5, 2,092)	
Sig.	p < .001		p < .001		p < .001		p < .001	

245

TABLE 10–4c. SUMMARY TABLE OF REGRESSION MODELS PREDICTING FHS DEPRESSION SCALE SCORES WITH *EDUCATION*

MULTIPLE REGRESSIONS

	Model 1		Model 2		Model 3		Model 4	
	b	Beta	b	Beta	b	Beta	b	Beta
Race	-2.71	-.12**	-.66	-.03	-.35	-.02	-.35	-.02
Education			-.50	-.23**	-.52	-.24**	-.52	-.24**
Age					-.03	-.07*	-.03	-.07*
Sex					-1.96	-.11**	-1.96	-.11**
R^2	.01		.06		.07		.07	
F, df	(31.80; 1, 2,096)		(68.25; 2, 2,095)		(42.85; 4, 2,093)		(42.85; 4, 2,093)	
Sig.	p < .001		p < .001		p < .001		p < .001	

whites, the mean score was 1.42. These differences were statistically significant (t = 2.98; p <.01). More important, race ceased to be a significant predictor in a regression analysis controlling simultaneously for SES (beta = -.03, b = -.10). Blacks, therefore, were not more likely than whites to be exposed to life-crisis events given similar levels of SES.

To assess the hypothesis of differential vulnerability by race, a series of multiple regression analyses were performed. First, depression scores were regressed on race after controlling for aggregate life-event scores. This provided a general test of whether blacks were more vulnerable than whites to life events. The data from these analyses (not shown) indicated that, given equal levels of exposure to life-crisis events, blacks had significantly higher FHS depression scores than whites (p < .001; beta = -.11; b = -2.45; F = 51.35).

Next, SES was introduced into a regression along with race and Life Crises Events (LCE) scores to determine whether differences in vulnerability could be accounted for by socioeconomic factors. Table 10–5 presents the findings from this analysis.

As demonstrated, the inclusion of SES negated, entirely, the effects of race on depression scores. The standardized coefficient for race was .04. Blacks, in other words, were found not to be differentially vulnerable compared to whites to the impact of life events once the effects of SES factors were controlled. This is further shown by the R-square change values. None of the variance in FHS depression scores was accounted for by race. SES accounted for most of the variance (10 percent). Life events accounted for only 2 percent.

DISCUSSION

This research was designed to address recent findings in the mental health literature regarding the relationships between race and depression. Kessler and Neighbors (1986) and Ulbrich and associates (1989) questioned over twenty years of psychiatric epidemiology by suggesting that blacks are more depressed than whites. More specifically, by simultaneously including interactions of race and factors of SES into empirical models regressing depression scores, these two research teams have determined that, given equal income (Kessler and Neighbors) or occupational status (Ulbrich et al.), lower-status blacks are more depressed than whites with similar SES characteristics.

In a reexamination of this proposition using the same survey data as Ulbrich and associates, the results of the current study suggest that these latest findings on the relationships between race, SES, and depression require

TABLE 10–5. RELATIONSHIP BETWEEN RACE AND FHS DEPRESSION SCORES CONTROLLING FOR LCE

	b	SE b	Beta	Sig	R^2 Change
LCE	1.12	.14	.18	**	.04
Race	-2.45	.47	-.11	**	.01
Constant	15.15	.48			

$R^2 = .05$
F, df = 51.35;   2; 2,095
p < .001

* p < .01
** p < .001
Sex   0 = female   1 = male
Race   0 = Black   1 = White

further interpretation. To be more precise, it was determined that an independent race effect was present only when the data were controlled for income, but not for occupational status, education, or a composite measure of SES. In short, the data here illustrate that the results one is likely to obtain depend more on the operationalization of socioeconomic status than on social reality. One possible explanation for the importance of SES on mental health can be drawn from psychosocial stress theory, which argues that lower socioeconomic status leaves an individual open to higher levels of exposure to daily hassles and negative life events that may precipitate psychological distress (Cannon 1929, Dohrenwend and Dohrenwend 1980, Holmes and Rahe 1967, Kessler and Cleary 1980, Lazarus and Folkman 1984, Lin et al. 1986, Pearlin 1989, Selye 1956, Warheit 1979).

The issues associated with differential vulnerability to life stressors may also be conceptualized as a function of socioeconomic status. When issues of support structures and response resources are considered, persons with higher socioeconomic status have been found to be better equipped to meet the demands posed by life-crisis events or other stressors posed by the social structure. While persons with low socioeconomic status may have a significant number of high quality relationships in their support network, the objective lack of instrumental resources may increase their vulnerability to depressive or other dysfunctional outcomes. Persons of higher SES tend to more readily adapt to meet the demands of comparable stressors.

While all of the above may be viewed within a racial perspective, the dynamics are clearly those of socioeconomic status. Social and psychiatric research associating race with the prevalence of various dysfunctions may often be artifacts not of ethnicity, but of economics. Race may be better considered an invisible proxy for low socioeconomic status due to the disproportionate distribution of resources in our society as a whole, and the overrepresentation of blacks among the poor. In short, what could be happening in the current social research on racial differences in mental health conditions may not be associated with issues of race at all, but rather the ultimate case of spurious causation.

An altogether different possibility for the findings in this chapter may be that the depression items being examined tapped into features of social status and perceived class differences as well as psychiatric symptomatology. Those items that consider variables of future outlook or optimism, eating or sleeping habits, even crying, may be culturally sensitive, and tap into the phenomenon of stratification in an indirect way. Although the FHS was developed from careful and intensive validation procedures over time, it is nonetheless important to note that systematic class biases may still be present.

It is still puzzling that when income was controlled for, blacks showed higher depression scores than whites. One possible explanation for this could be that the income variable is a household income figure, not adjusted for the number of persons residing in the household. The per capita income of black respondents could be lower than corresponding white respondents, thereby negating the stress mediating benefits of income. To examine this possibility, a separate post hoc analysis was performed examining average household size between black and white respondents. A significant mean difference was found between the mean black household size of 3.03 and a mean white household size of 2.67. While this analysis does not prove an argument of diminished per capita income explaining racial differences, it nevertheless lends support to the possible argument of income attenuation for black households.

While the findings in this chapter raise many questions, there are several theoretical, political, and pragmatic implications that should be mentioned. Perhaps the most important issue of significance to the literature is the unexpected power of SES as a predictor of mental health. The tenor of the literature, while recognizing the importance of socioeconomic factors, has usually conceptualized SES as a control variable mediating the impact of some free-standing independent variable. Perhaps the single most significant finding of this research is the implication that more research should be done examining socioeconomic status as a fundamental independent variable. While it was expected that the predictive power of race in the psychosocial dynamics in depression would be moderated by intervening factors such as SES, it was not expected that race would be relegated entirely to an artifact of this construct.

As was expected from a reanalysis of data used by Ulbrich and colleagues (1989), bivariate models found blacks to be significantly more exposed to and more vulnerable to the impact of life-crisis events than whites. Again, however, no statistically significant differences in exposure and vulnerability were found between these two racial groups when the data were controlled for SES. It would seem that a differential vulnerability hypothesis explaining race differences in depressive outcomes fails to take into account that SES is the overwhelming predictor in both exposure and vulnerability phenomena. The debate over racial differences of depressive prevalence being attributable to the factor of either exposure or vulnerability thus seems specious. If race were understood in such arguments as being a proxy for SES, such debate could be meaningful. Clearly, however, as explanations are being sought within the cultural and subcultural differences of minority family structure, urban community infrastructure, educational variables of race, and such racial and ethnically focused sociology, it is clear that race is still considered a significant independent variable.

The political and pragmatic significance of this research, especially as it could effect social policy, are fairly straightforward. The implications of the SES finding raise major questions of social stratification in our society. The most parsimonious understanding available of the current research, simply put, is that poverty is hazardous to one's mental health. In an era of ever diminishing social programs and ever increasing mental health needs, the finding that socioeconomic status may be more strongly related to depression than any of the endogenous or personal characteristics considered has disturbing implications. Social policy may ultimately be our most cost-effective means of addressing mental health protection and treatment. We may need a shift from the current state of neurobiological priorities to a more socially focused consideration of risk factors. A prospective outlook in maintaining mental hygiene may need to be adopted, rather than the retrospective attempt at damage control. Boldly stated, the results of this chapter underscore the concept of "casualties" of a stratified society. Finally, findings such as these, carelessly interpreted, could lead to the conclusion that minority mental health programs are unnecessary. Only by carefully and critically assessing the results of any social psychological research, with a view toward the potential limits of its methods and instruments, can the full picture of class and race dynamics emerge.

APPENDIX A: FHS DEPRESSION ITEMS

Affect—Mood

1. Do you feel in good spirits?
   ___ Very few times ___ Sometimes ___ Most of the time

2. How often do you have crying spells or feel like it?
   ___ Never ___ Seldom ___ Sometimes ___ Often ___ All the time

3. How often do you feel you don't enjoy things anymore?
   ___ Never ___ Seldom ___ Sometimes ___ Often ___ All the time

4. How often do you feel alone and helpless?
   ___ Never ___ Seldom ___ Sometimes ___ Often ___ All the time

5. How often do you feel people don't care what happens to you?
   ___ Never ___ Seldom___ Sometimes ___ Often ___ All the time

6. How often do you feel that life is hopeless?
   ___ Never ___ Seldom ___ Sometimes ___ Often ___ All the time

Body Complaints—Somatic

7. Do you tend to feel tired in the mornings?
   ___ Never ___ Sometimes ___ Often

8. Do you feel that you are bothered by all sorts of ailments in different parts of your body?
   ___ Never ___ Sometimes ___ Often

Psychological Patterns

9. Have you ever had periods of days or weeks when you couldn't take care of things because you couldn't get going?
   ___ Never ___ Seldom ___ Sometimes ___ Often ___ All the time

10. Do you have any trouble getting to or staying asleep?
    ___ Never ___ Sometimes ___ Often

11. How often do you have trouble with sleeping?
    ___ Never ___ Seldom ___ Sometimes ___ Often ___ All the time

12. Do you ever have loss of appetite?
    ___ Never ___ Sometimes ___ Often

continued

APPENDIX A: *(continued)*

Negative Self-Evaluation

13. When things don't turn out, how often would you say you blame yourself?
    ___ Never ___ Seldom ___ Sometimes ___ Often ___ All the time

14. How often do you think about suicide?
    ___ Never ___ Seldom ___ Sometimes ___ Often ___ All the time

15. Life has changed so much in our modern world that people are powerless to control their own lives.
    ___ Strongly disagree ___ Disagree ___ Undecided ___ Agree
    ___ Strongly agree

Future Outlook

16. Do you sometimes wonder if anything is worthwhile anymore?
    ___ Never ___ Sometimes ___ Often

17. How often would you say things don't turn out the way you want them to?
    ___ Always ___ Seldom ___ Sometimes ___ Often ___ All the time

18. How does the future look to you?
    ___ Bad ___ Poor ___ Fair ___ Good ___ Excellent

This appendix is used with the permission of George J. Warheit, Ph.D.

APPENDIX B: CHI-SQUARE COMPARISONS OF LIFE-CRISIS EVENTS BETWEEN BLACKS AND WHITES

	BLACKS (N = 450) %	*WHITES* (N = 1,648) %	*SIG*
Close friend died	33.7	25.2	***
Family member in trouble w/law	12.1	5.8	***
Family member died	36.3	21.1	**
Family member developed illness	10.2	15.3	**
Taken out a large loan	11.2	15.9	**
Unwanted pregnancy	3.8	1.0	**
Been in jail	1.3	0.3	**
Moved two or more times	2.0	4.4	*
Separated from spouse	4.6	2.2	*
Had an accident	6.0	5.5	
Broken a love relationship	7.3	7.6	
Stopped living with a lover	5.0	3.0	
Gotten divorced	2.1	1.9	
Been arrested	1.6	.7	
Fired from a job	3.2	1.7	
Had a miscarriage	2.1	1.0	
Lost a personal object	10.9	9.7	
Been a victim of a crime	6.2	8.9	
Developed a serious illness	5.8	7.0	
Been injured in an accident	6.7	7.4	
Forced to leave school	2.0	2.0	

* p.< .05
** p. < .01
*** p.< .001

REFERENCES

Aneshensel, C. S., Clark, V. A., and Frerichs, R. R. (1983). Race, ethnicity, and depression: a confirmatory analysis. *Journal of Personality and Social Psychology* 44(2):385–398.

Antunes, G., Gordon, C., Gaitz, C., and Scott, J. (1974). Ethnicity, socioeconomic status, and the etiology of psychological distress. *Sociology and Social Research* 58:361–368.

Beck, A. T. (1967). *Depression: Causes and Treatment.* Philadelphia: University of Pennsylvania Press.

Bevis, W. M. (1921). Psychological traits of the southern Negro with observations as to some of his psychoses. *American Journal of Psychiatry* 78:69–78.

Cannon, W. (1929). *Bodily Changes in Pain, Hunger, Fear and Rage.* New York: Appleton.

Comstock, G. W., and Helsing, K. (1976). Symptoms of depression in two communities. *Psychological Medicine* 6:551–563.

Cronbach, L. (1951). Coefficient alpha and the internal structure of tests. *Psychometrika* 16:297–334.

Diagnostic and Statistical Manual (1987). 3d ed. rev. Washington, DC: American Psychiatric Association.

Dohrenwend, B. P., and Dohrenwend, B. S. (1969). *Social Status and Psychological Disorder: A Causal Inquiry.* New York: Wiley-Interscience.

Dohrenwend, B. S. Life events as stressors: a methodological inquiry. *Journal of Health and Social Behavior* 14:167–175.

Dohrenwend, B. S., and Dohrenwend, B. P. (1980). Life stress and illness: formulation of the issues. In *Stressful Life Events and Their Contexts*, pp. 1–27. New Brunswick, NJ: Rutgers University Press.

Eaton, W. W., and Kessler, L. G. (1981). Of symptoms of depression in a national sample. *American Journal of Epidemiology* 114 (4):528–538.

——— (1985). *Epidemiologic Field Methods in Psychiatry: The NIMH Epidemiologic Catchment Area Program.* New York: Academic Press.

Frumkin, R. M. (1954). Race and mental disorders: a research note. *Journal of Negro Education* (23): 97–98.

Gove, W. R., and Tudor, J. F. (1973). Adult sex roles and mental illness. *American Journal of Sociology* 98:812–835.

Greene, E. M. (1914). Psychosis among Negroes—a comparative study. *Journal of Nervous and Mental Disease* 41:697–708.

Hollingshead, A., and Redlich, F. (1958). *Social Class and Mental Illness: A Community Study.* New York: Wiley.

Holmes, T., and Rahe, R. (1967). The social readjustment rating scale. *Journal of Psychosomatic Research* 11:213–218.

Iams, H. M., and Thornton, A. (1975). Decomposition of differences: a cautionary note. *Sociological Methods and Research* 3:341–351.

Jarvis, E. (1971). *Insanity and Idiocy in Massachusetts: Report of the Commission on Lunacy, 1855.* Cambridge, MA: Harvard University Press.

Kessler, R. C. (1979). A strategy for studying differential vulnerability to the psychological consequences of stress. *Journal of Health and Social Behavior* 20:100–108.

Kessler, R. C., and Cleary, P. D. (1980). Stress, social status, and psychological distress. *Journal of American Sociological Review* 45:463–478.

Kessler, R. C., and Neighbors, H. W. (1986). A new perspective on the relationships among race, social class, and psychological distress. *Journal of Health and Social Behavior* 27:107–115.

Kish, L. (1965). *Survey Sampling.* New York: Wiley.

Klerman, G. L. (1987). The nature of depression: mood, symptom, disorder. In *The Measurement of Depression*, ed. A. J. Marsella, R. M. A. Hirschfeld, and M. M. Katz, pp. 3–18. New York: Guilford.

Lazarus, R. S., and Folkman, S. (1984). *Stress, Appraisal, and Coping.* New York: Springer.

Lemkau, P., Tietz, C. and Cooper, M. (1942). Mental hygiene problems in an urban district. *Mental Hygiene* 26:100–119.

Leighton, D. C., Harding, J. S., Macklin, D. B., et al. (1963). *The Character of Danger.* New York: Basic Books.

Lin, N., Dean, A., and Ensel, W. (1986). *Social Support, Life Events, and Depression.* New York: Academic Press.

Lindenthal, J. J., Myers, J. K., Pepper, M. P., and Stern, M. S. (1970). Mental status and religious behavior. *Journal for the Scientific Study of Religion* 9:143–149.

Link, B. G., and Dohrenwend, B. P. (1989). The epidemiology of mental disorders. In *Handbook of Medical Sociology*, ed. H. E. Freeman and S. Levine, pp. 102–127. Englewood Cliffs, NJ: Prentice-Hall.

Lucas, W., and Adams, W. (1977). *An Assessment of Telephone Survey Methods.* Santa Monica, CA: Rand.

Malzberg, B. (1935). Mental disease among Negroes in New York State. *Human Biology* 7:471–513.

——— (1944). Mental disease among American Negroes: a statistical analysis. In *Characteristics of the American Negro*, ed. O. Klineberg, pp. 373–402. New York: Harper.

Mirowsky, J. and Ross, C. E. (1980). Minority status, ethnic culture, and distress: a comparison of blacks, whites, Mexicans and Mexican-Americans. *American Journal of Sociology* 86:479–495.

——— (1989). *Social Causes of Psychological Distress.* New York: Aldine de Gruyter.

Myers, J. K., Lindenthal, J. J., and Pepper, M. P. (1974). Social class, life events, and psychiatric symptoms: a longitudinal study. In *Stressful Life Events: Their Nature and Effects*, ed. B. S. Dohrenwend and B. P. Dohrenwend, pp. 191–206. New York: Wiley.

Nam, C. B., and Powers, M. G. (1983). *The Socioeconomic Approach to Status Measurement.* Houston, TX: Cap and Gown Press.

Neff, J. A. (1984). Race differences and psychological distress: the effects of SES, urbanicity and measurement strategy. *American Journal of Community Psychology* 12:337–351.

Neff, J. A., and Husaini, B. A. (1980). Race, socioeconomic status and psychiatric impairment: a research note. *Journal of Community Psychology* 8:16–19.

O'Malley, M. (1914). Psychoses in the colored race: a study in comparative psychiatry. *American Journal of Insanity* 71:309–337.

Paykel, E., Prusoff, B., and Uhlenhuth, E. H. (1971). Scaling of life events. *Archives of General Psychiatry* 25:340–347.

Pasamanick, B. (1959). *Epidemiology of Mental Disorder.* Washington, DC: American Association for the Advancement of Science.

Pearlin, L. (1989). The sociological study of stress. *Journal of Health and Social Behavior* 30:241–256.

Pettigrew, T. F. (1964). *A Profile of the Negro American.* Princeton, NJ: Van Nostrand.

Powell, T. (1986). The increase of insanity and tuberculosis in the southern Negro since 1860, and its alliance, and some of the supposed causes. *Journal of the American Medical Association* 27:1185–1188.

Prudhomme, C. (1938). The problem of suicide in the American Negro. *Psychoanalytic Review* 25:187–204.

Radloff, L. S. (1977). The CES-D scale: a self-report depression scale for research in the general population. *Applied Psychological Measurement* 1:385–401.

Regier, D. A., Myers, J. K., Kramer, M., et al. (1984). The NIMH epidemiologic catchment area program. *Archives of General Psychiatry* 41:934–941.

Robins, L. N., Helzer, J. E., Orvaschel, H., et al. (1985). The diagnostic interview schedule. In *Epidemiologic Field Methods in Psychiatry: The NIMH Epidemiologic Catchment Area Program,* ed. W. W. Eaton and L. G. Kessler, pp. 143–168. Orlando, FL: Academic.

Robins, L. N., Helzer, J. E., Weissman, M. M., et al. (1984). Lifetime prevalence of specific psychiatric disorders in three sites. *Archives of General Psychiatry* 41:949–958.

Schwab, J. J., Bell, R. A., Warheit, G. J., and Schwab, R. B. (1979). *Social Order and Mental Health.* New York: Brunner/Mazel.

Schwab, J. J., Bialow, M. R., Holzer, C. E., and Brown, J. M. (1967a). Sociocultural aspects of depression in medical inpatients: II. Frequency and social variables. *Archives of General Psychiatry* 17:539–543.

Schwab, J. J., Bialow, M. R., Holzer, C. E., et al. (1967b). Sociocultural aspects of depression in medical inpatients: I. Frequency and social variables. *Archives of General Psychiatry* 17:533–538.

Selye, H. (1956). *The Stress of Life.* New York: McGraw Hill.

Smirnov, N. V., ed. (1961). *Tables for the Distribution and Density Function of t-Distribution.* London: Oxford.

Snider, J. G., and Osgood, C. E. (1969). *Semantic Differential Technique.* Chicago: Aldine.

Srole, L., Langner, T. S., Michael, S. T., et al. (1962). *Mental Health in the Metropolis: The Midtown Study,* vol 1. New York: McGraw-Hill.

Stanton, W. (1960). *The Leopard's Spots*. Chicago: University of Chicago Press.

Star, S. A. (1950). The screening of psychoneurotics in the army: technical development of tests. In *Measurement and Prediction*, ed. S. A. Stouffer, L. Guttman, E. A. Suchman, et al., pp. 486–587. Princeton, NJ: Princeton University Press.

Ulbrich, P. M., Warheit, G. J., and Zimmerman, R. S. (1989). Race, socioeconomic status, and psychological distress: an examination of differential vulnerability. *Journal of Health and Social Behavior* 30:131–146.

Vega, W., Warheit, G., Buhl-Auth, J., and Meinhardt, K. (1984). The prevalence of depressive symptoms among Mexican Americans and Anglos. *American Journal of Epidemiology* 120:592–607.

Warheit, G. (1979). Life events, coping, stress and depressive symptomatology. *American Journal of Psychiatry* 136(4b):502–507.

Warheit, G. J., Auth, J. B., and Vega, W. A. (1985). Psychiatric epidemiologic field surveys: a case for using them in planning assessment and prevention strategies. In *Psychiatric Epidemiology and Prevention: The Possibilities*, ed. R. L. Hough, P. A. Gongla, V. B. Brown, and S. E. Goldston, pp. 165–190. Los Angeles: University of California Press.

Warheit, G. J., Holzer, C. E., and Arey, S. A. (1975). Race and mental illness: an epidemiologic update. *Journal of Health and Social Behavior* 16:243–256.

Warheit, G. J., Holzer, C. E., and Schwab, J. J. (1973). An analysis of social class and racial differences in depressive symptomatology: a community study. *Journal of Health and Social Behavior* 14:291–299.

Weissman, M. M, and Klerman, G. L. (1977). Sex differences in the epidemiology of depression. *Archives of General Psychiatry* 34:98–111.

Weissman, M., and Myers, J. K. (1978). Rates and risks of depressive symptoms in a United States urban community. *Acta Psychiatrica Scandinavia* 57:209–231.

Weissman, M. M., Sholomskas, D., Pottenger, M., et al. (1977). Assessing depressive symptoms in five psychiatric populations: a validation study. *American Journal of Epidemiology* 106:203–214.

11

Oppositional Behavior in Children

ARTHUR G. MONES

Childhood oppositional behavior is among the most prevalent and perplexing symptom patterns confronted by clinicians today (Forehand and McMahon 1981, Horne and Sayger 1990). Youngsters labeled "oppositional" are negativistic, defiant, and argumentative. They ignore rules at home and school. These children appear to be in a relational tug-of-war with parents, teachers, and, at times, their therapists. Oppositional defiant disorder is one of the few diagnoses in our current nosological system (*DSM-IV* 1994) that includes an interpersonal component, that is, one cannot be oppositional by oneself—this problem occurs in relationships. In this chapter I will review and critique existing models of childhood oppositionalism and then present an integrative model for understanding these children within their significant developmental contexts—family, school, community, and culture. The central thesis of this integrative model is that oppositionalism is a common thread that serves as an adaptive strategy for the central tasks of psychological development in childhood—maturity over time, connectedness to one's family, yet also the ability to evolve an independent and separate sense of self. I will argue that all childhood symptomatologies constitute attempts at coping with these central tasks of emotional development and that all have components that refer back to the intent of oppositional behavior—the preservation of the self. Thus it will be suggested that oppositional children, when viewed within multiple contexts, can be seen as adaptive and not pathological. Strategies for treating these children and their families will be presented, highlighted by case examples.

To begin with, two thumbnail sketches of oppositional children are offered:

Example A: Jason, age 10, is very bright but doing poorly in school and has poor peer relationships. He exhibits extremely controlling and defiant behavior at home: refuses to do his chores, refuses to do homework, bullies his younger brother, and ignores parental demands. Both parents are extremely frustrated and angry at the youngster so that a "toxic relationship" has developed, that is, there is a failure to be empathic. The child is viewed as "bad." A younger brother, age 7, is described as "a perfect angel."

Example B: Brenda, age 15, is of average intelligence and has been compliant until the onset of adolescence. She is currently doing poorly in school, listens to heavy metal music, socializes with older boys, is not heeding rules at home, stays out until all hours, and is sexually active with suspected drug experimentation. She alternates between depressive and explosive moods at home. There is intense sibling conflict.

A REVIEW AND CRITIQUE OF CURRENT THEORIES OF OPPOSITIONALISM

In the literature are models of oppositionalism and strategies for treating these children and their parents that can be grouped under three categories: trait theory, cognitive-behavioral theory, and psychodynamic theory. Recently, integrative models have combined psychodynamic and family systems thinking (Wachtel 1994) and a model, while not specifically addressing oppositionalism, that provides useful linkage of intrapsychic and family system dynamics that can be applied to the understanding of childhood oppositionalism (Schwartz 1995). I will attempt to capture the essence of each model and offer a critique of them, with suggestions about aspects that can be incorporated into the integrated model proposed here.

The Trait Model

Turecki (1985) has proposed the term *the difficult child* to describe oppositional youngsters. This theory makes the assumption that the child is born with a genetic predisposition or trait that includes a set of behaviors that can be grouped as oppositional. Such a child typically begins life as a colicky infant, is resistant to environmental change and transition, is demanding and controlling, and refuses to heed rules set forth by adults in his or her life. Consistent with Chess and colleagues (1968), when this basic disposition does not resonate with parental disposition, a "poorness of fit" occurs, leading to inadequate bonding and continuing tension. The focal point of treatment in this model consists of disengaging parents from patterns of blame of themselves and their children and helps them to accept the "character trait" of negativism. Parents take part in supportive group counseling that coaches them in more effective child management.

Critique of Trait Model

Turecki (1985) makes an important contribution to the understanding of oppositionalism by calling attention to the existence of "traits" or individual differences among children that exist from birth. If one observes neonates in the hospital nursery, one sees from the start that some babies are active, some seem to be passive, some seem to be responsive to the human voice and touch; others seem less responsive and perhaps even irritated with such input. It is very important for professionals in medical, mental health, and educational fields to help parents understand the normalcy of variability among children. Lack of acceptance of a child's particular traits can lead to an unproductive and even destructive struggle by parents to make their child into something that the child cannot be. (I will discuss the all-important issue of coercion later in this chapter along with how coercive interactions between parent and child—and between teacher and child—result in toxic oppositionalism.)

On the worrisome side, the focus on traits tends to have much in common with thinking that organizes around the definition of a problem-in-living as a "disease" entity. This thinking has been applied to a myriad of disorders including depression, schizophrenia, alcoholism, eating disorders, and gambling. While there is some literature that presents findings of physiological/genetic underpinnings for these behaviors, there is to date no definitive set of evidence. The danger here is that if a cluster of behaviors is labeled as "oppositionalism," and if this entity is assumed to be built into the child, parents and teachers may resign themselves to the belief that they have a handicapped child. On the one hand, this belief can be strategically useful in diminishing blame as it removes the issue of intentionality from the system, that is, how can a person be responsible for a trait? On the other hand, this belief can be destructive as it will likely limit the expectations for a given child and establish a self-view within the child of being defective. This view also promulgates the viewing of differences between parent and child or among siblings or peers as a judgmental endeavor, that is to say, if you are not like me (the person in power—parent, teacher, etc.) there must be something wrong with you. This belief then sets up a coercive interaction whereby the person in power forcefully attempts to change the child, resulting in the opposite of intentions—an escalation of defiant behavior.

The Cognitive-Behavioral Model

A burgeoning literature in recent years holds that oppositionalism is learned behavior, acquired via a negative reinforcement cycle established within parent–child interaction, resulting in an escalating cycle of coercive behaviors (Barkley 1987, Dadds 1987, Forehand and McMahon 1981, Horne and Sayger 1990, Patterson 1982, Webster-Stratton and Herbert 1994). A typical sequence would be as follows: parent gives command—child noncomplies, whines, yells—parent gives up/withdraws the command rather than listen to a whining and screaming child. The child is thereby reinforced for negativistic behavior. Another version might be as follows: parent gives command—child noncomplies, whines, yells—parent raises voice, repeats command—child noncomplies, yells louder, kicks chair—parent loudly repeats command, threatens child—child complies. Here, while oppositionalism is stopped in the short run, a coercive style of parenting is set in motion for the long run (Forehand and McMahon 1981). Treatment in this model consists of home-based and/or clinic-based programs aimed at educating parents (unfortunately, most emphasize mother-only training) regarding more effective patterns of reinforcement of their children's compliant behavior while extinguishing behavior that is defiant in nature.

Critique of the Cognitive-Behavioral Model

This model offers a more optimistic view of the child than does the trait model in its emphasis on oppositionalism as learned behavior. Treatment is aimed at the establishment of new interactive sequences with more positive outcomes for parents and children. Effective parenting strategies are promoted. This model assertively addresses the problem of coercive parenting, which, according to this author, is at the center of the oppositional struggle. This approach, however, is incomplete from a systems point of view. An important element is missing here, namely, the internal emotional experience of being a parent, being part of a parental team (mother–father), and the emotional experience of individuation for the child as well as the parents. Most of the books and articles promoting this model make note of its limited success beyond age 8. While little explanation for this limitation is offered, one could hypothesize that cognitive development of the growing child, rigid-ification of family structure as children mature, and the complexity of emo-tions in the family system make a straightforward linear approach based on learning principles unlikely to be successful with a large number of cases.

The Psychodynamic Model

Psychodynamic theorists look intrapsychically at the child and understand that the ability of the youngster to say "No" is a crucial step in psychological development (Mahler et al. 1975, Spitz 1957). This capacity reflects the all-important assertion of separateness of the child from the mother, a beginning of the establishment of a self or "I" position. The ability to oppose others, therefore, sets in motion the process of psychological individuation or differ-entiation, which constitutes the central journey of growth for a child. This model normalizes the process by which children assert their own separateness within their family of origin. According to other theorists (Kernberg and Chazan 1991), the process of self-assertion can become problematic when the child has very low self-esteem. In such cases the child enacts with others the drama of feeling bad or unworthy of love. Oppositional behavior can then be used to push others away or to unconsciously arrange/control the interper-sonal scenario so that it results in rejection, that is, "I feel worthless and expect to be rejected by others so I will push you away before you get the chance to reject me." Individual psychotherapy, including child play therapy focusing on the interpretation and working through of the child's intrapsychic conflicts, accompanied by parent counseling, are the mainstays in this model.

Critique of the Psychodynamic Model

This model views oppositionalism as serving a purpose for normal child development. Without stating so directly, oppositional behavior is seen as serving an adaptive purpose, namely, the role of becoming a separate self. One could extrapolate from this model and note a division between healthy oppo-sitionalism that promotes individuation and toxic oppositionalism that is based on blocked individuation. Psychodynamic theory emphasizes the inter-nal world of the oppositional child and links this behavior to the central task of separation-individuation or development of autonomy. Negativism and defiance are inextricably linked to the child's experience as a developing person and his/her sense of self-esteem. A treatment approach would thus need to address this intrapsychic pain as an important dimension of childhood oppositionalism. Unfortunately, the location of oppositionalism in the internal world of the youngster does not account sufficiently for the intricate relationship aspect of this behavior in which the child is embedded, that is, the parent–child struggle, intergenerational influence in the child's life, and self-esteem struggles in the parents that compound struggles experienced by the child. While classical psychoanalytic theory holds to the oedipal struggle as the central interpersonal triangle in a young child's development, there is little flexibility to include the father–child bond, parental conflicts, and their influence on children's behavior and sibling relationships.

Other Approaches

In her integrative model, encompassing psychodynamic and family systems models, Wachtel (1994) views oppositional behavior as a psychological defense. In this approach defiant behavior emanates from an intrapsychic sense of self-loathing and acute vulnerability. Oppositionalism is viewed as essential in normal child development as a central force in the establishment of a sense of autonomy. If the child feels threatened or controlled by others, the negativistic part of the child becomes an overworked defensive strategy that dominates the child's personality structure. Work with the symptomatic child, parents, and siblings attempts to restructure a family system that enhances the growth of self-esteem based on a respect for the child's developing autonomy. Schwartz (1995), while not specifically addressing oppositionalism in childhood, provides a useful Internal Family Systems model that recognizes how human beings create Parts within themselves that serve to protect and buffer stress and trauma to the psyche. Certain Managerial and Rescuer Parts develop to protect the Self of the individual from the experience of overwhelming sadness and vulnerability. Oppositionalism can be viewed as an overworked, sometimes dictatorial Part that can serve as protector against intrapsychic pain and as manager for gaining a sense of control in the interpersonal sphere.

AN INTEGRATIVE/ADAPTATIONAL MODEL OF CHILDHOOD OPPOSITIONALISM

The models reviewed and critiqued above contribute important ways to view and understand childhood oppositionalism. Each offers an important perspective and helpful concepts for application by the frontline clinician working with these cases. There are gaps in each model, however, and none presents a fully comprehensive view of such youngsters. In this chapter I will attempt to weave many of the concepts offered by other theorists into a cohesive, metatheoretical map that can prove useful in clinical work. Interestingly, whether the emphasis is on traits, learning history, or intrapsychic conflict, the common thread among treatment strategies that are highly effective is to disengage parents from patterns of blaming and coercion in their attempts to manage and change their children. This strategy can be extremely challenging. The interpersonal battle for control is very intense and seems to escalate as the child grows older. Missing from the literature is a view of oppositionalism that emphasizes such behavior as a dance of adaptation between child and parents. Once established, and because of its survival value, this choreography is difficult to interrupt. At its core this view posits that oppositionalism is embedded in the development of self that requires key ingredients from intrapsychic, interpersonal, and intergenerational spheres with significant influences from culture and community.

As stated above, one cannot be oppositional by oneself—this problem occurs in relationships. It is helpful, then, to view this perplexing behavior within the family systems context and to understand the adaptive nature of these behaviors in the life of a child and family. It is the thesis of this integrative/adaptational model that oppositionalism is a survival mechanism for children navigating through the challenging seas of growing up in a family. Normal oppositionalism is necessary for psychological growth. Toxic oppositionalism occurs when key systemic factors and conditions interfere with progressive psychological development. It is my view that oppositionalism is not a discrete diagnostic category as presupposed in *DSM-IV* (1994). Instead, oppositionalism pervades, in one degree or another and in variegated forms, all psychological symptomatology of childhood, which in turn are attempts at adaptation and preservation of the development of self (Mones 1998).

OPPOSITIONALISM AS ADAPTATION TO THE PROXIMITY-DISTANCE DIMENSION

To effectively understand oppositionalism, it is essential to place this cluster of aggravating behaviors within the context of the parent–child relationship. There is a "psychological dance," propelled by two very powerful emotional forces, that normally occurs in families. The first of these forces is *the need of children to feel connected* and attached to their parents. This has to do with feeling safe, protected, and loved. Connectedness is the emotional foundation from which a sense of belonging and self-esteem can develop. Equally strong is a second force called *individuation* (also called differentiation). This is the process by which children mature into people, separate from their parents. Individuation represents the journey toward fulfillment of the human potential in the biological, psychological, and social spheres (Bowen 1978, Bowlby 1973, Guerin and Gordon 1983, Mahler et al. 1975, Olson 1988, Spitz 1957).

The dance between connection and individuation varies in accordance with the age of the child and the life cycle stage of the family, but it is a necessary part of development. Children of all ages are aware (albeit unconsciously in most cases) of an existential "truth." They realize that they can never "escape" from their family; whether they remain home or move many miles away, they will always be a son or daughter to these particular parents and always be a sibling to their brothers and sisters. This is in contrast to all other human relationships in which making an exit from the relationship in effect defines the end of the connection. In a family the only option, from the child's point of view, is to regulate the degree of closeness and distance between themselves and their parents. Oppositionalism is a powerful strategy in this struggle. Defiant behavior pushes parents away (makes them angry and emotionally distant) and keeps them involved (managing the child) in one fell swoop. Thus we have a choreography that takes place on the spatial plane. Oppositionalism is a child's way of exercising control within the proximity–distance dimension. The result of this behavior is that the child can exert a semblance of control in the interpersonal sphere (child–parent relationship), thus affording protection and preservation of an autonomous self in the intrapsychic sphere. The self must be preserved at all costs for psychological survival. Oppositionalism, therefore, is a protective psychological strategy that appears to be noxious and disturbing on the surface, yet is essential for the survival of the child and in this very basic sense is adaptive. This can also account for the experience of parents, teachers, and therapists who try to challenge or wrestle with the oppositionalism: while they may win a battle in the short run they can never defeat the strategy of oppositionalism as it serves to protect the very existence of the person. Oppositionalism, in varying degrees, is part of growing at all stages, but it is especially strong during the "terrible twos" when the child may have tantrums and during adolescence when the young person, needing to be most emphatic about his or her statement of being a separate self, may stay out until all hours without calling home, among other worry-provoking behaviors.

Parents attempt to help their children navigate between the forces of connectedness and individuation. Their job description is to create an emotional climate of safety and protection while providing their children with enough space to think, feel, and act in ways that propel them forward on a path of continual growth and self-actualization. The ancient Native American proverb expresses this best: "We bequeath two things to our children. One is roots. The other is wings."

While trying to help their own children with this central life task of being connected and separate, parents themselves are dealing with their own tensions of connectedness and individuation with their own families of origin. The degree to which these forces are in or out of balance will profoundly affect their ability to guide their children.

In addition to the lifelong effects of one's family of origin, there is the impact that the current marital relationship has on the degree of individuation of each of the spouses. Each marital partnership will tend to nurture or obstruct the development and continued growth of each parent. Spouses who are stuck in a stage of disillusionment with each other will tend to blame their partner for their experience of unhappiness. Many couples try desperately to change each other rather than to experience the discomfort and pain of facing their own incompleteness and stunted individuation. As the partners blame and accuse one another, their relationship becomes increasingly polarized. This pattern of interpersonal coercion in the marital sphere becomes an unfortunate model and is often mirrored in the parent–child interaction: "You are to blame for my unhappiness. If I can get you to change and meet my needs I will be happy." Of course this never works. Instead, what results is that the partner digs in his or her heels even further (escalating oppositionalism) and both parents experience greater unhappiness (Nadelson et al. 1984, Scarf 1987). When parents bypass their own journey toward "selfhood" and instead attempt to forcefully shape the life course of their children, a tension will be created that converts the normal, self-affirming energy of the child's separateness into an oppositional struggle that is a no-win intergenerational battle of wills. When couples are able to reach a stage of *mutual acceptance* whereby they diminish their blame of their partner and let go of the coercive need to change them, they begin to experience an empathic connection and a relationship that can supersede and even at times embrace differences (Jacobson and Christensen 1996). When a marital relationship is in the acceptance mode there is great likelihood that each partner will be proceeding on his/her journey of individuation. As each spouse travels toward self-fulfillment, the capacity to parent will be increasingly free to release the need to control the strivings of their children and coercion in the parent–child sphere decreases while an empathic connection develops. The empathic parent–child relationship in which feelings are accepted and validated and differences are accepted and appreciated is rich soil in which healthy oppositionalism will propel unencumbered selfhood for the child.

OPPOSITIONALISM AS ADAPTATION
TO THE TIME DIMENSION

In addition to being inextricably bound to the proximity–distance dimension, families travel through the dimension of time. Once again, on biological, psychological, and social levels, children grow over time. The passage of time and the movement of each family through a life cycle represents another existential truth (Carter and McGoldrick 1989, Haley 1973, 1976, 1980). Children progress from small to large, young to old, immature to mature. This is inevitable. Once again, however, the human brain can apply behaviors, thoughts, and actions to regulate and shape this inescapable process. As examples, a child of 15 can display behavior of a 4-year-old. Also, parents can demand too much maturity from a young child, or can treat an older child in a babyish manner. To make the situation even more complex, most children (and adults) are, at any given time *oscillating* (Breunlin1988, Breunlin et al. 1992) between younger, older, and age-appropriate levels of psychological development. Take as an example a 12-year-old girl in a family whose parents are divorced. The older siblings have left home and the mother, with whom the girl resides, has a chronic illness. In her home context the girl is a devoted caregiver to her mother, taking on many adult responsibilities. At school the girl is out of the loop with her peer group and tends to behave in babyish and unstylish behavior in the social sphere. At the same time, she is an excellent writer and is achieving well in this academic area. We can see that at one cross section of time a child's competencies can be quite diverse given her/his emotional context at any developmental stage. Any given child and adult can be older, younger, or age-appropriate depending on what emotional parts need development and dominance (Schwartz 1995).

In addition, any given child displays maturity or immaturity in accordance with interactions with parents who are also oscillating in their own competencies/levels of maturity. A parent in his/her own struggle with emotional maturation can meet the responsibilities of adult life competently or incompetently. Just as a parent becomes engaged in his or her own struggle with connectedness and individuation, so he/she may be on multilevels within the time dimension. Drug abuse, alcoholism, gambling, and extramarital affairs are examples of short-term soothing strategies in parents who attempt to avoid the anxiety inherent in the assumption of full adult maturation. On the other extreme, some parents may handle the anxieties of life and responsibilities of family life by overmanaging their lives and the lives of their children. If this were not complex enough, the parent–child interactions are compounded by interactions with siblings who have their own competencies/levels of maturity that significantly impact on perceived degrees of freedom and choice for each individual child. (The significant impact of the sibling relationship will be discussed later in this chapter.)

Often, if not always, children who are displaying out of sync behaviors in accordance with developmental expectations—low school achievement, impulsive behavior, withdrawn behavior—will be defined as problem children or oppositional. We see that such oppositional behavior is, in actuality, behavior, thoughts, and feelings that serve as regulators of the time dimension. This behavior and accompanying modes of relating in the world serve to slow down or speed up the developmental clock. It is well documented that child symptomatology occurs most frequently at significant transition points in the family life cycle (Carter and McGoldrick 1989, Falicov 1988, Haley 1973, 1976, 1980). Ongoing change is the norm as time progresses. As children grow from infants to toddlers to school age to adolescence, the way we parent them must be flexible and fitting for the particular psychological needs at any given stage. When the adjustment and transition to new stages cannot be achieved successfully, psychological symptomatology, oppositionalism in its many forms, will likely emerge. Many families learn to regulate the speed and intensity of the interplay of connection and individuation over time as their life cycle unfolds. Successful families are able to apply the brake and accelerator to these forces as they navigate the difficult curves in the road on the way to growing up. Some families, however, have difficulty with this journey. Perhaps divorce, family illness, parental depression, or unemployment have put everyone on edge. As mentioned above, unresolved and out-of-balance issues in the parents' families of origin are powerfully operative at all times. In these families the forces of connection and individuation and maturity over time are out of balance (Beavers 1985, Becvar and Becvar 1988, Olson 1988).

OPPOSITIONALISM PERVADES ALL CHILDHOOD SYMPTOMATOLOGY

While it is treated as a discrete diagnostic category by traditional diagnosticians, it should be evident at this point that oppositionalism, a process utilized by the child to balance the forces of connection and individuation and to regulate the passing of time, is present in different forms in all of the diagnostic categories of childhood psychological symptomatology. It is the turbulence and toxicity of oppositionalism that leads parents and school personnel to refer children for treatment . Childhood symptoms tend to group themselves into two main clusters—symptoms of internalization or symptoms of externalization. Symptoms of internalization would include anxiety reactions, phobias, depression, and somatization. Symptoms of externalization would encompass conduct disorders, overt defiance, substance abuse, promiscuity, and a variety of antisocial behavioral patterns. It should be noted that some symptom pictures are not so clearly categorized. In fact, as discussed above, many children most likely contain multiple coping mechanisms, depending on their context. Most youngsters do demonstrate a dominant mode coping style and it can be useful to think in terms of these clusters as they tend to emanate from families with fairly predictable organization and structure, which then would lead the clinician to formulate treatment plans that can be effective with a particular case.

Families that are enmeshed, characterized by unclear or diffuse boundaries between parental and child generations along with overly sensitized emotional reactivity to one another, will tend to have children with symptoms of internalization (Minuchin 1974). These symptoms, while not typically considered oppositional, can be usefully viewed this way as anxieties or depression in childhood, which very powerfully serve as regulatory devices in an attempt to balance the forces of connectedness and individuation and rate of travel through the ongoing life cycle. For example, anxiety can lead to avoidance of situations and tasks that create discomfort. As a result a child may distance him- or herself from people or tasks, thereby regulating both spatial and competence-maturity (time) dimensions. Depression can serve a similar function when viewed from a systemic vantage point.

The therapist working with a family presenting a child with symptoms of internalization will note and experience an excess of connection in this system but insufficient allowance for individuation or selfhood. Treatment strategies, then, would be aimed at fostering an emotional climate wherein each member of the family is allowed to be heard with his/her "I" statement, that is, an individualized, assertive voice that is accepted and validated within the system. The clinician will pay close attention to the allowance of the expression of negative affect and ability of the family members to handle differences and conflict. Interventions would open up the family so that the individual selves of the family members can exist in a better balance with the holistic forces of the family system.

Families that are disengaged, characterized by an excess of separateness with a dearth of emotional bonding with one another, tend to produce children who manifest symptoms of externalization. The most extreme families in this category would be children without a sense of permanence from early childhood, for example, children placed in foster care or institutions. It should be noted that some intact families fail to achieve emotional bonding. These symptoms are in their way regulatory devices or "homeostatic maintainers" (Fishman 1988), other forms of the child's attempts to balance the forces of connection and individuation. Relationships in such families appear to be devoid of emotional reactivity to one another. Responsibility for behavior is largely externalized and actions appear to be hurtful and uncaring toward others.

For families with children who manifest symptoms of externalization, therapeutic interventions would be aimed at fostering emotional attachments by cultivating and strengthening the parental/executive system of the family so that clear leadership and rules of socialization can provide some glue for the cohesion of the family unit. Working to establish bonds of connection and loyalty within the sibling subsystem can reinforce this process.

COERCIVE FAMILY FORCES: A CLOSER LOOK

Thus far in this chapter we have reviewed the major models that conceptualize oppositionalism in childhood. A common theme throughout these models, at times emphasized and at other times assumed, is the interpersonal process of coercion between parents and children as a centerpiece of the family struggle. Coercion can be defined as the attempt of one person to force his/her will onto another human being. While in most human interactions there is the ability to cancel this exertion of power by exiting the interaction, in family systems, as mentioned above, there is no escape. As a result, the use of force either physically or mentally is a major factor influencing the degree of self-development in a family. Coercive parenting will settle the conflict in the short run: the more powerful usually dominate the less powerful. However, this disciplinary strategy robs a child of the means for establishing a regulatory style that is self-governing—the ultimate aim in child development that will allow a young person to be emotionally launched with success into the world. Parents with symptomatic youngsters tend to be either overly coercive in forcing their children to obey or inhibited and guilt-ridden regarding the assertion of their own views and values (Patterson 1982). Too much coercion or too little leadership/guidance will leave the child struggling with the inability to be or fear of being an assertive self (symptoms of internalization) or with the tendency to be a "bully" without regard for the rights of other selves with whom he/she interacts (symptoms of externalization). It appears that the key to successful parenting is the ability to respect the separate right to selfhood of one's children. This ability of capable parenting needs also to be embedded in contexts of mutual respect, equality, and noncoercion within the marital sphere and as an adult in one's family of origin.

It should be noted that parents are also the targets of coercion from their children. In fact, an operational definition of childhood oppositionalism in its concrete forms, such as temper tantrums, excessive demandingness, and refusal to cooperate, has at its core coerciveness on the part of the child. The dominance of this behavior on the part of the child is an exertion of power by an individual who most likely feels quite powerless and vulnerable but has not the means to fully experience or express such painful emotions.

SIBLING INFLUENCE ON CHILDHOOD OPPOSITIONALISM

In addition to the focus on the parent–child dimension of oppositionalism, it is important to mention the very powerful influence of sibling relationships on this behavior. The balance of connectedness and individuation is affected by and is regulated in this key family subsystem. To date there is little mention in the literature regarding the impact of sibling interaction on the development of oppositional tendencies. The family territory tends to get carved up by siblings whose selfhood appears to become skewed because of the space/identities already occupied. For example, if one sibling is "the athlete," the other sibling may need to distinguish herself by being "the student," and so on. Siblings can be extremely coercive with one another. Fighting between brothers and sisters can be powerful assertions of fairness and the right to be a separate person with a different point of view. It is not surprising that so many sibling relationships are complementary rather than symmetrical. The experience of one's family environment tends to be vastly different among siblings (Bank and Kahn 1982, Dunn and Plomin 1990). The proximity–distance and time dimensions are further regulated by the presence and forcefulness of one's brothers and sisters. In his clinical experience, the author has observed the profound impact that the privilege and power of an older sibling can have on a younger sibling with an accompanying dynamic of powerful-powerless interaction. Conversely to this dynamic is the sense of loss and threat felt by older siblings upon the arrival of younger brothers and sisters. According to Sulloway (1996), birth order appears to have a significant impact on whether an individual tends to join with the existing order of family life and societal values (predominantly older born) or will tend to question, challenge, and rebel against the existing order (predominantly younger born).

Once again, adding to even greater complexity, we need to consider that parents are also siblings in their respective families of origin. The experience of each parent as an older born, younger born, or only child will influence their responsiveness to one another (Toman 1976, 1993). This in turn will influence how differentially they respond to their own children. Within the marriage the recapitulation of sibling experiences of equality/inequality and power/powerlessness, and so forth will directly affect approaches to parenting in a cooperative or competitive manner.

Sibling position also has a powerful effect on the experience of gender. In a family, how a male child is treated differentially from a female child will have lifelong influences on each person that will inevitably become transmitted from their families of origin to their relationships with their own children. The definition of being a man or being a woman emanates from family-of-origin history and is conveyed from generation to generation in subtle and overt ways. This has important repercussions not only for each family but for our communities and society as well.

It should be noted that sibling relationships also contain a very positive potential for emotional growth. Sibling relationships can serve to compensate for deficiencies in the parent–child sphere. Where parents are unavailable for emotional bonding and attachment, siblings can sometimes rely on each other to provide these basic psychological needs. Sibling attachment can be very significant in single-parent families or families where parental resources are limited. While sibling fighting can be quite intense, as families allow for the successful resolution of such conflict, children can emerge with useful interpersonal tools that can foster their success in future relationships.

CULTURAL INFLUENCES AND CHILDHOOD OPPOSITIONALISM

Each family is embedded in a particular culture. The customs, beliefs, and values of that culture are transmitted to the child via the family filter. Families in which the current generation has recently arrived from another country face the daunting task of bridging their practices and beliefs with those of the American culture. Some aspects will be the same; some may be quite different. It can be stated that, with the exception of Native Americans, all Americans have experienced this challenge either recently or in generations past. Some came to this country of their own free will and others, notably

African-Americans and oppressed refugees fleeing for their lives, came here against their will or as a matter of basic survival (Breunlin et al. 1992, McGoldrick 1989). While cultures influence expectations of child development, it is this author's opinion that the job description of parents of all cultures is the same: to foster physical and emotional health, safety, and security in their children and to guide each child toward maturity and a sense of competence, that is, an ability to manage the tasks of living with a belief that what the person does will make a difference in the world.

Practices that interfere with these universal human rights occur in some families. Violation of the physical or emotional integrity of the person, such as physical or sexual abuse in children and marital violence, can never be excused, regardless of cultural background (Mones and Panitz 1994). More subtle practices such as male privilege over women are equally destructive. Thus there are two significant rules of thumb when considering cultural influence: first, therapeutic interventions, to be effective, must be applied with a careful understanding of cultural context. Second, any practices that diminish the status of an individual within a family system and serve to oppress another human being cannot be excused as culture bound and must be challenged by the therapist.

On a societal scale, oppression in the form of discrimination against minority cultures and policies that foster poverty lead to a sense of *powerlessness* in the family that can only block the development of competence, thereby disqualifying certain children from progressing on their journey of individuation (Fulmer 1989, Greene 1995, Hines 1989). The dimensions of proximity–distance and maturity over time will be severely restricted, leading to anger and hopelessness and eventually resulting in subgroups of families who will become primed for oppositionalism toward the larger society and whose children, having no other choice, will inherit oppositional modes of thinking, feeling, and behaving.

Clinicians working with families will need to be cognizant of the variety of beliefs and customs of many cultures and will need, on a case-to-case basis, to be clear and strong advocates for empowering families and ensuring that equality and respect are the rules that govern family systems.

SCHOOLS, FAMILIES, AND OPPOSITIONAL CHILDREN

Schools play a significant role in responding to difficult children. Most school systems are quite successful in dealing with children who are of average and above-average intelligence and who are compliant in behavior, adhering to the basic rules of the classroom. What distinguishes the really effective school is the ability of its administrators and teachers to work with children who are outside the norm either on an academic level or conduct level. Even with good intentions, school systems can often appear to be punitive toward children who are struggling and insensitive to the needs of families with troubled youngsters. Any attempt to shape up the child without at first working to understand the individual student and his/her emotional background will be experienced as yet an additional form of coercion by the child and parents and will be met, predictably, with escalating oppositionalism and noncooperation.

Schools have a special opportunity to help parents understand their challenging children and to foster ways that the family can receive help. The key to this opportunity is the creation of the school–family collaboration in which the school cultivates a *relationship* and *process* of meetings that include the parents and identified child along with school personnel who are knowledgeable about the youngster and about appropriate resources for problem solving (Sherman et al. 1994, Weiss and Edwards 1992). Engaging the family in information gathering and joining with them in problem solving closes the gap between an "us" versus "them" mentality that all too often exists between families and schools. This is an especially important structure for those families who experience a deep sense of powerless due to cultural differences or minority status.

This process is not especially difficult to organize; it is based largely on the philosophy of the leadership in each school and the willingness to provide the time (not exorbitant) to work in a humanistic manner with families who are often confused and, at times, ashamed of the difficulties being exhibited. The successful implementation of this process is also largely dependent on the belief system and tenacity of the family therapist to be insistent on advocating for the rights of the child and family. The reader will note the parallel theme of removing coercive interactions within the family and doing the same between family and the main societal institution with which their children interact—their school. Just as treatment is aimed at diminishing coercion and cultivating relationships in the family wherein empathy and understanding prevail, so schools can foster the same process toward empowering families.

A brief mention will be made at this point about the use of psychotropic medication with oppositional children. While medication can potentially be a short-term solution to settling down a difficult child, the result of this experience can be devastating to the child and family unless the decision making about medication is carefully discussed. Without a collaborative and educative process regarding this decision, the child will likely have a major blow to his or her self-esteem, feeling damaged and setting him or her and the family on a path of believing that they are dealing with a chronic illness. This belief will ultimately intensify the already gnawing feelings of power-lessness around the symptomatology and will likely set in motion a shame reaction that will pervade the family system. Decisions regarding medication and, for that matter, the need for special educational services or consideration to hospitalize a youngster, must be made carefully and rationally, always keeping in mind whether such a decision will ultimately foster or impede the central task of those guiding the child's development, that is, a continuing balance of connection and individuation. This is an extremely powerful deci-sion in a child's life and needs to be made with the participation of the child and family. If not, once again coercive forces will dominate and opposition-alism will intensify. The issue is not whether these decisions are right or wrong but whether the process of making the decision fosters emotional health. In other words, the means to the ends are as significant as the ends in themselves, or more so.

CASE EXAMPLES

Heather, age 10, was struggling in school with her academic subjects. She exhibited withdrawn behavior in the classroom and often clownish actions when interacting with her peer group. Heather displayed a depres-sive stance, looking sad and viewing herself as a failure. Her father, of Middle-Eastern extraction, had immigrated to the United States in late adolescence at a time when political upheaval engulfed his country of ori-gin. The father and his family had to leave abruptly, abandoning most of their worldly possessions and life as they had known it for many genera-tions. In America he had started a construction business that was currently in financial difficulty. The mother was American-born of a middle-class family and worked as a teacher in an elementary school. Heather had an older sister who was a high achiever in school and quite successful in the social sphere. She had a younger brother who had a winning personality and was coddled and doted upon by parents and grandparents alike.

Upon first encounter, Heather presented as a withdrawn, insecure child with little belief in her self-efficacy. Her mother hovered over her for sev-eral hours each evening attempting to monitor and help her with her homework. The mother read everything available on "special" children and attempted to micromanage Heather's life by trying strategy upon strategy to motivate her daughter. Many tutors were hired with very unproductive results. It appeared as though the mother was taking on a second career in trying to help her child. Periodically the father would vent his anger at Heather, calling her lazy and viewing her as disrespectful to her parents. He was also extremely angry at the school for not being able to educate his child adequately. The parents were divided in their approach to helping their daughter, which resulted in much tension. In a series of assessment sessions, the family was introduced to a systems approach to this problem. Placing the focus on the system as a whole and gradually defining the problem and hoped-for solutions as being in the realm of responsibility of the entire family relieved and engaged Heather, who heretofore felt that she was to blame for all of the difficulties. Parents, Heather, and siblings were enlisted to try to understand and point toward strategies for helping this youngster. The therapist asked the parents to place their frustration and anger on the sidelines so that they could hear the concerns of their child. Heather admitted being confused and having difficulty with fully grasping reading in several of her subjects. This resulted in her feeling bad about her abilities and led to a pattern of avoidance of schoolwork. She expressed that her mother was driving her crazy by her incessant attempts to manage her and to "fix" the problem and that her father was being a "bully," which made her madder and madder, resulting in less willingness to comply and do her work.

The therapist worked with the parents to revise their strategies, noting how devoted they were to their children but that their attempts at helping were actually backfiring and not allowing sufficient room for their daughter to develop her own separate self. They began to see that Heather struggled with the ability to tolerate frustration with her learning difficulties and that they were blocking their daughter's entitlement to express her own needs and emotions when they were not consonant with their own feelings. With Heather's newfound engagement in the process of being understood in a nonthreatening manner, the therapist and parents met with key school personnel to evaluate her learning needs. (Heather was invited to attend this meeting but requested that her thoughts be represented by the therapist and parents at this point, saying that she was "shy" about participating in a meeting with all adults. This request was respected and Heather's clear statement of her feelings was validated.) The school personnel were quite receptive to helping and pledged their commitment to this process. Heather cooperated in a subsequent learning evaluation, which resulted in recommendations for Resource Room assistance (one period per day of extra help with reading and receptive language skills). Over time, the therapist coached Heather's mother to disengage from the battle to "fix" her daughter. Much processing needed to be done to help the parents with their acceptance of the reality that their daughter had actual learning difficulties. As this process progressed (not always smoothly), the father softened his approach to his daughter and, with encouragement in therapy, began spending some enjoyable one-on-one time with her, doing some special projects around the house. The father's accusatory stance toward the school began to diminish as he observed their attempts to help his daughter. Heather steadily felt better about herself as a person, resulting in a less defensive stance interpersonally and in the cultivation of some close friendships.

Over time, Heather began to genuinely enjoy the school environment where, although not a high achiever, she completed her work without resentment and shame and was recognized by teachers and peers as being a caring and kind human being. The school would frequently give Heather special assignments, as a monitor, for example, which served to enhance her growing sense of self-esteem. Periodic school meetings were scheduled to monitor progress and family systems treatment continued over time to ensure Heather's progression along the road to psychological individuation and growth.

While the above case displays a summary of work done with a child with symptoms of internalization, the following example is of a family system that exemplifies a struggle with symptoms of externalization.

Jamie, age 7, typifies an aggressive youngster who displays overt defiance at home and at school. He is African-American and was born out of wedlock. A younger brother, age 4, born to this mother and a different father, had been placed in foster care at age 1. His mother was the older of two siblings in her family of origin, which was an intact family. Her younger sibling, a brother, was developmentally disabled. There was no contact between Jamie and his biological father.

The mother, age 22 and 25, respectively, at the birth of her sons, was severely depressed and very dependent on her parents for emotional and financial support. The mother had a history of abusing a whole range of drugs, including heroin.

At the point of referral, the grandparents were essentially raising Jamie. The mother had enrolled in an intensive drug rehabilitation treatment program. The school had referred Jamie as he was aggressive on the playground with other students, speaking disrespectfully to teachers, and doing little schoolwork. The initial treatment was working with the grandmother (the grandfather declined to be involved), coaching her regarding effective disciplinary strategies with Jamie and making a liaison with the school. Jamie was also engaged in individual therapy sessions aimed at fostering a consistent and trusting relationship in which he could be understood and his behavior could be monitored.

Over time, the mother successfully completed her rehab program and was employed part-time. At that point she expressed an interest in regaining her family and brought Jamie into her home. Shortly thereafter she brought her younger son to join them with the consent of the foster care agency. At this stage the task of therapy was essentially to build a family among a threesome where there was little basic emotional bonding. Therapy consisted of work with the mother and sons in various combinations. Involvement of the grandmother continued but began to taper off. Treatment was focused on helping the mother to become an effective parent to her children, inclusive of the application of effective disciplinary strategies. She learned that short-term, punitive measures to squelch Jamie's defiant behavior would be effective only within a relationship that was reliable and trusting. While the road to accomplishing this was quite stormy at times, progress occurred as the mother demonstrated greater stability and commitment to a leadership role in this family. At various points Jamie would challenge this leadership forcefully, stating in words and behavior both at home and at school, "Why should I trust the permanence of this parent?"

Interestingly, while the brothers were quite competitive with one another for their mother's attentiveness, they gradually became strongly connected and fiercely loyal and protective of one another. The mother became engaged in her own therapy regarding her continued individuation and completed a training program to become a counselor in the drug rehab program from which she graduated. She very cautiously rebuilt her social network, carefully monitoring her judgment. The school, upon the sustained effort of the therapist, served as a consistent and trusting context within which the boys and the mother could develop trust in the outside world. As the mother continued her self-development, while not perfect, Jamie's defiant behavior began to diminish. This family is committed to ongoing monitoring and therapy as they face the challenges of various stages of their life cycle.

CONCLUSION

This chapter attempted to present a conceptual map for understanding oppositional behavior as being embedded in the multifaceted contexts of the family system. Existing theories on defiant behavior were reviewed and critiqued and served as a foundation for the integrative approach offered here.

Oppositionalism is viewed as being part of the normal developmental challenge for a child who will need to stay connected and yet be a separate self within the family unit. This behavior and approach to life is viewed as adaptive, not pathological. The child, along with his/her parents and siblings, needs to navigate a course that includes the proximity–distance and time dimensions. Each family subsystem will exhibit a degree of coerciveness reactive to the anxiety attached to the struggle for self-development. The author attempted to demonstrate that oppositionalism is embedded in the full range of childhood problems, inclusive of symptoms of internalization and symptoms of externalization.

The model presented here recognizes the importance of the cultural context of each family and the need for the clinician and others interacting with the family to be mindful of influences of different cultures as well as the emotional interface of these influences that affect a family's sense of power and powerlessness within the dominant culture. This model also emphasizes the universal processes of equality and mutual respect that are prerequisites for healthy family functioning regardless of cultural influence. The important impact and therapeutic potential of inclusion of the school system in a family–school collaboration was discussed.

Treatment of families with oppositional children will aim at helping to interrupt coercive, no-win struggles and to help parents view the adaptational nature of their children's behavior. Psychotherapy for these families will need to tune in to the intrapsychic conflicts of family members and the beliefs and cognitions of each individual as well as the interactions among the members of a family unit, inclusive of intergenerational factors.

Disengaging parents from coercive interactions with their children is the centerpiece of work with oppositionalism. For children with internalized symptoms, this will take the form of allowing greater room for the child to be an assertive individual, able to disagree and still feel accepted. For children with externalized symptoms, greater leadership and executive functioning of parents will be encouraged as a safe, trusting backdrop for effective nurturing and discipline. Finding solutions for a better balance of the forces of connection and individuation and for propelling the family forward through the life cycle will most effectively involve work with the entire family system. Some oppositionalism will remain, but in tolerable, healthy doses.

The concepts and application of this model are consonant with the hopes of most parents—to see their children grow into happy and emotionally healthy human beings within the context of family balance and harmony.

REFERENCES

Bank, S., and Kahn, M. (1982). *The Sibling Bond*. New York: Basic Books.

Barkley, R. A. (1987). *Defiant Children: A Clinician's Manual for Parent Training*. New York: Guilford.

Beavers, W. R. (1985). *Successful Marriage*. New York: Norton.

Becvar, D. S., and Becvar, R. J. (1988). *Family Therapy: A System Integration*. Boston: Allyn & Bacon.

Bowen, M. (1978). *Family Therapy in Clinical Practice*. New York: Jason Aronson.

Bowlby, J. (1973). *Separation: Anxiety and Anger*. New York: Basic Books.

Breunlin, D. (1988). Oscillation theory and family development. In *Family Transitions: Continuity and Change over the Life Cycle*, ed. C. J. Falicov, pp.133–158. New York: Guilford.

Breunlin, D., Schwartz, R., and MacKune-Karrer, B. (1992). *Metaframeworks; Transcending the Models of Family Therapy*. San Francisco: Jossey-Bass.

Carter, B., and McGoldrick, M. (1989). *The Changing Family Life Cycle*. 2nd ed. Boston: Allyn & Bacon.

Chess, S., Thomas, A., and Birch, H. G. (1968). *Temperament and Behavior Disorders in Children*. New York: International Universities Press.

Dadds, M. (1987). Families and the origin of child behavior problems. *Family Process* 26:341–357.

Diagnostic and Statistical Manual of Mental Disorders. (1994). 4th ed. Washington, DC: American Psychiatric Association.

Dunn, J., and Plomin, R. (1990). *Separate Lives; Why Siblings Are so Different*. New York: Basic Books.

Falicov, C. J. (1988). *Family Transitions: Continuity and Change over the Life Cycle*. New York: Guilford.

Fishman, H. C. (1988). *Treating Troubled Adolescents*. New York: Basic Books.

Forehand, R., and McMahon, R. (1981). *Helping the Noncompliant Child: A Clinician's Guide to Parent Training*. New York: Guilford.

Fulmer, R. (1989). Lower-income and professional families: a Comparison of structure and life cycle process. In *The Changing Family Life Cycle*. 2nd ed., ed. B. Carter and M. McGoldrick, pp. 545–578. Boston: Allyn & Bacon.

Greene, B. (1995). African American families: a legacy of vulnerability and resilience. *National Forum* 75(3):26–29.

Guerin, P. J., Jr., and Gordon, E. M. (1983). Trees, triangles and temperament in the child centered family. *Compendium II, The Best of the Family, 1978–1983*. Rye, NY: Center for Family Learning.

Haley, J. (1973). *Uncommon Therapy*. New York: Norton.

——— (1976). *Problem-Solving Therapy*. San Francisco: Jossey-Bass.

——— (1980). *Leaving Home: The Therapy of Disturbed Young People*. New York: McGraw-Hill.

Hines, P. M. (1989). The family life cycle of poor black families. In *The Changing*

Family Life Cycle, ed. B. Carter and M. McGoldrick, 2nd ed., pp. 513–544. Boston: Allyn & Bacon.

Horne, A. M., and Sayger, T. V. (1990). *Treating Conduct and Oppositional Defiant Disorders in Children*. New York: Pergamon.

Jacobson, N. S., and Christensen, A. (1996). *Integrative Couple Therapy*. New York: Norton.

Kernberg, P. F., and Chazan, S. E. (1991). *Children with Conduct Disorders*. New York: Basic Books.

Mahler, M., Pine, F., and Bergman, A. (1975) . *The Psychological Birth of the Human Infant: Symbiosis and Individuation*. New York: Basic Books.

McGoldrick, M. (1989). Ethnicity and the family life cycle. In *The Changing Family Life Cycle*, ed. B. Carter and M. McGoldrick, 2nd Ed., pp. 69–90. Boston: Allyn & Bacon.

Minuchin, S. (1974). *Families and Family Therapy*. Cambridge, MA: Harvard University Press.

Mones, A. G. (1988). Oppositional children and their families: an adaptational chance in space and time. *American Journal of Orthopsychiatry* 68(1):147–153.

Mones, A. G., and Panitz, P. E. (1994). Marital violence: an integrated systems approach. *Journal of Social Distress and the Homeless* 3(1):39–51.

Nadelson, C., Polonsky, D. C., and Mathews, M. A. (1984). Marriage as a developmental process. In *Marriage and Divorce*, ed. C. Nadelson and D. C. Polonsky, pp. 127–141. New York: Guilford.

Olson, D. H. (1988). Family types, family stress and family satisfaction: a family developmental perspective. In *Family Transitions: Continuity and Change over the Life Cycle*, ed. C. J. Falicov, pp. 55–80. New York: Guilford.

Patterson, G. (1982). *Coercive Family Process*. Eugene, OR: Castalia.

Scarf, M. (1987). *Intimate Partners: Patterns in Love and Marriage*. New York: Ballantine.

Schwartz, R. (1995). *Internal Family Systems Therapy*. New York: Guilford.

Sherman, R., Shumsky, A., and Rountree, Y. (1994) *Enlarging the Therapeutic Circle: The Therapist's Guide to Collaborative Therapy with Families and Schools*. New York: Brunner/Mazel.

Spitz, R. (1957). *No and Yes: On the Genesis of Human Communication*. New York: International Universities Press.

Sulloway, F. (1996). *Born to Rebel*. New York: Pantheon.

Toman, W. (1976). *Family Constellation*. New York: Springer.

——— (1993). *Family Therapy and Sibling Position*. Northvale, NJ: Jason Aronson.

Turecki, S., with Tonner, L. (1985). *The Difficult Child*. New York: Bantam.

Wachtel, E. F. (1994). *Treating Troubled Children and Their Families*. New York: Guilford.

Webster-Stratton, C., and Herbert, M. (1994). *Troubled Families/Problem Children*. New York: Wiley.

Weiss, H. M., and Edwards, M. E. (1992). The family–school collaboration project: systemic interventions for school improvement. In *Home–School Collaboration: Enhancing Children's Academic and Social Competence*, ed. S. Christenson and J. C. Conoley, pp. 215–243. Colesville, MD: National Association for School Psychologists.

12

Is it Schizophrenia, Spirit Possession, or Both?

MIRIAM AZAUNCE

INTRODUCTION

"I am anxious and cannot sleep. My father wants me to leave my husband because he thinks that my husband has caused this upon me. He is a voodoo priest—that's how he knows."

"The devil is in me working against what God is trying to do for me. Once God takes the devil out of me (through divine healing), I will be well again."

"My problem is a spiritual problem. The spiritualist told me that my husband wants me out of the way to proceed with another relationship. What I need to do is stay away from him so that he is unable to 'put something on' me."

"My father's girlfriend, who is jealous of my success, put something in the black cake I ate and now I am sick."

The above statements are examples of chief complaints made by patients who presented for psychiatric treatment at a large urban hospital situated in an area where the largest number of Caribbean individuals living away from the Caribbean have settled. Many of these patients have been given the diagnosis of schizophrenia, which guides a treatment plan that is supposedly designed to promote improvement in functioning. It is a treatment plan that usually prescribes psychotropic medications and some form of talk and/or activity therapy. It is a treatment plan that is developed in the tradition of Western psychiatry and psychology.

Though in some sense most of these patients recognize that the behaviors that brought them to treatment are devalued, seen as negative, and are disrupting of their social lives, the explanations they offer for their own behavior reflect quite a different understanding of human suffering than that emphasized within the Western tradition. These patients employ a system of cultural symbols and meanings, usually learned and internalized during socialization, to explain the emergent disturbing and disruptive behaviors. They claim that, in some way, external, nonobservable, and nonmaterial forces—spirit possession and supernatural interference—have negatively impacted on their everyday lives. This viewpoint is reflective of a belief system about illness and wellness that draws from these individuals' religious and spiritual world views (Griffith and Young 1988). It is a belief system that is considered sacred, with social practices in accordance with this system, and with an accompanying method of mental health care that experts steeped in this tradition believe to be viable and effective.

Paradoxically, the problems discussed above are usually presented for alleviation of suffering at the doors of institutions that use a Western paradigm of diagnosis and treatment. Mental health professionals are therefore faced with the challenge of how to effectively diagnose and treat an affliction that is clearly defined by the patient from a different cultural and religious/spiritual frame of reference.

This chapter poses the question of whether the culturally determined phenomenon of spirit possession, a concept with a religious/spiritual base, is in fact a major symptom of a mental disorder such as schizophrenia and according, to Western tradition, should be treated as such—with psychotropic medication and psychotherapy—or if such behavior should be more accurately described as resulting from supernatural forces and treated from that perspective. Furthermore, is it possible that these two points of view can coexist and find expression within the same host? In other words, is it a psychiatric and/or psychological problem, a spiritual problem, or both? The two cultural frames of reference that produce these questions are explored below.

SCHIZOPHRENIA: BIOMEDICAL AND PSYCHOLOGICAL PERSPECTIVES

According to criteria given in the fourth edition of *Diagnostic and Statistical Manual of Mental Disorders* (*DSM-IV* 1994), schizophrenia is a clinical syndrome of unknown etiology and pathophysiology that is based on a pattern of characteristic signs, symptoms, and course of illness. Specifically, schizophrenia is characterized primarily by disturbances in feelings, thoughts and behavior, that is, delusions, prominent hallucinations, formal thought disorder such as incoherence or marked loosening of associations, abnormal affect (i.e., flat or grossly inappropriate), or psychomotor difficulties. At least two of these features must exist and last for at least six months for the diagnosis of schizophrenia to be given. Moreover, maladaptive behaviors as evidenced by educational and/or vocational dysfunction, and a deterioration in functioning in such areas as activities of daily living skills, and social relations, should be apparent. This description of schizophrenia reflects both positive signs (symptoms that are additions to, or distortions of, normal functioning, such as hallucinations) and negative signs (symptoms that are abnormal because of their absence, such as social withdrawal and poverty of speech).

Someone who has been diagnosed with schizophrenia is generally treated with antipsychotic medications found to be useful for eliminating delusions and hallucinations and ameliorating thought disorder. These medications influence brain chemistry, presumably correcting chemical imbalances in the brain. This treatment approach draws from the biomedical paradigm. Schizophrenia here is conceptualized as a disease process in the brain that involves some abnormalities in brain structures or neurochemistry.

Most investigators within this Western tradition subscribe to the view that the disease is triggered by an interaction between biological and environmental factors. Thus, in addition to antipsychotic medications, some form of social and psychological intervention is often prescribed for a person who is schizophrenic. This approach addresses environmental and psychological factors that may have contributed to the development of the disorder and draws from psychological paradigms for an understanding and treatment of the illness.

Social learning theorists, for instance, emphasize the disturbed early relationship between the child and caregiver. They believe that schizophrenia may develop in individuals who, as children, learned irrational ways of behaving and thinking by identifying with and imitating caregivers who display negative attitudes and may have their own emotional difficulties. Interpersonal problems, so noticeable in schizophrenics, are felt to be the result of poor learning models during childhood. The treatment of choice would be to provide the patient opportunities for new adaptive learning experiences that can promote more appropriate and desirable ideational behavior and affective responses.

Psychodynamic models emphasize the hypersensitivity to perceptual stimuli as a deficit that places stress on interpersonal relatedness. These models are based on the premise that psychotic symptoms have meaning in schizophrenia and can be understood as a defense against intrapsychic anxiety, for example, a victim of spousal abuse expressing paranoid ideations. Through some insight-oriented approach, therefore, the goal is to find meaning in the irrational behavior of the schizophrenic and to confront, explore, and understand the symbolic significance of these behaviors.

Whatever the theory that guides the treatment of schizophrenia, Western notions about the disease process assume that, as Fabrega (1989a) noted, the disorder erodes and undermines the organization and functioning of the self in a social system. Fabrega explained that schizophrenia alters and disturbs "an individual's customary sense of self, sense of boundaries between self and others, . . . and the ability of the self to relate meaningfully to the cultural world" (p. 278).

This perspective is guided by the understanding of the self, as described by Gaines (1982) and Landrine (1992), that recognizes a clearly defined distinction between the self and the nonself. In this conception, the self, referred to as the referential self, is understood to be separate and apart from—and independent of—the nonself. It is "the originator, creator, and controller of behavior" (Landrine 1992, p. 402). It has life and attributes of humanness and personness such as awareness, intention, and willed action, whereas the nonself is lifeless and nonhuman (Landrine 1992). Implicitly, not distinguishing between the self and the nonself constitutes psychopathology. For example, insinuating that the nonself has thoughts, feelings, and goals can be seen as pathological, as in the case of the idea that one's behavior is controlled by someone/something other than the self (e.g., demon possession). Moreover, to believe that events within the self such as wishes or feelings can create changes in the nonself, for example, make someone psychotic, is viewed as pathological and magical thinking or a thought disorder. In this tradition, diagnosis specifically looks at the form rather than the theme or content of the behavior. So, diagnostically, it does not matter that the symptom of thought withdrawal can be significant as a mode of experience and as a diagnostic hint. In other words, it is not important diagnostically whether it is the devil or some other person who withdrew the thoughts.

The biomedical and psychological perspectives follow the etic approach, which assumes universal parameters of human functioning that transcend specific cultural differences in human experience. According to this perspective, all human beings are, in some important respects, alike. As such, classifications are determined by external and observer-imposed conventions. This universalistic approach utilizes a scientific framework that is supposedly neutral and not influenced by the beliefs and practices of society for the understanding of psychotic behaviors (Gaines 1992). So the social, psychological, and behavioral properties of schizophrenia and, more generally, mental illness are seen as the same across cultures. Consequently, the techniques to counteract the illness are believed to be effective in any culture. This is an orientation that intentionally and unintentionally works against alternative approaches to the understanding and treatment of the illness and rejects such methods as spiritual healing as an approach to treating the afflicted. It is an orientation that, despite its aims at universal applicability, is in fact an outgrowth of a given cultural system—Western culture.

SPIRIT POSSESSION: A CULTURALLY DIFFERENT PERSPECTIVE

While it is not disputed that behaviors described as psychotic disturbances are universal in the human population, the same behaviors that characterize schizophrenia within the Eurocentric/Western tradition have often been explained and labeled differently in other cultures. Earlier in this chapter examples were given of the ways in which individuals have described their afflictions or personal states in terms of the influence of some external and supernatural force. The idea that one can be influenced by the supernatural or, more specifically, be possessed by a spirit, is not new. The belief in spirit possession has endured for centuries, has always been an integral part of African peoples, and is deeply rooted in religious thinking (Bourguignon 1991, Kiev 1961, Ward and Beaubrun undated). Instances of this phenomenon are still described in both primitive and advanced twentieth century societies (Bourguignon 1991, Ward and Beaubrun undated). Spirit possession is a belief that is also held in most contemporary Christian churches and at all social levels in society (Gopaul-McNicol 1993), though it is not always openly discussed, as Beaubrun (1975) notes in his description of Trinidadian society.

The spirit possession theory attempts to explain the origin of the new personality observed in the possessed and is often used to explain all kinds of misfortunes, for example, frustrations of life, symptoms of illness. One explanation posited is that cultural customs, beliefs, and traditions that may have supernatural premises, sometimes coupled with highly stressful situations, constitute the precipitating factors of possession. Some of the outward manifestations of possession are similar to behaviors observed in the mentally disturbed, for example, delusions, dissociation, or hallucinations. Individuals who are possessed may believe that their thoughts, feelings, and behavior can be controlled by other people or external forces of a supernatural nature. Kiev (1961) has defined the concept of spirit possession as the relationship between a human and a spirit when the human has been incorporated by the spirit. The behavior of the human is then taken to be the behavior of the spirit. Central to this concept is the idea that one is not responsible for one's behavior and is often made to act contrary to one's will.

Reformulated in terms of the self, the concept of spirit possession, in effect, describes how the self becomes connected to external, supernatural forces. This interpretation, which differs from the Eurocentric view, is rooted in the emic perspective, which assumes that behavior is culturally specific, unique, and local to the particular society. The idea that differing cultures, with their customs, traditions, and practices, provide the individual with different constructions of reality and categorizations of the self is well documented (Fabrega 1989a,b, Gaines 1995, Landrine 1992).

In the case of spirit possession, the self is not viewed as an independent entity, but is connected to relationships with others and exists only in this context. Gaines (1982) and later Landrine (1992), referred to this conceptualization of the self as the indexical self. The indexical self is not discrete, bounded, fully separated, or unique. It is conceptualized as a receptacle in social interactions, contexts, and relationships and can consist of persons and forces over which an individual has little control. This formulation, which perceives the self as not responsible for behavior, legitimizes the experience of spirit possession.

Within the Caribbean culture, strong religious and spiritual beliefs form a basis for understanding the concept of possession. These shared beliefs have a considerable hold on the conscious and unconscious life of the individual regardless of his or her level of sophistication. Lefley (1981) identifies Obeah, Voodoo, Espiritismo, and Santeria as prominent belief systems in the Caribbean that share certain commonalities with the Christian and West African religions. They cover a set of beliefs and practices that claim to deal with spiritual forces of the universe, and attempt to keep the individual in harmony with them as they affect his or her life.

In Santeria, for example, it is believed that the soul is immortal, does not expire upon death, and may remain earthbound to have profound effects on a person's life, events, thoughts, and behaviors. For proponents of Voodoo, the world contains two major categories: the visible world including humans, and the invisible world of the dead, spirits, and other supernatural beings (Lefley 1981). Such highly sanctioned beliefs are encouraged in their respective cultures and have been regarded as heavily institutionalized forms of expression that have important roles to play. For example, Garey (1991), looking at religious practices in Haiti, noted that, by possessing a member of a congregation, spirits might punish, admonish, reward, and encourage congregants as well as treat and cure their ills and worries.

The behaviors of the possessed may be perceived not only positively but also negatively. For instance, Rogler and Hollingshead (1961) made a distinction between culturally syntonic and pathological states of possession. They noted that, to those who believe in spirits, persistent hallucinations are not considered symptoms of psychosis. Rather, such behaviors demonstrate the development of psychic faculties that allow the individual to increasingly access the spirit world. On the other hand, "for those whose possessions last longer than the ceremonials warrant it is not legitimized and is considered a form of 'folie'" (Kiev 1961, p. 138). In these cases the individual is believed to be unwillingly possessed by intruding spirits and exhibits maladaptive behavioral responses attributable to the spirits' influence. This condition is characterized by a reduction of higher functioning, including a lack of social inhibitions, distortions in psychomotor behavior, and perceptual disturbances. This type of possession is usually referred to as demon possession.

According to folk belief, demon possession is not an enjoyable experience, can be harmful, and is something to be rid of. It is perceived as an attack upon the individual, often by an angry spirit or an angry individual who has the power to invoke such spirits to "put a curse" on the unsuspecting victim. It is not unusual to hear someone from the Caribbean culture who is afflicted with some malady say, "They must have put something on me." Some Hispanics believe the cause of their maladies to be a *brujeri*, a black magic curse, and possession by spirits who intend to harm or kill them (Garey 1991). It is the dysfunctional behavior often seen in this type of possession that, from a Eurocentric point of view, is ultimately included in the description of the clinical syndrome of schizophrenia. Schizophrenia can be interpreted, therefore, as being attributable to spiritual unrest or restlessness.

In response to this understanding of illness—that it is placed upon one—individuals who share these beliefs are more likely to turn to spiritual healers, such as an obeahman, shango leader, or voodoo priest, than to seek out Western forms of help. The spiritual healer takes into account various aspects of the presenting problem and puts them in the context of the cultural belief in spirits (Gopaul-McNicol 1993). He may act as a vessel through which the spirit world is accessed to determine which evil spirits are creating the individual's difficulties. He may engage in ritualistic behavior as spirits take over his body in an attempt to exorcise them. The spirits that possess these mediums are often identified by their appearance, behavior, and temperament and other human qualities and characteristics as they are manifested in their human agents. Through the medium, the spirit's messages are interpreted to the individual and herbs and ointments, spiritual baths, and prayers are prescribed, much as psychotropic medications used in biomedicine. These treatments are designed to alleviate the affliction and help the individual to gain spiritual strength. People may also seek to protect themselves and/or their property from harm through means such as "wearing a guard."

Spiritual healers who operate in the context of these religious rituals have often been characterized as having healing charisma. It is unclear whether this is so because of a mind-set that facilitates belief in the special powers of the healer or spiritualist or whether the individual may claim that the roots of his or her power reside in some supernatural being (Griffith and Young 1988).

DISCUSSION

Based on the above discussion, it can be concluded that determining whether behavior patterns are viewed as schizophrenia or demon possession depends on cultural and religious belief systems and on how the self is understood and defined. That is, different sets of cultural knowledge are brought to bear on the problem, which lead to different emphases and explanations. Based on this, the treatment of such afflictions can be accomplished by going either to the obeah man, exorcist, or voodoo doctor or to the psychiatrist and/or psychologist; treatment might be faith healing or bush medicine, or it might be psychotropic medication and psychotherapy.

One of the key points in this discussion is the importance of shared belief systems and how they impact on the lives of individuals. One's belief system provides a cognitive framework that gives meaning to behavior and guides how one thinks, behaves, and defines and explains events. It allows one to develop explanatory models about suffering and sickness. Moreover, it is extremely resistant to change "even in the face of flatly contradictory empirical evidence" (Gaines 1995, p. 286).

In the case of demon possession, for instance, the mental health professional is confronted with the need to bring about a cure in a person who believes he or she is possessed, a belief that might be strange and different from that of the professional. This individual not only needs relief from his distress, but also believes that the curative intervention that will expel the intruding spirits that envelop and besiege him or her can be mediated only through special and particular elements delineated in unique spiritual and religious rituals (Griffith and Young 1988). It is argued that those who believe they are possessed by evil spirits will fail to respond adequately to or grow with treatment that cannot give tangible proof that the evil has been extracted from their body. As long as these individuals continue to believe that evil spirits are dwelling in and tormenting them, the healing of a mental disease cannot proceed without assistance of a spiritual healer, who is the only one who can offer this kind of service.

Some clinicians, cited in Garey (1991), contend that belief in supernatural intervention offers a kind of faith that can cure. They suppose that it is what people believe that makes them ill and the reason for the success of exorcism is a shared belief system. Burke (1979), in a discussion of social psychiatry in the Caribbean, noted that, despite efforts to replace traditional therapeutic approaches with modern ones, it is significant that native healers are given more importance than Western ones because there is a persistence in the shared belief in their efficacy and in the belief that emotional problems have spiritual origins. Finkler (1985), discussing traditional healers in Mexico, makes a similar point. These investigators' observations are still relevant today.

Just as research has shown that the efficacy of psychotherapeutic approaches to treatment of mental illness is variable, an examination of the usefulness of spiritual healing offers mixed results. In their article on the therapeutic aspects of Christian religious rituals, Griffith and Young (1988) provided evidence of the usefulness of religious and spiritual practices as curative interventions in psychological healing to the extent that they suggested an incorporation of religious rituals into the context of a healing clinic. Alternatively, Finkler's (1985) investigation of the limitations and strengths of religious healing concluded that religious healing is neither a miraculous cure nor a hoax or sham. In her study, she demonstrated that patients responded differentially to the symbolic treatments of the religious healers. She also observed that they were less effective in dealing with severe psychiatric disorders. To conclude, therefore, that biomedical and psychological approaches to understanding and treatment of the disorder are more efficient than the others seems premature in the face of these research findings.

Nonetheless, primacy continues to be placed on Eurocentric notions of illness and treatment. The medical paradigm is commonly assumed to be "scientific, neutral and set apart from conventional beliefs and practices of the society in which they are found" (Gaines 1992, p. 5). However, Csordas (1992) notes that there is no universal psychiatric reality and that the biomedical paradigm and the spirit possession model should be recognized as belief systems that reflect a particular constructed world. In other words, to explain the religious phenomena of affliction in medical terms is merely to put one world view in place of another (Csordas 1992). Gaines (1992) further cautions that while the study of Western notions of illness and wellness is more formalized, it is not superior to other conceptions of illness and treatment.

As healing systems, spiritualism and biomedicine can be complementary approaches and do not necessarily have to be in competition with each other (Finkler 1985). In fact, Csordas (1992) also contends that demon possession and psychopathology are not necessarily mutually exclusive. Therefore, it is not farfetched to consider that demon possession and schizophrenia can coexist in the same host. Further investigation is required to confirm or reject this idea.

The *DSM-IV* makes an attempt to acknowledge the importance of a patient's cultural belief system by including a description of some culture-bound syndromes. The *DSM-IV* advocates that, as part of the psychiatric evaluation, the clinician take into account the individual's ethnic and cultural context: "The perceived causes or explanatory models that the individual and the reference group use to explain the illness, and current preferences for and past experiences with professional and popular sources of care" (*DSM-IV* 1994, p. 844). However, the *DSM-IV* falls short of legitimizing these syndromes as bona fide diagnoses by not giving codes for these categories of illness. These syndromes therefore will probably not be taken seriously when clinical treatment and managed care and the attendant fiscal considerations are taken into account. Further, while it is not the goal of the *DSM* to discuss treatment, it is unclear how this information informs the treatment of the patient: the question still remains regarding how one treats a culturebound syndrome after having made a cultural formulation. The literature lags behind in presenting appropriate treatment plans for such presentations. This reflects the continued hesitance of professionals to suggest that patients should seek treatment from native healers.

Clinical and Research Implications

Taking into account the individual's cultural and spiritual world views, and recognizing that therapeutic regimes, including biomedicine, are products of a given cultural system has implications for treatment. The healing process would be greatly enhanced if such belief systems are acknowledged and are used within or incorporated into the treatment process, and can be critical to this process (Cancelmo et al. 1990, Griffith and Young 1988). Lack of awareness and knowledge of how religious and spiritual beliefs may shape personality development can lead to misdiagnoses and failed treatment of patients.

Patients who fail to act in accordance with the clinician's culturally acceptable patterns of behavior may be diagnosed, erroneously, as having psychopathology. The diagnostic picture can also be complicated by the patient's rejection of the clinician's beliefs if they are alien and contrary to his or her tradition; for example, the belief that one is possessed by evil spirits may be so strong and powerful that it may render one highly resistant to biomedical and psychological treatment modalities. Further, the clinician's hesitating to pursue and explore the patient's belief system can be experienced by the patient as a devaluation of such beliefs and may also negatively impact on treatment outcomes.

The goal, therefore, should not be to change the patient's belief system or to dismiss or devalue it, but to help patients find an explanation for their own dysfunction and gain control over their lives (Gopaul-McNicol 1993) by interpreting behavior in the context of the culturally different patient's intended meaning. The effective cross-cultural clinician seeks to recognize and understand the various constructions of the self and to work within their framework; in this case the patient's sense of self as it is defined along spiritual and religious lines needs to be considered (Griffith and Young 1988). This approach to treatment helps patients to open up more about issues regarding their spiritual belief system and how it impacts on treatment. This is so particularly for those astute enough to recognize, as evident in their silence and "resistance," that such beliefs are not accepted by mainstream psychology.

A clinical assessment should include not only the individual's psychosocial, behavioral and cognitive functioning, but also an assessment of the patient's religious orientation and spiritual world view in order to facilitate effective treatment planning. For the clinician, accomplishing this requires increasing one's cultural knowledge and developing one's cultural dictionary through reading and consultation of indigenous people of the cultural community of which the patient is a part.

While some mental health professionals are beginning to view native healers as valuable assets for learning and referral purposes (Garey 1991, Lefley 1981), these indigenous clinicians are largely ignored by mainstream psychology. However, native healers in the community can serve as mental health resources akin to other resources normally accessed, such as schools and other social service agencies. They can be a valuable resource in interpreting behavior, particularly when they are known to the individual in question. And in the treatment process, they may serve as consultants or even as cotherapists. Gaines (1995) also suggests that one should rely more on the assessments of relatives of patients. They are the "experts in the logic of their own culture" (p. 283), and can inform the degree to which the individual's behavior is, in fact, culturally appropriate. Other resources, such as elders and leaders of the particular cultural community and cultural organizations (e.g., embassies, missions), can be accessed to develop a knowledge base of one's patients' cultural backgrounds. Doing so may help to legitimize the therapist's authority and credibility. One should not be fooled by the fact that a client may not be a member of an organized religion or church. Religion and spirituality are separate concepts. Many individuals, because of their socialization, may have an internalized sense of spirituality but may not be a member of an organized religious organization. As such, they may still have strong spiritual beliefs that may influence the way they think and behave and give meaning to behavior.

Striving toward an acceptance of other world views in a nonjudgmental manner also necessitates recognition that one's cultural beliefs as a clinician may conflict with the beliefs of those seeking care. It requires acknowledgment of one's own biases and prejudices, attitudes and values, and how they affect one's patients. This is essential if a clinician is to understand feelings regarding the differences between his or her cultural belief system and that of the patient.

From a research perspective, the study of abnormal behavior has been grounded in models derived from Western psychology rather than symbolic and culturally relevant parameters of social behavior (Fabrega 1992). The medical and psychological models have downplayed the importance of the phenomenon of possession and the relevance of non-Western healing methods as legitimate and viable alternative ways of defining and treating illness. This reluctance to engage in extensive exploration of the phenomenon of possession and the possible therapeutic value of alternative curative interventions comes even in the face of evidence of the efficacy of treatment of some problems by religious healers, suggesting a need for further research (Finkler 1985, Griffith and Young 1988).

Csordas (1992), citing the large gulf between the spiritual and psychological interpretations of human reality, noted that the difficulty in studying phenomena such as spirit possession lies in an inability to translate between these two radically different accounts of experience or healing systems. He calls for the recognition of demon possession and the medical description of human distress as interpretative processes that allow for parallel analyses of religious and medical accounts of distress. This will allow for "convergences and divergences of suppositions and interpretations [which] can be detailed systematically" (Csordas 1992, p. 164). Csordas offers the paradigm of "embodiment" as useful for comparing different cultural accounts of experience by providing a description of the existential common ground from which these accounts are abstracted.

If the field of psychology is to recognize that the world is a culturally constructed one, systematic research will need to be conducted that begins with genuine respect for alternative cultural world views, uses appropriate cultural meanings as guidelines for measuring constructs, and aims at providing insight and data both from Western and non-Western perspectives (Gaines 1992). This is the basis upon which valid research paradigms are developed. The efficacy of alternative healing methods should be examined not only with the aim of incorporating such treatments as a way of showing respect for the patient, but also because there is evidence that they are effective.

REFERENCES

Beaubrun, M. H. (1975). Mental health and the interaction of cultures in the Caribbean. *Proceedings, Tenth Biennial Conference of the Caribbean Federation for Mental Health, Caracas.*

Bourguignon, E. (1991). *Possession.* Prospect Heights, IL: Waveland.

Burke, A. (1979). Trends in social psychiatry in the Caribbean. *International Journal of Social Psychiatry* 25:110–117.

Cancelmo, J. A., Millan, F., and Vazquez, C. I. (1990). Culture and symptomatology—the role of personal meaning in diagnosis and treatment: a case study. *American Journal of Psychoanalysis* 50:137–149.

Csordas, T. J. (1992). The affliction of Martin: religious, clinical, and phenomenological meaning. In *Ethnopsychiatry: The Cultural Construction of Professional and Folk Psychiatries* ed. A. Gaines, pp. 125–170. New York: State University of New York Press.

Diagnostic and Statistical Manual of Mental Disorders (1994). 4th ed. Washington, DC: American Psychiatric Association.

Fabrega, H. (1989a). The self and schizophrenia: a cultural perspective. *Schizophrenia Bulletin* 15:277–290.

——— (1989b). On the significance of an anthropological approach to schizophrenia. *Psychiatry* 52:45–65.

——— (1992). The role of culture in a theory of psychiatric illness. *Social Science and Medicine* 35:91–103.

Finkler, K. (1985). *Spiritualist Healers in Mexico.* Westport, CT: Bergin & Garvey.

Gaines, A. (1982). Cultural definitions, behavior and the person in American psychiatry. In *Cultural Conceptions of Mental Health and Therapy.* ed. A. J. Marsella and A. White. London: Reidal.

——— (1992). Ethnopsychiatry: the cultural construction of psychiatries. In *Ethnopsychiatry: The Cultural Construction of Professional and Folk Psychiatries,* ed.

A. Gaines, pp. 3–49. New York: State University of New York Press.

———— (1995). Culture-specific delusions. *Psychiatric Clinics of North America* 18:281–301.

Garey, J. (1991). Templo spiritual luz Divina. *New York Newsday*, October 3, pp. 64, 65, 67.

Gopaul-McNicol, S. (1993). *Working with West Indian Families.* New York: Guilford.

Griffith, E. E. H., and Young, J. (1988). A cross-cultural introduction to the therapeutic aspects of christian religious ritual. In *Clinical Guidelines in Cross-Cultural Mental Health*, ed. L. Comas-Diaz and E. E. H. Griffith, pp. 69–89. New York: Wiley.

Kiev, A. (1961). Spirit possession in Haiti. *American Journal of Psychiatry* 118:133–138.

Landrine, H. (1992). Clinical implications of cultural differences: the referential versus the indexical self. *Clinical Psychology Review* 12:401–415.

Lefley, H. P. (1981). Psychotherapy and cultural adaption in the Caribbean. *International Journal of Group Tensions* 11:3–16.

Rogler, L. H., and Hollingshead, A. B. (1961). The Puerto Rican spiritualist as a psychiatrist. *American Journal of Sociology* 67:17–21.

Ward, C., and Beaubrun, M. B. (undated). *The psychodynamics of demon possession.* Unpublished manuscript.

13

Cross-National and Programmatic Differences in Outcome for Schizophrenia: Implications for the Process of Recovery

PHILIP T. YANOS, RAFAEL ART. JAVIER,
LOUIS H. PRIMAVERA, AND ANGELA M. MARTINEZ

INTRODUCTION

Psychiatry has historically viewed schizophrenia as a chronically disabling illness, with almost uniformly poor potential for improvement in functioning across the life span (Harding et al. 1987); for example, the *DSM-III* (1980) stated that "a complete return to premorbid functioning [in schizophrenia] is . . . so rare . . . that some clinicians would question the diagnosis" (p. 185). Recently, however, prominent psychiatric researchers have challenged this notion (Harding et al. 1987, 1992, P. Cohen and J. Cohen 1984). Citing evidence from longitudinal studies that suggests that in some locations, approximately 50 percent of individuals initially diagnosed with schizophrenia may eventually achieve unimpaired or mildly impaired levels of functioning (e.g., Bleuler 1978, Harding, Brooks et al. 1987), Harding, Zubin, and Strauss

(1987, 1992) have argued that the scientific evidence indicates that the traditional view regarding the prognosis for schizophrenia needs to be replaced with a more flexible attitude toward outcome.

A parallel development in the mental health field has been the ascendancy of the concept of recovery as a new perspective on possible outcome for serious mental illness. Within the past few years, recovery has been championed by researchers/clinicians (e.g., Anthony 1993, Carling 1995, Davidson and Strauss 1995) members of the mental health consumer advocacy movement (e.g., Deegan 1988, Lovejoy 1984), and has become something of a buzzword in policy circles (e.g., the Rockland Psychiatric division of the New York State Office of Mental Health made "hope and recovery from serious, complex mental illness" its mission statement in 1995). Anthony (1993), one of the architects of the influential psychiatric rehabilitation model, reflected much of the current enthusiasm about recovery in a recent paper that called on the mental health system to adopt recovery as its guiding vision in policy design and ultimate goal in service delivery. Though recovery is not often clearly defined, most authors (e.g., Anthony 1993, Deegan 1988) have stressed that achieving or being in recovery does not require one to be completely free of symptoms, but rather to have found "a way of living a satisfying, hopeful, and contributing life even with the limitations caused by illness" (Anthony 1993, p. 15). Thus the predominant opinion is that recovery reflects an individual's having learned to cope with and lessen the impact of psychiatric symptoms to the extent that they no longer seriously disrupt functioning.

Despite the current popularity of the recovery concept, and despite evidence from longitudinal research that a favorable course is not uncommon in schizophrenia, almost no quantitative research has addressed the question of why some individuals might recover from schizophrenia and related disorders while others do not. Nevertheless autobiographical reports by recovered individuals (e.g., Anonymous 1989, Deegan 1988, Lovejoy 1984) and qualitative studies (Davidson and Strauss 1992) have emphasized that psychological and environmental factors may facilitate recovery. Factors discussed as important in these writings include gaining a more integrated sense of self (Davidson and Strauss 1992), having positive expectations about the future (Lovejoy 1984), and using specific types of mental health services (Anonymous 1989, Deegan 1988). Although the role that such psychological and environmental factors play in recovery has yet to be systematically investigated, the importance of gaining a better understanding of variables that may facilitate recovery cannot be overstated, as findings from such research could have powerful implications for both mental health service delivery and policy. For example, determining that specific types of psychological changes facilitate recovery could have direct implications for how psychotherapy is conducted with individuals diagnosed with schizophrenia. Similarly, finding evidence supporting that specific types of psychosocial programs facilitate recovery could have important implications for how mental health resources are allocated.

Differences in Outcome: Clues to the Recovery Mystery?

Clearly, more direct research is needed to determine what role, if any, psychosocial variables play in facilitating recovery from schizophrenia. It is our view, however, that future inquiry into the environmental factors may be informed by an existing body of research on the long-term outcome for schizophrenia, which suggests that the prognosis of schizophrenia varies significantly by geographic location. We believe that this research carries clear implications for understanding recovery, following from the logic that, if good outcome for schizophrenia is significantly more common in certain geographic locations than others, environmental or treatment factors that vary systematically between these locations may play an important role in recovery. Two areas of outcome research seem particularly relevant in this regard: (1) research comparing differences in outcome for schizophrenia between industrialized and nonindustrialized locations, and (2) research comparing differences in outcome for schizophrenia between culturally similar locations that offer distinctly different mental health programs. Research in the first area may illuminate the existence of cultural or social factors that can influence recovery; research in the second area may demonstrate whether specific characteristics of a mental health program influence recovery when cultural and other social factors are held constant.

The purpose of this chapter, therefore, is to critically review the most important research that has been reported with regard to cross-national and programmatic differences in outcome for schizophrenia and related disorders. Its further goal is to discuss possible theoretical interpretations of findings from these studies, with an eye on the implications that these interpretations have for explaining the influence of psychosocial factors in facilitating recovery from serious mental illness.

CROSS-NATIONAL STUDIES OF OUTCOME FROM SCHIZOPHRENIA

While traditional psychiatric notions of chronicity in schizophrenia were based on outcome studies conducted in western Europe and North America, in the 1970s several studies began to address the question of whether prognosis for schizophrenia was similarly poor in Asia and other non-Western locations (Kulhara and Wig 1978, Lo and Lo 1977, Murphy and Raman 1971, Waxler 1979). Findings from two of these early studies (Murphy and Raman 1971, Waxler 1979) were initially interpreted as supporting the conclusion that the long-term prognosis for schizophrenia was significantly better in nonindustrialized settings (such as Africa and India) than the industrialized settings that predominate in the West.

Murphy and Raman's study consisted of a follow-up of ninety individuals diagnosed with schizophrenia on the island of Mauritius in the Indian Ocean, a setting considered to be almost completely nonindustrialized. At twelve-year follow-up, 64 percent of the sample was found to have achieved total recovery as defined by the absence of psychotic symptoms and the presence of good social functioning. After comparing these data with outcome data from earlier studies indicating that a substantially lower percentage of individuals diagnosed with schizophrenia achieved recovery in England, the authors concluded that their findings supported the view that schizophrenia has a more favorable prognosis in nonindustrialized than in industrialized settings.

Waxler (1979) conducted a follow-up study of a group of forty-four first-admission patients diagnosed with schizophrenia who presented at a hospital in Sri Lanka. At five-year follow-up the thirty-eight patients who could be recontacted were assessed for psychiatric symptomatology and social functioning; 45 percent were found to be completely asymptomatic, while 50 percent were found to be "normally" socially adjusted. After comparing her findings with outcome data from Western locations, Waxler also concluded that these data supported the view that the prognosis for schizophrenia is more favorable in nonindustrialized than in industrialized societies.

A problem with the interpretation of data from early follow-up studies conducted in the developing world, such as Murphy and Raman's (1971) and Waxler's (1979), is that these reports contrasted their own findings with findings from separate studies conducted in Western locations that frequently used different diagnostic criteria, different follow-up periods, and different outcome criteria (Lin and Kleinman 1988). As a result, it is difficult to draw any meaningful conclusions from such comparisons. Two large-scale investigations conducted by the World Health Organization (WHO), however, have all but eliminated this problem. The International Pilot Study of Schizophrenia (IPSS) (Leff et al. 1992, WHO 1979) and the more recent Determinants of Outcome of Severe Mental Disorder (DOSMD) study (Jablensky et al. 1992) were designed to investigate outcome for schizophrenia and other psychotic disorders in several international locations using standardized and rigorous diagnostic and outcome assessment procedures. As we discuss below, their findings have provided strong evidence of the existence of geographic differences in the prognosis for schizophrenia.

The IPSS

The IPSS (Leff et al. 1992, WHO 1979) studied individuals presenting with psychotic symptoms at sites in nine countries: Colombia, Czechoslovakia, Denmark, India, Nigeria, Taiwan, the Union of Soviet Socialist Republics (USSR), the United Kingdom (UK), and the United States. The authors of the IPSS categorized the different study sites as either industrialized or nonindustrialized based on the socioeconomic profile of each location; the Nigeria, India, and Colombia sites were categorized as nonindustrialized, while all other sites were categorized as industrialized. All patients presenting psychotic symptoms at psychiatric hospitals within specified catchment areas were approached for inclusion in the study. A total of 1,202 patients, 811 of whom met criteria for schizophrenia, were included in the initial phase of the study. Patients were assessed using the Present State Examination (PSE) (a structured diagnostic interview) and the CATEGO computer program (which has been demonstrated to provide reliable diagnoses according to International Classification of Diseases (ICD) criteria). Structured interviews were also used to assess premorbid history and social functioning. Both the PSE and the structured interviews of social functioning were readministered to patients who were recontacted at two- and five-year follow-up. In addition, to corroborate self-report data, interviews were conducted with family members and health professionals and hospital chart records were reviewed.

A two-year follow-up report on outcome for patients diagnosed with schizophrenia in the IPSS (WHO 1979) revealed striking differences in outcome for schizophrenia between the industrialized and nonindustrialized sites. Data on the two-year outcome of patients in each site are summarized in Table 13–1.

The IPSS authors (WHO 1979) classified patients into five outcome groups (ranging from "best" to "worst") based on the presence or absence of severe social impairment, the percentage of follow-up period spent in a psychotic episode, and type of remission after episodes. It was found that patients in two of the nonindustrialized sites (Nigeria and India) were significantly more likely than patients in the other centers to meet criteria for the best overall outcomes (e.g., 57 percent of the patients followed up in the Nigerian sample and 48 percent of the patients in the India sample were in the best outcome category, while only 6 percent of patients in the Denmark sample

TABLE 13–1. PERCENTAGE OF PATIENTS BY OUTCOME GROUP AND SITE IN THE IPSS AT TWO-YEAR FOLLOW-UP

Site	1 (best outcome)	2	3	4	5(worst outcome)
Denmark	6%	29%	17%	17%	31%
India	48%	18%	13%	6%	15%
Colombia	21%	32%	19%	13%	15%
Nigeria	57%	29%	7%	2%	5%
UK	24%	12%	23%	10%	31%
USSR	9%	39%	32%	9%	11%
Taiwan	15%	23%	27%	20%	15%
USA	23%	16%	16%	26%	19%
Czech.	14%	20%	27%	9%	30%

Source: World Health Organization (1979). *Schizophrenia: An International Follow-Up Study.* Chichester, UK: Wiley. Used with permission of the publisher.

were in this category). Patients in the Colombia sample were not significantly more likely to be in the best overall outcome category than patients in industrialized sites, but had the third highest percentage (after Nigeria and India) of patients in the two best outcome groups.

A report of data from a five-year follow-up of patients diagnosed with schizophrenia in the IPSS (Leff et al. 1992) revealed similar comparatively favorable outcomes for patients in Nigeria, India, and, to a lesser extent, Colombia. Data on the five-year outcome of patients in the IPSS are summarized in Table 13–2.

When judged according to the presence or absence of psychotic or other symptoms at five-year assessment, patients in Nigeria and India were significantly more likely to be judged currently asymptomatic than patients in the other centers (e.g., approximately 70 percent of patients in these centers were judged to be asymptomatic, while less than 10 percent of patients in Denmark, the USSR, and the United States met these criteria) (Leff et al. 1992). Furthermore, when judged according to the presence or absence of

TABLE 13–2. PERCENTAGE OF PATIENTS JUDGED
TO BE ASYMPTOMATIC OR NOT SEVERELY IMPAIRED
IN THE IPSS BY SITE AT FIVE-YEAR FOLLOW-UP
(DATA ON TAIWAN NOT AVAILABLE)

Site	% Asymptomatic	% Not Severely Impaired
Denmark	approx. 5%	50%
India	approx. 70%	97%
Colombia	approx. 25%	83%
Nigeria	approx. 70%	81%
UK	approx. 15%	73%
USSR	approx. 3%	77%
Czech.	approx. 40%	70%
USA	approx. 10%	75%

Source: Leff, J., Sartorius, N., Jablensky, A., et al. (1992). The International
Pilot Study of Schizophrenia: five-year follow-up findings. *Psychological
Medicine* 22: 131–145. Used with permission of the publisher.

severe social impairment, patients in the three nonindustrialized sites were
significantly less likely to be severely socially impaired than patients in industrialized settings.

Leff and associates (1992) attempted to address possible explanations for
the finding of better outcome for schizophrenia in the nonindustrialized centers in the IPSS. One possible explanation addressed was that the finding of
better outcome was related to selective attrition in the nonindustrialized sites.
Leff and associates agreed that the rate of patients lost at five-year follow-up
was high (41 percent) in the Nigerian sample, which would support this interpretation of the findings. However, these authors argued that the highest rate
of attrition was in the United States site (47 percent), and that attrition was
relatively low in the Indian and Colombian samples (26 percent and 8 percent, respectively), which does not support this interpretation of the results.

Another potential explanation addressed by Leff and associates (1992)
was the possibility that the finding of better outcome in the nonindustrialized
sites could be explained on the basis of other predictors (e.g., marital status,
premorbid personality, and type of onset) found to be related to better out-

come in previous research. The authors hypothesized that these predictors might vary systematically between industrialized and nonindustrialized locations, thereby accounting for differences in outcome between these locations. This possibility was examined by way of a log-linear analysis of the relationship between eleven predictors (including residence in a developing or developed site) and outcome status. It was found that the relationship between industrialization status and outcome remained statistically significant even when other variables were included in the equation. The authors concluded that the finding of a relationship between good outcome and residence in a nonindustrialized setting could not be accounted for on the basis of the variance of other, previously studied, factors. Leff and associates (1992) tentatively speculated that some other factor, possibly related to cultural differences between the locations, might be involved in the relationship.

A. Cohen (1992), however, suggested another possible artifactual explanation of the IPSS findings. He proposed that differences in outcome might have been related to differences in sample representativeness between industrialized and nonindustrialized sites. Cohen argued that, because patients included in the IPSS were recruited from admissions to psychiatric hospitals, there might be systematic differences in the representativeness of hospital-based samples between industrialized and nonindustrialized settings, and that this selection bias might have resulted in the observed differences in outcome. Leff and associates (1992) agreed that this interpretation of the IPSS could not be ruled out.

The DOSMD

A second study of the outcome of schizophrenia and other psychotic disorders in international settings, the DOSMD study (Jablensky et al. 1992), was designed to account for some of the methodological shortcomings of the IPSS. Notably, patients for this study were recruited not only from admissions to hospitals, but also from contacts made to several other types of helping agencies within each catchment area (including contact with the police, nonpsychiatric outpatient medical services, and traditional and religious healers). Along with several sites previously studied in the IPSS (in Denmark [Aarhus], Colombia [Cali], Czechoslovakia [Prague], Nigeria [Ibadan], India [Agra], and the U.S.S.R [Moscow]), additional sites were studied in the United States (Rochester, NY and Honolulu), Ireland (Dublin), the United Kingdom (Nottingham), Japan (Nagasaki), and India (Chandigarh, urban and rural). The Indian, Nigerian, and Colombian sites were classified as nonindustrialized or "developing," while all other sites were classified as industrialized or "developed." Diagnostic and assessment methods used were essentially the same as those employed in the IPSS.

A report of the two-year follow-up of patients in the DOSMD strongly supported the finding of a more favorable outcome for patients in developing countries, as previously reported in the IPSS. Data on the two-year outcome of patients in the DOSMD are summarized in Table 13–3.

With regard to psychiatric symptomatology, patients in developing sites on the whole were found to be significantly more likely to have spent between 76 percent and 100 percent of the follow-up period in complete symptom remission than patients in developed sites (38 percent versus 22 percent) (Jablensky et al. 1992). This distinction was especially marked for patients in the Nigeria and Agra (India) sites, of whom 73 percent and 63 percent, respectively, spent between 76 and 100 percent of the follow-up period in complete remission. Similarly, patients in developing countries were significantly more likely than other patients to have spent between 76 percent and 100 percent of the follow-up period at an unimpaired (i.e., as well as a "typical" person in the setting) level of social functioning (an average of 43 percent for the developing centers versus 31.6 percent for the developed centers). Once again, this difference was particularly marked for the Nigeria and Agra patients, approximately 65 percent of whom spent 76–100 percent of the follow-up period functioning socially at a level judged to be unimpaired.

As in the IPSS, Jablensky and colleagues (1992) tried to determine the relative importance of residence in a developing or developed country in relation to other established predictors of outcome using a logistical regression procedure. Predictors considered included gender, age, marital status, type of onset (i.e., acute versus gradual), social adjustment in childhood (i.e., good or poor), and drug use. Type of setting (i.e., industrialized versus nonindustrialized) was found to be a significant and strong predictor of outcome even when the statistical influence of the other variables was accounted for.

With regard to the possibility of selective attrition in nonindustrialized sites, which had been raised as a possible alternative interpretation of the IPSS findings, data from the DOSMD indicated that this interpretation would be implausible as attrition rates for the rural India sites were among the lowest in the study. In addition, the Africa sites' attrition rate in the DOSMD was substantially lower than its attrition rate in the IPSS, while findings of favorable outcome were strikingly similar to those found in the IPSS.

Jablensky and colleagues (1992) concluded that the more rigorous methodology of the DOSMD "replicated in a clear, and possibly conclusive way" (p. 88) the finding of a marked difference in prognosis for schizophrenia between developing and developed countries observed in the IPSS. Stating

TABLE 13–3. PERCENTAGE OF PATIENTS JUDGED
TO HAVE SPENT 76–100% OF FOLLOW-UP PERIOD IN
COMPLETE SYMPTOM REMISSION BY SITE IN THE
DOSMD AT TWO-YEAR FOLLOW-UP; PERCENTAGE OF
PATIENTS JUDGED TO HAVE SPENT 76–100% OF FOLLOW-
UP PERIOD AT UNIMPAIRED SOCIAL FUNCTIONING BY
SITE IN THE DOSMD AT TWO-YEAR FOLLOW-UP

Site	% Asymptomatic	% Not Severely Impaired
Aarhus (Denmark)	17.5%	31.3%
Dublin	21.4%	23.2%
Honolulu	14.3%	14.3%
Moscow	14.6%	14.3%
Nagasaki	7.3%	data not collected
Nottingham (UK)	39.5%	40.7%
Prague	39.1%	44.8%
Rochester, NY (USA)	29%	22.6%
Agra (India)	63.2%	65.8%
Cali (Colombia)	10.1%	21.7%
Chandigarh, rural (India)	30%	46.2%
Chandigarh, urban (India)	29.6%	32.4%
Ibadan (Nigeria)	73.1%	65.6%

Source: Jablensky, A., Sartorius, N., Ernberg, G., Anker, M., Korten, A., Cooper, J. E., Day, R., and Bertlesen, A. (1992). Schizophrenia: manifestations, incidence and course in different cultures. *Psychological Medicine* (Monograph Supplement 20). Used with permission of the publisher.

that artifactual interpretations of the data could be ruled out with confidence, the authors concluded that "a strong case can be made for a real pervasive influence of a powerful factor which can be referred to as 'culture'" (pp. 88–89). However, they conceded that no data were gathered that provided any clear

indication of how "cultural" factors might influence outcome from schizophrenia, and that the findings of the WHO studies could only indicate the
definitive need for future research in this area.

Theoretical Interpretations of WHO Study Findings

If one accepts that the relationship between geographic location and improved
prognosis for schizophrenia observed in the IPSS and DOSMD studies is
causal (as the evidence strongly suggests) and not artifactual, the question of
what mechanism or mechanisms might account for such a causal relationship
becomes essential. Though Jablensky and colleagues (1992) conceded that
they could not rule out the possibility that what presents as schizophrenia
within developing nations is genetically distinct from what presents as schizophrenia in developed nations, they argued that this interpretation seems
unlikely in light of the DOSMD's finding of a similar prevalence and initial
presentation for schizophrenia in all the locations they studied. The DOSMD
and IPSS findings therefore suggest that it is possible, if not likely, that environmental and psychological factors, which strict medical model conceptualizations of schizophrenia tend to downplay the importance of, become
strongly implicated in influencing the course of schizophrenia. Gaining an
understanding of these factors may therefore shed important new light on
environmental and psychosocial variables that can facilitate recovery from
schizophrenia.

An essential issue that interpretations of the findings of the WHO studies need to address is the assumption that the differences observed are necessarily attributable to cultural factors. The assertion of Jablensky and associates
(1992) that the findings of the DOSMD study indicated that "culture" influences outcome for schizophrenia was appropriately criticized by Edgerton and
A. Cohen (1994). They argued that the concept of industrialization as a cultural factor grossly oversimplifies the complex differences that exist between
similarly industrialized locations with different cultural makeups and culturally similar locations with different degrees of industrialization. This over-
simplification is borne out by the findings of the DOSMD themselves; for
example, the observed difference in outcome between industrialized and nonindustrialized locations was accounted for largely by vastly better outcomes
among patients in the Nigeria and rural India sites, while the outcome of
patients in the Colombia and urban India site was on the whole not substantially better than outcome for patients in the industrialized sites. It is difficult
to offer a plausible "cultural" interpretation of these findings, as it seems
inconsistent to suggest that the cultures of rural India and Nigeria are more

similar to each other than the cultures of rural and urban India. Yet the fact that prognosis was similarly superior in these rural India and Nigeria sites suggests that some broader factor common to these two settings might be involved in facilitating good outcome for schizophrenia. While this factor could be termed "cultural" in a more general sense, we believe that it should be distinguished from the more specific sense in which the word is usually imbued.

Lin and Kleinman (1988) discussed several possible explanations for the mechanisms that might underlie a relationship between geographic location and better prognosis for schizophrenia. Two of the possible explanations they suggested relate to culturally based differences in the quality of family and interpersonal relationships in industrialized and nonindustrialized societies. First, Lin and Kleinman proposed that developing societies might emphasize the value of social interdependence over the value of individualism that is generally stressed in Western societies. They reasoned that individuals suffering from a serious mental illness may therefore receive more social support and be less likely to become isolated in developing societies; improved social support may then facilitate better outcome. This argument is supported by evidence from the DOSMD indicating that social isolation is a significant predictor of poor outcome (Jablensky et al. 1992). A second, related explanation is that families in developing societies have lower levels of "expressed emotion" (EE) (which has been repeatedly demonstrated to be related to risk of relapse in schizophrenia) than families in industrialized society. This argument is partially supported by data from the DOSMD (Leff et al. 1987), demonstrating lower levels of EE in Indian than in Danish families.

Two other possible explanations proposed by Lin and Kleinman (1988) focused more on how industrialization might directly impact on behavioral and psychological factors that influence outcome (thus placing less of an emphasis on "culture" per se). First, they proposed that individuals suffering from schizophrenia may have more opportunity to resume working in nonindustrial societies, where jobs are likely to be assigned rather than sought, while work may be more difficult to resume in industrial societies, where the job market may be more competitive. Lin and Kleinman also speculated that the work environment of industrial societies may be relatively impersonal and unsupportive, making it more difficult for individuals suffering from mental illness to maintain work. The ability to find and maintain work could then affect outcome both directly (as work factors heavily in the measurement of social functioning) and by facilitating improvements in symptomatology. A second, related argument proposed was that mental illness may be more stigmatized in certain societies; this may impact on outcome by reinforcing negative beliefs among individuals labeled as schizophrenic and discouraging them from taking steps to improve their circumstances. This position was also argued in an earlier discussion by Waxler (1979). Limited evidence for this position exists in the form of ethnographic research that suggests that some non-Western cultures (such as those of sub-Saharan Africa) view mental illness as a transient, rather than chronic, condition (Patel 1995).

None of the possible explanations of the WHO findings discussed by Lin and Kleinman (1988) have been directly explored in research; it is our view, however, that their speculation that there is a more rapid resumption of work roles in nonindustrialized settings shows the most promise as a nonculture-specific explanation for better outcome. As the research of Bell and associates has recently demonstrated (Bell et al. 1996, Lysaker and Bell 1995), there is evidence that involvement in work facilitates improvements in both positive and negative symptoms for individuals diagnosed with schizophrenia. Furthermore, statements from the WHO researchers strongly suggest that it was quite common for patients in rural nonindustrial settings to return to work and other duties immediately after hospital discharge (e.g., the two-year IPSS follow-up report stated that "nearly all patients were found to be engaged in some form of work" in the Agra, India site [WHO 1979, p. 104]). Conversely, this rapid return to work has been described as less prevalent in urban than in rural Third World settings (Warner 1994), such as the urban Chandigarh DOSMD site, where good outcome was in fact less common than it was in rural nonindustrial sites. Thus it seems plausible that better outcome in rural nonindustrialized settings may be facilitated by a speedy return to work, possibly in combination with the presence of greater social support in the work environment. More definitive evidence of a more rapid resumption of the work role in rural nonindustrialized settings than in industrialized ones is still needed in support of this explanation, however.

The other possible explanations suggested by Lin and Kleinman (1988) are more problematic, though still worthy of future investigation. With regard to social support and EE, despite the well-demonstrated relationship between these factors and risk of relapse in schizophrenia, evidence that these factors are related to social functioning and symptomatology is weak. It therefore seems unlikely that they can account for the differences observed between patients in industrialized and nonindustrialized sites in these areas in the DOSMD. With regard to the issue of stigma, the view that primitive societies have less stigmatizing views of mental illness has been challenged (A. Cohen 1992), and has yet to be clearly demonstrated. More evidence is needed for this interpretation of the findings to be supported. Nevertheless, if it is true that nonindustrial societies do not regard schizophrenia as a chronic illness as it is viewed in the West, it does seem possible that this belief may influence outcome in a positive way, perhaps by making it more acceptable for formerly psychotic individuals to return to work.

Clearly, future transcultural research on outcome for schizophrenia needs to pay more attention to the importance of specific psychosocial factors such as work, social support, and stigma in determining outcome. On the basis of our review of existing research, however, we believe that the evidence points to the existence of a nonculture-specific factor leading to good prognosis for schizophrenia in rural, non-Western settings. We next turn to the possibility that such a factor may be further illuminated by research demonstrating differences in outcome between culturally-similar geographic locations.

PROGRAMMATIC DIFFERENCES IN OUTCOME

If, as suggested above, the differences in outcome observed in the WHO studies are not necessarily attributable to culture in the specific sense, another type of research that may shed light on the psychosocial variables that might facilitate recovery is research that examines outcome for schizophrenia in culturally similar geographic locations with distinct mental health programs. Only one study of this nature has been published to date.

DeSisto and colleagues (1995a, b) retrospectively compared the long-term outcome of seriously mentally ill individuals residing in Vermont and Maine. In the mid-1950s, 269 "back-ward," seriously mentally ill individuals residing in Vermont (the majority retrospectively meeting *DSM-III* criteria for schizophrenia) were released from a state hospital and enrolled in a pioneering rehabilitation program. This program placed particular emphasis on community reintegration with a goal of self-sufficiency, and provided services focused on vocational training, job placement, and alternative community residences (such as halfway houses). In the 1980s, 180 of the original subjects (97 percent of those still living) were interviewed and assessed for social and psychiatric functioning (average follow-up period was thirty-two years) (Harding, Brooks et al. 1987). In an attempt to assess the impact of the Vermont mental health program on outcome, DeSisto and colleagues (1995a) retrospectively selected a comparison group of 269 seriously mentally ill patients who were released from a state hospital in Maine during the same period. These patients were selected for comparison because Maine, though similar to Vermont in socioeconomic and ethnocultural composition, had had a more traditional mental health program that stressed psychiatric treatment but did not feature vocational rehabilitation or other alternative services. Maine patients were randomly selected from a pool of patients described in the hospital records who matched the Vermont patients on diagnostic, age, gender, and other demographic criteria. Of the 149 living patients selected from this cohort, 119 were successfully interviewed at an average of thirty-two years after initial discharge. A standard record review procedure was also conducted in order to assess any possible differences in outcome between deceased Vermont and Maine patients.

DeSisto and colleagues (1995a,b) reported data on the long-term outcome of interviewed individuals from both states that indicated that the Vermont patients had significantly better outcomes. With regard to global functioning, 68 percent of the Vermont subjects were rated as surpassing a cutoff on the Global Assessment Scale set to indicate the individual was functioning "pretty well, so that most untrained people . . . would not consider him [or her] sick" (Harding, Brooks et al. 1987, pp. 722–723); in contrast, 49 percent of the Maine subjects surpassed this cutoff. This difference was found to be statistically significant. Vermont subjects were also significantly more likely to be working (47 percent) than Maine subjects (26 percent), showed significantly better community adjustment, and displayed significantly fewer psychiatric symptoms at follow-up. DeSisto and colleagues (1995a,b) review of records from the deceased patients also indicated that the Vermont patients had had significantly better ratings of global functioning and community adjustment than the Maine patients.

In order to assess whether differences in outcome between the Vermont and Maine patients were due to the systematic variance of other factors, DeSisto and colleagues (1995a,b) examined whether the statistical impact of state residence on outcome would be eliminated when the variance of other predictors was considered. Factors studied included well-known predictors of outcome, including education, length of hospital stay, acute versus gradual onset, and diagnosis. A statistically significant effect for state residence in relation to the outcome variables of global functioning, community adjustment, work, and psychiatric symptomatology was observed even when the role of these other factors was statistically accounted for. The authors concluded that the better outcome for Vermont subjects was most likely related to the state's pioneering mental health program rather than to other factors.

Although the weight of the evidence suggests that the presence of a rehabilitation program in Vermont was related to the better outcome of its patients, several methodological issues preclude an unequivocal acceptance of this conclusion. First, the patients included in the Vermont sample were not randomly selected; rather, they were chosen on the basis of their moderate to poor response to neuroleptic drugs and their status as long-stay or "back-ward" patients. Thus the patients selected for inclusion in the Vermont program were individuals believed to be particularly severely disabled and nonresponsive to pharmacological interventions. Though the patients from Maine were matched with the Vermont patients on a number of demographic variables, "back-ward" status or poor response to medication were not factors in their selection. Differences in outcome between the Maine and Vermont samples may therefore have been partially the result of differences in sample selection.

Another important factor to consider is that initial diagnoses for patients in both samples were made using unreliable *DSM-II* criteria. Though retrospective rediagnoses with *DSM-III* criteria were conducted using a standardized chart-review procedure, considerable questions remain regarding the validity of the diagnostic makeup of the patient samples. It is possible that a number of patients who would today be diagnosed with affective or anxiety disorders may have been at that time diagnosed as suffering from schizophrenia. This problem impacts upon the extent to which the study findings can be considered generalizable to samples of seriously mentally ill individuals diagnosed according to current criteria.

Despite the limitations discussed, however, the findings of the Vermont study still provide strong evidence of the potential for environmental factors to influence outcome for schizophrenia and related disorders. Though the issue of sample selection is troubling, the fact that Vermont patients were selected on the basis of poor, rather than good, response to treatment argues against the view that these patients would be more likely to have a good outcome. (A recent meta-analysis of outcome studies found good initial response to neuroleptics to be a predictor of *good* outcome for schizophrenia [Pfeiffer et al. 1996].) Thus it seems unlikely that differences in sample selection could account for the differences in outcome observed between the Maine and Vermont samples.

As described by DeSisto and colleagues (1995b), the Vermont program featured a variety of experimental elements (both residential and vocational) that may have facilitated better outcome, but the degree or manner in which specific aspects of the Vermont mental health program may have influenced outcome is not clear. It seems plausible, however, that the vocational rehabilitation services offered by the Vermont program may have impacted on outcome; this is suggested by data indicating that a high percentage (47 percent) of the Vermont patients were engaged in work at follow-up.

Furthermore, as DeSisto and colleagues (1995b) suggest, the Vermont program was as much distinguished by the values of hope and optimism that drove it as by the specific treatments it offered. While no real data exist on the degree to which Vermont staff and patients absorbed these values, this assertion suggests that, in addition to offering services that may have facilitated better outcome, the Vermont program may have encouraged greater improvements by instilling staff and patients alike with an attitude of hopefulness. The view that hopefulness may have facilitated better outcome is consistent with statements made in several autobiographical accounts authored by recovering mental health consumers to the effect that hope and positive expectations may facilitate recovery (e.g., Lovejoy 1984).

SUMMARY AND CONCLUSIONS

What conclusions can be drawn from an integrated analysis of findings from both the WHO studies and the Vermont/Maine study? First and foremost, it can be concluded with some confidence that psychosocial variables *do* appear to influence the outcome of schizophrenia. In all studies, outcome for the disorder varied significantly between locations that differed on the basis of an essential environmental characteristic (either degree of industrialization or type of state mental health program) that can be reasonably presumed to be a proxy for a number of psychosocial differences. In each case the authors took care to consider possible confounding explanations, and found that the evidence did not support these alternative interpretations of the findings. Thus the evidence strongly suggested that environmental variables influenced outcome.

A second conclusion is that "recovery" from schizophrenia, whether defined according to symptom remission, unimpaired social functioning, or both, is not at all uncommon in certain settings. For example, in the Agra (India) and Nigeria sites of the two WHO studies, the proportion of individuals judged to be either socially unimpaired, in the best overall outcome category, or completely symptom free at follow-up was at or above 50 percent of the sample in each case. Similarly, in the Vermont/Maine study, 68 percent of the Vermont sample was judged to be functioning "pretty well" on the Global Assessment Scale at follow-up. On the other hand, in certain WHO centers, rates of recovery were extremely poor; for example, in the Danish center of the IPSS only 6 percent of the study sample met criteria for the "best" overall outcome group at two-year follow-up. These findings suggest that, under favorable environmental circumstances, at least half of individuals initially meeting criteria for schizophrenia or a related disorder may achieve outcomes that could be reasonably labeled "recovered," but that under less favorable circumstances considerably fewer may do so.

A third, more tentative, conclusion that can be drawn is that a common factor related to better outcome in both the WHO and the Vermont/Maine studies is a more rapid resumption of the work role. In the case of the Vermont study the relationship between work and good outcome seems relatively clear, as vocational rehabilitation was a major feature of the Vermont program; in the case of the WHO studies statements by the IPSS authors suggest that there was a rapid return to work in nonindustrial centers, but there is no direct evidence that work rates were higher than in industrial settings. The fact that work was implicated in both studies, however, supports the interpretation that work is related to better outcome in schizophrenia. Further evidence for the importance of work for recovery has been discussed by Warner (1994), who has argued that outcome for schizophrenia was significantly better in mid-nineteenth-century Europe and North America, when "moral treatment" (of which "work therapy" was a major feature) predominated, than in later years when custodial care became the norm. Warner has also argued that experimental mental health programs (such as the Vermont program) that arose in the United States and England in the late 1950s were very similar to nineteenth-century moral treatment.

An even more speculative conclusion relates to the implication from both the WHO and Vermont/Maine studies that positive expectations (or at least a lack of negative expectations) regarding the possibility of recovery may in some way facilitate better outcome. This possibility is implied by reports that certain cultures in which a more favorable outcome was observed tend to view psychosis as a transient, rather than chronic, condition (Patel 1995, Waxler 1979). In addition, the authors of the Vermont study (DeSisto et al. 1995b) suggested that the Vermont rehabilitation program placed a great emphasis on the values of hope, optimism, and community reintegration. Clearly, however, more concrete data are needed to support the speculation that these beliefs do or did prevail in these areas, and do indeed impact upon outcome for schizophrenia.

In summary, there is good evidence that recovery from schizophrenia does exist and is strongly influenced by psychosocial variables. Although more systematic research is needed to determine the extent to which specific variables relate to better outcome, it is our estimation that factors such as work and positive expectancies can be tentatively regarded as playing an important role in facilitating recovery. We hope that the mental health field will make use of this evidence as a guide for the conceptualization of future investigations as well as inspiration in the development of new forms of treatment and services aimed at maximizing chances of recovery for individuals suffering from schizophrenia.

REFERENCES

Anonymous. (1989). How I've managed chronic mental illness. *Schizophrenia Bulletin* 15:635–640.

Anthony, W. A. (1993). Recovery from mental illness: the guiding vision of the mental health service system in the 1990s. *Psychosocial Rehabilitation Journal* 16:11–23.

Bell, M. D., Lysaker, P. H., and Milstein, R. M. (1996). Clinical benefits of paid work activity in schizophrenia. *Schizophrenia Bulletin* 22:51–67.

Bleuler, M. (1978). *The Schizophrenic Disorders: Long-Term Patient and Family Studies.* New Haven, CT: Yale University Press.

Carling, P. J. (1995). *Return to Community: Building Support Systems for Persons with Psychiatric Disabilities.* New York: Guilford.

Cohen, A. (1992). Prognosis for schizophrenia in the third world: a reevaluation of cross-cultural research. *Culture, Medicine, and Psychiatry* 16:53–75.

Cohen, P., and Cohen, J. (1984). The clinician's illusion. *Archives of General Psychiatry* 41:1178–1182.

Davidson, L., and Strauss, J. S. (1992). Sense of self in recovery from severe mental illness. *British Journal of Medical Psychology* 65:131–145.

———— (1995). Beyond the biopsychosocial model: integrating disorder, health and recovery. *Psychiatry* 58:44–55.

Deegan, P. E. (1988). Recovery: the lived experience of rehabilitation. *Psychosocial Rehabilitations Journal* 11:11–19.

DeSisto, M. J., Harding, C. M., McCormick, R. V., et al. (1995a). The Maine and Vermont three-decade studies of serious mental illness, I: Matched comparison of cross-sectional outcome. *British Journal of Psychiatry* 167:331–338.

———— (1995b). The Maine and Vermont three-decade studies of serious mental illness, II: Longitudinal course comparisons. *British Journal of Psychiatry* 167:338–342.

Diagnostic and Statistical Manual of Mental Disorders (1980). 3rd ed. Washington, DC: American Psychiatric Association.

Edgerton, R. B., and Cohen, A. (1994). Culture and schizophrenia: the DOSMD challenge. *British Journal of Psychiatry* 164:222–231.

Harding, C. M., Brooks, G. W., Ashikaga, T., et al. (1987). The Vermont longitudinal study of persons with severe mental illness, II: Long-term outcome of subjects who retrospectively met DSM-III criteria for schizophrenia. *American Journal of Psychiatry* 144:727–735.

Harding, C. M., Zubin, J., and Strauss, J. S. (1987). Chronicity in schizophrenia: fact, partial fact, or artifact? *Hospital and Community Psychiatry* 38:477–486.

——— (1992). Chronicity in schizophrenia: revisited. *British Journal of Psychiatry* 161 (suppl. 18):27–37.

Jablensky, A., Sartorius, N., Ernberg, G., et al. (1992). Schizophrenia: manifestations, incidence and course in different cultures. *Psychological Medicine (Monograph Supplement 20)*.

Kulhara, P., and Wig, N. N. (1978). The chronicity of schizophrenia in North West India: results of a follow-up study. *British Journal of Psychiatry* 132:186–190.

Leff, J., Sartorius, N., Jablensky, A., et al. (1992). The international pilot study of schizophrenia: five-year follow-up findings. *Psychological Medicine* 22:131–145.

Leff, J., Wig, N. N., Ghosh, A., et al. (1987). Influence of relatives' expressed emotion on the course of schizophrenia in Chandigarh: III. *British Journal of Psychiatry* 151:166–173.

Lin, K-M., and Kleinman, A. M. (1988). Psychopathology and clinical course of schizophrenia: a cross-cultural perspective. *Schizophrenia Bulletin* 14:555–567.

Lo, W. H., and Lo, T. (1977). A ten-year follow-up of Chinese schizophrenics in Hong Kong. *British Journal of Psychiatry* 131:63–66.

Lovejoy, M. (1984). Recovery from schizophrenia: a personal odyssey. *Hospital and Community Psychiatry* 35:809–812.

Lysaker, P. H., and Bell, M. D. (1995). Work rehabilitation and improvements in insight in schizophrenia. *Journal of Nervous and Mental Disease* 183:103–106.

Murphy, H. B. M., and Raman, A. C. (1971). The chronicity of schizophrenia in indigenous tropical peoples: results of a twelve-year follow-up survey in Mauritius. *British Journal of Psychiatry* 118:489–497.

Patel, V. (1995). Explanatory models of mental illness in sub-Saharan Africa. *Social Science and Medicine* 40:1291–1298.

Pfeiffer, S. I., O'Malley, D. S., and Shott, S. (1996). Factors associated with outcome of adults treated in psychiatric hospitals: a synthesis of findings. *Psychiatric Services* 47:263–269.

Warner, R. (1994). *Recovery from Schizophrenia: Psychiatry and Political Economy* 2nd ed. New York: Routledge.

Waxler, N. E. (1979). Is outcome for schizophrenia better in nonindustrialized societies? The case of Sri Lanka. *Journal of Nervous and Mental Disease* 176:144–158.

World Health Organization (1979). *Schizophrenia: An International Follow-up Study*. Chichester, UK: Wiley.

Part III

Role of Ethnicity and Culture in Personality Development

14

The Development of Ethnic Identity

WILLIAM G. HERRON

The purpose of this chapter is to describe the development of ethnic identity from a psychoanalytic perspective. The current importance of doing this is emphasized by the increasing degree of ethnic strife and tension that appears in the world. Ethnic "hot spots" seem to be everywhere, as both the United States and the United Nations are continually discovering with growing discomfort. In the past, wars were fought primarily on political grounds, with democracy and freedom being the desired goals that were opposed by varieties of fascism and communism. Ethnic concerns were brought into these conflicts, but they were often thought of as means to political ends. However, as the political landscape has been revolutionized, ethnic hostility has intensified and fascist slogans of ethnic purity have resurfaced without their previous political umbrella. Political and economic systems may have operated to obscure ethnic differences, allowing no room for their expression, but as suppression lifted, ethnic identity took on a staggering and disturbing presence, particularly in areas that were believed to be working models of ethnic harmony, such as Bosnia.

To many people, the attraction and power of ethnic identification was a surprise. Although history attests to the repeated importance of maintaining ethnicity and the willingness of people to go to war and die for it, the hope of international acculturation appears to have turned into a belief that multiethnic democratic societies would prevail. Perhaps they will, but not easily, it seems, and it is clear that ethnocentrism is hardly a secondary issue in many parts of the world. Although it has been suggested that American society is not so vulnerable to ethnic disruption (Galatzer-Levy and Cohler 1993), the increasing multiethnic character of its population suggests that ethnic identity will become a very important issue. This concern is reinforced by the incidents of ethnic violence that have erupted in this country. Understanding more about ethnic identity becomes imperative, and psychoanalytic inquiry presents a promising opportunity.

Psychoanalysis has an ethnic identity of its own. Freud (1926) described himself as a Jew, and listed as one of his attachments to Jewry "a clear consciousness of inner identity" (p. 274). However, he lived in times and places that worked against Jewish ethnic pride, and he witnessed the negative results of ethnocentrism. His aims went instead in the direction of a universal psychology and panculturalism, and that has been the traditional mainstream approach of psychoanalysis since Freud. Unfortunately, that has resulted in neglecting the importance of the various ethnic identities, so that the current material represents relatively uncharted territory for psychoanalysis.

The discussion of the development of ethnic identity first requires the definition of ethnicity, followed by a consideration of identity as a psychoanalytic construct and specific consideration of ethnic identity.

ETHNICITY

There is often confusion between the terms *ethnicity* and *race*, which can, and often do, overlap. Race refers to genetic transmission, with people of the same race being descendants of a common ancestor and having inherited physical characteristics. Recognition is apparent through physical appearance. Race differs from ethnicity in that the latter has a common set of social characteristics as values, behaviors, and traditions, but people may be of mixed or pure race (Ocampo et al. 1993). In practice, ethnicity and race are frequently used as interchangeable terms (Jiobu 1990), although ethnicity is broader.

Because ethnic groups tend to be categorized by what they have in common, what they do not is often overlooked. Thus major ethnic minority groups, such as African Americans and Latinos, have considerable heterogeneity. As a result, ethnic groups have many subtypes and therefore cultural and personal variety within a category. Also, the categories tend to be based on descent from a cultural group as indicated by objective criteria, but psychological differentiation also has to be considered. The people in these ethnic categories will vary in the degree to which they consider themselves members of an ethnic group as well as the degree to which they behave according to ethnic customs and attitudes. Thus the meaning of ethnicity as perceived by the categorical observer, and the subjective ethnic experiences, often differ from each other.

Identity has been defined as "the relatively enduring, but not necessarily stable, experience of the self as a unique, coherent, entity over time" (Moore and Fine 1991, p. 92).

The psychoanalyst particularly associated with the concept of identity was Erikson (1982), who viewed identity development as the major psychosocial task of adolescence, but an evolution of integrating constitutional factors, drives, capacities, defenses, and identifications. Identity patterns emerge from a selection of certain childhood identifications as well as the roles fashioned by culture and society. Identity formation usually involves exploration of interests, abilities, potentials, and choices resulting in commitment to an identity that provides a direction for the future. Failure to do this results in identity confusion.

Depending on the degree of exploration of possible identities, and the degree of commitment to a personal identity, usually known as ego identity, four outcomes have been suggested (Marcia 1980). These are *identity diffusion*, where there is a lack of focus; *identity foreclosure*, which involves a premature commitment based on the opinions of others; *moratorium*, where options are still being explored; and, *identity-achieved*, where a secure sense of self has been developed. Although various patterns are possible through life, moratorium is generally considered a necessary developmental step and achieved identity as the desired outcome (Waterman 1984). A developmental pattern has been suggested of diffusion and foreclosure as more primitive stages of identity formation, followed by moratorium, with identity achievement as the final stage (Phinney 1993).

The content of identity includes intrapsychic structure, interpersonal relations, and a variety of social determinants such as religion, occupation, political affiliation, ethnicity, and sex roles. Identity is an interactive concept, involving a personal sense of being a specific person as well as continuity, and a fit between personal experience and group ideals. Thus identity is a personal-social construct that develops, exists, and solidifies within the contexts of self-recognition and recognition from others (Galatzer-Levy and Cohler 1993). It is the social-relational aspect of identity that is of particular interest in understanding the significance of ethnic identity.

Kernberg (1976) views *ego identity* as the most developed identification system of three levels of the internalization of object relations. The other levels are *introjection* and *identification,* and all these systems comprise object representations, self-representations, and affective states. These identification systems are defensively organized at first by splitting, which is in turn replaced by repression.

The relational development of identity appears first in introjection, the basic level of internalization. Introjection uses perception and memory to reproduce interaction with others, the reciprocal smiling response illustrating the process at about three months. Introjections taking place in the context of gratification result in the construction of good internal objects, including the beginnings of positive identity, whereas frustration has the opposite effect of promoting bad internal objects and negative features of identity. Thus the experiential material is provided for the subsequent fusion of good and bad into an integrated self with an established identity, and the influence of significant others on this process is made apparent, along with increasing self-awareness.

The next level is identification, essentially the ability to take on a role, a socially recognized function that is part of interaction. This requires increased perceptive and cognitive abilities resulting in learning values based on observing and remembering interactive functions. Memories include images of objects carrying out interactive roles with the self, as well as a clearer differentiation of self-images, and further affective specificity in regard to objects, the self, and social interaction. Both personal roles as well as the roles of others, and the corresponding behaviors, are learned in the process of identification, beginning between 10 and 12 months, and established during the second year.

The highest level is ego identity, the result of a synthesis of introjections and identifications so that there is both an organization of self-image components to form a self-structure that contains personal and social identities, and the development of a sense of continuity. Objects are also organized into a world of others that includes a sense of consistency in self–other interactions, and these consistent, though modifiable, interaction patterns are experienced as characteristics by the individual, and in turn confirmed by the interpersonal environment through recognition of the individual. Although object relations are continually internalized, earlier identifications are replaced by selective, partial identifications that fit with individual identity elaboration. Ego identity will be integrated in different ways during various developmental stages, with the identity crisis prominent in, though not restricted to, adolescence. The aim is an integrated, harmonious ego identity conceptualizing the representational world and the self.

This view of ego identity suggests that although identity, as in "this is who I am," emphasizes individuation, it is always a representational concept that is relative to another, or others, and it is external as well as internal due to the need for identity confirmation and the fit between personal and social roles. Identity emphasizes meaning in order to facilitate the understanding of self and others that will make consistency and continuity of the self possible. In its most developed form, identity represents the integrity of the self.

DeVos (1993) has described the formation of social identity as a function of three interactive ego operations: *exclusion, intake,* and *expulsion.* Exclusion is externally directed to boundary protection, and internally to self-consistency. It includes denial, repression, dissociation, and concentration, and is a facilitator of social adaptations. Intake is exemplified in social identification, and is facilitated by the growth of language, cognition, and locomotion. Effective introception involves the development of empathic responsiveness and selective experience facilitating both internal stability and socialization. Expulsion refers to internal control of external events as a response to the impact on the ego. This involves the development of a discrete self contrasted with outside forces and adaptive control of aggression, including the use of projection.

In normal development an interactive balance is achieved among exclusion, introception, and expulsion, although often one mechanism is relatively dominant to form a personality style that includes a social identity. For example, exclusion involves repression and identity foreclosure, with indiscriminate intake resulting in identity diffusion and explosion emphasizing marginality as social mobility. The three mechanisms are considered innate ego capacities evolving in relational contexts to result in a variety of identities as forms of social adaptations. Optimal identity development is considered unusual, with defensive adaptation the norm.

Actually, the degree of explicit psychoanalytic theory about identity is relatively limited, although the term gets considerable usage. Similar to the concept of "self," it has had more mention than definition. Identity is defined here as a person's sense of being that results from the integration of subjectively valued and desired self-images with externally designated self-representations. Identity formation requires the presence and formation of what are often designated as ego functions, particularly affective, cognitive, and relational capacities that can result in reflective self-awareness. Identity involves self-awareness as personalized experience, and as observations of the self in relation to others. The continuity and integrity of identity require an adaptive fit between these two types of self-awareness. Both identity formation and identity maintenance require that the person develops resolutions between internally focused and externally imposed perspectives of the self so that identity can be sufficiently flexible and yet consistent enough to be operative as the agent of the self. Identity develops within an interpersonal context, but has its origins with the inception of personal awareness. For example, identity has been described as "the earliest awareness of a sense of being, . . . It is not a sense of who I am but that I am; . . ." (Mahler et al. 1975, p. 8).

The emphasis in the preceding statement is on separateness and individuality. Complementary to this are the developmental stages suggested by Stern (1985) of emergent, core, subjective, and verbal selves, within domains of relatedness. Identity involves autonomy and dependence, narcissism (Auerbach 1993) and mutual recognition (Benjamin 1992). Identity guides the essential self that is developed through transformations of essential others, and ethnicity is one of those others that ultimately comprises individual identity.

ETHNIC IDENTITY

Ethnic identity is the personal conception of that individual's ethnic group membership. The components of ethnic identity include ethnic *self-identification*, ethnic *constancy*, ethnic *role behaviors*, ethnic *knowledge*, and ethnic *feelings* (Bernal et al. 1993).

Ethnic identity is part of the developmental process of identity formation, with definite ethnic awareness appearing around age 10. Prior to age 7, children appear ethnocentric, with bias decreasing between 7 and 10 (Aboud and Doyle 1993). In relation to overall identity, ethnicity appears as a major influence due to its probable effect on other identities, such as gender and family (Stryker 1987). Ethnic identity is seen as particularly significant for groups who are less powerful than others in any country where different ethnic groups coexist. In these situations assimilation raises the possibility of the loss of individuality through suppression, repression, or denial of significant aspects of the self. Learning situations that are not attuned to ethnic differences limit equality of achievement. Finally, multiculturalism offers the possibility of secure ethnic identities that could reduce prejudice toward other ethnic groups (Aboud and Doyle 1993).

Phinney (1990) categorized black, white, Mexican-American, and Asian-American tenth-graders in regard to ethnic identity development. White students tended not to see their ethnicity as a significant issue. The remainder of the sample was divided into unexamined, moratorium, and achieved. The unexamined group either saw themselves as very similar to whites and acted as if they were white, or wished they were white and accepted white values and beliefs. The moratorium group are in the search process, having begun to question cultural values of the dominant group as well as starting to understand their ethnicity. Ethnic identity achievement involves a distinct sense of one's personal ethnicity. However, most of the adolescents had not explored their ethnic identity significantly, with most of their notions coming from parents or society. At the same time, ethnic identity appears to show a developmental progression toward achievement that is most apparent as adolescence unfolds, but is also influenced by acculturation attitudes that come from parents, other adults, peers, and dominant and nondominant groups within the society.

The initial conveyors of ethnic identity to the child are the family members, particularly the parents. This is a socialization process in which both external and internal forces influence the degree to which parents want to instill ethnic identity in their children. The family is operating within an ecological context throughout the child's development, but the significance of their influence will vary with the child's development of an evaluated ethnic identity. Thus ethnic identity in the incorporative stage is being part of an externally confirmed identity, with accompanying learned behaviors in the identificatory stage along with cognitive and affective appraisals of the personal meaning of ethnic identity; subsequently there is the affirmation, to varying degrees, of a relatively consistent ethnicity as an integral part of one's identity.

Thus early ethnic identity has self-identification that begins with being identified ethnically by a significant other, such as the mother, rather than there being an understanding of an ethnic origin. Ethnic constancy, namely the permanence of many ethnic characteristics, is not comprehended. Ethnic roles are engaged in without being understood in their context. Ethnic knowledge is basic, and ethnic preferences are primarily family preferences. In school-age children shifts occur and continue through adolescence in the direction of establishing a meaningful ethnic identity that includes constancy, conception of the traits and values in ethnic roles, and marked preferences and feelings for ethnicity (Knight et al. 1993).

A major influence for the family is their position within a multicultural society. This is a political, economic, and cultural context that in a society tends to be structured with a dominant group (or groups) and acculturating groups. The formation of ethnic identity is primarily an issue for the acculturating groups, who have a number of options open to them. The viability of these options, however, is tied to the dominant group because they establish the broad guidelines for daily living in legal, political, economic, and educational policies. The society of the United States is clearly multicultural, but has emphasized assimilation as the best way to manage cultural diversity.

With *assimilation* the minority group does not want to maintain distinctive ethnicity, instead moving toward absorption into the larger society. In contrast, there could be a strategy of *separation* where ethnic identity is strongly maintained and there is as little participation with the larger society as possible. A variation on this is *marginalization*, which also avoids participation but lacks ethnic solidarity. A fourth possibility is *integration* where there is a definite multiculturalism that involves strong ethnic identities as well as having shared institutions that constitute the framework of the society for all its members.

These acculturation strategies tend to operate on continuous dimensions, and among ethnic groups they are subject to individual preferences within each group as well. A significant issue for the effectiveness of any one of them is how an operational core of society can be established while at the same time supporting diverse ethnic identities. Thus, in the United States, this attempt is symbolized in terms such as Mexican-American, African-American, and other hyphenated Americans. Also, the emphasis on assimilation can be viewed as an expression of a wish for mutuality that leads to a truly multicultural unity, or it can be seen as a persistent ideology that forces minorities into a mainstream that serves the interests of the dominant ethnic group.

An expansive multiculturalism, such as that represented by the population of the United States, increases the complexity of effectively encouraging cultural diversity. Even Berry (1993), in praising Canada for a national policy of multiculturalism and pointing a finger at the United States for its bias toward assimilation, endorses the necessity of official languages (French and English) in Canada, which is assimilative.

Families then will have adopted an acculturation strategy that will affect their approach to providing an ethnic identity for children. Marginalization provides the least support and separation the most, but the latter puts the person into potential conflict with the larger society. In this society assimilation and integration are the most likely attitudes. These prevailing attitudes are the functions of individual attitudes, and are subject to change. Thus, if assimilation turns out to be ineffective because it is coercive rather than desired, it is probable that integration may then gain in its impact. At issue, of course, is what is happening in some countries where there appears to be no room for ethnic separation. Many of these countries had a communist form of government that suppressed traditional ethnic identities. The result appears to have been increased covert ethnic identification that took a discriminatory form once it could be expressed. The saliency of ethnicity is influenced by the context of situations (Stryker 1987).

Major social ecology influences are represented by the family background, its structure, and the sociocultural environment (Knight et al. 1993). In regard to family background, parents who are newly arrived in the United States and have strong ethnic identities themselves are likely to try to foster similar identities in their children. Family structure, such as interdependence, patterns of status, and family size, also can play a significant role. These interact with the level of urbanization of the community, family and community socioeconomic status, and community and society reactions to a particular ethnic group. Then, in addition to the immediate family, there are extended family and other socialization agents, such as teachers, peers, neighbors, and the media. Ethnic identity is part of a social identity that is acquired through a socialization process of transmission of practices, attitudes, values, beliefs, and specific content from both the family and nonfamilial sources. A variety of patterns is possible, with the possibility of conflict arising due to different information coming from different agents.

Enculturation is a socialization process aimed at bringing an individual into accord with the beliefs, values, and behaviors of the person's ethnic group, resulting in an ethnic identity. *Acculturation* is a process of adaptation to the general society where beliefs, values, and behaviors of the dominant group are the norm. For nondominant groups there is a high probability of conflict between enculturation and acculturation, whereas the dominant group has identity congruence. Thus, for the dominant group, there is general consistency between the ethnic identity of enculturation and the social identity of acculturation. In contrast, nondominant groups have conflicts based on the degree of disparity between their ethnic and social identities. These conflicts are a function of both personality factors, such as the adherence to and manifestations of ethnic identity, and dominant group permeability for different ethnic identities.

An ethnic identity is part of the self concept, a self-representation that gives ethnicity personal meaning. Ethnic identity can be conceptualized as a schema that contributes to self activity by structuring experience and controlling behavior according to ethnic values. This schema evolves from memory structures. Cognitive and affective development affect the rate of acquisition of ethnic content, the assignment of meaning to ethnicity as both self and object representations, and in turn the relevance and complexity of ethnic identity as an adaptive function.

Ethnic identity has both integrative and defensive functions. The former are in place when ethnic identity is used as one type of essential other that provides meaning and coherence to the self (Galatzer-Levy and Cohler 1993). It can operate as what Kohut (1985) viewed as a cultural self-object that enhances morale and supports the vitality and continuity of the self.

The defensive aspects appear as reactions to threats to the self. Exclusionary defenses, such as denial, isolation, and repression, foster identity foreclosure and ethnic separation. Threats to the integrity of the self are reacted to by patterns of nonlearning. Minority children who find themselves dealing with unfamiliar social patterns in school may employ selective permeability (DeVos 1993) to alienate from peers, resulting in marginality to both their ethnic group and the larger society. Tension within the family may interfere with ethnic identification and result in children seeking external group support. Some ethnic identities have constrictive learning where identity is very narrowly depicted. In essence, exclusionary defenses may emphasize rigid ethnic identities to avoid the threat of alternate possibilities usually embodied in other contact groups who are discriminatory, or it may lead to rejection of ethnic identity as an attempt at adaptation based on perceived disadvantages of ethnicity.

Intake mechanisms tend to be involved as introjective defenses that stress superficiality and impermanence of identification. The result is diffusion of ethnic identity. One example is the imitation of others where boundaries are dissolved to the point of losing a sense of self. Another is the incapacity to understand similarities in people who are viewed as not sufficiently similar. Intake is defensively distorted to diffuse ethnic identity, leaving the individual vulnerable to external influences. There is a lack of regulation and balance of internalization that limits internal consistency.

DeVos (1993) suggests that the optimal solution is having identification and the capacity for empathy in harmony with experiential selectivity and contrastiveness illustrated in detachment and objectivity. Thus, for example, it is possible to remain a member of one ethnic group and still be empathic with other groups. When intake is out of balance, then there can be identity diffusion, or there may be exclusion and detachment to the point of imbalance with ethnic separation.

Expulsion as a defense splits the perceived good from the bad and projects undesired qualities of the self to others. Others are contrasted with the individual, and cognitive control is stressed relative to affective awareness and expression. The result is excessive social mobility and individuality, resulting in marginal ethnic identity.

Integration has tended to be viewed as the ideal ethnic identity policy in any pluralistic, multicultural society (Berry 1993, Berry et al. 1989, DeVos 1993). However, the relationship between bicultural identity and adjustment or self-esteem is a function of contextual factors, including the cultural and social situations as well as personal characteristics (Ratheram-Borus 1993). For example, in both traditional and segregated school settings exposure to ethnic diversity can negatively affect adjustment (Ramirez 1983). It has been suggested that for adolescents the value of ethnicity depends on dominant group attitudes, ethnic group strength, freedom of contact between groups, and family relationships (Rosenthal 1987). An overall bicultural context is both more receptive and facilitative of bicultural ethnic identities, so that ideal concepts of ethnic identity have to be referenced to their settings.

ETHNIC IDENTITY IN THE UNITED STATES

The formation of identity is a developmental process involving both intrapsychic and interpersonal elements. The intrapsychic component includes the use of cognitive and affective potentials to form self-representations and object representations that are involved in the creation of a self, as well as drive and structural integration. The interpersonal world supplies the interactions that are opportunities for integration and models for identification. Relations with significant others, persons as well as cultural and societal structures, provide mirroring, mutuality, and idealizing that lead to the formation of personal meaning within the self, namely an identity. Identity development involves integrating an egocentric self-perspective with an intrasubjective perspective of the self as an object.

Identity formation begins with the first experience of awareness, but the integrative capacity that involves reflection on the different perspectives of the self seems to come about during the second year of life (Auerbach 1993). Identity formation continues throughout the life cycle, with adolescence a particularly crucial time for the coherence and stability of identity, although identity may always have a certain fluidity due to the impact of different life-stage changes. Also, identity is subject to a variety of contextual features, particularly relational, but also constitutional, developmental, and cultural.

Initially, ethnic identity appears to be primarily the creation of the adult caregivers of children. This is affected by sources outside the family, particularly school, peers, and the media, so that there is an increasing awareness of the beliefs about ethnicity that exist in the larger culture as well as within one's own ethnic group. By adolescence ethnic identity is relatively self-determined, with ethnicity as an organizing construct that includes ethnic self-labels, knowledge of distinctive attributes of different groups, such as color and language, attitudes toward ethnic groups, and ethnically linked values, behaviors, and social expectations. A choice of a reference group tends to be made in adolescence, and is mainstream, or has a strong ethnic identification, or is bicultural. However, for most adolescents the identity process still has a way to go because many have not initiated the process of self-discovery that would lead to an achieved identity, although there is the developmental capability of making a commitment to ethnic roles (Phinney 1993). The frequent picture is the evolution of ethnic identity through adolescence with firm commitment established in adulthood (Ratheram-Borus 1993).

In the United States there is a mainstream American culture that is the product of many ethnic groups, although some have been more prominent than others. In the mainstream culture a number of factors have contributed to an American ethnic identity. One is a prevailing philosophy of assimilation based on the belief that such fusion and merger would be desired both by those who entered the country as well as those who were already here, and that it would provide the most effective way to operate the country. Then, many families had mixed ethnic backgrounds, so that the most efficient method of ethnic identity tended to be viewed as an American designation. Ethnic heritages and backgrounds appeared to be just that, background, as this country was primarily one of immigrants anyway. The Native Americans became a minority rather quickly and lost their power even more rapidly, so the nation of immigrants-turned-into-Americans tended to prevail. Although in the assimilated group there were status hierarchies linked to ancestry, many ethnic groups were blended and got a share of the power and pride by viewing themselves as particularly and primarily American and secondarily as having an ethnic background.

The precedence of polarity in the power structure, which may well be representative of a basic tendency to polarity in human personalities (Herron and Javier 1996), restricted the degree of assimilation into the power structure. For large minority groups ethnicity was used by the dominant group to discriminate against the minorities. The result has been a renewed emphasis on the significance of ethnicity as assimilation appears to offer only a paradoxical identity as an American rather than equal opportunities and equal rights. In some instances the result is to stress an ethnic identity that is distinct from being American. Children of parents who feel this way will be raised with a strong emphasis on their ethnicity in an environment that is separated as much as possible from other ethnic groups and the mainstream society. Such an identity is difficult to maintain in the United States, and attempts to foster it are likely to cause conflicts with other groups. At the same time, attempts to assimilate as ethnic denial or reaction formation can cause conflict with the family and others within one's ethnic group. Thus, emphasizing separation creates a potential for marginality in which the individual feels a lack of any ethnicity as well as anger and resentment at both one's own group and other groups.

Separation also can come from a source other than one's ethnic group, namely from other groups, particularly the dominant group, when there is prejudice and discrimination that emphasizes ethnic distinctions. Although this is not official policy in the United States, it often appears, resulting in enforced separation. The ethnic identity available in discriminatory situations is harder to stabilize for the minority group members because it is viewed negatively by the dominant group, and there are often status and power hierarchies between ethnic groups that are reinforced by the dominant group and foster discrimination among ethnic groups. Some minority groups may develop cohesive status around resisting their position in society, and this has helped alter the situation, but it also has limits in respect to its effectiveness with the rest of society. Fractionation and division based on attempts at assimilation are also possibilities where ethnic identity is ambivalent.

Assimilation appears to have limited success in making effective use of ethnic identity. The current trend appears to be toward integration through multiculturalism in which cultural diversity is viewed as an asset to be maintained and enhanced. Mainstream society and culture then need to be sufficiently porous to absorb a continuing variety of influences that reshape the American identity. National unity is first based on respect and pride for personal identity, of which ethnicity is a significant part. Accompanying this is respect for others and a desire to share feelings, thoughts, attitudes, and practices. There is an evolution of the effective degree of ethnicity that is mixed with national identity to result in an identifiable, distinctive nation. An existing model that illustrates multiple identities is that of residence, namely areas within a city, cities within a state, and states within a country, each providing its residents with an identity.

Undoubtedly, a fundamental issue is the distribution of power among the citizens of any country. True multiculturalism requires power sharing and equality of opportunity. This can be threatening to those already in power, and the process of change is often hampered by policies that inflict wounds as they attempt to create fairness and balance. Ethnic identities can be sources of difficulty as well as pride because, as with any aspect of identity, distinctive features can clash with the distinctive features of one or more other identities held by other people. Also, although ethnic identity has not been identified in the United States as the major source of a person's self-concept (Ratheram-Borus 1993), it is an increasingly significant source of conflict, both in regard to self-integration and integration with others. Multiculturation appears to be evolving out of these conflicts, but to be effective it will require special cultural blends of attitudes, values, and behaviors. All that means change, and the anxiety that usually accompanies life being different.

Psychoanalytic theory and practice, with their personal developmental understanding of change, offer opportunities to facilitate integrative ethnic identities and to defuse and prevent ethnic tension. For this to occur, however, psychoanalysis needs to give greater recognition to the significance of ethnicity as a part of the self as well as to its broader social significance. In addition, concentration must be given to understanding and reformulating the ethnic subjectivity of psychoanalysts so that multiculturalism is distinct from a rather singular middle-class pancultural theory of assimilation. The temptation is identity foreclosure around a comfortable, dominant-group national identity that still limits access to power. The goal is the formation of a national identity that integrates personal ethnicity, other group acceptance, and power sharing to form a union of equality.

REFERENCES

Aboud, F. E., and Doyle, A. B. (1993). The early development of ethnic identity and attitudes. In *Ethnic Identity*, ed. M. E. Bernal and G. P. Knight, pp. 47–59. Albany: State University of New York Press.

Auerbach, J. S. (1993). The origins of narcissism and narcissistic personality disorder: a theoretical and empirical reformulation. In *Psychoanalytic Perspectives on Psychopathology*, ed. J. M. Masling and R. F. Bornstein, pp. 43–110. Washington, DC: American Psychological Association.

Benjamin, J. (1992). Recognition and destruction. an outline of intersubjectivity. In *Relational Perspectives in Psychoanalysis*, ed. N. J. Skolnick and S. C. Warshaw, pp. 43–60. Hillsdale, NJ: Analytic Press.

Bernal, M. E., Knight, G. P., Ocampo, K. A., et al. (1993). Development of Mexican American identity. In *Ethnic Identity*, ed. M. E. Bernal and G. P. Knight, pp. 31–59. Albany: State University of New York Press.

Berry, J. W. (1993). Ethnic identity in plural societies. In *Ethnic Identity*, ed. M. E. Bernal and G. P. Knight, pp. 271–296. Albany: State University of New York Press.

Berry, J. W., Kim, U., Power, S., et al. (1989). Acculturation attitudes in plural societies. *Applied Psychology* 38:185–206.

DeVos, G. A. (1993). A psychocultural approach to ethnic interaction in contemporary research. In *Ethnic Identity*, ed. M. E. Bernal and G. P. Knight, pp. 233–268. Albany: State University of New York Press.

Erikson, E. H. (1982). *The Life Cycle Completed*. New York: Norton.

Freud, S. (1926). Address to the society of B'nai B'rith. *Standard Edition* 20:271–276.

Galatzer-Levy, R. M., and Cohler, B. J. (1993). *The Essential Other. A Developmental Psychology of the Self.* New York: Basic Books.

Herron, W. G., and Javier, R. A. (1996). The psychogenesis of poverty: some psychoanalytic conceptualizations. *Psychoanalytic Review* 83:631–640.

Jiobu, R. M. (1990). *City and Inequality.* Albany: State University of New York Press.

Kernberg, O. (1976). *Object Relations Theory and Clinical Psychoanalysis.* New York: Jason Aronson.

Knight, G. P., Bernal, M. E., Garza, C. A., and Cota, M. K. (1993). A social cognitive model of the development of ethnic identity and ethnically based behaviors. In *Ethnic Identity*, ed. M. E. Bernal and G. P. Knight, pp. 212–234. Albany: State University of New York Press.

Kohut, H. (1985). Idealization and cultural self-objects. In *Self Psychology and the Humanities: Reflections on a New Psychoanalytic Approach by Heinz Kohut*, ed. C. Strozier, pp. 232–243. New York: Norton.

Mahler, M. S., Pine, F., and Bergman, A. (1975). *The Psychological Birth of the Human Infant.* New York: Basic Books.

Marcia, J. (1980). Identity in adolescence. In *Handbook of Adolescent Psychology*, ed. J. Adelson, pp. 159–187. New York: Wiley.

Moore, B. E., and Fine, B. D., eds. (1991). *Psychoanalytic Terms and Concepts.* New Haven, CT: Yale University Press.

Ocampo, K. A., Bernal, M. E., and Knight, G. P. (1993). Gender, race, and ethnicity: the sequencing of social constancies. In *Ethnic Identity*, ed. M. E. Bernal and G. P. Knight, pp. 11–30. Albany: State University of New York Press.

Phinney, J. S. (1990). Ethnic identity in adolescence and adults: review of research. *Psychological Bulletin* 108:499–514.

——— (1993). A three stage model of ethnic identity development in adolescence. In *Ethnic Identity*, ed. M. E. Bernal and G. P. Knight, pp. 61–69. Albany: State University of New York Press.

Ramirez, M. III. (1983). *Psychology of the Americas: Mutizo Perspectives on Personality and Mental Health.* New York: Pergamon.

Ratheram-Borus, M. J. (1993). Biculturalism among adolescents. In *Ethnic Identity*, ed. M. E. Bernal and G. P. Knights, pp. 81–102. Albany: State University of New York Press.

Rosenthal, D. (1987). Ethnic identity development in adolescents. In *Children's Ethnic Socialization: Pluralism and Development*, ed. J. Phinney and M. Ratheram, pp. 156–179. Beverly Hills, CA: Sage.

Stern, D. (1985). *The Interpersonal World of the Infant.* New York: Basic Books.

Stryker, S. (1987). Identity theory: developments and extensions. In *Self and Identity: Psychosocial Perspectives*, ed. K. Yardley and T. Honess, pp. 89–103. Chichester, England: Wiley.

Waterman, A. (1984). *The Psychology of Individualism.* New York: Praeger.

15

The Ethnic Unconscious and Its Role in Transference, Resistance, and Countertransference

RAFAEL ART. JAVIER AND MARIO RENDON

A theory of the human condition that does not provide an adequate explanatory paradigm to understand the basic human dilemma and the motivational factors affecting our position in the world vis-à-vis ourselves and others is soon rendered ineffective and obsolete. Although a number of psychoanalytic thinkers have already provided a rich foundation in this regard (Erikson 1963, Freud 1894, 1905, 1924, Kohut 1971, Sullivan 1953, Winnicott 1965), the proliferation of violence in our society, international conflicts giving rise to wars within and among nations, the socioeconomic and sociopolitical realities that perpetuate poverty in its citizens, rape, child abuse, family violence, and the like are all in dire need of psychoanalytic attention. This is particularly the case with regard to the complex issues surrounding ethnic tension, a phenomenon that has become more and more prominent at the international and national level. Psychoanalysis is, indeed, in the best position to offer an in-depth understanding of the complex human motivations inherent in ethnic tension, racism and discrimination, and other prejudicial phenomena because of its unique set of formulations of mental function that are assumed to affect all human behavior (Altman 1993, Frosh 1989, Herron and Javier 1996, Javier 1990, Javier and Herron 1992, 1993, Perez Foster 1993, Thompson 1987).

In general, however, psychoanalytic formulations have focused in the main on the study of the individual's internal structure, the study of the mind as "a theater of conflict" (Kaplan 1984, p. 132), without much concern with the possible influence of ethnic components in the psychic structure. According to Kaplan, what makes psychoanalysis particularly powerful is its focus on the mental transformation of social forces, in which the mind in society is viewed as a vicissitude of object relations and society in mind is viewed as a process of internalization. Our interest at this point is to extend the study of the mind as "a theater of conflict" to also include the issue of ethnicity and ethnic tension. It is our goal to provide a psychoanalytic explanation for ethnic conflict by expanding some of the psychological mechanisms already proposed in psychoanalytic formulations.

Indeed, ethnic factors may define the very nature of the analytic dyad because ethnicity is an inescapable fact of life and one that permeates and determines the very nature of one's interaction in the world and the quality of one's psychic reality. And yet our understanding of the phenomenon is "limited to a condemnation of it as if it was just an undesirable, fictitious social phenomenon" (Javier 1994, p. 29). The problem with that position is that it tends to encourage a fragmented view of the issues surrounding ethnic tension between individuals and nations rather than to advance a psychological and psychoanalytic understanding of the phenomenon. Mystification is thus maintained.

ON PROVIDING A PSYCHOANALYTIC PERSPECTIVE ON ETHNIC TENSION: THE ETHNIC UNCONSCIOUS

What we are suggesting here is that the systematic study of ethnicity in psychoanalysis could offer a tremendous enrichment to the psychoanalytic formulation of psychic structure when it allows ethnic components to be part of the psychoanalytic equation. The nature of identification and introjection, as well as the nature of self-definition, projection, and projective identification could thus be affected. Only from that rich perspective are we in a position to provide a psychoanalytic explanation of what is going on in the former Yugoslavia, in what has been termed the "ethnic cleansing" of the Muslims by the Serbs and the Croats; or the tension in the Middle East between the Arab countries and Israel; the ethnic divisions in Russia; the implementation of legal mandates in Malaysia to ensure superiority of Malaysian citizens over the Chinese; the prejudicial treatment by Chinese against Taiwanese and Japanese against other Asian and non-Asian individuals (Roland 1989); the ethnic tension in South and Central America, or in the Caribbean Islands in which the color of the skin and whether you are of Indian or African descent could determine your social and political status (Javier and Yussef 1995); the Los Angeles riot following the Rodney King verdict, which became the catalyst for the expression of still unresolved racial discrimination problems that have historically characterized the lives of African Americans in the United States (West 1993); the killing of the hasidic students by the Arab militants at the Brooklyn Bridge; or the bombing of the World Trade Center and the tension in Crown Heights. All of these conflicts are clearly "ethnic." Although this may seem obvious, the unconscious influences fueling the conflict remain largely unknown. We are suggesting that while we can find clear socioeconomic and sociopolitical explanations for such events, the individual's personal psychology mediates the social event and can thus provide revealing and powerful perspectives.

The importance of ethnicity on psychological development is based on the fact that ethnic identity is psychologically governed by the same mechanism as the general identity. In fact, it is impossible to think about identity without its ethnic nature. Strongly grounded in each individual by a growing array of symbolic rituals in which specific cultural values are transmitted, a culturally influenced world view is thus established. Assumptions concerning causality, time, space, and human nature (Dana 1993, Kearney 1975), as well as basic belief systems and culturally specific styles of relating, are programmed in this manner and provide the foundation for the development of the self-identity. That is, it is in the context of our reference group that one develops a sense of self and others as "us and them" (Dana 1993, Knight et al. 1993, Roland 1989). Earlier identifications and introjections mediated by one's cultural and ethnic object world determine the structure and content of one's psychic reality (Javier and Yussef 1995). It is not surprising then that the nature of transference and countertransference can be so poignantly affected by these factors as the nature of the analyst's perception and the perception of the patient are affected by their respective psychic reality, which is in turn influenced by their idiosyncratic ethnic history. Freud was very much aware of these influences (Brunner 1991), and, although not fully discussed in his basic psychoanalytic conceptualizations, their presence was palpable in his conceptualization of superego formation, the process of internalization, identity formation and self-definition (Freud 1914, 1923, Herron 1992, Kernberg 1975,

Tyson and Tyson 1984). Freud thus explicitly refers to the problem in his "Group Psychology" (1921).

It is from this perspective that the concept of "ethnic unconscious" was proposed to refer to the individual's unconscious processes that can be explained only in reference to his or her specific cultural background. Although the concept is not a new one, its application by Herron (1995) to understand ethnic tension is novel. According to his formulation, the ethnic unconscious refers to "repressed material that each generation shares with the next and is shared with most people of that ethnic group" (p. 521). The nature of self-identity is thus determined. Ethnicity in this context is defined as "the degree of identification of a person with an ethnic group that in some way is his or her group of origin" (p. 524); and thus becomes part of the total self. For example, if an individual grows up in an Anglo-Saxon environment in which individualism, autonomy, independence, self-containment, egocentrism, and personal control are encouraged, then the self-concept (Dana 1993) and the nature of the psychic structure are likely to be characterized by these components. The nature of these individuals' transference is also likely to be colored by these components in which the verbal interaction will be characterized by direct eye contact, limited physical contact, and controlled emotion. Also important for these individuals are rigid time schedules, planning and delayed gratification (Dana 1993). In the case of individuals whose self-identity was influenced by a society that demands a very different level of interaction from its members, such as when concern for the others and collectivism take precedent over the need of the individual (Chan and Leong 1994), the nature of the self-concept and the transference will also be affected by these factors.

As is the case with any unconscious material, the ethnic unconscious for these individuals is viewed as a component of the personality to be analyzed as part of the total self. It is characterized by mental representations of folklore or heritage specific to the reference group and enduringly different and distinctive culturally colored fantasies. It also has to do with the patient's expectation that the analyst will be an expert authority and possibly belong to a different group. This is one of the central points made by Thompson (1995). She presented rich clinical material to illustrate not only the vicissitude of race and ethnicity in the development of self-identity, but the complications that such definition could introduce in the analysis of preoedipal and oedipal material. This is the case for one of her patients in which race was used as a shield to avoid the pain connected to early abandonment by his mother; for another with lighter skin color than others in her family, skin color was used to explain feelings of rejection by her own family as well as her own difficulty with achievement. For still another it was used to deny and split off important aspects of the self. The fact of the matter is that, to the extent to which the individual's relationship to his or her race, ethnicity, and linguistic dimensions is influenced by unconscious motivation of negative or positive valence, it may complicate the clinical picture at various levels. From the perspective of the patient, there could be an attempt to use race, ethnicity, and language as a repository and explanation of all the individual's anxiety and to deny important aspects of his or her experience with others. Such a posture limits the level of analytic inquiry and compromises the analytic stance. From the perspective of the therapist/analyst, it may result in what Judith Welles (1993) refers to in her paper of the same title as "Counterfeit Analyses: Maintaining the Illusion of Knowing," in which the individual's basic dynamic and unconscious motivations remain unknown and unanalyzed because of a collusion by the therapist/analyst with the patient. Thompson's paper speaks eloquently of the need to subject race and ethnicity to the same level of inquiry as other information that impedes the development of a productive and relatively happy existence in the patient. The analysis of mental representations and culturally colored fantasies could provide a window for the analysis of the ethnic unconscious of these individuals as it relates to the development of the self-representation and transference material. According to Herron (1995), these fantasies and representations are part of psychic dynamism of the individual and subject to what are considered the universals of psychoanalysis, "namely topographic, structural, dynamic, economic, genetic, adaptive, and social views of the personality" (p. 528).

A PSYCHOLOGICAL MECHANISM OF ETHNIC TENSION

An important point made by Herron (1995) and clinically elaborated by Thompson (1995), which has some bearing on the question regarding the psychoanalytic explanation of ethnic tension, is the idea that the integrity of the ethnic unconscious may be supported "by isolating some culture materials as distinctive fantasies. . . . [and/or by] relegating certain personal conflicts to the arena of ethnic differences, an acceptable social convention in some extent in many cultures" (p. 527). Since "every culture is viewed as having defensive hierarchies that result in cultural patterns and ethnic characters" (p. 526); when these defenses are incorporated as part of the ethnic person's psychic configuration, the result is the interplay of ethnic contents and more general personality characteristics. To the extent to which the resulting self-definition becomes embattled and "a self-identity is developed by opposition," as discussed by Thompson (1995, p. 533), ethnic tension will arise. Opposition is always part of identity, and ethnic opposition is no exception. This is the case because a self-definition developed in this manner is characterized by the primacy of exclusionary defenses—such as denial, isolation, and repression—which fosters identity foreclosure and ethnic separation, as amply discussed by Herron (1994) in another paper. The self-identity thus established is fraught with vulnerabilities, fears, and anxieties, which require the stubborn adherence to a narcissistic object choice and where a difference is viewed as undesirable and the cause of great personal anxiety. The megalomaniac quality of the psychic structure of these individuals makes what is different then the object of their negative projections, resulting in stereotyping; what has qualities assumed to be similar to theirs is endowed with a high level of desirability. Prejudice can thus be utilized as an attempt at buffering a more basic personal anxiety related to these individuals' self-definition. Thus the individual's need for stereotyping could be seen as a reflection of unresolved infantile material, a perspective advanced by Kaplan (1993) in his discussion of a paper on sexuality and race. In this paper he suggested that stereotypes "derive from infantile mythologies of power, sexuality, value, morality and much else that are mirrored in the social order as ideals to be conformed to or rejected in the cause of passing as normal to oneself and others" (p. 2). It is expected that, as the issues related to the "narcissism of minor differences" (Freud 1921, p. 101) involved in categorizing peoples are challenged by what Herron (1995) calls a "new version and aspects of the meaning of ethnicity to the individual" (p. 527), there could be a corresponding shift in self and object representations in which the process of adaptation and identification can resume a more positive course.

This is the basic point made by Moskowitz (1995). He postulates that, although the potential for racism is deep and universal, it can become actualized only in an atmosphere where stereotyping becomes a central component of the interaction. There is no ethnicity, he says. What there is "is hatred and the need to deny our own badness, and fear of our own hatred. Ethnicity and race are fantasies which we use to deny our own badness and display it onto others, as well as to protect ourselves against the very real hatred that others may have of us" (p. 553).

CONCLUSION

Herron (1995), Thompson (1995), and Moskowitz (1995) have advanced a number of important points related to the role of ethnicity, culture, race, and language in the development of self-definition as well as the nature of identification. The content of the unconscious is assumed to be affected by these materials, resulting in what is referred to as the "ethnic unconscious." The transference and countertransference implications related to this material are also amply discussed. It is our goal to encourage readers to engage in further discussion about the issue of ethnicity and culture in what pertains to psychoanalytic conceptualization and practice. We believe that the fact that ethnicity has been traditionally left out of psychoanalytic discourse as it regards identity and the unconscious is part of a secular trend that is being philosophically eroded by the so-called postmodern movement. Molecular issues, such as ethnicity, will increasingly gain an importance over molar issues as the "great narrative."

It is our belief that psychoanalytic formulation has a lot to offer with regard to finding psychoanalytic explanation for the tension (ethnic tension) in our society and the world at large. It is also our belief that only by including, in a systematic way, the role of ethnicity and culture in the nature and content of the psychic structure will we be able to appreciate at a much deeper and richer level the nature of the individual's psychic dilemma. To the extent to which we allow these dimensions to inform our analytic work, it is less likely that we will engage in counterfeit analysis in which we maintain the illusion of knowing the true nature of the patient's difficulties.

REFERENCES

Altman, N. (1993). Psychoanalysis and the urban poor. *Psychoanalytic Dialogues* 3:29–49.
Brunner, J. (1991). The(ir) relevance of Freud's Jewish identity to the origins of psychoanalysis. *Psychoanalysis and Contemporary Thought* 14:655–684.
Chan, S., and Leong, C. (1994). Chinese families in transition; cultural conflict and adjustment problems. *Journal of Social Distress and the Homeless* 3:263–281.
Dana, R. H. (1993). *Multicultural Assessment Perspectives for Professional Psychology.* Boston: Allyn & Bacon.
Erikson, E. H. (1963). *Childhood and Society.* 2nd ed.. New York: Norton.
Freud, S. (1894). The neuro-psychoses of defence. *Standard Edition* 3:45–61.
——— (1905). Three essays on the theory of sexuality. *Standard Edition* 7:130–254.
——— (1914). On narcissism: an introduction. *Standard Edition* 14:73–102.
——— (1921). Group psychology and the analysis of the ego. *Standard Edition* 18:67–143.
——— (1923). The ego and the id. *Standard Edition* 19:12–66.
——— (1924). The economic problem of masochism. *Standard Edition* 19:157–170.
Frosh, S. (1989). Psychoanalysis and racism. In *Psychoanalysis and Psychology,* pp. 229–244. New York: Macmillan.

Herron, W. G. (1992). *The development of the ethnic unconscious.* Paper presented at the Annual Convention of the American Psychological Association, Washington, DC, August.

—— (1994). *The development of the ethnic identity.* Paper presented at the APA Div. 39 Spring Meetings, Washington, DC, Spring.

—— (1995). Development of the ethnic unconscious. *Psychoanalytic Psychology* 12:521–532.

Herron, W. G., and Javier, R. A. (1996). The psychogenesis of poverty: some psychoanalytic conceptions. *Psychoanalytic Review* 83:611–620.

Javier, R. A. (1990). The suitability of insight-oriented psychotherapy for the Hispanic poor. *American Journal of Psychoanalysis* 50:305–318.

—— (1994). Committee on Multicultural concerns, ethnic tension, and the analytic situation. *Psychologist Psychoanalyst* 14:29–30.

Javier, R. A., and Herron, W. G. (1992). Psychoanalysis, the Hispanic poor, and the disadvantaged: application and conceptualization. *Journal of the American Academy of Psychoanalysis* 20:455–476.

—— (1993). *Personal reflections on the uneasy relationship.* Presented at the APA Div. 39 Spring meeting mini-conference on Psychoanalysis, Politics and the Good Society, New York, April.

Javier, R. A., and Yussef, M. (1995). A Latino perspective of the role of ethnicity in the development of moral values: implications for psychoanalytic theory and practice. *Journal of the American Academy of Psychoanalysis* 23:79–97.

Kaplan, D. M. (1984). "Thoughts for the times on war and death": a psychoanalytic address on an interdisciplinary problem. *International Review of Psychoanalysis* 11:131–141.

—— (1993). *Discussion of Dr. Stephen Tien's paper on Sexuality and Race: panel (with Dr. Homes and Lesser) on old lines, new boundaries.* Presented at the APA Div. 39 Spring meeting, New York, April.

Kearney, M. (1975). World view theory and study. In *Annual Review of Anthropology*, ed. B. J. Siegel, 4:247–270.

Kernberg, O. (1975). *Borderline Conditions and Pathological Narcissism.* New York: Jason Aronson.

Knight, G. P., Cota, M. K., and Bernal, M. E. (1993). The socialization of cooperative, competitive, and individualistic preference among Mexican American children: the mediating role of ethnic identity. *Hispanic Journal of Behavioral Sciences* 15:291–309.

Kohut, H. (1971). *The Analysis of the Self.* New York: International Universities Press.

Moskowitz, M. (1995). Ethnicity and the fantasy of ethnicity. *Psychoanalytic Psychology* 12:547–555.

Perez Foster, R. M. (1993). The social politics of psychoanalysis: commentary on Neil Altman's "Psychoanalysis and the urban poor." *Psychoanalytic Dialogues* 3:69–83.

Roland, A. (1989). *In Search of Self in India and Japan.* Princeton, NJ: Princeton University Press.

Sullivan, H. S. (1953). *The Interpersonal Theory of Psychiatry*. New York: Norton.

Thompson, C. (1987). Racism or neuroticism?: an entangled dilemma for the black middle class patient. *Journal of the American Academy of Psychoanalysis* 15:395–405.

——— (1995). Self-definition by opposition: a consequence of minority status. *Psychoanalytic Psychology* 12:533–545.

Tyson, P., and Tyson, R. L. (1984). Narcissism and superego development. *Journal of the American Psychoanalytic Association* 32:75–98.

Welles, J. K. (1993). *Counterfeit analyses: maintaining the illusion of knowing*. Paper presented at the APA Division 39 Spring meeting, New York, April.

West, C. (1993). *Race Matters*. Boston: Beacon.

Winnicott, D. W. (1965). *The Maturational Processes and the Facilitating Environment*. New York: International Universities Press.

16

Development of the Ethnic Unconscious

WILLIAM G. HERRON

This chapter introduces a concept, the ethnic unconscious, which is new in the way that it will be depicted here, yet has a history. In that regard it is a reintroduction, for the term has used before, and many of the issues involved have at least been touched upon in the past. For example, the relationship between culture in its vast expanse and psychoanalysis was, as noted recently by Wolfenstein (1991), there from the origination of a psychoanalytic way of thinking.

The generic concept of the unconscious has a similar, although clearly more prominent history. Thus in 1922 Freud stated, "The assumption that there are unconscious mental processes, the recognition of the theory of resistance and repression, the appreciation of the importance of sexuality and of the Oedipus complex—these constitute the principal subject matter of psycho-analysis and the foundation of its theory" (1923, p. 247). Of course, the unconscious had been discovered before that (Ellenberger 1970, Herron 1962), but it was Freud who invested it with unrelenting and persistent power.

In 1989 Gillespie elaborated the basics of psychoanalysis that have remained essential to its theory and practice. Six propositions were described in this context, and they all reflect the existence of the unconscious. Gillespie depicted the growth of psychoanalysis in a metaphor as the growth of a great tree with Freud providing the main trunk. The development of the unconscious can be viewed this way as well, with significant branches appearing in certain ways that ultimately reshape the tree and provide it with some of its more salient adaptive features. The development of the ethnic unconscious has the potential for being one of those branches.

The progression of psychoanalytic theory has in some ways facilitated the type of exploration described here, but in other ways has inhibited it. The facilitation has been in the expansions of the role of the unconscious. Thus, from a structural point of view the ego got more space. From a motivational point of view relational wishes reached for parity with, or supremacy over, libidinal and aggressive wishes. In this vein, Sandler (1989) describes the unconscious wish to establish certain types of relationships that are motivated by the control of feeling states, such as the restoration of security.

However, the issue of concern here is the content of the unconscious, which has always had a murky and mysterious flavor due to the defining characteristic of unawareness, and probably also due to the metaphorical language employed in turn to describe unconscious operations. A good example of the latter is projective identification (Welt and Herron 1990).

The unconscious itself, or the layered unconscious, represented various degrees of accessibility of material to awareness, and thus created the probability that much of what is unconscious will never see the light of day and what does will be idiosyncratic. Thus effort has seemed to go more in the direction of identifying expected themes, as the oedipal conflict, or trying to find out how the unconscious works. For example, Eagle (1985) contrasts the view that unconscious processes are neural activities, some of which get conscious representation, with the idea that unconscious motives are disclaimed actions in the domain of the person rather than the organism. Certainly these are important issues, and they involve content, but indirectly, particularly when it comes to what could be considered cultural, social, racial, or ethnic.

Nonetheless, the expansion in exploration of the unconscious should involve, directly or indirectly, growth in the knowledge of its potential and actualized contents, including more room for cultural components. Wolfenstein (1991) has noted that psychoanalysis is potentially the most comprehensive method of cultural knowledge available. However, the understanding and study of the unconscious has not yet reflected a major degree of interest in its cultural components. What has dominated has been individual motivation, whether couched in biological, interpersonal, or intersubjective terms.

Although an individual psychology does not have to be opposed to a social psychology, in psychoanalysis that has frequently been the case. At the same time, there is increasing acknowledgment that the content of the unconscious is always subject to cultural influences, but the history of psychoanalysis, and its current approaches, do not reflect the degree of probable impact. In the main, cultural components have been relatively homogenized into middle-class Westernized psychodynamics. Cultural diversity is acknowledged, but more in the service of comprehensive understanding than practical application.

A distinction also needs to be made here about what has been written concerning the content of the unconscious and the imputed causes of the content. In regard to the former, Greenberg (1991) comments on Freud's repeated reconstructions of the generic contents as impulses, fears, defenses, wishes: "These changes highlight the value of thinking of the unconscious as a container—one that Freud filled with whatever contents he found as his clinical experience grew" (p. 34).

In that sense the content is perhaps infinitely expandable, limited only by what people are unwilling to discover and to reveal. However, conceptions of the genesis of unconscious content have been far less expansive. Drive theorists have been internally focused on wishes that derived from structural conflicts centered around dyadic and triadic models, particularly the oedipal situation. Relational theorists are more struck by the centrality of interpersonal situations and the primacy of relatedness, so the role of social influence is notable. At the same time, it has been primarily person to person, with a nod given to broader concepts, such as society, culture, and ethnicity.

There are a number of reasons for this restriction in view. It is clear that psychoanalysts are aware of cultural diversity, but lean in the direction of minimizing its effects. This has been a traditional emphasis connected with a desire to indeed have as much universality as possible for what are already such complex situations. Thus the comments of Hartmann and colleagues (1951): ". . . if we keep in mind how fundamentally similar every human infant's situation in the adult world is; how limited the number of meaningful situations in which the infant invests with affect; how typical and invariant the infant's anxieties, and finally how uniform some of his basis perceptions and bodily sensations are bound to be" (p. 13).

The desire to reduce extensive variability is appealing in systematic, scientific enterprises, and psychoanalysis has often had aspirations to such an identity. The very process of psychoanalysis itself, expansive and freeing in regard to encouraging expression and exploration, nonetheless ultimately seeks a limited number of explorations as workable hypotheses. Thus Hartmann and colleagues certainly acknowledged that economic, social, and regional patterns did have an effect on personality. At the same time, they avoided the use of terms such as *national character* or *social character*, and wanted to keep their distance from conceptualizations such as the work of Erich Fromm that they saw as too focused on institutionalized behavior. They had an important concern, which is still an issue, that a dichotomy would appear between social science and psychoanalysis, even as they struggled with aspects of integration. Unfortunately, the attempted integration downplayed the social psychological aspect, reflected in their statement that ". . . it seems to be true that of the various factors in the analyst's personality which are bound to influence his work with any given patient, his cultural background is of comparatively minor relevance" (Hartmann, et al. 1951, p. 23).

This is increasingly doubtful, even for those who wish it were so. In fact it is very probable that a major effect is created by the ethnicity of psychoanalysis itself, from the perspective both of the majority of those who were and are being trained as analysts and the predominantly middle-class population they worked on and spun theories about. However, there are changes afoot. In the United States, immigration and migration have increased the cultural and ethnic mix, and in turn the applicability of psychoanalysis to ethnic groups that in the past were relatively uninvolved. For example, there is a considerable increase in the number of black families entering psychotherapy (Boyd-Franklin 1989). While psychoanalysis has by no means seized the high ground in working with this group, it has made initial attempts to work with those unfamiliar to both analysts and the analytic process. There will be an increasing need for psychoanalytic conceptualization and application with these less familiar groups of patients, and some of this is beginning to happen (Javier 1990, Javier and Herron 1991, 1992). This means greater interest in and understanding of concepts such as the ethnic unconscious.

In addition, this is now very much an international happening, as all over the world countries are being renamed, subdivided, and reshaped at what seems to be an incredible rate. There is a strong ethnic component in all this that cannot fail to escape notice, and can certainly be considered one of the conscious manifestations of an ethnic unconscious. As just one avenue of association, consider this headline for an article by Burns (1992b) in *The New York Times* of May 17, 1992: "The leader of Bosnia's Serbs is a psychiatrist who understands historical hatreds" (p. E7).

ETHNICITY

Ethnicity is operationally defined as the degree of identification of a person with an ethnic group that is in some way his or her group of origin. It is recognized that just as there is a danger of distorting any person's identity by denying or downplaying this identification, there is also a danger of stereotyping by categorizing. However, the value of the category lies in the opportunity to understand certain issues that are indeed inherent to it, and that is an essential starting point. Rather than being used as a restriction, the category is used as another of many possible avenues to understanding a person (McGoldrick et al. 1982).

Ethnicity is embedded in and influenced by developmental cultures, such as the various cultures of child rearing, but it is a more basic construct. In turn the ethnic unconscious is repressed material that each generation shares with the next and is shared with most people of that ethnic group. Ethnic categorization in the United States tends to be broad and relatively heterogeneous, although still categorical. Examples of this are Asian, African-American, and Hispanic.

The ethnic unconscious was prominent in the 1950s in the work of Devereux (1980), who equated it with a cultural unconscious as distinct from a biologically transmitted racial unconscious. The further distinction is made here, however, between ethnicity and culture, which is seen as a broader construct. Also, it is acknowledged that terms such as *race, culture, ethnicity*, and *society* have to be used with some reservation because it is difficult to define them with sufficient precision to avoid exceptions or disagreements as to their meaning. At the same time, they can be made operational by approximate description, so that is the path that will be followed here.

The ethnic unconscious refers to material that is derived from identification with a particular group of people who have sufficient characteristics in common to give themselves a categorical name, although they also have actual and potential individual differences. Territories of origin and lineage at one time simplified this categorization, but the expansion, migration, and increasing mixtures of population have altered this. Ethnic character has become a more complex construct, yet it remains a viable one that actually demands renewed attention.

In reporting on the tragedies that have been unfolding in the Balkans, Burns (1992b) has noted that Bosnia was thought to have an excellent potential for a peaceful multiethnic society. The ethnic groups are relatively balanced with approximately 44 percent Muslim Slavs, 31 percent Serbs, and 17 percent Croats, yet a furious civil war has raged. The causes appear to go beyond either historical programming or present injustices. As Burns (1992b) states, "But to an outsider traveling through the emptied, burnt-out villages, past the hostile, camouflaged men at roadblocks, and into communities where frightened refugees have found at last brief respite, the disaster's roots seem to lie more in the realm of carefully inflicted psychological wounds than of current wrongs demanding that they be avenged" (p. E1).

The psychological wounds involve using fears and mistrusts and hatreds that tap into ethnic nationalism. As ethnic groups turn toward or against each other, or struggle within themselves, there are always some visible signs of ethnicity, along of course with numerous other issues that have often been highlighted in respect to such struggles, as socioeconomic differences. However, underlying the ethnic consciousness is the ethnic unconscious, and that needs more attention.

ETHNIC UNCONSCIOUS

The existence, as well as the potentialities, of the ethnic unconscious have had both limited recognition and limited understanding. In particular, relatively little psychoanalytic attention has been devoted to the major minorities of our society, African-Americans and Hispanics, although the ethnic unconscious is a major factor in the psychic conflicts of these people, who are increasingly in need as the current society pressures and is pressured by their presence.

The unconscious ethnic component of personality is of interest as part of the total self that will be analyzed. Every culture can be viewed as having defensive hierarchies that result in cultural patterns and ethnic characters. These are complex in that although they appear to be overtly designed to maintain the culture, they do not always do so. In fact, in times of stress they may actually operate to undo or destroy the prevailing society.

Thus, in 1956, Devereux stated, "Every society not only has its 'functional' aspects by means of which it affirms and maintains its integrity, but also has a certain number of beliefs, dogmas, and tendencies that contradict, deny, and undermine not only the essential operations and structures of the group but at times its very existence" (1980, p. 30).

The understanding of the mix of any society's avowal and disavowal is always complicated, but certainly more so when the ethnic unconscious is rooted in cultural materials that reflect different patterns from the current surrounding environment. An example of this is the translation of the African legacy into the culture of the United States. An illustration of this legacy is the emphasis on kinship, a particular type of family unity that differs from what is usually depicted in traditional family psychodynamics. In kinship the emphasis is on the survival of the group rather than the individual (Nobles 1980), and thus ego boundaries may be viewed by the unfamiliar observer in seemingly unusual ways as African philosophy affects and is affected by Western philosophy. A tribal conception of family may be more dominant than a nuclear conception, or there may be conflicts about these conceptions and roles within a family that will be reflected in separation-individuation patterns that are different from mainstream approaches.

Also, whatever the level of sophistication of the individual, the cultural unconscious is vulnerable to what is essentially premature trauma relative to the structuralization of the personality. That is, despite the plasticity and resilience of the psyche, the ethnic component is contextual. Its adaptability has an attunement that is supported by the defenses made available by the culture. Thus, when slavery was operating in the United States, attempts were made to destroy the usual cultural supports of the people who were slaves, such as family and security, and black people had to develop their own methods of maintaining linkages by creating a culture with its own defenses within the existing prevalent culture.

Thus there is a stability of character that resists acculturation by others, even when it may be far less drastic than the degradation of slavery, yet that character trait has to be integrated with the flexibility required by whatever acculturation is needed and desired by all parties involved. The ego psychological principle of adaptation is going to be attempted in a variety of ways, but the nonmainstream ethnic character often does not have access to significant cultural possibilities, or is denied them, and in turn suffers a type of "stranger distress."

Self-actualization then will require access to the defenses of each culture inhabited by an individual, and certain transformations of the ethnic unconscious, as well as the possibility of the transformation of the new culture. In regard to the latter, the integrity of the ethnic unconscious may be supported by isolating some cultural material as distinctive fantasies that are enduringly different, and can remain so as fantasies, as well as relegating certain personal conflicts to the arena of ethnic differences, and acceptable social convention to some extent in many cultures. The ethnic unconscious is not a constant, however, as new versions and aspects of the meaning of ethnicity to the individual may be added with corresponding shifts in self and object representations.

Thus, although it is in one sense accurate to think of an ethnic component of the unconscious as having mental representations of folklore or heritage, as has been noted in regard to an African heritage, this history is being reshaped by the person to accommodate his or her self-image. Therefore it has to be understood in the context of what *has* happened as well as what *is* happening to the person. In addition, analysts are listening to the conscious derivatives of this material, not the original versions, so the experience is one of hearing a created memory that at the same time from the patient's view is probably thought of more as an actual event that is now being remembered. A probable discrepancy exists between reality and reconstructed reality that is usually more apparent to the analyst than it is to the patient, and at the same time can be expected in regard to any unconscious material.

In the preceding description nothing unusual may appear to be happening, but the ethnic material has some special qualities that do bear notice. One of these is that, in a relative and complex way, it tends to be more idiosyncratic than normative. For example, the description of a strict parent approaches a universal quality for the listening analyst, although it is specific to the patient. A description of a strict German parent adds an explanatory element from the patient's point of view that he or she may consider in the direction of normative for German parents and their children. At the same time, this description has now become either stereotypical or more individualized for the analyst because it is more dependent on the analyst's ethnicity and personal experience than on his or her knowledge of parental norms.

Of course, this is not beyond an analysts's conception and understanding, and it is similar to any experience of the patient that is unfamiliar to the analyst. However, it bears particular notice and examination as a significant added element in the patient's development of self and others. This points to a second distinctive quality of this type of material, namely, that the affective charge associated with it is not so predictable. The analyst cannot assume either the meaning or the directionality or the degree of ethnic identification from observable and conscious information. It is something that patients may play with, be deadly serious about, desire, insist on, use to denigrate or elevate the analyst and/or themselves—and these are only some of the possibilities. Transference and countertransference are bound to be shaped by the ethnic unconscious in that child rearing and parenting are generally set within an ethnic context, and ethnicity can be the tool of bias, prejudice, and stereotyping as well as pride, self-esteem, and the ego ideal. Ambivalence, in turn, is highly probable, because of the changing nature of feelings about identity.

The ethnic unconscious is also the raw material of myths and legends, as well as being replenished by fact and fiction. Nations and individuals rewrite their histories as the ethnic unconscious is both at work and being worked on.

The president of the Serbian Democratic Party of Bosnia, Radovan Karadzic, spent a year in the United States doing graduate work, and he is quoted as saying that from the Walt Whitman collection *Leaves of Grass*, he learned "the need of Americans for a national myth" (Burns 1992b, p. E7). Of course, it is not only Americans who have this need, but all people, as this is evidenced in the ethnic unconscious. It is also clear that this may be used as resistance in the analytic process, both in terms of feeling misunderstood when such is not the case and in not understanding and accepting the self in terms of the personal meaning of ethnic identity.

At the same time that the ethnic unconscious represents differences, it is subject to what are generally considered the universals of psychoanalysis, namely, topographic, structural, dynamic, economic, genetic, adaptive, and social views of the personality. The presence of an ethnic unconscious reflects content to be addressed in psychoanalysis, estrangement vulnerabilities to change, potentials as change agents, but all as structural components of the person. The neurotic conflict, the war between structures, the development of character, the psychotic break with reality, none of these are removed or inserted by the ethnic unconscious, but all are flavored by it.

The material in the ethnic unconscious would have been learned from caregivers as well as from the surrounding society and culture. It is certainly an example of adaptation to meet a variety of basic needs, whether couched primarily in classical drive theory or in relational theory. The material is part of the process of identification, of having a self and developing that self. Individuals within ethnic groups will vary in their degree of identification with ethnicity, from disavowal to nominal to complete. At the same time, perceptions of ethnicity will vary, as will ambivalence, even within groups of people who appear to have similar degrees of identification, but then their type of identification may also vary. People will also vary in their developmental patterns of exposure to and assimilation of ethnic experience. Thus there is a range of both core and secondary material that is repressed and in turn available for discovery, development, and actualization. In addition, the culture in which the ethnic unconscious does its work is very influential, and in turn is influenced by the ethnic character of the unconscious. For example, to identify oneself as Hispanic or Latino may have certain core unconscious derivatives, regardless of country, region, town, or city of origin, and certain variable unconscious characteristics influenced by the surrounding culture. The latter are more prone to shift if the culture and/or the person changes.

The repression involved is in service of the basic demands of the culture and society in which each individual develops. There are standards of living as well as opportunities for living. In one way then, the culture is an ideal and the ethnic characters within it are potentialities for expansion rather than constriction. This is the optimistic side for the 170 ethnic groups in the United States (Frohnmayer 1992). At the same time there are pathological cultures and societies, and pathologies within them, that distort and restrict both individuation and relatedness in the name of adaptation. In such situations the ethnic unconscious has a particularly heavy burden, either as a warped container of raw and unmodifiable impulses or as the repository of brittle and exaggerated defenses that strain under an ill-fitting accommodation to incongruence. The aspects of the representational world that are touched by the ethnic unconscious, including preconscious material, are conflicted because of their multiple determination. There are the original events with their affects, impulses, and objects, and now current circumstances that are not necessarily congruent with the original versions, even as remembered. Ethnic identity is strained, pushed, and pulled, and along with it, so is the ethnic unconscious.

THE ANALYTIC PROCESS

A particular concern is with the involvement of the ethnic unconscious in the processes of change, especially the psychoanalytic process. The United States is a multicultural, multiethnic society that has a declared commitment to diversity, yet at the same time has a relatively prevailing culture. As with any society certain degrees of external and internal adaptation are required for survival and growth. The repression creating the ethnic unconscious is essentially a defensive adaptation to the drives and relations, and their accompanying fantasies, that are complementary to the given culture. In that sense there is a commonality of defenses and conflicts that are provided and facilitated by the exigencies of the culture.

From the individual point of view the desired adaptation reflects what Pine (1990) has described as the "general tendency to maintain sameness" (p. 88). This means being as true as possible to the ego ideal of the ethnic unconscious, which is most easily accomplished in an open society. Concurrently developmental synchronicity with the prevailing culture can be a major facilitator of the healthy narcissism embodied in the existence of that ego ideal, but that is generally an imperfect possibility given the probabilities of life as conflict.

The movement from any one culture, whether direct or within a culture, and living with an ethnic unconscious that is not attuned to the prevailing culture are major stimuli for change. They are also situations that are very common in this society, and increasingly on an international level. These situations engender a great deal of stress and can be major aspects of conflicts presented by patients to analysts, regardless of whether the ethnic unconscious and its derivatives are indeed recognized.

What then are the tasks of the analyst in respect to this new but old component of the unconscious? They begin with recognition followed by understanding, which means that the analyst has an interest in all components of the unconscious. The expressions and repressions of ethnicity, the degree and types of ethnic identifications, are to be noted as the patient and analyst interact in the analytic process. This material is understood, interpreted, and worked through in a familiar analytic framework that now includes heightened recognition that ethnicity is part of the means for the actualization of human potentialities.

Analysts have become accustomed to analyzing patients from relatively similar social and cultural backgrounds, and this pattern has probably limited both their visions and their metapsychologies. The need for understanding cultural relativity and diversity as it is consciously displayed would be difficult to ignore in the world of today, and it certainly remains an issue both technically and in theory development. However, the ethnic unconscious is still another matter because it represents unfamiliar mixes of variation and catholicity, and it is generally defined inaccurately if left to supposition. One can imagine an ethnic unconscious, but it is in the telling that it assumes its best shape, and even then, distorted by the teller as well as the listener, it resides in the impressions that accompany most analytic material. This aspect of the unconscious was deflected by analyst–analysand contiguities and similarities. Ethnic values were cultural values mainstreamed into a familiar way of life. Their influence was accepted within a narrow range that aroused more "uh-huhs" than questions. This limited focus is even more striking in the light of this comment by Gillespie (1989) in regard to Freud's background, namely ". . . the fact that his family was a Jewish one was certainly of central importance in his life, and it had far reaching influences on his career and achievement . . ." (p. 38).

That is at least the whisper of the ethnic unconscious. It is quite probable that instead of hearing that voice grow louder, there has been a different type of listening. What appears to have been heard was the diversity among psychoanalytic schools and theories that too often raised the specter of fragmentation and disintegration. Thus diversity had the flavor of insecurity. There were also the demographics of psychoanalysts themselves, more homogeneous than their disputes would suggest, and again in a direction that would lend itself to mitigation of an ethnic unconscious as a major source of influence. Although certainly not always the case, it is probable that the result was too often the psychodynamic everyman, everywoman, everychild. Thus the ethnic unconscious as depicted here was not really postulated or it was not explored with sufficient intensity. It was, and has continued to be for the most part, an understandable case of complexity reduction in service of an also understandable desire for a viable working model.

However, the model was not intended to be that invariant and the emerging clinical facts suggest the need for changes. Thus the presence and influence of an ethnic unconscious arises with more vigor in the multiethnic societies that are on the increase and are replete with contradictions and confusions about autonomy, assimilation, and acculturation. The tools of analysis are definitely available, and the composition of the society and the patient population make it clear that now is the time for application.

REFERENCES

Boyd-Franklin, N. (1989). *Black Families in Therapy. A Multi-Systems Approach*. New York: Guilford.

Burns, A. F. (1992a). Understanding and letting loose, dark distrusts in the Balkans. *New York Times*, May 17, p. E7.

——— (1992b). Fear and unreason twist a spiral of death. *New York Times*, pp. E1, E4.

Devereux, C. (1980). *Basic Problems of Ethnopsychiatry*. Chicago: University of Chicago Press.

Eagle, M. N. (1985). Benjamin B. Rubinstein: contributing to the structure of psychoanalytic theory. In *Beyond Freud. A Study of Modern Psychoanalytic Theorists*, ed. J. Reppen, pp. 83–108. Hillsdale, NJ: Analytic Press.

Ellenberger, H. F. (1970). *The Discovery of the Unconscious*. New York: Basic Books.

Freud, S. (1923). Two encyclopedia articles. *Standard Edition* 18:235–259.

Frohnmayer, J. E. (1992). Is that what he meant? *New York Times*, June 14, p. E 19.

Gillespie, W. (1989). The legacy of Sigmund Freud. In *Dimensions of Psychoanalysis*, ed. J. Sandler, pp. 31–49. Madison, CT: International Universities Press.

Greenberg, J. (1991). *Oedipus and Beyond. A Clinical Theory*. Cambridge, MA: Harvard University Press.

Hartmann, H., Kris, E., and Loewenstein, R. M. (1951). Some psychoanalytic comments on "culture and personality." In *Psychoanalysis and Culture*, ed. G. B. Wilbur and W. Muensterberger, pp. 3–31. New York: International Universities Press.

Herron, W. G. (1962). The evidence for the unconscious. *Psychoanalytic Review* 49:70–92.

Javier, R. A. (1990). The suitability of insight-oriented psychotherapy for the Hispanic poor. *American Journal of Psychoanalysis* 50:305–318.

Javier, R. A., and Herron, W. G. (1991). *Urban poverty, ethnicity, and personality development from a psychoanalytic perspective*. Paper presented at the Inter-American Congress of Psychology, San Jose, Costa Rica, July.

——— (1992). Psychoanalysis, the Hispanic poor, and the disadvantaged: application and conceptualization. *Journal of the American Academy of Psychoanalysis* 20:435–476.

McGoldrick, M., Pearce, J., and Giordano, J., eds. (1982). *Ethnicity and Family Therapy*. New York: Guilford.

Nobles, W. (1980). African philosophy: foundations for black psychology. In *Black Psychology*, ed. R. Jones, 2nd ed., pp. 23–36. New York: Harper and Row.

Pine, F. (1990). *Drive, Ego, Object, and Self.* New York: Basic Books.

Sandler, J. (1989). Unconscious wishes and human relationships. In *Dimensions of Psychoanalysis*, ed. J. Sandler, pp. 65–81. Madison, CT: International Universities Press.

Welt, S. R., and Herron, W. G. (1990). *Narcissism and the Psychotherapist.* New York: Guilford.

Wolfenstein, E. V. (1991). On the uses and abuses of psychoanalysis in cultural research. *Free Associations* 24:515–547.

17

Blackness, Ethnicity, and the Fantasy of Ethnicity

MICHAEL MOSKOWITZ

THE ETHNICITY OF PSYCHOANALYSIS

Not too long ago, after a summer APA meeting, I went to pick up my son on his way home from his first summer away at camp. He was then 9. I looked forward to his return with more than eagerness. When we dropped him off, my wife and I had been sad and anxious. We tried halfheartedly and not very successfully to hide it. Our son seemed to be handling the departure much better than we were.

As we were walking away from the airport gate, my wife and I joked about our view of how we might handle this departure if we were upper-class British parents with stiff upper lips: "Cheerio. Ta-ta. See you at summer's end, or perhaps you'd rather continue directly on to boarding school" and the like. I don't know if people really talk like this anymore, or if they ever did.

But as we walked away I fantasized about how at least in the movies British parents cheerfully sent their sons off to war and adventure for the good and glory of Queen and Empire. I know I could never send my children off in this way, yet there is something of this ideal that is part of me; it is an ideal that I both admire and disdain; and it is an ideal that is contained in an ethnic fantasy.

Lawrence Stone (1979) persuasively argues that there were four causes for the development of what he calls an unfeeling culture. He writes:

> The lack of a unique mother figure in the first two years of life, the constant loss of close relatives, siblings, parents, nurses and friends through premature death, the physical imprisonment of the infant in tight swaddling cloths in early months, and the deliberate breaking of the child's will [through severe physical and mental punishment] all contributed to a "psychic numbing" which created many adults whose primary responses to others were at best a calculating indifference, and at worst a mixture of suspicion and hostility, tyranny and submission, alienation and rage. [p. 80]

These attributes may now seem negative in our eyes, but they were undoubtedly of value in building the adaptive, productive, and at times creative British empire. Only recently have we been able to acknowledge the downside of oppression and exploitation.

There has been very interesting recent work in psychoanalytic anthropology, such as detailed in Robert LeVine's chapter (1990), that looks at infant environments in different cultures from a psychoanalytic perspective. There is much to learn about the limits of an average expectable environment (Hartmann 1964), good enough mothering (Winnicott 1975), and their relationship to cultural types.

Now British values, ideals, and child-rearing practices have unquestionably changed (though some aspects of an unfeeling ideal remain). Winnicott's life and work are powerful examples of as well as agents of this continuing change. Winnicott was a product of British culture, but he was profoundly influenced by the work of Freud, a Jewish Austrian, and more profoundly by the work and the person of Melanie Klein, a flamboyantly Hungarian Jew. The complex ways in which Hungarian, Austrian, and Jewish culture came together in the British person of Winnicott to produce his work, which influences us all, would be difficult to disentangle, but he stands as an example to illustrate my first point that psychoanalysis is now and in fact has always been a deeply multicultural endeavor.

We have in current political debate sometimes equated multicultural with non-European, particularly Latino, African, and Asian cultures. I am here using it more broadly to refer to a blending of diverse cultures. I think a community that integrated Eastern European Jewish and British cultures deserves to be called multicultural. And yet to say that psychoanalysis is multicultural is not to say that it is omnicultural. Responding to cultural change is an ongoing process. As we absorb and transform the impact of new influences, so we are in turn transformed by them.

Wolf (1982) points out that most of the world, certainly the old world of Europe, Africa, and Asia, has been engaged in trade, including slaves, for millennia. (Until the fifteenth century, the slave trade was color-blind.) And Austria, at the very core of Europe, was at the center of trade between East and West along the Danube, and between the North and South through its alpine passes. Thus this European country that came to be seen by many as the center of Germanic culture had in fact, over centuries, absorbed Asian, African, Middle-Eastern, and other influences. I think it can reasonably be argued that "centers of culture," like Freud's Vienna or today's New York or Los Angeles, are often the melting pots or maelstroms of many cultures.

Vienna in Freud's time was the capital of Europe's largest empire, and probably the most cosmopolitan city in the world. It was also the most Jewish city in Europe (see Mitchell 1974). In 1910 the Jews made up 8.7 percent of its population, more than a third of its university students, and reputedly 75 percent of its journalists. The Jewish population was probably the most assimilated in history. Yet, as Juliet Mitchell points out, both Zionism and modern anti-Semitism were born in the Vienna of Freud's day.

No matter how assimilated and antireligious, there is no question that Freud considered himself a Jew, and felt that Jewishness placed him in opposition to mainstream culture and was a source of inspiration. He wrote:

> Nor is it perhaps entirely a matter of chance that the first advocate of psycho-analysis was a Jew. To profess belief in this new theory called for a certain degree of readiness to accept a situation of solitary opposition—a situation with which no one is more familiar than a Jew. [1924, p. 222]

And:

> Because as a Jew I found myself free from many prejudices which restricted others in the use of their intellect; [and] as a Jew I was prepared to join the Opposition and do without agreement with the "compact majority." [1926, p. 274]

I think there is increasing consensus that ego psychology, despite its profound contributions, has had a restrictive influence on American psychoanalysis. I think most psychoanalysts find something barren in it, something about its inability to talk about selves and passionate desires. It is my view that ego psychology as embedded in a conservative American medical culture was in part an attempt to "de-ethnize" psychoanalysis, and that its emphasis on adaptation was part of the ethos of an adaptable immigrant to U.S. culture trying to blend into the melting pot. We know that it is no accident that desexualizing and de-ethnizing go hand in hand.

Jacoby (1983) has powerfully documented the repression of psychoanalysis in the United States. He points out that many influential European analysts such as Fenichel, Edith Jacobson, and Annie and Wilhelm Reich were Marxists committed to social change. Simmel and Eitingon established the Berlin Clinic to provide therapy to the poor and working class.

While some analysts in the United States, perhaps most notably Fromm (1955, 1961) and others of the early interpersonalist school and Marcuse (1955, 1956) of the Frankfurt school, continued a commitment to social change, it must unfortunately be conceded that their impact on mainstream American psychoanalysis has not been great.

Though Freud was not a Marxist and thought many of Marx's assumptions psychologically naive, there is no question about his critique of mainstream culture. Freud wrote, in a letter to Putnam, that "the recognition of our therapeutic limitations reinforces our determination to change other social factors so that men and women shall no longer be forced into hopeless situations" (Turkle 1978, p. 142).

And in *The Future of an Illusion* he wrote:

> One thus gets the impression that civilization is something which was imposed on a resisting majority by a minority which understood how to obtain possession of the means to power and coercion. [1927, p. 6]

And:

> It is to be expected that these underprivileged classes will envy the favored ones their privileges and will do what they can to free themselves from their own surplus of privation. Where this is not possible, a permanent measure of discontent will exist within the culture concerned. . . . [I]t is understandable that the suppressed people will develop an intense hostility towards a culture whose existence they make possible by their work, but in whose wealth they have too small a share. In such conditions an internalization of the cultural prohibitions among the suppressed people is not to be expected. On the contrary, they are not prepared to acknowledge the prohibitions, they are intent on destroying the culture itself, and possibly doing away with the postulates on which it is based. . . . [1927, p. 12]

It seems to me that Freud was talking about himself, his own people, and psychoanalysis. This is in *The Future of an Illusion*, a book in which Freud is attempting to undermine one of the basic postulates of Western civilization, religion and the belief in God. Elsewhere he wrote: "Since we destroy illusion we are accused of endangering ideals" (1910, p. 147). For Freud the task of psychoanalysis was to liberate the individual not only from the illusions of childhood but also from the illusions of civilization.

It also appears that Freud is making explicit a motivation for revolution. He speaks to the futility of mainstream culture's attempt to force its values on those it oppresses. As Freud points out elsewhere, and historical and psychological studies have confirmed, the superego is a fragile and labile structure. Its maintenance requires the support of idealized leadership and community.

I dwell on these points because psychoanalysis often confronts the accusation that it represents or is the product of mainstream, middle-class European culture or the like. It may have become that in practice, but it is not in theory or origin. Our discipline in many ways has become comfortably mainstream, in part out of economic self-interest, but in large part out of internalized racism and fear: fear that our ethnicity will be discovered along with our sexuality and the potentially revolutionary nature of our endeavor.

BLACKNESS

This is a difficult topic, and in all circumstances, including the clinical situation, discussion must begin with the recognition of the reality of pervasive and oppressive racism.

Cheryl Thompson (1995) has poignantly portrayed the constant awareness that African-Americans and others designated black have of their blackness. It is astounding to hear that for many black families the question, "What color is the child?" precedes, "Is it a boy or a girl?" The questioner is asking, "What chance, what place, will your child have in the world?" As Thompson states for black patients, blackness permeates all aspects of their being.

This is the nature of trauma, that it permeates all aspects of being; and we must recognize that black people in this culture have been traumatized, many by the reality of poverty and discrimination, and all by the daily narcissistic assault of living in a racist society.

Freud was personally aware of the impact of this type of assault. When he was about 10 or 12 his father told him about an incident in which the elder Freud was walking along the sidewalk, all decked out and wearing a new fur cap, when along came a Christian man who knocked the cap into the muck and shouted, "Jew, off the sidewalk." Freud asked his father, "What did you do?" His father answered, "I stepped into the road and picked up my cap" (Gay 1988, p. 12).

Young Freud was deeply disillusioned and developed fantasies of revenge. He identified with the Semite Hannibal who had sworn to conquer the mighty Romans. He also came to see himself as part of a suppressed minority that must always be in opposition to mainstream culture.

What Freud did not come to conceptualize formally or at least to write about were the terrible costs in narcissistic injury paid by those who are traumatized by oppression. Chasseguet-Smirgel (1988) portrays the self-hatred, the internalized racism, borne by Jews in Freud's Vienna. Gilman (1991) writes how the modern nose job was invented by a Jewish surgeon practicing in Berlin in 1898 to efface the physical remnants of hated Jewishness.

As late as the mid-nineteenth century in Europe, Jews were thought of as black. One author wrote (quoted in Gilman 1991, p. 174), "The African character of the Jew, his muzzle-shaped mouth and face [remove] him from other races"; another, "the physiognomy of the Jew is like that of the black."

Freud needed to see himself as a conquering hero. This part of him has become part of psychoanalysis. But the unconscious aspects of his ethnicity, his self-hatred, I believe, also permeate psychoanalysis. Victims tend to blame themselves for their plight, and some versions of psychoanalysis express this self-blame through the wish and the hope that owning the reasons for one's misery will enable one to escape from it; Freud's discovery and assertion of the universality of humankind's base nature also contain a wishful proclamation of his commonality with the ruling class. Jews have always been accused of being too sexual and aggressive.

Malcolm X wrote:

> The Muslim's "X" symbolized the true African family name that he never could know. For me, my "X" replaced the white slavemaster name of Little which some blue-eyed devil named Little had imposed upon my paternal forebears . . . we would keep this "X" until God himself returned to give us a Holy name with his own mouth. [1965, p. 199]

Like many African Americans (Thompson 1995), Malcolm X is defining himself by what he is not. The X denotes an opposition, a negation of what is. X is not. But X is also what is. X is where it is. The point of departure and the point of buried treasure.

THERE IS NO ETHNICITY

Lacan (1982) has said that there is no sexual relation. By this he means that there is so much that is fantasy between two people engaged in a sexual relationship that what is real is largely beside the point.

As analysts we recognize that to call something a fantasy does not mean to diminish its power, but rather instead opens up the possibility of change via relationship and discourse. Fantasies are ideas and ideas by their nature can change.

It is noteworthy that other disciplines, such as history and anthropology, raise questions about the danger of reifying concepts like culture and ethnicity. Eric Wolf writes:

> The central assertion of this book is that the world of humankind constitutes a manifold, a totality of interconnected processes, and inquiries that disassemble this totality into bits and then fail to reassemble them falsify reality. Concepts like "nation," "society," and "culture" name bits and threaten to turn names into things. [1982, p. 4]

It is only in relatively recent history that "Tuscan," "Sicilian," "Venetian," and "Neapolitan" have been replaced by "Italian," and "Prussian," "Bohemian," and "Bavarian" replaced by "German." And who would have thought that "Yugoslavs" would become "Croats," "Serbs," and Muslim "Bosnians"? It is noteworthy that the Bosnian Muslims that have been "ethnically cleansed" by the Serbians are also Slavs, sharing looks and many customs—in many of the usual respects ethnically similar to their oppressors, their ancestors having converted from Christianity to Islam with the arrival of the Ottoman Turks in 1463. As of 1992, 16 percent of the children of Bosnia were offspring of so-called mixed marriages (Pfaff 1992). Once again a divisive ethnicity has been imposed by those who seek to exploit it.

Alba (1990), in a sociological study, concluded that for the vast majority of whites living in America ethnic identity had become a symbolic identity, a vestigial attachment to a few ethnic symbols imposing little cost on everyday life. Nearly two thirds of all native white Americans view themselves as having mixed ethnicity. However, on a not-quite-conscious level, a new ethnic identity is emerging, that of a European American. From that group, which has little real connection to the customs of Europe, Asians, Latinos, African Caribbeans, and African Americans are excluded. The new European-American identity becomes once again an ethnicity of privilege and exclusion.

For analysts it is time to more fully come to terms with the fact that ethnicity is an illusion of civilization, and to try to understand what unconscious purposes it serves. A psychoanalytic study group including Peter Neubauer, Martin Bergmann, and other distinguished analysts met for years trying to understand the sources of anti-Semitism. They concluded that anti-Semitism was unrelated to any particular pathology or character type, that it must derive from something deep and universal, like stranger anxiety. I too feel that the potential for racism is deep and universal, but is nurtured by context and leadership. Through my clinical work and study of German youth, I have come to see racism from a more Kleinian perspective. The depressive position, a position that entails owning one's hatred, is always a struggle to maintain. It is always easier to see badness in others than in ourselves. Owning our own hatred and potential for destruction requires the support of moral leadership and community, and the potential for making meaningful reparations.

There is no ethnicity. There is hatred and the need to deny our own badness, and fear of our own hatred. Ethnicity and race are fantasies we use to deny our own badness and displace it onto others, as well as to protect ourselves against the very real hatred that others may have for us.

It is especially important that we confront the fact that dividing the world into black and white is a delusion of civilization. People are not black or white (see Zuckerman 1990). Where the line is drawn is politically and psychologically motivated. There is *no* acceptable genetic basis for the concept of race (Cavalli-Sforza et al. 1994). That "race" is the only ethnic grouping in this culture that does not allow for the possibility of dual identity belies its delusional rigidity.

Freud wrote that psychoanalysis is a cure through love. We are limited in our ability to work psychoanalytically with people only by or in our inability to love or be loved by them. Anthropologists and soldiers have loved, been loved, and married across all boundaries of culture. Rendon (1992) reports that he could not work with someone he was ethnically identified with, but who was capable of betrayal. This is similar to what Thompson (1995) called her most obvious treatment failure. Issues of sameness and betrayal can lead to failure of empathy as powerfully as issues of difference.

Psychoanalysis is a discipline born in opposition and developed under conditions of oppression. I think for too long in the United States psychoanalysis and ego-psychology in particular have tried to deny its multicultural heritage in order to be part of a mainstream, supposedly non-ethnic, melting. As psychologists we can change that. But to do so we must now speak to those who are discriminated against and oppressed, not with the voice of an intellectual elite, as part of the medical-therapeutic establishment, or as a group that has "made it," but rather with a voice offering a tool for understanding the processes of oppression, subjugation, and their internalization.

REFERENCES

Alba, R. (1990). *Ethnic Identity: The Transformation of White America*. New Haven, CT: Yale University Press.

Cavalli-Sforza, L. L., Menozzi, P., and Piazza, A. (1994). *The History and Geography of the Human Gene*. Princeton, NJ: Princeton University Press.

Chasseguet-Smirgel, J. (1988). Some thoughts on Freud's attitude during the Nazi period. *Psychoanalysis and Contemporary Thought* 11:249–266.

Freud, S. (1910). The future prospects of psycho-analytic therapy. *Standard Edition* 11:139–152.

––––––– (1924). Resistances to psychoanalysis. *Standard Edition* 19:213–222.

––––––– (1926). Address to the Society of B'nai B'rith. *Standard Edition* 20:271–276.

––––––– (1927). The future of an illusion. *Standard Edition* 21:1–56.

Fromm, E. (1955). The human implications of instinctivistic "radicalism." *Dissent* II:342–349.

––––––– (1961). *Marx's Concept of Man*. New York: Continuum, 1988.

Gay, P. (1988). *Freud: A Life for Our Time*. New York: Norton.

Gilman, S. (1991). *The Jew's Body*. New York: Routledge.

Hartmann, H. (1964). *Essays on Ego Psychology*. New York: International Universities Press.

Jacoby, R. (1983). *The Repression of Psychoanalysis*. Chicago: University of Chicago Press.

Lacan, J. (1982). *Feminine Psychology*. New York: Norton.

LeVine, R. (1990). Infant environments in psychoanalysis: a crosscultural view. In *Cultural Psychology: Essays on Comparative Human Development*, ed. J. Stigler et al., pp. 454–476. Cambridge: Cambridge University Press.

Marcuse, H. (1955). *Eros and Civilization*. Boston: Beacon, 1966.

––––––– (1956). A reply to Erich Fromm. *Dissent* III:79–83.

Mitchell, J. (1974). *Psychoanalysis and Feminism*. New York: Vantage.

Pfaff, W. (1992). Reflections (The absence of empire). *New Yorker*, August 10, pp. 59–69.

Rendon, M. (1992). The ethnicity of psychoanalysis and the psychoanalysis of ethnicity II. APA Meeting, Washington, DC, August.

Stone, L. (1979). *The Family, Sex and Marriage in England 1500–1800, Abridged Edition*. New York: Harper.

Thompson, C. L. (1995). Self-definition by opposition: a consequence of minority status. *Psychoanalytic Psychology* 12:533–546.

Turkle, S. (1978). *Psychoanalytic Politics: Freud's French Revolution*. Cambridge, MA: MIT Press.

Winnicott, D. W. (1975). *Through Paediatrics to Psycho-Analysis*. New York: Basic Books.

Wolf, E. (1982). *Europe and the People without History*. Berkeley: University of California Press.

X, Malcolm (1965). *The Autobiography of Malcolm X*. New York: Grove.

Zuckerman, M. (1990). Some dubious premises in research and theory on racial differences. *American Psychologist* 45:1297–1303.

18

A Latino Perspective on the Role of Ethnicity in the Development of Moral Values

RAFAEL ART. JAVIER AND MARCELA B. YUSSEF

It is a rather complex and at times risky endeavor to make moral judgments about the acceptability of specific actions with regard to oneself and others. This is the case because doing so involves a definition of morality based on principles not always clearly evident to the observers or equally acceptable to the participants. It has been suggested that this is more likely to be true when the participants and observers are of different ethnic and cultural backgrounds and where the cultural mores that dictate their behaviors are based on different conceptions of reality and relationships.

It is our contention that morality, although assumed to have universal values, is intimately influenced in its development by culture and ethnicity. This is quite understandable if one accepts the notion that moral codes are developed in the context of one's relationships to others in the context of cultural surroundings. This is an idea widely accepted by philosophers, social scientists, and behavioral scientists interested in understanding human interaction. Indeed, according to these scholars, a full explanation of transactions among individuals needs to include an understanding of their level of moral development (Gilligan 1982, Haan 1975, Kant 1959, Kohlberg 1981, Piaget 1932, Rest 1973). In this context, morality can be defined with regard to its impact on behavior as a complex web of guidelines or a priori and a posteriori moral principles that permeate and influence all aspects of human existence, and is expected to determine the outcome of any human transaction (Kant 1959).

These principles are thought to have been developed out of the need to formulate rules that could serve as guidelines for the interaction toward oneself and others and to ensure the survival of members of society at large (Javier et al. 1992). According to Kohlberg and his associates (Kohlberg 1973, Kohlberg and Candee 1984), this is accomplished in the development of different levels of moral reasoning. The higher the level of moral reasoning individuals reach, the more likely it is that their actions will be guided by concern and respect for others' rights, thus determining the nature of moral actions. For Gilligan (1982), this is accomplished when affective components are also incorporated into the equation. Some of these conceptualizations, especially Kolhberg's, have met considerable criticism on theoretical and scientific grounds (Emler 1983, Hogan and Emler 1978). Nevertheless, the idea that individuals' actions are determined by their specific perception, appreciation, and judgment about an event, and that this perception and judgment are, in turn, influenced by their history and culture, cannot be refuted.

MORALITY AND CULTURE IN
PSYCHOANALYTIC THINKING

In spite of the pervasiveness of the assumed influence of cultural factors in moral behavior, these factors have received only limited attention in psychoanalytic theories, although they are implied throughout. For instance, they have been assumed in the conceptualization of superego function as the great heir of the oedipal dilemma, the processes of internalization, identity formation, self-definition, and the like, as well as the processes of transference and countertransference (Freud 1914, 1923, Herron 1992, Kernberg 1975, Tyson and Tyson 1984). They were referred to in the papers on "The Economic Problem of Masochism" (Freud 1924) and "The Ego and the Id" (Freud 1923). However, no concerted efforts are found to explain the extent to which cultural factors are relevant in the development of morality.

In a recent article by Brunner (1991), we see the reason for the lack of attention to this matter in Freudian conceptualization. He was much more concerned with developing a theory with universal appeal in his effort to deal with his political reality in Vienna. In the process, cultural factors were alluded to only in passing or were absent from the discussion altogether (Javier and Herron 1992).

Let us review briefly some of Freud's allusions to cultural factors in mental functioning referred to earlier. His definition of the superego, for instance, as a representative of the id and the external world and as a conscience, is, in fact, a reference to cultural influences. The superego is said to include the ideas of "right" and "wrong," initially related to the prohibitions associated with the expression of forbidden sexual and aggressive impulses toward the primary objects in the oedipal configuration. The transformation of these earlier object cathexes into identifications after they have ceased to be the objects of the libidinal impulses of the id makes possible the development of the conscience (Freud 1923, 1924). But to the extent to which these primary objects belong to the real external world, we see reference in Freud's thinking as to the role that cultural influences may have in superego formation. It is from there (from the external world) "that they were drawn; their power, behind which lie hidden all the influences of the past and of tradition, was one of the most strongly-felt manifestations of reality" (Freud 1924, p. 167).

It is in this context that the individual's morality is developed, the "source of our individual ethical sense" (Freud 1924, p. 168). It is assumed that to the extent to which the parents can teach to their children only what was taught to them in the context of their own development, and to the extent to which their development was influenced by culturally based norms, the content of their superego is also expected to have strong cultural ingredients. It retains essential features of the introjected persons, their strength, their severity, their view of the world, and their own sense of morality.

By placing morality in relation to superego formation, Freudian conceptualization does not allow for the development of morality until after the oedipal configuration has taken place. The implied reason for this is that a number of processes come into place at this developmental moment, without which the development of morality is not possible. These include neurological and physiological maturity (such as the completion of the myelination process of the neurons, the acquisition of motor-visual dexterity, and the acquisition of language) that allows the individual to progress cognitively and psychologically in the way elucidated by Piaget (1932) and Mahler and colleagues (1975). The development of cognitive schemes related to "I" and "you" or "them," the development of the sense of cause and effect, and the categorization of behaviors and experiences into "good" or "bad," "acceptable" or "unacceptable," are all possible when the child matures cognitively and accomplishes a progressively sophisticated state of self-differentiation (Mahler et al. 1975).

It is against this backdrop that the superego structure is developed. That is not to say that there are not superego precursors present in the earlier negotiations between a child and the primary object (Tyson and Tyson 1984). According to Daniel Stern's investigation (1985), children are much more actively involved in negotiating with their surroundings at a much younger age than has been suggested by earlier conceptualizations. They are much more alert, and their memory for events and objects in their surroundings is much more acute than earlier suggested (Fagen and Prigot 1993). This includes the ability to read their mothers' facial expression (e.g., pleasure, displeasure) and to process similarly loaded verbal communication. If this is the case, we could expect that, although narcissistically motivated, children do develop an early sense of good or bad and of avoidance of unpleasant situations so as to minimize tension and decrease anxiety (Sullivan 1953, Tyson and Tyson 1984). Cultural and ethnic influences will also be part of these early exchanges.

The development of a superego structure as structure with a universal appeal, however, was much more central to Freud's thinking than the importance of including in any systematic way the ethnic nature of its content as part of the moral equation. It is our contention that only by allowing the coexistence of the "Universals," including the "Categorical Imperatives" of Kant (1959), and the "Particulars" (culturally based norms) can a full moral meaning to the human equation be reached. By emphasizing the importance of the "Particulars," we are trying to resolve one of the greatest paradoxes in Freudian thinking: he believed that a person's cognitive and emotional experience could be explained through universal principles of mental functioning regardless of ethnic, cultural, socioeconomic, and sociopolitical status. By proving this is the case, it could be said that he became the greatest social reformer of our time, a social equalizer. However, by denying the proper positions of these factors in his theoretical formulations, he has contributed to the belief that psychoanalytic formulations and techniques are appropriate to the treatment of only a limited number of special individuals, the "new class" endowed with special qualities for analyzability (Eissler 1953, Javier and Herron 1992). With regard to Latino patients, such a position has influenced the extent to which psychoanalytic formulations are seen as relevant and applicable to the understanding of their reality (Javier 1990, Ruiz 1981).

The problem with understanding the world only from a position of "Universals" is that information that cannot be easily coded, say, within the Anglo-Saxon codes of conduct is normally delegated to a position of inferiority and does not allow room for the assessment of its contextual importance. The more divergent the information with regard to one's own belief, the more difficult it is to assimilate it within one's moral system. Take, for instance, the strong negative reaction one experiences when one hears reports (Rosenthal 1993, Walker 1992) about African and other customs in which a woman's clitoris or labia is removed at puberty as part of a traditional ceremony to become a full member of the tribe and a member of an age-set. It has been suggested that through this act, the circumcised girl can now enter into a more mature level of interaction in her society and become part of a group of women in her tribe, of similar age, who tend to act together for the rest of their lives. It is considered a joyous occasion for the girl and an opportunity to show, through her courage, that she is ready to be married. The assumed importance of this ceremony is briefly described in reference to the Kikuyu tribe by Professor Maynard H. Merwine in a recent letter to *The New York Times* (1993). In his description it is clear that the ceremony carries a tremendous meaning for the participants. Nevertheless, it is a disturbing practice from our (Western) perspective, and one that requires much greater sacrifices from the women than from the men. In the Western view it is a graphic and barbaric display of male dominance and from that perspective the concept "female mutilation" is applicable (Walker 1992). But what context are we to use to understand the morality of the practice? To call the practice "barbaric" or an act of "female mutilation" without an investigation of the actual reactions from the participants suggests the application of value judgments based on different sets of principles than what appeared to be meaningful to the Kikuyu tribe. Most important, it suggests that one set of moral principles is more desirable than another. And here lies the major problem facing behavioral scientists and the psychoanalytic community dealing with a population whose historical, cultural, and sociopolitical experience may be different from ours.

American psychoanalysts are used to calling those societies and individuals whose practices are not easily coded within the framework of the Anglo-Saxon ethical standards and psychoanalytic conceptualizations primitive or underdeveloped. The Latino community has also been victim of the same phenomenon. Such a tendency was explained by Freud in terms of "narcissism of the small difference" (Freud 1914). The stubbornness of this tendency was recently demonstrated in a series of commentaries by Pueblo Indian scholars and recently compiled by Jojola (1993) in response to Gutierrez's controversial book, *When Jesus Came, the Corn Mothers Went Away* (1991). According to these commentaries, even though Gutierrez is also of Pueblo Indian descent, his portrayal of the indigenous sexual customs and other codes of behavior, including gift giving, leaves the readers with a false perception of the Pueblo Indians as morally loose or without any moral principles. In addition, the book failed to recognize the great deal of diversity in customs among the Pueblo Indians. He was heavily criticized because his view was believed to suffer from the same level of inaccuracy in his description and interpretation of the Pueblo Indians' customs and behaviors as previously advanced by the Spanish Conquistadors and writers less sympathetic to, and knowledgeable of, Indian traditions.

ETHNIC AND CULTURAL INFLUENCES IN THE DEVELOPMENT OF MORALITY IN LATINO INDIVIDUALS

At this point we would like to discuss some of the cultural and ethnic characteristics that are assumed to impact on the development of morality in Latino individuals, affecting the nature of transference and countertransference. It is important to keep in mind that the characteristics referred to below are not applicable in the same way to all individuals of Latin descent. To begin with, there is a great deal of similarity in many aspects of their sociopolitical and socioeconomic histories; most Latin-American countries were under the control of the Spaniards for centuries (Gutierrez 1991) and were later governed by a repressive system of government. There are, however, a great many regional differences, ecological and linguistic, that militate against applying any of the comments made across the board (Javier 1993, Javier and Yussef 1992). Hence, great caution should be exercised to avoid sweeping generalizations leading to distortions of the Latinos' reality.

This is particularly relevant in the case of Latino people living in the United States whose moral codes may have been further influenced by their new reality as immigrants, with different levels of acculturation (Marin et al. 1987, Padilla 1980). Culture, traditions, and values, which have served as sources of identity for Latino individuals in their corresponding contexts of meaning, are now challenged by this new reality. Such factors begin to change gradually in the process of contact, conflict, and accommodation to the host culture (Salgado de Snyder 1987). Furthermore, it is important to keep in mind that a number of socioeconomic and sociopolitical influences in many Latin-American countries are currently affecting the old systems of interaction in substantial ways. For instance, women are now becoming more professionally oriented and involved in the work force. Similarly, grandmothers, the cradle of family tradition, are also returning to school and to the work force after finishing their responsibilities with their own children. Caring for their grandchildren is no longer a sure role.

The fact of the matter is that as a consequence of industrialization, with its accompanying increased mobility and fast pace of modern life, the culture is experiencing different degrees of change with regard to its influence on the moral values of Latin-American individuals. But for the purpose of this chapter, we will focus on traditional, although not necessarily equally applicable, codes of conduct, the nature of which may be present in different degrees in Latino people.

Thus, speaking in generality and emphasizing earlier traditions, Latino individuals could be defined as respectful, religious, hardworking, and family-oriented, people whose strong sense of "right" and "wrong" was instilled in their conscience from the early stages of development. Development occurs in the context of the influence of an extended family system. It includes grandparents, aunts and uncles, cousins, in-laws, and so-called second aunts and second uncles. The *compadres* (coparents) and *vecinos* (neighbors) subsystems, as well as all the major institutions such as school and church, are also part of this large system of moral influence that functions as an extension of the parental influence. They all contribute to set up the standards of acceptable behavior against which judgments about individual behavior are made. It is within this framework that traditions are formed and become the guiding code of conduct.

Through the example of the people around them, children learn to conform to norms of responsibility and appropriate behavior. *Respeto* is the backbone of the moral teachings transmitted to them. In addition, all the disciplinary techniques evolve as a function of respect. *Respeto* underscores the worth of the individual and entails special consideration for adults and older people (Canino and Canino 1980). The ultimate goal in the child-rearing process is to provide children with a structure that ensures the development of individuals with a solid moral character. Any transgression—at the level of actual direct action or simple thought—against any member of this large system is heavily condemned. Being a "good boy or girl," which is used as a reinforcer of good and desirable behavior, applies only to individuals who abide by, and are respectful to, traditional expectations. When children snap at their elders, verbally or otherwise, in defiance, give a dirty look (*pican los ojos*), lie, do not keep their word, or steal, they are expected to go to confession to expiate their sins. Unless they do this, children may have to carry the burden of a guilty conscience.

The mother may use her role of self-denying abnegation to her family to gain leverage, through guilt as a powerful negative reinforcer, to get her children to live up to set standards. When scolding, shaming, belittling, or punishing do not work, implanting the fear of the father may prove a successful means of control. While physical discipline is a condoned part of parental control directed toward teaching children behavior consistent with cultural standards of right and wrong (Reid 1984), both parents may also resort to withdrawal of love as their most powerful weapon to submit their children to their will. Other methods of reinforcement used with small children are the beliefs that God, the saints, and/or the Guardian Angel are always watching, or that the *cuco* (evil spirit in the dark or bogeyman), *duende* (gnome), or other evil spirits will get them for their bad deeds or thoughts.

Adults carry with them the internalized rules from their childhood and face additional external controls, such as running the risk of being sent to jail if found breaking the law. Nonetheless, the concern for what the *vecinos* (neighbors) and others will think or say and the importance of preserving the family's honor are, by themselves, a very strong deterrent to inappropriate actions. The negative social consequences of the community's disapproval contribute to its powerful influence as a means of social control. A "bad" reputation has a way of spreading very quickly and the individual may face the possibility of becoming a social marginal. The shame and stigma of having been in jail, for example, may carry a mark that stays with the individual. Friends know about it; prospective employers find out and react to it in a negative way. The family would show great hurt if they felt that the action of one of its members had resulted in denigration of the family reputation as a "serious and moral family." It is in this context that there is great reluctance to discuss family affairs with nonfamily members, including the therapist.

The Role of Religiosity in Moral Development

Religious beliefs, specially coming from the Catholic church, and popular myths are indeed very central in the development of morality for the Latino individual, even in individuals who consider themselves atheists (Ocampo 1989, Tejada et al. 1993). It is not unusual to hear someone saying *"si Dios quiere"* (God willing) or *"si mi Virgencita quiere"* (if my Lady's willing) after speaking of a future plan. Latinos are likely to present a more external locus of control than Anglos, which is characterized by a fatalistic view of the world where people's behavior is controlled by external natural and supernatural powers (Arce and Torres-Matrullo 1982). Thus the notion of supernatural intervention may be found in the traditions of most Latino groups, especially among individuals coming from the lower socioeconomic classes. As a consequence, some Mexican-Americans may seek the help of *yerberos* or *curanderos*, Cubans may pursue *santeros*, and Puerto Ricans may resort to the work of *espiritistas* (Argueta-Bernal 1990, Tejada et al. 1993). According to Tejada and associates, Dominicans will also rely on voodoo tradition in addition to the ones referred to above. Their usual goals may be to ensure the success of an important event in their lives, job, or relationships, or to purify themselves from the effect of a "*mal de ojo*"—evil eye (Ruiz 1981).

Latino people believe in and rely on prayer and the invocation of saints or spirits for a sense of safety and welfare. This may also be a way of decreasing the stress and tension that result from their precarious conditions of living (Argueta-Bernal 1990). These beliefs serve a very important role in the moral fabric of the Latino individual. They allow the individual to preserve a sense of self as basically good and moral. Serious transgressions may at times be ultimately justified as the work of evil power outside the individual's control. Prayers, *promesas*, and visits to the *espiritista* or *santero* (spiritual healers) are meant to counteract the impact of these negative forces or spirits.

To understand how religious beliefs became so central in the Latino reality, one has to look at colonial history in which, according to Tejada and colleagues (1993), the Catholic religion was used as a political tool to ensure obedience to the throne. The *santero* and *espiritista* practices evolved from the religious traditions of the African slaves brought to many Latin-American countries. Within the last few decades, pentecostal and evangelical groups have also become essential influential religious groups in the Latino moral fabric. Nevertheless, influences coming from the Catholic church and African religious traditions are still very prominent (Tejada et al. 1993).

Gender Differences in Moral Expectations

Women and men are guided by different and somewhat contradictory codes of conduct. Traditionally, females are expected to maintain a virginlike attitude with regard to sexual behavior and even in marriage are expected to demonstrate only a measured expression of pleasure in that regard. They are expected to be submissive and deferential to the male and suffer the partner's infidelity in silence. Women are socialized to believe that they are ultimately responsible for maintaining the integrity of the family.

Their sensuality and beauty are highly praised and admired by society at large. Even in that regard, though, their overall demeanor is expected to be guided by the code of *respeto*, "honor," and *honra* to their family and to the ideals of "a woman of moral character." Nonetheless, there is the cultural premise that they need to be watched over, since they are perceived as weak by nature and vulnerable to the sexual advances of males. Within this context it is important for a woman to avoid being alone with a man other than her spouse, avoid discussion of sexual content, and avoid staring in the eyes of members of the opposite gender. Otherwise she risks the label of "loose woman." Within that framework, when courting, the "chaperons system" has been used to provide the necessary supervision and protection of the young woman's name against temptation and "*el que diran*" (what people may say, gossip).

The male, on the other hand, is encouraged to express his masculinity in the conquering of female companions with or without ending in matrimony. Nonetheless, his family responsibility is expected to take precedence and he is to be a "*buen padre de familia*" (head of the family). This is done without precluding the possibility of extramarital affairs or having children outside the marriage. Again, the code of *respeto* and *honra* is used to describe the extent to which the male is able to maintain the family integrity by providing financially for its survival (Ghali 1982, Lauria 1964). Continued emotional involvement with his family affairs is not necessarily a part of this expectation.

DEFINING THE MORAL CHARACTER OF THE LATINO INDIVIDUAL

The cultural characteristics described above suggest that the nature of the superego structure and moral fabric of the Latino individual can be logically construed only as being influenced by severe and primitive content and the potential for sadomasochistic transformations. The expected transformations into identifications and the nature of the introjects of the Latino individual's early relationships are intricately and intimately related to the quality of these cultural influences. Subsequently, superego pathology of various forms is expected to define the mental health of the Latino individual.

Nevertheless, as it is true of any external influences on individuals' psychological development and the nature of their psychic structure (Arlow 1985), cultural influences are not processed in the same way by all individuals. And here lies a basic tenet in psychoanalytic thinking. That it is the nature of the individual psychic structure, the strength of the drives, the quality of the introjects, the nature of the identifications and adaptation level, and the quality of the id, ego, and superego organization that will ultimately determine the nature and extent of influence of the external (cultural) environment and how these influences are later processed (A. Freud 1936, Freud 1937). That was, in fact, the basic thesis of Freud's "Analysis Terminable and Interminable" (Freud 1937). Similar claims are ultimately maintained by, among others, Sullivan (1953), and by Fairbairn's (1941) and Winnicott's (1965) conceptualizations. Such a view is also closer to our own clinical experience with Latino individuals, in which, depending on the level of education and socioeconomic status, and the extent of acculturation to the cultural mores of this country, the impact of cultural expectations is felt differently in their psychological and moral development and functioning.

In the final analysis, the moral character of the Latino individual has to be defined in terms of the extent to which the contradictory cultural norms described above, such as gender differences in moral expectations, are dynamically integrated into a meaningful moral structure. The degree of meaningfulness of this moral structure depends on the extent to which it fosters psychological growth in the context of meaningful, respectful, and profitable relationships with a person's surroundings.

TREATMENT IMPLICATIONS

Culturally based moral influences present themselves in the treatment process of Latino patients in a number of ways, including the treatment of the most acculturated ones. It is truly a complex phenomenon and a tremendous challenge for clinicians because not all cultural factors are easily accessible to analysis. And yet they may still give a tremendous flavor to the Latino patient's personality structure. For instance, the effervescent manner of relating, with the concomitant high-spirited greeting style, hand movements, and frequent touching that characterize many Latino individuals' interpersonal relationships, may be organized around habitual structures and hence not be subject to psychoanalytic exploration. According to findings by Petri and Mishkin (1994) regarding the neuropsychology of memory, habits follow a very different organizational path than the traditional memory structure. It is this different cognitive organization that makes habitual information inaccessible to analysis. What may be subject to psychoanalytic explorations is cultural material organized around psychic dimensions, such as ego and superego structures. Only these dimensions are governed by the rules of consciousness and unconsciousness that also impact on the nature of the transference and countertransference. Nevertheless, the fact that some culturally sanctioned trait, such as *machismo* or the view of dreams as revelation, may have reached a certain level of habit does not mean that it is not also organized around the kinds of psychic dimensions suggested earlier. In the final analysis, and as suggested earlier, how cultural dimensions are organized, and the importance of these dimensions in explaining psychic formation, will have to be determined in the context of the individual psychology.

Thus the cultural influences described above with regard to moral development are expected to impact on the therapeutic process of Latino individuals in various degrees. For instance, the role of religion may sway a Latino patient to liken the therapeutic process to a "confession" and to perceive the therapist/analyst as a "priest." Similarly, for a Latino patient the content of the sessions may be influenced by the need to preserve and be loyal to family tradition. The patient may experience the revelation of family history and material of sexual content as "too personal," and hence would avoid exploring any experience that could lead into these kinds of discussions. Such behavior may give an impression of inaccessibility of important memories and hence affect the clinician's view of the nature of the patient's repression.

These behaviors are different for male and female patients. For instance, a female patient may find it easier to confide her sexual secrets to a female rather than to a male therapist/analyst. When discussing them with a male therapist/analyst, it may create additional anxiety around the concern that the therapist/analyst may see her as a "loose person" or erotically interested, which may be both a fear and a wish.

> An example of this phenomenon could be seen in the case of a 38-year old Latino woman. She sought treatment with the specific request that her sessions remain confidential and a promise that her husband would never know about her treatment. She was married to a pastor and felt very uncomfortable about seeking treatment outside her family and church instead of attempting to resolve her problems through prayers. Moreover, the fact that treatment was being conducted by a male therapist added further anxiety to an already intense situation. Indeed, she found it more difficult to ward off the intense erotic transference that quickly developed from the very beginning of her treatment and that disturbed her a great deal. She was concerned about the therapist's perception of her and what would happen should her husband find out about her secret arrangement. As these issues and her feelings of disloyalty toward her husband were being explored, she reported the following dream:

> She found herself at the beach with her therapist lying down by the water embracing each other, like the two main characters in the movie *Swept Away*. She felt a tremendous feeling of comfort, romance, love, and protection. In the next part of the dream, the therapist was now up in a mountain that extended from the beach. He was sitting reverently on a tall chair looking down. She saw him from the beach and knew that she was expected to come up to the mountain. The therapist was dressed in white religious attire as if in the middle of a ritual.

Following the dream, the patient reported feeling safer and less afraid about letting her husband know about her treatment. The therapist was invested with a priestlike quality and hence became less threatening. At this point in her treatment, this religious transformation of the therapeutic process could be seen as an effort to give herself permission to continue the therapeutic engagement.

In the case of a male patient, these same issues regarding sexual content may be present in various ways. Such content may become exciting or shameful, depending on the gender of the therapist and the nature of the conflict. One of the complications in the treatment of Latino males has to do with the expectation, in keeping with the macho code, that a man should rely only on himself to deal with his difficulties. It is, indeed, less likely that the Latino male patient will seek treatment unless conflicts in this area are somewhat resolved (Javier 1990, Javier and Herron 1992). His sexual escapades are seen as natural and hence not subject to exploration. That was in fact what a Latino male patient recently said with a broad smile in response to the therapist's inquiries about a series of extramarital affairs: "It is natural for a Latino man to have women on the side, don't you think?"

He was a well-dressed, college-educated young man who requested treatment because of feelings of emptiness and confusion around his marriage. He and his wife had decided to separate but he was not sure why. He felt an intense desire to be alone, but would find himself crying and longing for the company of someone once he was alone in his apartment after the separation. He had lost his alcoholic father five years before to cirrhosis and his mother in a car accident a couple of years later. His wife was described as beautiful and basically a good woman, with minimal education: "She would be perfect as the mother of my children . . . but she wants too much from me." He was referring to her constant questioning about his whereabouts when he would come home late and his lack of emotional involvement with her. "She shouldn't ask so many questions about my affairs." He reported having trouble feeling interested in his wife sexually, in spite of her beauty, but still feeling that he loved her very much. She apparently often complained that he treated her more like a sister or mother than a wife.

The multidetermined role served by his wife in terms of his basic dynamics emerged on several occasions, most recently around the issue of separation. As part of the separation, the patient agreed to provide financially for her at her new place, as he had also provided for his mother earlier upon his father's death. This was done to offset his sense of guilt associated with his feelings of failure as a husband. "A husband should always provide for his wife." Perhaps this was also a way of dealing with his feelings of guilt for his mother's death. With this arrangement he managed to keep himself connected to her even after the separation, which eventually contributed to a reconciliation. With regard to his brothers, his need to provide financially for them emerged. "I am supposed to be a parent to my brothers because I am better off financially." The patient had a very good job and drew a steady income while his brothers were either unemployed or earning minimal wages.

He felt, however, that his brothers' and wife's dependency on him, financially and emotionally, placed a heavy burden on him. It kept him ultimately trapped in the same kind of predicament he experienced while growing up in the ghetto. Taking care of a needy family member was indeed part of this patient's cultural code of behavior. It was part of being a "good" son and brother. Nevertheless, by depleting himself financially, he would also ensure that he was in fact not financially better off than his brothers and many of his ghetto friends. They could not then accuse him of having sold out to the white-collar world. Thus he would make sure to spend time with his friends drinking and using recreational drugs.

He, like his father before him, was described as a bright man with an excellent future. He graduated from an Ivy League school and was quickly employed by Wall Street. He always dated women with qualities very different from those of his wife and mother but was not sure why. Nonetheless, he selected as his wife a woman similar to his mother. When it was suggested to him that part of the reason for his attraction to her was his conflict around his self-definition as a successful Latino male as well as his fear related to his longing for his mother/father, he initially became defensive and later tearful. What emerged in response was his strong concern that if he became too successful, he would lose his connection with her and his family. Then he would no longer be his mother's and father's son and his brothers' brother. He also experienced "other" women as less demanding and sexually freer than his wife. With his wife, he felt trapped.

It is not our intention at this juncture to discuss the treatment of this patient in its entirety. Rather, we only want to provide some examples of the possible ways cultural expectations influence the treatment process and how cultural information can be used in the service of resistance. For this patient, his conflicted self-definition as a successful Latino individual, his rage and fear around abandonment issues, his unresolved range of feelings regarding his parents' death, and so on were all part of the therapeutic equation in the context of his cultural background. Culture-based expectations were used by this patient as a convenient device to avoid exploration of sensitive issues, including his hostility against and fear of the females in his life, and responsibility for his behavior. A successful treatment with these kinds of patients will occur only within a context that allows the respectful, and yet direct, exploration of cultural and personal dynamic factors in relation to the individual's personal psychology.

REFERENCES

Arce, A. A., and Torres-Matrullo, C. (1982). Application of cognitive behavioral techniques in the treatment of Hispanic patients. *Psychiatric Quarterly* 54:230–236.

Argueta-Bernal, G. A. (1990). Stress and stress-related disorders in Hispanics: biobehavioral approaches to treatment. In *Mental Health of Ethnic Minorities*, ed. F. C. Serafica, A. I. Shewebel, R. K. Russell, et al. pp. 202–221. New York: Praeger.

Arlow, J. (1985). The concept of psychic reality and related problems. *Journal of the American Psychoanalytic Association* 33:521–535.

Brunner, J. (1991). The (ir)relevance of Freud's Jewish identity to the origins of psychoanalysis. *Psychoanalysis and Contemporary Thought* 14:655–684.

Canino, I. A., and Canino, G. (1980). Impact of stress on the Puerto Rican family: treatment considerations. *American Journal of Orthopsychiatry* 50:232–238.

Eissler, K. R. (1953). The effect of the structure of the ego on psychoanalytic technique. *Journal of the American Psychoanalytic Association* 1:104–143.

Emler, N. (1983). Morality and politics: the ideological dimension in the theory of moral development, In *Morality in the Making*, ed. H. Weinreich-Haste and D. Locke, pp. 47–71. Chichester, UK: Wiley.

Fagen, J. W., and Prigot, J. A. (1993). Negative affect and infant memory. In *Advances in Infancy Research*, vol. 8, ed. J. Rovee-Collier and L. P. Lipsitt, pp. 169–216. Norwood, NJ: Ablex.

Fairbairn, W. R. D. (1941). A revised psychopathology of the psychoses and psychoneuroses. In *Essential Papers on Object Relations*, ed. P. Buckley, pp. 71–101. New York: New York University Press.

Freud, A. (1936). *The Ego and the Mechanisms of Defense*. New York: International Universities Press.

Freud, S. (1914). On narcissism: an introduction. *Standard Edition* 14:69–102.

———— (1923). The ego and the id. *Standard Edition* 19:1–66.

———— (1924). The economic problem of masochism. *Standard Edition* 19:155–172.

———— (1937). Analysis terminable and interminable. *Standard Edition* 23:209–253.

Ghali, M. A. (1982). The choice of crime: an empirical analysis of juveniles' criminal choice. *Journal of Criminal Justice* 10:433–442.

Gilligan, C. (1982). New maps of development: new visions of maturity. *American Journal of Orthopsychiatry* 52:199–212.

Gutierrez, R. A. (1991). *When Jesus Came, the Corn Mothers Went Away: Marriage, Sexuality, and Power in New Mexico, 1500–1845*. Stanford, CA: Stanford University Press.

Haan, N. (1975). Hypothetical and actual moral reasoning in a situation of civil disobedience. *Journal of Personality and Social Psychology* 32:255–270.

Herron, W. (1992). *The development of the ethnic unconscious.* Paper presented at the Annual Convention of the American Psychological Association, Washington, DC, August.

Hogan, R., and Emler, N. (1978). The biases in contemporary social psychology. *Social Research* 45:478–534.

Javier, R. A. (1990). The suitability of insight-oriented therapy for the Hispanic poor. *American Journal of Psychoanalysis* 50:305–318.

—— (1993). World of diversity: machismo/marianismo stereotypes and Hispanic culture. In *Human Sexuality in a World of Diversity*, ed. S. A. Rathus, J. S. Nevid, and L. Fichner-Rathus, pp. 166–167. Boston: Allyn & Bacon.

Javier, R. A., and Herron, W. (1992). Psychoanalysis, the Hispanic poor, and the disadvantaged: application and conceptualization. *Journal of the American Academy of Psychoanalysis* 20:455–476.

Javier, R. A., Konat, J., Smith, L., and Hernandez, A. (1992). *Promoting moral reasoning and psychological growth in a college student population.* Paper presented at the Annual Conference of the New York State Psychological Association, Bolton Landing, NY, May.

Javier, R. A., and Yussef, M. B. (1992). *A critical analysis of the therapeutic models used with Spanish-speaking patients.* Paper presented at the Ibero-American Congress of Psychology, Madrid, Spain, July.

Jojola, T. (1993). Commentaries: *When Jesus Came, the Corn Mothers Went Away: Marriage, Sex, and Power in New Mexico*, 1500–1846, by Ramon Gutierrez. *American Indian Culture Research Journal* 17:141–177.

Kant, I. (1959). *Foundations of the Metaphysics of Morals, and What Is Enlightenment?* Trans. L. W. Beck. New York: Liberal Arts Press.

Kernberg, O. (1975). *Borderline Conditions and Pathological Narcissism.* New York: Jason Aronson.

Kohlberg, L. (1973). The development of moral stages: uses and abuses. *Proceedings of the Invitational Conference on Testing Problems*, 1–8.

—— (1981). *The Philosophy of Moral Development: Moral Stages and the Idea of Justice*, 1st ed. San Francisco: Harper & Row.

Kohlberg, L., and Candee, D. (1984). The relationship of moral judgment to moral action. In *Morality, Moral Behavior, and Moral Development*, ed. W. M. Kurtines and J. L. Gerwirtz, pp. 52–73. New York: Wiley.

Lauria, A. (1964). "*Respeto*," "*relajo*," and interpersonal relations in Puerto Rico. *Anthropological Quarterly* 38:53–66.

Mahler, M. S., Pine, F., and Bergman, A. (1975). *The Psychological Birth of the Human Infant.* New York: Basic Books.

Marin, G., Sabogal, F., Marin, B. V., et al. (1987). Development of a short acculturation scale for Hispanics. *Hispanic Journal of Behavioral Science* 9:183–205.

Merwine, M. H. (1993). How Africa understands female circumcision, letter to the editor. *New York Times*, November 14, p. A 24.

Ocampo L. D. (1989). *Mitos Colombianos*, 2nd. Ed. Bogota, Colombia: Editorial Presencia.

Padilla, A. M. (1980). The role of cultural awareness and ethnic loyalty in acculturation. In *Acculturation: Theory, Models and Some New Findings*, pp. 47–84. Boulder, CO: Praeger.

Petri, H. L., and Mishkin M. (1994). Behaviorism, cognitivism and neuropsychology of memory. *American Scientist* 82:30–37.

Piaget, J. (1932). *The Moral Judgment of the Child*. Trans. M. Gabain. New York: Free Press.

Rest, J. (1973). The hierarchical nature of stages of moral judgment. *Journal of Personality* 41:86–109.

Reid, S. (1984). Cultural difference and child abuse intervention with undocumented Spanish-speaking families in Los Angeles. *Child Abuse and Neglect* 8:109–112.

Rosenthal, A. M. (1993). Female genital torture. *New York Times*, November 12, p. A33.

Ruiz, R. (1981). Cultural and historical perspectives. In *Counseling the culturally different*, ed. D. Sue, pp. 186–215. New York: Wiley.

Salgado de Snyder, S. (1987). Factors associated with acculturative stress and depressive symptomatology among married Mexican women. *Psychology of Women Quarterly* 11:475–488.

Sullivan, H. S. (1953). *The Interpersonal Theory of Psychiatry*. New York: Norton.

Stern, D. (1985). *The Interpersonal World of the Infant*. New York: Basic Books.

Tejada O. D., Sanchez M. F., and Mella M. C. (1993). *Religiosidad Popular Dominicana y Psiquiatria*. Santo Domingo, D.R: Corripio.

Tyson, P., and Tyson, R. L. (1984). Narcissism and superego development. *Journal of the American Psychoanalytic Association* 32:75–98.

Walker, A. (1992). *Possessing the Secret of Joy*. New York: Pocket Star Books.

Winnicott, D. W. (1965). *The Maturational Processes and the Facilitating Environment*. New York: International Universities Press.

19

The Role of Ethnicity in the Development of Moral Values

WILLIAM G. HERRON, LYDIA K. WARNER, AND SONJA M. RAMIREZ

The level of ethnic tension in the world challenges psychoanalysis to direct more attention to the influence on behavior of ethnic moral values. These values are essentially rules of conduct that have been developed by different groups of people throughout the world as structural supports for the growth and maintenance of societies. As such, ethnic moral values would appear to be symbols of civilization, yet they can be and have been discriminatory to the point of one group slaughtering others because one of the rules was ethnic purity.

Today there are many international "flash points" and "hot spots" that can and do explode into devastating conflicts that can be construed as rooted in disparate values. Even where the situation is not so drastic, as in the United States at this time, there is a dominant Anglo-American ethnic perspective that struggles with the demands of both the stated political philosophy of their country and the growing ethnic minority population to develop a viable multiethnic society. This requires the understanding and integration of ethnic moral values, a significant task for which psychoanalysis is well suited in its interest in the universe of human variations. However, the value of psychoanalysis is not going to be actualized unless the influence of ethnic moral values as a psychological force is truly acknowledged. Unfortunately, with some exceptions (Akhtar 1995, Antokoletz 1993, Grinberg and Grinberg 1989, Javier et al. 1995, Kakar 1995), it has not been. The purpose of this chapter is to highlight the challenge through one example, the effect of Anglo-American ethnic moral values in psychoanalytic theory and practice.

Some of the concepts involved in this presentation require definition. This will be followed by a discussion of the ways in which moral value development has been considered in the evaluation of psychoanalysis. The remainder of the chapter will emphasize the theoretical concerns and issues of practice that are involved in the Anglo-American psychoanalytic perspective of moral values.

DEFINITION

Although *ethnicity* and *race* are overlapping terms that some consider to be equivalent for practical purposes (Jiobu 1990), delineations are possible. *Race* refers to people descended from common ancestors with an inherited physical appearance, making that appearance a major cue to their identity. *Ethnicity* refers to people from a group having a common set of characteristics that include cultural values, traditions, and behaviors, but their race may be mixed, with their characteristics transmitted through socialization and heredity (Ocampo et al. 1993). Ethnic identity, or personal ethnicity, refers to self-identification as a member of an ethnic group due to the possession of attributes common to that group (Aboud 1987). Ethnic identity is depicted as having the five components of self-identification, constancy, role behavior, knowledge, and feelings and preferences that develop over time with a consolidation of ethnic awareness taking place in latency (Bernal et al. 1993). Shadings of confusion are likely to appear in regard to ethnicity, so it is best considered an approximate term.

The same is true for the category of Anglo-American. Ancestry produces considerable heterogeneity (Jiobu 1990), although European is most frequent. This group has a number of self-defining characteristics, such as combining the speaking of English (U.S. version) as a native language with being born in the United States, and being white. One of these categorical symbols is the WASP (white Anglo-Saxon Protestant), but this group is probably a minority within a majority. There are numerous divisions within Anglo-Americans, such as geographical (North and South) and religious (Christian and Jewish). With considerable variations the group represents the mainstream, a reference group for comparison and assimilation into the American culture. The specifics of this are often more easily described by what they are not in a given instance than by what they are. For example, Asians are not Anglos because of color and language, Africans because of color, and Hispanics because of language, yet they could all turn out to be classified as Americans. Although Anglo-Americans have this substantial diversity, they also have a sufficient core to represent a dominant value system that can be designated as the "American Way" (of doing things). This value system is connected to legislated principles, for example, the law of the land, but is subject to both interpretation and change.

VALUE DEVELOPMENT

In psychoanalytic theory, value development is generally designated as the primary work of a structural component of personality. The traditional structure has been the superego, with moral values developed through a series of identifications that are also processed by other personality structures, such as the ego and the id, and are a significant component of a relational system, or a self-system, depending on the context of conceptualization. Values are basically composed of material learned from significant others, as well as from the surrounding environment of society and culture, and are processed in reference to the narcissistic needs of each person as well. A constant shaping process has both consistency and sufficient elasticity to keep moral value systems within the context of reality. Distortions, extremes, and pathology are all at the service of moral values as well. For example, slavery and ethnic purity have both had their causes argued in terms of moral values.

Garza-Guerrero (1981) traced the history of the superego concept, and in turn the psychoanalytic theory of moral values, from Freud to the influence of object relations theory. In doing so, note is made of conceptual influences such as interpersonal relatedness and cultural factors, but limited note. In developing a relational model of the superego, Garza-Guerrero (1981/1982) depicts superego evolution as proceeding through the developmental phases of aggressively derived forerunners, then integration with the ideal self-object representations, oedipal derivation, and subsequent individualization, all set within the traditional family triad that has an implicit primary panculturalism. Mention is given to the possible influence of sociocultural factors, but the emphasis is on the universality of moral values as superego content (Ticho 1972). The degree to which personal narrative is ethnic narrative tends to be discounted in favor of more encompassing dynamics.

This trend continues in contemporary psychoanalytic theorizing. Self psychology (Kohut 1984) has given prominence to attunement, empathy, and the ideal self. The latter is a value system that develops as a differentiation from primary narcissism through internalization of parental ideals. The emphasis is on an interactive, dyadic systems point of view (Beebe et al. 1992). A similar trend is apparent in the melding of intrapsychic and inter-subjective systems in the development of mutual recognition (Benjamin 1992). All these relational approaches stress the influence of significant others, thus opening the door wider to consider ethnicity as a significant component of the content of learning from the others, but their focus, in being dyadic and "person" oriented, tends to contain the area of interactive influences to broad categories, as social relatedness. The pancultural nature of infant desires is reflected even in critical evaluation of the intersubjective expansion from one-person to two-person psychologies (Erreich 1993). Thus the wish list of infant desires includes empathy, along with feelings of intactness, pleasure, attention, support, and exclusive love. These add up to narcissistic motiva-tions that are prone to ethnic shadings, influences, and expressions, although this point has thus far been given limited attention. There seems to be an assumption that all individuals will essentially strive to move from concerns with the self to concern for others. It is an appealing assumption, but ethno-centrism poses a challenge to it, or at the very least, to the specifics of value representations within it. Cultural judgments about psychological maturity, for example, are openly embedded in what appear to be classed as universals, yet are the specifics of the Western imagination. The result is what Kohut has described as "health and maturity moralities" (1979, p. 12).

Cortese (1990) points out the restrictiveness of an Anglo social world model, suggesting instead that ethnic groups have different value systems designed for the moral vitality of their social worlds, whether they are in or out of this country. In this regard, Akhtar (1995) notes how for immigrants splitting may come into play between the "land of the mother" and the "land of the other." For example, an East-to-West immigrant denigrates the West, whereas the West-to-East reverses the process, and in each case the mother-land is glorified. The typical Western values listed are indeed part of the Anglo-American self-image, namely "industrious, conscientious, orderly, instinctually gratifying, and encouraging of self-actualization" (p. 1059).

THEORETICAL IMPLICATIONS

The Anglo-American perspective has stated ideals in regard to all people, sym-bolized primarily in the concept of equality, which in turn have to be integrated with its functional ideals, such as autonomy, rationality, and competition, which tend to reward those who help themselves. In commenting on our society, Perdue states, "It offers private solutions for public issues" (1986, p. 385). One of these private solutions is a relative ethnocentrism, which at its best clings to a melting pot approach, regardless of the desires of those to be melted, and at its most problematic breaks into ethnic hierarchies of power. In between, there is the possibility of an increasingly multicultural American society that appears to be given an ambivalent embrace by the Anglo community.

This ambivalence has been there in the inclusion of psychoanalytic theory in the fabric of the society. To the degree that it strove for universality and offered an ideal such as productivity, it fit well with a mainstream American ethic. It is, however, distant from the Anglo-American mainstream consciousness. It lacks the pragmatism of behaviorism, for example, that is more easily endorsed as a logical moral thrust. Its founders and major theorists have often been on the edge of the Anglo category, being foreign-born or Jewish. In this regard, it is of interest to speculate on the increasing popularity of relational theory in that its originator, Sullivan, was American-born, as were his parents. He was not a WASP, however, considering his Irish ancestry and Catholic background. In essence, psychoanalytic theory is not the home-grown product of an Anglo-American perspective. Nonetheless, it still stands as the most comprehensive theory of personality in this country, and represents a powerful Anglo subculture. The potential for greater effectiveness is there, provided that the comprehensiveness is actually going to increase. Thus far the major models for ethnic identity have been based on social learning and cognitive developmental theories (Bernal and Knight 1993) rather than coming from psychoanalytic theories. However, the relational tilt in analytic theory and the potential complementarity of intrapsychic and intersubjective systems are promising directions. Cortese concludes, "Relationships, not reason nor justice, are the essence of life and morality" (1990, p. 127).

IMPLICATIONS FOR PRACTICE

There has been an increasing recognition of the role of the analyst's subjectivity in analytic technique (Renik 1993). This understanding facilitates looking at the probability of an Anglo-American ethnocentrism as part of the analyst's personal motivations. This is transformed into an Anglo value system that provides a moral perspective for and about patients that can result in the imposition of personal truths as apparently universal standards.

However, in even achieving recognition of subjectivity, some content is harder to come by than other material, and the influence of the analyst's ethnic identity is often in the realm of the hidden or denied. There are a number of reasons for this, centering around a melding of the ideal of objectivity and the ethical and political incorrectness of even thinking about ethnic identity in any way that includes personal superiority.

The ideal of objectivity would put ethnocentrism into the countertransferential category, and because of the type of countertransference it would be classified as, it would be more difficult to take note of than sexual interests or the desires to be a savior, or any of the other countertransferences that are usually discussed in the literature. Analysts are more likely to be motivated to keep their own ethnic pride unconscious, with strong defenses against either its recognition or enactment in the analytic process. The enactment is a controversial issue in terms of technique, but the lack of awareness remains as a clear pattern. The result is a combination of self-deception and role-playing for the patient that undermines the authenticity of the therapeutic relationship.

Assuming an analyst is willing to acknowledge subjective feelings about being part of the Anglo-American ethnic tradition, then how may these feelings be utilized in service of therapeutic progress? Are they to be viewed as a countertransference that is to be thought about but never displayed? Or are they to be considered an "ineducible subjectivity" that can be used to further the process of change for the patient and the analyst?

In the main, the Anglo-American technique has reflected the ideal of objectivity and would decry any inevitability of ethnic differentiation that essentially insisted on the superiority, or stereotyping, of any ethnic group. The Anglo-American moral value is equality, but this is an ethnic group that has had the power. Is it not possible that their self-esteem rests upon perceiving a separateness, much as the duality has been maintained throughout centuries between the poor and those who are not poor (Herron and Javier 1996)?

Cortese (1990) has pointed out the familiarity one has with personal ethnic values that become translated into universal probabilities. That there are other ethnic values that are of equal probability is in turn neglected in deference to the anxiety of the in-group. In the Anglo-American value system that neglect should not continue, yet it is easier and safer to wait for assimilation than to really embrace multiculturalism. In the meantime, there is the hope that is supported by the research indicating that majority and minority children shift with age toward less bias (Aboud and Doyle 1993). However, in-group preferences remain.

Thus the possibility may be more of a probability that Anglo-American analysts have an ethnic pride that translates into a value system that can denigrate anyone other than Anglos. Granted that within this group there may be devaluing of subgroups, as Jews relative to Christians, but this may be minor relative to the Anglo overview. While it is unappealing and distasteful to consider an inevitable prejudicial subjectivity of personal morality, it bears consideration as reality. This translates into deciding how to constructively use the ethnic pride that defensively arises in an analyst when the patient is not an Anglo (or even not your kind of Anglo). Although not specifically focused on the ethnic morality that could be quite embedded in one's analytic technique, a number of analysts have been supporting the need for a practical blend of subjectivity with clinical intuition to produce a practical result as contrasted with a frustrating pursuit of objectivity (Hoffman 1992, Jacobs 1986, Renik 1993). Anglo-American morality is in theory an open door to freedom. Now it has to learn, operationalized in analytic techniques, what to do when strangers enter the room.

RECOMMENDATIONS

For an analyst who is identified with an Anglo-American moral value system to work effectively with patients who are not, it is first necessary for the analyst to recognize the signs of such a system that will be present in the analysis. A notable sign is language. The "usual" Anglo analyst (and we have to assume the existence of such a being for comparative purposes) will be fluent only in English and that will be the analyst's native language. Immigrant patients will have a different native tongue and will tend to be more adept in that language than in English. As a result there can be a communication barrier. Language can be used for defensive purposes by patient or analyst, but misunderstandings can also arise that are not due to resistance but to inabilities to communicate effectively with each other. To overcome this problem the analyst has to be alert to sorting out the defensive aspects from the unavoidable ones. The analyst also has to be willing to work on the clarity of an issue in terms of language as well as in terms of its affective content. Both patient and analyst can discuss throughout the analysis whatever means are needed to ensure effective communication. In particular, it is important that no superiority be attached to either analyst or patient based on linguistic ability or a relational tilt will occur that can distort the work. It would be easier if the analyst and the patient had the same native language, but when they do not, adaptations are to be made. In the case of the authors of this paper, one of them is fluent in languages other than English, but she also encounters patient situations in which she experiences a potential barrier. Another of the authors had a supervisee who learned to speak Spanish quite well, yet had trouble making interpretations in Spanish because she doubted her fluency. Akhtar (1995) has found that the majority of his patients do not choose him as an analyst because of a shared language. Thus, if patients who are not Anglos are willing to try to communicate with Anglo analysts, these analysts need to make sure that ethnic language pride does not get in their way.

There are other issues to this, such as the sense of time. In the United States, the time frame of a session tends to be viewed as a very significant feature. Patients and analysts are expected to be punctual and adhere to the stipulated time limits. There is a certain amount of flexibility in the time contract, but the latitude is limited. However, as Antokoletz (1993) has pointed out, there is considerable cultural and subcultural variation in the meaning and experience of time. For example, Pande (1968) has remarked that in the West, past, present, and future tend to be viewed as discrete entities, but in the Eastern world they are often merged. The result is a different valuing of a concept such as being "on time," and this different value needs to be understood by the analyst. Other aspects of the analytic situation, such as how the roles of patient and therapist are viewed, are subject to similar cultural influences.

The polyglottism of patients is an issue that requires continual attention and technical choices by the analyst. Whenever there are ethnic moral value differences between patients and the Anglo analyst, which there often are, the recognition of these differences must be followed by sorting out their impact on the analysis, which includes distinguishing the resistance, transference, and countertransference components from a customary cultural reaction. For example, if by virtue of the analytic frame the analyst is asking the patient to form a contract that will cause the patient to look at time in an unaccustomed way, the resistance aspect of punctuality needs to be viewed differently than if the analyst and patient shared cultural time values. In this vein, the analyst can have empathy for the patient's values, because the analyst is also being asked to understand a viewpoint that is "foreign." As a result, "stranger anxiety" exists for both patient and therapist and both will struggle in order to bring about a working alliance.

Also, the analyst is faced with the patient's loss of ethnic ties and therefore historical continuity, so that mourning and restitution are major issues. The analyst has to be attuned to the degree to which patients want to make value shifts, as well as adaptive necessities for the degree of acculturation desired. Depending on the analyst's own version of Anglo values, there will be feelings about the patient's differing ethnic values that can easily color the analyst's reactions. Awareness of these feelings can help the analyst examine their possible intrusion, and in turn the analyst can either reopen the interpersonal field if it has started to close, or keep it open if the countertransference has not already been displayed.

Theoretical differences will also be apparent, particularly in regard to the value of different family constellations. These issues appear in regard to the patient's view of separation-individuation, where patients may see themselves as individuated within a context of much stronger attachment to the family than the Anglo analyst usually associates with individuation (Roland 1988). Also, specific transferences can develop in both stereotyped ways, as black against white, and unexpected ways, as merged identities (Holmes 1992). In these instances, theoretical reformulations need to be considered because the conceptions are no longer based on traditional Western-world psychodynamics. At the same time, they are based on dynamic principles. Thus, while recognition and understanding/acceptance of ethnic moral values is a crucial factor for the Anglo analyst, who by virtue of position relative to non-Anglos in this country may have difficulties being apparently empathic, there is also a need to recognize the centrality of the analytic enterprise that can transcend even the apparently irreconcilable.

The latter point is well illustrated by Kakar (1995), who suggests that psychoanalytic practice is based on the acceptance by patients and analysts of a psychological modernity that permits the work to take place in relatively the same way across different societies. Internalization, viewed as internal animation rather than external, is considered the central aspect of modernity, and as a relatively cross-cultural recognition of subjectivity that is affectively disturbing or a result of personal thoughts and feelings. Thus, although different cultures will emphasize different intrapsychic and developmental issues, internalization makes possible a general culture of psychoanalysis that can work with varying ethnic moral values in both patients and their analysts.

As Akhtar notes, there is no set way to do this, yet there are indeed ways to accomplish the task and meet the challenges. Although focused on language differences, his comments suggest a path to overall effectiveness. "Technical choices . . . must derive not from rigid formulas but from the specific ebb and flow of the analytic material and the emotional ambience both of the relationship and of the particular session" (1995, p. 1074).

REFERENCES

Aboud, F. E. (1987). The development of ethnic self-identification and attitudes. In *Children's Ethnic Socialization*, ed. J. S. Phinney and M. J. Ratherava, pp. 32–55. Newberry Park, CA: Sage.

Aboud, F. E., and Doyle, A. B. (1993). The early development of ethnic identity and attitudes. In *Ethnic Identity*, ed. M. E. Bernal and G. P. Knight, pp. 47–59. Albany: State University of New York Press.

Akhtar, S. (1995). A third individuation: immigration, identity, and the psychoanalytic process. *Journal of the American Psychoanalytic Association* 43:1051–1084.

Antokoletz, J. C. (1993). A psychoanalytic view of cross-cultural passages. *American Journal of Psychoanalysis* 53:35–54.

Beebe, B., Jaffe, J., and Lachmann, F. M. (1992). A dyadic systems view of communication. In *Relational Perspectives in Psychoanalysis*, ed. N. J. Skolnick and S. C. Warshaw, pp. 61–81. Hillsdale, NJ: Analytic Press.

Benjamin, J. (1992). Recognition and detraction: an outline of intersubjectivity. In *Relational Perspectives in Psychoanalysis*, ed. N. J. Skolnick and S. C. Warshaw, pp. 43–60. Hillsdale, NJ: Analytic Press.

Bernal, M. E., and Knight, G. P., eds. (1993). *Ethnic Identity*. Albany: State University of New York Press.

Bernal, M. E., Knight, G. P., Ocampo, K. A., et al. (1993). Development of Mexican American identity. In *Ethnic Identity*, ed. M. E. Bernal and G. P. Knight, pp. 31–46. Albany: State University of New York Press.

Cortese, A. C. (1990). *Ethnic Ethics: The Restructuring of Moral Theory*. Albany: State University of New York Press.

Erreich, A. (1993). Review of *Diary of a Baby*. *Psychoanalytic Quarterly* 62:672–674.

Garza-Guerrero, A. C. (1981). The superego concept: Part I. *Psychoanalytic Review* 68:321–342.

——— (1981–1982). The superego concept: Part II. *Psychoanalytic Review* 68:515–546.

Grinberg, L., and Grinberg, R. (1989). *Psychoanalytic Perspectives on Immigration and Exile*. New Haven, CT: Yale University Press.

Herron, W. G., and Javier, R. A. (1996). The psychogenesis of poverty: some psychoanalytic conceptualizations. *Psychoanalytic Review* 83:631–640.

Hoffman, I. Z. (1992). Some practical implications of a social-constructivist view of the psychoanalytic situation. *Psychoanalytic Dialogues* 2:287–304.

Holmes, D. E. (1992). Race and transference in psychoanalysis and psychotherapy. *International Journal of Psychoanalysis* 73:U 1–11.

Jacobs, T. J. (1986). On countertransference enactments. *Journal of the American Psychoanalytic Association* 34:289–307.

Javier, R. A., Herron, W. G., and Yanos, P. (1995). Urban poverty, ethnicity, and personality development. *Journal of Social Distress and the Homeless* 4:219–235.

Jiobu, R. M. (1990). *Ethnicity and Inequality*. Albany: State University of New York Press.

Kakar, S. (1995). Clinical work and cultural imagination. *Psychoanalytic Quarterly* 64:265–281.

Kohut, H. (1979). The two analyses of Mr. Z. *International Journal of Psycho-Analysis* 60:3–27.

——— (1984). *How Does Analysis Cure?* Chicago: University of Chicago Press.

Ocampo, K.A., Bernal, M. E., and Knight, G. P. (1993). Gender, race, and ethnicity: the sequencing of social constancies. In *Ethnic Identity*, ed. M. E. Bernal and G. P. Knight, pp. 11–13. Albany: State University of New York Press.

Pande, S. K. (1968). The mystique of "Western" psychotherapy: an Eastern interpretation. *Journal of Nervous and Mental Disorders* 146:425–432.

Perdue, W. D. (1986). *Sociological Theory*. Palo Alto, CA: Mayfield.

Renik, O. (1993). Analytic interaction: conceptualizing technique in light of the analyst's ineducable subjectivity. *Psychoanalytic Quarterly* 62:553–571.

Roland, A. (1988). *In Search of Self in India and Japan: Toward a Cross-Cultural Psychology*. Princeton, NJ: Princeton University Press.

Ticho, E. (1972). The development of superego autonomy. *Psychoanalytic Review* 59:217–233.

20

Unconscious Ethnicity: Music, Early Development, and Psychotherapy

CORA L. DÍAZ DE CHUMACEIRO

Music is an inextricable part of our object world. The objective of this chapter is to propose that unconscious ethnicity reflected in the recall of music in treatment be included in the systematic study of ethnicity in psychoanalysis proposed by Javier and Rendon (this volume, Chapter 15). The results of analyzing unconsciously and consciously induced music evocations in clinical practice and everyday life indicate that there are powerful intrapsychic, unconscious reasons why individuals become attracted to or reject specific instrumental or vocal music (Díaz de Chumaceiro 1987, 1988, 1992, 1996a). To explore the origins of early musical experiences in the family, therefore, is of relevance. These data can provide new avenues for expanding understanding of the influence of music in general and ethnic music in particular in an individual's psychic structure and for formulating new hypotheses and theories. An overview of the growing literature on perinatal and neonatal auditory perception of music and the acquisition of musical behavior in childhood are discussed.

The role of ethnicity in psychoanalysis has recently been emphasized in the literature in a novel manner. Javier and Rendon (1995) suggested *the systematic study of ethnicity* that could provide an expansion of psychoanalytic assumptions of psychic structure by including ethnic variables in the psychoanalytic equation. They stressed that "the nature of identification and introjection, as well as the nature of self-definition, projection, and projective identification, could be thus affected" (pp. 514–515). What is the importance of ethnicity on psychological development? "Ethnic identity is psychologically governed by the same mechanisms as general identity. In fact, it is impossible to think about identity without its ethnic nature" (p. 515). Our culture and ethnic object world mediate early identifications and introjections and these determine our psychic reality's structure and content (Javier and Yussef 1995). It is hardly surprising, then, that these factors can deeply affect the nature of transference–countertransference because psychic reality, influenced by idiosyncratic ethnic history, affects the nature of the perceptions of patient and analyst (Javier and Rendon 1995). Furthermore, Herron (1995) reintroduced the concept of *the ethnic unconscious*—equated with a cultural unconscious in the work of Devereux (1956)—instead now meaning "repressed material shared by each generation with the next and with most people of that ethnic group. The material is derived from identifications that form ethnic character" (p. 521). He also called attention to the role and value of the ethnic unconscious for further comprehending transference, countertransference, and resistance in the psychoanalytic treatment process. Ethnicity was operationally defined as "the degree of identification of a person with an ethnic group that is in some way his or her group of origin" (p. 524). He stressed that major stimuli for change are movements from one culture to another, regardless of whether it is "direct or within a culture," or "living with an ethnic unconscious that is not attuned to the prevailing culture" (p. 530). High levels of stress can be provoked by these situations, which may be predominant facets of conflicts that patients present in treatment, in spite of recognition of the ethnic unconscious and its derivatives. (His caveat about using with reservation the terms *race*, *culture*, *ethnicity*, and *society* due to the difficulty of defining them precisely enough to avoid exceptions, conceptual misunderstandings, and disagreements is also applicable here.)

Introduction to music occurs at home. An individual is born into a family that is a member of a society within the general culture of a nation. In addition to directly teaching and indirectly projecting to the next generation the family's beliefs, values, morals, religion, ideals, fantasies, prejudices and hatreds, as well as other positive and negative factors, its members also consciously and unconsciously transmit their attitudes toward and preferences for different types of music that are valued or devalued in their own and previous generations. When children grow up, they may choose to migrate and change nationalities, or the parents may have made such a decision while a child was still in a dependent stage, or even in utero—an event not without its consequences, experienced by millions throughout generations, in different countries. Regardless of the circumstances of migration, the ethnic inheritance of the family of origin remains a constant factor in the individual's psychic structure—an indelible imprint—whether acknowledged or denied. Migration also affects music preferences. As Pollock (1989) has stressed, severance and loss are a consequence of leaving land or home by force or voluntarily, and often a reactive intensification of ethnic and national identities may result. For many, arrival at a new nation requires having to learn another language and, unavoidably, to listen to new songs and music. For children to decrease the resulting threat of loss and abandonment, or fears of the dark, for instance, a "transitional object" (Winnicott 1953) may be useful. Similarly, in the new milieu, groups stay together and converse in their "mother tongue," eating "mother foods," listening to "'mother lullabies' (music)" (Pollock 1989, p. 153). These and other such activities aid their transition and internal mourning process as well as facilitate their acculturation—if not for this generation, then for the next one and the grandchildren.

Since becoming a member of a particular family, individuals are exposed to their use of national and foreign music existing in their society and general culture, including the expansion that migration may afford. If and when children become adults, later marry and begin their own nuclear family, how these songs and instrumental music are used in the new home may be influenced by their positive or negative valence of the past family history. This usually unconscious ethnic-associative behavior with music can be readily observed, for example, when riding in taxicabs worldwide where passengers too often are forced to experience drivers' predilection for their ethnic music on the radio. These linking behaviors are also evident, though with less intensity, in many who travel abroad on vacations, particularly on special holidays such as Christmas. Latinos, for instance, often take with them traditional foods and music for Christmas and New Year's dinners, to be shared intimately with family and compatriots. The Spanish *aguinaldo* (also known as a *villancico*, *alabanza*, or *adoración*) typically sung at Christmas time in Latin America and favorite popular dance music are usually included.

Composers and lyricists create songs reflecting the music and themes of their personal issues mixed with those of the sociocultural milieu of the times. Listeners perceive and engrave in their memory songs according to affective needs and biopsychosocial limitations. Transitory music preferences and more permanent music tastes (Abeles 1980) have an ethnic component, overtly reflected in the nationality of the music per se as well as covertly in conscious and unconscious reasons for these selections. Because of these qualities, we can see how music recalled in treatment has transference–countertransference implications (Díaz de Chumaceiro 1990a,b, 1993a,b, 1996b, 1997, 1998, Freud 1901, 1916, Reik 1953, Rosenbaum 1963). But in order to understand this phenomenon further, let us look at the early development of music or sound appreciation as it relates to early communication between mother and child, even before birth. This is particularly important because specific music selection can become a powerful organizer of the experience later on, becoming affected by the same principle of repression as any other experience.

AUDITORY PERCEPTION AND ITS ROLE IN PSYCHIC DEVELOPMENT

In 1981 Verny's *The Secret Life of the Unborn Child* intrigued and stimulated many. While a series of studies by audiologist Michele Clements (1977) demonstrated the unborn child's distinct and discriminating musical likes and dislikes, Verny found that parents' fighting—loud, angry voices—causes even more distress to the fetus. Kicking is often triggered by such parental behavior and "furious kicking" has been identified as a consequence of the emotions of anger, fear, and anxiety in the mother. Such instances have been exemplified in Sontag's (1966) descriptions of "tragic babies" who suffered due to serious stress in their mother's life. On such occasions what stimulated babies to kick was frequently a mix of internal and external events. The fetus is affected by mother's behavior and emotions. Hypothetically, then, if the mother, for whatever reasons, upsets herself as a result of listening to certain types of music or to specific compositions that trigger distressing reactions, the fetus may react in similar fashion.

Verny (1981) also included a radio interview with Boris Brott, conductor of the Hamilton (Ontario) Philharmonic Symphony. When Brott was asked how his interest in music originated, after a moment of hesitation, he answered that although it might appear as strange to many, since before he was born, music had been a part of him. The interviewer, perplexed, requested an explanation. Brott obliged, revealing that when he was a young adult he had been mystified by his rare ability to perform some pieces he had never seen before: "I'd be conducting a score for the first time and, suddenly, the cello line would jump out at me; I'd know the flow of the piece even before I turned the page of the score" (p. 23). As his mother is a professional cellist, he commented to her one day about this phenomenon, thinking that she would be intrigued because what was so distinct in his mind was the cello line. She was curious. The mystery was rapidly solved when she heard which pieces they were. "All the scores I knew sight unseen were ones she had played while she was pregnant with me" (p. 23). Artur Rubinstein and Yehudi Menuhin have also made similar claims of having had their musical interests thus stimulated.

While many may be inclined to disregard such claims in biographical anecdotes as unscientific, others, fortunately, have no qualms with these data due to their interest in psychobiographies of musicians (see Burton 1968, Feder 1981, Ostwald 1985, among many). For the psychoanalytic exploration of the individual's psychic reality they are quite useful, in addition to providing validation of external reality. Nevertheless, nonmusician mothers rarely keep track of the music they repeatedly listened to or sang during their pregnancies and thus such correlations may not be available to many.

Olds (1985a) also discussed research on the presence of intelligence in the prenatal human being. He described differential responses to music to show the apparent presence of the unborn's preferences of specific music compositions and composers. Included was a discussion of the effects of the mother's prolonged emotional stress during pregnancy and uses of music to soothe the fetus and neonate. Later, Shetler (1990) reported that his findings support Olds' (1984, 1985b) speculations "that tempo—the temporal variation— may be the earliest and most primitive musical stimulus possible. Responses may be a predictor of personality and, eventually, of competent speech acquisition as well" (p. 54). Vocal production (singing or cooing) is one of the major musical behaviors Shetler was attempting to assess, in addition to early babbling or speech acquisition. Among his findings are "the early development of highly organized and remarkable articulate speech of those children who have been exposed to prenatal music stimulation" (p. 55).

More recently, Lecanuet and colleagues (1995) highlighted in a historical survey of the literature on fetal responsiveness to startling and nonstartling auditory stimulation that many significant findings already had been made in the 1930s. From their studies, they concluded that the discriminative abilities found suggested that fetuses in their third trimester could have benefits from being exposed to various sounds, including those of speech. Such early exposures may be a contributing factor for "the maintenance, tuning, and specification of the auditory abilities necessary for the neonate to process sounds that will be relevant postnatally" (p. 257). The fetus has "a variety of auditory perceptual capacities" (p. 257) and this information further supports and validates data that show prenatal auditory learning in postnatal infant studies. Newborns, 2–4 days old, were presented with stimuli from different categories to which they had been exposed systematically as fetuses during the last stage of gestation; they revealed "significant preferences" for stimuli that had been previously experienced, which included specific sequences of: (a) *music*

(Panneton 1985, Satt 1984); (b) *speech* (De Casper and Spence 1986); and (c) *the mother's native language* (Fifer and Moon 1995, Mehler et al. 1988, Moon et al. 1993) (Lecanuet et al. 1995, pp. 257–258).

The recent work of Fifer and Moon (1995) includes, first, a review of the studies in their laboratory that described the effects of fetal experience on the newborn's later behavior (DeCasper and Fifer 1980, Moon and Fifer 1990ab, Fifer and Moon 1989, Moon et al. 1992, 1993); second, the results of their research on newborns' cardiorespiratory responses to the stimulus of speech sounds; and finally, their findings on fetal responses to auditory stimulation. They suggested that a model for how the fetus's developing brain and behavior are shaped by very early experience may be seen in research on *the perinatal response to maternal voice:*

> The mother's voice is a naturally occurring and salient stimulus during a critical time period in which there is significant development in all areas of the brain. There appears to be immediate as well as enduring effects of this stimulation. Consequently, the response to voice may offer a unique probe for studying behavioral, cognitive, and autonomic capacities from the fetal through the newborn period. [p. 363]

Thus, one can also wonder about effects of the mother's singing voice on the fetus in general, and about professional singing in particular, which entails rigorous daily practice. There is so much that remains to be researched and observed that it seems noteworthy to mention another biographical report. About Dinu Lipatti, the famous Romanian pianist, son of a father-violinist and a mother-pianist, Gramajo Galimany (1993) wrote that during the pregnancy with Dinu, "her baby would rock to the rhythm of the tunes she played" (p. 385). According to Ricardo Turró, the music critic, when Anna Lipatti was expecting her firstborn child, she wanted and loved him so much that "she had already marked out the life of the child-to-be as being associated with music and the piano" (p. 385). She confessed that this child was worshipped long before he was born; "whenever she felt his little kicks, she would say to her husband: Dinu is kicking the piano, he is working with the pedals (he already had a name, that of his two grandfathers!). Oh no, he replied, he is angry and throwing his violin to the ground" (p. 385).

> The parents' satisfied wish is perhaps the "star on the forehead" which his godfather, the composer George Enesco [1881–1955], saw in his brilliant godson. Can a child subject to such pressures, and with exceptional musical gifts, escape his "destiny"? The continuity of transgenerational and social wishes was manifested in Lipatti. [Gramajo Galimany 1993, p. 385]

These biographical vignettes suggest that the musician parents transmitted, consciously and unconsciously, their ethnic-cultural musical attitudes and preferences to their gifted children. In both cases the child identified with the mother's musical instrument. Perhaps in their psychic reality these instruments represented mother and their early dyadic relationship with music since before birth, and this unit—mother-music—was reinforced afterwards during the acquisition and development of musical skills under her guidance and support. Furthermore, for the case of Lipatti, who died of leukemia when he was 43 years old while at the summit of his career (Gramajo Galimany 1993), McDougall's (1995) recent assertion is thought provoking. In her view, Morgan (1991) confirms with clinical observation that a role in the mother's contact with her unborn child is played by the parents' projections onto the fetus as well as by affectively charged external events that occur during the pregnancy. After these prenatal influencing factors, the mother–infant early transactions may together be a determinant of the tendency to react to internal and external stresses with somatization rather than with psychological reactions.

I thank Dr. Gerald M. Fishbein for calling my attention to the work of the child psychoanalyst Alessandra Piontelli, in Milan (personal communication, October 5, 1996). She studied prenatal life with ultrasound and followed neonates during the first year of life, underscoring the possibility of detection of early markers of character. Her work (1986, 1987, 1988, 1989) includes the study of twins in utero. Even though she does not address music per se, these studies can serve as an additional foundation for hypotheses for further explorations of the role of music on the internal world of the child before and after birth.

Turning now to research on postnatal life and music, Kessen and colleagues (1979) demonstrated that infants less than 6 months old could learn to imitate pitches with only a few sessions of training, and seemed to enjoy the process while working hard at it. The pleasure of listening and responding to music can be expedited by the baby's caregivers.

In 1984, more specifically, Trehub and associates summarized previous research on infant auditory perception of sequences, as follows:

> First, infants can detect changes in the component tones of a multitone sequence (Chang and Trehub 1977a,b, Kinney and Kagan 1976). Second, they can discriminate changes in the order of tones in such a sequence (Demany 1982, McCall and Melson 1970, Melson and McCall 1970). Third, they perceive changes in the temporal grouping or rhythm of tone sequences (Chang and Trehub 1977b, Demany, McKenzie and Vurpillot

1977). Fourth, they reorganize or group the component tones of a sequence on the basis of spectral or frequency similarity (Demany 1982). Finally, infants' encoding of information about frequency relations between tones allows them to "recognize" transpositions of simple melodies (Chang and Trehub 1977a). [p. 821]

As a result of their work, they then added a sixth point: infants have a global processing strategy that parallels the type used by adults with atonal or unfamiliar tonal melodies (Trehub et al.1984). Clearly, the past times when it was assumed and believed that infants were unaware and incapable of differentiating musical sound in their milieu could now be laid to rest as merely reflecting adults' ignorance of normal infants' innate capabilities in this area. Maurer and Maurer (1988), just a few years later, stressed that without linguistic meanings, the sound elements of timbre, intensity, duration, and pitch also form the elements of music. If these are isolated as music, it becomes clear that young infants appear to hear them as adults do. "Even newborns are more likely to respond to a sound with overtones than to a tone composed of only the fundamental frequency" (Hutt et al. 1968, p. 150). In their view, the young baby's adeptness with the sounds of music and language is one of the most surprising things about him or her.

Standley and Madsen (1990) also argued that while infant research in the music literature is hardly extensive, there is sufficient evidence that suggests that neonates' reactions to music may differ and they may begin to acquire other music skills more rapidly than previously assumed. (When Simons [1986] reviewed the early childhood development literature, fifty-four articles from 1971 to 1981 were identified.) These authors noted the difficulty of assimilating the wealth of data on infants' auditory response due to its rapid proliferation, complexity and diversity of research design and techniques, and the wide dissemination of results across various different areas and in many different forms. Consequently, they presented in table form a comprehensive review of the literature that included thirty-six studies on infant behavior and auditory stimuli conducted between 1961 and 1987, with a detailed analysis and comparisons of specific research variables. The authors also reported on their study that compared the preferences and responses of twenty-four infants aged 2 to 8 months to auditory stimuli of music, mother's voice, and other female voices, and found that infants do discriminate. They observed a significant interaction between age and preference—younger infants preferred the mother's voice while older ones equally preferred the mother and unfamiliar voices of other females—a finding inconsistent with previous research. "*Videotaped observation analyses showed that babies listened more intently to music than to the other stimuli*" (p. 54, italics added).

Standley and Moore (1993) then conducted a study on the effectiveness of music versus newborns' preferred auditory stimulus: mother's voice (see DeCasper and Fifer 1980). While infants with low birth weight who heard music had fewer occurrences of oximeter alarms as compared with those hearing mother's voice, very premature infants—of gestational age before 30 weeks—after music stimulation appeared to have an increase in episodes of apnea and bradycardia. Theoretically, this could be due to overstimulation of the most fragile infants as a result of music duration or decibel level. Thus their results support the notion that for music stimulation of the premature infant an important clinical consideration is to determine protocols of age, decibel levels, and presentation schedules (Schaefer et al. 1980, reported in Cassidy and Standley 1995). Incidentally, the mother's voice is recognized in the womb. By contrast, newborns demonstrate no similar preference for the voice of the father—even though they can distinguish between voices of two men (DeCasper and Prescott 1984). Newborns also recognize their own voices (Simner 1971).

Lorch and colleagues (1994) addressed the effects of stimulative and sedative music ("Sabre Dance" versus "Moonlight Sonata") on systolic blood pressure, heart rate, and respiratory rate in ten premature infants (33–35 weeks postconception) in an intensive care nursery. The authors' study found significantly different effects of stimulative and sedative music on specific physiological parameters. In their view, in the case of sick premature infants in the ICU, the effect, particularly of systolic blood pressure, might have an important impact on efforts to prevent intraventricular hemorrhage. Sedative music's calming and stabilizing effect might aid in reduction of the use of sedatives for infants on ventilators as well as the incidence of pulmonary barotrauma.

More recently, Cassidy and Standley (1995) focused on the effects of music listening on the physiological responses of oxygenated premature infants of 24 to 30 weeks gestational age in their first week of life in a neonatal intensive care unit. The music consisted of commercially recorded lullabies interpreted by a female singer, with orchestral accompaniment. "The selections included *Drift Away, Rhapsody in Baby Blue, Nightlights, I'll Love You Forever, Dreamship,* and *Loving My Baby Goodnight*" (p. 213). Their findings suggested that in the first week of life there was no contraindication for music for these infants of very low birth weight, usually restricted from sensory saturation. "In fact, music had noticeably positive effects on oxygen saturation levels, heart rate, and respiratory rate. No increase in apnea/bradycardia episodes following music treatment were observed" (p. 208). This lack of contraindication for the use of music may allow it to be a tool to facilitate bonding in situations where new parents cannot hold, feed, bathe, or touch their infants who are critically ill. The use of audiotapes of favorite music on a recorder, carefully controlling durations of stimuli, tempo, and volume, may give parents a way to partially control the infant's milieu. They added: "These infants also may respond positively long-term to the calming influence of familiar music as did the infants in the Polverini-Rey study [1992] who, as fetuses with similar gestational ages to the infants in this study, listened to lullaby music" (p. 223).

While research on the effects of music on the immunological system is still in its infancy, it is noteworthy that data on the neonatal and early infancy stages also converge with research in the fields of neurology and neuropsychology of music with adults. Harrer & Harrer (1977), in their extensive and detailed study of music, emotion and autonomic functions, found that autonomic response depends on: (1) reactivity—lability or stability of the autonomic regulatory processes, which in turn is affected by constitution (predisposition), age, sex, lifestyle, physical fitness and general state of health, and temporary factors (fatigue, drugs, alcohol and tobacco intake); (2) emotional reactivity; (3) attitudes toward music—importance of music in the person's life, immediate attitude in test situation; and (4) kind of music. With respect to the last variable Goldstein (1980) advocated that the "right kind" of music may trigger a "thrill response," which can affect the endocrine and immunological systems. At a cognitive level, instead, Makeig (1982) proposed that what a person experiences in the perception of music depends on the kind of interest, motivation, and imagination brought to the perception. Furthermore, Roederer (1982) suggested, as a lead to understanding the emotional response to music, that "motivation and emotion in man can be triggered with no relationship to the instantaneous state of the environment and the actual response of the organism to it" (p. 43). In simpler terms, then, affective responses to music depend on the degree of interchange between physical, organic, psychological, and experiential differences of the individual throughout his or her life cycle.

Sloboda (1992) made the point that in spite of various recent trials for constructing a theoretical perspective for taking into account emotions in music (e.g., Dowling and Harwood 1986), to study empirically the emotional responses to music is still at an infancy stage. Serious methodological and theoretical problems are posed when attempting to study this subject. "Since there is no generally accepted theory of the emotions and how they interact with cognition, [he believes] that open-ended empirical investigations with a strong element of natural history continue to be the most profitable way of exploring this area at this time" (pp. 43–44). Recently, Gregory and colleagues

(1996), after studying the development of emotional responses to music in young children, concluded that at least some of these responses are learned behavior and that 7–8 year olds have acquired the same level as adults of emotional associations to major-minor modes. (On affect in music, see Epstein 1993, Noy 1993, Rose 1980, 1993, Treitler 1993, among others.)

The studies in this section focused on different variables of auditory perception in prenatal and postnatal infants and they were briefly interfaced with research with adults. These works have been underscored because they advance appreciation of the tremendous innate receptivity at such a tender age to the influence of music, which linked with important people then becomes part of the individual's basic cognitive and emotional organization. Hence, these data may also serve as a basis for the formulation of psychoanalytic hypotheses and the development of theories for child, adolescent, and adult treatment. The importance of a loving and stimulating significant other in the child's environment cannot be overestimated. Early stimulation in a positive context may allow for the continuation of musical behavior into childhood, adolescence, and the rest of the life span as a vocation, a hobby, or as a pleasurable pastime of appreciating music performances of others. (For uses of music in medicine, see Aldridge 1993, Spintge and Droh 1992, Standley 1992.)

The individual in treatment may ignore details of musical experiences belonging to the prenatal and preverbal stages. Nevertheless, once one is curious and motivated to explore and ask older family members for information, new vistas may be opened for discussion on the impact of ethnic external reality in the family on the patient's psychic reality. Many have been delighted to rediscover, for instance, the specific favorite lullabies sung to them at bedtime, as well as other positive or negative anecdotes related to their early musical behavior, including music making in the family, which, for whatever reasons, had been forgotten or repressed in adulthood. Many a child has failed to develop an interest in the world of music due to negative criticisms of important others. A recent study by Davidson and colleagues (1996) on the roles of parents' influence in the development of musical performance found that, in effect, "the most successful children had parents who were the most highly involved in lessons and practice in the earliest stages of learning. . . . the most musically able children had the highest levels of parental support" (p. 399; also see Davidson et al. 1997). Such findings support common sense wisdom of the transmittal of parental preferences and tastes for art objects, in this case music, and also point to the interrelationship of emotional factors that underlie motivation and learning, of particular interest for the psychoanalytic study of unconscious ethnicity in treatment. A vista of how musical and intrapsychic behavior is acquired in early childhood further expands this horizon.

ACQUISITION OF MUSICAL AND
INTRAPSYCHIC BEHAVIOR

It is time to focus on the normal early development of the ability to play a musical instrument, including singing. These abilities, of course, also can be affected by psychological processes. As indicated earlier, it is in the context of interactions with the mother and other important persons in the environment that children learn to reproduce tunes with their internal musical instrument—the voice—and with external ones. Similar to the process of acquisition of language, normal children pass through different stages in early musical development.

In 1973, Ostwald presented, in broad strokes, the following sequences (which fifteen years later he still adhered to). Prenatal development includes the predetermined genetics of auditory sensitivity and musical ability as well as in utero experiences with vibrations, rhythms, and noises. The fetus usually has a response to acoustical stimulation by the third trimester. Singers have reported that when singing the fetus changes activity, usually seeming quieter. By contrast, mothers who are pianists or play other instruments have observed the fetus's increasing activity during the playing of music or soon after. At birth and during the first month of life, active musical behavior begins, represented in different tonal vocalizations, of which cries are predominant. Various distinct patterns, however, begin to emerge: "There is a regular sequence of tones, usually separated by an interval of about three or four notes. Typically, the melody pattern is one of rising-falling, and the maximum loudness (around 60 decibels) is achieved at the peak of the cry" (p. 368). Many influences can modify the musical form of the neonate's cries and thus they have diagnostic value (Ostwald et al. 1968). The duration, volume, and elevation of the pitch of the cries can be increased due to pain or distress as a result of various causes. In sharp contrast to crying, there is also humming—a softer vocalization linked with feelings of pleasure, especially satiation, initially heard during breast feeding. In between feedings, the baby "coos" or "squeaks" with his mouth open, and social interaction is characterized by musical vocalization and mutual smiles with the mother or other primary caregiver.

From the second to the sixth month, "vocal contagion" (Piaget 1951) is stimulated by converging the baby's vocalizations with those of another person. For the early development of vocal contagion, songs and lullabies are important because these tunes appear to comfort both the mother and the baby (see Kneutgen 1970). During the second half of the baby's first year, his or her capacity "to carry a tune" increases. To continue hearing the sounds in the milieu, the baby repeats with greater frequency the self-produced sounds and imitates those of others. Initially, such "circular reactions" are merely characterized by vocalizations. Common is singsong babbling, pitch slurs of a third or a fifth, and some intonation contours that are speechlike. However, even this early, a child occasionally evidences rare musical skills (see Platt 1933). Most babies have learned a few words by the age of 18 months, yet the making of sounds nonverbally is still predominant in their repertoire. Thus the playing with sounds—well described by Winnicott as a "*transitional phenomenon*" (McDonald 1970)—is of the highest importance. The child may develop a special attachment to musical instruments (e.g., the human voice, radio, record player, toy piano, drums, or machines that produce interesting rhythmical sounds).

During the second year, the toddler is increasingly able to sing song phrases even though all the words cannot be articulated and pitch cannot be maintained. Parts or all of some songs can be mastered well, and if encouraged to do this activity, the child may vocalize them spontaneously. In the third year and into nursery school, many toddlers can recognize different melodies and obtain acceptable scoring on tests for musical aptitude (Schuter 1968), including "absolute pitch." They already have the capacity to profit from individual and group music lessons.

McDonald (1970) coined the term "transitional tunes," and proposed a developmental line for the learning of music, which conforms closely to Suzuki's (1969) "talent education" methods and has many similarities with Anna Freud's (1965) work, "From the Body to the Toy and from Play to Work." Initially, the babbling of infants is considered "an autoerotic activity" that is accidentally rhythmic or musical. A transitional tune is later "created" by the child as his personal music, in the act of transfer of the musical properties of self and of mother (parents) to his "creation." As a transitional phenomenon in musical form, narcissistic and object libido cathect the tune. "It is the child's special lullaby (The child may also choose a musical toy for a transitional object . . .)" (p. 92). Subsequently, there is a broadening of interest in the world of music, as contrasted with the initial concern over a limited range of musical transitional phenomena. While the child's personal "lullaby" may keep its special purpose when going to sleep and during stressful times, it is only gradually that the transitional functions of the first musical interests fade away. After the third birthday, the child can be given the first musical instrument. It may appear to him as a new toy, or he may consider it a "successor" to a previous toy instrument—or to one that made music. Pleasure in a more organized ego activity evolves from the initial pleasure in disorganized play with the musical instrument. The child's productions on a musical instrument of harmony and rhythm are enjoyed together with the parents. An ability to achieve pleasure through "work" at music is evolved from the achievement of pleasure in "play" at music. "Greater impulse control, neutralization, sublimation, and the transition from the pleasure principle to the reality principle effect this change from play to work" (p. 93). Music may be an important sublimation for the adult personality. A passionate hobby or a full-time professional activity may be a consequence of such involvement with music.

As an example of evidence of transitional music phenomena in biographies and autobiographies, McDonald (1970) quoted Arazi (1969, p. 7) on an interview with the violist Ernst Wallfisch, on music's role in his life up to age 6. For Wallfisch, from the beginning, music played a very big part and he remembered a great deal about his father's big hobby: music, particularly chamber music. His father, a businessman and amateur violinist, had many friends who had similar musical interests and for whom a part of living was playing chamber music. Wallfisch could remember all of these individuals visiting his home—"talking, laughing, smoking cigars, and making music"—when he was a young boy. Initially, though, he recognized only the different sounds and the various moods of the music they played. When he grew older, he was able to start differentiating between composers, rhythms, and harmonies. Significantly, he stated:

> *I can remember being lulled to sleep by all these sounds*, and being put to bed with all these sounds swirling through my thoughts . . . *sometimes I would awaken a few hours later, and I could still hear music sounding through the house* . . . to this day, whenever I hear certain works played by a quartet, it brings back a flood of memories of many things and people . . . *yes, I was thoroughly imbued with the spirit of music from the cradle* so it seems. [McDonald's emphasis, p. 90]

Ostwald (1973) also addressed psychopathological aspects of musical development, pointing out that there are no guarantees of success in later life or of health as a result of having had early fixations on music, as evident in psychobiographical studies of famous musicians (see Díaz de Chumaceiro 1991, 1995, Ostwald 1985, 1993). Paradoxical responses to music can be observed in some children very early. Occasionally auguring a later abnormal development, they appear to have a hypersensitivity to sounds and other sensory stimuli (Bergman and Escalona 1949). Of diagnostic value, then, may be a baby's history of startling and crying when hearing ordinary sounds. These children prefer delicate and soft music, but regardless of special care, for the mother, soothing the baby and putting him to sleep is difficult. Noises and loud music trigger a greater amount of annoyance than is usual in others.

They specially hate banging and percussive noises and screaming; withdrawal can occur when anticipating stimuli that upset them. Included are autistic children and those with the idiot savant syndrome.

Last but not of least importance, Ostwald called attention to the emerging field of ethnomusicology, which aimed to demonstrate the relationships between culture and musical behavior. The carrying over of musical behavior into later childhood appears to him to be "a function of intense emotional involvement of the individual personality with music, its auditory enjoyment, or its motor performance, or both" (p. 374). Much later (1990), he stressed:

> No discussion of emotional development in childhood could proceed without a tribute to ethnomusicology. Clearly, we all must be aware of the enormous importance of culture as it dictates not only the sorts of musical instruments children learn to play and the styles of music they enjoy, but also the attitudes which are adopted toward music as a form of work, leading toward professional careers versus music as something simply to play and enjoy as an avocation. [p. 16]

In his commonsense view, he suggested that children who grow up in a Balinese village, with exposure in everyday life to Hindu ceremonies with the use of gongs, chimes, gamelan orchestras, and dances, for instance, are certainly going to develop different perceptions and cognitions than those of children who live in a metropolitan city, such as London, or a college town, such as Berkeley, California. This perspective finds support in the work of Deutsch and colleagues (1987, 1990) and Deutsch (1991, 1992), who studied the perception of "the tritone paradox"—the presentation of two tones separated by a half-octave (e.g., C followed by F# or D followed by G#)—which some hear as an ascending interval and others as a descending one. These differences demonstrate that perceptual agreement cannot be assumed as a given. To Deutsch's (1992) knowledge, these studies were the first to demonstrate correlates between the perception of a musical pattern and speech characteristics of the listener (speaking voice range of fundamental frequencies). In the 1987 study, Deutsch and associates reported significant differences in the distribution of peak pitch classes between two groups of listeners. One grew up in California and the other in the south of England: "Where the Californian group tended to hear the pattern as ascending the English group tended to hear it as descending, and vice versa. *These findings indicated that the same, culturally acquired pitch template influences both speech production and perception of this musical pattern*" (italics added, in Deutsch, 1992, pp. 132–133). Deutsch (1992) concluded:

Given that the differences obtained depended on linguistic dialect, we can assume that such differences are learned rather than innate. This may be contrasted with the strong handedness correlates that have been obtained with perception of the octave and scale illusions [Deutsch, 1974, 1975 a,b, 1983]. These handedness correlates indicate that differences in music perception can also be based on innate differences at the neurological level. [p. 136]

Some authors who have recently specifically addressed ethnic and cultural factors influencing music tastes include Gregory (1997), Russell (1997), and Stokes (1994), among others. It is a subject that needs to be discussed more frequently.

What do Western developmental theories have to say about music learning? In 1981, Funk and Whiteside discussed six developmental theories of five theorists—Howard Gardner, Jean Piaget (with two independent theories), Heinz Werner, Joachim Wohlwill, and Eleanor Gibson—in relation to their efficacy in creating a context for comprehending musical behavior in children. They found that there had been "little mutual overlap or influence" between empirical research on children's musical abilities and developmental theory. "Most research has not been founded on any of the major theories of perceptual or cognitive development and most theorists and their exponents have not attempted applications to the area of musical development" (p. 44).

Then, in the 1987 Denver Conference on Music and Child Development, Ostwald (1990) reiterated the concepts of the 1973 paper just reviewed and also drew attention to Stern's (1985) *The Interpersonal World of the Infant*, which he found very useful for understanding the development of musical emotions and cognitions of early childhood. In synthesis, Stern's four cumulative self-development stages range from birth to 3 years. During the first stage, called "the emergent self," from birth onwards, children establish their basic perceptual and motor organization. From 3 to 8 months, during the second stage of self-development, the "core self" is established by the child. It is the feeling of being a separate entity, with a separate will. From 8 to 15 months, in the third stage, called the "subjective self," the child starts to sense others' feelings about him or her, and vice versa. "Attunement" depicts the process of child and caregiver achieving empathy and mutuality—Stern's "evoked companionship," achieved via memory and fantasy. From 15 months to 3 years, in the fourth stage, is the development of the "symbolic self" with the learning of language and unspoken rules of nonverbal communications— needed for transcendence of reality: to dream, fantasize, and play-act. Ostwald (1990) believed that the basis of creativity and art is due to this change. After the child is 3 years old, music, to become relevant in a social sense, may leave the domain of the narcissistic personal component. During this stage, good role models (personal interactions with family members, neighbors, friends, or music teachers, and recordings or live concerts) are essential. This is the way to stimulate and achieve positive identifications pro music.

In the same conference, Rogers (1990) stressed that the problem encountered with the application of the major traditional Western theories of child development (based on Western culture) to the musical development of young children was that these theories "do not easily account for the proclivity with which young children learn the melody, rhythm, and lyrics of typical nursery songs and musical games, as well as more sophisticated musical skills" (p. 1). One reason these theories failed to address music learning is that Western theorists focused on what is of importance to the mind in the West: "logic, numbers, language, reasoning, information" (Gardner 1983, p. 1). (See Mussen 1983, with only one index listing about music.) Specific music skills in early development are unexpected and therefore not taught in Western culture; yet the development of musical skills is an area of importance that merits integration into a general theory of child development. Another reason is that for major theorists the *zeitgeist* demanded encompassing theories explaining big learning areas with as few elegant concepts as possible (such as those of Piaget, Skinner, and Erikson). According to Rogers (1990), "Musical ability is a more discrete area of ability than general concept formation, problem solving, or social learning" (p. 1). He concluded:

> None of the major theories of child development can account for the musical development which young children demonstrate. Humans appear to have a special aptitude for music learning which is maximally available for development when stimulated by the environment in early childhood. However, each of the current major global theories—psycho-dynamic, cognitive, and social learning theories—have important contributions to make as we try to uncover the emotional, perceptual, cognitive, and social experiences which form the core of early musical development. [pp. 8–9]

Furthermore, as Bjørkvold (1990) stressed, worldwide, children, in the initial, basic years of life, develop in similar ways. "*Child culture, therefore, seems to go beyond some of the boundaries of national cultures, manifesting cross-cultural traits*" (p. 119, italics added). After comparing children from the United States, the Soviet Union, and Norway, the author suggested that in spite of major differences of influence, these children appeared to share the following musical universals: "*a musical mother tongue* of clearly cross-cultural significance. Their spontaneous singing brought to life in everyday play and communication, clearly exhibits common patterns both in form, use and function" (pp. 119–120). The musical mother tongue is concerned with every level of identity formation, as is the child's verbal language, due to being so deeply rooted in the personality of the child.

> As one of the common codes through which child culture manifests itself, children's singing will obviously contribute to the constant consolidation of *cultural identity*. Sociometric analyses of the characteristic group dynamics of spontaneous singing can further explain how this singing also is important for establishing *group* identity as well as *sexual* and *individual* identity . . . [Italics in original, pp. 132–133]

Later, Unyk and colleagues (1992), and Trehub and associates (1993a,b) made several studies from a cross-cultural perspective that included lullabies, and maternal singing. More recently, Smith (1997) suggested that children 5 to 10 years old have knowledge of music intervals just by exposure to music in everyday life. (On procedural and declarative knowledge in music cognition, see Dowling 1993.) Finally, the recent work of Rauscher and associates (1997) suggesting that music training specifically causes long-term enhancement of preschool children's spatial-temporal reasoning has implications for standard curricula learning—of mathematics and science in particular.

What about children who do not sing and play as normal children generally do? As psychobiographical studies of famous musicians may provide additional insights, an extract of some of Burton's (1968) observations on the early childhood of Clara Wieck Schumann (also see Burton, 1985) seems appropriate to conclude this review with a note on failure of normal development that also addresses many points that have been discussed thus far.

Even before Clara's birth, her father, Friedrick Wieck, had made the decision that she was to become "the ideal child virtuoso" (Burton 1968, p. 100). Wieck's trade was in teaching, lending, and selling pianos, and he was considered, in the bourgeois art world of Leipzig, a prime mover—an exceptionally pragmatic, determined, dictatorial, and hypomanic man, who softened his stance only for Clara's study of music. About the emotional temperature of the Wieck household not much is known except that before Clara was 5 years old the parents divorced. Johanna Strobel, a remarkably taciturn maid, took care of Clara since her earliest age. De facto, Johanna's silent nature was blamed by Wieck as causal because, strikingly, Clara was unable to speak even single words until she was 4$^{1}/_{2}$ years old, and previously had not demonstrated evidence of understanding language. Wieck himself wrote the first entry in Clara's *Diary*, where this datum is contained—writing in the first person, as if he were his daughter—revealing important clues to his unempathic character and coarse taking over of the child's personality (Litzmann, 1913, Reich 1985).

Of interest in Clara's prenatal history is that she was conceived three months after the death of the first-born daughter of the Wiecks'. Then, before Clara was 17 months old and until she was 4 years and 2 months, her mother began a series of three pregnancies and four piano performances. Thus Burton presumed Clara's failure of development of verbal communication, a crucial ego function, to be a result of difficulties in the separation-individuation stage, following observations and clinical theories of Mahler and colleagues (1975). However, had her relationship with her father also suffered, her situation might have been worse.

The toddler had two nonverbal routes of communication: "her mother's music, and Johanna's silent mode of child rearing" (Burton 1968, p. 102). Burton wrote: "An innately gifted child whose not-too-available mother sings and practices the piano amidst the other sounds of a musical household is extremely likely to identify piano sounds with 'mother,' and to learn to hear and respond to elements of feeling in her mother's music" (Greenacre 1957, p. 102). It is normal for young toddlers who are or feel distant from their mothers to use sounds of speech as a way to keep contact. Treatment of autistic children gives evidence that an alternative and useful channel of communication may be provided with music. Burton reasoned, therefore, that it seemed highly probabilistic that Clara had had an early entrance into a musical space that meant "mother," and to an associative world connected with "mother," and that a psychological feeding had been derived from her languagelike understanding of ideas and feelings from this musical realm. In Burton's (1968) view, "this leads to the concept that her musical intuition and her lifelong need for music represented the continuance of a 'transitional process' begun in her first two years [Winnicott, 1953]" (p. 102). Moreover, contextually seen within childhood inner conflict, "hearing and 'thinking' music established a relatively safe surrounding; that is, one free of psychic conflict, and offering helpful possibilities of control and gratification. Musical thinking would thus acquire a valuable defensive function" (pp. 102–103).

CLINICAL IMPLICATIONS

The underlying theme in this presentation is that the use of sound is a central mode of communication between mother and child (A. Freud 1963) and, likewise, between patient and analyst. The symbolic function of these and other organizations can be used for therapeutic purposes. Music can function as an organizing structure of unconscious material and early experiences and, as Nass (1971) proposed, musical process can be comprehended in terms of contemporary ego psychology. In his view, a cognitive style may be developed from experiences of early hearing and listening that may be utilized by the ego for adaptation to and mastery of the external world. While these experiences may or may not have a relationship with music, "the art form of music provides a built-in vehicle through which this type of cognition may be developed and expanded" (p. 42). Musical experiences facilitate the emergence of less structured and ambiguous cognitive states side by side with concomitant drives. The presence of the primitive or early organizational modes of the ego (for which regressive processes need not be invoked) has a strong similarity with hearing and listening in the psychoanalytic experiences of patient and analyst (also see Nass 1975, 1984, 1989, 1993).

Different types of studies—empirical and anecdotal—have been compiled here to begin to arouse interest in various domains that may be of relevance for explorations of unconscious ethnicity in the recall of music. Patients and therapists, regardless of the ethnic mix of any dyad, dream, think, and talk about ideas and fantasies in conventional language. Yet they also may unwittingly displace such material into musical language, represented in songs or instrumental music that may be hummed, whistled, sung, or simply remembered, as has been sporadically reported in the psychoanalytic literature. In these unconscious and conscious displacements to music, ethnic issues are present, overtly and covertly, and music evocations have transference and countertransference implications for therapy. Music is a universal cultural experience and deserves further study of its roles in human development, from different interdisciplinary perspectives, for the advancement of psychological treatment.

REFERENCES

Abeles, H. F. (1980). Responses to music. In *Handbook of Music Psychology*, ed. D. A. Hodges, pp. 105–140. Lawrence, KS: National Association for Music Therapy.

Aldridge, D. (1993). Music therapy research I: a review of the medical research literature within a general context of music therapy research. *Arts in Psychotherapy* 20:11–35.

Arazi, I. (1969). One plus one equals one. *American String Teacher* 19:1, 6–10, 26.

Bergman, P., and Escalona, S. K. (1949). Unusual sensitivities in very young children. *Psychoanalytic Study of the Child* 3–4: 333. New York: International Universities Press.

Bjørkvold, J. R. (1990). Canto—ergo sum: musical child cultures in the United States, the Soviet Union, and Norway. In *Music and Child Development: Proceedings of the 1987 Denver Conference*, ed. F. R. Wilson and F. L. Roehmann, pp. 117–135. St. Louis, MO: MMB Music.

Burton, A. M. (1968). A psychoanalyst's view of Clara Schumann. In *Psychoanalytic Explorations in Music*, ed. S. Feder, R. L. Karmel, and G. H. Pollock, pp. 97–113. Madison, CT: International Universities Press, 1990.

———— (1985). Robert Schumann and Clara Wieck—a creative partnership. In *Psychoanalytic Explorations in Music*, ed. S. Feder, R. L. Karmel, and G. H. Pollock, pp. 441–463. Madison, CT: International Universities Press, 1990.

Cassidy, J. W., and Standley, J. M. (1995). The effect of music listening on physiological responses of premature infants in the NICU. *Journal of Music Therapy* 32(4): 208–227.

Chang, H., and Trehub, S. (1977a). Auditory processing of relational information of young infants. *Journal of Experimental Child Psychology* 24:324–331.

———— (1977b). Infants' perception of temporal grouping in auditory patterns. *Child Development* 48:1666–1670.

Clements, M. (1977). *Observations on certain aspects of neonatal behavior in response to auditory stimuli*. Paper presented at the 5th International Congress of Psychosomatic Obstetrics and Gynecology. Rome.

Davidson, J. W., Howe, M. J., Moore, D. G., and Sloboda, J. A. (1996). The role of parental influences in the development of musical performance. *British Journal of Developmental Psychology* 14:399–412.

Davidson, J. W., Howe, M. J. A., and Sloboda, J. A. (1997). Environmental factors in the development of musical performance skill over the life span. In *The Social Psychology of Music*, ed. D. J. Hargreaves and A. C. North, pp. 188–206. New York: Oxford University Press.

DeCasper, A. J., and Fifer, W. P. (1980). Of human bonding: newborns prefer their mothers' voices. *Science* 208:1174–1176.

DeCasper, A., and Prescott, P. (1984). Human newborns' perception of male voices: preference, discrimination and reinforcing value. *Developmental Psychology* 17:481–491.

DeCasper, A. J., and Spence, M. J. (1986). Prenatal maternal speech influences newborn's perception of speech sounds. *Infant Behavior and Development* 9:133–150.

Demany, L. (1982). Auditory stream segregation in infancy. *Infant Behavior and Development* 5:215–226.

Demany, L., McKenzie, B., and Vurpillot, E. (1977). Rhythm perception in early infancy. *Nature* 226:718–719.

Deutsch, D. (1974). An auditory illusion. *Nature* 251:307–309.

———— (1975a). Two-channel listening to musical scales. *Journal of the Acoustical Society of America* 157:1156–1160.

———— (1975b). Musical illusions. *Scientific American* 233:92–104.

———— (1983). The octave illusion in relation to handedness and familiar handedness background. *Neuropsychologia* 21:289–293.

———— (1991). The tritone paradox: an influence of language on music perception. *Music Perception* 8:275–280.

————— (1992). The tritone paradox: implications for the representation and communication of pitch structures. In *Cognitive Bases of Musical Communication*, ed. M. R. Jones, and S. Holleran, pp. 115–138. Washington, DC: American Psychological Association.

Deutsch, D., Kuyper, W. L., and Fisher, Y. (1987). The tritone paradox: its presence and form of distribution in a general population. *Music Perception* 5:79–92.

Deutsch, D., North, T., and Ray, L. (1990). The tritone paradox: correlate with the listener's vocal range for speech. *Music Perception* 7:371–384.

Devereux, C. (1956). *Basic Problems of Ethnopsychiatry*. Chicago: University of Chicago Press, 1980.

Díaz de Chumaceiro, C. L. (1987). *Induced song recall: a diagnostic and psychotherapeutic technique*. Dissertation Abstracts International 49/03B, p. 911. University Microfilms 8807026.

————— (1988). *La efectividad de la evocación inducida de Canciones en psicoterapia. [The effectiveness of induced song recall in psychotherapy] Master's Abstracts International*, 26/04, p. 454. University Microfilms No. 13–32884.

————— (1990a). Songs of the countertransference in psychotherapy dyads. *American Journal of Psychoanalysis* 50:75–89.

————— (1990b). La evocación inducida de canciones: una cuña comercial en psicoterapia [Induced song recall: a commercial jingle in psychotherapy] *Comportamiento* 1:49–56.

————— (1991). Sigmund Freud: on pianists' performance problems. *Medical Problems of Performing Artists* 6:21–27.

————— (1992). What song comes to mind? Induced song recall. Transference–countertransference in dyadic music associations in treatment and supervision. *Arts in Psychotherapy* 19:325–332.

————— (1993a). Parapraxes in song recall: a neglected variable. *American Journal of Psychoanalysis* 53:225–235.

————— (1993b). Transference–countertransference implications in Freud's patient's recall of Weber's *Der Freischütz*. *Psychoanalytic Review* 80:293–307.

————— (1995). Lullabies are "transferential transitional songs": further considerations on resistance in music therapy. *Arts in Psychotherapy* 22:353–357.

————— (1996a). Unconsciously induced song recall: the process of unintentional rather than so-called spontaneous evocations of music. *American Journal of Psychoanalysis* 56:83–91.

————— (1996b). "Dim spot": a variant in between countertransferential "blind" and "bright" spots. *Psychoanalytic Quarterly* 65:376–382.

————— (1997). Song synthesis: further neuropsychological assumptions of induced song recall. *American Journal of Psychoanalysis* 57(2):167–178.

————— (1998). Induced recall of a Broadway musical film revisited. *Arts in Psychotherapy* 25:51–55.

Dowling, W. J. (1993). Procedural and declarative knowledge in music cognition and education. In *Psychology and Music: The Understanding of Melody and Rhythm*, ed. T. J. Tighe and W. J. Dowling, pp. 5–18. Hillsdale, NJ: Lawrence Erlbaum.

Dowling, W. J., and Harwood, D. L. (1986). *Music Cognition*. New York: Academic Press.

Epstein, D. (1993). On affect and musical motion. In *Psychoanalytic Explorations in Music, Second Series*, ed. S. Feder, R. L. Karmel, and G. H. Pollock, pp. 91–123. Madison, CT: International Universities Press.

Feder, S. (1981). Charles and George Ives: the veneration of boyhood. In *Psychoanalytic Explorations in Music*, ed. S. Feder, R. L. Karmel, and G. H. Pollock, pp. 115–176. Madison, CT: International Universities Press, 1990.

Fifer, W. P., and Moon, C. M. (1989). Psychobiology of newborn auditory preferences. *Seminars in Perinatology* 13(5):430–433.

——— (1995). The effects of fetal experience with sound. In *Fetal Development: A Psychobiological Perspective*, ed. J. P. Lecanuet, W. P. Fifer, N. A. Krasnegor, and W. P. Smotherman, pp. 351–366. Hillsdale, NJ: Lawrence Erlbaum.

Freud, A. (1963). The concept of developmental lines. *Psychoanalytic Study of the Child* 18:245–265. New York: International Universities Press.

——— (1965). From the body to the toy and from play to work. In *Normality and Pathology in Childhood*, pp. 79–84. New York: International Universities Press.

Freud, S. (1901). The psychopathology of everyday life. *Standard Edition* 6:1–297.

——— (1916). Introductory lectures on psycho-analysis. *Standard Edition* 15:100–112.

Funk, J., and Whiteside, J. (1981). Development theory and the psychology of music. *Psychology of Music* 9(2):44–53.

Gardner, H. (1983). *Frames of Mind*. New York: Basic Books.

Goldstein, A. (1980). Thrills in response to music and other stimuli. *Physiological Psychology* 8(1):126–129.

Gramajo Galimany, N. N. (1993). Musical pleasure. *International Journal of Psycho-Analysis* 74:383–391.

Greenacre, P. (1957). The childhood of the artist: libidinal phase development and giftedness. *Psychoanalytic Study of the Child* 12:47–72. New York: International Universities Press.

Gregory, A. H. (1997). The roles of music in society: the ethnomusicological perspective. In *The Social Psychology of Music*, ed. D. J. Hargreaves and A. C. North, pp. 123–140. New York: Oxford University Press.

Gregory, A. H., Worrall, L., and Sarge, A. (1996). The development of emotional responses to music in young children. *Motivation and Emotion* 20:341–348.

Harrer, G., and Harrer, H. (1977). Music, emotion and autonomic function. In *Music and the Brain: Studies in the Neurology of Music*. ed. M. Critchley and R. A. Henson, pp. 202–216. London: Camelot.

Herron, W. G. (1995). Development of the ethnic unconscious. *Psychoanalytic Psychology* 12(4):521–532.

Hutt, S., Hutt, C., Lenard, H. G., et al. (1968). Auditory responsivity in the human neonate. *Nature* 218:888–890.

Javier, R. A., and Rendon, M. (1995). The ethnic unconscious and its role in transference, resistance, and countertransference: an introduction. *Psychoanalytic Psychology* 12(4):513–520.

Javier, R. A., and Yussef, M. (1995). A Latino perspective of the role of ethnicity in the development of moral values: implications for psychoanalytic theory and practice. *Journal of the American Academy of Psychoanalysis* 23:79–97.

Kessen, W., Levine, J., and Wendrich, K. (1979). The imitation of pitch in infants. *Infant Behavior and Development* 2:93–99.

Kinney, D. K., and Kagan, J. (1976). Infant attention to auditory discrepancy. *Child Development* 47:155–164.

Kneutgen, J. (1970). Eine Musikform und ihre biologische Function: über die Wirkungsweise der Wiegenlieder. *Zeitschrift für experimentale und angewandte Psychologie* 17:245.

Lecanuet, J. P., Granier-Deferre, C., and Busmel, M. C. (1995). Human fetal auditory perception. In *Fetal Development: a Psychobiological Perspective*, ed. J. P. Lecanuet, W. P. Fifer, N. A. Krasnegor, and W. P. Smotherman, pp. 239–262. Hillsdale, NJ: Lawrence Erlbaum.

Litzmann, B. (1913). *Clara Schumann: An Artist's Life*, ed. and trans. G. E. Hadlow, 2 vols., 4th ed. New York: Vienna House, 1972.

Lorch, C. A., Lorch, V., Diefendorf, A. O., and Earl, P. W. (1994). Effects of stimulative and sedative music on systolic blood pressure, heart rate, and respiratory rate in premature infants. *Journal of Music Therapy* 31(2):105–118.

Mahler, M., Pine, F., and Bergman, A. (1975). *The Psychological Birth of the Human Infant*. New York: Basic Books.

Makeig, S. (1982). Affective versus analytic perception of music intervals. In *Music, Mind, and Brain: the Neuropsychology of Music*, ed. M. Clynes, pp. 227–250. New York: Plenum.

Maurer, D., and Maurer, C. (1988). *The World of the Newborn*. New York: Basic Books.

McCall, R. B., and Melson, W. H. (1970). Amount of short-term familiarization and the response to auditory discrepancies. *Child Development* 41:861–869.

McDonald, M. (1970). Transitional tunes and musical development. *Psychoanalytic Study of the Child* 25:503–520; New York: International Universities Press. Also in *Psychoanalytic Explorations in Music*, ed. S. Feder, R. L. Karmel, and G. H. Pollock, pp. 79–95. Madison, CT: International Universities Press, 1990.

McDougall, J. (1995). *The Many Faces of Eros*. New York: Norton.

Mehler, J., Jusczyk, P., Lamperez, G., et al. (1988). A precursor of language acquisition in young infants. *Cognition* 29:143–178.

Melson, W. H., and McCall, R. B. (1970). Attentional responses of five-month-old girls to discrepant auditory stimuli. *Child Development* 41:861–869.

Moon, C., and Fifer, W. (1990a). Syllables as signals for 2-day-old infants. *Infant Behavior and Development* 13:377–390.

———— (1990b). *Newborns prefer a prenatal version of mother's voice*. Paper presented at biannual meeting of International Society of Infants Studies, Montreal, April.

Moon, C., Bever, T. G., and Fifer, W. P. (1992). Canonical and non-canonical syllable discrimination by two-day-old infants. *Journal of Child Language* 19:1–17.

Moon, C., Cooper, R. P., and Fifer, W. P. (1993). Two-day-olds prefer their native language. *Infant Behavior and Development* 16(4):495–500.

Morgan, C. (1991). *Dreams in the fetus and the newborn.* Paper presented to the Los Angeles Institute and Society for Psychoanalytic Studies, February.

Mussen, P. H., ed. (1983). *Handbook of Child Psychology.* Vol. 4. New York: Wiley.

Nass, M. L. (1971). Some considerations of a psychoanalytic interpretation of music. *Psychoanalytic Quarterly* 40:303–316. Also in *Psychoanalytic Explorations in Music,* ed. S. Feder, R. L. Karmel, and G. H. Pollock, pp. 30–48. Madison, CT: International Universities Press, 1990.

——— (1975). On hearing and inspiration in the composition of music. *Psychoanalytic Quarterly* 44:431–449. Also in *Psychoanalytic Explorations in Music,* ed. S. Feder, R. L. Karmel, and G. H. Pollock, pp. 179–194. Madison, CT: International Universities Press, 1990.

——— (1984). The development of creative imagination in composers. *International Review of Psycho-Analysis* 11:481–492. Also in *Psychoanalytic Explorations in Music,* ed. S. Feder, R. L. Karmel, and G. H. Pollock, pp. 179–193. Madison, CT: International Universities Press, 1990.

——— (1989). From transformed scream, through mourning, to the building of psychic structure: a critical review of the literature on music and psychoanalysis. *Annual of Psychoanalysis* 17:159–181.

——— (1993). The composer's experience: variations on several themes. In *Psychoanalytic Explorations in Music, Second Series.* ed. S. Feder, R. L. Karmel, and G. H. Pollock, pp. 21–40. Madison, CT: International Universities Press.

Noy, P. (1993). How music conveys emotion. In *Psychoanalytic Explorations in Music, Second Series,* ed. S. Feder, R. L. Karmel, and G. H. Pollock, pp. 125–149. Madison, CT: International Universities Press.

Olds, C. (1984). *A Sound Start in Life.* Wickford, Essex, UK: Runwell Hospital.

——— (1985a). The fetus as a person. *Birth Psychology Bulletin* 6(2):21–26.

——— (1985b). *Fetal Response to Music.* Wickford, Essex, UK: Runwell Hospital.

Ostwald, P. F. (1973). Musical behavior in early childhood. *Developmental Medical Child Neurology* 15:367–375.

——— (1985). *Schumann: The Inner Voices of a Musical Genius.* Boston: Northeastern University.

——— (1990). Music in the organization of childhood experience and emotion. In *Music and Child Development: Proceedings of the 1987 Denver Conference,* ed. F. R. Wilson, and F. L. Roehmann, pp. 11–27. St. Louis, MO: MMB Music.

——— (1993). Communication of affect and idea through song: Schumann's "I was Crying in my Dream" (op. 48, no. 13). In *Psychoanalytic Explorations in Music, Second Series,* ed. S. Feder, R. Karmel, and G. Pollock, pp. 179–193. Madison, CT: International Universities Press.

Ostwald, P. F., Phibbs, R., and Fox, S. (1968). Diagnostic use of infant cry. *Biologia Neonatorum* 13:68–82.

Panneton, R. K. (1985). *Prenatal auditory experience with melodies: effects on postnatal preferences in human newborns.* Unpublished doctoral dissertation, University of North Carolina at Greensboro.

Piaget. J. (1951). *Play, Dreams, and Imitation in Childhood.* New York: Norton.

Piontelli, A. (1986). *Backwards in Time.* Perthshire, Scotland: Clunie.

——— (1987). Infant observation from before birth. *International Journal of Psycho-Analysis* 68:453–463.

——— (1988). Pre-natal life and birth as reflected in the analysis of a 2-year-old psychotic girl. *International Review of Psycho-Analysis* 15:73–81.

——— (1989). A study on twins before and after birth. *International Review of Psycho-Analysis* 16:413–426.

Platt, W. (1933). Temperament and disposition revealed in young children's music. *Character and Personality* 2:246–251.

Pollock, G. H. (1989). On migration—voluntary and coerced. *Annual of Psychoanalysis* 17:145–158.

Polverini-Rey, R. A. (1992). *Intrauterine musical learning: the soothing effect on newborns of a lullaby learned prenatally.* Unpublished dissertation. California School of Professional Psychology, Los Angeles.

Rauscher, F. H., Shaw, G. L., Levine, L. J., et al. (1997). Music training causes long-term enhancement of preschool children's spatial-temporal reasoning. *Neurological Research* 19:2–8.

Reich, N. B. (1985). *Clara Schumann—The Artist and the Woman.* New York: Cornell University Press.

Reik, T. (1953). *The Haunting Melody: Psychoanalytic Experiences in Life and Music.* New York: Farrar, Straus & Young.

Roederer, J. G. (1982). Physical and neuropsychological functions of music: the basic questions. In *Music, Mind, and Brain: The Neuropsychology of Music,* ed. M. Clynes, pp. 37–43. New York: Plenum Press.

Rogers, S. J. (1990). Theories of child development and musical ability. In *Music and Child Development: Proceedings of the 1987 Denver Conference,* ed. F. R. Wilson, and F. L. Roehmann, pp. 1–10. St. Louis, MO: MMB Music.

Rose, G. J. (1980). *The Power of Form: A Psychoanalytic Approach to Aesthetic Form.* Expanded ed. New York: International Universities Press, 1992.

——— (1993). On form and feeling in music. In *Psychoanalytic Explorations in Music, Second Series,* ed. S. Feder, R. L. Karmel, and G. H. Pollock, pp. 63–81. Madison, CT: International Universities Press.

Rosenbaum, J. B. (1963). Songs of the transference. *American Imago* 20:257–269.

Russell, P. A. (1997). Musical tastes and society. In *The Social Psychology of Music,* ed. D. J. Hargreaves and A. C. North, pp. 141–158. New York: Oxford University Press.

Satt, B. J. (1984). *An investigation into the acoustical induction of intra-uterine learning.* Unpublished dissertation, California School of Professional Psychology, Los Angeles.

Schaefer, M., Hatcher, P., and Barglow, P. (1980). Prematurity and infant stimulation: review of the literature. *Child Psychiatry and Human Development* 10(4):199–212.

Schuter, R. (1968). *The Psychology of Musical Ability*. London: Methuen.

Shetler, D. J. (1990). The inquiry into prenatal musical experience: a report of the Eastman Project 1980–1987. In *Music and Child Development: Proceedings of the 1987 Denver Conference*, ed. F. R. Wilson and F. L. Roehmann, pp. 44–62. St. Louis, MO: MMB Music.

Simner, M. (1971). Newborn's response to the cry of another infant. *Developmental Psychology* 5:136–150.

Simons, G. (1986). Early childhood development: a survey of selected research. *Council for Research in Music Education* 12:212–226.

Sloboda, J. A. (1992). Empirical studies of emotional response to music. In *Cognitive Bases of Musical Communication*, ed. M. R. Jones, and S. Holleran, pp. 33–46. Washington, DC: American Psychological Association.

Smith, J. D. (1997). The place of musical novices in music science. *Music Perception* 14:227–262.

Sontag, L. W. (1966). Implications of fetal behavior and environment for adult personalities. *Annals of New York Academy of Sciences*, February 28, 134, part 2, pp. 782–786.

Spintge, R., and Droh, R., eds. (1992). *Music Medicine*. St Louis, MO: MMB Music.

Standley, J. M. (1992). Meta-analysis of research in music and medical treatment: effect size as a basis for comparison across multiple dependent and independent variables. In *Music Medicine*, ed. R. Spintge, and R. Droh, pp. 364–378. St Louis, MO: MMB Music.

Standley, J. M., and Madsen, C. K. (1990). Comparison of infant preferences and responses to auditory stimuli: music, mother, and other female voices. *Journal of Music Therapy* 27:54–97.

Standley, J. M., and Moore, R. (1993). *The effect of music vs. mother's voice on NBICU infants' oxygen saturation levels and frequency of bradycardia/apnea episodes*. Paper presented at the Tenth National Research in Music Behavior Symposium. Tuscaloosa, AL, April.

Stern, D. S. (1985). *The Interpersonal World of the Infant*. New York: Basic Books.

Stokes, M., ed. (1994). *Ethnicity, Identity, and Music: The Musical Construction of Place*. Oxford: Berg.

Suzuki, S. (1969). *Nurtured by Love: A New Approach to Education*. New York: Exposition.

Trehub, S. E., Bull, D., and Thorpe, L. A. (1984). Infants' perceptions of melodies: the role of melodic contour. *Child Development* 55:821–830.

Trehub, S. E., Unyk, A. M., and Trainor, L. J. (1993a). Adults identify infant-directed music across cultures. *Infant Behavior and Development* 16:193–211.

——— (1993b). Maternal singing in cross cultural perspective. *Infant Behavior and Development* 16:285– 295.

Treitler, L. (1993). Reflections on the communication of affect and idea through music. In *Psychoanalytic Explorations in Music, Second Series*, ed. S. Feder, R. L.

Karmel, and G. H. Pollock, pp. 43–62. Madison, CT: International Universities Press.

Unyk, A. M., Trehub, S. E., Trainor, L. J., and Schellenberg, E. G. (1992). Lullabies and simplicity: a cross-cultural perspective. *Psychology of Music* 20:15–28.

Verny, T. (1981). *The Secret Life of the Unborn Child*. New York: Summit.

Winnicott, D. W. (1953). Transitional objects and transitional phenomena. *International Journal of Psycho-Analysis* 34: 89-97.

PART IV

Evaluation, Treatment, and Supervisory Issues

21

The Delivery of Multicultural
Mental Health Services

WILLIAM G. HERRON, RAFAEL ART. JAVIER,
LYDIA K. WARNER, AND LOUIS H. PRIMAVERA

A multicultural model of society involves a complex interactive pattern in which all individuals can develop distinct positive identities as well as positive intergroup attitudes (Berry 1993). A favorable sociopolitical environment is necessary to develop a successful plural integrationist society in contrast to an assimilationist society with a mainstream minority emphasis that is more likely to promote acculturative stress (Berry et al. 1987). The United States has historically struggled with the development of policies that are more integrationist than assimilationist, but within the framework of a dominant ideology that has been rather assimilationist in nature. Such policies have resulted in the discrimination and isolation of various ethnic and social groups. Part of the reason for that is that the rules for assimilation into the dominant culture are imbued in socioeconomic and sociopolitical goals not easily attainable or impossible to attain for the culturally different and disenfranchised population. This is the paradox of the "melting pot" paradigm. An example of this dilemma can be seen in the recent controversy around the establishment of a national health care delivery system, which drew serious criticism from one or the other side of the isle on Capitol Hill. The nature of this criticism can be organized around political and financial grounds, but in the final analysis it has to do with the fact that we are not committed as a nation to make this a reality. In the meantime, a large sector of the population is left without adequate health care coverage. This situation is even more alarming with mental health services because of the additional prejudices and complications surrounding mental health needs (Padilla et al. 1975).

With regard to the issue of multiculturalism and health delivery in particular, a variety of policy perspectives need to be addressed if the country is to be successful in establishing a working, effective multiculturalism. A major one of these perspectives is the health of the population, both physical and mental, as well as their integration. This chapter focuses on the delivery of mental health services that are designed to suit the needs of a multicultural society, and includes the relationship between mental health and physical well-being.

HISTORICAL PERSPECTIVE

Issues with Mental Health Policies

A policy can be considered multicultural if it encourages distinctive groups to maintain their specialness and develop it at the same time that there is sharing between groups that is part of accepting other groups within a broad framework of national unity. The mental health policies of the past paid limited attention to this issue, and instead were caught up in developing a framework for service delivery that was primarily unicultural and categorical (Herron and Adlerstein 1994). Although mental health services were part of the general health services, they were never an equal part in respect to funding or status. A prevailing cultural belief was to both stigmatize and pathologize serious mental disorders, and to depreciate the impact of other emotional problems. Thus the legitimatization of all forms of mental disorders occupied most of the energy in the past, with limited attention given to the cultural characteristics of the people involved (Sue et al. 1991). The exception to that, and it is a notable one, was that the poor got public treatment if they became a problem to the society, whereas people who were economically advantaged had choices in getting services provided. To the degree that ethnic groups prevailed in disadvantaged social classes, their delivery systems became categorical. However, little thought or attention was paid to cultural differences within the categories, resulting in a unicultural pathology that turned class-conscious when treatment was to be delivered, essentially restricting multi-culturalism through denial and paradoxical selectivity.

An additional problem has been the erection of barriers for those who want to conform, or a definition of conformity that permanently categorizes the minority group as inferior. Health service delivery has been aligned accordingly so that minorities are likely to receive the least favorable care, despite legislative and policy initiatives that mandate a multicultural approach. Hence services are provided in which the ultimate possible outcome is the reinforcement of the status quo, in which the programmatic interventions are limited in nature or lack the necessary ingredients to encourage growth and/or are unresponsive to the basic needs of the clients (Javier et al. 1995, Padilla et al. 1975).

Problems with Institutionalization

An additional problem was an emphasis on institutionalization as a relatively uniform way for dealing with mental illness. Such an approach isolated people, thus working against societal integration. What was required to effect improvement was based on generalized views of psychopathology that ignored cultural differences as significant contributing factors to behavioral development. This is counter to the research findings by Sue (1988) and by Sue and associates (1991) that factors of class, ethnicity, language, and gender are important variables affecting premature termination from treatment, number of sessions attended, and treatment outcomes.

Although the past eventually saw changes that showed significantly greater understanding of mental health problems—for example, an emphasis on deinstitutionalization as well as greater funding and treatment opportunities for many more people—treatment delivery systems retained a class consciousness and psychopathology continued to be viewed with ethnic neutrality. In fact, as psychological factors were increasingly ignored as factors in the development of serious disorders, such as schizophrenia, a unitary culture of disease was in the making. Thus the foundation for unitary treatment, such as culture-blind psychotropic medication, has been constructed, insidiously favoring an assimilative view of society over an integrative one. Although the United States has always been a nation of immigrants and a pluralistic society, there has also always been a struggle concerning the method of working with diversity. In theory, multiculturalism appears as an ideal; in practice, minority groups have been expected to shape themselves to the mainstream or suffer unpleasant consequences.

TOWARD MULTICULTURAL MENTAL HEALTH: CURRENT CHALLENGES

Currently, the delivery of health services is a costly enterprise that can indeed provide quality care, yet still leave a significant proportion of the population without adequate access to such care (Frank 1993, Frank and VandenBos 1994). Cost reduction and improved access are both considered as goals for a national health policy, but it has proven so difficult to have them fit together that as of this writing national health care reform seems very unlikely. At the same time, cost cutting is increasing in popularity, and mental health services, particularly outpatient treatment, are frequently targeted so that access to these services is becoming more restricted (Herron et al. 1994). The growth of managed mental health care is producing a "one size fits all" delivery system that ignores the customized procedures needed to address multicultural concerns in psychotherapy (Boyd-Franklin 1989, Javier and Herron 1992). Despite the growing awareness of the importance of social, ethnic, and cultural factors in the development and treatment of psychopathology (Herron et al. 1992, 1994, Javier et al. 1994, Sue et al. 1991), the delivery of treatment disregards these issues. The result is *surface pluralism*, where the society acknowledges cultural diversity yet fails to respect it in designing essential services, such as mental health services.

Of course, there is a continuing struggle regarding inclusion of mental health in the essential category, as such services have been moved in and out of national health proposals, and even when they are in they are restricted relative to other health services. However, assuming mental health does get recognition as part of a national health policy, it is still necessary to have it provided within a multicultural context, and primarily emphasizing cost containment will not take care of the issue of cultural diversity. Current service delivery systems are unfortunately moving away from designs that recognize the complexity of the consumers' problems. This appears particularly disastrous for the society because it is happening at a time when ethnic tension is heightening throughout the world (Javier and Rendon 1995). Thus it is a time when multiculturalism deserves more consideration, particularly in regard to the fostering of mental health, yet service delivery continues to be limited and simplistic in reference to ethnic and cultural perspectives.

National Ambivalence

There is a persistent national ambivalence in regard to the provision of mental health care (Frank and VandenBos 1994, Herron and Adlerstein 1994).

On one side is an emphasis on individual responsibility, which is translated into a personal requirement to cope with mainstream systems that blur or ignore distinctive needs. On the other side is a need to be concerned with the needs of all individuals and to develop policies, such as ways to deliver mental health services, that are attuned to diversity. Current policies reflect compromises between these two sides, but the solution is too tilted in the direction of immediate cost savings and power preservation to effectively meet the needs of the society.

Deinstitutionalization is a good example of the problem. Institutionalization was seen as a costly and ineffective way to care for most of the mentally ill, whereas community-based approaches were seen as more effective. There is now considerable evidence to support the effectiveness of community care for severe mental disorders (Stein and Test 1980). However, there has been limited implementation of these community support systems. At the same time, institutions continue to be downsized or closed without appropriate coordination so that patients are too often "dumped" without adequate resources for their care.

The policy of deinstitutionalization in turn tends to be viewed as an unworkable good intention, although it appears to be continuing anyway in the name of fiscal exigency. For such a policy to be effective, it requires a matching, coordinated model of community support. This means comprehensive services such as crisis intervention as well as support for daily living in the way described by Padilla and his associates (1975). Patients have to be educated about the nature and management of their illnesses and to learn and implement psychosocial skills. Employment, housing, financial assistance, and medical and mental health care need to be made available. In reality, relatively few community support systems offer these necessary comprehensive services (Test and Scott 1990), and the prospects for improvements are limited (Rubin 1990).

Impact of Deinstitutionalization in the Minority Community

The deinstitutionalization situation, along with any program that results in limitations of care, is a multicultural issue because of the relationships between health, wealth, and minority status. It has been shown that there is a graded association between health and socioeconomic status, with individuals in lower status social groups being at the greatest health risk (Adler et al. 1994). Because large minority groups, such as African-Americans and Latinos, are majorities with low socioeconomic status, they are in greater need of health service delivery (Rogler et al. 1987, Sue et al. 1991). In general, this is a function of their lower status, and it is only being reinforced by market-driven systems that limit access to care. As cultural groups with lower socioeconomic status increase in numbers as mentally ill, they are less likely to improve because they will get inferior service relative to higher status groups. In turn, such a result reinforces negative stereotypes of these cultural groups. The problems of acculturation are being dismissed as irrelevancies in the current dominant policies of delivering mental health services, which essentially undercuts other efforts to effectively develop a multicultural society.

Barriers to the Development of Culturally Relevant Services

Funding. There are a number of barriers to creating culture-favorable delivery systems. For example, reducing the number of people who are hospitalized for mental illness would seem to cause the budgets of state mental hospitals to fall proportionately, but such has not been the case (Marmor and Gill 1990). Instead, it has been difficult to shift funds from hospitals to community care with the result that there is a mismatch between outpatient needs and funding. In addition, insurance reimbursements continue to favor hospitalization. Medicaid is a case in point because it allocates most of its budget for institutional treatment and pays low rates for outpatient services. Also, even where funds are made available they are often restricted to traditional treatments to the exclusion of social, educational, and rehabilitation services that are needed for comprehensive community care. Services are often fragmented, so that there is an unwieldy mix of government and private programs. Thus there may be overlap, or gaps, despite the presence of some services, and difficulty in establishing responsibilities for these services.

Sociodemographic, structural, and individual barriers. The service system is often a difficult entity for patients and their families to navigate. Communities themselves have negative reactions to the patients, and the various mental health disciplines have trouble adapting to the roles that are needed to make community care work. Three major classes of barriers or deterrents to care have been identified by Melnyk (1988), Padilla and his associates (1975), Rogler and associates (1987), and Sue (1988). Expanded on by Lia-Hoagberg and colleagues (1990), these include sociodemographic barriers such as poverty, unemployment, and lack of education; structural barriers such as organization of services and availability of care; and individual barriers such as knowledge of appropriate care, and feelings and attitudes about health care. It appears that all three types of deterrents operate to decrease access to care for minority groups. In particular, Lia-Hoagberg and colleagues (1990) cite child care and transportation as major structural barriers to obtaining health care for the women studied.

The limited implementation of community health care noted above directly reinforces sociodemographic, structural, and individual barriers to care. For example, child care and transportation would cease to be structural barriers if these services were available within community systems accessed by all members of our multicultural society, such as school-based or housing complex-based community clinics. Likewise, financial status and educational level could be eliminated as sociodemographic deterrents to use of health care if such care was equally available to all communities. Finally, individual barriers such as knowledge of appropriate mental health care could be overcome by the daily exposure to service availability that is possible only with a community model of health care.

The political-economic climate does not favor expansion in mental health service delivery. Less funding is being made available through insurance and government support, and shifts in emphasis in treatment, such as deinstitutionalization, have not led to a dividend that could be used for those less socially favored. However, there is always competition for need priority in the society, so the existence of the present constrictions and restrictions needs to be highlighted as a problem to be overcome. The task is harder because of the present mood, but there is also a strong push from the increasing plurality of the society to significantly increase multiculturalism, which in this case means changes in the delivery of mental health services. At the moment, the severity of this concern has not been recognized, but the degree of ethnic unrest that exists throughout the world suggests strongly that more attention must be paid to multicultural concerns. Clearly a major goal is to do this, which means political action for all who are concerned with this issue.

ESSENTIAL ELEMENTS FOR A MULTICULTURAL MENTAL HEALTH SERVICE

For a service to be multicultural it has to meet the needs of all the cultural groups who use it in an equal manner. Although this is an ideal that will be difficult to achieve either in theory or practice, nonetheless it is the goal. First, equality would mean equal access to the services, as opposed to discriminatory service based on the appeal of the groups to be served. Given the market-driven economy of the moment, groups that can afford to pay more have greater appeal in general to service providers. Thus services to the poor require an economic subsidy, usually from the government, to give them parity with services to the middle and upper classes. The achievement of such parity usually requires a national policy because there can be uneven distribution of resources when there is more local control. At present, service access is not equal for all segments of the society, despite policies designed to facilitate parity, such as Medicare and Medicaid. However, limitations or even failures of existing policies should not mean abandonment of the concept. As of this writing the political mood in the country appears to be moving in the direction of restrictive social policies, based both on economic concerns and interest in greater localization of service policies, so it will be more of a struggle to develop an approach that ensures viable multiculturalism.

There are important factors that have been suggested and demonstrated in the literature as having different degrees of success with culturally diverse groups (Padilla et al. 1975, Rogler et al. 1987, Sue et al. 1991).

What is required is a certain level of customization of services, a situation that could be quite challenging within the current managed care environment. In the final analysis, it is a question of providing service for each cultural group equal to that available for the dominant group. As indicated earlier, past practices have tended to mainstream the services in regard to diagnosis and treatment, often leading to errors in both. Cultural factors that contribute to behavior, if ignored or misunderstood, can lead to the apparent presence of a mental disorder when such is not the case and to apparent resistance to treatment when that is not a patient's intention. The use of language and conceptions of time and space often reflect cultural differences that if not understood create distorted impressions of people's level of mental health (Javier and Herron 1992). The fact is that patients from minority backgrounds are more likely to seek services, stay in treatment longer, and show improvement in their psychological and psychiatric conditions when these services are offered in a context that is sensitive to their language, ethnic, gender and socioeconomic needs (Padilla et al. 1975, Rogler et al. 1987). For instance, ethnic matching of patients with therapists was important for Asian and Mexican Americans who did not speak English as their primary language in terms of premature termination, number of sessions, and outcomes. For English-speaking patients, matching was not as important except for the number of sessions among the Asian-American clients. The combination of ethnic matching and language was very important for clients whose primary language was not English, particularly in reference to premature termination and number of sessions (Sue et al. 1991). Thus, for service delivery to be culturally sensitive, or what Rogler and associates (1987) refers to as "isomorphic," these elements have to form an essential part of the intervention. It is important for the services to be linguistically accessible and ethnically relevant, and to include nontraditional approaches. In this regard, the roles of the clergy, the healer, and interpreters should be clearly defined in response to specific patients' needs. It is important to recognize in this context that not all patients need these approaches, and traditional approaches may also be beneficial for some of them. According to Sue and his colleagues (1991), generalization of services to all ethnic groups is difficult and is ". . . influenced by local policies and programs, as well as by characteristics of the ethnic populations" (p. 538).

Training for Providers

Customizing service delivery is not particularly expensive, depending primarily on the sensitivity of the clinician rather than on any elaborate treatment. It does require different training patterns for clinicians, but that is more a matter of emphasis than cost. Also, in designing services there is an awareness of a mainstream culture and the need for people to develop an adaptation to it. At the same time, there is recognition that cultures change and are the products of all the people within them. Thus acculturation involves both shaping and being shaped. Individual identities are integrated products of cultural forces that significantly include all cultural components experienced by an individual (Herron 1995). Everyone needs to come to terms with the dominant culture, but it is crucial to understand that there are many ways to do this. Having trained providers that are sensitive to these tensions could facilitate the development of a working alliance in which the patients could experience the services as more culturally syntonic (Padilla et al. 1975). Padilla and his associates suggested that indigenous staff and paraprofessionals from the community, who are familiar with the community and its members, could have a crucial role in the delivery of mental health services, provided that they are trained in the provision of these types of services.

   Unfortunately, the two principles of equal availability and equal variability of mental health services have been difficult to develop. Equal availability requires that access be available based on need rather than on the patient's ability to have an appeal for the service providers. Some patients have an appeal for services based on their disorder, but this is less true in mental health services than it is in a number of other health services where the patient's problem—liver, heart, lungs, and so on—becomes separated from personality. Mental health services, in contrast, are provided with greater eagerness to personality types who are viewed in advance as better to work with, such as favoring neurotics over psychotics, or people who are from similar socioeconomic and cultural backgrounds as the providers. Because providers are generally part of the mainstream culture, there is a significant probability of ignorance and prejudice when working with a multicultural population. However, this issue can be addressed and remedied over time through education for providers.

The need for doing this is increasing. The 1990 Census (U.S. Bureau of the Census) shows that the ethnic minority population is increasing rapidly, now being approximately one quarter of the total population. To effectively provide services to these groups, clinicians need knowledge regarding pertinent practice and research concerns as well as an understanding of clients' values, beliefs, customs, and language. Training to prepare providers to serve multicultural clients has increased (Bernal and Castro 1994), but the need remains for some improvement in training for multicultural competence that will involve greater numbers of multicultural trainers and trainees who will become providers. Overcoming prejudice and going beyond superficial, politically correct statements is certainly a difficult task so that it is essential that training programs renew or increase their efforts to ensure a viable supply of providers who have both the interest and abilities to serve diverse ethnic and cultural groups.

Financial Considerations

The problem of developing funding for services is serious, particularly with respect to establishing equal access to quality services. It is clear that there is a need to provide services to the economically disadvantaged. Private insurance coverage, while generally not available to lower socioeconomic groups, has nonetheless provided a model for public financing that emphasizes higher funding for hospitalization and limited mental health benefits, with managed care further restricting outpatient services. At the same time, there is a greater need for community care that tends to be effective only if it is also comprehensive. Thus the unpleasant facts are that providing adequate mental health services for the increasing multicultural population that also contains a large number of economically disfavored people is going to be expensive. There is considerable resistance to restructuring the financing of mental health services in ways that would increase immediate expenses, yet it is apparent that just such an increase will occur if even an appropriate balance of community and inpatient programs is put into place to serve a multicultural population (Mechanic and Aiken 1989).

Need for Professional Role Redefinition

Cooper (1990) has pointed out additional problems found in the type of innovative, specialized delivery systems that would be considered multicultural. In essence, they are difficulties in developing a provider style that is a multidisciplinary team effort. For community care to be effective there will be a blurring in the distinct roles of the providing disciplines, which threatens professional identities and territories. Traditional patterns of responsibility and authority may be altered. Clinical skills are certainly involved, but so are other less customary skills, such as advocacy. Thus the barriers within and between mental health professionals need to be eliminated so that emphasis can be placed on doing what works though that may be quite a change from the past. Furthermore, the field needs to be marketed in a fashion that makes it more attractive than it has been, which again brings up the need for adequate funding.

FINAL COMMENTS

Constriction in mental health delivery systems has been fostered based on the impression that services are inefficient already. It is true, they are inefficient, not in their expansiveness, or even their current costs, but in their failure to understand the potential impact of mental illness on the health and growth of the society. There is an intense fear of violence in the streets without a corresponding concern about the mental status of the violent people. The most serious problems faced by societies, such as violence, always have major psychological components, yet the funding for their solution pays limited attention to the enhancement of psychological well-being.

This country is increasingly pluralistic, and it has a stated commitment to multiculturalism. Assimilation has not solved the problem of ethnic tension, so that if the country is to thrive through acculturation, it must support true multiculturalism. This means policy shifts that foster equal access and equality of service to all, and mental health service delivery is in dire need of gaining priority status.

REFERENCES

Adler, N. E., Boyce, T., Chesney, M. A., et al. (1994). Socioeconomic status and health: the challenge of the gradient. *American Psychologist* 49, 15–24.

Bernal, M. E., and Castro, F. G. (1994). Are clinical psychologists prepared for service and research with ethnic minorities? Report of a decade of progress. *American Psychologist* 49:797–805.

Berry, J. W. (1993). Ethnic identity in plural societies. In *Ethnic Identity: Formation and Transmission among Hispanics and Other Minorities*, ed. M. E. Bernal and G. P. Knight, pp. 271–296. Albany: State University of New York Press.

Berry, J. W., Kim, V., Minde, T., and Mok, D. (1987). Comparative studies of acculturative stress. *International Migration Review* 21:491–511.

Boyd-Franklin, N. (1989). *Black Families in Therapy. A Multisystems Approach*. New York: Guilford.

Cooper, J. E. (1990). Professional obstacles to implementation and diffusion of innovative approaches to mental health care. In *Mental Health Care Delivery: Innovation, Impediments and Implementation*, ed. I. Marks and R. Scott, pp. 233–253. New York: Cambridge University Press.

Frank, R. G. (1993). Health care reform: an introduction. *American Psychologist* 48:258–260.

Frank, R. G., and VandenBos, G. R. (1994). Health care reform: the 1993–1994 evolution. *American Psychologist* 49:851–854.

Herron, W. G. (1995). The development of the ethnic unconscious. *Psychoanalytic Psychology* 12:521–532.

Herron, W. G., and Adlerstein, L. K. (1994). The dynamics of managed mental health care. *Psychological Reports* 75:723–741.

Herron, W. G., Javier, R. A., and Cicone, J. (1992). Etiological patterns of child abuse and neglect. *Journal of Social Distress and the Homeless* 1:273–290.

Herron, W. G., Javier, R. A., McDonald-Gomez, M., and Adlerstein, L. K. (1994). Sources of family violence. *Journal of Social Distress and the Homeless* 3:213–228.

Herron, W. G., Javier, R. A., Primavera, L. H., and Schultz, C. L. (1994). The cost of psychotherapy. *Professional Psychology: Research and Practice* 25:106–110.

Javier, R. A., and Herron, W. G. (1992). Psychoanalysis, the Hispanic poor, and the disadvantaged: application and conceptualization. *Journal of the American Academy of Psychoanalysis* 20:455–476.

Javier, R. A., Herron, W. G., and Bergman, A. (1994). Introduction to the special issue of the multicultural view of domestic violence. *Journal of Social Distress and the Homeless* 3:1–5.

Javier, R. A., Herron, W. G., and Yanos, P. T. (1995). Urban poverty, ethnicity, and personality development. *Journal of Social Distress and the Homeless* 4:219–235.

Javier, R. A., and Rendon, M. (1995). The ethnic unconscious and its role in transference, resistance, and countertransference: an introduction. *Psychoanalytic Psychology* 12:513–520.

Lia-Hoagberg, B., Rode, P., Skovholt, C. J., et al. (1990). Barriers and motivators to prenatal care among low-income women. *Social Science Medicine* 30:487–495.

Marmor, T., and Gill, K. (1990). The political and economic context of mental health care in the United States. In *Mental Health Care Delivery: Innovation,*

Impediments and Implementation, ed. I. Marks and R. Scott, pp. 137–153. New York: Cambridge University Press.

Mechanic, D., and Aiken, L., eds. (1989). *Paying for Services: Promises and Pitfalls of Capitation*. San Francisco: Jossey-Bass.

Melnyk, K. A. M. (1988). Barriers: a critical review of recent literature. *Nursing Research* 37:196–201.

Padilla, A. M., Ruiz, R. A., and Alvarez, R. (1975). Community mental health services for the Spanish-speaking/surnamed population. *American Psychologist* 30:892–905.

Rogler, L. H., Malgady, R. G., Constantino, G., and Blumenthal, R. (1987). What do culturally sensitive mental health services mean? The case of Hispanics. *American Psychologist* 42:565–570.

Rubin, J. (1990). Economic barriers to implementing innovative mental health care in the United States. In *Mental Health Care Delivery: Innovation, Impediments and Implementation*, ed. I. Marks and R. Scott, pp. 220–232. New York: Cambridge University Press.

Stein, L. I., and Test, M. A. (1980). Alternatives to mental hospital treatment: I. Conceptual model, treatment program, and clinical evaluation. *Archives of General Psychiatry* 37:392–397.

Sue, S. (1988). Psychotherapy services for ethnic minorities: two decades of research findings. *American Psychologist* 43:301–308.

Sue, S., Fujino, D. C., Hu, L., et al. (1991). Community mental health services for ethnic minority groups: a test of the cultural responsiveness hypothesis. *Journal of Consulting and Clinical Psychology* 59:533–540.

Test. M. A., and Scott, R. (1990). Theoretical and research bases of community care programs. In *Mental Health Care Delivery: Innovation, Impediments and Implementation*, ed. I. Marks and R. Scott, pp. 11–16. New York: Cambridge University Press.

U.S. Bureau of the Census (1990). *Census of Population and Housing Summary* (Tape file IC, CD-ROM). Washington, DC: Government Printing Office.

22

Psychosocial and Psychotherapeutic Issues in Working with Immigrants

SHARON-ANN GOPAUL-McNICOL

Migration can be defined as the more or less permanent movement of persons or groups over a significant distance (Fabrega 1969). Berry and colleagues (1987) define acculturation as a "culture change which results from continuous first hand contact between two distinct cultural groups" (p. 491). This really involves a "shift in the cultural emphasis," involving "people in a relationship to an environment that is changing or changed" (Fabrega 1969, p. 316). Acculturation can be examined from many perspectives, including educational, economic, class, cultural, psychological, and behavioral. To some extent all immigrants face a period of adjustment, for immigration itself is "a process that stimulates mixed and varied responses at unpredictable periods of time" (Arredondo-Dowd 1981, p. 372). One can experience a sense of loss, sadness, and confusion, as well as feelings of happiness and elation. The processes of acculturation therefore play a major role in migration and in one's assimilation into the host society.

Because there is much diversity within immigrant families, assessing their acculturation and adaptation should be done cautiously. Lee (1982) suggested that therapists should determine the number of years immigrants have been in the United States because a third generation person may be more

"Westernized" than a newly arrived immigrant. Likewise, age at the time of immigration should also be considered, since younger people tend to assimilate more readily than older migrants. Moreover, one's country of origin is also important to explore since the economic, political, and educational background of the immigrant will also determine the rate of acculturation. In addition, the immigrant's professional affiliation may help to expedite the assimilation process since it can give one greater access to nonimmigrant Americans and other avenues that can accelerate the process of acculturation. Education appears to be a consistent predictor of low stress among immigrants (Berry et al. 1987), offering some acculturation prior to actual contact with the new country.

The matter of legality also helps to determine how quickly an individual assimilates into a new culture. Gopaul-McNicol (1993) emphasized that legal immigrants have more access to social support networks than illegal ones, who have to establish their own support networks. Therefore, being legal in the United States aids in better assimilation. Gopaul-McNicol also highlighted that children of mixed (immigrant-American) marriages tend to assimilate more quickly because one parent is familiar with the workings of American culture. Similarly, fluency with the language also aids in the assimilation process.

Berry and associates (1987) propose five stages of acculturation:

1. *Physical changes.* The individual must cope with living in a new place, including such elements as increased population density and more pollution. Prior intercultural experiences, such as having lived in an urban setting, play an important role. West Indians who migrated first to England, then to the United States, tend to assimilate better because of the prior experience of living elsewhere.

2. *Biological changes.* The individual encounters, for example, a new nutritional status, and new diseases.

3. *Cultural changes.* Political, economic, technical, linguistic, religious and social institutions become altered, or new ones take their place. People who were forced to leave their native countries (push factor) in order to escape from unpleasant situations, such as poverty, political repression, or personal problems, tend to have greater difficulty in adjusting. Those who left to study abroad or for personal growth (pull factor) tend to experience less acculturational stress.

4. *New sets of social relationships.* The individual must function within new social networks, both ingroup and outgroup. In most cases parents are separated from their children for several years prior to

coming to the host country, and many families are going through a readjustment period because they may not have seen each other for extended periods of time. Parents may not have significant background information, such as medical records and other developmental milestones. Therapists may view parents as uncaring because of their ignorance of such important information. Due to prolonged separation, children may view their grandparents as their primary caregivers which may lead to resentment by the natural parents. Social support factors have also been found to correlate with low stress in acculturation. Churches serve as a good support system in the areas of interpersonal, emotional, and religious needs. Moreover, people who have been able to establish contact with and participate in the larger society tend to have less stress in acculturation.

5. *Psychological and behavioral changes.* An alteration in mental health status due to culture shock often occurs in some form as individuals attempt to adapt to their new milieu. However, not all families are unable to negotiate the acculturation process. Oberg (1972) proposes five stages in the process of culture shock with respect to immigrants: (i) One feels euphoria about the exciting new culture; (ii) failure to succeed leads to extreme dissatisfaction with the host culture. This is a period of psychological transition from back-home values to host-home values; (iii) persons begin to understand the host culture and feel more in touch with themselves; (iv) the host culture is viewed as offering both positive and negative alternatives; (v) the immigrant returns home and experiences reverse culture shock.

In summary, most immigrants initially "have two lives, one back home and one here. It adds up to almost no life" (Rimer 1991, p. B6-L). In other words, physically arriving in the United States is not the same as emotionally arriving. For many immigrant families, the initial goal upon arrival in the United States is to "save money, buy a house back home and go back and start a business" (Rimer 1991, B6-L). However, going back is harder than anticipated because it is quite difficult attaining these goals; many immigrants are responsible for repaying family members back home who assisted in their migration. Some migrants, especially undocumented ones, must work two jobs to meet their responsibilities both back home and in the new country. Their children may have enormous problems because their parents have little time to assist in their adjustment. Children are expected simultaneously to assimilate and to maintain and respect their parents' traditional cultural values; they too are expected to live in two worlds. In addition, some families live in crowded conditions, because they live with relatives or friends, making it difficult for children to concentrate on their studies.

Given the many factors that can affect an individual's ability to assimilate into a new culture, it is vital that a therapist determine the stage of acculturation an individual is in before providing treatment to such an individual.

DETERMINING THE STATE OF ACCULTURATION/CULTURAL IDENTITY

Sluzki (1979) stated categorically that in working with migrant families, "in the course of the first interview the therapist should establish which phase of the process of migration the family is currently in and how they have dealt with the vicissitudes of previous phases" (p. 389). Helms (1985) outlines three phases of cultural identity that can be used to assess one's stage of acculturation.

The first stage, the preencounter stage, is the phase before an individual's cultural awakening. In this stage the individual is enmeshed in the Eurocentric/American view, in that he or she idealizes white culture and feels negative toward his or her own culture of origin. Poor individual and group self-esteem is the affective state associated with this stage.

The second stage is the transitional phase, which occurs when the individual realizes that he or she is not accepted absolutely by the white world. The individual goes through a period of withdrawal and cultural reassessment, and finally becomes a member of his or her own cultural group. The individual becomes ethnocentric and sees his or her cultural group as superior to other cultural systems. The affective state is experienced as one of rebirth as the individual tries to identify with his or her culture of origin. This rebirth results in a sort of euphoria. However, confusion may also ensue if the individual realizes that he or she is no longer fully able to identify with his or her culture of origin, since he or she has taken on some of the values of the host society.

The transcendent stage is the final stage. This occurs when a person becomes bicultural and uses experiences from both cultural groups to adjust to his or her more realistic circumstances. The individual accepts the advantages and disadvantages of both cultures and does not idealize either group. The individuals's affect is more temperate and the experience is one of identity resolution. Since a broader perspective is endorsed, one's self-esteem is improved. Generally, it takes a form of an identity transformation, via educational and cultural socialization experiences and personal readiness, for this stage to be attained.

A MODEL FOR WORKING WITH IMMIGRANT FAMILIES TO AID IN THEIR ACCULTURATION PROCESS

Many therapists, irrespective of ethnic orientation, have been educated and socialized with respect to middle-class values. Therefore, unless he or she is from a social class background similar to that of his or her therapist, an immigrant client may be expected to distance him- or herself from early cultural experiences. With immigrant families, distancing oneself from one's traditional values can result in anxiety. Weidman's (1979) concept of the "culture broker," and Bowen's (1978) concept of the "coach," calls for a friend of the family or a more neutral member of the family to serve as a mediator between the family in transition and the new culture. With the help of the coach, the therapist suggests ways to accommodate without expecting the family to take on the therapist's values. The therapist must accept the family from their vantage point and validate their position. Thus it is important for the therapist to become knowledgeable about the dominant values of the particular cultural group of the family he or she is working with.

At times a single family member may be able to serve as a "coach" to assist the therapist in providing a link between the therapist and the family (McGoldrick et al. 1982). This technique, known as link therapy, involves the training and coaching of one family member to serve as a therapist to his or her family system (Landau 1981). The link member receives treatment from the therapist and goes back to the family to initiate interventions. In the meantime, he or she receives continued supervision and guidance from the family therapist. Landau (1982) suggested that the link therapist be a family member who is also in the process of cultural transition. Landau (1982) cautioned against selecting the most acculturated member of the family as the link therapist. The link therapist can also be a peripheral member of the family who is generally not a complainant. In Gopaul-McNicol's (1993) multicultural/multimodal/multisystems model, several techniques (one of which is link therapy) are suggested in working with immigrant families.

THE MULTICULTURAL/MULTIMODAL/MULTISYSTEMS APPROACH TO WORKING WITH IMMIGRANTS

The multicultural/multimodal/multisystems approach (Multi-CMS) (Gopaul-McNicol 1993) is composed of four phases based on the concept of circularity (rather than linearity). Each component of each phase can recur repeatedly at various levels throughout the treatment process. The therapist must be flexible enough to intervene at whatever level is needed at whichever phase in therapy. With this in mind, the flow of treatment for the Multi-CMS approach is as follows:

Phase I. Assessment Process
> Step 1. Initial assessment
>> A. Explaining the process
>> B. Establishing trust
> Step 2. Gathering information
> Step 3. Determining the stage of acculturation
> Step 4. Outlining the goals

Phase II. Educational Treatment Process

Phase III. Psychological Treatment Process

Phase IV. Empowerment Treatment Process

Phase I. Assessment Process

Step 1. Initial Assessment

The initial assessment stage, which occurs in the first therapy session, is broken into two subphases: (i) explaining the process and (ii) establishing trust.

In an effort to establish a relationship, the therapist must explain the therapeutic process as clearly as possible because many immigrants view psychotherapy as a visit to a medical doctor. Many believe that therapy will last for only one session and that only the identified patient (in most cases a child) will be involved. At this juncture the process of psychotherapy should be explained. It must be pointed out that many immigrants believe that a person is either "normal" or "crazy" and only "crazy" people seek psychotherapy. Therefore, it is necessary to explain that a therapist also works with "normal, healthy" people who are simply experiencing adjustment difficulties, not just "crazy" people. This will help to mitigate anxiety surrounding psychotherapy. The therapist should also explain that each therapy session usually lasts approximately one hour (although the initial session can take as long as two hours) and that at times it may be necessary to see the entire family, not only the identified patient. Many families are not aware that they are expected to pay and even become angry when told this. This can result from the belief that a visit to a doctor involves a one-time payment, and that informal, community, social support is usually free. Examining the health insurance or any other medical plans of such families can alleviate some of the anxiety regarding full payment. The first fifteen minutes of therapy should be used to clear up misconceptions about psychotherapy and explain the process of treatment.

The next stage of this initial assessment process is the establishment of trust. Giving a gift (empathic understanding and/or sensitivity to culturally relevant issues) to the client early in treatment can give the client the impression that something was gained from the therapeutic encounter.

Step 2. Gathering Information

In the second stage of the assessment process, it is necessary to gather as much information as possible. For immigrant families this can begin very early in the treatment process since most families want to get on with whatever is necessary so that they can be finished with therapy. Therapists should be aware that copious note taking can be quite intimidating and distracting, and that some families will feel that a therapist who takes copious notes is not paying attention to them.

The genogram, a tool derived from anthropology but quite commonly used in psychology, is a sort of family tree. It can be quite useful to the therapist working with immigrant families as many family members and friends are often directly or indirectly involved in the problems presented. If nothing else, a genogram allows the individual or family to visually represent their support systems. Once a picture has been drawn, the therapist can encourage the family to bring in some or all of the family members who are impacting on the life of the identified patient.

Step 3. Determining the stage of acculturation (see discussion above)

Step 4. Outlining the Goals

In establishing credibility, it is necessary to outline very briefly what the individual or family will gain from therapy before the end of the first session. This is important because any discrepancy between the clients' and the therapist's perception of the clients' problems can lead to a conflict in the development of the goals for treatment. This can result in diminished therapist credibility and mistrust. As a matter of practice, at the end of every session it is wise to reevaluate progress and see if the goals of therapy are being accomplished.

Phase II. Educational Treatment Process

In working with immigrant families, much of therapy may be educational in nature, since many adjustment difficulties may be due to cultural differences or a lack of knowledge about United States educational, social, legal, and political systems. If, after the assessment process is completed, it is determined that the family members lack basic knowledge about systems they have to deal with every day, the therapist may find it necessary to educate them.

If the assessment shows that the individual is in the preencounter stage described above, then the therapist can expect him or her to endorse a Eurocentric view and to feel ashamed of his or her parents, accent, clothes, foods, and so on. Parents in turn may feel rejected, frustrated, angry, and confused. In this stage therapy has to focus on both the parents and the children. Parents must be taught the social/emotional adjustment stages that children go through. The goal of therapy is still educational at this point, since the therapist needs to assist the parents in understanding:

1. The causes of childhood misbehavior and the principles and concepts underlying the social learning of such behavior
2. The cultural differences in values and discipline as they affect their children's adjustment
3. The emotional stress and fears that emerge in a child as a result of migration and adjustment to a new family and the difference between an emotional disturbance and cultural adjustment
4. The differences in the school structure, school expectations
5. The criteria used by the school system in placing children in special programs and their parental rights
6. How parents can build positive self-esteem and self-discipline in their children via a home study program, so that their children will be empowered to maintain a positive self-image in this race-conscious society
7. How to communicate more effectively with their children and to be critical without affecting their child's self-esteem
8. The impact of peer pressure and how it can be monitored

In this preencounter stage therapy for immigrant children would be both educational and psychological, since they ought to be taught:

1. To understand the sociocultural differences between their native country and the United States (educational)
2. To cope with peer taunts about their accents, mode of dressing, foods, family, and so forth (psychological)
3. To communicate more effectively with their families (educational and psychological)
4. To acquire social skills and assertiveness skills needed to survive (psychological)

5. To improve study skills and to understand cultural differences in test taking, school structure, school expectations, and language factors (educational)
6. To cope with the emotional stress and fears that accompany migration (psychological)
7. To understand the psychology of being an immigrant in American society (psychological)
8. To understand the concept of self-esteem, its relation to performance and success, and the sources, institutions, and images that affect self-esteem (educational and psychological)

The child who is in stage two, the transitional phase, realizes his or her lack of absolute acceptance by the white world and tries to identify with the culture of origin. This is the most difficult stage for both parents and children. They all have to acknowledge racism and discrimination. The main affect is one of frustration and anger, and behavior is generally militant. Interpersonal relations tend to become limited mainly to one's own cultural group. Therapy has to be both extensive and intensive, tapping many modalities (affective, interpersonal, educational, behavioral, cognitive, structural) and many systems (individual, family, extended family, church, and community).

The child who is in the final or transcendent stage of acculturation will probably not need psychological therapy as such (at least not for acculturation matters), because he or she will have become bicultural and will use experiences from both cultural groups to best fit his or her own circumstances.

Phase III. Psychological Treatment Process

The greater the cultural difference between therapist and client, the greater the challenge to maintaining the therapeutic relationship. These cultural differences can dominate the therapeutic relationship and affect therapeutic progress. With an immigrant family, a therapist's efforts to "cross over" may have to be greater than they would be for a family with values and customs similar to those of the therapist. Gopaul-McNicol (1993) found that a combination of Lazarus's (1976) broad-based, multimodal approach, Minuchin's (1974) structural approach, and Bowen's (1978) family dynamics approach is most helpful in addressing the psychological problems faced by immigrant families and in easing the "joining" or "crossing-over" process. As has been demonstrated above, the initial stages of therapy with immigrant families tend to be very educational, unless there is a crisis due to some traumatic incident. However, if the individual or family is familiar with the various social systems they need to know about and the problem persists, then a more psychological approach to treatment is needed.

Applying Multimodal Therapy with Immigrant Families

Multimodal assessment, with its multilayered approach, focuses on behaviors that are impeding the acculturation of immigrant families. The therapist observes and asks what makes an individual sad, frightened, angry, anxious, timid, and so on, in addition to observing what types of behaviors the individual displays when feeling these emotions. Generally, when maladaptive behaviors are present, behavior therapy will need to be implemented.

With respect to the affective domain, Domokos-Cheng Ham (1989a, b) discussed how the therapist can "join" with immigrant families in an empathic manner. Domokos-Cheng Ham discussed the interactive process of therapy, the diadic relationship between therapist and client, and the therapist's ability to convey emotional sensitivity. Gladstein (1983), Rogers (1975), and Aspy (1975) all emphasized the value of having the therapist listen for feelings. The important factor to note here is that, while the therapist may be affectively empathic, he or she must maintain "cognitive empathetic skills in perceiving, categorizing and making sense" of the client's feelings (Domokos-Cheng Ham 1989a, p. 38). The idea, then, is not merely to *feel* what the client is feeling, but to *comprehend* and *act on* what the client is feeling. Gopaul-McNicol (1993) recommended that affective therapy be introduced somewhere around the middle to end phase of the therapeutic process. However, if the need arises earlier, the therapist should assist the client in amplifying his or her feelings.

Exploring how thoughts influence emotions and behavior, the therapist may try to examine the client's belief systems. Ellis's (1974) rational emotive therapy (RET), which is a cognitive, behavioral, and affective approach to treatment, is quite relevant to immigrant families. The important thing to keep in mind is that, by using this cognitive approach to therapy, many of a client's irrational thoughts can be examined. Therefore, parents who simply expect their children to like cultural change merely because they did, or to do well because opportunities exist, or to acculturate with minimal difficulty can benefit from Ellis's rational emotive therapy.

Interpersonal relations is the area in which immigrant children experience the most difficulty in school (Gopaul-McNicol, 1993). Teaching alternative ways of coping with problem situations via role play, assertiveness training, and social-skills training should aid in addressing this problem. In addition, teaching children to cope with peer taunts and to understand the sociocultural differences between their native countries and the United States are some ways to improve their interpersonal relationships.

In order to improve self-esteem (a problem commonly seen in immigrant children), it can be helpful to explore how children perceive themselves and their body and self-image with questions such as "What do you dislike or like about yourself," and then observe how these images influence their moods, sensations, and behaviors. A child may persistently complain about unpleasant sensations, such as aches and pains. This may often be the child's way of communicating stress in dealing with the cultural transition.

What can be seen in examining the multimodal approach to therapy is that when dealing with behavior, affect, sensation, imagery, cognition, and interpersonal factors, the emphasis is essentially educational. The therapist offers guidance, displays caring, modifies faulty styles, corrects misconceptions, provides information, and delivers the support necessary for the client to attain his or her goals. In selecting which problems and which modality to address first, Lazarus (1976) recommends starting with the most obvious problem and using the most logical procedure.

Phase IV. Empowerment Treatment Process

The final stage of the treatment process is the empowering of the family via a multisystems approach. Boyd-Franklin (1989) examines the importance of intervening at various levels—individual, family, extended family, church, community, and social services. There is little doubt that this approach can be quite effective, because it provides a flexible set of guidelines for intervention with immigrants. It also recognizes the adage, "It takes a whole community to raise a child." Immigrant families are generally not aware of a number of systems that they can use (e.g., educational, legal, community), and empowering them to use all of the support systems available to them is crucial to the acculturation process. The use of these systems can be implemented at any stage in therapy, but families must be aware of all potential systems before therapy is terminated so that they can readily tap into them if the need arises.

Encouraging an individual to embrace the support of their extended family and friends in their communities in areas such as child care and education may help in preventing personal difficulties. The use of the church in therapy with immigrant families is also very relevant, because of the importance religion plays in the life of many migrant families. Boyd-Franklin (1989) recommended that therapists keep a file on these different services so they can mobilize them when necessary. This kind of tapping of available resources is sometimes the single most important interaction in facilitating the possibility of treatment.

In addition, the therapist needs to be knowledgeable about the legal system as it applies to immigration policies and to be familiar with at least one immigration attorney, because of the illegal immigration status of many immigrant families. Knowing about immigration laws is important in order to be sensitive to the family's fears surrounding their immigrant status.

In using the Multi-CMS approach to treating immigrant families, a therapist can explore a broad spectrum of techniques to address the needs of this population.

REFERENCES

Arredondo-Down, P. (1981). Personal loss and grief as a result of migration. *Personnel and Guidance Journal* 58:376–378.

Aspy, D. (1975). Empathy: let's get the hell on with it. *The Counseling Psychologist* 5:10–15.

Berry, J. W., Kim, U., Minde, T., and Mok, D. (1987). Comparative studies of acculturative stress. *International Migration Review* 21:491–511.

Bowen, M. (1978). *Family Therapy in Clinical Practice*. New York: Jason Aronson.

Boyd-Franklin, N. (1989). *Black Families in Therapy*. New York: Guilford.

Domokos-Cheng Ham, M. A. (1989a). Empathetic understanding: a skill for joining with immigrant families. *Journal of Strategic and Systemic Therapies* 8:36–40.

——— (1989b). Family therapy with immigrant families: constructing a bridge between different world views. *Journal of Strategic and Systemic Therapies* 8:1–13.

Ellis, A. (1974). *Humanistic Psychotherapy: The Rational Emotive Approach*. New York: McGraw-Hill.

Fabrega, H. (1969). Social psychiatric aspects of acculturation and migration. *Comprehensive Psychiatry* 10:314–326.

Gladstein, G. (1983). Understanding empathy: integrating counseling, developmental and social psychology perspective. *Journal of Counseling Psychology* 30:467–482.

Gopaul-McNicol, S. (1993). *Working with West Indian Families*. New York: Guilford.

Helms, J. (1985). Cultural identity in the treatment process. In *Handbook of Cross-Cultural Counseling and Therapy*, ed. P. Pedersen, pp. 36–48. Westport, CT: Greenwood Press.

Landau, J. (1981). Link therapy as a family therapy technique for transitional extended families. *Psychotherapeia* 7:382–390.

——— (1982). Therapy with families in cultural transition. In *Ethnicity and Family Therapy*, ed. M. McGoldrick, J. K. Pearce, and J. Giordano, pp. 123–133. New York: Guilford.

Lazarus, A. A. (1976). *Multimodal Behavior Therapy*. New York: Springer.

Lee. E. (1982). A social system approach to assessment and treatment for Chinese American families. In *Ethnicity and Family Therapy*, ed. M. McGoldrick, J. K. Pearce, and J. Giordano, pp. 123–133. New York: Guilford.

McGoldrick, M., Pearce, J. K., and Giordano, J. (1982). *Ethnicity and Family Therapy*. New York: Guilford.

Minuchin, S. (1974). *Families and Family Therapy*. Cambridge, MA: Harvard University Press.

Oberg, P. (1972). Model for culture shock. *The Personnel and Guidance Journal* 2:376–378.

Rimer, S. (1991). Between two worlds: Dominicans in New York. *New York Times*, September 16, p. B6-L.

Rogers, C. (1975). Empathetic: an unappreciated way of being. *The Counseling Psychologist* 5:2–10.

Sluzki, C. E. (1979). Migration and family conflict. *Family Process* 18:379–390.

Weidman, H. (1979). Falling-out: a diagnostic and treatment problem viewed from a transcultural perspective. *Social Science and Medicine* 13:95–112.

23

The Impact of Acculturation on the Adjustment of Immigrant Families

TANIA N. THOMAS-PRESSWOOD

INTRODUCTION

Migration is stressful. It demands emotional, social, cultural, educational, and economic adjustments. The migration of individuals and families, for temporary purposes or permanent resettlement, has occurred throughout history, and, like numerous countries in the world, the United States is largely a land of immigrants (Westermeyer 1989). Foreign immigration to the United States continues to outstrip every other country in the world; in fact, about 3,000,000 illegal aliens now reside in the U.S. (Westermeyer 1989). There have been numerous studies of the effect of migration on mental health, most of which pursued the idea that, due to the stress involved in migration, immigrant families are at risk for various psychiatric disorders and social maladjustment (Faris and Dunham 1960, Golding and Burnham 1990, Van Deusen 1982, Westermeyer 1989). The impact of stress on the individual is thought to be manifested in psychological disturbances such as depression and physical ailments such as cardiovascular disease (Cleary 1987). The type of stress considered to be an inherent aspect of the immigrant experience is often referred to as "acculturative stress." This chapter discusses the types of stressors typically experienced by immigrant families in the process of acculturation and in learning the customs of a new society.

Acculturation has been defined as the process by which the attitudes and/or behaviors of persons from one culture are modified as a result of contact with a different culture (Moyerman and Forman 1992). Acculturation is a multidimensional process whereby acculturating individuals may attain a bicultural or monocultural orientation (Berry 1986, Moyerman and Forman 1992). Acculturation is thought to encompass several phases. Berry (1986) described a three-phase course of acculturation: (1) contact—encounter of two groups of people; (2) conflict—a state of dissonance between giving up valued features of one's culture and accepting the values of the host culture; (3) adaptation—a variety of ways in which to reduce or stabilize conflict. In the adaptation phase, Berry (1986) identified four distinct varieties of acculturation: (1) assimilation—relinquishing cultural identity and moving into the larger society; (2) integration—the maintenance of cultural integrity as well as the movement to become an integral part of a larger societal framework; (3) rejection—self-imposed withdrawal from the larger society (when imposed by the larger society, it is segregation); and (4) deculturation—characterized by striking out against the larger society and by feelings of alienation, loss of identity, and stress. Mendoza and Martinez (1981) introduced a two-dimensional model of acculturation that includes a modalities dimension, with cognitive, affective, and behavioral components, and a types dimension, consisting of the following six levels: (1) cultural assimilation, (2) native cultural extinction, (3) cultural resistance—active or passive resistance to dominant cultural patterns as depicted by lack of assimilation, (4) cultural shift—substitution of one set of practices with alternate cultural characteristics as exhibited by simultaneous assimilation and extinction, (5) cultural incorporation—adaptation of patterns representative of both cultural groups as demonstrated by assimilation without extinction, and (6) cultural transmutation—alteration of certain elements of both cultures to create a third and unique subcultural entity (Kagan and Cohen 1990).

Oberg (1960) focused on the concept of "culture shock," which is precipitated by the anxiety that results from losing all familiar signs and symbols of social intercourse (Furnham and Bochner 1986). Perhaps a more accurate term for this phenomenon might be "migration readjustment experiences" (Westermeyer 1989). The concept of culture shock refers to the idea that entering a new culture is potentially a confusing and disorienting experience (Furnham and Bochner 1986). Five stages in the process of culture shock were presented by Oberg (1960): (1) the immigrant feels euphoria about the exciting new culture, (2) failure to succeed leads to extreme dissatisfaction with the host culture (this represents a period of psychological transition from back-home values to host-home values), (3) the immigrant begins to understand the host culture and feel more in touch with his/herself, (4) the host culture is viewed as offering both positive and negative alternatives, and (5) the immigrant returns home and experiences reverse culture shock. Researchers since Oberg have seen culture shock as a normal reaction, as part of the routine process of adaptation to cultural stress and the manifestation of a longing for a more predictable, stable, and understandable environment (Furnham and Bochner 1986). All these models emphasize the importance of a certain degree of cognitive restructuring in the process of culture shock. Indeed, Ramirez, and colleagues (1974) and Kagan and Cohen (1990) found that cognition plays a major role in defining acculturation levels. Moreover, a high external decision-making style predicts low adjustment, while a low external decision-making style predicts high adjustment (Kagan and Cohen 1990).

Changes on all levels are necessary in immigrant family life to facilitate acculturation. Berry and associates (1987) noted several types of changes that commonly occur: (1) physical changes—the person must cope with living in a new place, including such elements as increased population density, pollution, and a different climate; (2) biological changes—the individual encounters dietary differences and propensity to diseases (e.g., hay fever, allergies) (Westermeyer 1989); (3) cultural changes—political, economic, technical, linguistic, vocational/educational, religious, and social institutions become altered, or are exchanged for new ones; (4) social changes—the immigrant family must function within new social networks, both ingroup and outgroup; and (5) psychological and behavioral changes—alteration in mental health status resulting from cultural readjustment experiences almost always occurs in some form or other as individuals attempt to learn the ways of the new environment. Immigration and the process of adaptation to the host culture can be considered important life event changes (Salgado de Snyder 1987). These changes are accompanied by stress. Central Americans and other immigrants in the United States experience the stressful effects of exposure to an unfamiliar and sometimes hostile environment. Moreover, stressors associated with the experience of dislocation through migration include lack of language skills, lack of familiarity with cultural norms and values, and lack of information about social systems in the host country (Cervantes et al. 1989).

Stress is generally conceptualized as an altered state of an organism produced by agents in the psychological, social, cultural, and/or physical environment (Salgado de Snyder 1987). It is the result of the simultaneous confluence of environmental demands and inadequate resources for adaptation (Dressler 1991). Acculturative stressors include behaviors and experiences that are generated during acculturation and that can be mildly pathological and disruptive to the immigrant and his or her family (e.g., depression, feelings of marginality, substance abuse, anxiety, psychosomatic symptomatology, adjustment disorders, deviant behaviors) (Berry 1986). In other words, acculturation stress refers to the pain and suffering that accompany one's adaptation to a new environment. The greater the dissimilarity with the host culture, the greater the acculturative stress in the immigrant (Berry 1986).

The life-events literature has demonstrated that numerous stressors operating simultaneously or in sequence have greater impact than stressors that occur separately because the behavioral and adaptive capabilities of an organism tend to drop dramatically when confronted with such an overload (Canino et al. 1980). Some studies (Padilla et al. 1985) have indicated that individuals who migrate after the age of 14 experience higher levels of stress than those who migrate before that age (Salgado de Snyder 1987). Among late immigrants (after age 14), the combination of self-imposed pressure to succeed in the new country and a lack of communication and other skills provides a high-risk situation for the development of psychosocial conflicts (Salgado de Snyder 1987). Five stressors that impact on the immigrant families' effort to acculturate and learn the new culture are language, employment and economic status, education, family life, and sociopolitical and immigration status.

LANGUAGE

The lack of language skills has often emerged as a major stressor for immigrants. Padilla and colleagues (1988) found that a language barrier can present a difficult obstacle to overcome for several reasons. First, many immigrant adults have little formal education and are intimidated by formal methods for learning English. Second, immigrants tend to have few financial resources with which to sustain themselves and their families and no alternative but to find employment quickly, leaving no time to acquire English skills (Padilla et al. 1988). However, with greater English-language proficiency come increased opportunities, economic enhancement, and associated feelings (i.e., self-esteem) about one's ability to function in society (Padilla et al. 1988). The acquisition of a limited number of everyday expressions and the ability to shop and travel can take months (Westermeyer 1989). Middle-aged immigrants may never reach social fluency, but can usually attain adequate language for work and ordinary social functions (Westermeyer 1989). Elderly immigrants often do not reach a level adequate even for self-sufficiency using a new language (Westermeyer 1989). Children and adolescents generally master the English language faster than their parents, and often become translators for their parents. When made to be dependent on their children to communicate their needs, parents develop feelings of inadequacy and children are placed in a difficult role. Often, many immigrants who feel alienated from the mainstream because of limited English proficiency find comfort in remaining in the immigrant communities or enclaves where they can function in their native language, at the expense of a second language.

Children confront other difficulties stemming from the natural processes involved in second-language acquisition. They must face having to learn a second language while being expected to function academically at grade level. The research on second-language acquisition indicates that it takes approximately five to seven years to acquire language skills that can support academic learning (Cummins 1982, 1984). Learning a new language may interfere with a child's academic progress. According to Esquivel and Keitel (1990), problems may stem in part from fears of needing to speak standard English in a group situation; in addition, anxiety, limited exposure and opportunities to use English, lack of literacy skills in the native language, and community and parental attitudes toward learning a second language may play a role (Hamayan and Damico 1991). These problems are reflected by the high incidence of "elective mutism" among bilingual children (Esquivel and Keitel 1990).

Multiple factors influence the process of second-language acquisition: (1) cognitive factors, (2) attitudinal and motivational factors, (3) personality factors, (4) native language proficiency, (5) home characteristics—such as literacy and attitudes, (6) community characteristics, and (7) curricular factors (Hamayan and Damico 1991). These factors interact to affect academic achievement. Many public schools have special academic programs to address the language needs of bilingual children (i.e., English as a Second Language and bilingual classes). Nevertheless, Cummins (1982) noted that often these children achieve at comparably lower levels than do their monolingual peers, particularly in the areas of reading and language arts. Similarly, immigrant children from the English-speaking Caribbean Islands who speak English-Creole or West Indian Creole also experience difficulty adjusting to the American pattern of speech and vocabulary (Thomas 1992).

EMPLOYMENT AND ECONOMIC STATUS

The U.S. Immigration and Naturalization Services indicated in their Statistical Yearbook (1982–1987) that the majority of those who migrate to the United States are from lower socioeconomic levels and are usually unskilled workers. Consequently, immigrant adults must settle for menial, low-paying jobs due to limited education, lack of English skills, illegal immigration status, or professional training not recognized by the U.S. (e.g., medical doctors, lawyers, teachers). It is not uncommon to find immigrants trained as medical doctors in their countries of origin working as nurse's aides or driving taxis because they are unable to pass the "boards" due to lack of English language proficiency or U.S. requirements that may demand further college preparation.

Since 1960, migration from the West Indies to the United States has been dominated by females. The types of jobs available—for example, jobs as domestics, nurse's aides, and health aides—are female-dominated occupations (Gopaul-McNicol 1993). However, in some countries males still migrate more often than women. In the decade of 1970–1980, 44.3 percent of those who migrated from Mexico between the ages of 20 and 29 were women, with a mean of 6.9 years of education (Portes and Bach 1985, Tienda et al. 1984). It is common for immigrant parents to obtain several jobs in order to support their family—a practice that tends to have a negative effect on family life and the parents' availability to their children.

In some Central American communities, several families may pool their financial resources to buy a house that they subdivide into several apartments with very little privacy, and later rent to completely unknown people. The renters tend to be males who immigrated without their families. Obviously, financial gains are the basis for this decision; in some instances, however, this practice has resulted in devastating experiences for children and families (e.g., sexual abuse of children by strangers, statutory rape, conflicts between families).

The social network of the immigrant can help secure contacts important to obtaining employment. Padilla and colleagues (1988) found that employment was frequently secured through contacts that a person was able to make because of family acquaintances in the United States. It appeared that the immigrant's network is the single most important factor in assisting the transition to a new way of life for recent Latin American arrivals (Padilla et al. 1988). Vocational training and counseling are generally required to help immigrant adults obtain adequate employment and financial security. However, since these types of services are rarely available, many immigrants obtain employment in factories that overwork them, pay them low wages, and provide little or no health insurance.

EDUCATION

Limited education creates great impediments to the accessibility of good paying jobs for immigrant adults, which then impacts on the economic status of the family. According to O'Hare and colleagues (1991), although the socioeconomic status of most ethnic groups has improved over the past several decades, there is still a significant gap between these groups and whites. Socioeconomic status has an effect on the goods, services, opportunities, and power available to individuals from immigrant groups (Aponte and Crouch 1995).

Illiteracy may further complicate one's ability to function adequately in the host culture. In many countries, only the very privileged are formally educated. Gopaul-McNicol (1993) noted that, because of the limited resources in most West Indian countries, high schools can accommodate only a minority of students. For example, in Jamaica, only 25 percent of potential students obtain a free high school education (Gopaul-McNicol 1993). For the other islands, the percentages range from 30 percent to 40 percent, except for small islands where all students receive a free high school education due to their small population (Gopaul-McNicol 1993). It must be noted that the remaining 60 percent or so of students in the West Indian Islands attend schools where the focus is on vocational skills training (Gopaul-McNicol 1993). A number of immigrants from countries like the Dominican Republic and El Salvador formerly lived in rural areas where schools are miles away from their homes, and in some cases they simply did not attend school because they had to help their families financially or domestically. Hispanics are the least likely of all immigrant groups to have a high school education (O'Hare 1992).

The states with the fastest growing immigrant populations include California, New York, Texas, Florida, Illinois, New Jersey, and Pennsylvania (Goodstein 1990). Immigrants to these states often settle in the most densely populated and poorest areas of the community while their children are enrolled in already overcrowded and underserved schools (Goodstein 1990). Once in school, the adjustment can be overwhelming for immigrant children; they must contend with a cultural clash between the norms of their country and the expectations in the U.S. Many of them have minimal, if any, education in their native language, much less English. Most come from homogeneous nations and are unaccustomed to the racial and ethnic diversity of the U.S. (Goodstein 1990). Academic stress is usually related to a discrepancy between the child's cultural values and those encouraged in the U.S. school system (Esquivel and Keitel 1990), and to difficulties associated with second-language acquisition processes.

FAMILY LIFE

A typical reaction for most immigrants is the disorganization they experience as a result of the differences between native and new ways of life (Adler 1987, Ramos 1980, Regis 1988). In Latin America and the West Indies, families are usually extended families. Aunts, uncles, grandparents, godparents or *comadres* or *compadres* (*comadre* is a godmother while *compadre* is a godfather, or these could be close family friends in Latin families) are all actively involved in raising each other's children and sharing resources at times. When a family migrates, they often must learn to function as a nuclear family, which is a new phenomenon involving a great degree of adjustment (e.g., baby-sitting arrangements must be made, daily meals must be prepared, children must assume more or new responsibilities). The family must now function as an independent unit with little support from extended family members.

Family life is generally affected by parents' unavailability to their children as a consequence of working long hours or several jobs. Parents are unable to attend school conferences or help with homework, or to provide emotional support for the acculturating child. In many instances mothers or fathers migrate first, leaving their children under the care of relatives (Thomas 1992). The children are usually separated from the parents for several years, during which time they may become attached to the relative assuming the role of parent and caregiver while the true parents may have missed important developmental milestones (Thomas 1992). When children are reunited with the parents, conflicts often result around family relationships, communication, and discipline of the children (Sewel-Coker et al. 1985).

Intergenerational conflicts often emerge when children acculturate at a faster rate than their parents (Esquivel and Keitel 1990, Sue and Chin 1983). When this occurs, the parent–child relationship usually changes. As a result of the Western influence, children become more vocal, express their opinions more freely, and are more independent, like their U.S. counterparts (Yao 1985). According to Yao, the quality of the parent–child relationship could also decline because immigrant children can adapt to an English-speaking environment much faster than their parents, creating a communication gap. The bilingual proficiency of parents and children differs because their primary language may not be the same (Yao 1985). Subsequently, poor communication between parents and their children frequently leads to learning and behavioral problems in schools (Yao 1985). Immigrant children often receive messages that are at odds with their parents' expectations (Goodstein 1990). For example, in American schools children are expected to speak up and participate in class, while at home this is unacceptable. In school, individual work is commended—it is often considered cheating to help another student. At home, children are expected to cooperate with their brothers and sisters. Parents tell their children that the teacher is the most important person next to the priest and nun; in school they find out otherwise (Goodstein 1990). The immigrant child may not be allowed to socialize with the mainstream child because the immigrant parent fears the child may adopt the values and behaviors of his or her mainstream counterpart, losing an appreciation for his or her cultural roots and values.

In some immigrant communities great emphasis is placed on achievement. Children are expected to excel academically. There is little tolerance for failure or grades that do not reflect excellence. Some parents emphasize achievement and neglect building a nurturing relationship with their children. The overwhelming pressure to succeed and the child's perception that he or she cannot be less than perfect have led to highly dysfunctional behaviors in immigrant children (e.g., depression, suicide attempts, acting-out behaviors, running away). Many immigrant parents view what it means to be a parent as culturally different from the mainstream culture. Many feel that a good parent is one who provides shelter, food, clothes, and educational opportunities to his or her children. Very little emphasis is placed on building communication skills and understanding the child's emotional and social needs.

Discipline and other parenting skills generally must change after immigration. In the West Indies and Latin American countries, for instance, corporal punishment is often used as a means of disciplining children. Parents soon learn that this is not an acceptable form of punishment in the United States and that there are laws condemning these practices. Parents with few parenting skills tend to feel that their power as parents to discipline their children has been usurped.

Marital relationships also change and in some instances these changes can be disturbing to the marriage. Men may be unable to find employment, and former homemakers may have to enter the workplace (Westermeyer 1989), assuming the role as the breadwinner of the family. Husbands tend to become resentful of their wives' apparent new independence, viewing it as a challenge to their patriarchal authority (Espin 1987). Thus, culturally based conflicts may develop when newly encountered patterns of gender roles combine with greater access to paid employment for women and new economic, social, and emotional options, creating an imbalance in the traditional power structure of the family (Espin 1987, Torres-Matrullo 1980). Even though the pace of acculturation tends to be slower for females in all other aspects, they tend to acculturate faster than males when it comes to gender roles (Ginorio 1979).

SOCIOPOLITICAL AND IMMIGRATION STATUS

The status of the illegal entrant entails additional stresses created by the fear of being apprehended by immigration authorities and being returned to politically dangerous circumstances in the country of origin (Cervantes et al. 1989). Certainly, under the status of illegal alien, it is more difficult to obtain employment, and hence, even more difficult to provide for a family. Illegal aliens often have to work under deplorable conditions (e.g., long working hours, little pay, and no protection under labor laws or from unions) in order to survive.

Although in recent years the political climate in many Latin American countries has been relatively stable, the political turmoil of the '70s and '80s in countries such as El Salvador, Guatemala, Nicaragua, Argentina, Panama, and Chile resulted in extreme violence, including kidnappings, disappearances, shootings, and torture (Cervantes et al. 1989). Many immigrants from these regions enter the U.S. as refugees. Central Americans fleeing political unrest do not hold legal immigrant status in this country because they are not covered by the Refugee Act of 1980 (Arredondo et al. 1989). The United States has refused to give Central Americans legal immigration status, instead considering them economic refugees (Arredondo et al. 1989). Refugees experience even more stress than other immigrants. First, they are not voluntary immigrants. They have been forced to leave their country, possessions, and loved ones, and are thus both physically and psychologically displaced (Cervantes et al. 1989). Second, refugees have experienced varying kinds and degrees of psychological trauma due to prolonged exposure to violence and war (Cervantes et al. 1989). Researchers have reported a relationship between refugee status and increased psychiatric disturbances such as posttraumatic stress disorder, severe depression, conversion and dissociative disorders, reactive psychosis, paranoid psychosis, and even organic brain disorder (Lin 1986).

Race also affects the process of acculturation and adaptation for immigrants. Light-skinned immigrants usually encounter a more favorable reception in the United States than the dark-skinned (Espin 1987). Espin pointed out that, when an immigrant comes from a country where he or she belongs to the racial majority or where, as in Latin countries, racial mixtures are the norm, the experience of turning into a minority in the United States and losing political power can be a disorienting experience. In a study conducted by Padilla and associates (1988), respondents indicated that part of the stress they experienced was related to discrimination against Latinos. For example, many indicated that U.S citizens treated them unfairly and had negative stereotypes of them.

Gopaul-McNicol (1993) noted that racial self-perception plays an important role in the overall adjustment of immigrants of color from the West Indies. Those who perceive themselves as black before they migrate tend to adjust more easily with respect to the European or American definition of "black." Those who perceive themselves as white (people of mixed descent— European and African—and East Indians) usually go through a period of denial when they are termed "black" by the European or American society (Gopaul-McNicol 1993). In many West Indian countries, light-skinned blacks have a higher status than dark-skinned blacks. However, when light skinned West Indian blacks migrate to the U.S., they are also subject to racial discrimination and prejudice.

Immigrants who have not become U.S. citizens through the process of naturalization have very little political power because they cannot vote. This certainly interferes with their ability to lobby for special services and resources for their communities.

SUMMARY

Acculturative stress is an inherent aspect of acculturation and adaptation to a new culture. A number of changes in the immigrant family are demanded in order to acculturate and adapt. These changes create stress. Stressors include learning a new language, having a limited education, difficulty obtaining adequate employment, low socioeconomic status, stressed family life, and changed sociopolitical and immigration status. While acculturative stress is common and expected, it does not have to be negative or devastating. The recognition of these stressors and subsequent education of the immigrant would help ameliorate negative effects and provide the immigrant family with more efficient coping skills. Via workshops, educational programs, counseling services, vocational counseling, and training directly aimed at the immigrant family and delivered in nonthreatening settings (e.g., school, education centers), mental health workers, school counselors, and teachers can educate these families regarding the stressors involved in acculturation.

REFERENCES

Adler, S. (1987). Maslow's need hierarchy and the adjustment of immigrants. International Migration Review, 11: 444–451.

Aponte, J. F., and Crouch, R. T. (1995). The changing ethnic profile of the United States. In *Psychological Interventions and Cultural Diversity*, ed. J. F. Aponte, R. Y. Rivers, and J. Wohl, pp. 1–18. Boston: Allyn & Bacon.

Arredondo, P., Orjuela, E., and Moore, L. (1989). Family therapy with Central

American war refugee families. *Journal of Strategic and Systemic Therapies* 8:28–35.

Berry, J. W. (1986). The acculturation process and refugee behavior. In *Refugee Mental Health in Resettlement Countries,* ed. C. L. Williams and J. Westermeyer, pp. 25–37. Washington, DC: Hemisphere.

Berry, J. W., Kim, U., Minde, T., and Mok, D. (1987). Comparative studies of acculturative stress. *International Migratory Review* 21:491–511.

Canino, I. A., Earley, B. F., and Rogler L. H. (1980). *The Puerto Rican child in New York City: stress and mental health. Hospital and Community Psychiatry.* New York: Fordham University, Hispanic Research Center Monograph 4.

Cervantes, R. C., Salgado de Snyder, V. N., and Padilla, A. M. (1989). Posttraumatic stress in immigrants from Central America and Mexico. *Hospital and Community Psychiatry* 40:615–619.

Cleary, P. D. (1987). Gender differences in stress-related disorders. In *Gender and Stress,* ed. R. C. Barnett, L. Biener, and G. K. Baruch, pp. 39–72. New York: Free Press.

Cummins, J. (1982). Test achievement and bilingual students. *Focus* 1–7.

——— (1984). *Bilingualism and Special Education: Issues in Assessment and Pedagogy.* San Diego, CA: College-Hill.

Dressler, W. W. (1991). *Stress and Adaptation in the Context of Culture.* Albany, N.Y: State of New York Press.

Espin, O. M. (1987). Psychological impact of migration on Latinas. *Psychology of Women Quarterly* 11:489–503.

Esquivel, G., and Keitel, M. (1990). Counseling immigrant children in the schools. *Elementary School Guidance & Counseling* 24:213–221.

Faris, R. E. L., and Dunham, H. W. (1960). *Mental Disorders in Urban Areas.* New York: Hafner.

Furnham, A., and Bochner, S. (1986). *Culture Shock: Psychological Reactions to Unfamiliar Environments.* New York: Methuen.

Ginorio, A. (1979). A comparison of Puerto Ricans in New York with native Puerto Rican and Caucasian- and Black-Americans on two measures of acculturation: Gender role and racial identification. Doctoral dissertation, Fordham University. *Dissertation Abstracts International* 40:983B–984B.

Golding, J. M., & Burnham, A. (1990). Immigration, stress, and depressive symptoms in a Mexican-American community. *Journal of Nervous and Mental Disease* 178:161–171.

Goodstein, C. (1990). American societies: the new immigrants in the schools. *Crisis* 98:17.

Gopaul-McNicol, S. (1993). *Working with West Indian Families.* New York: Guilford.

Hamayan, E. V., and Damico, J. S. (1991). *Limiting Bias in the Assessment of Bilingual Students.* Austin, TX: ProEd.

Kagan, H., and Cohen, J. (1990). Cultural adjustment of international students. *American Psychological Society* 1:133–137.

Lin, K. (1986). Psychopathology and social disruption in refugees. In *Refugee Mental*

Health in Resettlement Countries, ed. C. L. Williams and J. Westermeyer, pp. 70–89. Washington, DC: Hemisphere.

Mendoza, R. H., and Martinez, J. L. (1981). The measurement of acculturation. In *Explorations in Chicano Psychology*, ed. A. Baron, Jr., pp. 50–60. New York: Praeger.

Moyerman, D. R., and Forman, B. D. (1992). Acculturation and adjustment: a meta-analytic study. *Hispanic Journal of Behavioral Sciences* 14:163–200.

Oberg, K. (1960). Cultural shock: adjustment to new cultural environments. *Practical Anthropology* 7:177–182.

O'Hare, W. P. (1992). America's minorities—The demographics of diversity. *Population Bulletin* 47:1–47.

O'Hare, W. P., Pollard, K. M., Mann, T. L., and Kent, K. M. (1991). African-Americans in the 1990s. *Population Bulletin* 46:1–40.

Padilla, M. A., Cervantes, R. C., Maldonado, M., and Garcia, R. E. (1988). Coping responses to psychosocial stressors among Mexican and Central American immigrants. *Journal of Community Psychology* 16:418–427.

Padilla, A. M., Wagatsuma, Y., and Lindholm, K. J. (1985). Acculturation and personality as predictors of stress in Japanese and Japanese-Americans. *The Journal of Social Psychology* 125:295–305.

Portes, A., and Bach, L. R. (1985). *Latin Journey: Cuban and Mexican Immigrants in the United States*. Berkeley: University of California Press.

Ramirez, M., Castaneda, A., and Harold, P. L. (1974). The relationship of acculturation to cognitive style among Mexican-Americans. *Journal of Cross Cultural Psychology* 9:424–433.

Ramos, R. (1980). A preliminary look at an alternative approach to the study of immigrants. In *Sourcebook on the New Immigration: Implications for the United States and the International Community*, ed. R. S. Bryce-Laporte, pp.12–35. New Brunswick, NJ: Transaction Book.

Regis, H. (1988). A theoretical framework for the study of the psychological sense of community of English-speaking Caribbean immigrants. *Journal of Black Psychology* 15:57–76.

Salgado de Snyder, V. N. (1987). Factors associated with acculturative stress and depressive symptomatology among married Mexican immigrant women. *Psychology of Women Quarterly* 11:475–488.

Sewel-Coker, B., Hamilton-Collins, J., and Fein, E. (1985). Social work practice with West Indian immigrants. *Social Casework: The Journal of Contemporary Social Work* November, 564–568.

Sue, S., and Chin, R. (1983). The mental health of Chinese-American children: stressors and resources. In *The Psychosocial Development of Minority Group Children*, ed. G. F. Powell, pp. 385–397. New York: Brunner/Mazel.

Thomas, T. N. (1992). Psychoeducational adjustment of English-speaking Caribbean and Central American immigrant children in the United States. *School Psychology Review* 21:566–576.

Tienda, M., Jensen, L., and Bach, R. L. (1984). Census-based qualitative analyses of female immigrants and their labor market characteristics: an international comparison. Immigration, gender and the process of occupational change in the United States, 1970–1980. *International Migration Review* 18:1021–1044.

Torres-Matrullo, C. (1980). Acculturation, sex-role values and mental health among Puerto Ricans in mainland United States. In *Acculturation: Theory, Models and Some New Findings*, ed. A. M. Padilla, pp. 120–132. Boulder, CO: Westview.

U.S. Department of Justice, Immigration, and Naturalization Services (1982–1987). *Statistical Yearbook.*

Van Deusen, J. M. (1982). Health/mental health studies of Indochinese refugees: a critical review. *Journal of Medical Anthropology* 6:231–252.

Westermeyer, J. (1989). *Mental Health for Refugees and Other Migrants.* Springfield, IL: Charles C Thomas.

Yao, E. L. (1985). Adjustment needs of Asian immigrant children in the schools. *Elementary School Guidance and Counseling* 19:222–227.

24

Overcoming Cultural and Linguistic Bias in Diagnostic Evaluation and Psychological Assessment of Hispanic Patients

GIUSEPPE COSTANTINO AND
ROBERT G. MALGADY

INTRODUCTION

In 1993 an estimated 23 million Hispanics/Latinos were living in the United States, an increase of more than 50 percent between 1980 and 1990 (U.S. Bureau of Census 1994). This growth rate is more than seven times that of any other ethnic population and is attributed to high birth rates, young age distribution, and high numbers of immigrants. These figures do not include the Spanish-speaking population missed by the 1990 census (U.S. Bureau of

The research reported in this chapter was supported by the National Institute of Mental Health Grants ROI-MH33711, ROI-MH30569, and ROI-MH45939 to the Hispanic Research Center, Fordham University.

the Census 1991), undocumented Hispanic/Latino immigrants (Warren 1994), and the population of the Commonwealth of Puerto Rico.

Warren (1994) estimates that there were 2.4 million undocumented immigrants from Latin America as of October 1992, principally from Mexico (1.3 million), but including a substantial number of other Latin American countries heavily represented in the New York area. The U.S. Bureau of the Census (1991) estimates that 5 percent of the Hispanic population nationally was missed in the 1990 census, over twice the level for the general population (2.1 percent). However, estimates for major cities like New York are much higher, due in part to concentrations of young Hispanic populations and because the level of differential undercount by race and Hispanic origin is high and actually has grown in recent decades (New York City Department of City Planning 1988, U.S. Bureau of the Census 1988). Considering these estimates, the number of Hispanics/Latinos living in the U.S. may well be over 30 million. The annual growth rate of the Hispanic/Latino community has been estimated at 4.8 percent compared with the 1.8 percent for blacks and .06 percent for whites (U.S. Bureau of the Census 1990).

The 1990 Decennial Census and the annual Current Population Surveys for the post-1990 period indicate that the Hispanic population is markedly diverse in national origin and becoming increasingly more diverse over time. The most important change in the composition of the Hispanic population in the past twenty years has been in the influx of "other Hispanics," primarily immigrants from the Dominican Republic, Central and South America (U.S. Bureau of the Census 1994), the fastest growing segments of the Hispanic population in the U.S. Diversity means much more than differentiation by birthplace. The socioeconomic level of individual Hispanic groups varies dramatically, although all Hispanic subgroups are at levels lower than those of the non-Hispanic white population. For instance, data from the 1993 Current Population Survey indicate that 84 percent of non-Hispanic white persons nationally have graduated from high school compared to 46 percent of Mexicans, 60 percent of Puerto Ricans, 62 percent of Cubans, and 63 percent of Central/South Americans (U.S. Bureau of the Census 1994). Median incomes for Mexicans, Puerto Ricans, Cubans, and Central/South Americans were 69, 57, 78 and 68 percent that of non-Hispanic white households ($33,400), respectively.

Hispanics in New York City

The 1990 census counted 1,783,511 Hispanics in New York City, more Hispanics than in any other city in the U.S., representing 24.4 percent of the city's recorded total population (New York City Department of City Planning 1992). In New York City the Hispanic population has increased by 27 percent over the past decade. Puerto Ricans increased by 4 percent, while non-Puerto Rican Hispanics increased by 63 percent. In 1992, however, Puerto Ricans still constituted half of all Hispanics in the City (Salvo et al. 1994). The New York region is a major U.S. settlement area for Puerto Ricans, Dominicans, and South Americans. One out of every two Puerto Ricans on the U.S. mainland resided in the New York region in 1990, which was also home to 78 percent of all Dominicans in the nation, 62 percent of Ecuadorians, and 43 percent of Colombians. This pattern of Hispanic settlement has led to a major diversification of the Hispanic population in the region over the past two decades. New York City alone receives 45 percent of all Dominicans who enter the nation, half of all Ecuadorians, and 40 percent of all Colombians (Salvo and Ortiz 1992).

According to Salvo and Ortiz, the population of Dominicans in New York City increased by 165 percent in the last decade, from 125,000 to 333,000. The Dominican population of New York City is currently conservatively estimated to be in excess of 400,000 persons, the largest number outside of the Dominican Republic and the largest non-Puerto Rican Hispanic component in the region. In absolute size, two other major components of the newest Hispanic communities in the New York region are Colombians and Ecuadorians, numbering 161,000 and 119,000, respectively. Between 1980 and 1990 these populations in New York City have increased by 87 percent for Colombians and 95 percent for Ecuadorians. There has also been a significant increase in the number of Mexicans. In 1990 the Mexican population in New York City numbered some 62,000 persons, an increase of 173 percent from 1980.

The 1990 Census Data for New York City show that Puerto Ricans and Dominicans have generally lower socioeconomic status (SES), while the Colombians and Ecuadorians have generally higher SES. In 1989 there were 156,000 Hispanic households in New York City receiving some form of public assistance. Hispanics accounted for a greater percentage of all public assistance households in 1989 than they did ten years earlier; 42 percent of all households with public assistance income were Hispanic in 1989, compared to 34 percent in 1979. Homelessness is another indicator of socioeconomic distress among Hispanics, who made up 30 percent of the persons in emergency shelters for the homeless, and 35 percent of persons designated as homeless visible in street locations (U.S. Bureau of the Census 1991).

Hispanics and Mental Health

The disadvantaged socioeconomic position of Hispanics has serious implications for their mental health since an inverse relationship between SES and mental illness has been established in several early studies (Rogler et al. 1989) and recently reconfirmed (Kessler et al. 1994). More direct evidence is provided by recent population estimates that project higher levels of serious mental illness for Hispanics than for other population groups. For example, it has been estimated that the prevalence of schizophrenic disorders among Hispanics will grow by 27 percent during this decade compared to projected increases of 1.42 percent among whites and 12 percent among blacks (Kramer 1990). Puerto Ricans appear to be at particularly high risk of certain psychological disorders (e.g., depression) even in comparison to other Hispanic groups (Moscicki et al. 1987). The recent report of lifetime and twelve-month prevalence of selected *DSM-III-R* (1985) disorders from the National Comorbidity Survey (NCS) (Kessler et al. 1994) has revealed unexpectedly high prevalence rates of disorder and comorbidity, particularly with regard to major depression and alcohol dependence. Kessler and associates reported that Hispanics have a significantly higher prevalence of affective disorders (i.e., major depression, manic episode, dysthymia, and other affective disorders) and a higher prevalence of active comorbidity compared to non-Hispanic whites and blacks. The problem is compounded by the fact that the "safety net" for Hispanics in times of crisis is insufficient to support their mental health care needs. For example, national data from the Survey of Income and Program Participation for the fourth quarter of 1990 indicated that 28 percent of all Hispanics nationally had no health insurance coverage, a figure well above the average for whites and blacks (Short 1992). When the criterion for coverage was calculated as continuous coverage for a twenty-eight-month period, 46 percent of Hispanics were uninsured.

Migration from Latin America has been deploying large numbers of Hispanic immigrants, mostly Spanish monolingual or limited-English proficient (LEP), into major urban areas in the United States (Rogler 1994). Coupled with the already substantial numbers of resident Hispanics, most of whom are Spanish-dominant (U.S. Bureau of the Census 1991), members of this growing population must cope not only with stressors associated with lower socioeconomic status, but also stress associated with the language and cultural demands of the host American society. When limited-English proficient, unacculturated Hispanics turn to organizations delivering mental health services, they often face a common problem of language and cultural distance from mental health service providers because of the severe shortage of bilingual/bicultural clinicians in the mental health service system (Dana 1996,

Padilla et al. 1975, Rogler et al. 1989). During the last decade, Hispanics have faced the problem of diminishing access to general health care (Rogler et al. 1989), thus becoming an increasingly underserved population. Hispanics, paradoxically, are at high risk of mental disorder, but are proportionally infrequent utilizers of mental health services (Rogler et al. 1989). Those who make initial contact with traditional services are likely to drop out from treatment prematurely. The mental health services literature indicates that the cultural distance between Hispanic clients and non-Hispanic service providers is an impediment to the utilization and effectiveness of mental health services.

Moreover, cultural conflicts emerge not only in the relationship between the Hispanic client and the nonculturally competent therapist, but also when the therapy modality is not culturally sensitive to the client's language and cultural and religious values and beliefs (Costantino et al. 1994). Gomez and colleagues (1985) have referred to Hispanic patients in the mental health services system as constituting a "linguo-cultural minority." In the Hispanic mental health literature, there has been considerable speculation and concern that biases in psychiatric diagnosis occur when Spanish-dominant Hispanic patients are interviewed in English by non-Hispanic mental health clinicians, even when a translator is utilized (e.g., Javier and Alpert 1986, Javier and Marcos 1989, Malgady et al. 1987, Marcos 1994, Vazquez and Javier 1991). Despite the importance of accurate psychiatric diagnosis in the delivery of mental health services, empirical research on this topic has been historically equivocal, while theoretical formulations have been limited (Malgady et al. 1992). Given the attention to the consideration of cultural and linguistic diversity in the formulation of diagnostic criteria in the *DSM-IV* (1994) (e.g., "ethnic and cultural considerations," and its glossary of "culture-bound syndromes"), there is a critical need to understand the diagnostic process in the light of such considerations. Moreover, our own recent research (from an NIMH-funded study of Puerto Ricans) indicates that the ethnic match between patient and diagnostician, level of patient's acculturation, and the language spoken during the diagnostic interview (English only, Spanish only, or bilingual) influence perceived symptom severity. In addition, interviewing Spanish-dominant patients in English, especially by an Anglo clinician, also tends to disturb diagnostic sensitivity and specificity. However, since previous research has been largely atheoretical, there has been no attempt to systematically model the dynamic interpersonal process by which language and ethnic matching affect the behavior and communication of patients during the psychiatric interview, and how these in turn affect the diagnostic impression of mental health clinicians. Much like the psychotherapeutic treatment literature on racial and ethnic matching of patient and therapist, it is not clear whether language and ethnic matching has a direct or "proximal" effect on diagnostic outcomes or whether the effect is "distal" or mediated by interpersonal process variables emergent during the patient–clinician interaction (Sue and Zane 1987).

These problems are compounded by Hispanics' underutilization of mental health facilities and high dropout rate after initial contact with service providers (Rodriguez 1987, Sue and Zane 1987). The high rate of comorbidity among Hispanics poses a further impediment to the provision of effective mental health services (Kessler et al. 1994). A variety of sociocultural factors have been implicated as responsible for the underutilization of traditional mental health services, among them, cultural distance between patient and clinician (Rogler et al. 1989). Consequently, critics of mental health policy assert that clinical services must be responsive to the Hispanic client's culture (Cohen 1972, Rosado 1980). Thus it is important to understand the influence of cultural diversity on the process of diagnostic decision making, given the increased attention accorded to culture in the *DSM-IV*.

CULTURAL AND LINGUISTIC BIAS IN PSYCHIATRIC DIAGNOSIS OF HISPANICS

Rogler and colleagues (1983, 1989) present a framework for research on mental health services with Hispanics. The most central phase of this proposed framework is the psychodiagnosis and evaluation of Hispanics' mental health status. The reason for such emphasis is vividly apparent, because the diagnosis rendered should clarify the nature and extent of psychological distress that initially gives rise to help-seeking behavior and should also structure the path of psychotherapeutic treatment and subsequent follow-up efforts to facilitate readjustment within the community setting.

Psychologically distressed individuals' early contacts with a mental health agency are likely to be diagnostic in nature whether the assessment performed is formal or informal, brief or intensive. The procedure might include a mental status examination, psychological tests, a neurological screening, and a social history to place test and interview data in proper context. At the end of this process, an admitting or provisional diagnosis may be formulated, a disposition for a specific therapy modality may be rendered, and an individual treatment plan (ITP) may be developed according to the problems, needs, and strengths of the client.

The question of whether the instruments used in assessment and even the interview process itself are culturally biased against ethnic minorities has been widely debated, but the presence of differences between ethnic groups attributable to the psychological assessment process is indisputable. Psychiatric epidemiological studies have revealed that the incidence of psychotic diagnoses among ethnic minority populations was substantially higher compared to nonminority populations, and particularly so for Hispanics (Gross et al. 1969). According to their survey (1989), ethnic minority patients were more likely to be diagnosed as schizophrenic and treated in a psychiatric emergency room than were nonminority patients, who in turn tended to be more often classified as neurotic and subsequently referred for outpatient psychiatric services. Similar trends toward increased prevalence rates of psychological disorder have been reported in epidemiological surveys of black and Hispanic patients, as contrasted with white patients, at large community mental health centers and psychiatric hospitals (e.g., Baskin et al. 1981). Still other differences have been reported in varying comparisons between members of Hispanic and other ethnic groups. To name but a few, Durrett and Kim (1973) found that Mexican-American preschool children were less behaviorally mature than their Anglo-American peers. Haberman's (1976) field studies have indicated that Puerto Ricans consistently reported more psychiatric symptoms than other groups. Kagan and Romero (1977) found that assertive behavior was more prominent among Anglo-American than Mexican-American children.

One interpretation of such alarming cross-ethnic comparisons is that something other than the qualities that psychological assessment is designed to assess is being revealed. The evaluation of Hispanic patients' psychopathology may be tainted by bias within the majority culture's mental health service system. Such bias may intrude on clinical judgment and decision making when nonminority clinicians use standardized psychological tests that lack sensitivity to the cultural values of behavioral norms and the linguistic variability of Hispanic people (e.g., Malgady et al. 1987).

Interview Language and Individual Differences

Research suggests that the misdiagnosis of bilingual Hispanic patients may stem from the language and behavior used to express distress during a psychiatric interview (Gomez et al. 1985, Marcos et al. 1973, Price and Cuellar 1981). Language and behavior influence the bilingual patient's ability to express thoughts, feelings, and emotions, and the diagnostician's interpretation of the patient's verbal and nonverbal responses. Unbiased assessment of a patient's orientation, presenting symptoms, judgment, and other mental functions requires accurate communication; hence biases may intrude into the diagnostic process to the extent that the interview language promotes misinterpretations of the patient's verbal and nonverbal responses to diagnostic inquiry.

Previous research with Hispanics has examined the impact of language spoken during psychiatric interviews on judgments of severity of pathology. However, the findings were equivocal regarding which language—English or Spanish—spoken by Spanish-dominant patients leads to clinical judgments of greater or lesser pathology. In a case study report, Del Castillo (1970) described several clinical episodes in which Spanish-speaking patients appeared overtly psychotic during a Spanish interview, but much less so when interviewed in English. Del Castillo speculated that when the patients were interviewed in English, their nondominant language, they exerted more effort to communicate, which produced greater vigilance and control over their emotions. On the other hand, Marcos (1976, Marcos et al. 1973) reported findings opposite to those of Del Castillo: the symptomatology of Spanish-dominant schizophrenics was rated as more severe when they were interviewed in English. Although Marcos conducted a more controlled study than Del Castillo's, a critical problem was that interview language and ethnicity of the clinician were confounded: a non-Hispanic clinician evaluated the English interviews and a Hispanic clinician evaluated the Spanish interviews. In an attempt to eliminate such confounding, Price and Cuellar (1981) investigated the effect of interview language on symptom severity ratings, but held clinician ethnicity constant, using bilingual Hispanic clinicians to evaluate both the English and Spanish interviews. Their results contradicted Marcos's findings and supported Del Castillo's: symptoms were rated as more pathological in the Spanish interviews. In a related study Gonzalez (1978) did not find a direct effect of clinicians' ethnicity on judgments of severity of symptomatology, but Hispanic clinicians offered more pessimistic prognoses than Anglo clinicians.

Several studies have demonstrated that clinicians of diverse ethnicity render significantly different diagnoses to similar patients (Baskin et al. 1981). Lopez and Nunez (1987) have remarked that the *DSM-III* did not provide guidelines for taking cultural factors into consideration in formulating a diagnosis, and that practicing clinicians do not concur on what cultural factors are crucial in the diagnostic process (Lopez and Hernandez 1987). The *DSM-IV* now provides greater attention to culture than its predecessors; however, there is limited empirical and virtually no theoretical basis for understanding how to make a culturally sensitive diagnosis.

There is a paucity of research on this topic, which is not surprising since the major interest in the literature has been the effect of language, which is usually spoken by a bilingual Hispanic clinician and thus is naturally confounded with ethnicity. Thus there is a need to assess the independent and possible interactive effects of the language of the interview and the ethnicity of the clinician in the mental health evaluation process.

A Current Study of Language and Ethnic Matching

In order to assess the effects of language and culture and the psychiatric diagnoses of Puerto Rican and Dominican mental health patients, Malgady and colleagues 1992, Malgady and Costantino (in press) are conducting a project in a large community mental health center in the New York metropolitan area. This NIMH-funded study was designed to overcome the methodological limitations of previous studies on language and ethnic matching identified by Vazquez (1982). The first phase of the study was based on 156 in vivo, diagnostic interviews of adult Hispanics upon intake as administered routinely at two psychiatric hospitals in New York City. Patients were screened by a panel of expert psychiatric diagnosticians for three target disorders (schizophrenia, major depression, anxiety disorder), and further stratified by gender, place of birth, and level of acculturation. They were interviewed by a clinical psychologist or psychiatrist blinded to the target diagnosis. Matched groups of patients were randomly assigned to interview situations by either a Hispanic or non-Hispanic white clinician, either in Spanish only, English only, or bilingually. Clinicians indicated any Axis I and II *DSM-III-R* disorders, Axis V global assessment of functioning, assessment of symptom severity on the Brief Psychiatric Rating Scale, and recommended psychotherapeutic and/or pharmacological treatment plans. Patients were interviewed twice by independent clinicians within a 48-hour period in order to assess diagnostic concordance. Results indicated, first of all, that there were no differences in diagnostic accuracy, concordance, or rated symptom severity between clinical psychologists and psychiatrists. Hispanic psychiatrists and psychologists consistently rated symptoms as more severe than non-Hispanic white clinicians. Symptom severity was rated highest in bilingual interviews, followed by Spanish interviews, and least in English interviews. Diagnostic sensitivity, specificity, and concordance with the "expert" gold standard were best in bilingual interviews by a Hispanic clinician, followed by Spanish interviews by a Hispanic clinician. Overall, these effects were greatest on rated symptom severity and diagnostic sensitivity and concordance. Differences in specificity were weakest. Specificity was lower for depression and anxiety disorders than for schizophrenia. Treatment decisions varied largely as a function of the diagnosis. Diagnosis-appropriate medication was recommended for all disorders; psychotherapy, for anxiety disorders and, less often, depression.

PERSONALITY ASSESSMENT OF HISPANICS

A ubiquitous issue in psychological testing is the questionable practice of assessing ethnic, socioeconomic, or linguistic minorities with instruments conceived, standardized, and validated from a nonminority, middle SES English-speaking, Anglo-American perspective (e.g., Costantino and Malgady 1995). Historically, the majority of debate about this issue has focused primarily on intelligence-testing practices with black minority examinees. Here we will briefly revive the issue of test bias in relation to personality testing practices with Hispanic minority examinees.

The difficulties involved in testing a non-English-speaking client cannot be denied. When a Hispanic client who speaks little or no English is being assessed by an English-speaking clinician, an interpreter's services are often solicited—unfortunately, often from any available person, such as a family member or convenient bystander. Consequently, interpreter-related distortions may give rise to misconceptions about the patient's mental health status. These distortions are most frequently associated with defective linguistic or translation skills of the interpreter or the interpreter's self-imposed role and attitude toward either the patient or clinician (Marcos 1980). In a related article, Sabin (1975) discussed two case histories of Spanish-speaking clients who had been evaluated by English-speaking clinicians aided by interpreters. Sabin's intensive analysis of these case histories revealed that the patients' emotional problems were selectively underestimated and that their anxiety was inadequately translated to the clinicians.

Important as the issue of language is, it is surrounded by the more generic issue of biculturalism. Although some attempts have been aimed at developing personality tests specifically geared toward Hispanic cultures, these instruments unfortunately have not weathered critical psychometric scrutiny (e.g., Oakland 1977). Over two decades ago, Padilla and Ruiz (1973) maintained that psychometric research had yet to offer valid testing procedures (particularly projective techniques) for personality assessment of Hispanics. Scattered research and commercial efforts have emerged over the years, yielding reliable Spanish translations of paper-and-pencil tests of mental health constructs such as self-esteem (e.g., Fitt's Tennessee Self-Concept Scale, Alvarez and Barrientos 1969), depression (e.g., National Institute of Mental Health Center for Epidemiological Studies Depression Scale, Radloff 1977), and state-trait anxiety (e.g., Spielberger's State-Trait Anxiety Inventory, Villamil 1973). Although the parallel Spanish forms of these tests demonstrate acceptable correlations with their corresponding English forms when administered to bilingual examinees, independent evidence of criterion-related validity for Hispanics has not been established, nor has it been shown that the internal factor structure of such tests is invariant between forms. Moreover, these tests have been used primarily for research purposes but not as components of conventional psychodiagnostic test batteries in clinical settings.

Perhaps the most comprehensive self-report inventory widely used for clinical assessment is the Minnesota Multiphasic Personality Inventory (MMPI), which has spawned multilingual translations. The MMPI, of course, is not beyond reproach in the test bias literature that focuses on black-white comparisons, and there is a rift in opinion on whether separate norms are required as a function of ethnicity (cf. Gynther and Green 1980, Pritchard and Rosenblatt 1980). In reviewing the recent literature (1975–1985) on the MMPI as a function of ethnicity, Malgady and colleagues (1987) located thirty-seven articles in psychology journals, five pertaining to whether Hispanics differed from whites or blacks. One study concluded, on the basis of a sample of eleven Hispanics (Page and Bozlee 1982), that separate Hispanic MMPI norms are not called for, whereas the remaining studies, on the basis of substantially larger sample sizes, reported significant differences between Hispanics and other ethnic groups on selected MMPI scales (Fuller and Malony 1984, Holland 1979, McCreary and Padilla 1977, McGill 1980).

Such differences between Hispanics and the standardized white norm may be due to cultural bias in the MMPI. Because items are keyed to reflect psychopathology on an empirical basis, many items indicative of pathology from standardization on Anglo-American diagnostic groups may not necessarily be pathological, and may even be customary behaviors, feelings, and beliefs in different Hispanic subcultures (Padilla and Ruiz 1973). For example, in Puerto Rican culture, it is commonplace to practice *espiritismo*, or spiritualism, independent of religious affiliation (Rogler and Hollingshead 1985). This belief posits that we are surrounded by an invisible world of good and evil spirits who may penetrate this world to influence human lives (e.g., cause mental illness). Persons who have gained *facultades*, or psychic faculties, over the spirits are often sought out as folk healers to cure emotional problems. When certain MMPI items—for example, "Evil spirits possess me at times"—are viewed in the context of the spiritualistic aspects of Hispanic culture, certainly a pathological symptomatology cannot be indiscriminately inferred about the respondent.

Turning to more open-ended tasks, traditional projective tests such as the Thematic Apperception Test (TAT) and the Children's Apperception Test (CAT) have often characterized both Hispanics and blacks as less verbally fluent (and at times, more pathological) than nonminority examinees (e.g., Ames and August 1966, Booth 1960, Costantino and Malgady 1983, Costantino et al. 1981). Levine and Padilla (1980) listed a number of personality tests on which Hispanics' performance differed from that of other ethnic groups, concluding that projective tests tap personality factors as they vary with cultural and social milieu, and that cultural ideology and acculturation level may affect choices made on objective personality measures.

Quite apart from the usual psychometric reservations often voiced about projective techniques with nonminority examinees (e.g., Anastasi 1981), it is difficult to reconcile why such assessment practices prevail with ethnic and linguistic minorities when it is widely acknowledged that the validity of projective techniques is impugned by using them with inarticulate examinees (Anderson and Anderson 1955, Entwisle 1972). One exception, however, is a new ethnically pluralistic thematic apperception test entitled TEMAS (an acronym for "Tell-Me-A-Story," also meaning "themes" in Spanish). This test has been shown to enhance self-disclosure of Hispanic examinees in comparison to traditional projective tests and also has rudimentary evidence of reliability and criterion-related validity (Malgady et al. 1984). This test is widely used in clinical practice, with separate norms for Hispanics, blacks, and whites (Costantino et al. 1988).

On the basis of considerations such as these, it is not surprising that the use of conventional self-report personality inventories and projective tests for psychodiagnosis of Hispanics has prompted incisive indictments of minority testing practices (e.g., Olmedo 1981, Padilla 1979) and, even more broadly, of the mental health care system in this country (e.g., Rogler et al. 1983). It is heartening, however, that the American Psychological Association's *Standards for Educational and Psychological Testing* (1985) includes numerous recommendations for the development and revision, validation, and use of tests with diverse ethnic groups. In addition, a chapter is devoted to testing linguistic minorities.

Projective Testing with Minority Children

Traditionally, in clinicians' analyses of responses to projective personality tests, Hispanic and black children have been evaluated as being less verbally fluent, less behaviorally mature, and more psychopathological than their nonminority counterparts (Ames and August 1966, Durrett and Kim 1973). This is a particular problem because it has been widely acknowledged that the validity of projective techniques is impugned when administered to examinees who are verbally inarticulate (Anderson and Anderson 1955, Reuman et al. 1983).

In contrast, minority children are more articulate when tested with culturally sensitive instruments (Bailey and Green 1977, Costantino and Malgady 1983, Costantino et al. 1981, Thompson 1949).

Projective techniques, especially the Rorschach and the TAT, have been used to probe the cognitive, affective, and personality functioning of individuals from different cultural backgrounds. From early cross-cultural investigations using projective tests in the 1940s, it was observed that the TAT (Murray 1943) stimuli had limited relevance to individuals of different cultures; hence, culturally sensitive TAT stimuli were developed to study such groups as Mexican Indians, Ojibwa Indians, Southwest Africans, and South Pacific Micronesians (Henry 1955). However, such early efforts to provide a culture-specific and sensitive interpretive TAT framework have not been eagerly pursued by psychometricians (Dana 1986a,b).

More recently, the work of Monopoli (1984, cited in Dana 1986a) indicated that culture-specific stimuli were necessary for personality assessment of unacculturated Hopi and Zuni Indians, whereas the Murray TAT was deemed more useful with acculturated individuals. Avila-Espada (1986) found that, following the development of an objective scoring system and norms, the standard TAT seems to have only a modest clinical utility for personality assessment of European Spaniards. Dana (1993a) has argued that most personality tests are assumed to be genuinely etic or culturally general and universal in their assessment. Consequently, the use of an etic orientation in assessing multicultural groups has erroneously minimized cultural differences and hence has generated inappropriate inferences from an Anglo-American personality construct viewpoint. This has created unfavorable psychological test results and unfair clinical dispositions of culturally diverse individuals (Costantino 1992, 1993, Dana 1993b, Malgady 1990, 1996). Dana (1993b) further emphasizes that a correct etic orientation needs to be used to demonstrate multicultural construct validity. He evaluates the TEMAS test, which was "developed to salvage the Thematic Apperception Test . . . as a landmark event for multicultural assessment because it provides a picture-story test that has psychometric credibility" (p. 10). In the same vein, Ritzler (1993) writes that TEMAS "represents a milestone in personality assessment. It also represents the first time a thematic apperception assessment technique has been published in the United States with the initial expressed purpose of providing valid personality assessment of minority subjects" (p. 381). Ritzler (1995) writes that only the Rorschach Comprehensive System, the TEMAS test and the Early Memory Procedure "have established reliability and validity for multicultural assessment" (p. 116).

Development of TEMAS

Based on these considerations, the TEMAS test was developed as a multicultural thematic apperception test for use with Puerto Rican, other Hispanic, black, and white children. TEMAS is different from previous thematic apperception tests in a number of ways. The test was developed specifically for use with children and adolescents; it has two parallel sets of stimulus cards, one set for minorities and another for nonminorities; it has extensive normative data for both minorities and nonminorities; it has an objective scoring system of both thematic content and structure. The TEMAS pictures embody the following features: structured stimuli and diminished ambiguity to pull for specific personality functions; chromatically attractive, ethnically and racially relevant and contemporary stimuli to elicit diagnostically meaningful protocols; and representation of both negative and positive intrapersonal and interpersonal functions in the form of conflicts that require a solution (Costantino 1987, Costantino et al. 1988).

The principal rationale for the development of TEMAS was the acknowledged need for a psychometrically sound and multicultural thematic apperception test designed specifically for use with children and adolescents. It can be used normatively with children and adolescents aged 5 to 13 and used clinically with children and adolescents up to the age of 18.

The theory underlying TEMAS incorporates the dynamic-cognitive framework, which conceives of personality development as occurring within a sociocultural system. Within this system, individuals internalize the cultural values and beliefs of family and society (Bandura and Walters 1967). Personality functions are learned initially through modeling (Bandura 1977) and are then developed through verbal and imaginal processes (Paivio 1971, Piaget and Inhelder 1971). When a test's projective stimuli are similar to the circumstances in which the personality functions were originally learned, these functions are readily transferred to the testing situation and are projected into the thematic stories (Auld 1954). Moreover, personality is a structure comprising a constellation of motives that are learned and internalized dispositions and that interact with environmental stimuli to determine overt behavior in specific situations. Because these dispositions are not directly observable in clinical evaluation, projective techniques prove to be useful instruments in probing beneath the overt structure or "phenotype" of the personality, thereby arousing the latent motives imbedded in the personality "genotype." Hence it is assumed that projective tests assess relatively stable individual differences in underlying motives, which are exposed in narrative or storytelling. Atkinson (1981) emphasized that the analysis of narrative (thematic content) has a more solid theoretical foundation and is the most important and virtually untapped resource we have for "developing our understanding of the behavior of an animal distinguished by its unique competence in language and use of symbols" (p. 127).

The TEMAS Stimulus Cards

The settings, characters, and theme in the TEMAS stimulus cards were created by Costantino (1978), and the artwork was rendered by Phil Jacobs, an artist who worked closely with the author. Several hundred pictures were drawn before the twenty-three standardized pictures were selected.

There are two parallel versions of TEMAS pictures: the minority version consisting of pictures featuring predominantly Hispanic and African-American characters in an urban environment, and the nonminority version consisting of corresponding pictures showing predominantly white characters in an urban environment. The themes depicted in the two parallel sets of pictures were created to assess the same personality functions.

Both the minority and nonminority versions have a Short Form comprising nine picture-cards and a twenty-three-picture-card Long Form. Of the nine Short Form picture-cards, four are administered to both genders and five are gender-specific. Of the twenty-three Long Form picture-cards, twelve are for both genders, eleven are gender-specific, and one is age-specific. Furthermore, there are four picture-cards showing pluralistic characters, which can be used interchangeably for both the minority and nonminority versions.

The theme that we have discussed is that traditional psychological testing and psychiatric evaluations have been challenged with regard to their appropriateness for Hispanics and other linguistically and culturally diverse groups. Despite several decades of rhetoric and scattered research, there is some empirical consensus that cultural factors do indeed impact on the outcomes of standardized testing and psychiatric diagnosis. There is a need to develop culturally sensitive psychological tests for reliable and valid personality assessment and equally culturally sensitive psychiatric evaluations of culturally and linguistically diverse children, adolescents, and adults. To this end, the TEMAS test has not only contributed to the revival of the TAT technique in general, but constitutes a landmark event in the development of culturally sensitive and competent tests, because it provides a picture story test that has both emic and etic validity (e.g. Costantino and Malgady 1995, Dana 1996).

CONCLUSIONS

Hispanics are a rapidly growing, underinsured, and underserved population with increased mental health needs. Psychological assessment and psychiatric diagnosis are critical to the effective disposition of Hispanic and all other patients in the mental health system. Research and clinical practice have raised serious concerns about the accuracy of psychiatric diagnosis when patients are interviewed in their nondominant language by a clinician who lacks or has limited Spanish-language proficiency. Concerns have also been raised about the reliability and validity of standardized psychological tests and assessment techniques used to understand the underlying psychopathology and thus inform psychiatric diagnosis with culturally and linguistically diverse patients.

The literature on mental health services delivery is replete with references to the linguistic, socioeconomic, psychosocial, and geographic access barriers confronting Hispanic patients as well other linguistically and culturally different patients (Costantino and Malgady 1994, Rogler et al. 1987, 1989). Moreover, research has emphasized the cultural distance between Hispanic clients and non-Hispanic clinicians or clinicians lacking competence in Hispanic culture and Spanish language (Malgady et al. 1987, Rogler et al. 1987). Cultural dissonance emerges not only in the client–therapist relationship, but also when traditional therapy modalities clash with the cultural and religious values and beliefs of the Hispanic clients and all other culturally and linguistically different individuals. The need for a culturally competent mental health delivery system with culturally competent assessments and treatments becomes urgent in a managed care environment where speedy access and shortened treatment is the golden norm.

Urging the development of new valid instruments, Gallagher (1979) lamented "We often curse the quality of the tools we have. But we are trapped by them" (p. 997). The research literature has also emphasized the need to develop psychological tests for reliable and valid diagnosis and personality assessment of minority children (Padilla 1979) and to create culture-specific norms for projective tests (Dana 1986a, Exner and Weiner 1982).

REFERENCES

Alvarez, B., and Barrientos, G. (1969). *Escala Tennesee de autoconcepto* (The Tennessee Self-Concept Scale). Chihuahua, Mexico: Instituto Interamericano de Estudios Psicologicos Sociales.

Ames, L. B., and August, J. (1966). Rorschach responses of Negro and white 5 to 10-year olds. *Journal of Genetic Psychology* 10:291–309.

Anastasi, A. (1981). Diverse effects of training on tests of academic intelligence. In *Issues in Testing: Coaching, Disclosure, and Ethnic Bias*, pp. 5–20. San Francisco: Jossey-Bass.

Anderson, H., and Anderson, G. (1955). *An Introduction to Projective Techniques*. New York: Prentice-Hall.

Atkinson, H. W. (1981). Studying personality in the context of advanced motivational psychology. *American Psychologist* 36:117–128.

Auld, F. (1954). Contribution of behavior theory to projective testing. *Journal of Projective Techniques* 18:129–142.

Avila-Espada, A. (1986). *Manual operativo para el Test de Apercecion Tematica*. Madrid: Ediciones Piramide, S.A.

Bailey, B. E., and Green, J., III (1977). Black thematic apperception test stimulus material. *Journal of Personality Assessment* 4:25–30.

Bandura, A. (1977). *Social Learning Theory*. Englewood Cliffs, NJ: Prentice-Hall.

Bandura, A., and Walters (1967). *Social Learning and Personality Development*. New York: Holt, Rinehart & Winston.

Baskin, D., Bluestone, H., and Nelson, M. (1981). Ethnicity and psychiatric diagnosis. *Journal of Clinical Psychology* 37:529–537.

Booth, L. J. (1960). A normative comparison of the responses of Latin American and Anglo American children to the Children's Apperception Test. In *The CAT: Facts About Fantasy*, ed. M. R. Haworth, pp. 84–85. New York: Grune & Stratton.

Cohen, R. E. (1972). Principles of preventive mental health programs for ethnic minority populations: acculturation of Puerto Ricans to the United States. *American Journal of Psychiatry* 128:1529–1533.

Costantino, G. (1978). *TEMAS, a new thematic apperception test to measure ego functions and development in urban black and Hispanic children*. Paper presented at the Second Annual Conference on Fantasy and the Imaging Process, Chicago, November.

——— (1987). *TEMAS (Tell-Me-A-Story) Pictures*. Los Angeles: Western Psychological Services.

——— (1992). Overcoming bias in educational assessment of Hispanic students. In *Psychological Testing of Hispanics*, ed. K. F. Geisinger, pp. 89–98. Washington, DC: American Psychological Association.

——— (1993). School dysfunctions in Hispanic children. In *School Dysfunctions in Children and Youth*, ed. E. H. Wender, pp. 206–112. Report of the 24th Ross Roundtable on Critical Approaches to Common Pediatric Problems. Columbus, OH: Ross Product Division.

Costantino, G., and Malgady, R. G. (1983). Verbal fluency of Hispanic, black and white children on TAT and TEMAS, a new thematic apperception test. *Hispanic Journal of Behavioral Sciences* 5:199–206.

—— (1994). Storytelling through pictures: culturally sensitive psychotherapy for Hispanic children and adolescents. *Journal of Clinical Child Psychology* 23:13–20.

—— (1995). Development of TEMAS, a multicultural thematic apperception test: psychometric properties and clinical utility. In *Multicultural Assessment in Counseling and Clinical Psychology*, ed. G. R. Sodowsky and J. C. Impara, pp. 85–137. Lincoln, NE: Buros Institute of Mental Measurements, University of Nebraska.

Costantino, G., Malgady, R., and Rogler, L. H. (1988). Folk hero modeling therapy for Puerto Rican adolescents. *Journal of Adolescence* 11:155–165.

—— (1994). Storytelling through pictures: culturally sensitive psychotherapy for Hispanic children and adolescents. *Journal of Clinical Child Psychology* 23:13–20.

Costantino, G., Malgady, R., and Vazquez, C. (1981). A comparison of the Murray TAT and a new thematic apperception test for urban Hispanic children. *Hispanic Journal of Behavioral Sciences* 3:291–300.

Dana, R. H. (1986a). Personality assessment and native Americans. *Journal of Personality Assessment* 50:480–500.

—— (1986b). Thematic Apperception Test used with adolescents. In *Projective Techniques for Children and Adolescents*, ed. A. I. Rabin, pp. 14–36. New York: Springer.

—— (1993a). *Multicultural Assessment Perspectives for Professional Psychology*. Boston: Allyn & Bacon.

—— (1993b). *Cross-cultural personality assessment: a model for practice*. Paper presented at the 14th International Congress of the Rorschach and other projective methods, Lisbon, Portugal, July.

—— (1996). Culturally competent assessment practices in the United States. *Journal of Personality Assessment* 66:472–487.

Del Castillo, J. (1970). The influence of language upon symptomatology in foreign-born patients. *American Journal of Psychiatry* 127:242–244.

Diagnostic and Statistical Manual of Mental Disorders (1985). 3rd ed., rev. Washington, DC: American Psychiatric Association.

—— (1994). 4th ed. Washington, DC: American Psychiatric Association.

Durrett, M. E., and Kim, C. C. (1973). A comparative study of behavioral maturity in Mexican American and Anglo preschool children. *Journal of Genetic Psychology* 123:55–62.

Entwisle, D. R. (1972). To dispel fantasies about fantasy-based measures of achievement motivation. *Psychological Bulletin* 77:377–391.

Exner, J. E., and Weiner, I. B. (1982). *The Rorschach: A Comprehensive System: Vol. 3. Assessment of Children and Adolescents*. New York: Wiley.

Fuller, C. G., and Malony, N. H. (1984). A comparison of English and Spanish (Nunez) translations of the MMPI. *Journal of Personality Assessment* 48:130–131.

Gallagher, J. J. (1979). Research centers and social policy. *American Psychologist* 34:997–1000.

Gomez, R., Ruiz, P., and Rumbaut, R. (1985). Hispanic patients: a linguo-cultural minority. *Hispanic Journal of Behavioral Sciences* 7:177–186.

Gonzalez, J. R. (1978). Language factors affecting treatment of bilingual schizophrenics. *Psychiatric Annals* 8:68–70.

Gross, H., Knatterud, G., and Donner, L. (1969). The effect of race and sex on the variation of diagnosis and disposition in the psychiatric emergency room. *Journal of Nervous and Mental Disease* 148:638–642.

Gynther, M., and Green, S. (1980). Accuracy makes a difference, but does a difference make for accuracy? *Journal of Consulting and Clinical Psychology* 48:268–272.

Haberman, P. W. (1976). Psychiatric symptoms among Puerto Ricans in Puerto Rico and New York City. *Ethnicity* 3:133–144.

Henry, E. W. (1955). The Thematic Apperception Technique in the study of group and cultural problems. In *An Introduction to Projective Techniques and Other Devices for Understanding the Dynamics of Human Behavior*, ed. H. H. Anderson and G. L. Anderson, pp. 230–278. New York: Prentice-Hall.

Holland, T. R. (1979). Ethnic group differences in MMPI profile pattern and factorial structure among adult offenders. *Journal of Personality Assessment* 43:72–77.

Javier, R. A., and Alpert, M. (1986). The effect of stress in the linguistic generalization of coordinate bilinguals. *Journal of Psycholinguistic Research* 15:419–435.

Javier, R. A., and Marcos, L. R. (1989). The role of stress on language-independence and code-switching phenomenon. *Journal of Psycholinguistic Research* 18:449–472.

Kagan, S., and Romero, C. (1977). Non-adaptive assertiveness of Anglo-American and Mexican-American children of two ages. *Interamerican Journal of Psychology* 11:27–32.

Kessler, R. C., McGonagle, K. A., Zhao, S., et al. (1994). Lifetime and 12-month prevalence of *DSM-III-R* psychiatric disorders in the United States. *Archives of General Psychiatry* 51:8–19.

Kramer, M. (1990). *Population changes, schizophrenic and other mental disorders, 1990, 2000, and 2010: their implications for mental health programs.* Based on a paper presented at the National Symposium on Schizophrenia of the Sheppard Pratt National Center for Human Development, Baltimore, MD, November 15–16.

Levine, E. S., and Padilla, A. M. (1980). *Crossing Cultures in Therapy: Counseling for the Hispanic.* Monterey, CA: Brooks/Cole.

Lopez, S., and Hernandez, P. (1987). When culture is considered in evaluation and treatment of Hispanic patients. *Psychotherapy* 24:120–126.

Lopez, S., and Nunez, J. A. (1987). Cultural factors considered in selected diagnostic criteria and interview schedules. *Journal of Abnormal Psychology* 96:270–272.

Malgady, R. (1990). *Issues of bias in assessment of Hispanics.* Paper presented at the meeting of the American Psychiatric Association, New York, May.

——— (1996). The question of cultural bias in assessment and diagnosis of ethnic minority clients: let's reject the null hypothesis. *Professional Psychology: Research and Practice* 27:101–105.

Malgady, R. G., and Costantino, G. (in press). Effects of language and culture on psychiatric evaluation of Hispanics. *Psychological Measurements.*

Malgady, R., Costantino, G., and Rogler, L. H. (1984). Development of a Thematic

Apperception Test (TEMAS) for urban Hispanic children. *Journal of Consulting and Clinical Psychology* 52:886–896.

Malgady, R., Rogler, L. H., and Costantino, G. (1987). Ethnocultural and linguistic bias in mental health evaluation of Hispanics. *American Psychologist* 42:228–234.

Malgady, R., Rogler, L. H., and Marcos, L. (1992). *Culture and Behavior in the Psychodiagnosis of Puerto Ricans*. Grant No. RO1 MH45939. Rockville, MD: National Institute of Mental Health.

Marcos, L. R. (1976). Bilinguals in psychotherapy: language as an emotional barrier. *American Journal of Psychotherapy* 30:552–560.

——— (1994). The psychiatric examination of Hispanics across the language barrier. In *Theoretical and Conceptual Issues in Hispanic Mental Health*, ed. R. Malgady and O. Rodriguez, pp. 144–154. Melbourne, FL: Krieger.

Marcos, L., Alpert, M., Urcuyo, L., and Kesselman, M. (1973). The effect of interview language on the evaluation of psychopathology in Spanish American schizophrenic patients. *American Journal of Psychiatry* 130:549–553.

McCreary, C., and Padilla, E. (1977). MMPI differences among Black, Mexican American, and White male offenders. *Journal of Clinical Psychology* 33:171–177.

McGill, J. (1980). MMPI sex differences among Anglo, Black, and Mexican American welfare recipients. *Journal of Clinical Psychology* 36:147–151.

Monopoli, J. (1984). *A culturally-specific interpretation of the thematic apperception test for American Indians*. Unpublished master's thesis, University of Arkansas, Fayetteville.

Moscicki, E. K., Rae, D., Regier, D. A., and Locke, B. Z. (1987). The Hispanic health and nutrition examination survey: depression among Mexican Americans, Cuban Americans, Puerto Ricans. In *Health Behavior: Research Agenda for Hispanics*, ed. M. Gaviria and J. D. Arana, pp.145–149. Simon Bolivar Research Monograph No. 1. Chicago: University of Illinois at Chicago.

Murray, H. (1943). *The Thematic Apperception Test*. Cambridge, MA: Harvard University Press.

New York City Department of City Planning (1988). Selected data on differential underenumeration by race and Hispanic origin, 1970–1990. Unpublished tabulations.

——— (1992). Demographic profiles: a profile of New York City's community districts from the 1980 and 1990 censuses of population and housing. No. 92–32.

Oakland, T. (1977). *Psychological and Educational Assessment of Minority Children*. New York: Brunner/Mazel.

Olmedo, E. L. (1981). Testing linguistic minorities. American Psychologist 36:1078–1085.

Padilla, A. M. (1979). Critical factors in the testing of Hispanic Americans: a review and some suggestions for the future. In *Testing, Teaching and Learning: Report of a Conference on Testing*, ed. R. Tyler and S. White, pp. 219–243. Washington, DC: National Institute of Education.

Padilla, A., and Ruiz, R. (1973). *Latino mental health: a review of the literature*

(DHEW Publication No. HSM 73-9143). Washington, DC: U.S. Government Printing Office.

———— (1975). Personality assessment and test interpretation of Mexican Americans: a critique. *Journal of Personality Assessment* 39:103–109.

Padilla, A., Ruiz, R., and Alvarez, R. (1975). Community mental health services for the Spanish-speaking/surnamed populations. *American Psychologist* 30:892–905.

Page, R. D., and Bozlee, S. (1982). A cross-cultural MMPI comparison of alcoholics. *Psychological Reports* 50:639–646.

Paivio, A. (1971). *Imagery and Verbal Processes*. New York: Holt, Rinehart & Winston.

Piaget, J., and Inhelder, B. (1971). *Mental Imagery in the Child*. New York: Basic Books.

Price, C. S., and Cuellar, I. (1981). Effects of language and related variables on the expression of psychopathology in Mexican American psychiatric patients. *Hispanic Journal of Behavioral Sciences* 3:145–160.

Pritchard, D., and Rosenblatt, A. (1980). Reply to Gynther and Green. *Journal of Consulting and Clinical Psychology* 48:273—274.

Radloff, L. (1977). The CED-D scale: a self-report depression scale for research in the general population. *Applied Psychological Measurement* 1:385–401.

Reuman, D. A., Alwin, D. F., and Verof, J. (1983). *Measurement models for thematic apperception measure of achievement motive*. Paper presented at the American Psychological Association Convention, Anaheim, CA, August.

Ritzler, B. (1993). TEMAS (Tell-Me-A-Story): a critique. *Journal of Psychoeducational Assessment* 11:381–389.

———— (1995). Projective methods for multicultural personality assessment: Rorschach, TEMAS, and the Early Method Procedure. In *Handbook of Multicultural Assessment*, ed. L. A. Suzuki, P. J. Meller, and J. J. Ponterotto, pp. 114–135. San Francisco, Jossey-Bass.

Rodriguez, O. (1987). *Hispanics and Human Services: Help-Seeking in the Inner City*. Monograph No. 14. Hispanic Research Center. New York: Fordham University.

Rogler, L. H. (1994). International migrations: a framework for directing research. *American Psychologist* 48:701–708.

Rogler, L. H., and Hollingshead, A. (1985). *Trapped: Puerto Rican Families and Schizophrenia*. Maplewood, NJ: Waterfront Press.

Rogler, L. H., Malgady, R., Costantino, G., and Blumenthal, R. (1987). What do culturally sensitive mental health services mean? The case of Hispanics. *American Psychologist* 42:565–570.

Rogler, L. H., Malgady, R., and Rodriguez, O. (1989). *Hispanics and Mental Health: A Framework for Research*. Melbourne, FL: Krieger.

Rogler, L. H., Santana-Cooney, R., Costantino, G., et al. (1983). *A Conceptual Framework for Mental Health Research on Hispanic Populations*. Hispanic Research Center Monograph No. 10. New York: Fordham University.

Rosado, J. W. (1980). Important psychocultural factors in the delivery of mental health services to lower-class Puerto Rican clients: a review of recent studies. *Journal of Community Psychology* 8:215–226.

Sabin, J. E. (1975). Translating despair. *American Journal of Psychiatry* 132:197–199.

Salvo, J. J., and Ortiz, R. J. (1992). *The Newest New Yorkers: An Analysis of Immigration to New York City in the 1980s.* New York City Department of City Planning.

Salvo, J. J., Ortiz, R. J., and Lobo, A. P. (1994). *Puerto Rican New Yorkers in 1990.* New York City Department of City Planning.

Short, K. (1992). *Health Insurance Coverage: 1987–1990.* Current Population Reports, Household Economic Studies, Series P–70, No. 29.

Standards for Educational and Psychological Testing (1985). Washington, DC: American Psychological Association.

Sue, S., and Zane, N. (1987). The role of culture and cultural techniques in psychotherapy: A critique and reformulation. *American Psychologist* 42:37–45.

Thompson, C. E. (1949). The Thompson modification of the Thematic Apperception Test. *Journal of Projective Techniques* 17:469–478.

U.S. Bureau of Census (1988). *The Coverage of the Population in the 1980 Census, Evaluation and Research Reports.* PHC80–E4, February. Washington, DC: U.S. Government Printing Office.

———— (1990). The Hispanic population in the United States: March 1990. (Serial P-20, No. 449). Washington, DC: U.S. Government Printing Office.

———— (1991). 1990 Census of Population and Housing (Summary Tape File 1A, Data User Services Division). Washington, DC: U.S. Government Printing Office.

———— (1992). Current population reports, population characteristics, March. Washington, DC: U.S. Government Printing Office.

———— (1993). Hispanic Americans today. *Current Population Reports,* Series P23–183. Washington, DC: U.S. Government Printing Office.

———— (1994). *Current Population Reports, Population Characteristics.* Washington, DC: U.S. Government Printing Office.

Vazquez, C. (1982). Research on the psychiatric evaluation of the bilingual patient: a methodological critique. *Hispanic Journal of Behavioral Sciences* 4:75–80.

Vazquez, C., and Javier, R. A. (1991). The problem with interpreters: communicating with Spanish-speaking patients. *Hospital and Community Psychiatry* 42:163–165.

Villamil, B. (1973). *Desarrollo del Inventario de Ansiedad Estado y Rasgo para niños.* (Development of the State-Trait Anxiety Inventory for children). Unpublished master's thesis, University of Puerto Rico.

Warren, R. (1994). *Estimates of the unauthorized immigrant population residing in the United States, by country of origin and states of residence.* Paper presented at the California Immigration 1994 Conference, Immigration and Naturalization Service, Statistics Division, August.

25

Developing and Evaluating Culturally Sensitive Mental Health Services for Hispanics

ROBERT G. MALGADY, GIUSEPPE COSTANTINO, AND SONIA PARDOE MATTHEWS

INTRODUCTION

Three broad approaches to the development of culturally sensitive therapy programs have emerged in the mental health literature on Hispanic populations: first, rendering traditional treatments more accessible to Hispanics; second, selecting available therapeutic modalities according to the perceived features of Hispanic culture; and third, extracting elements from Hispanic culture to modify traditional treatments or to use them as an innovative treatment modality (Costantino et al. 1985, 1994, Rogler et al. 1987). This chapter

Research reported in this chapter was supported in part by grants from the National Institute of Mental Health (Grant Nos. RO1–MH30589 and RO1–MH33711), services Research Branch, and by the W. T. Grant Foundation (Grant No. 83-0868).

raises a fundamental question concerning how the relationship between culture and therapy is conceived by clinical practitioners and how it ought to be
conceived. Must the content of culturally sensitive/competent therapies stand
in isomorphic, mirrorlike relationship to the client's culture? Research seeking to evaluate a culturally sensitive therapy modality for children examines
this question and invites more appropriate formulations relating culture to
therapy.

The need for mental health services addressing the special problems of
Hispanic adults and youngsters is a widely acknowledged issue in the minority mental health literature (e.g., Costantino et al. 1994, Rogler et al. 1989).
At the root of this issue, the cultural distance experienced by Hispanic clients
when seeking mainstream mental health services has prompted efforts to
increase the sensitivity of services to Hispanic culture. Indeed, mental health
services have become more culturally sensitive in several ways: by matching
clients with Spanish-speaking Hispanic therapists, by matching the theoretical orientation of therapy to therapists, by matching the theoretical orientation of therapy to clients' cultural values, and by introducing culture directly
into the therapeutic process (Costantino et al. 1985, Rogler et al. 1987, 1993).
There is scattered empirical evidence that such efforts, which are largely limited to adults, result in less premature treatment dropout, increased participation, and more effective treatment outcomes (Sue et al. 1991). Our program
of culturally sensitive treatment research has developed and evaluated experimental mental health interventions for Hispanic children and adolescents.
These studies were preventive interventions developed on the basis of narrative therapy using cultural role modeling (varying the narrative modality by
age cohort) to impact on high-risk indicators such as anxiety symptomatology, acting out behavior, and poor ethnic and self-concept (e.g., Costantino et
al. 1985, 1994, Costantino and Malgady 1996a,b, Malgady et al. 1990a,b).

In the 1960s attention was focused on the need for culturally sensitive
mental health services for economically disadvantaged minority populations.
The nationwide development of community mental health programs was
expanded to cover new, economically disadvantaged service areas with populations that had never before received adequate professional mental health services. Thus many of the deficiencies of traditional service systems and
therapies became evident. Traditional therapeutic modalities were based on
the mental health needs of middle-class clients, and therefore often proved to
be of questionable effectiveness with minority persons living in inner-city
neighborhoods. This prompted pleas for culturally sensitive modalities.

Culturally sensitive mental health services are especially important for
Hispanics, because they are the most rapidly growing minority population in

the United States. According to census figures, the Hispanic population was 23 million in 1993, and it has had higher annual growth rates since 1970. The annual growth rate of Hispanics in the U.S. has been estimated at 4.8 percent compared with 1.8 percent for blacks and .06 percent for non-Hispanic whites (U.S. Bureau of the Census 1994). Moreover, demographic studies of the Hispanic population indicate that Hispanics are younger, less educated, poorer, and more likely than the general population to live in inner-city neighborhoods. In addition, language problems and acculturative stress are common among Hispanics. These characteristics put Hispanics at high risk of mental health problems requiring assessment and treatment interventions.

During the past two decades there has been extensive growth in the literature focusing on Hispanic mental health. This literature is pervasively critical, documenting multiple barriers that, despite massive need, keep Hispanics from receiving adequate mental health care (Rogler et al. 1983, 1989). At the core of the literature's criticism is the charge that mental health services targeted for Hispanics are not culturally sensitive. To answer this question, we examined the use of the concept by mental health practitioners and researchers in their work with Hispanics. This process revealed the three approaches to cultural sensitivity (increasing accessibility of treatments, selecting treatments according to the perceived features of Hispanic culture, and infusing treatments with elements of Hispanic culture). This chapter describes the components of cultural sensitivity within each of the three approaches mentioned above. In addition, we examine the relationship between culture and therapy in the literature on Hispanics by posing a fundamental question: Must culturally sensitive/competent therapies have an isomorphic, mirrorlike relationship to the client's culture?

INCREASED ACCESSIBILITY OF TREATMENT

The first and most fundamental approach to culturally sensitive mental health services involves increasing the accessibility of treatments for Hispanic clients. This approach follows Freidson's (1970) argument that two characteristics of an ethnic group are likely to influence its utilization of the professional health care system. The first involves the level of congruence between the client's and the professionals' understanding of illness and treatment. The greater the level of congruence, the more likely a client is to use health care services. The second characteristic involves the ethnic group's lay referral system, which ranges from allowing the individual great flexibility in personal health decisions to pressing the individual to act according to the values of the culture. The least use of health services occurs in communities that have a marked incongruence between cultural and traditional professional values. A constricted lay referral system is likely to inhibit the use of mainstream professional services and to provide alternative routes to coping with mental health needs in a culturally congruent way.

Research suggests that many Hispanics fit into this categorization (Rogler et al. 1989). Therefore, a treatment program for Hispanics should increase the congruence between mainstream professional mental health values and indigenous Hispanic values and also incorporate elements of the lay referral system in order to increase the mainstream programs' accessibility.

A variety of attempts have been made to develop more accessible treatment programs for Hispanics in diverse mental health settings. Karno and Morales (1971), for instance, described the development of a mental health clinic tailored to the perceived needs of Hispanic mental health prevention services where consultation with community agencies and crisis intervention was incorporated into the program along with routine clinical services. Karno and Morales stated that Mexican Americans respond just as well to traditional treatment as Anglos when they are treated in a context of cultural and linguistic familiarity.

Scott and Delgado (1979) presented issues arising during the development of a mental health program for Hispanics within a community clinic. They reported that the program became effective after the recruitment of a bilingual/bicultural staff, integration of the program into the infrastructure of the host facility, and coordination of the program's effort with the needs of the Hispanic community. Similarly, Abad and colleagues (1974) established a mental health clinic in a community mental health center. They emphasized the need to gain support from local religious and political leaders prior to commencing the effort. The clinic's success was based on the maintenance of a credible presence in the institutional structures affecting the Puerto Ricans' lives. Other successful programs were developed by Cuellar and associates (1981) in an inpatient setting and by Normand and colleagues (1974) and Rodriguez (1971) on a small-group basis within large hospital settings.

For many culturally sensitive treatments the primary effort has been focused on recruitment of bilingual/bicultural staff in order to overcome the greatest communication barriers between clients and staff. The importance of such efforts is illustrated by the use of paraprofessionals in Acosta and Cristo (1981). Based on the assumption that Hispanics' needs for mental health services would likely continue to exceed the availability of Hispanic therapists, Acosta and Cristo developed a bilingual interpreter program in a psychiatric clinic. Interpreters were recruited from the same neighborhoods as the clients and were trained in key concepts of psychotherapy and the terminology used in clinical settings. They also acted as cultural consultants, explaining to English-speaking therapists the meanings conveyed by patients during therapy. The success of this program in increasing accessibility of the mental health services was evident by the fact that the percentage of Spanish-speaking patients admitted to the clinic doubled after this program was established. Moreover, there is other longitudinal and cross-sectional evidence that such innovations increase utilization rates in Hispanic communities (Bloom 1975, Trevino et al. 1979). In order to reduce the many barriers associated with the delivery of mental health services to Hispanics, in 1984 the Sunset Park Mental Health Center was converted from a medical model clinic to a culturally competent mental health center by hiring a large percentage of bilingual/bicultural clinicians, administrators and clerical staff and by introducing newly developed programs such as Cuento therapy and the TEMAS test. Within a few years, the patients' census increased from 1,000 to about 2,500, and annual visits increased from about 30,000 to 70,000. The center has been evaluated as a model of delivery of culturally competent mental health services (American Psychological Association 1994, personal communication).

By reaching out to the ethnic community's network, the mental health services system has found that it can attract Hispanics to use and retain its services, advance professional conceptions of mental health, and supplement alternative coping patterns indigenous to Hispanic culture. At the same time, by incorporating members of the ethnic network into the mental health services system, key elements of the lay culture are incorporated into its infrastructure. These ways of increasing accessibility represent the first approach to providing culturally sensitive mental health services.

SELECTION OF TREATMENTS TO FIT HISPANIC CULTURE

Another area of concern for cultural sensitivity has been the treatment Hispanics receive when they do use the mental health system. The second approach to cultural sensitivity is the selection of a therapy modality to coincide with perceived Hispanic cultural characteristics.

Some researchers and therapists have argued that treatment decisions ought not to preclude the use of psychoanalytic concepts and techniques with ethnic minority clients. Madura and Martinez (1974) argued that "more self-aware individuals are needed to confront insidious social realities in the outer world, as well as unconscious themes in the inner world" (p. 461). They asserted that Jungian dream analysis is congruent with Mexican culture because folk healers often specialize in the interpretation of dreams. Such traditional analytic treatments are accessible and appropriate to their Hispanic clientele. However, mental health practitioners working in inner-city, economically depressed Hispanic neighborhoods were among the first to criticize insight-oriented psychoanalytic therapy as both uneconomical and irrelevant to the context of Hispanic life (Ruiz 1981, Sue and Sue 1977). A pervasive view developed that insight-oriented techniques were too esoteric to respond to the massive socioeconomic and acculturative barriers that impinged on many Hispanic clients.

Bluestone and Vela (1982) proposed a series of culturally informed adaptations in the use of insight-oriented therapy with low SES Puerto Ricans. Nevertheless, they recognized that suitable candidates for insight-oriented intervention must be relatively free from severe stress to be motivated to remain in therapy, have a long-term outlook on life, and show insight. Therefore, traditional psychoanalytic insight therapy would be an inappropriate modality for most members of economically disadvantaged, inner-city Hispanic communities. Ruiz (1981) emphasized this conclusion in reference to the treatment of inner-city Hispanic clients: "Do they need brilliant insights into the etiology of . . . paranoia? Do they need to become more introspective or psychodynamically oriented? The answers to these questions are negative" (p. 202).

As an alternative to insight-oriented therapies, others have suggested individualized treatment modalities. That is, culturally sensitive therapy must be congruent with the mental health needs of the individual client. However, in broadly discussing cultural traits, one can easily fall into the trap of stereotyping and of disregarding the substantial differences between Hispanic subcultures (Malgady 1994). Ruiz (1981) identified the diversity of subcultures that fall under the catchall phase "Hispanic" or "Latino" and pointed out the difficulty of differentiating Hispanics who are bicultural or sufficiently assimilated to be considered Anglo-American. Clearly, treatment dispositions cannot be based on a criterion such as a Spanish surname alone. Ruiz believed that culturally sensitive treatment plans should be based on the objective assessment of the degree of biculturalism that the individual client manifests. Prior to selection of a therapy modality for a given client, his or her linguistic skills in English and Spanish (both dominance and preference) and general level of acculturation should be assessed. Ruiz discussed integrated treatment plans that range from the "most Hispanic" to the "most Anglo" client.

Acculturation refers to the process by which the behaviors, attitudes, and values of the migrant change toward the host society as a result of exposure to a cultural system that is significantly different (Cortes et al. 1993). A variety of acculturation measures have been published for diverse Hispanic subcultures, including Mexican Americans (Cuellar et al. 1980), Cubans (Szapocznik et al. 1978), and Puerto Ricans (Cortes et al. 1994). Following the assessment of acculturation the therapist is able to make a more judicious decision about which treatment modality is most appropriate.

Acculturation signifies a multifaceted process. Some components change more rapidly than others. Rogler and Cooney (1984) investigated internationally linked Puerto Rican families. Thus treatment decisions based on the client's level of acculturation were ambiguous. In such situations, a transcultural orientation may be needed to address issues pertaining to the client's traditional culture, the culture of the host society, or some emergent product of both cultures. Nevertheless, individualizing the treatment process is the primary and preferred mode of dealing with the problem.

The second approach to the delivery of culturally sensitive mental health services involves distinguishing between acculturated and bilingual Hispanics who can be treated as if they were Anglo-Americans and less acculturated and limited English proficient Hispanics who require a special treatment modality. Treatment of the latter group would possibly be in Spanish and congruent with Hispanic cultural values. The need for treatment of the latter clientele thus prompts the third approach to culturally sensitive treatment.

MODIFYING TREATMENTS TO
FIT HISPANIC CULTURE

Aspects of the psychotherapeutic modalities can be adapted to fit the client's culture. A clear example of using an element from the client's ethnic culture to complement and modify the provision of therapy is apparent in Kreisman's (1975) account of treating two Mexican-American female schizophrenics who thought of themselves as bewitched. Kreisman's treatment modification began by concurring that they were indeed bewitched. Their therapist's acknowledgment of bewitchment and of the need for folk remedies encouraged the rapport that could not be established in conventional therapy, thus facilitating therapeutic progress. In this context the clients' culture was incorporated into the treatment without compromising the therapist's chosen modality.

Another example of using an element of the client's culture is the language-switching technique employed by Pitta and colleagues (1978). They argued that emotional expression is freer and more spontaneous in one's native tongue, whereas the use of a second language fosters intellectual defenses and control. Accordingly, the language in which therapy is conducted is chosen according to patient characteristics and phase of treatment, and language switching is used as a therapeutic technique. The modality into which this technique was incorporated was traditional insight-oriented psychotherapy. Neither the conception of therapy nor the therapeutic role was altered, but an ethnic characteristic of the client was introduced to enhance the cultural sensitivity of the treatment modality.

A programmatic effort to adapt treatment modalities to the traits of a Hispanic population has been made by Szapocznik and his collaborators (Szapocznik et al. 1979, 1994). They developed measures of Cuban value orientations and acculturation and then structured therapeutic interventions. According to their theory of intrafamily tension and stress, the greater the disparity in acculturation between family members, the greater the family tension and stresses. Szapocnzik and associates (1978) maintained that the treatment of the mental health problems of Cuban families should have an isomorphic, mirrorlike relationship to the clients' cultural background: "Cubans' value structure must be matched by a similar set of therapeutic assumptions" (p. 116). The selection of family therapy as the treatment of choice was predicated on the notion that Cubans are very family oriented. Having determined through their research that the Cuban value system prizes lineality, Szapocznik and colleagues (1979) had the family therapist assume a position of authority to restore or reinforce parental authority over the children. These researchers have outlined a detailed sequence of therapeutic interventions deduced from their findings on the cultural characteristics of Cuban clients, and have implemented these interventions following the assumption that therapeutic content should mirror the culture.

Subsequently, Szapocznik and colleagues (1980) recognized that treatment modifications with Hispanic clients need not follow a rigid isomorphic pattern with respect to the culture. Sometimes the objective of treatment is to change culturally prescribed behavior. Similarly, Boulette (1976) observed the ubiquity among Mexican-American women of the "subassertiveness" pattern, which is judged to be psychologically dysfunctional. This became the target for a therapeutic intervention to train Mexican-American women to be more assertive. The ultimate purpose was for the women to overcome somatic complaints and symptoms of depression and anxiety, which were thought to result from culturally prescribed submissiveness. Other Hispanic groups have similar cultural patterns (Rogler and Hollingshead 1985). These therapeutic approaches raise important issues when placed in the context of the lives of persons who are rooted in first-generation, traditional ethnic culture and who are of low socioeconomic status. In such a context, Hispanics often experience role segregation by gender, (Rogler and Cooney 1984). Among spouses there is a sharp distinction between *trabajo de hombre* (men's work) and *trabajo de mujer* (women's work) as well as gender role differences in leisure patterns and inequities in power. How does the development of assertiveness interact with such role segregation? Will the women's assertiveness clash with the culturally prescribed submissiveness embedded in role segregation? The questions can be raised, but the research required to answer them is not available.

Nonetheless, contrasted with earlier accounts that prescribed that therapeutic activities and structure should mirror Hispanic culture, the view that some cultural behaviors are dysfunctional in American society raises intriguing questions. Once the cultural characteristics of a minority ethnic group have been adequately documented, how should they be incorporated into treatment? Is effective therapy necessarily therapy that attempts to preserve traditional cultural elements, or should acculturation, assimilation, or adaptation to the host society sometimes take priority? Perhaps advocacy on behalf of preserving traditional cultural elements, no matter how well intentioned, ought not always or exclusively shape the nature of therapeutic interventions. On the other hand, neither should the values of the host society be idealized as reflecting universal standards of mental health.

It is our contention that when therapy modalities are modified to address the needs of Hispanic clients, the adapted therapy need not isomorphically reflect the client's cultural characteristics. We suggest that therapeutic gains can be made when traditional cultural patterns are redirected according to predetermined therapeutic goals. Thus the first step in the process of treatment modification is to determine the ethnic group's traits of likely therapeutic relevance and then employ them directly or transform them as needed. Isomorphic reinforcement of cultural traits implies that they are necessarily adaptive, whereas departures from this assumption imply that some cultural traits serve as an obstacle to therapy and that acculturation of the values of the host society is an additional and valid standard of adjustment. It also assumes that cultural elements can be modified within the treatment without impugning their value and purpose as functional cultural traits in the immigrant's society of origin. The modifications imply the development of hypotheses reflecting the intricacies of the many possible connections between various cultural traits and the therapies administered. The ultimate goal should be relief from psychological distress and the adaptation of the Hispanic client to the new host society in such a way that ethnic identity and pride are not negated or belied.

DEVELOPING A CULTURALLY SENSITIVE
TREATMENT MODALITY WITH CHILDREN

The third approach to cultural sensitivity, modification of treatment, is also in evidence when specific elements from the client's culture are used as the vehicle for therapeutic intervention. *Cuento* or folktale therapy, a recent innovation (Costantino et al. 1986), provides an illustration. Cuento therapy is a modeling technique based on the principles of social learning theory, but it takes as its medium the folktales of Puerto Rican culture and focuses them on psychologically distressed Puerto Rican children and mothers.

Although much of the aforementioned literature has dealt with the mental health of Hispanic adults, little attention has been directed to second-generation Hispanic children who, trapped between two cultures, are at high risk of mental disorder. For this reason we developed the program of cuento therapy. This culturally sensitive therapy was administered by bilingual/bicultural therapists in a mental health clinic with a service area that is predominantly Hispanic. The objective in telling folktales to the children was to transmit cultural values, foster pride in the Puerto Rican cultural heritage, reinforce adaptive behavior within the American culture, and bridge the gap between the two cultures.

To conduct the therapy, the therapist read the folktales aloud in both English and Spanish and led the children in a group discussion on the meaning or moral of the story, highlighting the "good" and "bad" behaviors of the characters. The stories quickly captured the attention of the children, who identified readily with the characters portrayed and imitated their behaviors. In the next step of the intervention, the group participants role-played the various characters in the story. The therapist and eventually peer group members reinforced adaptive imitated behavior. This activity was videotaped, and afterward the children viewed themselves on tape and discussed the role-playing activities with the therapist in relation to their own problems. The therapist then proposed new scenarios for role playing, and the children acted out solutions to problems presented in the scenarios. The therapist verbally reinforced adaptive behavior and corrected behavior that was maladaptive.

To examine the question of whether therapy should isomorphically reflect the culture, some of the children were told folktales, thus replicating cultural elements without changing them. Departing from the isomorphic assumption, other children were told folktales that had been changed to convey the knowledge, values, and skills useful in coping with the demands of the sociocultural environment of the host society's inner-city neighborhoods. In the adaptation of stories, moral issues were retained from the original story, but other changes were made: cultural objects constituting the setting changed from a rural tropical scene to an urban Hispanic neighborhood; culturally based interpersonal patterns also were changed: for example, authoritarian control of a younger sibling by an older one was transformed into the problem of maladaptive influences from peers in an urban setting and the overcoming of fear in resisting such influences.

Thus there is empirical justification for the development of both therapies that take elements unchanged from the client's culture and those that adapt such elements to the host society.

Our program of culturally sensitive treatment research has been conceptualized in the narrative process and rooted in social learning theory principles (modeling) (Bandura 1977). Narrative psychotherapy is rapidly gaining acceptance as a culturally sensitive treatment modality (Howard 1991). Cognitive psychologists such as Bruner (1986) and Mair (1988) have affirmed that identity development occurs as a result of life-story construction. Howard (1991) conceptualizes psychopathology as an incoherent story with an incorrect ending; psychotherapy presents a coherent story with a correct ending. Further, he describes the techniques of storytelling as the most adept process in understanding culturally diverse individuals and in conducting cross-cultural psychotherapy.

EVALUATING CULTURALLY SENSITIVE INTERVENTION OUTCOMES

Despite considerable attention to problems attending the delivery of mental health services to Hispanics, such as underutilization of services (Rodriguez 1987), premature dropout rates from psychotherapy (Sue et al. 1991), and allegations of ineffective treatment modalities (Padilla et al. 1975, Rogler et al, 1987, 1993), there has been little research evaluating the effectiveness of psychotherapy for Hispanics and even less attention to outcomes of services for children or adolescents. The more general literature on Hispanics, largely focused on Mexican-American adults, implicates cultural distance between the typically low SES, Spanish-dominant Hispanic client and the middle-class, English-speaking non-Hispanic therapist as the root of psychotherapeutic calamity. The cognition of cultural conflict not only between the client and therapist, but also conflict between Hispanic clients' cultural values and the orientations embodied in mainstream health care services, has prompted considerations of cultural "sensitivity" (Rogler et al. 1987, 1993) or cultural "responsiveness" (Sue 1988) in the provision of mental health services, or culturally "competent" care (APA Guidelines 1993).

It is important not only to develop culturally sensitive interventions, but also to evaluate treatment outcomes. In cuento therapy we compared the intervention to traditional group therapy and nonintervention. Significant reduction in anxiety symptomatology was evident. Moreover, the therapy group with cuentos adapted to American society evidenced a greater reduction in anxiety symptoms, and this effect remained stable one year after the intervention.

A related modeling intervention appropriate for adolescents was based on "heroic" adult role models (Malgady et al. 1990a,b). A major consideration in developing this modality was the frequency of young single-parent households, indicating that Puerto Rican adolescents often lack appropriate adult role models with whom they can identify, and therefore adaptive values and behaviors to imitate during the critical adolescent years. National figures indicate that 41 percent of Hispanic households are headed by females (U.S. Bureau of the Census 1991); estimates specific to Puerto Ricans in New York City are somewhat higher (44 percent, according to Mann and Salvo 1985); and our own samples drawn from New York City public schools in Hispanic communities had rates of female-headed households exceeding 60 percent. Consequently, Puerto Rican adolescents appeared to be suitable candidates for a modeling therapy that fulfills their need for adaptive role models in a culturally sensitive way. We developed and evaluated a modeling therapy using biographical stories of heroic Puerto Ricans in an effort to bridge the bicultural, intergenerational, and identity conflicts faced by Puerto Rican adolescents. This modality endeavored to enhance the relevance of therapy for adolescents by exposing them to successful male and female adult models in their own culture, fostering ethnic pride and identity as Puerto Ricans, and modeling achievement-oriented behavior and adaptive coping with stress common to life in the urban Hispanic community. The content of the biographies embodied themes of cultural conflict and adaptive coping with stress. This intervention was also considered preventive because, although the adolescents were screened for behavior problems in school, they did not meet DSM-III-R (1987) diagnostic criteria. Treatment outcomes were assessed relative to an attention-control group participating in a school-based dropout prevention program. Evaluation of treatment effectiveness revealed that the culturally sensitive modeling intervention generally decreased anxiety symptomatology and increased ethnic identity. However, treatment interacted with household composition and participants' gender. Consistent with the intention of the intervention, the role models promoted greater ethnic identity in the absence of a male adult in the adolescents' households—but only among male adolescents. Female adolescents had stronger Puerto Rican identities than males regardless of treatment, possibly because of stable maternal identification. Similarly, the role models promoted greater self-esteem among male and female adolescents from female-headed households; however, although females from intact families felt "more Puerto Rican," their self-image diminished in the process. Thus the role models presented in treatment may have been perceived as idealized and aroused conflict concerning their real parents such that parental identification led to lower self-esteem. This process may have operated only among females because the female role models presented in treatment often represented untraditional female sex-roles.

The interactions impacting on treatment outcomes call attention to the importance of adolescents' social context in considering the mental health value of culturally sensitive interventions. This implicates the need to investigate both the integrity and quality of intrafamilial relations as potential mediators or moderators of treatment outcomes. The introduction of cultural sensitivity into the treatment process is a promising approach to impacting on the special mental health needs of Hispanic adolescents; however, further research is warranted inquiring how culturally sensitive services can be implemented more effectively given that dynamic processes may intervene to enhance or impugn their effectiveness. One objective of this research program will be to investigate the dynamic interplay between a culturally sensitive modeling intervention and the familial context of male and female Hispanic adolescents to make gender- and family-specific refinements in treatment protocols.

The third intervention developed in this program of treatment outcome research was also a narrative modality with older children and young adolescents, including Puerto Ricans and Dominicans, and a small group of Central and South Americans (Costantino et al. 1994). The participants were screened for *DSM-III-R* symptomatology; the most symptomatic were included in the study (though none reached caseness). The most prevalent symptoms were associated with conduct, anxiety, and phobic disorders. The intervention consisted of a storytelling modality based on pictorial stimuli depicting Hispanic cultural elements (e.g., traditional foods, games, gender role), family scenes, and neighborhoods (e.g., bodegas) in urban settings. The pictures portrayed multiracial Hispanic characters interacting in a variety of home, urban, and school settings. The therapy sessions were conducted in three phases. In the first, group members collaborated to develop a composite story about a particular picture, identifying the characters, setting, what is happening, and the resolution of the plot. In the second phase, group members shared their personal experiences as related to the composite story and the therapist verbally reinforced themes in their personal narratives that were adaptive resolutions of interpersonal conflicts. This phase engaged the youths in self-disclosure of personal conflict in their lives and how they coped, seeking to reinforce and internalize adaptive models of coping with stress. In the third phase, participants dramatized the composite story by performing the roles of the characters in the pictures. Verbally supportive reinforcement of imitative target behaviors was administered by the therapist and by peers. The psychodrama was videotaped and played back for critical review and discussion of appropriate behavior. The narrative intervention was compared to an attention-control group who engaged in discussion sessions with a psychoeducational purpose. Results indicated that although there was no effect on depression symptoms, there was significant reduction of conduct disorders and phobic symptoms, especially among the younger adolescents.

CONCLUSIONS

The three approaches to cultural sensitivity have been viewed metaphorically as a pyramidal structure (Rogler et al. 1987). At the base lie the numerous programs that endeavored to improve the accessibility of mental health services to Hispanic populations. Moving up the pyramid, we find fewer programs that have gone further in this process and that choose treatments according to the cultural characteristics of Hispanics. At the top are those scant programs modifying traditional therapy modalities according to an understanding and evaluation of ethnic characteristics or creatively deriving the therapeutic vehicle from the cultural milieu. Szapocznik and colleagues (1994) refer to only two such programs of research with Hispanics. Although our analysis of culturally sensitive treatment was prompted by Hispanic concerns, in principle we believe that this pyramidal structure can be extended to other migrant and culturally different groups.

The development of new therapeutic modalities out of specifically relevant cultural traits is always an ambitious and difficult task. Efforts to render therapeutic modalities culturally sensitive/competent, no matter how persuasive or attractive they are, must ultimately attend to the final objective of relieving the client of psychological distress and of improving his or her level of psychosocial functioning in society. It should no longer be sufficient for a clinician merely to assert cultural sensitivity/competence on the basis of good intentions alone. As an alternative, we invite our colleagues to situate their clinical innovations in the pyramidal framework developed here. From our attempt to order conceptually the many uses and meanings of cultural sensitivity/competence, it is the concept of therapeutic isomorphism that emerges as a major contribution to the field. Thus we also invite our colleagues to attend to the distinction we have drawn between isomorphic reinforcement and departures from isomorphism in the interest of the clients' well-being, not only in working with Hispanic clients but with any culturally and linguistically different clientele.

To attend to such issues, evaluative research must be conducted. As Padilla and associates (1975) stated, "An innovative treatment program is self-defeating unless validating research is conducted . . . to guide the development of programs with the greatest probability of success" (p. 900). It is particularly important that innovative modalities such as cuento therapy not become part of the vast pool of untested therapies, but the task of validation should not deter us from creating new, culturally sensitive therapeutic programs.

Perhaps the most fundamental question that should be faced in culturally sensitive psychotherapy research is whether the attenuation of cultural distance is consequential to treatment outcome (Malgady 1994). In a recent review of two decades of cross-cultural psychotherapy research on ethnic minority populations, Sue (1988) identified two competing conclusions pertinent to this fundamental question. The first is that ethnic or cultural mismatch decreases the likelihood of favorable treatment outcomes; the second is that cultural differences are, for the most part, irrelevant to treatment outcomes. Sue (1988) and Sue and Zane (1987) have proposed an interesting hypothesis that synthesizes these apparently contradictory conclusions. This hypothesis is that cultural factors may have a "distal" rather than "proximal" effect on treatment outcomes. Consideration of a client's culture in treatment planning may not necessarily have a direct link to outcome, but may enhance the process of therapy, which in turn is more directly linked to outcome. This reasoning calls attention to the need for process-oriented research on culturally sensitive treatment outcomes. Process research is needed to determine the extent to which treatment outcomes are a direct or indirect function of culture introduced into the modality and the extent to which outcomes are a result of mediating responses to culture.

A related but unexamined question is whether culture-specific interventions enhance treatment outcomes in the cultural target group more than in other ethnic or cultural groups. For example, an intervention based on Hispanic role models who are black may produce similar treatment outcomes among non-Hispanic African Americans. Similarly, given role models of low SES, similar effects might be found with low SES non-Hispanic whites. Thus, similar to the refined questions that can be posed about whether culture's effects are direct or indirect through intervening processes, the potential moderating effects of clients (e.g., culture, race, SES, gender, family structure) also need to be experimentally investigated.

REFERENCES

Abad, V., Ramos, J., and Boyce, E. (1974). A model for delivery of mental health services to Spanish-speaking minorities. *American Journal of Orthopsychiatry* 44:584–595.

Acosta, F., and Cristo, M. (1981). Development of a bilingual interpreter program: an alternative model for Spanish-speaking services. *Professional Psychology* 12:474–482.

American Psychological Association (1993). Guidelines for providers of psychological services to ethnic, linguistic and culturally diverse populations. *American Psychologist* 48:44–48.

———— (1994). Personal communication.

Bandura, A. (1977). *Social Learning Theory*. Englewood Cliffs, NJ: Prentice-Hall.

Bloom, B. (1975). *Changing Patterns of Psychiatric Care*. New York: Human Sciences.

Bluestone, H., and Vela, R. (1982). Transcultural aspects in the psychotherapy of the Puerto Rican poor in New York City. *Journal of the American Academy of Psychoanalysis* 10:269–283.

Boulette, T. (1976). Assertive training with low income Mexican American women. In *Psychotherapy with the Spanish-speaking: Issues in Research and Service Delivery*, ed. M. R. Miranda, pp. 67–72. Los Angeles: University of California, Spanish Speaking Mental Health Research Center.

Bruner, J. (1986). *Actual Minds, Possible Worlds*. Cambridge, MA: Harvard University Press.

Cortes, D. E., Rogler, L. H., and Malgady, R. G. (1993). *Assessing biculturality among Puerto Rican adults in the United States*. Manuscript submitted for publication.

Costantino, G., and Malgady, R G. (1996a). Culturally sensitive treatment: cuento and hero/heroine modeling therapies for Hispanic children and adolescents. In *Psychosocial Treatment Research of Child and Adolescent Disorders: Empirically Based Strategies for Clinical Practice*, ed. P. Jensen and E. Hibbs, pp. 639–697. Washington, DC: American Psychological Association.

———— (1996b). Cuento and folk hero modeling therapies for Hispanic children and adolescents. In *Jahrbuch fur transkullturelle medizin und psychotherapie* (Yearbook of Cross-Cultural Medicine and Psychotherapy), ed. W. Andritzky, pp. 273–296. 1993. Berlin, Germany: Verlag fur Wissenschaft und Bildung.

Costantino, G., Malgady, R. G., and Rogler, L. H. (1985). *Cuento Therapy: Folktales as a Culturally Sensitive Psychotherapy for Puerto Rican Children*. Hispanic Research Center Monograph No. 12. Maplewood, NJ: Waterfront.

———— (1994). Storytelling through pictures: culturally sensitive psychotherapy for Hispanic children and adolescents. *Journal of Clinical Child Psychology* 23:13–20.

Cuellar, I., Harris, L., and Jasso, R. (1980). An acculturation scale for Mexican-American normal and clinical populations. *Hispanic Journal of Behavioral Sciences* 2:199–217.

Cuellar, I., Harris, L., and Naron, N. (1981). Evaluation of a bilingual bicultural treatment program for Mexican-American psychiatric inpatients. In *Explorations in Chicano Psychology*, ed. A. Baron, pp. 165–186. New York: Praeger.

Diagnostic and Statistical Manual of Mental Disorders (1987). 3rd ed. rev. Washington, DC: American Psychiatric Association.

Freidson, E. (1970). *Profession of Medicine.* New York: Dodd, Mead.

Howard, G. S. (1991). Culture tales: a narrative approach to thinking, cross-cultural psychology and psychotherapy. *American Psychologist* 46:187–197.

Karno, M., and Morales, A. (1971). A community mental health service for Mexican-Americans in a metropolis. *Comprehensive Psychiatry* 12:116–121.

Kreisman, J. (1975). The *curandero's* apprentice: therapeutic integration of folk and medicinal healing. *American Journal of Psychiatry* 132:81–83.

Madura, R., and Martinez, C. (1974). Latino dream analysis: opportunity for confrontation. *Social Casework* 55:461–469.

Mair, M. (1988). *Between Psychology and Psychotherapy.* London: Routledge.

Malgady, R. (1994). Hispanic diversity and the need for culturally sensitive mental health services. In *Theoretical and Conceptual Issues in Hispanic Mental Health*, ed. R. Malgady and O. Rodriguez, pp. 227–246. Melbourne, FL: Krieger.

Malgady, R. G., Rogler, L. H., and Costantino, G. (1990a). Hero/heroine modeling for Puerto Rican adolescents: a preventive mental health intervention. *Journal of Consulting and Clinical Psychology* 58:469–474.

——— (1990b). Culturally sensitive psychotherapy for Puerto Rican children and adolescents: a program of treatment outcome research. *Journal of Consulting and Clinical Psychology (Special Series on Treatment of Children)* 58:704–712.

Mann, E. S., and Salvo, J. J. (1985). Characteristics of new Hispanic immigrants to New York City. *Research Bulletin* (Hispanic Research Center, Fordham University), 8: No. 1–2.

Normand, W., Iglesias, J., and Payn, S. (1974). Brief group therapy to facilitate utilization of mental health services by Spanish-speaking patients. *American Journal of Orthopsychiatry* 44:37–42.

Padilla, A., Ruiz, R., and Alvarez, R. (1975). Community mental health services for the Spanish-speaking/surnamed populations. *American Psychologist* 30:892–905.

Pitta, P., Marcos, L., and Alpert, M. (1978). Language switching as a treatment strategy with bilingual patients. *American Journal of Psychoanalysis* 38:255–258.

Rodriguez, I. (1971). Group work with hospitalized Puerto Rican patients. *Hospital and Community Psychiatry* 22:219–220.

Rodriguez, O. (1987). *Hispanics and Human Services: Help-Seeking in the Inner City.* Hispanic Research Center Monograph No. 14. New York: Fordham University.

Rogler, L., and Cooney, R. (1984). *Puerto Rican Families in New York City: Intergenerational Processes.* Hispanic Research Center Monograph No. 11. Maplewood, NJ: Waterfront.

Rogler, L. H., Cortes, D. E., and Malgady, R. G. (1993). The mental health relevance of idioms of distress among Puerto Ricans in New York City. *Journal of Nervous and Mental Disease* 40:335–342.

Rogler, L. H., and Hollingshead, A. (1985). *Trapped: Puerto Rican Families and Schizophrenia.* Maplewood, NJ: Waterfront.

Rogler, L. H., Malgady, R. G., Costantino, G., and Blumenthal, R. (1987). What does culturally sensitive mental health services mean? The case of Hispanics. *American Psychologist* 43:565–570.

Rogler, L. H., Malgady, R. G., and Rodriguez, O. (1989). *Hispanic and Mental Health: A Framework for Research.* Malabar, FL: Krieger.

Rogler, L. H., Santana-Cooney, R., Costantino, G., et al. (1983). *A Conceptual Framework for Mental Health Research on Hispanic Populations.* Hispanic Research Center Monograph No. 10. New York: Fordham University.

Ruiz, R. (1981). Cultural and historical perspectives in counseling Hispanics. In *Counseling the Culturally Different,* ed. D. Sue, pp. 186–215. New York: Wiley.

Scott, J., and Delgado, M. (1979). Planning mental health programs for Hispanic communities. *Social Casework* 60:451–455.

Sue, D. W., and Sue, D. (1977). Barriers to effective cross-cultural counseling. *Journal of Counseling Psychology* 24:420–429.

Sue, S. (1988). Psychotherapeutic services for ethnic minorities. *American Psychologist* 43:301–308.

Sue, S., Fujino, D. C., Hu, L. T., et al. (1991). Community mental health services for ethnic minority groups: a test of the cultural responsiveness hypothesis. *Journal of Consulting and Clinical Psychology* 59:535–540.

Sue, S., and Zane, N. (1987). The role of culture and cultural techniques in psychotherapy: a critique and reformulation. *American Psychologist* 42:37–45.

Szapocznik, J., Kurtness, W., and Fernandez, T. (1980). Bicultural involvement and adjustment in Hispanic-American youths. *International Journal of Intercultural Relations* 4:353–365.

Szapocznik, J., Kurtness, W., and Santisteban, D. A. (1994). The interplay of advances among theory, research and application in family intervention for Hispanic behavior-problem youth. In *Theoretical and Conceptual Issues in Hispanic Mental Health,* ed. R. G. Malgady and R. Orlando, pp. 155–180. Malabar, FL: Krieger.

Szapocznik, J., Scopetta, M., Hervis, O., et al. (1979). The Spanish Family Guidance Center of Miami. *Research Bulletin,* 4. (Available from Fordham University, Hispanic Research Center, Thebaud Hall, Bronx, NY 10458)

Szapocznik, J., Scopetta, M., and King, O. (1978). Theory and practice in matching treatment to the special characteristics and problems of Cuban immigrants. *Journal of Community Psychology* 6:112–122.

Trevino, F., Bruhn, J., and Bunce, H. (1979). Utilization of community mental health services in a Texas-Mexican border city. *Social Science and Medicine* 13:331–334.

United States Bureau of the Census (1991). 1990 Census of Population and Housing, Summary Tape File 1A, Data User Services Division, Washington, DC, September.

——— (1994). Current Population Reports, Population Characteristics, March.

26

The Hispanic Elderly

CARMEN I. VAZQUEZ AND LYDIA P. BUKI

The gerontologic literature on Hispanics has expanded in the past twenty years in the areas of health and social problems (Cuellar 1990, Sotomayor 1989, Vazquez and Clavijo 1995). There has been limited attention, however, focused on understanding the mental health needs of the older Hispanic-American population.

Demographic trends point to a graying of the population, largely fueled by the baby-boomer generation that began to turn 50 years old in 1996. Aging projections for the Hispanic population are not only consistent with these demographic trends, but are in fact more dramatic. The Hispanic-American elderly population grew by 75 percent between 1970 and 1980. The number of Latinos ages 65 and older is expected to increase 53 percent by the year 2005 and to triple its current number by the year 2050. Projections for Latinos ages 85 and older are similar for the short run and more pronounced for the long term. This group is expected to increase by 54 percent by the year 2005 and to more than quadruple by the year 2020. By the year 2050, however, the number of Latinos in this age category will be almost twenty-five times greater than it was in 1995 (Cheesman-Day 1996).

Policymakers and mental health professionals need to understand these trends and realize that it is time to implement preventive programs that will help the aging segment of the population. The accelerated growth indicates that, unless the needs and issues of the Hispanic elderly are identified and faced, problems within the population will also grow exponentially. Too many needs of older Latinos, ranging from health care and housing to mental health and employment, are not being met. Recent legislation threatens to further jeopardize the livelihood, health care access, and overall quality of life for older Latinos.

The Hispanic elderly are likely to have very little education, to earn low salaries, and to have long periods of underemployment and unemployment (Sotomayor 1989). In 1991 the poverty rate was 28.7 percent for Hispanics and 9.4 percent for non-Hispanic whites (García 1993). As Hispanics age, their sources of income are more limited than those of non-Hispanic whites, because most have worked in low-paying, hourly rate jobs that do not provide a retirement pension. Therefore, Hispanics are more likely to rely on Social Security and to be affected by inflation than their white counterparts (García 1993, Sotomayor 1989).

This chapter will look at some of the preventive and culturally appropriate clinical considerations applicable to the provision of mental health services for Hispanic elderly. These considerations are based both on clinical and research experiences. Counselors and therapists need to (1) understand the steps that are required to provide culturally sensitive preventive services, (2) recognize and learn how to work with the great heterogeneity of this population, and (3) know how to measure the effectiveness of their interventions. Preventive and culturally relevant services should aid the Hispanic elderly to better their quality of life and improve their knowledge of available services, and should result in greater access to culturally relevant interventions.

CLINICAL ISSUES

Empirical evidence suggests that approximately 7 million elderly Americans are in need of professional mental health services; that is, between 15 percent and 25 percent of the 28 million elderly in the United States suffer from significant mental health problems (Flemming et al. 1986). Although corresponding statistics are not available for the Hispanic elderly, many factors lead us to believe that the need for mental health services in this population is at least the same, if not greater.

There are stressors common to all elderly, such as losses relating to deteriorating health, diminishing memory, waning physical strength, and a shrinking support system (e.g., friends and family members of the same age cohort passing away). However, the minority elderly also often experience what

Miranda (1991) refers to as "multiple jeopardy." Multiple jeopardy encompasses being elderly, a member of a minority group, and poor. For the Hispanic elderly, issues such as language usage, religious beliefs, socioeconomic factors, level of education, migration, immigration, and acculturation are overrepresented. These issues must be explored and understood in order to determine the most appropriate and applicable treatment modality.

It is not unusual for older Latinos to present with a variety of needs ranging from mental health needs to the need for a referral to a dentist that charges on a sliding fee scale. Clinicians need to be very familiar with the community resources available for this population and need to triage situations that are not always in their area of expertise. Often, clinicians who treat this population become advocates for their clients in areas such as medical access, housing, and employment. Professionals recognize that institutional barriers need to be broken in the interest of their client's mental health.

Counseling the elderly also necessitates an understanding of the client from a holistic point of view (Clark 1995). There may be times when a treatment of choice would work well with a younger person but would not be warranted for an older person because the everyday lives and needs of individuals in the two groups are different. Mental health professionals need to assess carefully, with the client, what is best, given the client's life context.

The range of behavioral possibilities and self-perception on the levels of energy, health, and usefulness varies among many elderly individuals. There is not necessarily a one-to-one correlation between age and being infirm. In fact, the elderly can be productive and have a steady level of health and energy despite the presence of a chronic health condition. If we consider that the elderly population currently comprises 12 percent of the United States population and that so called "old age" can span twenty to thirty years, we must look at clinical needs from this perspective. A multidimensional conceptualization of psychopathology includes psychological and physical disorders as well as a preventive component aimed at maintaining a better quality of life. The goal is to promote autonomy, higher self-esteem, and a healthier individual overall.

Mental health services are underused by the Hispanic population in the U.S. Studies with ethnic elders in general report findings of the highest level of underutilization of services overall (Blendon et al. 1989). Some of the barriers to service access include poverty, lack of health insurance, lack of knowledge about available services, lack of culturally sensitive programs, limited English language fluency, distrust of the system, lack of transportation, belief in nontraditional healing practices, and a limited number of ethnically similar counselors. Lack of consideration of the heterogeneity of the elderly could be another explanation for the often reported underutilization of services.

Providers of services to the Hispanic elderly are confronted with the challenge of offering culturally sensitive treatments that include values, traditions, and beliefs that may be more ingrained and may hold more power within the Hispanic elderly population. Exploring cultural values and beliefs that include concepts such as *respeto* and *familismo* are essential for the provision of mental health treatment to older Latinos.

Respeto refers to the way people are expected to relate and react toward others. It has overtones of obedience, duty, and deference. *Respeto* serves as a guide within interpersonal relations recognizing individual power and achievements such as wealth, age, or other gains (Marin and VanOss 1991). *Respeto* also is a concept that values the innate worth of the individual regardless of concrete achievements. It recognizes the individual as a sole and valuable component and member of the universe. Unless you demonstrate otherwise, this philosophy presupposes that you are worthy of respect, as a human being.

Familismo is a cultural value that refers to significant (strong and valued) identifications with nuclear and extended families. These identifications hold strong beliefs of loyalty, solidarity, and reciprocity among members of the same family (Triandis et al. 1982). This value serves as a buffer and offers protection against physical and emotional stress (Sotomayor 1989, Valle and Martinez 1980). *Familismo* includes perceived obligations to provide support for family members, particularly in times of crisis, and to be loyal to other members. It also carries expectations of reliance on close family members as well as the extended family (Sabogal et al. 1987).

At the moment, there is an understanding that many of the treatment approaches with the elderly are often best offered within the community, such as senior centers, churches, schools, and community centers. Therefore, we propose a close connection between outpatient clinics that treat the elderly and schools, churches, and other relevant institutions. These connections would help in the planning and delivery of comprehensive interventions directed at the various aspects of the older person's life. Collaboration among various community agencies would significantly help the clinician to offer optimum treatment modalities for existent pathologies and to design carefully targeted and relevant preventive programs.

DIVERSITY ISSUES

It has been estimated that the Latin-American population will reach in excess of 500 million by the end of the century, approximately twice the number of

English-speaking people in North America (Lambert 1967, World Bank 1993). If we include Haiti, Latin America is composed of twenty-one republics plus Puerto Rico and cannot be seen as a single culture, but rather as a variety of cultures, with specific beliefs, mores, values, and political, socioeconomic, and cultural differences.

At present, Hispanics make up 9.5 percent of the U.S. population (Labovitz 1996); projections indicate that they will surpass 31 million by the year 2000 (Cheesman-Day 1996). According to the Bureau of the Census, *Hispanic* is a person of Mexican, Puerto Rican, Cuban, Central or South American, or other Spanish culture or origin, regardless of race. At 62 percent, Mexican Americans are the largest Hispanic subgroup in the United States, followed by Puerto Ricans (12 percent), Central and South Americans (12 percent), and Cubans (5 percent).

The heterogeneity of the Hispanic elderly population in the United States extends from individual, socioeconomic, religious, and geographical differences to variations related to country of origin, reasons for immigrating into the United States, incentives for remaining in this country, and level of acculturation (Aranda 1990, Sabogal et al. 1987). For example, a number of Mexican Americans can trace their origins to areas of the Southwest that later became part of the U.S.; their ancestors helped build this country, particularly cities in the Southwest, where Hispanics were the majority population until the building of the railroads (Luckingham 1994, Muller and Espenshade 1985). The majority of recent arrivals from Central America, on the other hand, immigrated to flee untenable political situations. Some have experienced traumatic events such as torture or have watched violent acts against another, and are in great need of psychological counseling. The importance, therefore, of understanding a person's past and current life context is paramount for service delivery to be culturally sensitive, appropriate, and effective.

SOCIOCULTURAL ISSUES

It is important to recognize that some of the differences that have been reported for the Hispanic elderly can be decisive in determining what type of assessment and/or treatment to conduct. The diversity in terms of education, for example, becomes clear when we compare the level of education attained by three major Hispanic subgroups in the United States. The percentage of older Latinos with less than an eighth grade education is highest for Puerto Ricans (77 percent), a bit lower for Mexican Americans (75 percent), and lowest for Cubans (57 percent). Although there is great variation within each subculture, the different levels of education attained by the immigrant groups must be determined routinely before any assessment or research can proceed with the older generation. As the statistics suggest, most older Hispanics have a very low level of education; sometimes, depending on their country of origin, they may not have learned how to read and write. Many individuals are very embarrassed to volunteer this information.

A low level of education can contribute to being a poor historian, resulting in inaccuracies in the assessment process. Older Hispanics may not understand the level of the language or terminology used by providers or be able to read or write instructions. The elderly may also have no experience performing tasks that require a certain level of cultural and educational learning. Their penmanship can appear uncoordinated, when in reality it is more a result of poor education than physiological deficit. Older Hispanics may also appear slower or more depressed than they are in reality, due to linguistic difficulties as a result of their limited knowledge of the English language. These demographic, sociocultural, and psychological characteristics of the Hispanic elderly influence their use of clinical services. These factors need to be recognized so that clinicians work within a framework that respects the client's right to sensitive and effective mental health treatment.

ACCULTURATION IMPACT

Generation in the U.S., length of residence in this country, age at arrival, and ethnic self-identification are important variables found to influence a person's mental health, willingness to seek mental health services, and choice of counselor. The experiences of a 78-year-old Central American woman who has been in the U.S. for five years and spends most of her time with Spanish-speaking family members will be different from those of a similarly aged woman who has lived in the U.S. for twenty years and has had a chance to develop greater bicultural skills. Acculturation is a difficult process for most individuals, particularly if added stressors such as poverty and discrimination exist.

The mental health of older Hispanics is affected not only by their own process of acculturation, but also by the similar stressors and changes that other family members experience (Garza and Gallegos 1995). Acculturation and adjustment to new economic realities contribute to a changing family structure in which the family role of the older generation may require flexibility and skills that differ from those in traditional cultures. For example, a

Spanish-speaking grandparent may need to care for the grandchildren if both parents need to work outside the home. This task can be difficult enough for grandparents who were raised in the culture in which their grandchildren are growing up; however, many Hispanic grandparents may have had little or no exposure to the values held by the dominant culture in the U.S., particularly if they received their schooling in another country (Miranda and Ruiz 1981), making their grandparenting efforts all the more challenging. In fact, because of limited access to transportation, low socioeconomic status, and language barriers, members of the older generation are the most isolated from societal changes. Language not only acts as a communication barrier with younger family members, particularly grandchildren, but also affects the elders' ability to receive information through the media (Becerra and Shaw 1984, Butler et al. 1991). The impact of these social changes on the elderly is profound, as they are often associated with other risk factors such as poverty and discrimination (Miranda 1991).

ASSESSMENT

Within and between Hispanic ethnic subgroups is a wide variation in English proficiency among the elderly. For example, Mexican-American elderly are the most likely to speak English, in contrast to Cuban Americans who are the least likely (Gallegos 1991). How does this translate into assessment? First of all, there is a dearth of standardized psychological tests in Spanish needed to evaluate the most common syndromes found among the elderly. Evaluation of memory and language, depression and cognitive functions, and family life is often done from a direct translation of an English test, without taking into account the lack of standardization or the accuracy of the translation. Norms for older Hispanics are also often lacking. These factors need to be taken into account when determining the need for, and choosing, a test that will yield useful information.

Adding to this complexity, when the professional administering the test is English monolingual, and there is no alternative, an interpreter must be used for assessment purposes. In this case it is highly recommended that only a trained interpreter—someone who has been formally and professionally trained in interpretation techniques—be used. Often a janitorial or clerical member staff is used for formal assessment, creating serious problems, including misdiagnosis, minimization of existing pathology, pathologizing of a normal situation, and contributing to miscommunication between patient and clinician. It is important to recognize that interpreters should have a minimal level of education, and preferably a formal education obtained in both Spanish and English. They should be familiar with colloquial expressions used in the client's country of origin, and be aware of limitations inherent in translations, particularly in translations that involve material of a psychological nature. The difficulty in translating the words *upset* and *angry* in a family assessment measure from English into Spanish illustrates this problem. Members of the translation panel were completely bilingual and bicultural; three of the five obtained their high school diploma in Spanish-speaking countries and had master's degrees obtained in the United States. This group in fact debated for days how to translate the words *upset* and *angry*. In Spanish there is no word that exactly connotes the concept *upset* as it is used in English. Instead, a Spanish speaker will express a specific feeling rather than use a generic term like *upset* to convey a general sense of discomfort. In searching for an adequate translation, the panel considered using *molesto* and *enojado*, but *molesto* has a connotation of having been bothered, and *enojado* has the connotation of being angry. Whichever word was chosen, the translation would not convey in Spanish the meaning that *upset* has in English (Buki and Cañive 1994). Mental health professionals, especially those who are English monolingual, need to realize that the translation of psychological language is not always a straightforward task.

If a translated test must be used, the clinician should ascertain the adequacy of the translation and the cross-cultural equivalence of the scale. For a discussion of translation techniques and the assessment of test equivalence, the reader may refer to Karno and associates (1983) and McKay and colleagues (1996). The importance of this discussion is underscored because the translation is the foundation upon which any conclusions about Spanish-speaking individuals are built (Buki and Cañive 1994). The clinician must exercise extreme caution in interpreting findings of a written report or a treatment plan. It is essential for inexperienced clinicians to consult with more experienced and culturally competent colleagues when test equivalence has not been shown in a satisfactory manner. A misdiagnosis may result in the mishandling of a psychological condition at best, and in aggravation of the presenting problem with severe consequences at worst.

The clinician should also bear in mind that cross-cultural issues are at play even when language is not a barrier. Group norms and values differ not only between Hispanic Americans and members of other cultures, but also within Hispanic subgroups. Given the task at hand in assessment, which involves comparing behaviors and scores against a "norm," it is important for the mental health professional to be aware of the cultural values held by an individual and how they differ from others in the same group (Carter 1991).

RESEARCH ISSUES

A direct application of an approach incorporating members of three generations in a study of Mexican-American grandparents was conducted by Strom and associates (1997). In their research, nonconsanguineal grandparents, parents, and grandchildren provided information about grandparents' strengths and needs. One hundred and eighty-one grandparents, 148 parents, and 173 school-age grandchildren were recruited from senior centers, public schools, community organizations, and churches that serve Hispanic families in metropolitan Phoenix, Arizona. Each grandchild selected a grandparent to evaluate. Likewise, grandparents chose a child, and parents identified both a child and a grandparent to keep in mind while answering the questions on the Grandparent Strengths and Needs Inventory (GSNI) (Strom and Strom 1993a). Given the population under study, grandparents and parents were given the choice of filling out the questionnaire in English or Spanish. Standard back-translation methods were employed for translation of the GSNI. An English-Spanish bilingual team of faculty and staff at one of the participating elementary schools discussed the items and their meaning to ensure comparability across cultures. After the team had agreed upon the translation, the items were discussed with grandparents and parents who could read Spanish. After minor corrections, the Spanish version was considered ready for administration.

Thirty-one percent of grandparents and 25 percent of parents chose to complete a Spanish version. When data were ready for analysis, a preliminary test was conducted to test the equivalence of Spanish and English answers. A finding that English and Spanish answers are equivalent would suggest that all answers could be pooled for subsequent analyses; a finding that the answers are significantly different would suggest that analyses should be conducted separately for each language. Because statistical differences were found as a function of language of test, subsequent multivariate analyses were conducted separately for each language.

Interesting differences emerged between groups. Spanish-speaking grandparents appear more isolated from mainstream information than English-speaking grandparents because they reported a greater need for information about their grandchildren's upbringing than the latter group. In fact, their need for information was very great, suggesting that programs for this population should address this issue. Spanish-speaking grandparents also reported more frustration than their English-speaking counterparts when dealing with adolescent grandchildren. This finding is not surprising, because the older grandchildren tend to be the most acculturated members of the family, and the Spanish-speaking grandparents the least acculturated; relationships between the two groups are often fraught with miscommunication and misunderstanding, and cultural issues are at the core of these conflicts.

For English-speaking grandparents, grandchildren reported a lower need for information about grandchildren's upbringing than the younger grandparents themselves. This indicates that, although younger grandparents may feel a need for additional knowledge, this deficit does not adversely affect grandchildren's perceptions of their knowledge. In addition, members of the three generations agreed that grandparents who spent more than five hours a month with their grandchildren were more effective in a number of grandparenting tasks than those who spent less time. This finding may suggest that grandparents who spend more time with their grandchildren get to know them better and consequently set more reasonable expectations for them. It may also suggest that grandparents who have more interest or talent choose to spend more time with their grandchildren.

The above discussion of research is meant to illustrate a strategy for conducting cross-cultural research with Latino grandparents. It is not meant to be a comprehensive review of the study. For further information, the reader is referred to the original manuscript. This research, although limited to nonconsanguineal grandparents, illustrates the usefulness of a specific approach that could incorporate members of different generations and the community at large.

TREATMENT APPROACHES

The clinical needs of the Hispanic elderly have been neglected in the literature (Vazquez and Clavijo 1995). The studies that exist today are focused primarily on Mexican-Americans (Cuellar 1990, Sotomayor 1991). In this respect, as previously stated, caution should be exercised when extrapolating from one Hispanic subpopulation to another, taking into consideration the differences surrounding immigration and acculturation. There are, however, stressors associated with the acculturation process that could apply to most older Hispanics.

Hispanic elderly, like other minority groups, have a lower institutionalization rate and a higher level of need than the majority population (Damron et al. 1994). This is one of the most dramatic differences between minority and nonminority elderly populations, and suggests the need for community support treatment facilities.

Treatment of the elderly in psychotherapy, including different modalities such as dynamic psychotherapies and groups, is viewed differently these days than it used to be. It is no longer believed that the elderly population is not amenable to treatment, but unfortunately the bulk of the available literature is based on the needs of an educated and resourceful older population. Because the majority of the Hispanic elderly do not hold high levels of education or have little awareness about how to navigate the system, innovative approaches need to be employed. Currently, experts agree that older Hispanics are faced with the reality of a shortage of services.

Traditional Hispanic culture puts great emphasis on respect of the elderly and family interdependency (Gallegos 1991). Older Hispanic patients may react more strongly to cultural issues such as *respeto*, particularly when they are working with a younger therapist. They may feel that the therapist is asking embarrassing questions. When therapists feel that there is a need for therapeutic confrontations and/or interpretations, it is essential that they keep cultural values such as *respeto* in mind. Therapy may necessitate different modalities of treatment that require the inclusion of cultural values and beliefs, including a deeper involvement on the part of the therapist and the incorporation of psychoeducational approaches.

The client's values can be included in the planning of culturally sensitive treatments. For example, the closeness of the family and the traditional family helping role can be used in the development of preventive strategies. Because self-esteem and health are influenced by a person's sense of usefulness and purpose in life, efforts need to be made to enhance older individuals' ability to contribute to their families and communities (Starrett et al. 1989). For example, child care can provide much needed help to parents, loving attention and teaching to grandchildren, and enhanced sense of purpose in life for grandparents. It is important to remember, however, that grandparents may need additional tools to be a good resource for their grandchildren. It is very likely that older Hispanics' grandchildren are growing up in a world much different from that in which the older generation was raised. Educational programs for African-American and Caucasian grandparents have shown that grandparents can enhance their grandparenting skills by revising their role. Grandparents attending such programs indicated that instruction has helped them (1) gain awareness on how to be more helpful to their children and grandchildren, (2) improve their outlook on family affairs, (3) increase mental stimulation, (4) gain better communication skills necessary for intergenerational communication, and (5) improve family relations (Strom and Strom 1993b, 1996).

Hispanic elderly often share in the care of children in the family. This is more prevalent today because of a combination of technological development and economic realities, which compel more parents to work outside the home, and sociocultural factors. The lengthening of the life span has also presented an unprecedented opportunity for older relatives to be of help to their children and grandchildren for a longer period of time (Aldous 1985). The proportion of children living with their grandparents is highest among blacks (13 percent), lower among Hispanics (6 percent) and lowest among Whites (3 percent).

Grandparents are stepping in as a support system for their grandchildren in times of family crisis, such as when an unmarried grandchild becomes a parent; or when a parent gets divorced, becomes unemployed, is unable to pay for child care, is addicted to alcohol or drugs, has committed child abuse, is in jail, suffers from illness, or is deceased (Burton 1992, Burton and Bengtson 1985, Cherlin and Furstenberg, Jr. 1986, Hagestad 1985, Minkler and Roe 1993, Norton and Glick 1986, Scherman et al. 1988, Strom and Strom 1993c, Thomas 1990). Although these circumstances are present in all segments of society, some of them are more prevalent among ethnic minority groups.

In the last decade the number of households headed by grandparents increased by 40 percent (Strom and Strom 1993c). It is estimated that 3.5 million children are being cared for by their grandparents (U.S. Bureau of the Census 1991). Parenting classes for younger generations are commonplace, yet grandparenting classes for the older generations are not. There is a growing literature, however, on grandparenting education (e.g., Strom and Strom 1989, 1990, 1991a,b,c), which includes a comprehensive grandparenting curriculum that has been found successful with white and African-American populations. Information is available on ways to adapt this curriculum for use with Mexican-American grandparents (Strom et al. in press). In addition, efforts are underway to identify the needs of grandparents in other Hispanic subgroups. Because Hispanic grandparents have a prominent role in their families, grandparenting education could be included in the planning of mental health services, particularly in preventive interventions. By helping grandparents become better resources for their grandchildren, Hispanic families can be empowered and strengthened, capitalizing on the strong extended family networks already in place for this group.

CONCLUSION

In light of the above, treatment approaches that take into account the older person's values, degree of acculturation, preferred language, and role in the family are imperative. Therapies that promote self-confidence and a feeling of control over inevitable losses, and that reduce feelings of isolation and alienation would be indicated. The use of support groups, group therapy, psychoeducational approaches, and intergenerational interventions is suggested.

REFERENCES

Aldous, J. (1985). Parent–adult child relations as affected by the grandparent status. In *Grandparenthood*, ed. V. L. Bengtson and J. F. Robertson, pp. 117–132. Beverly Hills, CA: Sage.

Aranda, M. P. (1990). Culture-friendly services for Latino elders. *Generations Counseling and Therapy*, Winter, 14(1):55–57.

Becerra, R. M., and Shaw, D. (1984). *The Hispanic Elderly: A Research Reference Guide*. New York: University Press of America.

Blendon, R. J., Aiken, L. H., Freeman, H. E., and Corey, C. R. (1989). Access to medical care for black and white Americans: a matter of continuing concern. *Journal of the American Medical Association* 216:278–281.

Buki, L. P., and Cañive, J. (1994). Evaluating test equivalence of a family assessment measure. In *Group and Family Therapy Research with Hispanic Adolescents*. Symposium conducted at the Annual Convention of the American Psychological Association, Los Angeles, CA, August.

Burton, L. M. (1992). Black grandparents rearing children of drug-addicted parents: stressors, outcomes, and social service needs. *The Gerontologist* 32:744–751.

Burton, L. M., and Bengtson, V. L. (1985). Black grandmothers: issues of timing and continuity of roles. In *Grandparenthood*, ed. V. L. Bengtson and J. F. Robertson, pp. 61–78. Beverly Hills, CA: Sage.

Butler, R. N., Lewis, M. I., and Sunderland, T. (1991). *Aging and Mental Health: Positive Psychosocial and Biomedical Approaches*, 4th ed. New York: Merrill.

Carter, R. T. (1991). Cultural values: a review of empirical research and implications for counseling. *Journal of Counseling and Development* 70:164–173.

Cheesman-Day, J. (1996). *Current Population Reports: Projections of the United States by Age, Sex, Race, and Hispanic Origin: 1995 to 2050*. Bureau of the Census. Series P–25, No. 1104. Washington, DC: U.S. Government Printing Office.

Cherlin, A., and Furstenberg, F. F., Jr. (1986). Grandparents and family crisis. *Generations* 10:26–28.

Clark, L. H. (1995). Issues and concerns of the elderly: implications for counselors. In *Counseling Diverse Populations*, ed. D. R. Atkinson and G. Hackett, pp. 190–206. Madison, WI: Brown & Benchmark.

Cuellar, J. B. (1990). Geriatric education curriculum development for selected health professionals. In *Minority Aging: Essential Curricula Content for Selected Health and Allied Health Professions*, ed. M. S. Harper, pp. 365–413. DHHS Publication No. HRS P–DV–90–4. Washington, DC: U.S. Government Printing Office.

Damron, J. A., Wallace, S., and Kington, R. K. (1994). *Service Utilization and Minority Elderly: Appropriateness, Accessibility and Acceptability*. New York: Haworth.

Flemming, A. S., Richards, L. D., Santos, J. F., and West, P. R. (1986). *Report on a Survey of Community Mental Health Centers*, vol. 3. Action Committee to Implement the Mental Health Recommendations of the 1981 White House Conference on Aging. Washington, DC: American Psychological Association.

Gallegos, J. S. (1991). Culturally relevant services for Hispanic elderly. In *Empowering Hispanic Families: A Critical Issue for the '90s*, ed. M. Sotomayor, pp. 173–190. Milwaukee, WI: Family Service America.

García, C. (1993). What do we mean by extended family? A closer look at Hispanic multigenerational families. *Journal of Cross Cultural Gerontology* 8:137–146.

Garza, R. T., and Gallegos, P. I. (1995). Environmental influences and personal choices. a humanistic perspective on acculturation. In *Hispanic Psychology: Critical Issues in Theory and Research*, ed. A. Padilla, pp. 3–14. Thousand Oaks, CA: Sage.

Hagestad, G. O. (1985). Continuity and connectedness. In *Grandparenthood*, ed. V. L. Bengtson and J. F. Robertson, pp. 31–48. Beverly Hills, CA: Sage.

Karno, M., Burnam, M. A., Escobar, J. I., et al. (1983). Development of the Spanish-language version of the National Institute of Mental Health diagnostic interview schedule. *Archives of General Psychiatry* 40:1183–1188.

Labovitz, P. (1996). Immigration just the facts. *The New York Times*, March 25, OP-ED A15.

Lambert, J. (1967). *Latin America Social Structures and Political Institutions*. Trans. Helen Katel. Berkeley: University of California Press.

Luckingham, B. (1994). *Minorities in Phoenix: A Profile of Mexican American, Chinese American, and African American Communities, 1860–1992*. Tucson: University of Arizona Press.

Marin, G., and VanOss, M. B. (1991). Hispanics: Who Are They? In *Applied Social Research Methods Series: Vol. 23. Research with Hispanic Populations*, pp. 1–17. Newbury Park, CA: Sage.

McKay, R. B., Breslow, M. J., Sangster, R. L., et al. (1996). Translating survey questionnaires: lessons learned. *New Directions for Evaluation* 70:93–104.

Minkler, M., and Roe, K. N. (1993). *Grandmothers as Caregivers: Raising Children of the Crack Cocaine Epidemic*. Newbury Park, CA: Sage.

Miranda, M. (1991). Mental health services and the Hispanic elderly. In *Empowering Hispanic Families: A Critical Issue for the '90s*, ed. M. Sotomayor, pp. 141–153. Milwaukee, WI: Family Service America.

Miranda, M. R., and Ruiz, R. A. (1981). Research on the Chicano elderly: theoretical and methodological issues. In *Chicano Aging and Mental Health*, ed. M. Miranda and R. A. Ruiz, pp. 269–279. Rockville, MD: National Institute of Mental Health.

Muller, T., and Espenshade, T. J. (1985). *The Fourth Wave: California's Newest Immigrants*. Washington, DC: Urban Institute.

Norton, A. J., and Glick, P. C. (1986). One parent families: a social and economic profile. *Family Relations* 35:9–17.

Sabogal, F., Marin, G., Otero-Sabogal, R., et al. (1987). Hispanic familism and acculturation: What changes and what doesn't? *Hispanic Journal of Behavioral Science*
9:397–412.

Scherman, A., Goodrich, C., Kelly, C., et al. (1988). Grandparents as a support system for children. *Elementary School Guidance and Counseling* 23:16–22.

Sotomayor, M. (1989). The Hispanic elderly and the intergenerational family. *Journal
of Children in Contemporary Society* 20:55–65.

——— (1991). Introduction. In *Empowering Hispanic Families: A Critical Issue for the
'90s*, ed. M. Sotomayor, pp. xi–xxiii. Milwaukee, WI: Family Service America.

Starrett, R. A., Todd, A., Decker, J. T., and Walters, G. (1989). The use of formal
helping networks to meet the psychological needs of the Hispanic elderly.
Hispanic Journal of Behavioral Sciences 11:259–273.

Strom, R. D., Buki, L. P., and Strom, S. K. (1997). Intergenerational perceptions of
English speaking and Spanish speaking Mexican American grandparents.
International Journal of Aging and Human Development 45:1–21.

Strom, R. D., and Strom, S. K. (1989). Grandparents and learning. *International
Journal of Aging and Human Development* 29:163–169.

——— (1990). Raising expectations for grandparents: a three-generational study.
International Journal of Aging and Human Development 31:161–167.

——— (1991a). *Becoming a Better Grandparent: A Guidebook for Strengthening the
Family*. Newbury Park, CA: Sage.

——— (1991b). *Becoming a Better Grandparent: Viewpoints on Strengthening the
Family*. Newbury Park, CA: Sage.

——— (1991c). *Grandparent Education: A Guide for Leaders*. Newbury Park, CA:
Sage.

——— (1993a). *Grandparent Strengths and Needs Inventory Manual*. Chicago, IL:
Scholastic Testing Service.

——— (1993b). Grandparent education to enhance family strength. In *Encyclopedia
of Adult Development*, ed. R. Kastenbaum, pp. 186–194. Phoenix, AZ: Oryx.

——— (1993c). Grandparents raising grandchildren: goals and support groups.
Educational Gerontology 19:705–715.

Strom, R., Strom, S., Collinsworth, P., et al. (1996). Black grandparents: curriculum
development. *International Journal of Aging and Human Development*
43:119–134.

Thomas, J. L. (1990). The grandparent role: a double bind. *International Journal of
Aging and Human Development* 31:169–177.

Triandis, H. C., Marin, G., Betancourt, H., Lisansky, J., and Chang, B. (1982).
Dimensions of Familism among Hispanic and Mainstream Navy Recruits. Chicago:
University of Illinois Press.

U.S. Bureau of the Census (1991). *Current Population Reports: Marital Status and
Living Arrangements*. Series P–20, No. 450. Washington, DC: U.S. Government
Printing Office.

Valle, R., and Martinez, C. (1981). Natural networks of elderly Latinos of Mexican heritage: implications for mental health. In *Chicano Aging and Mental Health*, ed. M. Miranda and R. A. Ruiz, DHHS Publication No. (ADM) 81–952. Rockville, MD: National Institute of Mental Health.

Vazquez, C. I., and Clavijo, A. (1995). The special needs of elderly minorities: a profile of Hispanics. In *Mental Health Services for Older Adults: Implications for Training and Practice in Geropsychology*, ed. B. G. Knight, L. Teri, P. Wohlford, and J. Santos, pp. 93–99. Washington, DC: American Psychological Association.

World Bank (1993). *Human Capital Development and Operations Policy HCO* Dissemination Notes.

27

Common Errors by Interpreters in Communicating with Linguistically Diverse Patients

RAFAEL ART. JAVIER, CARMEN I. VAZQUEZ, AND LUIS R. MARCOS

Language is the primary, although not the only, mode by which our experiences are organized and communicated cognitively and emotionally (Piaget 1955, Vygotsky 1962). It is intimately connected with many aspects of human interaction (Cassirer 1953, Javier 1989, Whorf 1956). Thus it is not surprising that linguistic manifestations are frequently seen as accurate reflections of emotional processes.

Mental health professionals make particular use of these linguistic manifestations because it has been observed that language is vulnerable to the effect of pathological conditions (Krapf 1955, Marcos 1976, Marcos et al. 1973). Buxbaum (1949) and Hartmann (1958) suggested that language is one of the functions of the ego that deteriorates when the ego is impaired. This has been repeatedly reported by Javier (1989), Mahl (1959), and Marcos (1976) with monolingual and bilingual individuals suffering from various degrees of psychopathology.

The problem with dealing with individuals who possess two or more linguistic modes of communication is that linguistic deficiencies do not always reflect pathological disturbance. It may only indicate linguistic deficiencies or, at the very least, an interactive condition. Marcos (1976) and Marcos and colleagues (1973) demonstrated that the linguistic deficiencies manifested in the second language by schizophrenic bilingual individuals who are deficient in second-language processing (subordinate linguistic organization) can be viewed by clinicians unfamiliar with the impact of bilingualism as reflecting the deteriorating effect of a psychotic process. These patients were evaluated as sicker when interviewed in the second language. Del Castillo's (1970) patients, on the other hand, demonstrated more pathology in the primary language. Although Marcos's studies and Del Castillo's observations have been criticized from a methodological perspective (Price and Cuellar 1981, Vazquez 1982), the fact that the nature and extent of emotional difficulties can be reflected linguistically is strongly emphasized by both authors. The success in distinguishing between these deficiencies will improve the nature and quality of the evaluation and treatment of these individuals.

This task is further complicated when interpreters are routinely incorporated as part of the evaluation and treatment process. This is particularly the case in many urban psychiatric centers that, as a solution to the shortage of bilingual/bicultural professionals, are now including untrained interpreters as an essential part of the evaluative process. To complicate matters to an even greater extent, these untrained interpreters are usually janitors, clerical helpers, other staff professionals, and even patients or relatives of patients (Marcos 1979). Although practical considerations are usually cited as the reason for this occurrence, such a practice represents a tremendous danger to the process of communication. It certainly puts in doubt the accuracy of the evaluation and treatment given to these patients. It may reflect only an inaccurate translation or a vague interpretation of the patient's difficulties. Furthermore, such a practice demonstrates a lack of appreciation of the complexity inherent in the process of communication. In this chapter we will address the crucial role played by interpreters in the evaluation of psychopathology and will briefly outline the complex nature of the interpretation process. Descriptions of the common errors in interpretation will also be provided.

COMMUNICATION PROCESS

Communication between two individuals involves the process of transmitting (decoding and encoding), both verbally and nonverbally, different perceptions, experiences, beliefs, and thought processes as well as the affective components associated with these perceptions, experiences, beliefs, and thoughts (Vazquez and Javier 1991). When the communication occurs between individuals whose worlds have developed in different geographical, cultural, and linguistic contexts (Ervin 1963, Whorf 1956), it is even more difficult to gauge accurately what is being communicated. The likelihood for misconception, therefore, depends on the personal cultural and linguistic histories of the individuals involved in the communication. When such histories diverge greatly from one another, the possibilities for misunderstandings and gaps in the communication increase (Dale 1972). However, this communication gap can be reduced provided that there is an appreciation, respectful awareness, acceptance, and sensitivity not only at the linguistic level but also at the cultural, political, and socioeconomic level between the clinician and the patient. This nonjudgmental attitude, which has been described in the psychoanalytic literature as "evenly suspended attention" (Freud 1912) and "listening with a third ear" (Reik 1958), and more amply described by Freedman (1983) in terms of its components, allows for not-easily-understood data to become part of the information bank.

Psychiatric patients present an additional challenge to clinicians because their communications are frequently fraught with tangentiality and other cognitive distortions (Vazquez and Javier 1991). Problems for these patients are compounded when clinicians come to the interaction with a preconceived notion that "psychiatric patients do not make sense" and thus are less inclined to try to obtain accurate information from these patients. As indicated earlier, such a bias or distortion may be further intensified when the individuals being evaluated come from a culture and linguistic community that is different from that of the interviewer (Marcos et al. 1973). The communication process is therefore dependent upon the clinician's ability to maintain the necessary flexibility in order to take the perspective of his or her patient. Only in this way can the patient's true levels of difficulty be accurately ascertained.

INTERPRETATION PROCESS

The previous section emphasized the communication between two individuals. Here, we focus on the interpretation process, which by definition requires three individuals, one functioning as the mediator of the communication between the two main actors. The process of interpretation is not just a linguistic exercise but requires an appropriate knowledge and appreciation of the culture, geographical characteristics, sociopolitical and sociolinguistic realities, regionalism, and educational background, as well as the logic systems of interpersonal communications of both the speaker and the receiver of the message. That is to say, it requires a process of interpretative transposition of the message. This allows for the intended meaning of the communication to retain its accuracy to a greater extent.

However, the process of interpretation refers to a very specific process often confused with translation. A definition distinguishing these terms is relevant to our discussion. In this chapter we will use the concept of interpretation to refer to the process of communicating orally across linguistic/cultural barriers (Arjona 1977). It does not involve a literal linguistic transposition of the message but, instead, the oral translation of the intended meaning. A translation, on the other hand, is the communication of information from one language into another in written form. According to Arjona (1977), it refers to the interlingual, sociolinguistic, and cultural transfer of any message from one individual to another, through written, oral, or mechanical means or combination thereof. It is a specialized discipline of academic studies.

Of great importance is the clarification that fluency of language alone is not sufficient for the quality of interpretation and/or translation. It is also important to recognize that these processes are not automatic within individuals. In fact, it is believed that they require an innate ability (Grosjean 1982). Nevertheless, the complexity of the process of translation and interpretation skills can be developed through training (Acosta and Cristo 1981, Arjona 1977). A good interpreter is one who is able to render the original message into the necessary meaningful linguistic and paralinguistic symbols and codes of the listener's culture and language (Arjona 1977). It is not surprising from this perspective that the interpretation provided by the unsophisticated and untrained interpreters, such as those routinely used by hospitals and clinics, may be fraught with inaccuracies and distortions; hence the question of whether you are communicating with your patients, especially when the interaction between the clinician and the patient is mediated by an interpreter.

Interpretation of the psychiatric patient's verbalizations requires, in addition to the cultural and linguistic issues referred to above, knowledge of the professional jargon, specific concepts, including understanding of blocking, derailment, tangentiality, and other indications of thought disorder or markers for psychopathology (Bellak and Faithorn 1981, de Zulueta 1984). Failure to do so could render the interview meaningless because the clinician is not getting an accurate picture of what the patient presents. For example, if a patient is blocking a thought or using convoluted structure of language, an untrained interpreter might construct the utterance to make sense, thus injecting a personal meaning. Doing this type of reconstruction for the patient distorts and minimizes the actual pathology for the clinician. Similarly, distortion can occur when the interpreter misconstrues the patient's verbalizations and thus increases the perception of pathology.

Regarding the role of culture in the interpretation process, it is important to clarify a common confusion. In determining the nature of biculturalism of an interpreter or patient, it is normally assumed that a bilingual person is automatically bicultural and a monolingual individual is automatically monocultural. Such a confusion could not be further from the truth. This can easily be demonstrated in some African nations using a lingua franca that has shown that bilingualism and biculturalism are not automatically coexistent. Similarly, French-speaking Britons or English-speaking Scots who are bicultural demonstrate that you can have one language and two cultures (Grosjean 1982). In the United States we can find many English-speaking native Americans and second and third generation immigrants who share more than one culture, but might speak only one language, English. This suggests the importance of accurately determining the cultural and linguistic characteristics of the individuals involved in the communication without making assumptions based on linguistic or cultural characteristics alone. It questions, for instance, the assumed similarities within the different ethnic groups (e.g., blacks, Latin Americans, Asians, and so forth from different geographical locations) and calls for an appreciation of the ways their similarities and differences may impact on their linguistic and psychopathological behaviors.

METHODS OF INTERPRETATION

The complexity of the interpretation process notwithstanding, distortions of communication can be greatly minimized when interpreters are properly selected and trained (Acosta and Cristo 1981). Two main methods of interpretation have been suggested: simultaneous and consecutive. Namy (1977), Arjona (1977), and Longley (1977) suggested simultaneous interpretation as the best method to apprehend and communicate the message in its entirety. During this process, the interpreter renders the interpretation of the material concurrently or in very close proximity to the speaker's verbalization. It does not give much room for the interpreter to inject personal meaning or to evaluate the nature of the message.

Consecutive interpretation, on the other hand, lends itself to much more distortion of the message because the interpreter provides the interpretation after the speaker has completed part of or the whole message. Thus the possibility for the injection of personal meaning and reorganization of the message is greatly enhanced. Implied in this formulation, therefore, is the idea that simultaneous interpretation provides the best condition when non-English-speaking patients have to be evaluated/treated by a monolingual English-speaking professional.

It is not the scope of this chapter to provide a detailed description of or endorsement for a specific interpretation method. It suffices to say that the simultaneous interpretation method was found to be effective in a pilot study conducted by Luis Marcos and Palma Valverde (personal communication). According to Namy, Arjona, and Longley, simultaneous interpretation allows the speaker optimal access to verbal and nonverbal aspects of the communication more directly and clearly (e.g., body language, tone of voice, etc.) in a manner not provided by the other method. This is true because the simultaneous interpretation method requires the interpreter to be physically positioned unobtrusively outside the visual field of the individuals involved in the communication (e.g., behind the patient). Typical training for this kind of interpretation normally includes role-playing exercises regarding the actual interpretation process, listening process, and adequate facial and bodily movements. The training also provides information on the cultural, linguistic, and sociopolitical characteristics of the speaker and the listener as well as training concerning psychiatric concepts. Attention is given to the accuracy of the interpretation, language proficiency, vocabulary usage, and recognition of psychiatric terminology in the languages involved in the interpretation (Namy 1977).

COMMON ERRORS

There are many ways in which an interpreter can render a message inaccurate and confusing (Marcos 1979). The errors referred to here usually occur when an interpreter takes shortcuts or "literary liberty" because of a lack of familiarity with specific concepts, colloquial regionalism, slang, and so forth; a lack of appreciation of the importance of accurate interpretation; or a lack of interest. The latter may be particularly present in the case of unwilling interpreters who experience interpreting for patients as an additional burden to their already arduous job. In situations where the demand for bilingual/bicultural professionals cannot be met, there is a tendency to overwork not only the few professionals with bilingual/bicultural backgrounds, but also the paraprofessionals and support staff. This in turn may contribute to an early burnout syndrome for these individuals.

Although the emphasis of this chapter is on the description of common errors in the communication process and the importance of using trained interpreters in the field of mental health, we cannot emphasize enough the role played by the clinician in this regard. Indeed, many times interpreters are faced with the almost insurmountable task of having to interpret communication from clinicians whose idiosyncratic and peculiar linguistic behavior is not easily understandable. Such a condition may contribute to communication errors, with the subsequent impact on the evaluation of the patient's pathology and treatment plan.

In the following paragraphs we will describe the most common errors observed with untrained interpreters. We will use the abbreviations C, P, and I to refer to the clinician, patient, and interpreter, respectively. Parentheses will be used to provide a more accurate interpretation when the one offered is inaccurate.

Omission

Omission is a process by which an interpreter may completely or partially delete a message sent by a speaker. Examples of this can be seen in the following exchanges between a patient and a clinician mediated by an interpreter.

Exchange 1
C. Well, it seems to me that it is difficult for her to talk about the family and how everybody is feeling.
I. El ... tenemos la impresión de que le es un poco difícil hablar de la situación de la familia y cómo se está sintiendo con la familia. [He ... We have the impression that it is a little difficult for you to speak about the family situation and how you are feeling with the family.]
P. ¡Aha! (*not translated*)
C. I noticed that she [patient] smiled. Could she tell me why?
I. ¿El nota que se sonríe, le puede explicar por qué?
P. Es que le estoy explicando lo de mis hijas. [It is that I am explaining about my daughters.]
I. She said something, I don't know if I should go on ...

Exchange 2
C. OK and how is she feeling about that plan?
I. ¿Y que usted opina sobre ese plan?
P. Bueno, según ella me dijo, que era para ayudarme a mi, para darme la misma receta, para ayudarme al tratamiento que me daba ella. No me

acuerdo. [Well, according to what she—social worker—told me, it was to help me, to give me the same prescription medication, to help me in the treatment she was providing for me. I don't remember.]

I. OK she says basically it was to help her to continue her medication and to help her with the housing problem.

Exchange 3

C. Yes, were things ever different between her and her son?

I. ¿Usted, en algun momento, ha tenido una relación distinta con su hijo? Las cosas eran distintas antes con el?

P. ¿Cómo? (*not interpreted*) [What?]

I. Cómo Ud. se llevaba con su hijo anteriormente? [How did you get along with your son before?]

P. Bien. Lo que lo hicieron asi eran las malas amistades . . . esta vacio. [Well, what made him like that was the bad company. He is empty.]

I. He wasn't really like that but maybe he changes from his bad friends, wrong friends.

P. Y No va a la escuela. No quiere ir a la escuela, no. [He does not go to school, he refuses to go to school, no.]

C. I see, so that must be very painful for her.

I. (*not interpreted*)

Although these three exchanges demonstrate different kinds of errors, the most prominent ones are errors of omission. In Exchange 1, for instance, the interpreter failed to relate to the clinician the patient's response to the question about her smile. Similarly, in Exchange 2, not only is the patient's communication condensed, but the fact that the patient responded with "I don't remember" was never related to the clinician. In Exchange 3, the clinician's attempt to be empathic with the patient ("I see, so that must be very painful for her") was not communicated to the patient. It is possible that the smile is inappropriate or that "I don't remember" is irrelevant or that the patient may ignore the clinician's attempt to be empathic; however, the clinician is not given all the information provided by the patient and the patient is not provided with all the communication from the clinician, which further diminishes the patient's opportunity to respond coherently.

Additions

This refers to an interpreter's tendency to include information not expressed by the speaker. It normally occurs in conjunction with a partial or complete omission of a message.

Exchange 4

C. Likewise, how her . . . could she tell me how she perceives the problem now, with her son?

I. El ha leido sobre eso en su expediente, pero usted puede decir un poco más sobre cómo están los cosas con su hijo? ¿Explicarle un poco mas sobre su relacion con su hijo? [He has read about this in your record, but could you say more about how things are going with your son? Explain more about your relationship with your son?]

P. ¿Qué es lo que paso? aha! [What happened? aha!] (*not interpreted*)

I. ¡Si, exacto! [Yes, exactly.]

P. Pues, yo tengo un hijo de 14 años y me da muchos problemas por cuestión de malas amistades que tiene, éste . . . ha cogido vicios con ellos y se busca problema en un hotel en que yo vivo, éste . . . . no respeta, no hace caso, en eso yo me he descontrolado los nervios. [Well, I have a 14-year-old son who gives me a great deal of trouble due to his bad company. He . . . . has picked up vices from them and gets himself in trouble at a hotel where I live, he . . . does not show any respect, he does not pay attention, in that I have lost control of my nerves.]

I. She has a 14-year-old who has been giving her a hard time. He's been hanging around with wrong people. He's been now picking a lot of different kinds of vices, drugs, sounds like drug problems. She lives in a hotel and he's been giving problems there, getting into a lot of trouble.

In this exchange we can see how the interpreter's personal bias is added to the patient's message (". . . drugs, sounds like drug problems") while also condensing the patient's verbalization about her experience with her son. Her feeling that her son shows no respect and does not pay attention to her is not related to the clinician and hence the clinician may miss the interpersonal/cultural nature of patient–son conflict.

Condensation

Condensation refers to an interpreter's tendency to simplify and explain a message sent by a speaker. It usually occurs when omission and addition has taken place. It is clearly demonstrated in Exchange 2 when the patient's long response to the clinician's question is summarized with ". . . she says basically. . . . ." Similarly, in Exchange 4 the same condensation process takes place with regard to the patient's experience with her son. As indicated earlier, the part of her message that is deleted, coupled with the elements added, can only contribute to an inaccurate appraisal of the patient's experience.

Substitutions

This error refers to an interpreter's tendency to replace concepts in a message sent by a speaker with the purpose of embellishing or condensing it. A change in the meaning of the message usually occurs. The errors resulting from substituting aspects of the communication are related to omission, addition, and condensation errors described above.

Consider the following exchange:

Exchange 5

C. Since you were started in the medicine, which was about three weeks, have you, eh, been, ah, experiencing anything unusual like feeling that somebody is talking to you and there will be nobody else there?

I. Mientras estaba sobre la medicación, mientras estabas cogiendo la medicación, tu oido "voices," ¿te has sentido distinto, diferente, o de otra forma? [While you were on the medication, while you were taking the medication, did you hear voices, or have you felt different . . . or in a different way?]

P. No, igual, siempre igual.

I. He says, always the same.

C. What does that mean?

I. ¿Cómo, qué es igual? [How, what is the same?]

P. ¡Bien, bien!

I. He says, fine, fine!

In this exchange we can see that the patient's response is not to the clinician's question but to the interpreter's verbalization, resulting in confusion. In addition to condensation and addition errors, the interpreter substituted "somebody is talking to you and there will be nobody else there" as "hearing voices" and "what does that mean?" for "what is the same?" The interpreter's verbalization ". . . or felt different . . . ?" resulted in the patient's "inappropriate" response (". . . always the same") to the clinician's question regarding the presence of "auditory hallucinations." Consequently, the issue of the auditory hallucinations could not be assessed.

Role Exchange

This error refers to the interpreter's tendency to take over the interaction and replace questions from the speaker with his or her own set of questions as if assuming the role of the clinician or the patient.

The following exchange demonstrates this error:

Exchange 6
C. And who . . . was anyone else in the household?
P. No.
C. Do you have any other family besides your mother?
I. ¿Tiene otra familia fuera de su mamà?
P. ¡Sí, sí! [Yes, yes.]
I. ¿Quienes? [Who?]
P. Mis hermanos. [My brothers.]
I. ¿Sus hermanos? Cuanto? [Your brothers? How many?]
P. Quince. [Fifteen.]
I. ¿Quince? ¿Pero no viven todos juntos? [Fifteen? But do you all live together?]
P. No, en frente. [No, across the street.]

Although this particular exchange may not have serious consequences for the patient, consider what could happen in a situation where an assessment of suicidal or homicidal potential is being performed. Since interpreters are not always knowledgeable of the crucial components necessary for such an assessment, they may fail to relate important information related by the patient to the clinician. Indeed, interpreters who make this kind of mistake usually tend to condense the message and include his or her view about the speaker's message. This occurred in Exchange 4 when the interpreter indicated that it ". . . sounds like drug problems" even though the patient never reported this. A similar situation was described in an earlier paper (Vazquez and Javier 1991) in which the evaluation of a patient's level of suicidality was seriously compromised by a family member's inability to communicate to the clinician the patient's true psychiatric state. The family member failed to mention to the clinician the patient's depression or the fact that the patient was hearing her dead mother's voice.

CONCLUSION

These issues regarding the negative consequence of communication errors cannot be sufficiently underlined. The different exchanges presented here attempt to demonstrate the deleterious effect of errors that an interpreter can make. They play a crucial role in rendering the communication between a patient and clinician either clear and accurate or confusing. The interpreter serves as a liaison, or bridge, between two worlds, each with its own history, geography, belief systems, culture, language, and logic systems of interpersonal communication. Adequate interpretation poses a heavy burden for the interpreter, as the nature and quality of the interpretative activity may make a difference between life and death for some patients and for the public at large. The nature and quality of the treatment patients receive are also significantly impacted by poor interpretation. This is particularly the case with psychiatric patients who may have lost, partially or completely, the capacity to organize a fluid and chaotic subjective experience.

To avoid complications resulting from inadequate interpretations provided by untrained interpreters, it is strongly recommended that individuals serving this role be properly trained (Acosta and Cristo 1981, Arjona 1977, Longley 1977, Namy 1977). Only in this manner will the intended meaning of the communication have a chance to retain its accuracy. Individuals functioning as interpreters and lacking proper training tend to add, omit, condense, and/or substitute important information in the communication as delineated above. Similarly, they tend to take on the role of the clinician and/or the patient (role exchange) and encourage the relationship between patient and clinician to remain detached and impersonal (e.g., using the third person pronoun—"The patient or the doctor said that . . .").

The deleterious impact of these types of errors on the evaluation of psychopathology was assessed systematically in a previous study by Marcos (1979). He concluded that distortions in communication can occur when the interpreters have:

1. Insufficient language competence and deficient interpretative skills
2. Insufficient psychiatric sophistication
3. Questionable attitude toward the patient and/or the clinician

This issue of personal attitude is particularly problematic when using family members or other interpreters with strong personal views, as demonstrated by Marcos (1979) and Vazquez and Javier (1991). For example, Marcos described the reaction of a daughter who expressed strong negative feelings about the medication the clinician had just prescribed, and encouraged the mother not to take it. It is in these kinds of situations that pre- and postinterview meetings of the clinicians and interpreters are strongly encouraged. According to Marcos, these meetings should focus on a discussion of the goals of the evaluation, the focal areas to be assessed, and the interpreter's attitude regarding any aspect of the process.

There are different components to objectively assess in training interpreters. The goal of training is ultimately to prepare better listeners who are able to render the original message into the necessary meaningful linguistic and paralinguistic symbols and codes of the listener's culture and language. The training of interpreters, however, is only an interim and partial solution to the problem. The more adequate and ethical solution to this problem is the training and hiring of professionals with bilingual and bicultural backgrounds who have an appreciation of the patient's cultural and linguistic characteristics.

REFERENCES

Acosta, F. X., and Cristo, M. H. (1981). Development of a bilingual interpreter program: an alternative model for Spanish-speaking services. *Professional Psychology* 12(4):474–482.

Arjona, E. (1977). Intercultural communication and the training of interpreters at the Monterey institute of foreign studies. In *Language Interpretation and Communication*, ed. D. Gerver and H. W. Sinaido. New York and London: Plenum Press.

Bellak, L., and Faithorn, P. (1981). *Crisis and Special Problems in Psychoanalysis and Psychotherapy*. New York: Brunner/Mazel.

Buxbaum, F. (1949). The role of a second language in the formation of ego and superego. *International Journal of Psychiatry* 18:279–289.

Cassirer, F. (1953). *Language and Myth*. New York: Dover.

Dale, P. S. (1972). *Language Development, Structure and Function*. Hinsdale, IL: Dryden.

Del Castillo, J. (1970). The influence of language upon symptomatology in foreign-born patients. *American Journal of Psychiatry* 127:242–244.

de Zulueta, F. I. S. (1984). The implications of bilingualism in the study and treatment of psychiatric disorders: a review. *Psychological Medicine* 14:541–557.

Ervin. S. (1963). Language and TAT content in bilinguals. *Journal of Abnormal and Social Psychology* 68:500–507.

Freedman, N. (1983). On psychoanalytic listening: the construction, paralysis, and reconstruction of meaning. *Psychoanalysis and Contemporary Thought* 6(3):405–434.

Freud, S. (1912). Recommendations to physicians practising psychoanalysis. *Standard Edition* 12:109–120.

Grosjean, F. (1982). *Life with Two Languages: An Introduction to Bilingualism*. Cambridge, MA: Harvard University Press.

Hartmann, H. (1958). *Ego Psychology and the Problem of Adaptation*. New York: International Universities Press.

Javier, R. (1989). Linguistic considerations in the treatment of bilinguals. *Psychoanalytic Psychology* 5(1):87–96.

Krapf, E. E. (1955). The choice of language in polyglot psychoanalysis. *Psychoanalytic Quarterly* 24:343–357.

Longley, P. (1977). An integrated programme for training interpreters. In *Language Interpretation and Communication*, ed. D. Gerver and H. W. Sinaido. New York/London: Plenum.

Mahl, G. F. (1959). Measuring the patient's anxiety during interviews from "expres-
    sive" aspects of his speech. *Annals of the New York Academy of Sciences* 21:249–257.
Marcos, L. R. (1976). Bilinguals in psychotherapy: language as an emotional barrier.
    American Journal of Psychiatry 30:552–560.
——— (1979). Effects of interpreters on the evaluation of psychopathology in non-
    English-speaking patients. *American Journal of Psychiatry* 136(2):171–174.
Marcos, L. R., Alpert, M., Urcuyo, L., and Kesselman, M. (1973). The effect of inter-
    view language on the evaluation of psychopathology in Spanish-American
    schizophrenic patients. *American Journal of Psychiatry* 29:655–659.
Namy, C. (1977). Reflections on the training of simultaneous interpreters: A metalin-
    guistic approach. In *Language Interpretation and Communication*, ed. D. Gerver
    and H. W. Sinaido. New York/London: Plenum.
Piaget, J. (1955). *The Language and Thought of the Child*. Cleveland: Meridian.
Price, C., and Cuellar, I. (1981). Effects of language and related variables on the
    expression of psychopathology in Mexican Americans. *Hispanic Journal of
    Behavioral Sciences* 3:145–160.
Reik, T. (1958). *Listening with the Third Ear: The Inner Experience of a Psychoanalyst*.
    New York: Farrar, Straus.
Vazquez, C. A. (1982). Research on the psychiatric evaluation of the bilingual patient:
    a methodological critique. *Hispanic Journal of Behavioral Sciences* 4:75–80.
Vazquez, C. A., and Javier, R. A. (1991). The problem with interpreters: communi-
    cating with Spanish-speaking patients. *Hospital and Community Psychiatry*
    42(2):163–165.
Vygotsky, L. S. (1962). *Thought and Language*. Cambridge, MA: MIT Press.
Whorf, B. (1956). *Language, Thought and Reality*. Cambridge, MA: MIT Press.

28

Psychotherapy with Asian Immigrant Populations: Psychoanalytic-Narrative and Constructivist Cognitive Approaches

WILLIAM BRACERO AND ELLEN C. TSUI

INTRODUCTION

Although Asian Americans have been described as a model minority with favorable demographic statistics such as high academic performance and a median family income above the national median, it has been documented that prevalence of mental illness among Asian Americans is not significantly lower than the general American population. In an interview study with adults in a large Chinatown community, Loo and colleagues (1989) found that 33 percent of the adult subjects they surveyed reported emotional tension, while 40 percent expressed depressed feelings. Other investigations also reported similar rates of psychological disorders among different Asian-American groups across the country (Hurh and Kim 1988, Kinzie et al. 1990, Kuo 1984, Kuo and Tsai 1986). In addition, research conducted in various Asian nations has shown that Asians experience the same symptoms of mental illness as other ethnic groups, albeit with lower prevalence rates, as reported in the study by Lee and colleagues (1990a). Nevertheless, Asian Americans are less likely to use mental health services than other ethnic groups, according to Sue and Morishima (1982). These researchers hypothesize that factors contributing to Asians' underutilization of mental health services include language barriers, stigma toward mental illness, and therapists' inability to deliver culturally responsive forms of treatment (Sue and Zane 1987).

With the advent of the postmodernist movement in Western philosophy, along with a growing awareness of cultural diversity in the United States, psychological research has begun to explore Asian Americans' unique cultural traits and mental health needs in order to facilitate service delivery. Among Asian Americans, there are disparate groups who experience distinct acculturation processes and psychological stressors, and who have different socioeconomic characteristics, expectations of mental health treatment, and service needs. To deliver effective services, one needs a thorough understanding of the diverse characteristics and needs of Asian Americans.

Composition of Asian Americans

Chinese began immigrating to the United States in the eighteenth century; numbers were initially small, though, as the Chinese Exclusion Act of 1882 allowed only men to enter the country to take up hard labor jobs such as mining and railroad construction. In 1965 the immigration law changed and families were able to immigrate more freely. As a result, the number of Asian immigrants started to expand, with Chinese and Japanese the two largest groups. This new pool of Chinese immigrants was mainly from Taiwan and Hong Kong. While many still had only limited education, some came from better educated and more affluent economic backgrounds and spoke different Chinese languages.

Since the diplomatic relationship between Mainland China and the U.S. resumed in the early '70s, a new wave of immigrants from Mainland China arrived in the U.S. under the Family Reunification bill. Many of these new immigrants came from rural backgrounds and have limited education, partly due to the denunciation of education during the Cultural Revolution in China during the '60s. Chinese now constitute the largest Asian-American subgroup.

The Japanese initially moved to Hawaii in the 1880s as contract laborers on plantations, and in the 1890s to work on farms on the U.S. mainland. Among the Japanese whose immigration to the U.S. was not restricted by the

Exclusionary Act, many have stayed in this country for several generations: Issei (first generation, emigrated prior to the Immigration Act of 1924), Nisei (second generation, born between 1910 and 1940), Sansei (third generation, born between 1940 and 1965), and Yonsei (fourth generation, born between 1965 and 1995). Overall, they have achieved higher education and income levels than other Asian immigrants, but at no little cost to their Japanese heritage, which became the object of national vilification and racist U.S. government policies during the period of World War II and the notorious internment camps (Nagata 1991).

Along with the Chinese and Japanese immigrations, Koreans, Filipino, and Indochinese populations have also increased dramatically since 1965.

Due to the Spanish-American War and the Treaty of Paris (1899), America owned the Philippines until the Tidings-McDuffie Independence Act. By 1985, Filipinos had become the largest group of Asian Americans in the United States, the majority being servicemen on American naval bases. Some of them were students and professionals with Catholic backgrounds, but many of the early Filipino professionals have not been able to obtain licenses to practice in the U.S. and thus experience financial hardship.

Among Korean immigrants, a large percentage were Christians sponsored by American missionaries in Korea, beginning in 1903. The political division of Korea in 1945, followed by the American "police action" during the Korean Conflict of 1950–1953, saw the arrival of college students, Korean wives of American servicemen, and Korean war orphans adopted by American families. Since the 1965 amendment to the Immigration and Nationality Act, the easing of restrictive quotas has resulted in a veritable explosion of immigrants from Asia. Hurh and Kim (1984) report that the Korean rate of immigration is surpassed only by Mexicans and Filipinos. The Korean-American population has seen an increase in family violence, substance abuse, and suicide (Kim 1995) with recent epidemiologic studies of four Asian-American groups in the Seattle area showing Korean Americans to have the highest prevalence of depression (Kuo 1984), followed by Filipino, Japanese, and Chinese Americans.

Korean immigrants, many of whom are well educated, often experience a negative reversal of their fortunes and expectations upon arrival in the U.S. Min (1984, 1990) has documented the plight of the prototypical Korean-American small-business owner in a higher crime neighborhood who must contend with usurious landlords and explosive racial tensions. Acculturation appears to be slower in this population, with an increasing communication gap between Korean-born parents and their children, who have recently been referred to as the 1.5 generation, typically fluent in neither Korean nor English, caught between two countries, alienated from both (Uba 1994).

Significant numbers of Southeast-Asian refugees from Vietnam and Cambodia started to arrive in the U.S. in 1975. Refugees were forced to leave their countries abruptly due to a series of wars and political upheavals. They had already experienced trauma, as in the case of the Cambodians who suffered tremendously during the Pol Pot regime when thousands of people were tortured to death. These prior traumatic experiences compounded their psychological difficulties in adapting to new life in the U.S.

These diverse immigrant groups have had to adjust or acculturate to the new country in addition to coping with developmental changes and psychosocial crises common to any human experience. Marin (1992) defined acculturation as "a process of attitudinal and behavior change undergone by individuals who reside in multicultural societies . . . or who come in contact with a new culture due to colonization, invasion, or other important political changes" (p. 239). Thus mental health issues are intensified by language barriers, clashes of cultural values, financial constraints, and emotional difficulties.

MENTAL HEALTH ISSUES

The Confucian Coping Style

Asian cultures have been profoundly influenced by Confucius, a world-renowned Chinese philosopher and educator during the Spring and Autumn Period (551 to 491 B.C.) of ancient Chinese history; throughout history, Confucian philosophy has provided Asian families and citizens with a well-defined, structured sociopolitical environment (Hsu 1972). In the Confucian system, there are five basic relationships in society: those between a ruler and his subjects, father and son, husband and wife, elder and younger siblings, and friends (Keyes 1977). Political and psychosocial stresses are reduced by an emphasis on maintaining interpersonal harmony with decorum/etiquette rather than exercising personal rights, creating interpersonal conflicts, and confronting others. Familial relationships supersede individual needs. Individuals are expected to constrain their own personal impulses, desires, emotions, and the like for the good of the family and state. Each member of the family and society knows what role to assume and how to fulfill it. Devereux (1980) and Lin (1983) reported slightly lower mental disorder rates among Chinese populations in contrast with other cultural groups and suggested that this "Confucian coping style" may be prominent among the contributing factors.

It is worth considering how these cultural themes are given a "voice" within a culture. One facet of Chinese society where they are quite evident is in the classic Chinese children's stories, such as the twenty-four stories of Filial Piety, told by adults to children since ancient times. In a thematic exploration of these "culture tales," Tseng and Hsu (1972) assert:

> The children's story, like the myth, is a variety of projected cultural material in which the salient personality characteristics and values of a people are expressed, the covert conflicts among its members are revealed, and ways of coping with problems provided by that culture are shown . . . Chinese children were more often offered tales of filial piety and other moral teaching. Chinese parents tell stories to their children to educate rather than to entertain them. [p. 28]

The twenty-four stories were grouped by the authors according to certain main themes. In the biggest group are stories in which a child obtains food for the mother and is duly rewarded. Another thematic grouping centers around adult children who, regardless of high social status, continue to take personal care of their mothers. Yet, another thematic group concerns children who sacrifice themselves and endure physical suffering for their elderly parent. Other stories reviewed illustrated themes of "psychosocial" development, including transition from fantasy to reality, triangular conflicts between adult children and parents, and interference by authority with the alliance of a young couple. Common outcomes, and moral lessons contained in them, are that defiance of parental authority invariably leads to punishment or even death, with surviving transgressors given the opportunity to atone for their sins against the family, where the elders must always triumph in the end.

ASIAN-AMERICAN ACCULTURATION PROBLEMS

Far East Asian Americans: The Chinese Example

Asians are typically family oriented and interdependent, but when they immigrate to the U.S. they face difficulties in (1) lack of knowledge and basic skills to function in a new culture, (2) disruption of family structure and support system, (3) economic hardship, (4) clashes of cultural values, and (5) prejudice and racial tension.

As new members in a society, immigrants lack basic skills and knowledge to negotiate daily routines. Language barriers present the major difficulties for most Asians. For example, many Asian parents are not aware that children younger than 12 have to be supervised, and they might let children stay home without supervision after school. They become embarrassed when school or social services accuse them of negligence. It becomes frustrating and depressing when an adult has to relearn basic social skills.

Asians used to rely on their family members or extended family for emotional support and practical help, but often such a support network disappears in the process of migration. Among Chinese, many come to the U.S. in "chain immigration," that is, one sponsors an extended family member to come to this country, and in time this extended family member sponsors his or her entire family. For instance, decades ago many Chinese men went back to China to find their brides. These Chinese brides became citizens and they sponsored their siblings to immigrate to the U.S. Later on, the siblings were able to sponsor their adult children but not their immediate families, who stayed in China until they became qualified to immigrate. As a result, many families have been disrupted. Some new immigrants have not been able to reunite with their immediate families for several years, leading to mental disorders that are easily triggered when one has to go through such severe emotional stress.

Asians are typically self-reliant, and expect to contribute to the family as productive members. Many Chinese immigrants cannot find gainful employment because of language barriers, although they may be professionals in their home countries. Some may find it difficult to make ends meet. Their self-esteem dissipates with feelings of failure and worthlessness. Uba (1994) reported that the loss of a job is a common precipitating factor in mental illness, an observation noted also by the present authors among their patients in a community outpatient mental health clinic.

It is not an exaggeration to state that Asian values are often totally opposite to Western values. Asian cultures emphasize self-control of emotion and verbal expression (Chew and Ogi 1987), avoidance of talking about personal accomplishment or opinions (Brower 1989), and humility to the extent of making self-deprecating remarks (Tung 1985). For example, it is not uncommon to hear Chinese parents call their child "my little dog." It does not create any emotional difficulties among Chinese children when they live in the original culture because every child is a "little dog." However, Chinese children are likely to feel hurt when their parents address them in deprecating remarks and then compare themselves to American children whose parents give praise and affectionate remarks openly. Parent–child conflicts occur as a result. The infestation of youth gangs is a serious problem in all Chinese communities across the country. Marital discord frequently occurs when one spouse is significantly more acculturated. Traditionally Asian males take the more dominant role as breadwinner and decision maker (there are exceptions in some Chinese families where the wives are more dominant). However, it is almost impossible for immigrant families to have just one income. In some cases a husband may fear losing face because his wife has to work, and the wife may assume more responsibility in decision making with newfound earning power and a more assertive, Americanized sense of individual female identity. Many Asians find that they have difficulties competing in the workplace because they have not been brought up to compete overtly. Uba (1994) also described a "syndrome among Asian Americans that involves a particular type of reserve, reticence, deference, and humility" (p. 17), which can often be a hindrance in an aggressively competitive work environment. Clashes of cultural values occur in almost every aspect of an immigrant's life.

In addition to coping with acculturation issues, immigrants may have to endure prejudice and discrimination. Although Asian Americans have been positively labeled as a "model minority," and one might think that they are accepted by the mainstream culture, Uba (1994) has described how Asians have to cope with personal experiences of racism, such as hate crimes and even police brutality. For example, in 1994, a Chinese female film director successfully sued the New York police for harassment and an illegal "strip" search (personal communication with members of the Asian American Education and Legal Defense Fund in New York). She responded to the police, "This is a free country!" when the police told her to get back inside her car in a traffic jam. Many people got out of their cars. The police yelled only at her and came back to issue her two tickets for disobedience of police directives and a "non-violent, non-moving traffic violation." The police then took her to the precinct for a strip search.

Not only do Asians have cultural values that are often opposite to those of Westerners, their presentation of illness also frequently differs. For example, Chinese express their mental distress differently from Westerners who subscribe to the Cartesian separation of body and mind (Kleinman 1980, 1982). In the Chinese medical system there is an interrelationship between psychological and physiological functions (K. Lin 1981, R. Lin 1983). Asian patients often make somatic complaints intermixed with affective complaints, a syndrome that corresponds to the Western psychiatric definition of the disorder termed neurasthenia, which is characterized by headaches, lack of energy, weakness, insomnia, and dizziness (Kleinman 1980).

Two arguments have been suggested to understand Asians' presentation of psychobiological distress. Ots (1990) contends that, according to the Confucian tradition of inhibition of emotions, somatic complaints are more acceptable metaphors for expressing emotions. Tseng (1973) explained that health is seen as the balance between positive and negative forces, Chi. The basic five emotions correspond to internal organs (heart–sorrow, liver–anger, lung–worry, kidney–fear, spleen–joy). Illnesses are understood as Chi being disturbed in a corresponding internal organ. It is common for a parent to express that "my heart pains" when mishaps occur to their family members.

Southeast Asians

Most of the Vietnamese, Laotians, and Cambodians came to the U.S. as refugees after the collapse of South Vietnam in 1975 and civil war in Cambodia in the '70s. The U.S. 1980 Refugee Act, which is based in part on U.N. policy guidelines, describes refugees as "people who flee persecution or the fear of persecution." As refugees they have suffered atrocity and survived. Many of them experienced severe mental illnesses for several years, but assumed a traditional Asian attitude toward their suffering of denial, delay of treatment, and stoic endurance (Chan and Leong 1994) and thus would not report their symptoms to government authorities out of a sense of shame as well as a pervasive mistrust of all "legal" authority.

Chambon (1989) discussed three major problems from a family perspective that Southeast Asians experience: family disruption, violence and trauma, and acculturation and adaptation. The constellation of the Asian family is usually comprised of an extended family. Many Southeast-Asian refugees may not be able to leave their country as a "whole family" (Chambon 1989). Family members were often separated during their flight from danger, as happened during the final American airlift in South Vietnam, the escape route for "boat people" on the high seas, and refugee camps throughout Southeast Asia. Surviving members not only lost their family support, but often experienced guilt and depression.

A Vietnamese legend, the Land of Bliss (Forrest 1971) appears to deal with the ambivalence of the immigrant, both with his country of origin and his newly adopted country. In brief, the legend speaks of the ambition of a certain Mandarin, over 500 years ago, to visit this lost paradise, said to be a land of eternal youth, beautiful women, and timeless pleasure. He eventually found this land, married the daughter of the Fairy Queen, and lived happily there for some time. But he began to yearn for his native village and family, and decided to go there, promising to return soon. However, upon his return to the village he saw that all had changed and his relatives were long dead, as a year on earth was only a day in the land of bliss. Dejected, he sought to return to his paradise, but whether he found it again, no one knows.

The legend illustrates, in our view, the lure of the American Dream, and how even its attainment eventually becomes meaningless if it cannot be shared with family. Even in the land of plenty, the dutiful son should never forget his relatives, lest he be abandoned in turn by them. The Mandarin reaches the end of this story alone, out of time and out of place, connected to no one—a veritable ghost, a victim of his own personal ambitions. This sense of anomie and rootlessness among certain Asian-American immigrant clients can be quite powerful, and a precursor of more severe psychopathology.

Case 1

The Troung brothers were in their early and late teens and had already spent a couple of years in refugee camps in Thailand and Singapore before they arrived in the United States. The family gathered enough gold to send the two oldest sons of the family to a refugee boat. The older brother had to work long hours to support both of them while the younger brother went to college. Without much emotional support, they had to cope with cultural shock, depression, and guilt in addition to learning new skills in this country. The older brother finally had a psychiatric episode and had to be hospitalized.

While Bemak (1989) suggests that, "What is common among the different cultural [Southeast-Asian] refugee family groups is the loss of country, community, customs and frequently family members" (p. 22), Chambon (1989) asserts that their difference from "traditional" immigrant families lies in their distinct identity as "exile family" or "survivor family." Chambon suggests that they enact different family legacies of violence and trauma, and can readily be compared to the families of World War II Holocaust survivors, who transmit not only strategies of survival, but stories of unspeakable acts of terror and unforgettable moments of horror. Mollica and Lavelle (1988), of the Indochinese Psychiatry Clinic (IPC) in Boston, have termed these legacies of horror "trauma stories" (pp. 287–291), and assert that "the trauma story is a living reality and is present for every patient" (p. 289), and that "the trauma story emerges as the centerpiece of any treatment approach" (p. 287) with this Southeast-Asian refugee population.

It has been documented that these refugees display posttraumatic stress disorder at higher rates than other Asian groups (Ying and Hu 1994) as a result of their victimization (an example being the unexplained loss of eyesight among Cambodian women in California). During the Pol Pot era, there was rampant rape, murder, and kidnapping in Cambodia. Ngor (1987) vividly described the unthinkable torture that Cambodians were forced to watch and suffer. It is hypothesized that avoiding the place, thoughts, feelings, and activities that are associated with these traumatic events might not be sufficient to cope with the horror of having seen them. Therefore, such individuals have to become blind so as not to "see" all the atrocities they have witnessed or undergone themselves.

Unfortunately, violence does not disappear after Southeast-Asian refugees have resettled in the U.S. Many new Southeast-Asian immigrants live in inner cities where they are vulnerable to robbery, harassment, and violence that revive their fear and feeling of helplessness and may lead to flashbacks, if not reenactments, of their particular "trauma story."

Bemak (1989) suggests there are three phases that make up the developmental acculturation process for Southeast-Asian refugee families. Phase I concerns issues of security and safety, as the family learns the basic coping skills of the host society. Phase II describes the process of integration of the family with the new cultural identity and its psychosocial demands. Phase III concerns are related to a search for meaning as to the outcome and purpose of the immigrants living in America, with a focus on the future.

Every immigrant has to go through acculturation, but may not do so at the same rate. Acculturation triggers intrafamilial conflicts when family members adapt to the host country at different paces. Intergenerational and marital conflicts are not uncommon. In many cases the children learn the new language and adopt American values much faster than their parents, who have to rely on their children to translate when the family has to navigate the systems, such as schools, immigration, and social service offices. This pattern of role reversal minimizes the authority of parents, who traditionally enjoy filial piety from children in Asian culture. Children who adopt elements of American culture that value freedom of dressing, dating, and leisure activities may not seek approval from parents as a way to show respect. As a result, parent–child conflicts surface.

TREATMENT WITH ASIANS

Anecdotes and research have shown underutilization of mental health services among Asians. Furthermore, Asians do not seek treatment until they experience more severe and disabling disorders (Sue et al 1991). Sue and colleagues proposed the cultural responsiveness theory, which argues that when therapy is culturally responsive, clients' participation and outcomes in treatment will improve. Sue and Zane (1987) proposed that there are distal and proximal variables in cultural responsiveness. Ethnic or language matching between therapist and client is a "distal" variable, because it does not guarantee commonality between client and therapist in cultural attitudes toward mental health services. Proximal variables are beliefs and treatment about mental illness, which are more pertinent to cultural responsiveness and therefore affect utilization and outcomes more than distal variables. However, Sue and Zane also argued that a therapist's cultural sensitivity or knowledge of a culture does not necessarily lead to culturally competent treatment strategies, and the psychological community continues to search for more effective treatment for ethnic minority groups.

Flaskerud and Hu (1994) analyzed the treatment and outcomes of Asian patients seen in an outpatient clinic for major depression in a California county for five years. They concluded that "treatment with medication had a significant relationship to total number of treatment sessions (participation) and improvement in the admission-discharge Global Assessment Scale (GAS) score (outcome)" (p. 289). Furthermore, ethnicity matching between therapist and client affected only the number of treatment sessions but not GAS score improvement. When traditionally trained clinicians worked with Asian clients who did not require drug therapy in a psychodynamic model, they found many of the basic tenets did not apply. For example, Tang (1991) argued that Winnicott's (1960) conceptualization of true self versus false self did not fit with the striving for an ideal self in the Chinese belief system. Yi (1995) and Tung (1991) also argue how the Chinese sense of self is distinct from the concept of self in the dynamic model. Among the Chinese, the concept of self is a merger of individual and family. They also caution against misuse (overuse) of transference interpretations with Asian patients. (Later we will focus on treatment with Chinese clients to illustrate techniques that might be more culturally sensitive, consistent, and competent.)

Shon and Ya (1982) report cognitive responses that many immigrants experience as follows: (1) cultural shock and disbelief at the disparity between what was expected and what actually exists, (2) disappointment at what exists, (3) grief at the separation from and loss of what was left behind, (4) anger and resentment, (5) depression because of the current family situation, (6) some form of acceptance of their situation, and (7) mobilization of family resources and energy. The following case vignette is an example of how a Chinese family experienced "culture shock" upon their arrival in the U.S.

Case 2

Peter, a 10-year-old child who came to the U.S. with both parents and an older sister from Hong Kong, was referred for therapy due to behavioral problems in school. He did not pay attention to teachers and often got into fights. Upon several meetings, Peter tearfully expressed his sadness at missing his friends in Hong Kong. Without directing his resentment toward his parents, he stated that he would not have come to this country had it been his choice. At the same time, his mother also reported depressed feelings that she did not expect that the daily struggling would be so severe. The parents were office clerks in Hong Kong and able to maintain a stable home. Now they had to perform manual labor as factory workers, twelve hours a day and six or seven days a week. In therapy, both parents and children mourned their loss of cultural and familial networks, learned to be empathetic about each other's experience, explored resources to improve their situations, and finally talked about their common goals to "stick it out because there was no way back."

The family described in Case 2 had to cope with all the typical difficulties of immigrants in addition to daily living tasks of any family and the developmental crises of the children. Their psychosocial stressors were thus intensified and they became more vulnerable to emotional disorders. Studies have documented that Chinese, Korean, and Japanese Americans have all reported higher rates of depression than European Americans (Aldwin and Greenberger 1987, Chan 1991, Hymes and Akiyama 1991). In most cases it is probably more effective to strengthen immigrant family members' emotional support of each other, developing positive attitudes and goals for the future and acquiring practical skills to achieve their goals together rather than helping them to explore their individuality.

THE CHALLENGE OF CROSS-CULTURAL PSYCHOTHERAPY: INTEGRATING PSYCHOANALYTIC AND COGNITIVE APPROACHES

The present work presents an approach to therapy with Asian immigrant populations that links psychoanalytic and cognitive therapy concepts: the Sampson-Weiss Control-Mastery method. The term "cognitive" is used not in the traditional, rationalist sense, but in the more recent "constructivist" model of cognitive-behavioral therapy (CBT) as explicated by Donald Meichenbaum (1996). The constructivist CBT model, while providing access to Asian clients (in that several of its techniques and strategies appear to be consistent with traditional Asian cultural values), does not sufficiently address the internalized conflicts of the Asian immigrant who is experiencing the many challenges inherent in the acculturation process. The psychoanalytic approach allows us to explore these issues, but its traditional focus on the "autonomous" individual self has been problematic for clients from cultures emphasizing a collectivist world-view perspective. We outline an approach to therapy that expands upon the Eurocentric principles of psychoanalytic Control-Mastery theory, elaborating more on how its constructions of therapeutic goals and pathogenic adaptations may be modified to become more sensitive to Asian immigrants' needs and expectations. Our approach combines both the constructivist features of CBT and the Control-Mastery method, with culturally sensitive modifications that allow for effective resolution of acculturation dilemmas and the beginnings of bicultural competence.

This project requires that we first lay these two perspectives side by side in order to explore how they have each begun to address the issue of cultural diversity as it pertains to the Asian immigrant population. We advocate an understanding of this cross-cultural encounter within the context of each model, placing emphasis on the opportunities and dangers of a straightforward application of these therapies as usually practiced upon an Asian client population. We shall then present an extended case example illustrative of the proposed combined therapeutic approach.

The Constructivist CBT Perspective

The rise of what has been variously termed the constructivist/narrative or "postmodern" movement in psychotherapy during the 1990s has had a profound impact upon both cognitive-behavioral and psychodynamic schools of thought. Perhaps the most eminent spokesperson for the constructivist perspective in CBT has been Donald Meichenbaum, considered a founder of the "cognitive revolution" in psychotherapy for the past twenty years. Rather than continuing in the CBT "rationalist" stance, which strives toward disconfirmation or disputation of the "irrationality" of the client's belief system (i.e., cognitive schema), Meichenbaum (1996) proposes that:

> there are multiple realities and one of the tasks of therapy is to help clients appreciate how they go about constructing their realities; how they "author their stories." In contrast to standard forms of cognitive therapy, the constructivist approach:
> - places greater emphasis on the developmental history
> - targets deeper core beliefs and processes
> - explores the behavioral impact, emotional toll and personal price of the client's holding certain "root metaphors"; and
> - engages the patient in a discovery-oriented process. [pp. 18–19]

Recently, cognitive-behavioral therapists have also begun to explore applications of their theory and techniques with Asian clients (Iwamasa 1993, Iwamasa and Lam 1996, Kleinknecht et al 1994). Iwamasa (1993) has argued that several CBT techniques and strategies appear to be consistent with traditional Asian values; these would include CBT's task orientation, focus on cognition and rational behavior, focus on goal specificity and problem solving, and CBT's educational focus, which tends to minimize the stigma of mental illness. In addition, the time-limited and structured format of CBT sessions can be of considerable value for Asian clients, who may object to the traditionally loose structure and potential high cost and time commitment of more emotionally expressive and introspective psychodynamic therapies.

Cognitive-behavioral therapy may therefore be more culturally consistent with traditional Chinese culture. Their similarities are listed as follows in Table 28–1.

A therapist may find it more effective to work with Asian clients within a CBT framework, particularly in the beginning phase with new immigrants who experience anxiety, depression, and intrafamilial conflicts due to the stressful situation of immigration. A CBT therapist may work with clients and their families to negotiate their way through the host country and obtain skills to cope with situational problems.

In this sense the therapist becomes very much of a "culture broker" for the immigrant and his or her family, assuming some of the supportive and educative functions of the "family sponsor" role common in the history of Asian chain-migration. The successful negotiation of such a "mentoring" or "sponsoring" relationship between the mental health clinician and Asian immigrant client becomes a central task of such cross-cultural counseling and psychotherapy. Meichenbaum and Fitzpatrick (1993), however, caution against too literal an application of the "mentoring" role relationship within the practice of a constructivist CBT:

> [T]his entire "narrative repair" effort is conducted in a collaborative inductive fashion and not imposed upon, nor didactically taught, to distressed individuals. The distressed client must come to develop and accept a reconceptualization of the distress that he or she has helped concrete. [p. 698]

Iwamasa and Lam (1996) have noted how many cognitive-behavioral therapists mistakenly believe their principles of treatment can be applied universally to culturally diverse clients because "it is assumed that a comprehensive functional analysis of a given individual will render an understanding of cultural values and issues unnecessary" (p. 137).

Table 28-1: Thematic Parallels of CBT and Chinese Traditions

Chinese Culture	CBT
Views life as a learning	Educative focus and process, homework
High respect for teachers	Therapist "coaching" role
Self-reliant and reluctant to dwell on negative thoughts	Capitalize on positive and rational (Ellis) thinking
View problems as situational events in life	Emphasis on situational factors and short-term treatment
Focus on appropriate behavior	Focus on measurable behavioral outcomes
Pragmatic orientation	Solution orientation
Traditional coping techniques: meditation, focused breathing	Behavorial techniques: relaxation breathing, visual imagery
Emphasis on proper interpersonal relations	Social skills training

Another potential for misapplication of CBT techniques concerns the dangers inherent in the therapist's directive stance and the issue of "core beliefs" (Childress and Burns 1981), defined as fundamental beliefs underlying and influencing the development of cognitive schema, defined as a set of intermediate assumptions and attitudes about self and others (Beck 1995). What may seem to be an irrational personal belief to a Western therapist may be a long-cherished cultural value that profoundly influences the Asian person. Attempts at "disconfirmation" of such core beliefs, whether from a psychodynamic or CBT clinician, would be counterproductive and counter-therapeutic (Corey 1990). Such dangers can be avoided if, as Iwamasa and Lam (1996) suggest, "to determine the function of a behavior in its environment, one needs to understand the cultural context in which the behavior is practiced . . . [in relation to] . . . the protective as well as the risk factors related to cultural values and practices among Asian Americans and their level of mental health" (p. 137).

A recent example of a nearly "culture-blind" application of CBT principles to the case formulation of a young Asian "depressed" male client (Persons et al 1991) had only one sentence stating that the client's view of his parents' needs overriding his own personal needs "are to some degree a product of his Asian heritage" (p. 613). Otherwise, the case formulation focused on the client's fears of abandonment and criticism in areas of social and occupational achievement, which the CBT therapist categorized as negative "automatic thoughts" that were thus unrealistic, illogical, and distorted, and when taken together, form a maladaptive "cognitive schema," or set of underlying assumptions, which were perceived as the basis of the client's low self-esteem and social isolation.

Meichenbaum has also emphasized the importance of being culturally sensitive in the formulation of a CBT treatment: "[B]eing sensitive to cultural differences should influence the nature and form of the intervention. When I am in doubt, I spell out the treatment options and collaborate with the client in formulating, implementing, and evaluating the therapeutic options" (Hoyt 1996, pp. 133–134).

The Psychoanalytic Control-Mastery Perspective

The past sixteen years have witnessed a growing interest in the application of psychoanaltyic theory and technique to Asian immigrants and Asian-American clients (Bracero 1994, 1996a, b, Chin 1994, Mollica and Lavelle 1988, Persons et al 1991, Roland 1988, 1995, Takermoto 1989, Tang 1991, Tung 1981, 1991, Yi 1995). The aforementioned article by Persons and colleagues (1991) may also be seen as an example of how traditional psychoanalytically oriented clinicians tend to address issues of cultural diversity: the authors' psychoanalytic case formulation covertly but thoroughly pathologized the client and his parents by negatively interpreting expressions of unrecognized (or perhaps recognized and devalued?) Asian cultural values such as filial piety, middle-position virtue, and ideals of emotional restraint and self-control, and in general proposing therapeutic goals and "insights" that had the potential to further alienate the client from his family of origin and his cultural heritage (Bracero 1994). Notably absent from the case formulation were any references to relevant demographics such as specific ethnic or national origin, level of acculturation, ethnic community residence, immigration status, or socioeconomic situation.

Central to our thesis is our assertion that both the CBT and psychoanalytic approaches are culturally biased against the Asian immigrant client in that they are inherently value-laden with Western Eurocentric concepts of an autonomous self that is geared toward the attainment of "healthy" separation-individuation. E. E. Sampson, in a seminal 1985 article, presented a post-modernist critique of this Western ideal of personhood: "[A] central theme in our culture is its underlying belief that order and coherence are achieved by means of personal control and mastery. Our culture's ideal of personhood reflects this theme in portraying a character designed to be the architect of control and mastery" (p. 1203).

This conceptualization of an encapsulated self struggling for autonomy becomes the basic assumption for a psychological theory that constructs its own narrative model of a human being who is profoundly motivated to reenact elements of unresolved past traumatic life events with significant others in order to control their damaging effects of the present, and thus pursue mastery of normative psychosocial developmental life tasks. This is one of the central organizing themes of a model of psychotherapy that utilizes principles of cognitive theory and learning applied within the psychoanalytic paradigm of unconscious mental processes and the dynamics of transference relationships. Under development for the past twenty-five years, principally in psychoanalytic circles in the San Francisco Bay area, the model has become known as the Sampson-Weiss Control-Mastery theory (Weiss et al. 1986). Weiss's (1993) theory proposes that:

> traumatic life experiences create pathogenic beliefs which the ego utilizes in the service of creating a safe environment for the whole person. However, motivational processes towards control and mastery pressure the person to unconsciously disconfirm such pathogenic beliefs and master their related warded-off impulses, affects and memories in significant interpersonal relationships through a gradual unconscious process of "testing" the "danger" of such beliefs. The manner in which this is done in a professional therapeutic relationship has been named the client's Unconscious Plan. [Bracero 1996a, b, p. 95]

It should be recognized that, from the CBT perspective, the Unconscious Plan is a particular instance of a cognitive schema, though, of course, CBT theorists would object to the term *Unconscious*. It should also be recognized that, from the constructivist/narrative perspective, the above quote is a summary of a "master-narrative" that places the individual in a meaningful context *within which* to enact their life story. Bracero has argued elsewhere (1994, 1996a) that the Eurocentric individualist "master-narrative," or metapsychological assumptions, of Control-Mastery theory (implied in the very name) need modification in order to make an otherwise effective clinical technique less biased against the traditional "mental health" goals and strategies-for-living of Asian cultures, operating out of their own "master-narratives" or "culture tales" (Howard 1991). Bracero (1994, 1996a, b) has proposed that Asian cultures have traditionally motivated their members toward values of intersubjective Harmony, attained through practices of interpersonal Negotiation, at both macro and micro levels of society, within both internal and external realms of experience.

Rapaport (1996) should be credited in this connection with his recent introduction of the term *pathogenic adaptation*, which is meant to replace the term *pathogenic beliefs*. He rightly argues that pathogenic beliefs are not the same as the client's fundamental or core beliefs, but are instead personalized adaptations to past trauma, where the client seeks out the interpersonal and intrapsychic "safe space" within which to disconfirm and relinquish beliefs that are no longer adaptive. "Control-Mastery theory does not allow for the possibility of unhealthy goals," Rapaport (1996, p. 3) states, and, by extension, asserts that there are no pathogenic fundamental cultural beliefs. The proposed Harmony–Negotiation perspective toward traditional Control-Mastery theory (actually a manner of "restorying" the theory) thus reformulates Western individualist therapeutic goals and metapsychology in order to be more consistent with and supportive of collectivist Asian cultural norms and family-structured dynamics, referred to by the present authors as the "Confucian coping style."

> In fact, viewed from an Asian perspective, the client–therapist relationship becomes not so much of a transferential "testing-ground" for the client's efforts at a self-control based on mastery of warded-off "dangerous" impulses, affects and memories through the repudiation of pathogenic beliefs about them, but rather becomes a "testing-ground" for client efforts at re-establishing an emotional connectedness and group-based identity, through the therapist's supportive interpretation of and management of experiences of disharmony and disconnection in the transference and "real" relationships. [Bracero 1996b, pp. 95–96]

The Teacher Transference: Dovetailing the Two Frameworks

The present authors propose that, for most if not all sessions of short-term psychotherapy, and also for at least initial sessions of long-term psychotherapy, therapist treatment strategies should be focused less on attending to "parent–child" transference enactments and more on the establishment and maintenance of optimal "teacher–student" therapeutic alliances with Asian immigrant clients. Even in this connection, potential misunderstandings exist if the therapist assumes that Eurocentric traditions of educational philosophy and practice are readily applicable to Asian populations. Cross-cultural differences exist in expectations of proper behavior and teacher–student interaction in and out of the classroom, and these may readily be "transferred" to the consulting room and therapist–client interaction.

A means of conceptualizing such differences in expectations was offered by Hofstede (1986) in his seminal study of the cultural norms of fifty different countries—specifically, the collectivist versus individualist dimension, which is represented by Asian versus Western societies, respectively. Hofstede distinguishes between collectivist attitudes toward education, wherein students expect to learn how to do, rather than how to learn; where harmonious learning situations, rather than differences in opinion, should be encouraged; where neither teacher nor student should be made to lose face or suffer embarrassment; and where acquiring status and certificates is as important as acquiring competence, if not more so. Transferred to the consulting room, such expectations would appear to favor an intensely hierarchical transference relationship, where conflict and confrontation are to be avoided, and the therapist is expected to actively lead the client in the search for solutions to problematic life situations and guide the client on the "correct" way to live.

It would be a gross misunderstanding to assume that such a teacher transference would lack much emotional depth and/or meaning for the traditional Asian immigrant. What literature exists on the subject suggests that the teacher transference is very much an idealized transference, culturally prescribed and often experienced subjectively at a preconscious level of awareness. Takermoto (1989) writes movingly of his own teacher transference in relation to his American analyst: "As far as I am concerned, the primary preconscious context of my positive transference to my analyst was this teacher transference. My concern over how he regarded me, my respect for him, my attachment to him, as well as the caring concern I could not help but experience for him: all this must be understood primarily in this context" (p. 431).

Takermoto went on to assert that the preconscious teacher transference "should be considered as a possible part of the context for transference in any transcultural analysis, whatever the cultural interface" (p. 448). In further developing this thesis from a Harmony–Negotiation perspective, Bracero (1996b) has presented an integration of elements of the prototypical Asian therapeutic relationship, as conceptualized by Sue and Zane (1987) and Roland (1988). In the present discussion, the concept of the hierarchical transference appears relevant, in that the "teacher–student" relationship should be understood as having a dual nature for the Asian client/student, which is representative of superior-subordinate relationships throughout Asian societies. The discussion thus far has described what Roland (1988) has termed the dynamic of *structural* hierarchy, communicated through verbal expressions of deference, loyalty, and subordination on the part of the client/student, with expectations that the therapist/teacher will respond with supportive/educative interpretations and expressions of concern and a sense of responsibility for his or her "charge." Yet another manifestation of the hierarchical transference is a *qualitative* hierarchy, communicated nonverbally and often affectively, through client/student expressions of veneration, respect, and even idealization of personal qualities of the therapist/teacher and through the art of gift giving. The therapist/teacher response in such a relationship is simply to be oneself, and not discourage such idealization, but to remain accepting and tolerant. The senior author's first experience of this qualitative aspect of the hierarchical transference was during a predoctoral internship therapy experience with a Japanese immigrant client, who, when informed of my being unable to comply with requests for teaching "correct thinking" on certain life situations, responded, after a thoughtful pause, "Well then, perhaps you can inspire me!" This search for both inspiration and guidance on the part of Asian clients has been met with time and again in the consulting room, and is not to be minimized, regardless of theoretical orientation.

One may well ask then if there is any kind of "teaching methodology" that would be culturally consistent with the role expectations of Asians? We believe the "teaching method" most familiar to Asians and other non-Western peoples is to be found in the narrative tradition, that is, in storytelling. Storytelling, used as a means of presenting moral lessons or prescriptions for "correct" thinking or behavior, is of course not alien to Western culture by any means, as can be seen in the ancient fables of the Greek poet Aesop and in the Biblical tradition of the various teaching parables of Jesus. We are interested here not just in the stories told by a culture to its people, the "culture tales" (Howard 1991), but also in the stories told by our clients about their own lives, and how these personal and cultural narratives intersect (Parry and Doan 1994).

Storytelling therapy, whether directed by the therapist or the client, has had a long and venerable history as a therapeutic tool with a variety of populations (Bettelheim 1987, Costantino et al 1986, Howard 1991, Laird 1989, Ucko 1991, White and Epston 1990). More recently, psychoanalytic writers have become aware of the reparative possibilities inherent in narrative construction (Siegler 1994, Spence 1982), and along with cognitive-behavioral practitioners (Hoyt 1996, Meichenbaum 1996) have begun to practice one or another form of "story-repair" or "restorying" of the presenting problem-saturated client life-stories (Omer 1993a, b). However, the reluctance of many Asian immigrant groups to engage in intensive self-disclosure, within or outside the family, often makes the sharing of the trauma story quite difficult for the therapist to facilitate. Many Asian groups believe that mental health is attainable through mental discipline and sheer willpower, and focusing on serene and pleasant topics; thus, dwelling on problems and emotional distress is perceived as a morbid self-indulgence and is itself a sign of personal weakness and probably a result of poor family upbringing, if not inheritance (Flaskerud and Soldevilla 1986).

Nevertheless, it is clear that clinical assessment of Asian clients, and particularly Chinese and Indochinese refugee clients, requires an exploration of "(1) language; (2) current and past stressors to the immigration or refugee experience; (3) assessment of family strengths, cultural beliefs, and responses to mental health problems; (4) assessment of the differences between cultural traits vs. clinical pathologies" (Chan and Leong 1994, p. 277). Such areas of exploration imply use of a comprehensive assessment package that would include a variety of clinical instruments and procedures, but such an assessment package would prove unwieldy and even counterproductive for Asian immigrants, who expect benefits even from a first clinic visit. Clearly, assessment and treatment must be ongoing and *concurrent* processes.

Given these constraints, it is recommended that clinicians employ the circular interviewing technique developed as part of the Milan approach to systemic family therapy (Boscolo et al. 1987, Selvini-Palazzoli 1980). This interview technique constrains both therapist and client to view the presenting problem at the relational system level, which in practice assumes a mutual feedback quality. The questions are essentially contextual—who, what, where, and when—and can be answered only in relational terms, by eliciting the client's "standpoint," or unique perspective and position in relation to their interpersonal experiences. Having attained this understanding of the client's unique experience, clinical judgments become much more grounded in the client's life world, and thus become more treatment-relevant and culturally sensitive, and become the basis of a co-created CTP (Contextualized Treatment Plan). Table 28-2 offers a list of open-ended questions from which the therapist may choose during the initial therapy session. Not all of the questions need to be asked as they tend to overlap in form, but they are designed to elicit information concerning help-seeking behaviors and the interpretive constructions not only of the client, but of the client's family and community. This is consistent with the concept of the extended self or "We/Self" referred to by Roland (1988). Needless to say, such questions can be asked over and over as new "problem situations" arise during the course of treatment and its "therapeutic conversations."

Sampson (1985), in his postmodernist critique of Western ideals of personhood, presents another issue that is relevant to the constructivist/narrative perspective. It is, paradoxically, a critique of the narrative metaphor itself as a tool for Western concepts of the masterful individual:

TABLE 28-2. MULTICULTURAL INTERVIEW QUESTIONS

1. What made you decide to seek treatment at this time?
2. Was anyone else involved in the decision to come here for treatment?
3. When was this problem first noticed?
4. Who besides yourself noticed that there was a problem?
5. What do you think is the cause of the problem?
6. Do you think it is natural to have such a problem?
7. Who else was involved at the start with this problem?
8. What do people around you think about why this problem began when it did?
9. What do you think this problem does to you? How does it work? Do you think it will have a short or long course?
10. How does this problem affect others close to you?
11. How severe is this problem? What would happen if this problem went untreated?
12. What kind of treatment do you think you should receive?
13. Who else should be involved in your treatment/recovery?
14. How long do you expect the treatment/recovery to last?
15. How would others close to you know the problem is over?

> One of the most striking metaphors to describe our culture's personhood ideal derives from the notion of authorship. People are encouraged to take charge and become the authors of their own life stories. To be a character in another's story is to have lost authority over one's own life . . . because we seek mastery by means of the authority of authorship. [pp. 1207–1208]

Sampson (1985, 1993) suggests that a personal narrative, like any text in print, is open to the reinterpretation of any and all readers, and thus the narrative's "final meaning," long considered the exclusive right of authorship, becomes the final right of the reader, or, in postmodern terminology, the "language community" of the narrative's initial "author." It therefore becomes the community, over and above the client or clinician, who exercises the "authority" to make the "final reading" or even "the final analysis." From this standpoint, then, it is not enough to have the individual client construct a more meaningful, positive narrative, regardless of cultural context. It becomes necessary then to consider the cultural context not only as part of the story, but as the final authority on the story thus constructed—the enigmatic "third force" in the triadic co-construction of narrative in the clinical consulting room.

This consideration of the power of the culture to both constitute and critique the narratives it contains leads to the inclusion in our constructivist/cognitive/psychoanalytic therapeutic framework of the work of Mollica and Lavelle (1988), of the New England-based Indochinese Psychiatry Clinic, who proposed that a major therapeutic intervention strategy with Asian refugee clients is "to allow the trauma story to emerge gently and become a familiar and acceptable theme within the clinic, and ultimately within the patient's family and community" (p. 290). IPC clinicians suggested that attempts at classical abreaction and catharsis may do more harm than good, intensifying symptoms and intrusive trauma-related thoughts. They noted that "a gentle sharing and acceptance" of the patient's narrative of pain and torture, at a pace determined by the patient, would often lead to a reduction of shame, fear, and incompetence, as well as help give their suffering a socially acceptable meaning within the context of their own family and community norms and values.

Indeed, Wigren (1994) has theorized that clients with traumatic life histories suffer from an *interrupted* life narrative, disrupted by the considerable destructive impact of the traumatic event, which thus remains unintegrated and unfinished in the client's psyche. This disruption can be overcome only by a rebuilding of the social connections and supports that the trauma victim has lost, in order to again "organize affect and make sense of experience by creating stories to contain it" (p. 417). Until then, the trauma is recalled mostly through intrusive, fragmented "flashbacks," which Mollica and Lavelle (1988) have termed "pre-narrative."

The present authors conclude this work with a clinical case presentation illustrative of this eclectic but culturally sensitive approach to Asian immigrant clients in short-term therapy.

Case 3

TH was a 26-year-old Vietnamese male with a negative past psychiatric history. He was referred to our community mental health center through the medical center, where he had presented with complaints of headaches and chest pain. When asked about emotional problems, he spoke of his inability to control his own anger toward his girlfriend, a fellow Vietnamese refugee whom he had known for several years.

In addition, despite being in his senior year of college, he expressed feeling lost and uncertain about his future and admitted to vague suicide ideation, though without plan or intent.

As is common with many Indochinese refugees, he was able to pinpoint the day and hour of his depression and irritability. He remembered with great vividness his confused feelings when he saw North Vietnamese tanks and soldiers entering his neighborhood from the vantage point of his bedroom window in his father's house. He had witnessed the fall of Saigon, and overnight neither he nor his world were ever the same. He had been, he recalled, not a model of filial piety, indulging in drunkenness and petty crimes that angered and humiliated his merchant-class father and mother and concerned his siblings. Before long, his loose conduct brought him to the attention of the North Vietnamese, and he was placed in "reeducation" camps deep in the countryside and far from the city life he knew. He had met a young teenage girl there, and despite the brutal treatment and conditions, fell in love with her, and swore his eternal affections. Shortly thereafter, his father had managed to bribe some guards, and the client was allowed to leave the compound. In addition, his father had paid for arrangements to have him leave the country immediately by sea, in secret and without being able to say farewell to anyone, even his father.

He survived the perilous journey across the waters, as well as the endless months in refugee detention centers, and eventually managed to arrive in the United States, sponsored by relatives who had already been living in America for a few years. His parents remained in Vietnam, and he never saw his girlfriend again. In the States he drifted from job to job and college to college, never staying long in one place. Then he met MC, a pretty, single, Vietnamese clerical worker, who showered him with affection and advice. At first, they were happy, but his refusal to marry her after ten years together strained their relationship to the breaking point, again and again. They argued, they came to blows, they separated, they reunited, unable to stay apart or stay together with any degree of harmony or peace. He longed to escape his present existence, but felt he could do so only through death. Life seemed meaningless and empty to him. He had no feelings for his girlfriend, or even for himself.

The following discussion relates to the ten months of TH's twice-a-month treatment, paralleling the school year. TH worked on three goals of treatment, established in the initial session. First, he wanted to regain a sense of control over his own angry feelings and establish more harmonious relations with his girlfriend. Second, he wanted to resolve intrusive doubts as to his father's decision to rescue him from the North Vietnamese. Why did he do it? He was neither the eldest nor the most favored son. (Here one may recognize classic "survivor guilt" syndrome.) Third, he wanted, albeit ambivalently, to establish a sense of belonging and virtue in this new country, despite his chronic feelings of emptiness and boredom. It should be evident that TH was embroiled in Bemak's (1989) Phase III of the acculturation process, wherein he struggles to place his survival and migration into some meaningful narrative, the "point" of which escapes him, but thus exemplifies the difficulties that occur when narratives remain incomplete.

At first hearing, TH's story appears to be almost exclusively about survivor guilt. He did not understand why his father would sacrifice himself and endanger the entire family for him, a less-than-deserving son who showed little filial piety. The debt owed to his father was more than he could bear. Similarly, his separation from his girlfriend in the reeducation camp—his only one true love—was perceived as abandonment by him, and he refused to abandon his "new" girlfriend, no matter what the cost, perhaps as some form of "atonement" for the debt he felt he owed his family and significant other. Last, he felt himself lost and abandoned in this new country, perhaps not so much rescued as exiled, unable to return home, and yet afraid to do so, fearing what might await him. He felt no sense of "homeplace" in America, and may have felt it to be a betrayal to his true homeplace to attempt to construct a life for himself here. He remained very much the refugee, fleeing from one maturational challenge and call for social connection to the next, refusing to make commitments and accept responsibilities. Still on the run, the major insight that he needed to attain was that his story is about hope yet to be fulfilled—his father's hope that his son would have a better life in America and not have his body and spirit crushed in a bleak reeducation camp. Is the son worthy of the father's hopes? Through his actions the father has already decided that. It is now up to the son to make good on the father's hopes to make a life for himself, and thus, in the spirit of Confucian family ethics, to make a life for the continuing family narrative in a new land.

Such insights were not offered immediately, but were allowed to emerge at the client's own pace, which was determined by whether or not the therapist passed appropriate transference tests in which the client tested the limits of the therapist's interest in him as a person, rather than as an extension of his own interests. The manner in which this was done at first was interesting as an example of "coaching," a way of preparing the therapist to pass particularly "difficult" transference test situations. In TH's case, he early on gave the therapist a manuscript he was working on (he was majoring in journalism), the narrative of which centered on a Vietnamese refugee who is interviewed by an American journalist interested in the "refugee experience." It becomes clear that the journalist is interested only in the story and not in the person telling the story, whom he quickly abandons once the story is told. The therapist's comments about how cold and uncaring the interviewer was, and how it would have been entirely appropriate for the interviewee to let this be known to him, were apparently enough to pass the test.

Attempts to initiate some form of family intervention or couples therapy were politely discouraged by the client, and a referral to a local Vietnamese-speaking counseling center was allegedly rebuffed by the girlfriend. It was clear the client wanted all therapeutic conversations to be between himself and the therapist.

TH and the therapist were able to work through the client's issues gradually in an atmosphere of safety and nurturance, as the therapist came to assume more of a mentoring role to this young man without a father figure in this strange land. Over time, TH's mood brightened and he reported no recurrence of violent behavior toward his girlfriend, but their relationship was far from harmonious. This was quite evident even in manifest dream content, which the client was intrigued by due to his readings in college psychology courses and thus offered up in the therapy as a sort of "gift giving." One dream occurring midway through the treatment depicted him walking through the streets of New York with his girlfriend, but he was oblivious to her complete nakedness, yet well aware of the lewd stares and laughter of passers-by. This dream was pivotal in the therapist's decision to refer TH to an Asian therapy group being conducted at the time with the co-author (ET). The client's lack of empathy for his girlfriend's naked shame, and his inability to "see" what was so plainly obvious to "peers" in the community, were interpreted within a supportive context, as was the recommendation for group therapy. The therapist saw the referral as an opportunity for a corrective emotional (and cognitive) experience, both as a therapeutic enactment of being "sent away" by the father and yet remaining in touch with him as a mentor in a new social situation, and also as an opportunity for him to practice "bridging" and "expanding" his Asian identity relating to a small "co-ed" group of bilingual/bicultural Asian immigrants, each struggling with issues of acculturation and Asian-American identity formation. Headed by an American male therapist and Asian female cotherapist, the group presented each of its members with a "second-chance family" of surrogate peers and parents with whom to work through unresolved issues of racial discrimination, sexism, sibling rivalry, and other vicissitudes of living in America.

The resulting combination of group and individual therapy enabled the client to confront his divided sense of self and his ambivalent feelings about being both Asian and American, and, most importantly, about his feelings for Asian women and his conflicted sense of obligation. The understanding and support he received from the women in the group, and the empathic connection he felt from the other Asian male peers in the group, helped him to resolve his feelings about his girlfriend and to begin a process of disengagement from her, which she, surprisingly, responded to with relief and understanding.

The interpretation the therapist offered in this context was that TH had in fact been relating to his girlfriend not as a lover, but as a sister, in an effort to make amends for what he perceived as his abandonment of family in Vietnam. What he had done was noble, but it was unnecessary so far as his family of origin was concerned. Nevertheless, he could continue the relationship with the woman, but with a clear understanding between them that the relationship would be "as if" they were brother and sister, not lovers, and with the mutual respect and affections common to such "fictive" kin. This interpretation was readily accepted by the client, and appears to parallel traditional Vietnamese conceptualizations of quality of relationships between a husband and wife, which are predicated on Confucian role models of the relations between brother and sister (Forrest 1971).

Apparently, both of them knew their relationship as lovers was fated to end, but neither had felt safe enough to begin to let go. Soon after, the client was able to tearfully express, in individual session, his sense of unworthiness for all the attention and help the therapist had given him. The therapist recognized this as an expression of the "teacher transference," and it was then that he felt it was "safe" to share with the client the "insights" mentioned earlier in this case discussion. The client relaxed visibly and nodded in agreement. Soon after this he graduated from college and found a job in his field out of state. By that time he had already announced he was leaving group therapy, and now it had come time for us also to terminate treatment. He told the therapist it was time for him to stop running. "No more refugee," he said.

REFERENCES

Aldwin, C., and Greenberger, E. (1987). Cultural differences in the predictors of depression. *American Journal of Community Psychology* 15:789–813.

Beck, J. (1995). *Cognitive Therapy: Basics and Beyond.* New York: Guilford.

Bemak, F. (1989). Cross-cultural family therapy with Southeast Asian refugees. *Journal of Strategic and Systemic Therapies* 8: 22–27.

Bettelheim, B. (1987). *The Uses of Enchantment: The Importance and Meaning of Fairytales.* New York: Vintage.

Boscolo, L., Cecchini, G., and Hoffman, L. (1987). *Milan Family Systemic Therapy.* New York: Basic Books.

Bracero, W. (1994). Developing culturally sensitive psychodynamic case formulations. The effects of Asian cultural elements on psychoanalytic control–mastery theory. *Psychotherapy* 31, 525–532.

———— (1996a). The storyhour: narrative and multicultural perspectives on managed care and time-limited psychotherapy. *Psychotherapy Bulletin* 31:59–65.

———— (1996b). Ancestral voices: narrative and multicultural perspectives with an Asian schizophrenic. *Psychotherapy* 33: 93–103.

Brower, I. C. (1989). Counseling Vietnamese. In *Counseling American Minorities: A Cross-Cultural Perspective,* ed. D. R. Atkinson, G. Morten, and D. W. Sue, pp. 129–147. Dubuque, IA: William C. Brown.

Chambon, A. (1989). Refugee families's experiences: three family themes-family disruption, violent trauma and acculturation. *Journal of Strategic and Systemic Therapies* 8:313.

Chan, D. W. (1991). Depressive symptoms and depressed mood among Chinese medical students in Hong Kong. *Comprehensive Psychiatry* 32:170–180.

Chan, S., and Leong, C. W. (1994). Chinese families in transition: cultural conflicts and adjustment problems. *Journal of Social Distress and the Homeless* 3:263–281.

Chew, C. A., and Ogi, D. C. (1987). Asian American college student perspectives. *New Directions for Student Services* 38:39–48.

Childress, A. R., and Burns, D. D. (1981). The basics of cognitive therapy. *Psychosomatics* 22:1017–1027.

Chin, J. L. (1994). Psychodynamic approaches. In *Women of Color: Integrating Ethnic and Gender Identities in Psychotherapy,* ed. L. Comas-Diaz and B. Greene, pp. 194–222. New York: Guilford.

Corey, G. (1990). *Therapy and Practice of Group Counseling* 3rd ed. Pacific Grove, CA: Brooks/Cole.

Costantino, G., Malgady, R., and Rogler, L. (1986). Cuento therapy: a culturally sensitive modality for Puerto Rican children. *Journal of Consulting and Clinical Psychology* 54:639–645.

Devereux, G. (1980). *Basic Problems of Ethnopsychiatry*. Chicago: University of Chicago Press.

Flaskerud, J. H., and Hu, L-T. (1994). Participation in and outcome of treatment for major depression among low income Asian-Americans. *Psychiatry Research* 53:289–300.

Flaskerud, J. H., and Soldevilla, E. Q. (1986). Filipino and Vietnamese clients: utilizing an Asian mental health center. *Journal of Psychosocial Nursing* 24:32–36.

Forrest, D. V. (1971). Vietnamese maturation: the lost land of bliss. *Psychiatry* 34:111–139.

Hofstede, G. (1986). Cultural differences in teaching and learning. *International Journal of Intercultural Relations* 10:301–320.

Howard, G. (1991). Culture tales: a narrative approach to thinking, cross-cultural psychology and psychotherapy. *American Psychologist* 46:187–197.

Hoyt, M. F. (1996). Cognitive-behavioral treatment of a posttraumatic stress disorder from a narrative-constructivist perspective: a conversation with Donal Meichenbaum. In *Constructive Therapies* 2nd ed., M. F. Hoyt, pp. 124–147. New York: Guilford.

Hsu, F. (1972). *American Museum Science Book*. Garden City, NY: Doubleday.

Hurh, M. H., and Kim K. C. (1984). *Korean Immigrants in America: A Structural Analysis of Ethnic Confinement and Adhesive Adaptation*. Rutherford, NJ: Associate University Press.

Hurh, W. M., and Kim, K. C. (1988). *Uprooting and Adjustment: A Sociological Study of Korean Immigrants' Mental Health. Final Report to the National Institute of Mental Health*. Macomb, IL: Western Illinois University, Department of Sociology and Anthropology.

Hymes, R. M., and Akiyama, M. (1991). Depression and self-enhancement among Japanese and American students. *Journal of Social Psychology* 131:321–334.

Iwamasa, G. Y. (1993). Asian Americans and cognitive behavioral therapy. *The Behavior Therapist* 16:233–235.

Iwamasa, G. Y., and Lam, C. (1996). Asian American issues in behavior therapy: current status, future directions, and resources. *The Behavior Therapist* 19:136–138.

Keyes, C. (1977). *The Golden Peninsula*. New York: Macmillan.

Kim, M. T. (1995). Cultural influences on depression in Korean Americans. *Journal of Psychosocial Nursing* 33:13–18.

Kinzie, J., Boehnlein, J. K., Leung, P. K., et al. (1990). The prevalence of posttraumatic stress disorder and its clinical significance among Southeast Asian refugees. *American Journal of Psychiatry* 147:913–917.

Kleinknecht, R. A., Dinnel, D. L., Tanouye-Wilson, S., and Lonner, W. J. (1994). Cultural variation in social anxiety and phobia: A Study of Taijin Kyofusho. *The Behavior Therapist* 17:175–178.

Kleinman, A. (1980). *Patients and Healers in the Context of Culture*. Berkeley: University of California Press.

―――― (1982). Neurasthenia and depression: a study of somatization and culture in China. *Culture, Medicine, and Psychiatry* 6:117–190.

Kuo, W. H. (1984). Prevalence of depression among Asian-Americans. *Journal of Nervous and Mental Disease* 172:49–457.

Kuo, W. H., and Tsai, Y. M. (1986). Social networking, hardiness, and immigrants' mental health. *Journal of Health and Social Behavior* 27:133–149.

Laird, J. (1989). Women and stories: restorying women's self-constructions. In *Women in Families: A Frame for Family Therapy*, ed. M. McGoldrick, C. M. Anderson, and F. Walsh, pp. 426–450. New York: Norton.

Lee, C. K., Kwok, Y. S., Yamamoto, J., et al. (1990a). Psychiatric epidemiology in Korea. Part I: Gender and age differences in Seoul. *Journal of Nervous and Mental Disease* 178:242–246.

―――― (1990b). Psychiatric epidemiology in Korea. Part II: Urban and rural differences. *Journal of Nervous and Mental Disease* 178:247–252.

Lin, K. M. (1981). Traditional Chinese medical beliefs and their relevance for mental illness and psychiatry. In *Normal and Abnormal Behavior in Chinese Cultures*, ed. A. Kleinman and T. Lin, pp. 357–369. Dordrecht, Netherlands: D. Reidel.

Lin, R. Y. (1983). Psychiatry and Chinese culture. *Western Journal of Medicine* 139:862–867.

Loo, C. K., Tong, B., and True, R. (1989). A bitter bean: mental health status and attitudes in Chinatown. *Journal of Community Psychology* 17:283–296.

Marin, G. (1992). Issues in the measurement of acculturation among Hispanics. In *Psychological Testing of Hispanics,* ed. K. F. Geisinger, pp. 235–251. Washington, DC: American Psychological Association.

Meichenbaum, D. (1996). *Mixed Anxiety and Depression: A Cognitive-Behavioral Approach (A Viewers Manual).* New York: Newbridge Professional Programs.

Meichenbaum, D., and Fitzpatrick, D. (1993). A constructive narrative perspective on stress and coping: stress inoculation applications. In *Handbook of Stress,* ed. L. Goldberger and S. Breznitz, pp. 695–710. New York: Free Press.

Min, P. G. (1984). A structural analysis of Korean business in the United States. *Ethnic Groups* 6:1–25.

——— (1990). Problems of Korean immigrant entrepreneurs. *International Migration Review* 24:436–455.

Mollica, R., and Lavelle, J. (1988). Southeast Asian Refugees. In *Clinical Guidelines in Cross Cultural Mental Health,* ed. L. Comas-Diaz and E. Griffith, pp. 262–293. New York: Wiley.

Nagata, O. (1991). Transgenerational impact of the Japanese-American internment: clinical issues in working with children of former internees. *Psychotherapy* 28:121–128.

Ngor, H. (1987). *A Cambodian Odyssey.* New York: Warner.

Omer, H. (1993a). Quasi-literary elements in psychotherapy. *Psychotherapy* 30:59–66.

——— (1993b). Short-term psychotherapy and the rise of the life-sketch. *Psychotherapy* 30:668–673.

Ots, T. (1990). The angry lover, the anxious heart, and the melancholy spleen. *Culture, Medicine, and Psychiatry* 14:21–58.

Parry, A., and Doan, R. E. (1994). *Story Re-visions: Narration Therapy in the Postmodern World.* New York: Guilford.

Persons, J. B., Curtis, J. T., and Silberschatz, G. (1991). Psychodynamic and cognitive-behavioral formulations of a single case. *Psychotherapy* 28:608–617.

Rapaport, A. (1996). The structure of psychotherapy: control-mastery theory's diagnostic plan formulation. *Psychotherapy* 33:1–10.

Roland, A. (1988). *In Search of Self in India and Japan: Toward a Cross-Cultural Psychology.* Princeton, NJ: Princeton University Press.

——— (1995). Value issues involving Western psychoanalysts with Asian patients. *Journal of the American Academy of Psychoanalysis* 23:283–292.

Sampson, E. E. (1985). The decentralization of identity: toward a revised concept of personal and social order. *American Psychologist* 40:1203–1211.

——— (1993). Identity Politics: Challenges to psychology's understanding. *American Psychologist* 48:1219–1230.

Selvini Palazzoli, M., Boscolo, L., Cecchini, G., and Prata, G. (1980). Hypothesizing–circularity–neutrality: three guidelines for the conductor of the session. *Family Process* 19:3–12.

Shon, S., and Ya, D. (1982). Asian families. In *Ethnicity and Family Therapy*, ed. M. McGoldrick, J. Pearce and J. Giordano, pp. 208–229. New York: Guilford.

Siegler, A. (1994). The boy with two kingdoms: ontogeny of a narrative. *Psychoanalytic Psychology* 11:309–328.

Spence, D. (1982). *Narrative Truth and Historical Truth: Meaning and Interpretation in Psychoanalysis*. New York: Norton.

Sue, S., Fujino, D., Hu, L., et al. (1991). Community mental health services for ethnic minority groups: a test of the cultural responsiveness hypothesis. *Journal of Consulting and Clinical Psychology* 59:533–540.

Sue, S., and Morishima, J. (1982). *The Mental Health of Asian Americans*. San Francisco: Jossey-Bass.

Sue, S. and Zane, N. (1987). The role of culture and cultural techniques in psychotherapy. *American Psychologist* 42:37–45.

Takermoto, Y. (1989). An American-Japanese transcultural psychoanalysis and the issue of teacher transference. *Journal of the American Academy of Psychoanalysis* 17:427–450.

Tang, N. M. (1991). Some psychoanalytic implications of Chinese philosophy and child-rearing practices. *Psychoanalytic Study of the Child* 47:371–389. New Haven, CT: Yale University Press.

Tseng, W. (1973). The development of psychiatric concepts in traditional Chinese medicine. *Archives of General Psychiatry* 29:569–575.

Tseng, W. S., and Hsu, V. (1972). The Chinese attitude toward parental authority is expressed in Chinese children's stories. *Archives of General Psychiatry* 26:28–34.

Tung, M. (1991). Insight-oriented psychotherapy and the Chinese patient. *American Journal of Orthopsychiatry* 61:186–194.

Tung, T. M. (1981). On being seen as a "Chinese therapist" by a Caucasian child. *American Journal of Orthopsychiatry* 58:136–142.

——— (1985). Psychiatric care for Southeast Asians: How different is different? In *Southeast Asian Mental Health: Treatment, Prevention, Services, Training, and Research*, ed. T. Owan, pp. 5–40. Washington, DC: U.S. Department of Health and Human Services.

Uba, L. (1994). *Asian Americans: Personality Patterns, Identity and Mental Health*. New York: Guilford.

Ucko, L.G. (1991). Who's afraid of the big bad wolf? Confronting wife abuse through folk stories. *Social Work* 36:414–419.

Weiss, J. (1993). *How Psychotherapy Works: Process and Technique*. New York: Guilford.

Weiss, J., Sampson, H., and The Mount Zion Psychotherapy Research Group (1986). *The Psychoanalytic Process: Theory, Clinical Observation and Empirical Research*. New York: Guilford.

White, M., and Epston, D. (1990). *Narrative Means to Therapeutic Ends*. New York: Norton.

Wigren, J. (1994). Narrative completion in the treatment of trauma. *Psychotherapy* 31:415–423.

Yi, K. (1995). Psychoanalytic psychotherapy with Asian clients: transference and therapeutic considerations. *Psychotherapy* 32:308–316.

Ying, Y. W., and Hu, L. T. (1994). Public outpatient mental health services: use and outcome among Asian Americans. *American Journal of Orthopsychiatry* 64:448–455.

29

The Supervision of Psychotherapy for African-American and Culturally Diverse Patients

DOLORES O. MORRIS

SUPERVISION IN THE CONTEXT OF CULTURAL DIVERSITY

Supervision is recognized as a vital component in preparing competent therapists for the process of dynamic psychotherapy; it should increase the proficiency with which the supervisee uses complex therapy procedures. The literature on dynamic supervision addresses the supervisory process from a variety of theoretical approaches (Beutler and Kendall 1995, Bongar and Beutler 1995, Caligor et al. 1984, Goldberg 1995, Gordan 1996, Herron et al. 1995, Jacobs et al.1995, Rodenhauser 1995, Singer 1995, Traunt and Lohrenz 1993, Watkins 1993).

For the past two decades, cross-cultural counseling literature has made significant contributions toward identifying the characteristics and needs of culturally diverse populations with emphasis on what makes them responsive to mental health services (Atkinson et al. 1993, Comas-Díaz 1988, Sue et al. 1982). Nevertheless, there is a shortage of empirical literature that addresses supervision for culturally diverse patients (Williams and Halgin 1995, Yutrzenka 1995). Most of the existing literature has examined the match and mix between the supervisee and patient, with less frequent attention to the match and mix between supervisor and supervisee (Bradshaw 1982, Grier 1967, Griffith 1977, Holmes 1992, Hunt 1987, Remington and DaCosta 1989, Schacter and Butts 1968, Williams and Halgin 1995).

Racial issues are not usually raised in supervision with sufficient frequency and specificity to allow for the development of technical competence and ease in their exploration (Bradshaw 1982, Yutrzenka 1995). Race/ethnicity is a highly charged subject for the supervisor, the supervisee, and the patient, and tends to provoke strong reactions. This combination of insufficient attention and intense unconscious material related to race/ethnicity ensures that the combination of supervisor, supervisee, and patient will be affected by these factors; consequently, the supervision of psychotherapy for culturally diverse patients requires the supervisor to make a special effort to consider the existence of cultural factors in the working alliance, resistance, transference, and countertransference.

There is a common misconception that ethnic American patients and/or patients who come from poor circumstances lack motivation and are unable to introspect. The belief that they are deficient in processing their inner world, thereby rendering them poor candidates for psychoanalytic psychotherapy or psychoanalysis, is a stereotypical response that interferes with an objective evaluation of individuals' capacity to respond to treatments (Altman 1995, Dana 1993, Javier and Herron 1992, Minuchin 1968, Sue 1988). This erroneous notion has reduced effective and efficient service delivery, resulting in high dropout rates and an underserved population of ethnic Americans. Culturally diverse patients often deviate from stereotypical expectations of the analytic/therapeutic culture that often blames the victim (Foster 1996, Javier 1996, Whitson 1996). As a result of such preconceived notions and biases, most professionals come to supervision without adequate educational preparation, ill equipped to work effectively with a diverse population of patients. The increasing proportion of culturally diverse patients and supervisees in America makes it imperative to provide supervision that will address these issues.

The two most critical components in the supervision of psychotherapy for culturally diverse patients are the supervisor's ability (1) to provide a sense of comfort with diversity and (2) to mediate the world-view difference between the supervisee and patient, increasing the fit between them. In this process, the supervisor must make a meticulous inquiry regarding the responses of the patient and the supervisee and of the interaction between them. One major goal of the supervisory function is to educate and enable the supervisee to make the patient feel understood in order to remain in treatment and make a better life adjustment.

The focus of this chapter will be the intricacy of the supervisor–supervisee–patient triad and the critical nature of the interface between culture and psyche in providing psychotherapy to culturally diverse or ethnic American patients. The fundamental principles of psychotherapy will be applied in a cultural context. The terms *culturally diverse* or *race/ethnicity* will be used interchangeably to describe broad groupings of Americans on the basis of both race and culture of origin. Race/ethnicity denotes a group of people who share a common ancestry and cultural heritage (Atkinson, et al. 1993). The U.S. Bureau of Census includes as five basic groups Hispanic, non-Hispanic white, black, Native American, and Asian/Pacific (Phinney 1996). Thus, this discussion will address the needs of Hispanic, black, Native American, and Asian/Pacific patients. Blacks will be referred to as African Americans, Hispanics as Hispanic Americans, Asian/Pacific as Asian Americans, and non-Hispanic whites as European Americans. These terms will be used as they are inclusive of the American culture and are more accurate descriptors. Native Americans will be so referred to.

Ethnic membership has important psychological implications for the individual, yet knowledge of a person's ethnicity does little to explain specific social, emotional, cognitive, and mental health outcomes. The boundaries of ethnicity and race are indistinct and flexible. Culture, ethnic identity, and minority status are three aspects of ethnicity that have been identified as psychologically important in understanding the context of the individual (Dana 1993, Phinney 1996). The individual's world view encompasses group identity, individual identity, beliefs, values, and language. These components are the underpinnings for the perceptions of reality as experienced by individuals who share a common culture. The world view of a culture functions to make sense of life experiences (Dana 1993, Kearney 1975).

PARTICIPANTS IN THE PSYCHOTHERAPEUTIC PROCESS

The Patient

The patient represents a cross section of the culturally diverse population and may be a member of any one of the ethnic American groups under discussion. There are more differences within ethnic groups than between them; consequently, any attempt to make generalizations about each of the groups would be misleading and could result in stereotypical notions. There is disagreement about the best term to use when referring to a specific racial/ethnic group. Therefore, it is important that the supervisee find out the preference of the patient. For instance, an African-American patient may prefer to be called black or Afro American or African American. See Atkinson and colleagues (1993) and White (1997) for a full discussion of differentiation of preferences.

The world view of each group reveals some common, but relative, concepts that may be culturally based, such as the patient's feeling that the therapist has an understanding of the patient's culture and the importance of family, spirituality, and building a trusting relationship. The issue of trust is the most prominent for ethnic Americans due to their minority status and the tradition of racial, religious, ethnic, and class prejudices in this country. It is not surprising that the literature describes a readiness for mistrust, an expectation of mistreatment, and a defensive posture (Bradshaw 1982, Dana 1993, Sue and Zane 1987, Uba 1994, Wohl 1989, Wu 1994, Yi 1995).

In addition, the following culturally linked factors must be understood by both the supervisee and the patient: for Hispanic Americans and African Americans, issues of language (Dana 1993, Foster 1992, Williams and Halgin 1995); for African Americans, skin color and physical characteristics (Goodman 1964, Mitchell 1970, Myers 1977, Williams 1996, Williams and Halgin 1995), for Hispanic Americans and Native Americans, reliance on alternative treatment modalities such as their use of folk medicine and medicine men (Dana 1993); and for Asian Americans, culturally linked role relationships in which age, gender and expertise are primary considerations (Uba 1984, Wu 1994, Yi 1995). The patient's relationship to these cultural factors will influence the treatment process.

Knowledge of the literature regarding a particular ethnic group is not sufficient to make one competent in addressing the issues of the culturally diverse patient. Cultural experience is unique to the individual and is influenced by life's vicissitudes. An African American may identify as such, but may have had significant experiences with other ethnic Americans, such as European Americans, Hispanic Americans, and/or Asian Americans, which will make the world view different from that of other individual African Americans. What this may or may not mean to this individual, if relevant, would have to be understood in the context of treatment. Each group is heterogeneous, manifesting diversity in attitudes, values, behavior, education, income, acculturation, and race/ethnic identity.

The degree of assimilation into the mainstream culture varies. Attitudes may range from a wish to be totally assimilated into the dominant culture to a rejection of it and a wish to be totally immersed in the minority culture (Parham and Helms 1981, Ruiz and Padilla 1977, Sue and Sue 1971, Uba 1994). Each member of any ethnic group has a unique and distinguishing set of characteristics that go beyond the group.

According to Atkinson and colleagues (1993), acculturation is a measure of within-group diversity; the therapist should be aware, not only of the patient's ethnic background, but the extent to which the patient identifies with its practices, that is, the practices of generations before them. Atkinson and colleagues describe a bicultural socialization model that applies to all racial/ethnic groups. The individual is simultaneously socialized with his or her own group culture and the dominant culture. They also refer to a body of research that ascertains the relationship between acculturation and counseling practices for Asian Americans, Native Americans, and Hispanic Americans. The culturally diverse patient also brings an array of problems that parallel those of patients in the mainstream population. The supervisor and the supervisee learn about the culture of the patient through experience, by familiarity with the relevant literature, and by taking the journey with the patient. While there has been a focus on an increased sensitivity to culturally diverse patients, attentiveness to cultural determinants is invaluable in the treatment of any patient.

The Supervisor and the Supervisee

A scarcity of ethnic diversity among supervisees is caused by consistent underrepresentation of ethnic Americans in training programs for more than two decades (Bernal and Padilla 1982, Boxley and Wagner 1971, Moses 1990) and because they are choosing other professions. The supervisor and supervisee are therefore most likely to be European-American. The combinations of participants in the therapeutic triad are usually mixed and not matched; in dyads they may be mixed and matched.

A small body of literature that grows out of counseling psychology indicates patient preference for a mental health worker from the same group across race/ethnicity categories (Atkinson et al. 1993, Clarkson 1995). On the other hand, research linking race/ethnic similarity to outcome has had ambiguous results. While some patients may request a mental health worker of similar ethnicity, it has not been shown to be linked to therapeutic effectiveness on a consistent basis (Clarkson 1995). Norcross and Goldfried (1992) point out that the assignment of ethnically similar supervisees to ethnically similar patients may fail to account for more important sources of diversity, such as age, gender, and socioeconomic status. Another consideration comes from Carney and Kahn's (1984) observation that European-American mental health workers tended to ignore or minimize the importance of race/ethnic differences.

PREPARATION FOR SUPERVISION

Critical Concepts in Providing Service to Culturally Diverse Patients

To successfully treat ethnic American patients, the supervisor must prepare the supervisee to work with the social and personal concepts that influence the behavior of the patient. Seven critical concepts are cited in Table 29-1. These concepts should be integrated for a better understanding of the patient so as to determine the direction of the inquiry, decide on the necessary interventions, and execute appropriate services effectively and efficiently. It is anticipated that these critical concepts will enhance the supervisee's knowledge and comfort with diversity, thereby helping him or her to understand the particular needs of the patient. While these concepts are relevant to all patients, the application of them to culturally diverse patients individualizes the work with them. Table 29-1 makes clear the dichotomy between the social and the personal influences that impact on adjustment.

Assessing the Organization

Since treatment for culturally diverse patients usually occurs within an organizational setting, a supervisor's attention to organizational context and constraints is imperative. Supervision, whether in a private or public agency, constitutes only one component in a complex system that influences the quality of care. The degree of versatility that the organization has in the use of its resources and the framework within which the supervisor can insist on good conditions for therapy has to be kept in mind and assessed by the supervisor. It is more likely that the supervision of psychotherapeutic work with culturally diverse patients will be with supervisees who are employed by public clinics, community mental health centers, or hospital clinics. Supervisors must also be aware of the laws and ethics that apply to the practice of psychotherapy and that govern supervisory practices in their jurisdiction (Kalous 1996). This knowledge must be integrated in their supervisory practices. Supervisees may be so focused on the clinical aspect of their work that they may overlook

TABLE 29-1. CRITICAL CONCEPTS IN PROVIDING SERVICE TO CULTURALLY DIVERSE PATIENTS

Influences	Critical Concepts
Social Influences	Impact of socioeconomic and political factors on psychological development and sociocultural identification
	• culture, race, class, gender, and sexual orientation
	• cultural values, attitudes, behaviors, and language differences that distinguish each ethnic group
	• family as the carrier of culture and the subjective experience of the family
Personal Influences	• Impact of experiences associated with minority status (i.e., powerlessness, discrimination, and prejudice)
	• Personal/private identities vs. social/communal identities
	• Subjective sense of ethnic group membership (i.e., ethnic identity)

important legal and ethical issues. It is the responsibility of the supervisor to bring these matters to the supervisee's attention.

A larger number of patients, especially culturally diverse patients, are covered by managed care or government-sponsored programs such as Medicaid or Medicare. These programs often face the possibility of cutbacks in the frequency and duration of therapy sessions and premature case closings. Many of these patients may be at high risk because of stressful reality situations and may not meet the criteria for continued medical necessity. The supervisor must be prepared to set priorities for these at-risk cases by overseeing cost-effective case management while maintaining quality of care. Kalous (1996) recommends that the supervisor keep progress notes that meet the needs of both the supervisor and the organization. The supervisor also should be willing to promote time-limited therapy. Cummings (1996) points out that preparation for brief, short-term, problem-focused therapy is crucial in a clinic situation and is the reality in the current climate of managed care. He cites research that demonstrates that short-term focused interventions are more effective than long-term treatment. Some of the strategies of time-limited therapy are compatible with the values and expectations of culturally diverse patients who come from poor circumstances. In time-limited therapy the solution is focused on (1) why the patient chooses to come to therapy at this time, (2) what the patient's expectations are, (3) establishing clear objectives for interventions with emphasis on the patient's strengths and coping skills, and (4) increasing empowerment rather than on personality change. The patient should feel in control of the change process, understand that therapy may be brief and intermittent, and be aware that resources outside of treatment may be used (Cummings 1996, Kalous 1996).

The supervisor should remember that the supervisee is dependent on the organization's goals, the treatment ideology, and the resources as they affect the chances of meeting the expectations of how good psychotherapy should be conducted (Altman 1995, Gordon 1996). The supervisor must assess three categories—attitudes, resources, and policies of the organization—in preparation for work with the supervisee. Critical questions have been developed for these three categories and are presented in Table 29-2. Attitudes, the first category, includes management and staff's attitudes toward patients, the theoretical orientation of supervisors and supervisees and managed care policies. The second category is the delineation of policies regarding treatment, payment, supervision, and paperwork. The third category covers resources available to the supervisee and the patient.

These critical questions will enable the supervisor to develop realistic expectations for the supervisee in the supervisory relationship and will provide further clarity when cultural issues arise.

The inherent conflicts regarding the goals of an organization will influence the conditions of the supervisee's psychotherapy and supervision. The supervisor must be attuned to these factors and incorporate them in the supervisory process. In most public clinics supervisees are expected to fulfill multiple roles in relation to their patients. They may be expected to function as advocates for their patients with social service agencies and schools; make decisions about whether their patients are entitled to emergency care, food, or carfare; work with more than one member of a family; or function as both individual and group therapist to a patient. Decisions to deal with the external circumstances of the patient are an important part of the treatment plan and can provide the necessary conditions for a good therapeutic alliance. In some instances these management activities may be offered before psychotherapy begins or during the course of it. The supervisee and the supervi-

TABLE 29-2. CRITICAL QUESTIONS FOR ASSESSING THE ORGANIZATION IN PREPARATION FOR SUPERVISION

Category	Questions
Attitudes	• What is the attitude toward culturally diverse patients? • What is the attitude toward culturally diverse therapists? • What is the ethnic mix of the professional staff? • Are the supervisor's attitudes and theories about care and psychotherapy compatible with those of the organization? • How do insurance plans and managed care impact on care and attitudes?
Policies	• How flexible are the options for treatment interventions? • Who is accepted for psychotherapy? • Is there a time limit for treatment? • How long are therapy sessions? • What is the policy for missed appointments? • How is payment received? • What are the expectations regarding report writing and paperwork? • Is supervision conducted on site or in the supervisor's private office?
Resources	• What training resources are available for the supervisee? • What treatment modalities and resources are available for the patient within and outside of the organization?

sor's attitudes toward these expectations will affect the execution of these duties and their outcome. They may feel put upon and resentful that such demands are being made and would need to probe these feelings in the context of the interaction between the supervisee, supervisor, and patient as well as the organization.

Establishing Goals

The supervisor and supervisee should collaborate on the goals of the overall supervision and establish the treatment plan for the patient. One aspect of this planning should include class, race, culture, and ethnicity. The primary goal of supervision is to enable the supervisee to integrate insights about self with theoretical and practical experience with the patient.

Supervisor's Assessment of Self

Self-analysis of the supervisor is central to the supervisory process and to an interpersonal approach. The supervisor must be especially attentive to personal race/ethnic biases and countertransference resistances that could interfere with or distort the process (Bradshaw 1982, Remington and DaCosta 1989, Whitson 1996, Wohl 1989). In the process of this self-analysis, the supervisor may consider society's influences as delineated in Table 29-1. Consideration should be given to the supervisor's awareness of the historical and current experience of being a culturally diverse individual in this society, to the way that the supervisor's personal values influence how the therapy is conducted, to the way that the presenting problem and the goals for therapy are viewed, and to the match between the value system of the patient and the goals for therapy (Wilson and Stith 1993). These considerations should put the supervisor more in touch with some of the personal views and biases that may impede the process, as indicated in the description below.

Both supervisee and supervisor, notwithstanding their cultural background, may mutually reinforce stereotypes of the patient by either being the bearer of myths that influence diagnostic assessment or by making presumptive conclusions and premature closure relating to the patient's pathology and strengths (Atkinson, et al 1993). For instance, the supervisee and/or supervisor may subscribe, uncritically, to the myth that lower-class patients are invariably difficult to treat because they view all their problems as being caused by external events. They may underinterpret in cases in which they share the erroneous belief that the patient is too fragile to tolerate interpretive activity or that interpretation will increase the patient's overt aggressiveness. The supervisee and supervisor may project their own anxiety and aggression. Their anxiety may make it difficult for them to see how the patient's resistances and defenses cause him or her to make references to race or subcultural language differences and to act out racial stereotypes. Another circumstance is when the supervisor considers the possibility that culturally diverse supervisees are an "exception to the rule" or that their success is attributable to having been given certain compensatory privileges (Pettigrew 1979).

Transference phenomena are encountered in any supervisor–supervisee relationship; transference may be intensified in the supervision of supervisees of culturally diverse patients. Ethnocultural differences between supervisor

and supervisee can play a significant role. The supervisor should actively identify and pursue a discussion of these differences and pertinent issues as early
as possible, recognizing that race/ethnicity is one of the defining features of
the relationship (Bradshaw 1982, Chin et al. 1993, Remington and DaCosta
1989, Williams and Halgin 1995). In some instances attempts to deal directly
with the differences within the supervisory relationship may be responded to
with denial and hostility; in other instances the supervisee may be receptive
to a mutual exploration of the differences. At the same time, ethnocultural
differences may be relatively benign and deserving of at best a brief comment.
Failure to acknowledge these issues can adversely affect the supervisory relationship, the supervised therapy, and the overall education of the supervisee,
as well as the treatment of the patient.

A process-oriented model of supervision that examines the nature of the
supervisory relationship as well as the supervisee–patient dyad diminishes the
chance that ethnocultural factors will be overlooked. Every set of training circumstances will present a new challenge by openly addressing ethnocultural
issues from the beginning, thus making the learning alliance more effective
and productive. The values and belief system of both the supervisor and
supervisee are major determinants of what is chosen for inquiry and interpretation and what are viewed as important goals for the patient. The supervisee's
capacity to understand and communicate to the supervisor the patient's values and beliefs will affect intervention strategies. These factors in turn will
shape the growth of the supervisee and the patient.

As pointed out earlier, the supervisor can open the work of supervision
by wondering about the effects of the supervisee's racial and ethnic background on the therapeutic process, by confronting issues early in the treatment, and by dealing with countertransferences tied to the supervisee's
feelings about social taboos, class, and other biases (Bradshaw 1982, Hunt
1987, Wong 1978).

Assessing the Supervisee

The assessment of the supervisee is an ongoing process that occurs informally
and formally throughout the supervisory relationship. The supervisor must
consider how the supervisee thinks and learns, and what elements may get in
the way of learning and how these obstacles can be overcome. The supervisor
may want to pay attention to how the supervisee relates and note the progress
in learning (Jacobs, et al. 1995). All of these factors will enable the supervisor
to make the necessary adjustments in supervision. Outcome studies of psychotherapy have demonstrated that the relationship between the supervisee

and the patient is one of the most significant factors in successful therapy (Clarkson 1995, Strupp 1996) and more important than theoretical orientation (Clarkson 1995). As a result, the supervisor must assess the supervisee's potential or skill in managing or developing a therapeutic alliance.

The supervisor may not have been involved in the selection of the supervisee, but in preparation for the supervisee, an assessment of the supervisee's background and experience should be made. Consideration must also be given to the context in which supervision takes place, such as the degree of disturbance and complications in the patient's condition, the supervisee's experience, and the supervisor's competence in working with the culture of the patient. The supervisor is ultimately responsible for the supervisee's professional development and most often the patient's welfare (Gordan 1996, Kalous 1996). The initial interview with the supervisee should include a discussion of the relevant factors in the above section.

SUPERVISORY PROCESS

Developing the Learning Alliance

The learning alliance is built on mutual trust and respect. Trust and respect develop as the supervisee begins to experience the supervisor as genuinely responsive to observations made about the patient as they collaborate on a dynamic understanding of the patient and as they determine therapeutic interventions for the patient. In the coparticipant model, the supervisor is an observed as well as an observing member of the dyad. The supervisor's willingness to be self-aware even in the face of potential anxieties may encourage the supervisee to do the same. The supervisor's awareness and direct expression of interests, concepts, and values may allow the supervisee to become clearer about the importance of a particular viewpoint and its consequences on the supervisee's work (Lesser 1984). The more comprehensible the supervisor makes the patient's behavior to the supervisee, the less likely the supervisee is to have severe negative countertransferences based on race (Bradshaw 1982, Remington and DaCosta 1989, Williams and Halgin 1995). Under the tutelage of the supervisor, the supervisee, as participant-observer with a detailed inquiry, explores the sociocultural historical context of the lifelong vicissitudes of the patient and recognizes that the impact of culture is mediated by the individual's temperament and private experience. In this endeavor the therapist enables the patient to begin to question values and conventional views.

Managing Transference and Countertransference

In a process-oriented model of supervision, an understanding of the patient's and the supervisee's transference and countertransference reactions is important. These reactions are also valuable instruments in the investigation of the patient's problems and a way to model a treatment approach for the supervisee. The supervisee brings to the supervisory situation emotional attitudes toward both the patient and the supervisor. There can be a mutual exploration of these attitudes as they surface to the benefit of all parties involved. Marshall and Marshall (1988) note that it is not uncommon for supervisees to withhold information from their supervisors and embellish what transpired in the interaction; consequently, there is a transference potential that is not always recognized and discussed. A strong learning alliance and a coparticipant model should diminish this transference potential and motivate the supervisee to report the interaction and the patient's productions as accurately as possible.

The mutual inquiry of the supervisee's countertransference to the patient is considered by some authors as an intrusion that goes beyond the boundaries of proper supervision and is more appropriate for the supervisee's personal analysis. The question is whether the supervisor's primary function is to help the supervisee understand the patient or to identify those instances in which the countertransference impedes the work (Lesser 1984). This is a compelling issue that is a judgment call for the supervisor and involves complicated factors surrounding the learning alliance, such as the willingness of the supervisee, the stage of the treatment, and the level of experience. The supervisee may be responsive or accept interpretations given in relation to behavior toward the patient and even toward the supervisor. Jacobs and colleagues (1995) present arguments in favor of a didactic supervision.

This raises another concern regarding the development of the parameters or boundaries of supervision. Many culturally diverse supervisees found themselves in a constant struggle to learn their profession without annihilating their historical sense of themselves. The supervisor can be central in enabling culturally diverse supervisees to integrate their professional and personal identities by acknowledging this conflict and by working through some of the issues that are germane to their alliance.

Cultural Countertransference

Cultural countertransference recognizes that both supervisee and patient are equally caught in their cultures. It is the cultural dimension in the mutual enactment of all the feelings, both conscious and unconscious, that are aroused by virtue of the attitudes, values, morals, biases, and prejudices that each party brings to the relationship (Chin et al. 1993, Grey 1993, Ticho 1971, Whitson 1996).

The differences in values and attitudes may stimulate a multiplicity of responses in the matched and mixed combinations. These differences may come up in new ways as treatment progresses. Below are descriptions of some of the defenses and anxieties that may transpire between these combinations (Bradshaw 1982, Comas-Diaz and Jacobsen 1991, Gottesfeld 1978, Grier 1967, Holmes 1992, Schacter and Butts 1968, Ticho 1971, Tsui and Schultz 1985, Wohl 1989).

Matched Pair

Each person in a matched pair seemingly carries a distinctive view of the same culture. Supervisors and supervisees with common ethnic identities may make assumptions about the patient that are not justified or may ignore and fail to inquire about certain material because it seems self-evident. There may be collusion between them to sidestep certain areas. Race/ethnic prejudices can occur regarding color and class when supervisee and supervisor share the same ethnic group. For instance, there may be negative reactions to manifestations of class differences, such as accent, pronunciation, dress, or even a marked difference or sameness in skin coloring (Bradshaw 1982, Hunt 1987, Williams 1996, Williams and Halgin 1995). Overidentification with the patient as oppressed and a victim of racial discrimination can result in overlooking internal conflicts by favoring external circumstances.

Mixed Pair

The participants in a mixed pair are more likely to be self-conscious about their differences and the biases and prejudices attendant to them. The supervisee may use racism as resistance to deflect legitimate questions about a supervisee's work. Real or imagined fears that the supervisor is judgmental, unenlightened, or even racist may inhibit an open dialogue about the patient. The supervisee's projections regarding race/ethnicity may also be reflected in defensive distancing or an overcompensating indulgence toward the patient. The supervisor may be overcautious and uncritical toward the culturally diverse supervisee to protect against a criticism of bias. The supervisor and supervisee may overcompensate for anxiety and prejudices by viewing most of the patient's productions in terms of racial conflict and negative feelings toward race/ethnicity, which deprives the patient of the opportunity to work through conflicts related to other issues.

Bradshaw (1982) describes a countertransference phenomenon in a mixed triad where the supervisor is European-American, the supervisee, an African American with a strong ethnic identity; and the patient, African-American. The countertransference develops in which the supervisee overidentifies with the patient and views the supervisor as a representative of some destructive and arbitrary authority. The supervisee believes that the patient's productions or behavior would reinforce the supervisor's negative stereotypes of African Americans. According to Bradshaw, more African-American patients unwittingly provoke this reaction in African-American supervisees than do their European-American counterparts. The history of racial discrimination and the minority status of the patient and the supervisee probably motivate the supervisee to be protective of the patient and the "race." It is not surprising that the supervisee may unconsciously withhold material, fearing that it would confirm the supervisor's already stereotyped view of African Americans. The supervisor's knowledge of the patient's subculture and a positive attitude toward the patient, with a willingness to keep an open mind regarding the patient, could preclude this type of countertransference phenomenon.

Illustrations

The consequences of the earlier described defenses and anxieties in the matched and mixed pair on the productiveness of the treatment makes it imperative to examine in detail some of the situations that may occur in the learning and treatment environment. The following illustrations attempt to incorporate the critical concepts delineated earlier and recognize some of the variables that affected the learning/treatment alliance in supervision. In order to achieve clarity regarding diversity and how it is expressed by the supervisor–supervisee–patient triad, the illustrations and case material will focus on the cultural and racial/ethnic factors in the treatment.

Learning Climate of the Organization

A climate that invites a free give and take and that is safe for the participants to reveal themselves is critical in preparing supervisees for effective psychotherapy. Supervision must be sensitive and supportive of the issues of ethnic combinations in the therapeutic dyad and the content that is germane to it. An atmosphere in which the participants can grow and learn from one another is required. The following two situations illustrate the point.

Illustration 1

Two analysts, one European-American and the other African-American, were sharing their experiences about their patients. The European-American analyst mentioned that in the four-year treatment of an African-American patient, the subject of ethnicity never came up. When the African-American therapist expressed surprise and suggested that both the patient and therapist might be avoiding differences, the therapist dismissed the possibility. Several months later, the European-American therapist indicated that there were, in fact, dynamics that both she and the patient had denied. The therapist recognized that she had been denying any significance of the race/ethnic difference between them because it meant investigating her own attitudes and possible biases. It was more comfortable for her to see a reasonably accomplished middle-class woman who was suffering from episodes of depression and profound feelings of isolation and aloneness than to look at her in a cultural context. The therapist had had very little interaction with African Americans and the patient was nothing like the stereotyped African Americans she had read about. The therapist was surprised to learn that the patient, who had even greater economic and educational advantages than she, had experienced discrimination and prejudice. She even failed to link the patient's preference for a European-American therapist, or her choice of European Americans for all other professional services, because both she and the patient believed that whites were better prepared and would provide better services. The patient had learned that blacks had to be twice as good to make it, and even then would be regarded as inferior. As their work progressed, the patient and the therapist were able to see how the patient's racial beliefs were influencing her view of herself. They began to understand how this contributed to the patient's depression and low self-esteem. The therapist learned that her own inability to recognize the racial roots of the patient's problems was due to a threat to her view of herself as a color-blind liberal person.

In this illustration, neither the patient nor the therapist saw their race/ethnic difference as an important defining feature of their professional relationship. They both denied the salience of race, and in so doing failed to explore an aspect of their belief systems that was interfering with the therapeutic work. The earlier dialogue between the two therapists contributed to the European-American therapist's interest in the cultural and ethnic component of her work with her patient. The same productive outcome may occur in supervision.

Illustration 2

In an ongoing case seminar, an African-American male, the only African American in the seminar, presented a case that had come to an impasse. The patient was an obese European-American female who was in treatment three times a week. She had indicated a preference for a male therapist and said that it did not matter that he was African-American, remarking, parenthetically, that her parents would be alarmed. She had developed an idealized transference and had resisted any efforts to interpret it. Dreams and other symbolic material had not revealed any concerns about the racial/ethnic differences. The matter had been discussed on several occasions in supervision and it was felt that the patient's overwhelming need for acceptance and approval blinded her from seeing the therapist as a person.

The supervisor advised the therapist to be sensitive to symbolic productions related to cultural issues that might be forthcoming as treatment progressed. Several of the therapists took exception to the point, insisting that the ethnic difference between the therapist and the patient was being denied. They felt that the therapist should be more active in generating a discussion with her about the difference. The African-American therapist said if turnabout is fair play, then the other therapists should have pressed their patients to discuss ethnic differences as well, and they had not.

When the African-American therapist looked to the supervisor for support, the supervisor talked only about the dynamic issue between the therapist and the patient and said nothing explicitly about the controversial group process. While it was important for this therapist to gain more insight about dynamics, it was equally important for the participants in the seminar to gain some understanding about their strong reactions to this case and the dynamics that were being played out in the seminar. Thus all the therapists were left with information that failed to enhance their awareness of an important cultural issue. The therapist felt misunderstood and attacked by the group. He also was frustrated by his inability to engage his European-American colleagues in a dialogue that considered their countertransferential issues. He also felt quite miffed that the European-American therapists were taking a protective attitude toward his European-American patient and did not feel similarly toward their African-American patients. The European-American therapists believed that the African-American therapist was defensive and resisting their insights.

In both illustrations, strong feelings were evoked and reflect the resistance to open discussion regarding issues of ethnicity in the mixed therapeutic dyad.

Clinic Setting

Case 1 Mixed Triad

In a clinic, a poor Irish-American Catholic female entering her senior year in college was assigned to an African-American female therapist for twice-a-week therapy. She appeared surprised when the therapist called her name and brought her to the treatment room. During the initial interviews, her feelings about having an African-American therapist and what it meant to be in treatment were explored. She replied by saying it did not matter to her. However, she added, "My folks would die if they knew I was seeing a shrink, and a black one at that." The difference was discussed again as part of the transference when the patient had an affair with an African-American male. She talked about profound feelings of guilt and shame regarding this relationship and was preoccupied with fear that her parents might find out.

The initial stages of the supervision of this supervisee centered around the ethnic and class difference between them. The supervisee had never had any experience with the culture of poor Irish Catholics. In this case there were strong family ties and identification with an Irish heritage. The expectation was that the children would remain in the community and marry Irish Catholics, raising their children to do the same. They had difficulty accepting people who were not Irish and made disparaging and bigoted remarks about them. This family was extremely intolerant about blacks, viewing them as inferior. The patient's parents drank alcohol excessively and fought frequently, using nasty and foul language. The parents had lived in very poor circumstances as had the patient's grandparents. During sessions, the patient habitually used foul language and made insulting remarks about people with whom she worked. The therapist made the observation to the patient that she was mirroring her parents. The patient remarked that the therapist flinched and flushed when she spoke in this manner. The supervisee was embarrassed and took it up in supervision.

The supervisor recognized the supervisee's conflict and discomfort with the patient and pointed out that there was something about the patient that made her feel uneasy. The supervisee was puzzled by her own reaction to the patient's foul language since it was something with which she was familiar. She had believed that it was the intensity and the frequency that bothered her. Instead, her introspection revealed that what was making the supervisee uneasy was that the patient was expressing contempt toward her. Readings were suggested for the supervisee to broaden her perspective on the patient's cultural background. The inquiry was focused by the supervisor to elicit a clearer understanding of the psychodynamics. The supervisee and patient were able to get in touch with their transference–countertransference reactions. For this patient, who felt like a social outcast, having a boyfriend and a therapist whose racial affiliation had a low status in her mind made her feel more valued and preferred than at home or in the outside world. The supervisee and the supervisor discussed how these prejudicial attitudes protected the patient from dealing with some of the core issues in her treatment.

As the supervisee and the patient got more in touch with what it meant to be in treatment in general and with an African-American therapist in particular, the two began to understand more about the meaning of the patient's interaction with her family. She felt tied to explicit and implicit expectations, that is, what it meant to live in a family with alcoholic parents who had low aspirations and whose daughter would be the first to graduate from college and move out of the community. The patient was then able to make adjustments in her values and experience herself as separate from her family. She moved from home and started a life separate from her family.

This case illustrates how the prejudices that the supervisee and the patient brought to the treatment served as a catalyst that enabled them to expand their understanding of themselves.

Case 2: Mixed Triad

An Asian-American female in her mid-twenties, married to a European American and working in the mental health profession, abruptly terminated treatment, giving notice at the beginning of the session after three months in once-a-week therapy with an African-American therapist. The therapist was surprised because she believed that some progress was being made in establishing an alliance with this patient who had issues regarding trust and gaining access to her emotional life. The patient had already seen two female therapists: the first an Asian American who she believed did not grasp the depth of her despair, telling her how she should not take her problems so seriously. She spent a brief time with her second therapist, a European American, but terminated because she "could not afford the fees." The patient was referred to an African-American therapist by a low-cost referral service. Upon meeting the therapist, the patient indicated that for the first time she felt that she was being heard and that her ethnic/racial issues would be understood.

The patient's initial complaint concerned her obsessive preoccupation with a traumatic experience. While pledging a sorority where, according to her belief, her race was an attraction for scapegoating, she was accused by the group of being insincere and manipulative. She felt humiliated, misunderstood, and ostracized. The patient presented herself as well assimilated and sophisticated about mental health practices but gave evidence of self-consciousness and rejection of her Asian appearance and identity. She was brought to this country over twenty years before by her family. She acquired her education in an upper middle-class European-American community and in an Ivy League college and graduate school. So when she asserted that she did not know what to expect in therapy, did not want to discuss earlier life experiences, and was not sure that the process would be beneficial, the therapist took it to be resistance to the treatment rather than a difference in world view.

On the surface she was agreeable and compliant as a result of adhering to the mores and customs of Asian culture. She avoided conflict and deferred to an older authority figure and expert in the person of the therapist. Thus she went through the process, explored issues, kept appointments on time, and was a "good patient." At the same time, however, she became increasingly more guarded and defensive until a considerable amount of rage had accumulated. She could do nothing with this rage except escape the situation by terminating treatment.

In supervision it was pointed out that this patient was outraged that her therapists, her projected parents, were not able to provide her with the support and protection she wanted as she ventured out into the Western world. She responded by denying and rejecting her heritage, by identifying with and attempting to become a part of the world that did not understand her. But she was bound by the culture of her birth and upbringing to protect her family even from her own inquiry and certainly from her anger. Thus she was unable to get to the depth of her despair. Her compliant manner misled the therapist into thinking that a therapeutic alliance was being developed when it was not. Consequently, the therapist failed to convey to the patient that she and her culture were understood. The patient in turn felt that the therapist could not be trusted. All of this increased the patient's doubts about the usefulness of the treatment process.

The alliance with this patient might have been strengthened had the therapist acknowledged with the patient a possible conflict between their therapeutic process and the exposure of unacceptable feelings about her family members or her sense of betrayal of the values with which she was raised.

This case illustrates how the cultural values instilled in such patients coexist with their exposure to the Western values in which they were educated. The conflict between these values needs to be considered openly. Therapists should not be blinded by the overt sophistication presented by the most educated, long-term, well-exposed person who was nurtured in another culture.

Case 3: Mixed Triad

In a clinic, a 5-year-old intellectually gifted but frightened and sexually traumatized light-skinned African-American female was assigned to a white Hispanic female therapist for twice-a-week dynamic play therapy. The supervisee expressed a special interest in cultural differences to her African-American female supervisor as they were establishing the learning alliance. This interest grew out of her own disturbing personal experiences. She was sensitive to the affects and the pain associated with race/ethnic prejudice and discrimination. Rapport between the patient and supervisee was established easily, as it was with the parents, who looked to the supervisee for support and direction. The parents were seen every six weeks to discuss the patient's progress.

Six months into the treatment, the patient remarked about the skin color difference between the dolls, the supervisee, and herself by grouping the white dolls next to the supervisee. The patient joined the group of dolls, showing the palm of her hand and stating that she was white. The supervisee was alarmed and believed that it meant that the patient was denying her ethnic identity. She wanted to intervene immediately by talking with the patient about the difference between them, but decided to bring it to supervision. The supervisor felt that an intervention would be premature and that this was a playful experimental activity that suggested that the patient was merely accepting the therapist and wanted to be like her. It was felt that to intervene would be making too much out of the action; it was important to wait and see what would transpire in the future. Readings in the area of development of racial awareness were recommended.

The patient's school adjustment improved and she began to develop a more differentiated sense of self and others, with an ability to better tolerate boundaries. A year later, the patient again remarked about color differences, but this time in the context that her sister's African-American therapist was going to have a baby and she wondered whether it would be a black baby. The patient also commented on the difference in hair texture between herself and the supervisee and wanted to know why there was such a difference. She went on to sing the first lines of a song that has been made popular by an African-American singer, connoting pride in her color.

The supervisor pointed out that there were two separate issues, the first having to do with the patient's desire to be the therapist's daughter and the second that the patient was in the process of developing her ethnic identity. The patient was attempting to reconcile the difference between them.

During this same period, the parents expressed dissatisfaction with the predominantly Hispanic parochial school to which the patient had transferred with the help of the supervisee. The parents had been happy with the school, but believed that the teachers favored the other children over the patient, who was the only African American in the class. These beliefs grew out of a criticism of the teacher regarding the patient's performance and the request that the parents become more active with homework assignments and other activities.

The supervisee felt frustrated and overcome by the parents' sabotage of her therapeutic interventions with the patient and the family. She was unable to recognize that some of her frustrations were also related to the derogatory comments they were making about the Hispanics at the school. These parents had difficulty accepting what they viewed as criticism; they had been overwhelmed with managing other stresses in their lives and were unable to undertake another responsibility. They were using race/ethnicity as a defense to avoid looking at the issues.

This case illustrates how a supervisee can be overly attentive to race/ethnic issues and the importance of redirecting the therapist to the process of racial/ethnic identity in preschoolers and more specifically to this patient. It also demonstrates how the attitudes and values of the parents can influence the course of treatment.

Case 4: Mixed Triad

A depressed and anxious African-American female in her early twenties from a working class background was assigned to a European-American male therapist. In the first session the patient began to talk about the pride she felt in her African heritage and began to display her knowledge. In supervision, the supervisee declared that the patient required an African-American therapist and asked that she be reassigned to one.

The supervisor inquired about the reasons for the supervisee's request. The supervisee expressed concern that he did not know anything about African heritage, that he did not feel prepared to work with her, and that he believed an African American would better suit her "needs." As the supervisor and the supervisee began to mutually explore their reactions to the supervisee's wish, it became apparent to them that the supervisee was distancing himself from the situation and was rejecting the patient before she rejected him. The patient in turn was using her knowledge about "her people" to keep the therapist at a distance. Both were feeling anxious and were reacting to stereotypical notions about a "white male with a black female."

The supervisor directed the discussions and the supervisee began to understand what the patient was stimulating in him and what he was probably stimulating in her. The patient stirred in him a feeling of inadequacy and he was threatened by her assertiveness. It became apparent that the patient was afraid to reveal herself to the therapist, a "white man"; to tell her family secrets felt like a betrayal. Once his anxiety was allayed, he was able to engage the patient and began to clarify for himself and his patient what had brought her to treatment. The patient was one of a few of members in her community to complete college. During high school and college she did not feel accepted by her peers in the community, who accused her of wanting to be "white." She felt caught between two worlds and felt alienated from both.

The supervisor also realized that he and the supervisee had not talked about what their ethnic and ideological differences were and what it meant to them; more importantly, how the supervisee felt about working with culturally diverse patients. The supervisee felt isolated as one of only a few European-American supervisees in the clinic, fearing that he would not be supported by his African-American supervisor who may have had a different outlook on treatment and who appeared to be protective of culturally diverse patients. As they talked, they became aware of their biases and prejudices. They also discovered that many of their values and attitudes were compatible. The supervisor learned from their discussions that he had tended to overidentify with many of the patients. As a result of this experience, the supervisor listened more carefully to the supervisee and had continuing educational opportunities that specifically dealt with identity issues for both patients and supervisees in the treatment of culturally diverse patients.

In most clinics, patients and therapists have no choice in the selection process; they may only be able to indicate a preference and hope for the best. In this situation it was a reflection of the supervisee's anxiety about his competence to handle the case. What does it mean when a patient makes such a request or when confronted with the difference indicates that it does not matter? Very often patients may say such a choice doesn't matter, but someone else they're close to would object. Exploring this sort of denial, if pursued, can be the beginning of productive racial/ethnic dialogue. It can also blossom into a journey of exploration where both parties began to learn more about themselves.

This case illustrates how supervisory triads have ramifications that go beyond the patient and therapist match. All three participants were bringing their biased expectations to the treatment. The supervisor's intervention allowed participants to benefit from the process.

Case 5: Matched Triad

An African-American male supervisee in his early twenties presented a case of a chronically depressed African-American female patient in her mid-forties to an African-American female supervisor. The patient's physical complaints consisted of a heart condition, anemia, chest pains, asthma, and arthritis. A former drug addict in recovery for three years, she had been without a home for over a year. She lived with a friend who provided a small room for the patient and her two grandchildren. She was overwhelmed with the responsibility of the care of her grandchildren, with visits to her hospitalized daughter, with the burden of a disabled son, and with responding to the requests of her friend. She had not been able to keep appointments in a timely fashion and often neglected to call or cancel. The supervisee had been helping the patient to negotiate the welfare system for housing and the court system for neglect charges. The supervisee was pleased about the patient's progress and admired her "energy" in accomplishing so much in a day. However, he was concerned that the patient failed to keep appointments.

The supervisee usually provided a full physical description of his patients and while he indicated that this patient was attractive and neat in appearance, he neglected to mention her weight. The supervisor inquired about the patient's weight because of concern about her poor health. The supervisee expressed surprise and mumbled that she was heavy, but well built. When the supervisor pressed the issue about how heavy, he continued to deny the issue of obesity, stating that she was shapely. In defense, the supervisee referred to the psychiatric interview and remarked that even the psychiatrist did not note the patient's weight. Finally, when asked about her height and weight, he indicated that she was about five feet and about 190 pounds. The supervisor pointed out that 190 pounds is obese.

The supervisee understood what the supervisor was telling him; consequently, the inquiry had to be redirected to the supervisee's perception of the patient and the reality of the size of the patient. What was there about this patient that distracted him from seeing her as she was, an obese women with a heart condition, anemia, chest pains, asthma, and arthritis? He immediately saw how he overlooked her weight as a critical factor in her treatment and how she had never talked about losing weight. The supervisor's inquiry was more than the supervisee could tolerate. He felt put upon and overwhelmed with paperwork and other matters with this patient. How could he be expected to record and see these things? The supervisor pointed out that these were separate issues.

This illustration raises the issue of how values and biases can interfere with perception. Had this been a middle-class patient or a younger patient where "slim and trim" are a high priority, this would have been one of the major topics of exploration. The supervisee felt unsupported and unrecognized in the day-to-day demands being made on him by the agency, the supervisor, and the patient. He, like the agency itself, had begun reacting to managed care's increasing demand for paperwork, reduced session frequency, and shortened treatments. The supervisor's request for introspection and consideration of the needs of the patient was too much to ask of a supervisee who felt neglected himself. The patient had the energy to mobilize herself but could not take the time to acknowledge the supervisee by calling to cancel appointments. The supervisee was beginning to question his ability to provide quality service to his patients. The supervisor realized that she must begin to talk more about his expectations of his patients and his feelings about the agency.

This case illustrates how, unwittingly, the expectations of the agency can impact on the therapeutic process.

REFERENCES

Altman, N. (1995). *The Analyst in the Inner City: Race, Class, and Culture through a Psychoanalytic Lens.* Hillsdale, NJ: Analytic Press.

——— (1996). The accommodation of diversity in psychoanalysis. In *Reaching Across Boundaries of Culture and Class: Widening the Scope of Psychotherapy,* ed. R. M. Perez Foster, M. Moskowitz, and R. A. Javier, pp. 195–209. Northvale, NJ: Jason Aronson.

Atkinson, D. R., Morten, G., and Sue, D. W., eds. (1993). *Counseling American Minorities: A Cross-Cultural Perspective.* Madison, WI: Brown & Benchmark.

Bernal, M. E., and Padilla, A. M. (1982). Status of minority curricula and training in clinical psychology. *American Psychologist* 37:780–787.

Beutler, L. E., and Kendall, P. C. (1995). Introduction to the special section: the case for training in the provision of psychological therapy. *Journal of Consulting and Clinical Psychology* 63:179–181.

Bongar, B., and Beutler, L. E. (1995). *Comprehensive Textbook of Psychotherapy: Theory and Practice.* New York: Oxford University Press.

Boxley, R., and Wagner, N. N. (1971). Clinical psychology training programs and minority groups: a survey. *Professional Psychology* 2:75–81.

Bradshaw, W. H. (1982). Supervision in black and white. In *Applied Supervision in Psychotherapy,* ed. M. Blumenfield, pp.190–220. New York: Grune & Stratton.

Caligor, L., Bromberg, P. M., and Meltzer, J. D., eds. (1984). *Clinical Perspectives on the Supervision of Psychoanalysis and Psychotherapy.* New York: Plenum.

Carney, C. G., and Kahn, K. B. (1984). Building competencies for effective cross cultural counseling: a developmental view. *Counseling Psychologist* 12:111–119.

Chin, J. L., Liem, J. H., Ham, M. D. and Hong, G. K. (1993). *Transference and Empathy in Asian American Psychotherapy.* Westport, CT: Praeger.

Clarkson, P. (1995). *The Therapeutic Relationship: In Psychoanalysis, Counseling Psychology and Psychotherapy*. London: Whurr.

Comas-Diaz, L. (1988). Cross-cultural mental health treatment. In *Clinical Guidelines in Cross-Cultural Mental Health*, ed. L. Comas-Diaz and E. E. H. Griffith, pp. 337–361. New York: Wiley.

Comas-Diaz, L., and Jacobsen, F. (1991). Ethnocultural transference and counter-transference in the therapeutic dyad. *Journal of the American Orthopsychiatric Association* 61:392–402.

Cummings, N. A. (1996). The impact of managed care on employment and professional training: A primer for survival. In *Surviving the Demise of Solo Practice: Mental Health Practitioners Prospering in the Era of Managed Care*, ed. N. A. Cummings, M. S. Pallak, and J. L. Cummings, pp. 11–26. Madison, CT: Psychosocial Press.

Dana, R. H. (1993). *Multicultural Assessment Perspectives for Professional Psychology*. Needham Heights, MA: Allyn & Bacon.

Foster, R. M. P. (1992). Psychoanalysis and the bilingual patient: some observations on the influence of language choice on the transference. *Psychoanalytic Psychology* 9:61–75.

––––––– (1996). What is a multicultural perspective in psychoanalysis? In *Reaching Across Boundaries of Culture and Class: Widening the Scope of Psychotherapy*, ed. R. M. Perez Foster, M. Moskowitz, and R. A. Javier, pp. 3–20. Northvale, NJ: Jason Aronson.

Goldberg, F. H. (1995). Contemporary issues in and approaches to psychoanalytic supervision. In *Psychoanalytic Approaches to Supervision*, ed. R. C. Lane. Monographs of the Society for Psychoanalytic Training No. 2. New York: Brunner/Mazel.

Goodman, M. E. (1964). *Race Awareness in Young Children*. Reading, MA: Addison-Wesley.

Gordan, K., (1996). *Psychotherapy Supervision in Education, Clinical Practice, and Institutions*. Northvale, NJ: Jason Aronson.

Gottesfeld, M. (1978). Countertransference and ethnic similarity. *Bulletin of the Menninger Clinic* 42:63–67.

Grey, C. (1993). Culture, character, and the analytic engagement: toward a subversive psychoanalysis. *Contemporary Psychoanalysis* 29:487–502.

Grier, W. (1967). When the supervisee is Negro; some effects of the treatment process. *American Journal of Psychiatry* 123:1589–1592.

Griffith, C., and Delgado, A. (1979). On the professional socialization of black psychiatric residents in psychiatry. *Journal of Medical Education* 54:471–476.

Griffith, M. S. (1977). The influences of race on the psychotherapeutic relationship. *Psychiatry* 40:27–40.

Herron, W. G., Javier, R. A., and Intranuovo, L. R. (1995). Issues in supervision (psychoanalytic) at the graduate discipline training level. *Clinical Supervisor* 13:121–131.

Holmes, D. E. (1992). Race and transference in psychoanalysis and psychotherapy. *International Journal of Psycho-analysis* 73:1–11.

Hunt, P. (1987). Black patients: implications for supervision of trainees. *Psychotherapy* 24:114–119.

Jacobs, D., David, P., and Meyer, D. J. (1995). *The Supervisory Encounter: A Guide for Teachers of Psychodynamic Psychotherapy and Psychoanalysis.* New Haven, CT: Yale University Press.

Javier, R. A. (1996). Psychodynamic treatment with the urban poor. In *Reaching Across Boundaries of Culture and Class: Widening the Scope of Psychotherapy,* ed. R. M. Perez Foster, M. Moskowitz, and R. A. Javier, pp. 93–113. Northvale, NJ: Jason Aronson.

Javier, R. A., and Herron, W. (1992). Psychoanalysis, the Hispanic poor, and the disadvantaged: application and conceptualization. *Journal of the American Academy of Psychoanalysis* 20:455–476.

Kalous, T. D. (1996). Conducting psychotherapy supervision in the managed care era. In *Surviving the Demise of Solo Practice: Mental Health Practitioners Prospering in the Era of Managed Care,* ed. N. A. Cummings, M. S. Pallak, and J. L. Cummings, pp. 93–116. Madison, CT: Psychosocial Press.

Kearney, M. (1975). World view theory and study. *Annual Review of Anthropology* 4:47–270.

Lesser, R. (1984). Supervision: illusions, anxieties, and questions. In *Clinical Perspectives on the Supervision of Psychoanalysis and Psychotherapy,* ed. L. Caligor, P. Bromberg, and J. Meltzer, pp. 143–152. New York: Plenum.

Marshall, R. J., and Marshall, S. V. (1988). *The Transference-Countertransference Matrix: The Emotional-Cognitive Dialogue in Psychotherapy, Psychoanalysis and Supervision.* New York: Columbia University Press.

Minuchin, S. (1968). Psychoanalytic therapies and the low socioeconomic population. In *Modern Psychoanalysis: New Directions and Perspectives,* ed. J. Marmor, pp. 532–550. New York: Basic Books.

Mitchell, M. (1970). *Not by the Color of Their Skin: The Impact of Racial Differences on the Child's Development.* New York: International Universities Press.

Moses, S. (1990). Sensitivity to culture may be hard to teach: APA approves practice guidelines. *APA Monitor,* December, p. 39.

Myers, W. (1977). The significance of the colors black and white in the dreams of black and white patients. *Journal of the American Psychoanalytic Association* 35:163–181.

Norcross, J. C., and Goldfried, M. R. (1992). *Handbook of Psychotherapy Integration.* New York: Basic Books.

Parham, T. A., and Helms, J. E. (1981). The influence of black students' racial identity attitudes on preference for counselor's race. *Journal of Counseling Psychology* 28:250–257.

Pettigrew, T. F. (1979). The ultimate attribution error: extending Allport's cognitive analysis of prejudice. *Personality and Social Psychology Bulletin* 5:173–176.

Phinney, J. S. (1996). When we talk about American ethnic groups, what do we mean? *American Psychologist* 51:918–927.

Remington, G., and DaCosta, G. (1989). Ethnocultural factors in resident supervision—black supervisor and white supervisees. *American Journal of Psychotherapy* 43:398–405.

Rodenhauser, P. (1995). Experiences and issues in the professional development of psychiatrists for supervising psychotherapy. *Clinical Supervisor* 13:7–22.

Ruiz, R. A., and Padilla, A. M. (1977). Counseling Latinos. *Personnel and Guidance Journal* 55:401–408.

Schacter, J., and Butts, H. (1968). Transference and countertransference in interracial analyses. *Journal of the American Psychoanalytic Association* 16:792–808.

Singer, J. L. (1995). The supervision of graduate students who are conducting psychodynamic psychotherapy. In *Psychoanalytic Approaches to Supervision*, ed. R. C. Lane. Monographs of the Society for Psychoanalytic Training No. 2. New York: Brunner/Mazel.

Strupp, H. H. (1996). The tripartite model and the consumer reports study. *American Psychologist* 51:1017–1024.

Sue, D. W., Bernier, J. E., Durren, A., et al. (1982). Position paper: cross-cultural counseling competencies. *Counseling Psychologist* 10:45–52.

Sue, S. (1988). Psychotherapeutic services for ethnic minorities: two decades of research findings. *American Psychologist* 43:301–308.

Sue, S., and Sue, D. W. (1971). Chinese-American personality and mental health. *Amerasia Journal* 1:36–49.

Sue, S., and Zane, N. (1987). The role of culture and cultural techniques in psychotherapy. *American Psychologist* 42:37–45.

Ticho, G. (1971). Cultural aspects of transference and countertransference. *Bulletin of the Menninger Clinic* 35:313–326.

Traunt, G. S., and Lohrenz, J. G. (1993). Basic principles of psychotherapy I. Introduction, basic goals, and the therapeutic relationship. *American Journal of Psychotherapy* 47:8–17.

Tsui, P., and Schultz, G. L. (1985). Failure of rapport: why psychotherapeutic engagement fails in the treatment of Asian clients. *American Journal of Orthopsychiatry* 55:561–569.

Uba, L. (1994). *Asian Americans: Personality Patterns, Identity, and Mental Health.* New York: Guilford.

Watkins, C. E. (1993). Development of the psychotherapy supervisor, concepts, assumptions, and hypotheses of the supervisor complexity model. *American Journal of Psychotherapy* 47:58–74.

White, J. E. (1997). "I am just who I am": Race is no longer as simple as black or white. So what does this mean for America? *Time*, May 5, 149, pp. 32–36.

Whitson, G. (1996). Working class issues. In *Reaching Across Boundaries of Culture and Class: Widening the Scope of Psychotherapy*, ed. R. M. Perez Foster, M. Moskowitz, and R. A. Javier, pp. 143–157. Northvale, NJ: Jason Aronson.

Williams, A. L. (1996). Skin color in psychotherapy. In *Reaching Across Boundaries of Culture and Class: Widening the Scope of Psychotherapy*, ed. R. M. Perez Foster, M. Moskowitz, and R. A. Javier, pp. 211–224. Northvale, NJ: Jason Aronson.

Williams, S., and Halgin, R. P. (1995). Issues in psychotherapy supervision between the white supervisor and the black supervisee. *Clinical Supervisor* 13:39–61.

Wilson, L. L., and Stith, S. M. (1993). Culturally sensitive therapy with black clients. In *Counseling American Minorities: A Cross-Cultural Perspective*, ed. D. R. Atkinson, G. Morten, and D. W. Sue, pp. 101–111. Madison, WI: Brown & Benchmark.

Wohl, J. (1989). Integration of cultural awareness into psychotherapy. *American Journal of Psychotherapy* 43:343–355.

Wong, N. (1978). Psychiatric education and training of Asian and Asian-American psychiatrists. *American Psychiatric Association* 135:1525–1529.

Wu, J. (1994). On therapy with Asian patients. *Contemporary Psychoanalysis* 30:152–168.

Yi, K. (1995). Psychoanalytic psychotherapy with Asian patients: transference and therapeutic considerations. *Psychotherapy* 32:308–316.

Yutrzenka, B. (1995). Making a case for training in ethnic and cultural diversity in increasing treatment efficacy. *Journal of Consulting and Clinical Psychology* 63:197–206.

30

Assessing Workplace Disruptions in a Multicultural Context

WAYNE J. WARREN, RAFAEL ART. JAVIER, AND FATIMAH EL-JAMIL

Workplace violence has become increasingly problematic in our society, carrying with it tremendous psychological and economic implications for recipient and perpetrator, whether an individual or an institution (Bulatao and VandenBos 1996). These violent acts range anywhere from the sensational post-office carnage reported on television and in newspapers to less sensational and newsworthy disruptions, such as property damages, absenteeism, and the like. Regarding the most severe incidents, according to the National Institute for Occupational Safety and Health (1993), an average of twenty employees are murdered each week and 18,000 employees are assaulted. The Bureau of Labor Statistics data for 1993–1994 reported homicide to be the second leading cause of job-related deaths and was approaching the frequency of job-related deaths in motor vehicles (cited in Bulatao and VandenBos 1996). Of all the job-related fatalities in 1994, 16 percent were homicides. In 1992, however, of all job-related injuries, only 1 percent was due to violent acts.

Similarly alarming statistics are reported in the 1993 survey by Northwestern National Life Insurance (Northwestern National Life Employee Benefits Division 1993). They found that 2 million employees suffer physical attacks at work each year and more than 6 million are in some way threatened at work (cited in Barling 1996). Men are the most likely victims of violence, accounting for 80 percent of workplace homicides between 1980 and 1992. Overall, women have the highest rate, considering their smaller proportion in the workplace. Women accounted for 42 percent of occupational injury deaths as compared to 11 percent for men. Additionally, the risks for homicide among minority groups were found to be high, accounting for a fourth of homicide victims, although they make up only an eighth of the workplace population (Bulatao and VandenBos 1996). As disturbing as these numbers are, they are considered an underrepresentation as many incidents are not reported, particularly the less severe disturbances.

PROBLEM WITH DEFINITION

It is difficult to predict under what conditions one is more likely to become a victim of a crime, but some employment situations have been found to be of higher risk than others. For instance, individuals identified as more likely to become a victim of a crime are those working in retail trade (38 percent), service industries (17 percent), taxicab services (41.4 percent), liquor stores (7.5 percent), detective and protective services (7.0 percent), gasoline service stations (4.8 percent), and jewelry stores (4.7 percent), when compared to individuals working in other occupations. Postal service industries or postal occupations are not among the groups at high risk, accounting for only a small percentage of incidents. Multiple murders, however, are reported in these incidents (Bulatao and VandenBos 1996). "Going postal" has become a vernacularism used to denote multiple murders.

Can the phenomenon of violence in the workplace in general be understood and is it possible to predict it? Can potential violence in the workplace be identified and prevented? What role do cultural factors have in understanding and prevention of this phenomenon? Barling (1996) and Bulatao and VandenBos (1996) suggested that answers to these questions depend largely on how we define the phenomenon. For instance, Buss (as cited by Folger & Baron [1996]) distinguished between workplace aggression that is flagrant and active and that which is more passive in terms of physical aggression (e.g., *Active*: homicide, assault, sexual assault, obscene gestures, etc. *Passive*: intentional work slowdowns, refusal to provide needed resources, delaying work, etc.); and verbal aggressions (e.g., *Active*: threats, yelling, sexual harassment, sarcasm, spreading rumors, and transmitting damaging information, etc. *Passive*: failure to return phone calls, giving target the "silent treatment," and failure to deny false rumors, etc.) (cited by Folger and Baron 1996). Although it is clear that there is less likelihood that a blatant act of aggression would be misunderstood, the problem occurs in less clearly defined situations. This is particularly the case when the individuals involved come from diverse cultural backgrounds and with different perceptions of violence and disruptive behaviors. From this perspective the assessment of workplace disruption and development of appropriate interventions are made a more complex task. There is less ambiguity concerning the economic impact of disruptive behaviors in the workplace (Barling 1996).

Our society is becoming increasingly diverse and the workplace is no exception. With the socioeconomic and geopolitical changes, more and more individuals from South and Central America and Caribbean countries are immigrating into many metropolitan cities in the United States. Similarly, Asians and individuals from the former Soviet Union are making the United States their home. We now have a work force that is becoming increasingly diverse, and a consumer population reflecting these characteristics. Many companies are paying close attention to these developments because of the great economic potential, and have begun to develop products targeted specifically to these new consumers.

In order to understand how confusion regarding problem definition is possible, one has to consider how an individual develops his or her value systems. Who we become is influenced by our own history, our relationship with family, friends, teachers, and environment. We then organize our experience with others based on attributes acquired in the context of these experiences and define ourselves accordingly. Thus the rest of the world is processed in terms of the degree of familiarity with what we know best—our world. Our world becomes the point of reference for everything we do with ourselves and with others (Dana 1993). Prejudice occurs when one considers his or her personal views the most important, and relegates to inferior and undesirable the positions of those who hold different views and come from different cultural and socioeconomic backgrounds (Lichtenberg et al. 1997). In the case of a work situation, one can see how serious problems could emerge whenever one's personal reference point to understand others' behavior is no longer valid. Mislabeling of a behavior could occur in terms of the quality and nature of its phenomenological manifestation and motivational characteristics. Since one's perception of the event determines what courses of action are followed, then it is likely that the selected intervention may cause additional problems for the corporation.

For instance, the case of two co-workers, an African-American female who recently joined the company and a Korean male who already was enjoying a great reputation in the company: they had met earlier in the day and exchanged pleasantries, and were now by the soda machine during a morning break. The African-American woman decided to get a soda but realized that she did not have enough change. She requested change from a Korean co-worker who had already gotten his beverage and was sitting at a table with other friends not far from the soda machine. She held her dollar bill in an extended hand while he eagerly went into his pocket and searched for change. He counted a dollar's worth of change and proceeded to place it on the table, bypassing the extended hand of the African-American woman. She became visibly upset and, throwing the dollar bill on the table, proceeded to count the change. The Korean co-worker became upset when he saw her counting the change. At the end, the tension between these two individuals mounted to such a level that each was accusing the other of discrimination and prejudice. She felt that he was avoiding touching her because of her skin color, and he felt that it was clear that she had questions about his character, enough to count the change. The danger with this situation is that once a specific perception about a motivation of a behavior sets in, it tends to affect every other aspect of the interaction. It is likely to affect future interactions between these two individuals who unintentionally ended up offending each other. We can see how misperceptions of motives are likely to occur in situations where the cultural scripts guiding individuals' behavior are unfamiliar to the participants. The cultural script of the Korean individual expects that he places money in a receptacle and not in the individuals' hands, out of respect. For the African-American individual, it is expected that she counts her change right away to avoid future problems in case there is an honest mistake.

For our purposes, we will refer to *workplace violence* as *workplace disruptions* because such a definition better encompasses a variety of situations. This term was chosen because the term *workplace violence* is associated with the sensational incidents that make headlines, those in which individuals from the outside enter with a gun and shoot one or more people. While these situations do occur, we suggested earlier that the more serious and subtle threats to corporations are the less sensational situations in which a workplace disruption could include verbal threats, assaults, and destruction of property, as described earlier. Furthermore, workplace violence may be perceived as unpredictable, unpreventable, and caused largely by emotionally disturbed individuals or individuals from a cultural or ethnic background different from the majority group. The fact is that these views are misperceptions and the phenomenon is more complex. There are many causes for workplace disruptions.

It is also true that employers and employees can take steps to make the workplace safer.

In this chapter we will attempt to address the following questions: (1) Why has violence increased in the workplace and what role does the growing diversity play in this increase? (2) What is the difficulty in assessing workplace violence when there are people from various cultural and ethnic backgrounds present? (3) What are the warning signs and predicting factors that are crucial in order to better cope with workplace disruptions? and (4) Can such workplace disruptions be prevented?

ASSESSMENT OF WORKPLACE DISRUPTIONS

Assessment of workplace disruptions has only recently begun to receive attention from corporations, which are now more aware of the tremendous financial liabilities (e.g., lost wages and time, medical costs, legal fees, demoralization) of not having adequate strategies to make the work site a safe place for their employees. The multiplicity of contributing factors normally associated with violence are made even more complicated by the increasing diversification in the workplace population. Cultural differences with differing perceptions and behavioral displays of emotions can make assessment of potential workplace disruptions more difficult. When assessing the potential for workplace disruption, an evaluation of the person's actions within the norms of his or her culture is crucial. Ignorance about cultural norms can affect the assessment in either direction. In other words, an over- or underassessment of risk could occur if cultural norms are not taken into consideration. (This issue will be discussed later in this chapter.)

Consider the following workplace situation. Joe works for a large company. He has been employed there for the past five years and supervises a small group of employees. The last two months he has been coming in five to twenty minutes late most days although previously he was always quite punctual. He has been looking tired, and even though he was never very friendly, he has been glaring at and giving menacing stares to other employees. Joe was always somewhat of a complainer, but lately his complaints have been more threatening, albeit vague. The other day he was seen kicking and cursing at the copying machine. His team's productivity has been good and his division is profitable. Is Joe a problem? The question can be answered only if an assessment of his behavior is made in the context of clear company policies and procedures regarding assessment of workplace disruptions and ways to handle them and in the context of an appreciation of the cultural characteristics of employees. We will now focus our attention on a specific discussion of general and culturally specific assessment strategy that corporations could include as part of their policies and procedures.

Typical Profile

There has been some question about whether it is possible to determine a typical profile that could allow companies to predict workplace disruptions. The safest approach is to consider that anyone could be involved in a disruptive situation under the right set of circumstances. Any combination of work stress, personal problems, family problems, illness, and conflicting cultural perceptions and needs could propel someone into a disruptive condition (Gutierres et al. 1994). Consider the classic study by Zimbardo (1972) in which he demonstrated that the situational context can radically change a person's behavior. In his experiment he divided student volunteers into prisoners and guards. He considered the students to be typical highly educated, middle-class people. Within a few days of role-playing, some "guards" became hostile and sadistic toward the "prisoners." In fact, the change was so dramatic that after only a few days the experiment had to be cut short. Given the right set of circumstances interacting with personal issues, almost anyone could act in a violent or disruptive manner.

With this caveat in mind, the following is suggested as a typical profile of a potentially violent employee:

- a Caucasian male between the ages of 30 and 40
- with a history of drugs and/or alcohol usage
- who tends to be an externalizer (blaming others for his problems)
- with a history of military service
- who holds a fascination with and usually owns weapons
- who is usually described as argumentative
- who is a loner
- with a history of violent behavior
- whose job is the most important part of his world and, finally,
- with few, if any, outside interests

Some of these characteristics have also been described by Barling (1996) and Folger and Baron (1996) as important in determining potentially violent behaviors. These characteristics comprise the essential elements in the assessment of potential violent and disruptive behaviors. Let's look at these elements more closely in terms of warning signs employers should pay careful attention to.

Warning Signs

The most important element in preventing workplace disruptions is to have managers who are good observers. Managers have to know their employees in order to assess the potential for disruptive behavior. A good manager is one who takes time to know an employee and the employee's work habits as well as his or her general behavior. The only way to be aware of a change in behavior is to have a baseline against which to compare. This is time consuming but critical in preventing workplace disruptions. The manager who views his or her job as merely assigning work tasks and evaluating work performance is not an adequate manager. Only by really knowing the work habits as well as the personal aspects of an employee can someone be in a position to manage them. This does not mean that a manager has to know the intimate details of an employee's life or personal problems. However, the relationship should be such that an employee would let an immediate supervisor know if there is a particular problem that he or she is facing. In addition, managers have to be informed and educated regarding warning signs related to violent or disruptive behavior. Workplace disruptions do not occur in a vacuum and, in almost every situation, some warning sign is given. Below we will address some of the warning signs to look for. The more warning signs evidenced by an employee, the higher the risk of a workplace disruption.

Change in the Employee's Behavior

The most important warning sign is a change in the employee's behavior for no apparent reason. This change could be in any direction; a quiet employee, for example, starts acting loud, or a loud one becomes quiet. The important factor is a change in behavior for no explainable reason. In the case example presented earlier, if Joe's spouse recently had a baby, then his lateness and tiredness might be accounted for by his not getting enough sleep at night with a new baby in the house. A manager has to know the employee to adequately assess the behavioral change. Managers should not accept simple answers to their inquiry. In our example, if Joe says, "My alarm clock didn't go off," this should not be accepted as an adequate explanation because of the pattern of lateness that has been observed. Managers have to be willing to pursue more plausible explanations.

Change in Work Habits

A related warning sign is a change in the employee's work habits. An employee who always met deadlines and now is falling behind and is late with assignments should be viewed by a manager as a potential warning sign for possible disruptive behavior. Again, no simple explanation of the changed behavior should be accepted. In most situations of workplace disruptions, the employee makes some sort of threat prior to the incident. People have an unconscious wish to reveal what they are about to do. Their motivations could be many, including a wish to be stopped, a narcissistic need to inflate their self-esteem, or a need to reduce their guilt. Nevertheless, each and every threat has to be taken seriously. Dismissing a threat as "that's just Joe" is ignoring a predictive warning sign that can have serious results. In the above example, Joe's threatening complaints must be taken seriously.

Direct or Indirect Threats

A change in behavior and direct or indirect threats are the two most predictive indicators of potential disruptive behavior. Except for these two, no one single warning sign is a significant predictor of disruptive behavior. However, the other important warning signs should also be considered when making an assessment of potential workplace disruptive behavior. If an employee is evidencing several of these behaviors, then the potential for disruptive behavior has to be considered.

Presence of Emotional Upheaval

There are other, more personal, signs that should be considered in making a determination of the potential for workplace violence as follows:

Severe personal problems. These could include serious illness in the family, marital problems, financial problems, mental illness, and addictions, such as gambling. When someone is under personal stress, there is an increased potential for acting-out behavior. In the example of Joe, his manager would have to know him well enough to know if Joe was having any severe personal problems that might account for his changed behavior. It must be taken into consideration that individuals who belong to backgrounds different from the majority in the workplace will also encounter different kinds of stress. For instance, the plight of the minority and immigrants who feel disenfranchised and disconnected from their homeland and family members left behind must be considered. It is more likely that stress will occur in this case because a mismatch between the employee and the corporation is more likely. Stress normally occurs when an individual's attributes and the environment configuration are found to be incongruous (Gutierres et al. 1994).

History of complaints. Another important warning sign is a history of complaints against an employee. Indeed, the best predictor of future behavior is past behavior. For example, if one wanted to know how well a student would do in the spring semester at school, the best predictor would be how he or she did in the fall semester. The same is true in predicting disruptive behavior. If an employee has a history of complaints that includes harassment, verbal threats, difficult behavior, or the like, then that person is more likely to engage in workplace disruptions in the future. It is important for a manager to address all complaints against an employee in a thorough and timely manner. To ignore what might be considered trivial infractions could set the stage for more disruptive behavior in the future.

Romantic obsession. An often overlooked but important warning sign of disruptive behavior is a romantic obsession in the workplace. A distinction should be made between true feelings of friendship or love and an obsession. An obsession is usually one-sided: an individual thinks and ruminates about another person without the other person's reciprocating these feelings. The person who is obsessing can feel very possessive and jealous. This can lead to office confrontations. The situation is particularly troublesome if it is part of a triangle at work. Managers have to be sensitive to triangles developing and take necessary steps to prevent violent behavior. Related to this is the increase in domestic violence that has been shown to spill over to the workplace (Bulatao and VandenBos 1996). An abusing spouse will sometimes come into the workplace either to attack the abused spouse or because of paranoid or jealous suspicions that the abused spouse is involved with someone at work. Proper security measures need to be in place to handle these situations.

Psychotic behavior. Another cause for concern is an employee who may be exhibiting odd or psychotic behavior. Apparent breaks in reality thinking are not always dramatic and can in fact be subtle. Delusional thinking can account for someone acting in a destructive way. Any such behavior that comes to the attention of a manager needs to be handled immediately. However, contrary to media headlines, most workplace disruptions are not caused by someone who is psychotic. Some more blatant warning signs include a fascination with weapons as well as obvious drinking or drug problems. If the employee brags about weapons or brings them to work, the manager needs to see that as a potential problem. If a person has access to weapons, the likelihood increases that a weapon will be used in a workplace situation. Also, if an employee has a drinking or drug problem, its use can lower inhibitions and impair judgment with resulting disruptive behavior (Barling 1996). For many reasons, once a manager becomes aware of an employee's addictive behavior, a referral to an employee assistance program or other rehabilitation program is essential.

As with any organization, there exists some corporate paranoia. However, corporations need to be mindful of how the culture of the organization either increases or minimizes this paranoia. People vary in their personal level of paranoia. Individuals of cultural or ethnic minorities may also perceive certain situations or actions as harmful, while others may not. If the organization is very secretive, this may increase employees' level of paranoia. A manager who observes an employee verbalizing many paranoid comments needs to address the matter immediately. Corporations have to be mindful of the psychological needs of their employees (Kluckhohn 1968, 1986), as well as the different needs and expectations of cultural and ethnic minorities.

Related to corporate paranoia is the degree of stress that exists within an organization. Contemporary corporate life has changed. Long-term commitments from organizations to employees or from employees to corporations are no longer the norm. "Downsizing" or "rightsizing" have become euphemisms for being fired. Employees are considering themselves "individual corporations" whereby they can stay with a company for a few years and then take their skills and experience elsewhere. More and more companies are hiring consultants and outsourcing work rather than employing permanent full-time workers. All such actions reduce loyalty and, in a sense, inhibitions against acting-out behavior. In the past corporate life meant starting out in the mail room and working your way up to CEO, at least in commitment. Such corporate culture fostered security and loyalty. The employee who became angry would not express it at work for fear of losing his or her job. While loyalty still exists to some extent, it is not nearly as important and hence there is increased chance of disruptive behavior.

Many people look for their security and dependency needs to be met by the corporation they work for (Levinson, 1976). The Person–Environment Fit Model (Caplan 1983, Gutierres et al. 1994, Van Harrison 1985) demonstrates the need for a congruency between personal attributes and the environment, while stress develops where there is a lack of fit. For example, job-related tension often arises when one feels unqualified to handle a job, believes that one's needs are not met, doubts the likelihood of personal attainment of important outcomes, has too little authority to carry out responsibilities (little decision latitude), and/or has to do things that are against his or her personal judgment (Bhagat et al. 1994, Gutierres et al. 1994). When such needs are threatened, people sometimes act violently.

CULTURAL ISSUES IN ASSESSING WORKPLACE VIOLENCE

Aggression and violence often result from a misunderstanding or an incongruence in the way individuals are perceiving and reacting to a given event (Gutierres et al. 1994). Assessment of predictors associated with potential violence becomes a challenging task with the understanding that different cultural groups hold different perceptions that shape their emotional and behavioral displays. With the awareness that there is a need for understanding how individuals' cultural backgrounds shape perceptions, we would like to further delineate the factors that contribute to one's perception and that are likely to produce additional stress among employees coming from diverse cultural backgrounds.

Difference in World View

In a recent book, Dana (1993) described the complexity surrounding the psychological evaluation of individuals coming from diverse cultural backgrounds. It is his belief that the individual is heavily influenced by his or her world view that in turn determines his or her cognitive process and the way information around him or her is processed. The quality and nature of this world view are determined by the extent and nature of group membership, the self-concept derived from that membership, and the degree to which the individual adheres to the value/belief systems and language characteristics of his or her reference group. In the case of immigrant and minority workers, the more rigid the adherence to the beliefs and cultural and linguistic characteristics of the original reference group, the more likely tension is to occur. The possibility of experiencing acts of prejudice and discrimination often arising from differences in language, dress, musical interest, skin color, social class, religion, and country of origin could serve as a potential for stress in the workplace.

    The fact that one's cultural background affects one's world view was demonstrated by Kluckhohn (1960) who described the ways five major ethnic groups differ along five value dimensions. She emphasized that Anglo-American, African-American, Asian-American, Hispanic-American, and

Native American people differ in their views of human nature, the person–nature relationship, time, social relationships, and activity. Anglo Americans' view of human nature was described as "evil," whereas to the African American, the Hispanic, and the Native American it was described as "good/evil." For the Asian American it was described as "good." Regarding their view of relationships with others, there was again a clear difference, with the Anglo American and the African American being more individualistic. The Asian American and Hispanic are more lineal in their views of relationships while the Native Americans are more collateral. Their views of activity and work also varied from construing activities as "Doing" (e.g., Anglo American and African American), "Being" (e.g., Hispanic), "Being-in-Becoming" (e.g., Asian American), and "Being/Doing" (e.g., Native American). The Anglo American's and African American's time focus is oriented toward the future, while for the Hispanic and Native American it is toward the present. For the Asian American the focus is toward the past. In the case of each group's relationship to nature, the Anglo American is described as more concerned with mastery, while the African American and Native American are more concerned with harmony with nature. The Asian American and the Hispanic American are more concerned with their subjugation to nature.

Such difference in viewpoints can serve as a potential for misunderstanding in the workplace as different groups enter the workplace with different expectations. While these cultural minorities initially expect an extension of trust from their fellow workers, Anglo Americans are more likely to be suspicious and distrustful, eliciting feelings of inferiority, inadequacy, and further distrust in the minority individual. This view reflects the need or desire for control, which may also spill over into the workplace and strain interactions between peoples of different cultural backgrounds. Regarding the concept of time, when people tend to be motivated for the future, they may find it easier to cope with or ignore present occupational stress; however, for those whose present circumstances are the most important determinants of their mood and behaviors, they may find it more difficult to deal with work stress when their needs are not being met.

With regard to the different views of relationships, complication in the workplace could emerge when, for example, a Native American's preference to work in a group setting and rely on group opinions will contrast with the preference of the Anglo and African Americans to work alone in order to fulfill individual goals more efficiently. The preference of Asian Americans to consider the help or opinions of an older generation may also cause complications. These different views may cause disagreements among co-workers when organizational goals are the same for all the workers alike yet different peoples use different processes to achieve their goals.

Beliefs

Shared beliefs among cultural and ethnic groups include the nature of health and illness, responsibility and control, and spirituality and religion. In some groups of non-European origin, the cause of illness is directly related to influences of magic, dreams, spirits, forces of nature, the will of God, or the "evil eye." Concepts such as the "evil eye" can be brought into the workplace and promote suspicion and distrust toward others. Furthermore, concerning religion and issues of control, individuals of certain cultures hold a more deterministic view of life and may therefore undermine the amount of control they have over their present situations. A belief in such a lack of control can actually increase stress and frustration both in and out of the workplace.

Group Identity

Group identity is a cultural consciousness that includes the history and cultural heritage of the group (Dana 1993), most often existing in the form of a predominant or modal personality, more clearly described as the "traditional personality." Some individuals do not choose to identify with their traditional cultural group but rather with the dominant "out-group." Phinney (1991) points out that such discontent or dissatisfaction with one's ethnic identity is often viewed as a denial of one's identity, and thus viewed as an indicator of psychopathology. Therefore, even racial or cultural minorities who choose to acculturate as much as possible are faced with further issues of loyalty to the collective group. Individuals may be forced to adopt one set of behaviors for the workplace, such as individual decision making, and then to return to a home life based on a more collectivist orientation, hence stirring individualistic-collectivistic conflict. Such social identity processes were shown not only to aggravate work stress but were also associated with poor health outcomes (James 1994).

The most stressful adaptation in the workplace seems to occur when minority individuals find difficulty interacting with the majority group but also have a weak identification with their in-group (Phinney 1991). This lack of connection causes minorities even greater strain as they may be viewed as outcasts by an entire organizational group and in turn become distrustful and angry. Any misunderstanding or setback may then easily trigger workplace disruptions of verbal or physical aggression.

Self-Concept

The self-concept is regarded as one's personal or individual identity. The self-concepts of Anglo Americans have characteristically encompassed a sense of individualism, egocentrism, and personal control (Dana 1993). However, the self-concept of cultural groups of non-European origins is most often based on responsibility and obligation to family and/or one's people. These qualities are then made part of all decision-making and problem-solving situations. Often, cultural minorities, for reasons of responsibility and obligation, will withstand high levels of occupational stress and work longer hours so as to fulfill family honor and pride and to retain a job or position. If the motivation behind such behavior is not understood by the majority group or Anglo Americans, then there is a high possibility of the group's being mislabeled as passive, submissive, or weak. Such a misconstrued characterization may exaggerate differences among the groups and create an atmosphere of unfamiliarity and discomfort between the individuals.

Language

Language is one of the vehicles for structuring experience and imposing one's perceptions on reality (Dana 1993). Language also plays a significant role in labeling emotions and expressing the salient characteristics of a particular culture. Tension in the workplace may occur during the communicative interaction between two individuals of different cultures when one or both of these individuals do not speak the target language well. It is likely, however, that misunderstandings will occur even when language proficiency is not much of an issue. One's accent or dialect may make communication difficult to follow. In some situations, one's accent may become the subject of prejudice by a native speaker of English and thus contribute in those individuals to a feeling of rejection and social isolation. Such remarks may be perceived as an attempt at superiority in the native speakers and to inferiority in the other individuals.

Prejudice

According to the Social Identity Theory, a desire to maintain a positive identity is viewed as a major motivating force behind individuals' cognitions, emotions, and behaviors and can enhance the ability to cope with stress. A positive identity is more difficult to maintain when one is frequently surrounded by prejudice from groups that are culturally and/or racially different. The detrimental effect of a culturally hostile work environment has been well documented. For instance, perceptions of discrimination in the workplace were found to contribute to increased stress levels in minorities (Erlich and Larcom 1992, Frone et al. 1990, James et al. 1984). The presence of discrimination can include exclusion from informal networks, being placed in dead-end jobs, or having to work harder to get ahead (Gutierres et al. 1994).

It can also include open or subtle criticism regarding dress style, food, musical interests, religious practices, and personal styles of different ethnocultural groups. These ethnocultural characteristics can serve as triggers for prejudice and discrimination (Greenberg et al. 1986, Katz and Hass 1988). Remarks may be directed toward the lunch one brings to work, the music one listens to during break, or a more traditional attire one chooses to wear. Pictures of their country of origin and family members back home may be different or unfamiliar to those who have lived only in America; again, such unfamiliarity may trigger feelings of prejudice. An expression of such prejudice can also be found in the form of jokes made at the expense of the cultural groups, which have resulted in anger and even violent behavior in some situations (Marsella 1994). A hostile environment has been found to have a deleterious impact on an individual's emotional and physical well-being. It has been found to trigger feelings of inferiority, low self-concept, depression, anger, and fear, with its concomitant physical, psychological, and social implications (e.g., illness or disease; substance abuse; family, marital, or social-functioning problems; and even physical violence) (Bulatao and VandenBos 1996).

Cultural behaviors pertaining to physical space, greetings, and eye contact may also trigger prejudice or misunderstanding. For some cultural groups eye contact is vital to communication and acceptance of others, and those who do not view eye contact with as much importance may be mislabeled as inconsiderate or disrespectful. With regard to greetings and physical space, many cultural minorities greet each other with physical contact and feel comfortable in standing close to the person to whom they are speaking. Individuals of Anglo-American heritage, on the other hand, may view such behavior as a violation of their personal space. Such miscommunication can quite easily trigger misunderstanding and strain in the interaction between these individuals.

PREVENTION

What can corporations do to reduce workplace disruptions? Employee education is the most effective way to prevent or reduce the likelihood of workplace disruptions. While it is necessary for managers to be aware of warning signs, profiles, and an employee's behavior, fellow workers can also be good observers. Educating them regarding the warning signs can help them become more aware of potentially dangerous situations. Education can also help overcome the stumbling blocks to observations. Many employees will not report a fellow employee they are concerned about because when they hear a threat, for example, they may well feel Joe is just expressing what they all feel inside. Aggressive fantasies are part of everyone. However, verbalizing them to other employees or management is not. There is a distinction between feeling and thinking on the one hand and acting on the other. In fact, much clinical work is based on helping clients see the distinction between having all kinds of fantasies and feelings and actually engaging in those behaviors. Not being able to make that distinction is often an indication of a psychological disorder (Kernberg 1980).

Another inhibiting factor as to why problem behavior might go unreported is that no one wants to be responsible for someone else losing a job. Guilt can be a powerful inhibitor. Employees need to realize that reporting warning signs will be of benefit to everyone, including the person with the problem. Employees may also feel that threats or verbal abuse is part of the job. In certain occupations, particularly ones that involve manual labor, displaying a *machismo* attitude is seen as being part of the group. Acting "tough" is considered within the norm and is expected both in certain jobs and in certain cultures.

Another factor inhibiting employees from reporting one another is the externalization and rationalization of violence, that is, society is at fault for the fact that we live in a violent society (Bulatao and VandenBos 1996). The extent of violence seen in the workplace is considered only a reflection of what goes on in society in general. Here a certain complacency or resignation can set in, which then permits disruptive behavior to go unreported.

Employees need to know that management will take workplace safety seriously. Written policies confronting the problem of workplace disruptions are necessary to instill a sense of security. Employees have to know that, if a problem is reported, some action will take place. Also, having a written policy that the company adheres to will help protect it from possible legal claims of bias if some action is taken. A well-thought-out policy communicates the corporation's commitment to preventing workplace disruptions and providing a safe and secure work environment. Employee education is one ingredient of the written policy. Education should include the warning signs of a potential disruptive employee, the profile of a typical violent employee, and the procedures for reporting a problem. It should also include cultural awareness and sensitivity training regarding cultural differences in behavior in order to reduce misunderstandings with respect to certain behaviors.

It is also crucial that all employees be aware of the policy. Too often corporations have written policies but the only people aware of them are the human resource personnel. To have an effective policy a company should do a comprehensive assessment of what policies are already in place. Input from all employees would help them feel part of the process as well as provide information that may not be received any other way. It will also give employees the feeling that management is taking their concerns seriously. Managers need their own training as well. They have to be trained to be good observers. They have to be educated about warning signs and how to recognize them. Many times managers are unaware of what resources are available to help a troubled employee. The earlier an intervention is made once problem behaviors become known, the more likely a successful outcome will take place. Getting an employee help through the company's EAP, for instance, can make a difference in how that employee copes with whatever might be causing the problem behavior. Unfortunately, managers often manage by denial. What this means is that they consciously or unconsciously ignore a problem in the hope that it will either go away or get worked out in some fashion. Sometimes it does go away, but more likely it does not and then there are consequences for unrecognized problems.

In the example given at the beginning of the chapter, Joe was clearly evidencing a change in behavior. If his behavior was allowed to go on without any intervention, the chances for a disruptive outcome increase. However, if Joe's manager addressed his concerns about Joe, there could be an effective intervention that would then decrease the chances for a disruptive outcome. Prevention is the most effective tool for decreasing workplace disruptions. There are no foolproof measures to ensure that workplace disruptions will not happen, but education and training can make a difference.

In this example, the manager should specify exactly what behaviors were observed that are of concern. These behaviors should be recorded in case Joe has any questions about the validity. He should be given an opportunity to give his input. Together Joe and the manager have to develop a plan to address the problem behaviors. The plan can be imaginative and include almost any intervention that could make a difference, depending on what Joe gives as reasons for his behavioral change. If the problem is family or personal, a referral to the EAP or psychotherapy may be indicated. If the problem is financial, the company may have financial planners as part of the EAP. If the problem is work related, then the problem has to be addressed with either Joe and/or other employees if necessary. A manager has to be aware of what company benefits are available and be willing to be creative in seeking solutions to a problem.

Issue of Termination

Termination and its impact on an employee, as well as how it is handled by a corporation, makes it one of the most likely situations where a disruptive reaction could result. Termination therefore deserves particular attention regarding training and policy. Baron (1993) recommends the following procedures regarding termination:

- All employees should be treated with dignity and respect.
- All termination procedures should apply equally to all employees.
- Adverse actions by the corporation should be avoided whenever possible if the employee is under particular personal stress that includes family illness, pregnancy, or recent death of a family member as well as certain cultural issues regarding responsibility and obligation to family.
- More than one person should be present and the expectation should not be that the employee will act rationally.
- The reasons given for dismissal should be business related and handled in an honest and confidential manner.

Employees join a corporation with a "personal contract" that they have in mind about themselves and their relationship to the corporation. This is similar to the underlying contract people have when they get married. Often this contract is not spoken but is held onto as though both parties discussed it and agreed to it. An example of such a contract might be, "If I am a good worker, you [the corporation] will take care of me and treat me well." If an employee is fired because of "rightsizing," for instance, that employee may believe that the personal contract was broken and feel betrayed. The result could be a disruptive one. Termination is therefore a very sensitive and significant aspect of an employee's work life. It is an area that requires good training, cultural sensitivity, and a strong policy.

Workplace Disruptions

What happens when a workplace disruption occurs in a corporation? The corporation should have a policy that includes procedures for addressing what to do in the event of a disruption. A "trauma response team" needs to be in place that includes management, human resource personnel, a security person, medical doctor, lawyer, and psychologist or other mental health professional. These members might be on staff or hired as consultants depending on the size of the corporation. A spokesperson may be necessary, again depending on the size of the corporation as well as the nature of the workplace disruption. People vary in their ability to cope with stress. The corporation needs to assess the degree of trauma experienced. Trauma is measured not only by the scope of the event itself, but also by the individual's perceptions or beliefs and reactions about the event. What employees say to themselves about the event will determine the degree of trauma they experience (Ellis and Harper 1975). For example, in the case of an armed bank robbery, if one employee believed she was going to be killed and another believed the gun was a fake, the former employee was more likely to be traumatized by the event. Corporations need to respond in a direct and calm manner to the event. Someone from the response team needs to assess what happened and where it happened. All people involved should be questioned about the incident and a written record should be kept. An assessment of what services are needed—hospitalization, police called, families called—should be made. Again, the extent of the disruption will determine the level of response. More severe events—for example, those involving homicide or destruction of property—will require more extensive intervention. Less severe disruptions usually involve fewer members of a response team.

Again, depending on the severity of the disruption, a critical incident debriefing may need to be done. This consists of meeting with the affected employees to discuss the event. It is a time for the employees to express any fears or concerns they may have and for a mental health person to assess each person's individual reaction to the disruption. The critical incident debriefing facilitates a sense of community about what happened and conveys to the employees that management cares about how they are doing. It also allows for information to be disseminated about what services and benefits are available. A critical incident debriefing can be done on an individual basis if necessary, but is usually done in small groups depending on the size of the group affected by the disruption. Debriefers also need to be sensitive to different reactions people have about asking for help and expressing distress. Cultural differences are particularly relevant here. People vary in terms of the degree of prior trauma or stressors they have experienced, which influences how they respond to the current event. People of different backgrounds may also have some specific core beliefs or perceptions that can determine their response to trauma.

Employees must feel that the corporation is concerned about them and their welfare. Any disruption changes the dynamics and feel of the workplace.

The goal of intervention is not to return to pretrauma functioning, but rather to establish a new workplace culture. In some situations what had existed previously may not have been healthy for the organization in that the corporate culture may have contributed to the disruption. For example, there might not have been a policy in place or managers may never have been trained to be good observers.

Prevention is the best way for a corporation to address this escalating problem. Education and training can make a difference in reducing the likelihood of workplace disruptions. Training should include managers and employees and should be sensitive to cultural differences. In the event of a workplace disruption, the corporation needs to respond quickly and compassionately to address any general problems or issues specific to cultural or ethnic minorities and to offer the services necessary to restore a new sense of security and safety in the workplace.

REFERENCES

Barling, J. (1996). The prediction, experience, and consequences of workplace violence. In *Violence on the Job: Identifying Risks and Developing Solutions*, ed. G. R. VandenBos and E. Q. Bulatao, pp. 29–49. Washington, DC: American Psychological Association.

Baron, S. A. (1993). *Violence in the Workplace*. Ventura, CA: Pathfinder.

Bhagat, R. S., O'Driscoll, M. P., Babakus, E., et al. (1994). Organizational stress and coping in seven national contexts: a cross-cultural investigation. In *Job Stress in a Changing Workforce: Investigating Gender, Diversity, and Family Issues*, ed. G. P. Keita and J. J. Hurrell, Jr., pp. 93–105. Washington, DC: American Psychological Association.

Bulatao, E. Q., and VandenBos, G. R. (1996). Workplace violence: its scope and the issues. In *Violence on the Job: Identifying Risks and Developing Solutions*, ed. G. R. VandenBos and E. Q. Bulatao, pp. 1–23. Washington, DC: American Psychological Association.

Caplan, R. D. (1983). Person-environment fit: past, present, and future. In *Stress Research: Where Do We Go from Here?* ed. C. L. Cooper, pp. 35–77. New York: Wiley.

Dana, R. H. (1993). *Multicultural Assessment Perspectives for Professional Psychology*. Boston: Allyn & Bacon.

Ellis, A., and Harper, R. A. (1975). *A New Guide to Rational Living*. Englewood Cliffs, NJ: Prentice Hall.

Erlich, H. J., and Larcom, B. E. K. (1992). *The effect of prejudice and ethnoviolence on the workers' health*. Paper presented at the 2nd American Psychological Association and National Institute of Occupational Safety and Health Conference on Work Stress and Health, Washington, DC, November.

Folger, R., and Baron, R. A. (1996). Violence and hostility at work: a model of reactions to perceived injustice. In *Violence on the Job: Identifying Risks and Developing Solutions*, ed. G. R. VandenBos and E. Q. Bulatao, pp. 51–85. Washington, DC: American Psychological Association.

Frone, M. R., Russell, M., and Cooper, M. L. (1990). *Occupational stressors, psychological resources, and psychological distress: a comparison of black and white workers.* Paper presented at the annual meeting of the Academy of Management, San Francisco, August.

Greenberg, J., Pyszczynski, T., and Solomon, S. (1986). The causes and consequences of need for self-esteem: a terror management theory. In *Public Self and Private Self*, ed. R. F. Baumeister, pp. 189–212. New York: Springer-Verlag.

Gutierres, S. E., Saenz, D. S., and Green, B. L. (1994). Job stress and health outcomes among white and Hispanic employees: a test of the Person-Environment Fit model. In *Job Stress in a Changing Workforce: Investigating Gender, Diversity, and Family Issues*, ed. G. P. Keita and J. J. Hurrell, Jr., pp. 107–125. Washington, DC: American Psychological Association.

James, K. (1994). Social identity, work stress, and minority workers' health. In *Job Stress in a Changing Workforce: Investigating Gender, Diversity, and Family Issues*, ed. G. P. Keita and J. J. Hurrell, Jr., pp. 127–145. Washington, DC: American Psychological Association.

James, S. A., LaCroix, A. Z., Kleinbaum, D. G., and Strogatz, D. S. (1984). John Henryism and blood pressure differences among Black men: II. The role of occupational stressors. *Journal of Behavioral Medicine* 7:259–275.

Katz, I., and Hass, R. G. (1988). Racial ambivalence and American value conflict: correlational and priming studies of dual cognitive structure. *Journal of Personality and Social Psychology* 55:893–905.

Kernberg, O. F. (1980). *Internal World and External Reality*. New York: Jason Aronson.

Kluckhohn, F. R. (1960). A method for eliciting value orientation. *Anthropological Linguistics* 2(2):1–23.

——— (1968). *Executive*. Cambridge, MA: Harvard University Press.

——— (1976). *Psychological Man*. Cambridge, MA: Levinson Institute.

——— (1986). *Ready, Fire, Aim: Avoiding Management by Impulse*. Cambridge, MA: Levinson Institute.

Lichtenberg, P., van Beusekom, J., and Gibbons, D. (1997). *Encountering Bigotry: Befriending Projecting Persons in Everyday Life*. Northvale, NJ: Jason Aronson.

Marsella, A. J. (1994). Work and well-being in an ethnoculturally pluralistic society: conceptual and methodological issues. In *Job Stress in a Changing Workforce: Investigating Gender, Diversity, and Family Issues*, ed. G. P. Keita and J. J. Hurrell, Jr., pp. 147–160. Washington, DC: American Psychological Association.

National Institute of Occupational Safety and Health. (1993). *Preventing Homicide in the Workplace*. Washington, DC.

Northwestern National Life Employee Benefits Division. (1993). Fear and violence in the workplace: a survey documenting the experience of American workers. Minneapolis, MN.

Phinney, J. S. (1991). Ethnic identity and self-esteem: a review and integration. *Hispanic Journal of the Behavioral Sciences* 13:193–208.

Van Harrison, R. (1985). The person-environment fit model and the study of job stress. In *Human Stress and Cognition in Organization: An Integrated Perspective*, ed. T. A. Beehr and R. S. Bhagat, pp. 23–55. New York: Wiley.

Zimbardo, P. G. (1972). Pathology of imprisonment. *Society*, April.

31

Sexual Identity in Sociocultural Context: Clinical Implications of Multiple Marginalization

SUSAN (SHANEE) STEPAKOFF
AND LISA BOWLEG

The aim of this chapter is to enhance awareness about psychological issues that emerge among culturally diverse lesbians, gay men, and bisexuals as they engage in the process of claiming a sexual minority identity. In particular, we consider the variety of sociocultural variables that shape the manner in which these individuals negotiate important domains of experience. Although mental health professionals who treat sexual and ethnic minorities may have separately considered each dimension of identity, in this chapter we focus on the ways in which multiple identities interact and exert combined effects. We hope that the chapter will serve as an introduction to some key issues worthy of exploration in the therapeutic process and to the variety of culture-specific meanings that gay, lesbian, or bisexual identity may carry.

The chaper is designed to provide practitioners with a deeper understanding of sexual minority clients' day-to-day dilemmas and concerns. We begin by examining some of the political and sociocultural realities that affect the thoughts, feelings, and behavior of culturally diverse sexual minorities. We go on to consider some basic clinical issues that tend to arise in work with this population.

THE REALITIES OF DISCRIMINATION: STONEWALL VERSUS BRICK WALL

Psychology, in both theory and practice, has traditionally emphasized individual experience without considering the ways in which experiences are shaped—indeed, often determined—by contextual factors. For sexual minorities, however, political and sociocultural realities profoundly influence cognitions, emotions, and behavior. Without adequate appreciation of these realities, therapists will have only a very limited capacity to empathize with and interpret the day-to-day experiences of sexual minority clients.

In June 1969, a group of predominantly black and Latina drag queens in Greenwich Village, New York City, fought back against a police raid, sparking four nights of riots. These riots, known as the Stonewall Rebellion, marked the beginning of the modern gay rights liberation movement in the United States. Since then, sexual minorities have witnessed many social and legal victories such as more tolerant societal attitudes and limited antidiscrimination protections. In the same time period, however, sexual minorities have also experienced many social and legal defeats. For example, at present only eleven states[1] and the District of Columbia have laws prohibiting discrimination based on sexual orientation (Human Rights Campaign [HRC] 1997a). Sexual minorities seeking equal rights often encounter a "brick wall" of legally permitted and socially sanctioned discrimination.

Employment

Many sexual minorities choose to remain invisible because of concerns about employment discrimination. These fears are not unfounded. Openly gay Congressman Barney Frank (D-MA) has noted that "the single most important thing people can do is to come out, and one of the obstacles to coming out is the fear that you're gonna lose your job" (Frank 1997). To date, most states and the federal government do not prohibit employment discrimination

---

1. California, Connecticut, Hawaii, Maine, Massachusetts, Minnesota, New Hampshire, New Jersey, Rhode Island, Vermont, and Wisconsin.

against sexual minority employees (HRC 1997a, National Gay & Lesbian Taskforce [NGLTF] 1997). In June 1997, 180 members of Congress introduced the Employment Non-Discrimination Act of 1997 (ENDA) into the 105th Congress. If passed, the bill would prohibit employment discrimination based solely on sexual orientation and would provide remedies for discrimination such as those provided under Title VII of the Civil Rights Act of 1964. Employers with fewer than fifteen employees and religious institutions would be exempt from ENDA provisions, however (NGLTF 1997).

Individuals who already face job discrimination because of their race, ethnicity, or other devalued aspects of their identity may be less willing to risk additional hardships and mistreatment by revealing their sexual orientation. A Puerto Rican lesbian has explained her decision to prioritize job security over disclosure of her sexual identity:

> I try to remain invisible as far as being a lesbian. I am afraid that being "out" will jeopardize my employment—it is hard enough to be Puerto Rican and be employed or promoted. . . . It took me a long time to get where I am. . . . I have worked too hard to be accepted by the staff and I don't want to spoil that now by coming out. [Hidalgo 1995, p. 25]

In contrast to white sexual minorities who often naively trust the efficacy of antidiscrimination laws and policies, sexual minorities who also belong to racial and ethnic minority groups may have a more realistic view of the limited effectiveness of such measures and the persistence of discriminatory practices despite official prohibitions.

Housing, Public Accommodations, and Credit

In the District of Columbia and most of the eleven states that specifically prohibit employment discrimination on the basis of sexual orientation, antidiscrimination laws cover not only employment but also areas such as housing, public accommodations, and credit (HRC 1997a). States that lack these legal protections—that is, the vast majority of states—permit sexual minorities to be denied housing, access to public accommodations, health care, and credit with no legal recourse. For example, in states that provide no legal protections against housing discrimination or that have laws prohibiting sodomy, sexual minority tenants who reside in a building in which the rental agreement prohibits "illegal or immoral behavior" or "association with undesirable people" may risk eviction (Curry et al. 1994, pp. 2–8).

The federal Americans with Disabilities Act (ADA), signed into law in

1990, prohibits discrimination against people with HIV infection and AIDS. Thus sexual minorities with HIV infection and AIDS (as well as other mental and physical disabilities) have some protections against discrimination in employment, public accommodations, and transportation. This law, however, does not protect individuals from discrimination based on sexual orientation, and in states that offer no legal protections nondisabled sexual minorities remain quite vulnerable .

Many sexual minorities risk discrimination in public accommodations, housing, and access to credit. Intersections among sexual orientation, race, class, and gender influence the circumstances under which discrimination occurs. Poor and working-class gay, lesbian, bisexual, and transgendered people typically have limited options about where to live and often have a greater reliance on public accommodations than those who are middle or upper class. Although people with economic privilege are not entirely safe from discrimination based on sexual orientation, their class affords them wider options. Thus gay men, lesbians, bisexuals, and transgendered individuals who are also marginalized as a result of their race, ethnicity, gender, or socioeconomic status may view invisibility as a necessary protective strategy.

Sodomy Laws

In 1986, in the case of *Bowers v. Hardwick*, the U.S. Supreme Court upheld the constitutionality of Georgia's law against sodomy. More than a decade later, at least thirteen states have laws that prohibit private consensual sodomy (whether same-sex or heterosexual), and approximately seven have laws specifically prohibiting same-sex sodomy (Curry et al. 1994). Although modern-day officials may enforce sodomy laws with less rigor than in the past, the mere existence of these laws serves as a potent reminder that same-sex sexual behavior is illegal. Moreover, in actuality these laws are almost never enforced with regard to heterosexual couples, and seem to be aimed primarily or exclusively at same-sex practices. These laws have led Curry and associates (1994) to quip, "If [gay, lesbian, and bisexual people] feel like outlaws, it may very well be because [they] are" (p. viii).

Although the possibilities for practical enforcement are minimal, sodomy laws present major obstacles to visibility for gay and bisexual men. As with many of the other legal issues that affect sexual minorities, sodomy laws may have a particularly strong psychological impact on gay and bisexual men from racial and ethnic minority backgrounds. Regardless of their sexual identity and social class, most black men in the United States report countless experiences of being viewed with suspicion on the basis of their race and gender, particularly by whites. Many have been subjected to intrusions and humiliations such as being followed in stores, questioned by authorities for no legitimate reason, and unjustly arrested. Thus it is understandable that many gay and bisexual men of color may be unwilling to invite further harassment by making their sexual orientation known.

Violence and Hate Crimes

The ever-present threat of homophobic violence is a significant barrier to sexual minority visibility. The 1990 Hate Crime Statistics Act mandates that the Justice Department collect data on crimes that "manifest prejudice based on race, religion, sexual orientation, or ethnicity" (as cited in HRC 1997b). States may provide further protections against hate crimes. Twenty[2] states and the District of Columbia now have hate crime laws that specifically cover sexual orientation (HRC 1997c). Despite these protections, according to recent data collected by the Federal Bureau of Investigation, hate crimes against sexual minorities are on the rise (HRC 1997d). More specifically, whereas in 1991 hate crimes against lesbians, gay men, and bisexuals accounted for roughly 9 percent of all hate crimes reported, in 1995 this figure had risen to approximately 13 percent (HRC 1997d).

Fear of visibility may be especially acute for sexual minorities who emigrate from countries with state-sanctioned policies of violence. For example, in many Latin American countries people who engage in same-sex practices are subjected to extensive and severe violence; many sexual minorities in these countries live in mortal dread of being discovered (Trujillo 1997a). In Peru, lesbians and gay men have received the death penalty for their sexual identities or same-sex sexual behavior. Human rights organizations have reported that death squads in Mexico have murdered sexual minorities with government approval. In Brazil, between 1980 and 1985, unidentified groups of people murdered more than 1,500 people perceived to be gay or lesbian. Since 1987, more than 100 gay men in Ecuador have been murdered. Conscious or subliminal awareness of a history of violence against gay, lesbian, bisexual, and transgendered people in one's culture of origin is likely to affect individual decisions about disclosing a sexual minority identity.

---

2. Arizona, California, Connecticut, Delaware, Florida, Illinois, Iowa, Louisiana, Maine, Massachusetts, Minnesota, Nebraska, Nevada, New Hampshire, New Jersey, Oregon, Utah, Vermont, Washington, and Wisconsin.

FAMILY ISSUES IN THE ERA OF "FAMILY VALUES"

Same-Sex Couples

In 1993, the Supreme Court of Hawaii ruled that denying same sex couples the right to marry may violate the state's constitution (Curry et al. 1994). The case is now on appeal with a ruling expected in 1998. The issue of same-sex marriage and the prospect that a U.S. state might permit it has initiated a flurry of public debates among people on both sides of the gay rights issue. The case has also prompted policymakers to pass laws prohibiting the recognition of same-sex marriages in the event that the Hawaiian Supreme Court's ruling stands. Thus, on September 21, 1996, President Clinton signed the Defense of Marriage Act into law. As a result, same-sex couples continue to be prohibited from obtaining the psychological, social, and economic benefits of an intimate, committed partnership that is legally recognized and publicly affirmed.

In recognition of the growing number of nontraditional families, several municipalities, counties, organizations, companies, and universities have adopted domestic partnership benefits[3] for couples of the same sex, as well as those who are heterosexual and unmarried (Curry et al. 1994). Although a sign of progress, these benefits are not comparable to those provided for legally married heterosexual couples. The latter include the right to file joint income tax returns; recover damages based on injury to one's partner; receive survivor's benefits; enter hospitals, jails, and other places restricted to "immediate family"; live in neighborhoods zoned "family only"; obtain health insurance, dental insurance, bereavement leave, and other employment benefits; gain residency status to avoid deportation of a noncitizen spouse; collect unemployment benefits upon leaving a job to accompany a partner who has obtained a job in a different location; automatically make medical decisions if one's partner is injured or incapacitated; and automatically inherit one's partner's property if he or she dies without a will (Curry et al. 1994). Whereas few would question the right of a member of a heterosexual couple to spend time with a seriously ill or incapacitated partner who has been hospitalized, sexual minority couples who find themselves in this predicament must weigh the benefits and risks of visibility. Faced with the prospect of being refused the opportunity to visit a partner who has been hospitalized, members of sexual minority couples often prefer to conceal the nature of their relationship by

---

3. Domestic partnership benefits include health insurance, sick and bereavement leave, accident and life insurance, death benefits, parental leave, housing rights, tuition reduction, and use of recreation (Curry et al. 1994).

pretending to be biological relatives. For sexual minorities with physical and psychiatric disabilities, these realities affect decisions about disclosure.

Decisions about being visible in a same-sex dyad are inevitably shaped by the intersections among sexual orientation and other dimensions of difference. For example, although the existence of domestic violence in same-sex relationships is beginning to be acknowledged, racism within the lesbian community may deter lesbians of color who are in violent relationships from seeking help (Kanuha 1990). Lesbians of color may remain in battering situations longer than white lesbians do because they feel isolated in the predominantly white support networks for battered women and/or they feel obliged to protect the image of their racial or ethnic community.

Additional issues emerge for interracial same-sex dyads. There is evidence that many ethnic minority lesbians, gay men, and bisexuals have partners of another race. A recent survey of intimate relationships among African-American lesbians and gay men indicated that 30 percent of the women and 42 percent of the men reported that their current partners were of another race (Peplau et al. 1997). Often those partners were white. For those who can voluntarily conceal their sexual orientation, interracial same-sex relationships may be a clue to sexual minority identity. Whereas most people are likely to perceive same-race same-sex dyads as "just good friends," de facto racial segregation typically renders cross-race same-sex dyads suspect. Barbara Smith, an African-American lesbian, has described her experiences of being part of an interracial couple in public:

> I think it's easier for two Black women who are lovers to be together publicly than it is for a mixed couple. To me, that's a dead give-away because this is such a completely segregated society. Whenever I had a lover of a different race, I felt that it was like having a sign or a billboard over my head that said—"These are dykes. Right here." Because you don't usually see people of different races together in this country, it was almost by definition telling the world that we were lesbians. I think the same is true for interracial gay male couples. [Gomez and Smith 1991, p. 50]

Thus choices about how visible or vocal to be with regard to one's same-sex relationship are determined by a complex interplay among individual personality, dimensions of identity, and sociocultural context.

Parenting: Cultural Resonances and the Risks of Visibility

These are no precise statistics on the number of parents who are gay, lesbian, bisexual, or transgendered. Researchers estimate, however, that the number of gay, lesbian and bisexual families with children is steadily rising (Curry et al. 1994, Kantrowitz 1996). Lee Badgett (1997), an economist at the University of Maryland, has used several national probability samples to estimate the number of families in which at least one parent is a gay man or lesbian. Her analyses of data from the annual General Social Survey found no significant differences between the percentages of heterosexual women with children and lesbians with children. Gay men, on the other hand, were half as likely as heterosexual men to have children. Badgett has also used data from the Voters News Service survey and the Yankelovich Monitor (a large marketing survey) to examine parenting rates among sexual minorities (as cited in DeAngelis 1996). Results from the 1993 surveys replicate her findings from the General Social Survey. Specifically, lesbians reported living with the same proportion of children under the age of 18 as did heterosexual women. Gay men were half as likely as their heterosexual male counterparts to live with children under the age of 18. Although the number of families in which at least one parent is a sexual minority appears to be growing, numbers are not synonymous with societal acceptance (Kantrowitz 1996). Many Americans remain uncomfortable with the idea of sexual minority parents and rationalize this discomfort by means of religious doctrine or professions of concern for the welfare of the children (Kantrowitz 1996), despite the fact that research has consistently shown that children raised by lesbians or gay men are at least as psychologically well-adjusted as children raised in heterosexual families (Patterson as cited in American Psychological Association 1997a, Patterson 1995, Tasker and Golombok 1995).

No statistics exist on the percentage of sexual minorities who have been heterosexually married and divorced, but according to most estimates the number is "certainly large" (Curry et al. 1994). Attorneys who focus on legal issues for gay and lesbian couples have consistently found that when a (heterosexually) married person comes out as a sexual minority and seeks a divorce, child custody is by far the most difficult issue (Curry et al. 1994). The challenges involved in trying to gain custody of a child in most United States courtrooms are so daunting that "many gay parents have remained in unfulfilling heterosexual marriages, or lived secretive, guarded gay lifestyles after separation, out of fear of losing their children" (Curry et al. 1994, ch. 8, p. 11).

In 1996, Sharon Bottoms, a white lesbian from Virginia, lost custody of her 2-year old son Tyler Doustou to her mother, the child's biological grandmother. Sharon's mother had sued for custody of Tyler on the grounds that her daughter's lesbian relationship and cohabitation with her partner had harmed or would harm Tyler. In his opinion, Henrico County Circuit Court Judge Parsons ruled that "the mother's conduct is illegal and immoral and renders her unfit to parent" (as cited in Pratt 1997, p. 278).

Threatened or actual loss of custody of one's children as a result of coming out as gay, lesbian, or bisexual is profoundly traumatic for all sexual minority parents. For sexual minority parents (or prospective parents) who are marginalized in additional dimensions of identity, however, the threat of losing one's child may carry particular psychological resonances that are rooted in racial and ethnocultural histories of oppression. For example, African Americans may retain conscious and unconscious images of the horrors of slavery, when children were torn from their mothers and sold to distant slaveowners. Similarly, for sexual minorities of Native American ancestry, the threat of losing custody of a child may be experienced as highly salient in light of the historical practices of white Christian missionaries who endeavored to "civilize" American Indian and Alaskan people by kidnapping their children (sometimes at gunpoint) and placing these children in federal boarding schools that deprived the children of their culture, language and traditions. Several boarding schools for Native American children still exist (Tafoya 1997). Likewise, many Jewish parents faced traumatic separation from their children during the Holocaust as a result of having to place them in Christian homes or orphanages to increase the children's chances for survival. In ninteenth-century Russia, moreover, young Jewish boys were routinely removed from their mothers and forced into the Czarist army where all ties to family and cultural background were severed.

A group history of coercive removal of children from their families may contribute to a decision to remain silent and invisible with regard to one's sexual minority status. This dilemma may be experienced with particular acuteness by lesbians, gay men, and bisexuals from oppressed racial or ethnic communities. In psychotherapy with sexual minority clients it is important to be aware of these cultural resonances and to recognize the ways in which current emotions and cognitions may be shaped by historical memory.

Collective Memory and Child-Bearing Choices

Feelings about parenting are complex for any lesbian, gay man, or bisexual, in light of widespread societal disapproval of same-sex parents, lack of a socially sanctioned role for the coparent (i.e., the partner of the biological parent), and legal barriers to child custody and adoption. Nevertheless, decisions and feelings about parenthood are even more complex for sexual minorities who are members of marginalized racial or ethnic groups, particularly those that are demographically at risk as a result of attempted genocide (e.g., Native Americans, Jews). For members of such groups, the decision to bear (or not bear) and/or raise a child carries meanings and psychological implications that differ from those faced by members of nonmarginalized cultures.

Greene (1994a) has argued that for groups such as African Americans and Native Americans who have suffered histories of physical and cultural assaults, "reproductive sexuality is viewed as the means of continuing the group's presence in the world. . . . hence. . . , sexuality that is not reproductive may be viewed by group members as instruments of genocide" (p. 244). Specifically, the combined forces of racism, sexism and heterosexism often result in the scapegoating of lesbians of color as a source of "decline" of the traditional family and as a threat to racial and cultural continuity (Greene 1994b). Gay and bisexual men of color have been similarly attacked. Clarke (1983) has recounted her experience of attending the First National Plenary Conference on Self-Determination in 1981, a gathering proclaimed as a "historic meeting of the Black Liberation Movement" (p. 199), only to discover the following statement on a flyer left on every seat: "Homosexuality is a genocidal practice. . . . Homosexuality does not produce children. . . . Homosexuality does not birth new warriors for liberation. . . . The practice of homosexuality is an accelerating threat to our survival as a people and as a nation" (as cited in Clarke 1983, p. 199).

Likewise, Native American sexual minorities may harbor strong feelings about the importance of bearing children to replenish lost lives and ensure the survival of their nations. In addition to being subjected to the genocidal policies and practices of white settlers, Native American populations were decimated by exposure to European diseases for which they had no immunity. Tafoya (1997) has estimated that approximately 80 percent of the Native population in the Pacific Northwest died within two generations of having had contact with European settlers. Similar issues exist for Jews who faced threats to group survival as a result of the Nazi genocide. Traditionally, Jewish cultures have socialized women to feel personally responsible for the continuity of the Jewish people, and many Jewish people believe that having children is the surest way to ensure Jewish survival (Dworkin 1997).

Of course, being a sexual minority and perpetuating one's race or culture are hardly mutually exclusive. The biological ability to reproduce bears little relation to sexual behaviors or identity. This point is underscored by a study of 530 black lesbians in which fully a third were mothers (Mays and Cochran 1988). Ironically, statements denouncing black lesbians and bisexual women for failing to propagate the black race are reminiscent of the racist antiabortion appeals of whites in the 1800s who believed that allowing white middle-class women to have abortions would jeopardize the "future well-being of the [white] race" (Smith-Rosenberg 1985, p. 227).

Historically marginalized racial, ethnic, and cultural communities may exert strong social pressures for procreation. There are various reasons, other than biological, that sexual minorities may be unable to have children. These include legal prohibitions against adoption, lack of financial resources for alternative insemination, and social sanctions against sexual minority parenting. Gay, lesbian, and bisexual members of oppressed communities who wish to have children but cannot may experience deeper levels of mourning than do sexual minorities from more mainstream cultures. This deeper mourning may stem from the fact that in addition to individual or familial mourning (e.g., failure to carry on the family name), there is also a reawakening of mourning for the demographic and cultural losses suffered by one's racial/ethnic group.

Despite the challenges that inhere in bearing and rearing children as a sexual minority individual or couple, the notion that sexual minorities do not have children remains more myth than reality. Moreover, the myth that same-sex attraction precludes parenthood may lead multicultural sexual minority clients (and their families of origin) to feel unnecessary anxiety and distress. Lorde (1991) has offered a strong reminder not to equate sexual minority status with the relinquishment of the option of having children:

> I have heard it said—usually behind my back—that Black Lesbians are a threat to the Black family. But when 50 percent of children born to Black women are born out of wedlock, and 30 percent of all Black families are headed by women without husbands, we need to broaden and redefine what we mean by family. I have heard it said that Black Lesbians will mean the death of the race. Yet Black Lesbians bear children in exactly the same way that other women bear children, and a Lesbian household is simply another kind of family. Ask my son and daughter. [p. 95]

DIMENSIONS OF DIFFERENCE

Race, Ethnicity, and Culture

In a society that is intolerant of any form of same-sex sexual behavior or gender nonconformity, coming out as a gay, lesbian, or bisexual is a complex and challenging process regardless of race or ethnicity. This process is even more complex, however, for sexual minorities who are members of historically marginalized racial or ethnic groups. Unlike racial and ethnic minorities who are visible by virtue of their skin color or facial features, sexual minorities can sometimes choose to avoid the consequences of discrimination by staying in the closet (Swigonski 1995). People who are members of visible minority groups may have a stronger desire to remain in the closet because they can exert control over the terms of their self-revelation or self-concealment (Greene 1994a). Indeed, their sexual minority status may be one of the few features that they can choose to conceal. According to Smith (1997), the choice to conceal one's sexual minority status may be a psychologically adaptive strategy:

> For African American lesbians, discrimination based on sexual orientation adds yet another burden and level of jeopardy to these women's life experiences. . . . Having survived the battles of other forms of oppression over which she has no control or choice, a Black lesbian may proactively choose not to take on yet another hardship by coming out. . . . Exercising control over the disclosure of a stigmatized aspect of her identity that she can control may be adaptive. [p. 288]

Decisions about whether to disclose one's sexual minority status to others also carry particular meanings and nuances for sexual minorities who are Jewish. Gay men, lesbians, and bisexuals who have encountered social exclusion and condemnation with regard to their Jewish identity may be reluctant to risk further societal rejection by being open about their sexual orientation. Throughout history, being identified as a Jew has constituted life-threatening danger. As a result, Jews often harbor unconscious associations between visibility and peril. Beck (1982), a Jewish lesbian, has explored the ways in which her identity as a Jewish Holocaust survivor has shaped her feelings about coming out as a lesbian: "In Vienna in 1938, when I was five years old and Hitler came to power, visibility was not safe. Schools were closed to me, as were parks, stores, restaurants. Once I was sent to buy butter because I was blonde and did not look Jewish" (p. xvi).

Chan (1997) has argued that cultural background plays a decisive role in the process of gay or lesbian identity development, and even in whether such an identity can be imagined or "owned." Chan maintains that Western models of sexual identity development are not necessarily applicable to individuals from non-Western cultural backgrounds. For example, East Asian cultures may not have concepts of sexual identity comparable to the concepts found in the West. She notes that "there are considerable cultural differences in the extent to which sexuality is available for discussion and display, and cultures vary in the degree of prohibitions against public expressions of sexuality" (p. 241). In a recent study of Asian-American lesbians and gay men (Chan 1989), respondents revealed that they were more likely to come out to non-Asians than to other Asians. Chan argued that this finding reflected the value placed on privacy in Asian cultures. Chan (1997) has discussed this issue at length:

> A crucial distinction between traditional East Asian culture and Western culture is the concept of sexuality and sexual expression as a private matter. Any direct and open discussion of sexuality is unusual in Asian cultures, as sexuality is considered to be a very sensitive subject. Even among one's closest friends, a discussion about sexuality is considered to be awkward and highly embarrassing at best, and at worst, strictly taboo. . . . In . . . cultures such as Chinese, Japanese, and Thai, sexuality would rarely be expressed in the context of the public self; it is usually expressed only within the private self. Especially for women, the private self is never seen by anyone other than an individual's most intimate family and friends. [p. 244]

For ethnic minority lesbians, gay men, and bisexuals, the history of acceptance or rejection of sexual minorities within one's own racial or ethnic group is likely to influence individual attitudes toward coming out. Individuals may retain conscious or unconscious memories of how sexual minorities in their particular ethnic group have traditionally been treated. Such memory traces may exert powerful effects on day-to-day decisions and behavior. For example, according to Tafoya (1997), a Native American gay man:

> The majority of Native American tribes classified members as having more than two genders. The 16th-century Spanish explorer Balboa declared individuals who were not considered male or female to be "sodomites," and literally had them torn apart by his dogs. Thus from the very beginning of European contact, Native people learned not to discuss openly matters of sexuality and gender with the European newcomers, because they could be killed for being "different." [p. 3]

Additional issues emerge with regard to sexual minorities who are immigrants or refugees. Often such individuals were raised with a parental emphasis on "blending in" and not calling attention to one's difference from the mainstream. Compared to white, middle-class, American-born sexual minorities, lesbians, gay men, and bisexuals who are also immigrants, refugees, or members of other marginalized groups may feel that their social status is more precarious or vulnerable. Leung (1991), a lesbian of Chinese ancestry who emigrated from Trinidad to Canada at age 6, states:

> As Chinese immigrant parents, my mother and father wanted desperately to protect me with . . . middle class stability. . . . I was not, under any circumstances, to make waves; to make a spectacle of myself; to do anything

that would anger the gracious white hosts who had allowed us into their country. In other words, the only protection I had against deportation and racism was the cloak of middle class invisibility. [p. 108]

Heterosexuality as Privilege

Individuals who are oppressed as a result of their race, ethnicity, or culture may wish to cling to the one vestige of privilege available to them: the appearance of heterosexuality. Greene (1994b) has observed that African-American women, who are viewed as "low status" on the dimensions of race and gender, may feel that appearing heterosexual is the one identity dimension in which they can be treated with respect. This desire to hold on to heterosexual privilege also affects the attitudes of heterosexual African-American women toward African-American lesbians. More specifically, there may be a kind of displaced aggression or "horizontal oppression." Fanon (1968) has argued that members of oppressed groups often deflect their rage from its appropriate target (the oppressor) onto members of one's own group or highly similar groups, thereby engaging in "auto-colonial" behaviors that entail the betrayal of one's own people (Bulhan 1985). Fanon's ideas may help to explain why African-American lesbians are especially derided by African-American heterosexual women. Lorde (1984) has remarked:

> Black women . . . now insist that Black lesbians are a threat to Black nationhood, are consorting with the enemy, are basically un-Black. These accusations, coming from the very women to whom we look for deep and real understanding, have served to keep many Black lesbians in hiding, caught between the racism of white women and the homophobia of their sisters. [p. 274]

Gender-Specific Aspects of Sexual Identity

The official stance of the American Psychological Association (1997b) is that sexual orientation is involuntary. Some psychologists have criticized this stance, however, for privileging gay men's experiences and obscuring those of lesbian and bisexual women (Golden 1994). In particular, psychologists who study sexual orientation have tended to disregard the factor of choice because they "fail to consider the feminist movement when theorizing about the nature and origins of sexuality" (Golden 1994, p. 58). Golden has noted that the feminist movement of the 1970s and 1980s "had a powerful influence on how many women conceptualize and make choices about their sexuality"

(p. 62). Indeed, in the 1970s, many feminist organizations "defined [lesbian-ism] as a political choice and as the ultimate form of solidarity between women" (Golden 1994, p. 57).

In 1978, Ponse identified two groups of lesbians: "primary" and "elec-tive." The former group consisted of women who felt that they were born les-bians and had always been attracted to women; the latter group comprised women who felt they had chosen their lesbian identity after first identifying as heterosexual or bisexual. According to Golden (1994), "the elective lesbians described themselves as having made a conscious decision to consider les-bianism. . . , [which was] prompted by their developing feminist conscious-ness" (p. 59). It is virtually unheard of for a man to self-identify as gay as part of a program to attain political liberation from women, because in a patriar-chal society—that is, a society in which institutional power is held by men—men do not require political liberation from women. By contrast, for some women—particularly white, middle-class women—the experience of coming out as a lesbian is grounded in a commitment to the political ideology of les-bian feminism, an ideology expressed in the statement "feminism is the the-ory, lesbianism is the practice" (Ti-Grace Atkinson, as cited in Abbot and Love 1972, p. 117). Based on numerous interviews with lesbian-identified women, Golden has concluded that many women experience the process of self-identifying and living as a lesbian to be an active, fundamentally political choice rather than a biological mandate. Whereas for men the awareness of same-sex attraction is typically accompanied by feelings of fear and self-loathing, for many women (specifically, those who fit the definition of elective lesbians) there is often an exhilarating, celebratory quality to the discovery of same-sex attraction. This is because passionate relationships with their own sex are viewed as a path to self-liberation and women's liberation. For exam-ple, a 1990 international conference on women's issues featured a workshop entitled "Two Women Together: Intensive Relationships between Women and How They Can Develop," in which the stated aim was to encourage the participants to actively consider the possibility of choosing other women as sexual and life partners (Golden 1994).

Thus, in considering the experience of coming out as a sexual minority and the feelings that accompany this process, it is important to consider the ways in which the experience is gender-specific. Models and assumptions that apply to the gay male experience are not necessarily applicable to the experi-ences of lesbians and bisexual women. Women, who are marginalized in patri-archal society by virtue of their gender, may experience the renunciation of sexual relationships with men and development of erotic partnerships with women as a form of self-emancipation. Moreover, some women may view same-sex relationships as the only form of partnership that provides the possibility for equality and empowerment.

Issues of choice may be particularly relevant to women with physical disabilities. As a result of society's reluctance to consider sexuality in general and heterosexuality in particular as options for women with disabilities, women with disabilities may be more willing to embrace a lesbian or bisexual identity. Kate, a lesbian with a physical disability, has articulated the liberatory aspects of claiming a sexual minority identity:

> I have a strong sense of my accident having liberated me when it comes to relationships. I was 19 when I had my accident and I'd grown up with an unthinking expectation of getting married and having numerous children. My immediate reaction in hospital, and for months and years afterwards, was of feeling neutered and completely rejected as a sexual being by men. But I also remember the glimmers of feeling real freedom from Society's expectations of me. Society had rejected me, but that also meant it didn't have any power over me, either. I didn't have to achieve the role of wife and mother any more. . . . Eventually I was able to have my first relationship with a woman without any of the traumas that many of my gay women friends have gone through. I haven't had to face family reactions of "Why haven't you gotten married?" or Society's reaction of "Why haven't you got a man?" because I'm not expected to have one! [Cited in Appleby 1993, p. 267]

Cultural Specificity in Gender Role Expectations

Culture-specific gender expectations, stereotypes, and myths have important psychological implications for sexual minority individuals. Different cultures have differing degrees to which identifying as gay, lesbian, or bisexual represents a violation of accepted gender roles. According to Greene (1994b), understanding the meaning of being an ethnic-minority gay man or lesbian in a given culture requires a careful exploration of the "nature and . . . relative fluidity or rigidity of the culture's traditional gender stereotypes" (p. 392). For example, Greene has asserted that in Latin-American culture, "women are expected to be overtly submissive, virtuous, respectful of elders, willing to defer to men and . . . to reside with their parents until they are married, [while] men are expected to provide for, protect, and defend the family" (p. 394). Espin (1987) has noted that in labeling themselves lesbian, Latina women "force a culture that denies the sexuality of women to confront it" (as cited in Greene 1994b, p. 411). Similarly, Anzaldua (1987) has argued that by rejecting the traditional roles ascribed to women in patriarchal Mexican culture (wife, mother, virgin, or whore), Chicana lesbians violate moral prohibitions not only against homosexuality but also against women's sexuality in general.

Gender roles are inevitably shaped by experiences of racial and ethnocultural oppression. Silvera (1991), a Jamaican lesbian who immigrated to Canada, has analyzed the ways in which the history of slavery and colonialism in her native country contributed to a contemporary emphasis on heterosexuality:

> Under slavery, production and reproduction were inextricably linked. Reproduction served not only to increase the labour force of slave owners but also . . . facilitated . . . a focus . . . on those aspects of life in which they could express their own desires. Sex was an area in which to articulate one's humanity, but, because it was tied to attempts to "define oneself as human," gender roles, as well as the act of sex, became badges of status. To be male was to be the stud, the procreator; to be female was to be fecund, and one's femininity was measured by the ability to attract and hold a man, and to bear children. [p. 23]

The gender myths associated with a given culture are likely to affect one's feelings about claiming a marginalized sexual orientation and the response one receives from other members of one's cultural group. For example, Asian women are often stereotyped as being meek, exotic, and subservient (Leung 1991). Asian-American families tend to be characterized by expectations of unquestioning obedience to one's parents and a sharp delineation of gender roles. Chan (1989) has argued that in Asian cultures being gay or lesbian is viewed as a rejection of the most important roles for women and men: that of being a wife and mother for women, and that of being a father and dutiful son for men. In addition, for gay men and lesbians from Asian backgrounds, the development of a sexual identity may be complicated by the fact that sex is considered a "taboo topic, to be avoided, and shameful if discussed openly" (p. 18). Lee (1991) has commented: "My father expected me to grow up to be a 'nice Chinese girl.' This meant that I should be a ladylike, submissive, obedient, morally impeccable puppet who would spend the rest of her life deferring to and selflessly appeasing her husband" (p. 116).

These views contrast sharply with the gender myths of some other groups. For example, Jewish women are often stereotyped as being loud, aggressive, dominating, and pushy (Kaye/Kantrowitz 1982). Gender expectations in (and about) one's culture of origin are likely to affect feelings, attitudes, and behavior with regard to claiming a sexual minority identity.

Cultural norms also influence the degree of rigidity and polarization in sex-role socialization. For example, many Native American cultures have traditionally enjoyed greater freedom and flexibility with regard to gender roles than most white American cultures. Tafoya (1997) has noted that of the approximately 250 Native American languages still spoken in the United States, at least 168 have terms for people who are viewed as neither male nor female. Similarly, Greene (1994a) has described the relative fluidity of gender roles that characterizes African-American culture and the historical origins of this fluidity:

> Gender roles in African-American families have been somewhat more flexible than their White and many of their ethnic-minority counterparts. This flexibility is . . . in part . . . a derivative of the value of interdependence and somewhat more egalitarian nature of some precolonial African cultures. It is also a function of the need to adapt to racism in the United States, which made it difficult for African-American men to find work and fit the ideal of the Western male provider. Hence, rigid gender role stratification was somewhat impractical. [p. 245]

Other cultures may exhibit far less flexibility in gender roles. For example, Trujillo (1997b) has argued that in Chicana culture "lesbians are perceived as a greater threat to the Chicano community because their existence disrupts the established order of male dominance, and raises the consciousness of many Chicanas regarding their own independence and control" (p. 255). Latino men who have sex with men may also be perceived as a threat to the established order, particularly if they claim a sexual minority identity by openly self-identifying as "gay" or "bisexual."

Socioeconomic Class

People in the United States are generally reluctant to recognize class differences (Langston 1988). Nevertheless, socioeconomic class is fundamental to the experience of negotiating the world as a sexual minority individual. Opponents of civil rights for sexual minorities typically note that most gay men and lesbians are economically secure; thus, giving them any other rights amounts to special rights (Badgett 1997). This view, however, obscures important gender, racial, and ethnic distinctions. For example, gender has been found to be more salient for personal income and personal and household earnings than is sexual minority status. Badgett's analysis of the annual General Social Survey data found no significant differences between the earnings of lesbians and heterosexual women. She found that on average

lesbians had an annual income of $15,000 compared to $18,000 for heterosexual women. Gay men had annual incomes of $26,000; heterosexual men
had average incomes of $28,000 (DeAngelis 1996). As for household
income, Badgett's review of 1990 Census Data found that two-women
households had incomes of approximately $45,200 per year; heterosexual
households, approximately $47,000 per year; and two-male households,
approximately $58,400 per year. Moreover, in the United States, socioeco-
nomic status intersects with race and ethnicity. Thus ethnic minority lesbians, gay men, and bisexuals are likely to have fewer economic resources
than their White counterparts.

Class is also about having choices. For lesbians, gay men, and bisexuals,
social class background will influence a host of factors related to daily living.
As we have discussed previously, class will determine whether a person can
"afford" to be visible and risk discrimination in employment, housing, public
accommodations, and credit. Class will influence whether one has access to
resources such as support groups or the time to attend gay-sponsored social
and recreational events that provide opportunities for sexual minorities to
meet friends and potential partners, and gain information and support. Class
is a key determinant of the option to seek alternative insemination and/or to
intentionally raise a child alone as a gay, lesbian, or bisexual parent. If one is
HIV infected or has AIDS, race and class often determine one's access to
costly drug therapies that can dictate whether one lives or dies.

Sexual Minorities with Disabilities

Lesbians, gay men, and bisexuals who have disabilities encounter numerous
barriers to visibility as sexual beings in general, and visibility as sexual minorities in particular. Marginalization in the larger society as a result of having a
physical disability is likely to influence feelings about claiming a sexual minority identity. Chan (1990), an Asian-American heterosexual woman with a
physical disability, has noted that many East Asian cultures have "strong folk
beliefs that a person's physical state in this life is a reflection of how morally
or sinfully he or she lived in previous lives . . . and that the fate of one [fam-
ily] member can be caused by the behavior of another" (pp. 162–163).

Cultures that hold such moralistic beliefs may be doubly reluctant to
accept a member of their community who has a disability and is also gay, lesbian, or bisexual. Chan (1990) has written about how her family often felt
that her legs should be covered to hide her disability. Thus issues of conceal-
ment and disclosure carry multiple resonances for sexual minorities who are

physically disabled. Experiences with regard to others' perceptions of one's body and one's physical disability are likely to influence emotions and attitudes about disclosing a minority sexual orientation.

Moreover, lesbians, gay men, and bisexuals who are able-bodied have greater access to resources and support than do sexual minorities with disabilities (Appleby 1993, Hearn 1989). For example, a vision-impaired individual may not have the same opportunities to become familiar with gay-affirmative literature and movies that an able-bodied person would have. In recent years, however, many organizations for sexual minorities have begun to provide information and outreach for people with disabilities. Nevertheless, Appleby (1993) has maintained that these efforts are insufficent:

> Access to information does not guarantee entry into the lesbian community. I contacted six lesbian lines [in the United Kingdom] to find out what was wheelchair accessible in their area. . . . Of the six lines that were contacted only one was able to offer a partially accessible venue. All the women I spoke to . . . explained that it was very difficult to find somewhere that accepted lesbian bookings at affordable prices and those that did were often in basement or in upstairs rooms and not accessible. [p. 268]

Similarly, sexual minorities who are hearing impaired may lack access to important resources for information, education, and social support. Hoffmann (1993), a deaf gay man, has remarked: "Deaf people's knowledge of the world is limited compared to hearing people's, who can pick up what's new by listening to the radio, so deaf people's understanding of gay people is limited" (p. 88). Bernstein (1993) has noted: "When you're deaf, being left out of even the most mundane experiences can make you feel cut off and out of touch" (p. 186). Moreover, people who use American Sign Language (ASL) are often more conspicuous than their hearing counterparts. Consequently, gay men, lesbians, and bisexuals who use ASL may be reluctant to risk further exclusion and visibility by claiming a sexual minority identity.

Historically, the gay, lesbian, and bisexual community has been reluctant to meet the needs of hearing-impaired sexual minorities (Hoffman 1993). "In the past," Hoffman has written, "the hearing gay community didn't have much interest in sign language, nor a lot of patience for writing back and forth with a gay person" (p. 87). As sexual minority communities have gained greater sensitivity to the needs of hearing impaired individuals, however, efforts to provide sign-language interpreters and other services have increased.

FAMILY AND COMMUNITY:
TIES THAT BIND, LINES THAT DIVIDE

Individuals who are members of marginalized racial, ethnic, and cultural groups typically evince a stronger reliance on familial and community ties than do individuals whose identity is not devalued or rejected in the mainstream society. Thus the costs associated with coming out as gay, lesbian, or bisexual may be greater for persons who are marginalized in other aspects of their identity. When society at large is experienced as hostile, dangerous, and rejecting, it is psychologically important to have people to whom one can turn for solace and a place where one's culture is accepted and valued. Moreover, the family may be the only setting in which one's ethnicity is recognized and affirmed. As a result, in comparison to their white counterparts, ethnic minority lesbians, gay men, and bisexuals may be less willing to risk the disruption in familial and community ties that often accompanies the process of coming out. Aguilar-San Juan (1991), a Filipina American lesbian, has described the importance of family in the lives of many Asian Americans: "For those of us who are Asian, losing connections to our family represents one of our greatest fears, since in this White society, our cultural identity depends precisely on family links. Some of us are forced to conclude that coming out is simply not worth that price" (p. 191).

Similarly, the aphorism "Separate not from the community" is a strong message instilled in Jews early in life (Dworkin 1997). According to him, Jewish lesbians often feel they must conceal or relinquish part of their identity, depending on the situation: "Either they pass as single heterosexual women subject to community pressures to get married, remaining invisible as lesbians, or they come out as lesbians and are tolerated but not fully accepted as Jews . . . and . . . alienate themselves from necessary familial/religious supports" (p. 72).

The literature on gay men, lesbians, and bisexuals of color is replete with expressions of these pressures and dilemmas. Moreover, in cultures where familial identity and affiliation are prominent, bisexual men and women may face strong family pressure to marry (Rust 1996). Rust has cautioned counselors to be aware that married men from certain cultures may identify as heterosexual even though they engage in extramarital same-sex relations. Their identification as heterosexuals does not represent a repudiation of bisexuality but rather the fact that "their primary identity is derived from family [and cultural] roles, not sexual behavior" (p. 59).

There are considerable cultural variations with regard to attitudes toward same-sex attraction. Jack Chan, a Chinese immigrant father of a gay man, commented on the ways in which his response to his son's coming out as gay were influenced by cultural proscriptions: "Shame, that's a big factor. Shame brought upon the family. You have to remember [that for] the Chinese, the name, the face of the family is everything" (as cited in Hom 1996, p. 45).

In light of the tensions and even ruptures in one's family and community of origin that may accompany coming out as a sexual minority, social support networks for sexual minorities from ethnic minority backgrounds serve important psychological and practical functions. Lahkana (1994) has expressed her joy at finding another Cambodian lesbian:

> Before I met her I was the only Cambodian I knew of who is lesbian. I looked for a sense of family and community to the gender Asian and Pacific Islander lesbian and bisexual community but felt invisible. I longed to meet someone with a similar historic and cultural background. Someone who felt and still feels the pain from the atrocities and crimes that were and are still being committed against and in Cambodia, my homeland. Someone who would understand the confusion, fragmentation, and fear of being bicultural. Someone with whom I can share an unspoken commu-nality. [p. 156]

Arnesen, an African-American bisexual Vietnam veteran, has described similar feelings of elation at attending a conference for bisexual men and women: "I left the conference on cloud nine. Very rarely have I ever felt so comfortable with such a diverse group of people. My bisexual brothers and sisters filled me with a feeling of empowerment and affirmation by their acceptance, love and visibility" (1991, p. 239).

Social networks in which participants share important identity charac-teristics may offer particular promise for psychologically bolstering multicul-tural sexual minorities who face oppression on multiple fronts.

RELIGION AND SPIRITUALITY

In addition to family and community, religion and spirituality tend to strongly influence the lives of many racial and ethnic minority individuals in the United States. Thus decisions about visibility and silence on the part of cul-turally diverse sexual minorities may be shaped by religious affiliation. For example, cultures in which the Catholic church is a prominent force may hold more intolerant attitudes toward homosexuality and bisexuality than do cultures with more liberal religious doctrines. Trujillo (1997b) has explored these issues in her work on Latina lesbians:

> Chicana lesbians who confront their homosexuality must, in turn, confront (for those raised in religious households) religion, bringing to resolution some compromise of religious doctrine and personal lifestyle. Many choose to alter, modify, or abandon religion, since it is difficult to advocate something which condemns our existence. This exacerbates a sense of alienation for Chicana lesbians who feel they cannot wholly participate in a traditional religion. [p. 258]

Religious institutions often play a core role in the lives of multicultural sexual minorities. In addition to fulfilling spiritual needs, the church also provides its members with access to a large network of social support (Icard 1986). Historically, the African-American church's homophobia has denied black lesbian, gay, bisexual, and transgendered people access to this support. Elias Farajaje-Jones, a black bisexual associate professor in Howard University's Divinity School, has asserted that much of the black community's homophobia and biphobia can be traced to the black church (as cited in Mundy 1993). Although churches of all races and ethnic groups selectively interpret biblical passages to bolster their opposition to homosexuality, Farajaje-Jones has argued that homophobia in the black church is particularly pronounced in that ministers openly preach against homosexuality. Farajaje-Jones notes: "In the African-American tradition, [ministers] don't mince their words—at all" (cited in Mundy 1993, p. 33). West has echoed this theme: ". . . there were sermons preached against homosexuality, and the gay church organist or the lesbian singer could not live an 'out' life. It was an understood contract: if you kept it to yourself and sat there quietly listening to the preacher haranguing homosexuality, you were allowed to participate fully in community life" (hooks and West 1991, p. 84).

In response to the homophobia that characterizes many religious organizations, sexual minorities of all races and ethnicities have turned to nontraditional religious groups and organizations to fulfill their religious and spiritual needs. Increasingly, a number of racial and ethnic sexual minorities have begun to seek out religious institutions that recognize and affirm their sexual as well as their racial and ethnic identities. Tinney (1986) has documented the existence of black gay churches in urban areas such as Chicago, New York City, and Washington, DC. Similarly, several major cities now have special synagogues for gay and lesbian Jews, and a growing number of mainstream synagogues affiliated with the Reform and Reconstructionist branches of Judaism have openly gay or lesbian rabbis.

MEDIA IMAGES OF MULTICULTURAL SEXUAL MINORITIES

For sexual minority individuals, decisions about visibility and silence may be strongly affected by the presence of positive role models in the mass media. Although there is a general lack of accurate media representations of same-sex relationships, this absence is particularly extreme with regard to gay men and lesbians of color. Moreover, apart from stereotypic portrayals in which they are blamed for the AIDS epidemic, bisexuals "have been rendered virtually invisible and unnewsworthy in the women's, straight, and gay media" (Hutchins and Kaahumanu 1991, p. 217).

Media portrayals of lesbians and gay men have increased in recent years. Nevertheless, with the exception of two African-American television actors who portray gay male characters (Michael Boatman plays a Director of Minority Affairs on the ABC comedy *Spin City*, and Vondie Curtis-Hall plays a doctor on the CBS drama *Chicago Hope*), there is a dearth of television images of multicultural sexual minorities (Gay and Lesbian Alliance Against Defamation [GLAAD] 1997). In comparison to their gay, lesbian, and bisexual counterparts, transgendered people have become popular television icons in recent years (Bornstein 1997, MacKenzie 1994). Talk shows have been major purveyors of information and, often, misconceptions about transgendered people (MacKenzie 1994).

Like television and movies, books written by and about sexual minorities are a further factor that may influence decisions about visibility. According to Holly Fogleboch (personal communication, 1997), a bookseller at a lesbian, gay, and bisexual bookstore in Washington, DC (Lambda Rising), anthologies written by multicultural sexual minorities have flourished over the past decade. To date, multicultural anthologies by bisexual and lesbian women have outpaced those written by men. Fogleboch believes that the gender difference in multicultural anthologies can be explained by two factors. First, women have been socialized to feel more comfortable about expressing and sharing their experiences and emotions. Second, women have access to and may be more likely to submit their manuscripts to small feminist and women's publishing presses. These presses are often more amenable to publishing lesbian, gay, bisexual, and transgendered themes than are more mainstream presses (personal communication, Holly Fogleboch, December 17, 1997). The gender discrepancy in publications about sexual minority identity is consistent with issues of gender specificity in the coming-out process alluded to in an earlier section of this chapter. After multicultural women, black men have been at the forefront in the publishing of gay anthologies, a trend that began with the publication of *In the Life: A Black Gay Anthology* (Beam 1986).

For many lesbians, gay men, and bisexuals, the experience of claiming a sexual minority identity is shaped by the availability of personally and culturally relevant literature. Books and articles by members of one's own cultural group may fulfill the individual's need for a cognitive framework within which to understand his or her experiences. At the same time, such materials may also serve a "mirroring" function by providing the individual with role models and objects for identification and idealization. Lahkana (1994) has discussed how her process of coming out as a Cambodian lesbian was rendered more difficult by the absence of such material or role models:

> It would have been easier for me if I had picked up a book about lesbians and there was a Cambodian lesbian writer in it. Or if I had picked up an anthology of women of color or lesbians of color and I had seen that then. I think I would have come out sooner. I think that's part of the reason why I'm out and visible. Hopefully my experience can support another sister's process and make it a little bit easier. [p. 160]

In this section we focus on three issues that tend to arise in psychotherapy with multicultural sexual minorities. These issues may be regarded as key therapeutic tasks in work with this population: (1) recognition of resilience, (2) integration of multiple identities, and (3) maintenance of self-esteem.

MULTIPLE MARGINALIZATION AND IDENTITY INTEGRATION

Sexual minorities from historically oppressed racial and ethnic groups are subjected to multiple forms of marginalization. Lorde (1984) has eloquently described the difficulties that inhere in this situation: "I find I am constantly being encouraged to pluck out some aspect of myself and present this as the meaningful whole, eclipsing and denying the other parts of the self. But this is a destructive and fragmenting way to live" (p. 120).

Multicultural lesbians, gay men, and bisexuals face compounded stress as a result of simultaneous and interlocking experiences of oppression such as racism, sexism, and heterosexism. According to the "minority status as stressor" model, "stressful stimuli such as prejudice, discrimination and attendant hostility from the social environment as a function of minority status" serve to intensify psychological stress (Moritsugu 1983, p. 164). Gonsiorek (1982) has posited that intense anxieties associated with coming out as a sexual minority may at times be misconstrued as individual psychopathology. Some multicultural sexual minorities may alleviate this stress through healthy practices such as mobilizing social support or obtaining psychotherapy. Others, however, may internalize aspects of the hatred and devaluation they experience in the dominant culture and turn to self-destructive practices such as substance abuse, battering (Island and Letellier 1991; Kanuha 1990), or sexual risk-taking behaviors. Findings from the National Lesbian Health Care Survey suggest there may be a relationship between multiple oppression and substance abuse (Bradford and Ryan 1988). More specifically, although a third of the overall sample reported regularly using alcohol, black and Latina lesbians reported greater use of substances such as alcohol and cocaine than did their white counterparts.

Concerns that the label "gay" or "lesbian" will subsume or obliterate other important aspects of identity shed further light on the reluctance of some members of racial, ethnic, and cultural minority groups to be visible as sexual minorities. Among sexual minorities who wish to be "out," most want not only their sexual identity but also their racial/ethnic/cultural identity to be validated. Many, however, have found that after their sexual orientation was made known, others subsequently viewed them primarily in terms of their sexuality, thereby denying the centrality of their racial, ethnic, or cultural identity. Consequently, members of racial or ethnic minority groups may choose not to identify as part of a sexual minority group because they experience their racial or ethnocultural identity as "a more salient or primary locus of oppression than their sexual orientation" (Smith 1997, p. 288). Chan (1997), an Asian-American lesbian, has provided important insights on this issue:

> Given the assumption of heterosexuality as the norm, it is an inherent political statement to acknowledge a sexual identity. Even if it is one identity among several, and one is not prioritizing it over racial, ethnic, gendered, and professional identities, individuals who declare a sexual identity may become identified primarily in terms of their sexual identity. Perhaps it is because of this "primacy effect" of transgressive sexual identity that lesbians of color may be reluctant to take on a label of a sexual identity. When they do, it can overshadow their racial/ethnic identity, which affords a sense of social belonging and group cohesion. [p. 241]

Similarly, Beck (1982) has described the difficulties that Jewish lesbians encounter as they seek recognition and validation for both dimensions of their identity:

> It was as if the juxtaposition Jewish/lesbian were just too much. . . . I began to understand the limits that the dominant culture places on "otherness."

> You could be a Jew and people would recognize that as a religious or eth-
> nic affiliation *or* you could be a lesbian and some people would recognize
> that as an "alternative lifestyle" or "sexual preference," but if you tried to
> claim both identities—publicly and politically—you were exceeding the
> limits of what was permitted to the marginal. You were in danger of being
> perceived as ridiculous—and threatening. [p. xv]

Likewise, Farajaje-Jones (1995) has described the difficulties of identity
integration and the persistent sense of "otherness" encountered by lesbians,
gay men, and bisexuals of African descent:

> In our experience of Otherness, we are doubly or triply the ultimate Other,
> the Different One. As a black queer man, I am oppressed as a man of
> African descent, I am oppressed as a queer, and I am oppressed as a queer
> of African descent. My oppression comes not only from the dominating
> culture, but also from within my own communities: In the black commu-
> nity, I am oppressed for being queer; in the queer community, I am
> oppressed because I am a man of color. [p. 123]

Often, multicultural sexual minorities feel pressure to compromise or
relinquish some part of the self. Clough (1991) has acknowledged this
quandary: "I am legally a Canadian, and emotionally a Jamaican . . . and that
means I . . . carry inside me an empty space which little in this culture, climate
and geography can fill" (pp. 8–9).

RECOGNITION OF RESILIENCE

So far, we have emphasized the ways in which the process of self-identifying
as a sexual minority may be made more difficult by one's membership in additional marginalized groups. Yet in many instances the experience of growing
up with a marginalized racial or ethnocultural identity may actually help to
prepare one for the process of identifying as gay, lesbian, or bisexual, perhaps
through fostering resilience or an "inoculation" type of effect with regard to
social hardships. Although most theorists have emphasized the risks and
stressors associated with multiple minority status, the experience of coping
with racism and sexism may actually foster resilience that aids in the subsequent struggle to live openly as a sexual minority. For example, Greene
(1994a) has maintained that multicultural sexual minorities bring unique
resources and resiliencies to the task of managing multiple identities, honed
in earlier encounters with racial and ethnic oppression. Clough (1991) has

remarked, "perhaps . . . 'coming out' as a woman of color . . . has something to do with [my] being able to come out as a lesbian. . . . Being outside of the mainstream as a woman of color and a lesbian feels like the authentic place for me" (p. 9). Similarly, Beam (1991) has posited that experiences of marginalization may actually serve as a source of self-empowerment: "It was imperative for my survival that I did not attend to or believe the images that were presented of Black people or gay people. Perhaps that was the beginning of my passage from passivisim to activism, that I need to create my reality, that I needed to create images by which I, and other Black gay men to follow, could live this life" (p. 262).

Romo-Carmona (1995) has maintained that her initial experience of becoming visible and vocal as a politically active Latina contributed to her subsequent ability to come out as a sexual minority:

> The women who . . . were clearly visible as Latina lesbians were also active in Latin American feminist organizations, in pro-Puerto Rican independence and Latin American solidarity movements, labor, the Left, reproductive rights, human rights, housing, anti-racist movements. . . . In New York City, this broad political consciousness existed before Latinas were ready to organize specifically as Latina lesbians. . . . Active participation in the civil rights movements of the sixties and seventies served as a training ground for Latina lesbians, many of whom were in leadership positions in these organizations. [pp. 88–90]

Thus, in some instances, rather than constituting a liability to one's physical and mental health, one's experiences as a member of a racial, ethnic, or cultural minority may strengthen one's capacity to openly claim a sexual minority identity.

MAINTENANCE OF SELF-ESTEEM

We live in a society that routinely rejects and devalues people who are not heterosexual. Thus questions related to preserving, facilitating, or strengthening self-esteem are important for all sexual minorities. Nevertheless, the process of maintaining a positive self-image as a gay, lesbian, or bisexual person is rendered even more complicated for those who are also members of other oppressed groups. For gay men, lesbians, and bisexuals from marginalized ethnocultural backgrounds, there is a "persistent sense of 'otherness'" and a heightened feeling of having to "'prove' one's acceptability on multiple levels" (Swigonski 1995, p. 13). Greene (1994b) has used the phrase "triple jeopardy" to describe the experience of African-American lesbians who are simultaneously devalued at the level of race, gender, and sexual orientation. Ethnic minority gay men, lesbians, and bisexuals often are deprived of role models, mirroring, and mentorship. Moreover, in their exposure to television, film, and other aspects of popular culture, they do not typically encounter positive representations of people with whom they can identify simultaneously on ethnic and sexual orientation levels. These factors may contribute to feelings of inferiority, self-doubt, or self-deprecation. Thus clinicians working with this population may need to devote particular attention to issues of self-acceptance. Bruining (1995), a lesbian who as a Korean orphan was adopted by a white American family and raised in a white neighborhood, has remarked:

> My childhood and adolescence were filled with constant overt and covert experiences of racism . . . [which] included the subtle stares of young children, name-calling by older children, verbal harassment, verbal threats of violence. . . , stone-throwing . . . [being] asked offensive, intrusive and inappropriate questions. These years of racism, in the form of verbal abuse, ostracism, and blatant hatred caused profound psychic wounds and scars. The repercussions of society's intolerance and rejection of my Asian appearance were internalized feelings of alienation, rage, despair, sadness, self-hatred, low self-esteem, and loneliness. [p. 62]

Obviously, men and women who already harbor feelings of low self-worth as a result of racial, ethnic, or class oppression may find it even more difficult to maintain a positive self-image after self-identifying as a sexual minority. The task of maintaining a positive self-image may be influenced by the extent to which one's cultural group has (or lacks) positive models of people with nontraditional sexual orientations. There are significant cultural variations in the presence (or absence) of such models. For example, in *Sexuality and Eroticism among Males in Moslem Societies*, Schmitt and Sofer (1992) have noted that some cultures have no linguistic terms for same-sex practices and suppress all knowledge about such practices. Gaspar de Alba (1993) has asserted that "nothing in . . . Chicana culture nor in the dominant culture validates or even acknowledges lesbian existence" (p. 958). Similarly, Clough (1991), a Jamaican lesbian who immigrated to Canada, stated, "When I was growing up and going to an all girls' school, I never heard the word 'lesbian.'" (p. 9). By contrast, in some cultures gay men, lesbians, and bisexuals have been well regarded. In Native American cultures, for example, gay men, lesbians, bisexuals, and transgendered people were treated with respect and even reverence. Likewise, Gomez (in Gomez and Smith 1991) notes that "there have always been acceptable places for gay Black men to retreat and escape from the danger, i.e., the 'choir queen'" (p. 55).

A creative example of a culturally syntonic role model is found in a fascinating essay by Alice Lee (1989) entitled "Spinsterhood and the Chinese Lesbian Group." Lee has discussed the popular spinsterhood associations that arose in the Canton Delta from the end of the nineteenth century until the 1930s in connection with the flourishing silk-weaving industry. According to Lee, women's labor was important in all stages of silk production, and the sisterhood associations that formed around the industry were an accepted part of village life. Lee has explored how her discovery of these associations strengthened her sense of self-esteem as a Chinese-American lesbian: "Talking to my aunts made me realize that I came from a strong tradition of marriage-resisting women. As Chinese lesbians, we have very few role models to go by. Just knowing about the sisterhood is a kind of validation" (p. 5).

In addition to being influenced by the existence (or absence) of role models and mentors, the ability to maintain self-esteem as a "multiply marginalized" lesbian, gay man, or bisexual may also be affected by the question of whether one's native language contains a word for persons who are attracted to members of their own sex, and if so, what connotations that word carries. For example, among Latinos there are men who eschew the labels "gay" or "bisexual" but will readily self-identify as a "man who has sex with men." Pamela H. (1989) has noted that "most Asian languages do not have a word meaning 'lesbian'" (as cited in Trujillo 1997a, p. 270). In many Native American nations, by contrast, lesbians and gay men were traditionally referred to as "two-spirit" people, a term that was positive and respectful. Silvera (1991), a Jamaican-born lesbian, has remarked:

> I . . . managed to hear snippets of words, tail ends of conversations about women together. In Jamaica, the words used to describe many of these women would be "Man Royal" and/or "Sodomite." Dread words. So dread that women dare not use these words to name themselves. They were names given to women by men to describe aspects of our lives that men neither understood nor approved. . . . The word "sodomite" derives from the *Old Testament*. Its common use to describe lesbians . . . is peculiar to Jamaica, a culture historically and strongly grounded in the Bible. [pp. 15–16]

Thus, in psychotherapy with culturally diverse sexual minorities, it is important for clinicians to inquire about the specific words or terms used to describe gay men, lesbians, and bisexuals in the client's culture of origin. Further, the therapist should elicit and explore the client's cognitive and affective associations to these terms. In oppressed and marginalized communities, the task of maintaining self-esteem is typically fulfilled in one's family and ethnocultural community, because the larger society tends to be dismissive and hostile. As we have discussed earlier, claiming one's sexual minority identity may lead to rejection by family and community, thereby depriving the individual of a potential source of self-esteem. Thus the maintenance of self-esteem may be a greater challenge for ethnic minority lesbians, gay men, and bisexuals than for sexual minorities whose racial, religious, or ethnocultural backgrounds are valued in the society at large.

CONCLUSIONS

Throughout this chapter we have focused on a variety of contextual factors that influence the thoughts, feelings, and behavior of multicultural sexual minorities, particularly in regard to questions of visibility and silence. Clinicians who work with sexual minority clients must be cognizant of the sociocultural context in which individual lives and meanings unfold. For clients who are marginalized not only as a result of their sexual orientation but also because of additional dimensions of difference, this sociocultural context includes specific historical and contemporary experiences of oppression and survival. Sexuality inevitably intersects with gender, race, ethnicity, culture, and additional categories of identity in shaping the client's self-image, strengths, vulnerabilities, coping strategies, fears, fantasies, and realities.

REFERENCES

Abbot, S., and Love, B. (1972). *Sappho Was a Right-On Woman: A Liberated View of Lesbianism*. New York: Stein & Day.

Aguilar-San Juan, K. (1991). Exploding myths, creating consciousness: some first steps toward Pan-Asian unity. In *Piece of My Heart: A Lesbian of Colour Anthology*, ed. M. Silvera, pp. 185–192. Toronto, Canada: Sister Vision Press.

American Psychological Association (1997a). Brief of *Amici Curiae* in *Bottoms vs. Bottoms*, 94–1166. Retrieved December 14, 1997, from http://www.apa.org/pi/bottoms.html.

——— (1997b). Answers to your questions about sexual orientation and homosexuality. Media information retrieved December 14, 1997, from http://www.apa.org/pubinfo/orient.html.

Anzaldua, G. (1987). *Borderlands/La Frontera: The New Mestiza*. San Francisco: Spinsters/Aunt Lute.

Appleby, Y. (1993). Disability and "compulsory heterosexuality." In *Heterosexuality: A Feminism and Psychology Reader*, ed. S. Wilkinson and C. Kitzinger, pp. 266–269. London: Sage.

Arnesen, C. (1991). Coming out to Congress. In *Bi Any Other Name: Bisexual People Speak Out*, ed. L. Hutchins and L. Kaahumanu, pp. 233–239. Boston: Alyson.

Badgett, L. (1997). *Economic issues for lesbians*. Paper presented at the Institute of Medicine Workshop on Lesbian Health Research Priorities, Washington, DC, October.

Beam, J. (1986). *In the Life: A Black Gay Anthology*. Boston: Alyson.

———— (1991). Making ourselves from scratch. In *Brother to Brother: New Writings by Black Gay Men*, ed. E. Hemphill, pp. 261–262. Boston: Alyson.

Beck, E. T. (1982). Why is this book different from all other books? In *Nice Jewish Girls: A Lesbian Anthology*, pp. xv–xxxviii. Boston: Beacon.

Bernstein, A. (1993). Of bread, love. In *Eyes of Desire: A Deaf Gay and Lesbian Reader*, ed. R. Luczak, pp. 184–187. Boston: Alyson.

Bornstein, K. (1997). The hard part. In *In Our Own Words: Readings on the Psychology of Women and Gender*, ed. M. Crawford and R. Unger, pp. 170–175. New York: McGraw Hill.

Bradford, J., and Ryan, C. (1988). *National Lesbian Health Care Survey*. Washington, DC: National Lesbian and Gay Health Foundation.

Bruining, M. O. (1995). A few thoughts from a Korean, adopted, lesbian, writer/poet, and social worker. In *Lesbians of Color: Social and Human Services*, ed. H. Hidalgo, pp. 61–66. Binghamton, NY: Harrington Park.

Bulhan, H. A. (1985). *Frantz Fanon and the Psychology of Oppression*. New York: Plenum.

Chan, C. S. (1989). Issues of identity development among Asian-American lesbians and gay men. *Journal of Counseling and Development* 68:16–20.

———— (1990). You're short besides. In *Making Face, Making Soul: Haciendo Caras: Creative and Critical Perspectives by Feminists of Color*, ed. G. Anzaldua, pp. 162–168. San Francisco: Aunt Lute.

———— (1997). Don't ask, don't tell, don't know: the formation of a homosexual identity and sexual expression among Asian American lesbians. In *Ethnic and Cultural Diversity among Lesbians and Gay Men*, ed. B. Greene, pp. 240–248. Thousand Oaks, CA: Sage.

Clarke C. (1983). The failure to transform: homophobia in the black community. In *Home Girls: A Black Feminist Anthology*, ed. B. Smith, pp. 197–208. New York: Kitchen Table: Woman of Color Press.

Clough, A. (1991). Leaving home, coming home. In *Piece of My Heart: A Lesbian of Colour Anthology*, ed. M. Silvera, pp. 8–10. Toronto, Canada: Sister Vision Press.

Curry, H., Clifford, D., and Leonard, R. (1994). *A Legal Guide for Lesbian and Gay Couples*. 8th ed. Berkeley, CA: Nolo.

DeAngelis, T. (1996, October). Better research being done on gay men and lesbians. *APA Monitor*, pp. 1–2. Newspaper; selected stories on line. Retrieved December 14, 1997, from http://www.apa.org/monitor/oct96/improve.html.

Dworkin, S. H. (1997). Female, lesbian, and Jewish: complex and invisible. In *Ethnic and Cultural Diversity among Lesbians and Gay Men*, ed. B. Greene, pp. 63–87. Thousand Oaks, CA: Sage.

Espin, O. (1987). Issues of identity in the psychology of Latina lesbians. In *Lesbian Psychologies: Explorations and Challenges*, ed. Boston Lesbian Psychologies Collective, pp. 35–51. Urbana, IL: University of Illinois Press.

Fanon, F. (1968). *The Wretched of the Earth*. New York: Grove.

Farajaje-Jones, E. (1995). Fluid desire: race, HIV/AIDS, and bisexual politics. In *Bisexual Politics: Theories, Queries, and Visions*, ed. N. Tucker, pp. 119–130. New York: Haworth.

Frank, B. (1997). *Barney Frankley on E.N.D.A.* Public service announcement. Retrieved December 14, 1997, from http://members.aol.com/barneyenda/barney.html

Gaspar de Alba, A. (1993). Tortillerismo: work by Chicana lesbians. *Signs* 18(4):956–963.

Gay and Lesbian Alliance Against Defamation (1997). GLAAD TV scoreboard. Retrieved December 30, 1997, from http://www.glaad.org/glaad/scoreboard.html.

Golden, C. (1994). Our politics and choices: the feminist movement and sexual orientation. In *Lesbian and Gay Psychology: Theory, Research, and Clinical Applications*, ed. B. Greene and G. M. Herek, pp. 54–70. Thousand Oaks, CA: Sage.

Gomez, J. L., and Smith, B. (1991). Taking the home out of homophobia: black lesbian health. In *Piece of My Heart: A Lesbian of Colour Anthology*, ed. M. Silvera, pp. 40–57. Toronto, Canada: Sister Vision Press.

Gonsiorek, J. (1982). The use of diagnostic concepts in working with gay and lesbian populations. In *Homosexuality and Psychotherapy: A Practitioners Handbook of Affirmative Models*, pp. 9–20. Beverly Hills, CA: Sage.

Greene, B. (1994a). Ethnic-minority lesbians and gay men: mental health and treatment issues. *Journal of Consulting and Clinical Psychology* 62(2):243–251.

———— (1994b). Lesbian women of color: triple jeopardy. In *Women of Color and Mental Health*, ed. L. Comas Diaz and B. Greene, pp. 389–427. New York: Guilford.

Greene, B. (1997). Ethnic minority lesbians and gay men: mental health and treatment issues. In *Ethnic and Cultural Diversity among Lesbians and Gay Men*, ed. B. Greene, pp. 216–239. Thousand Oaks, CA: Sage.

Hearn, K. (1989). A woman's right to cruise. In *Out the Other Side: Contemporary Lesbian Writing*, ed. C. McEwen and S. O'Sullivan, pp. 48–52. Freedom, CA: Crossing Press.

Hidalgo, H. (1995). The norms of conduct in social service agencies: a threat to the mental health of Puerto Rican lesbians. In *Lesbians of Color: Social and Human Services*, pp. 23–41. Binghamton, NY: Harrington Park.

Hoffmann, E. (1993). Leaving South Dakota. In *Eyes of Desire: A Deaf Gay and Lesbian Reader*, ed. R. Luczak, pp. 86–89. Boston: Alyson.

Hom, A. Y. (1996). Stories from the homefront: perspectives of Asian American parents with lesbian daughters and gay sons. In *Asian American Sexualities:*

Dimensions of the Gay and Lesbian Experience, ed. R. Leong, pp. 37–49. New York: Routledge.

hooks, b., and West, C. (1991). *Breaking Bread: Insurgent Black Intellectual Life*. Boston: South End Press.

Human Rights Campaign (1997a). *Non-discrimination in the Workplace*. Issue brief. Retrieved December 14, 1997, from http://www.hrc.org/issues/workplac/nd/index.html.

———— (1997b). *Hate Crimes Laws*. Issue brief. Retrieved December 14, 1997, from http://www.hrc.org/issues/antigay/fedlaws.html.

———— (1997c). *State Hate Crimes Laws*. Issue brief. Retrieved December 14, 1997, from http://www.hrc.org/issues/antigay/hatestat.html.

———— (1997d). *Responding to Anti-Gay Hate Legislation and Issues*. Issue brief. Retrieved December 14, 1997, from http://www.hrcusa.org/issues/antigay/index.html.

Hutchins, L., and Kaahumanu, L. (1991). Overview. In *Bi Any Other Name: Bisexual People Speak Out*, pp. 216–222. Boston: Alyson.

Icard, L. (1986). Black gay men and conflicting social identities: sexual orientation versus racial identity. Special issue: social work practice in sexual problems. *Journal of Social Work and Human Sexuality* 4(1–2):83–93.

Island, D., and Letellier, P. (1991). *Men Who Beat the Men Who Love Them: Battered Gay Men and Domestic Violence*. New York: Haworth.

Kantrowitz, B. (1996). Gay families come out. *Newsweek*, November 4, pp. 50–52, 53–56, 57.

Kanuha, V. (1990). Compounding the triple jeopardy: battering in lesbian of color relationships. *Women & Therapy* 9(1/2):169–183.

Kaye/Kantrowitz, M. (1982). Some notes on Jewish lesbian identity. In *Nice Jewish Girls: A Lesbian Anthology*, ed. E. T. Beck, pp. 34–50. Boston: Beacon.

Lahkana, P. (1994). Tha phi neah yeung the . . . ? (Only the two of us. . . ?) In *The Very Inside: An Anthology of Writing by Asian and Pacific Islander Lesbian and Bisexual Women*, ed. S. Lim-Hing, pp. 156–161. Toronto, Canada: Sister Vision Press.

Langston, D. (1988). Tired of playing monopoly? In *Race, Class, and Gender: An Anthology*, ed. M. L. Andersen and P. H. Collins, 2nd. ed. pp. 100–110. Belmont, CA: Wadsworth.

Lee, A. (1989). Spinsterhood and the Chinese lesbian group: a visit to my aunts. In *Out the Other Side: Contemporary Lesbian Writing*, ed. C. McEwen and S. O'Sullivan, pp. 4–7. Freedom, CA: Crossing Press.

Lee, C. A. (1991). An Asian lesbian's struggle. In *Piece of My Heart: A Lesbian of Colour Anthology*, ed. M. Silvera, pp. 115–118. Toronto, Canada: Sister Vision Press.

Leung, P. (1991). On iconography. In *Piece of My Heart: A Lesbian of Colour Anthology*, ed. M. Silvera, pp. 108–109. Toronto, Canada: Sister Vision Press.

Lorde, A. (1984). Age: race, class, and sex: women redefying difference. In *Sister Outsider*, pp. 114–123. Freedom, CA: Crossing Press.

———— (1991). I am your sister: black women organizing across sexualities. In *Piece of My Heart: A Lesbian of Colour Anthology*, ed. M. Silvera, pp. 94–99. Toronto, Canada: Sister Vision Press.

MacKenzie, G. O. (1994). *Transgender Nation*. Bowling Green, OH: Bowling Green State University Popular Press.

Mays, V., and Cochran, S. (1988). The black women's relationship project: a national survey of black lesbians. In *The Sourcebook on Lesbian/Gay Health Care*, ed. M. Shernoff and W. Scott, 2nd ed., pp. 54–62. Washington, DC: National Lesbian and Gay Health Foundation.

Moritsugu, J., and Sue, S. (1983). Minority status as a stressor. In *Preventive Psychology: Theory, Research and Practice*, ed. R. D. Felner, pp. 162–174. New York: Pergamon.

Mundy, L. (1993). Black and bi. *Washington City Paper*, February 5–11, pp. 28–35, Washington, DC.

National Gay and Lesbian Task Force (1997). *Employment non-discrimination bill introduced*. Press brief. Retrieved December 14, 1997, from http://www.ngltf.org/Press/enda2.html.

Pamela H. (1989). Asian American lesbians: an emerging voice in the Asian American community. In *Making Waves: An Anthology of Writings by and about Asian American Women*, ed. Asian Women United of California, pp. 282–290. Boston: Beacon.

Patterson, C. J. (1995). Lesbian mothers, gay fathers, and their children. In *Lesbian, Gay and Bisexual Identities over the Lifespan*, ed. A. R. D'Augelli and C. J. Patterson, pp. 262–290. New York: Oxford University Press.

Peplau, L. A., Cochran, S. D., and Mays, V. M. (1997). A national survey of the intimate relationships of African American lesbians and gay men: a look at commitment, satisfaction, sexual behavior, and HIV disease. In *Ethnic and Cultural Diversity among Lesbians and Gay Men*, ed. B. Greene, pp. 11–38. Thousand Oaks, CA: Sage.

Ponse, B. (1978). *Identities in the Lesbian World*. Westport, CT: Greenwood.

Pratt, M. B. (1997). One good mother to another. In *In Our Own Words: Readings on the Psychology of Women and Gender*, ed. M. Crawford and R. Unger, pp. 277–279. New York: McGraw-Hill.

Romo-Carmona, M. (1995). Lesbian Latinas: organizational efforts to end oppression. In *Lesbians of Color: Social and Human Services*, ed. H. Hidalgo, pp. 85–93. Binghamton, NY: Harrington Park.

Rust, P. C. (1996). Managing multiple identities: diversity among bisexual women and men. In *Bisexuality: The Psychology and Politics of an Invisible Minority*, ed. B. Firestein, pp. 53–83. Thousand Oaks, CA: Sage.

Schmitt, A., and Sofer, J., eds. (1992). *Sexuality and Eroticism among Males in Moslem Societies*. New York: Haworth.

Silvera, M. (1991). Man royals and sodomites: some thoughts on the invisibility of Afro-Caribbean lesbians. In *Piece of My Heart: A Lesbian of Colour Anthology*, pp. 14–26. Toronto, Canada: Sister Vision Press.

Smith, A. (1997). Cultural diversity and the coming out process: implications for clinical practice. In *Ethnic and Cultural Diversity among Lesbians and Gay Men*, ed. B. Greene, pp. 279–300. Thousand Oaks, CA: Sage.

Smith-Rosenberg, C. (1985). The abortion movement and the AMA, 1850–1880. *Disorderly Conduct: Visions of Gender in Victorian America*. New York: Oxford University Press.

Swigonski, M. E. (1995). The social service needs of lesbians of color. In *Lesbians of Color: Social and Human Services*, ed. H. Hidalgo, pp. 67–83. Binghamton, NY: Harrington Park.

Tafoya, T. (1997). Native gay and lesbian issues: the two-spirited. In *Ethnic and Cultural Diversity among Lesbians and Gay Men*, ed. B. Greene, pp. 1–10. Thousand Oaks, CA: Sage.

Tasker, F., and Golombok, S. (1995). Adults raised as children in lesbian families. *American Journal of Orthopsychiatry* 65:203–215.

Tinney, J. S. (1986). Why a Black gay church? In *In the Life: A Black Gay Anthology*, ed. J. Beam, pp. 70–86. Boston: Alyson.

Trujillo, C. M. (1997a). Sexual identity and the discontents of difference. In *Ethnic and Cultural Diversity among Lesbians and Gay Men*, ed. B. Greene, pp. 266–278. Thousand Oaks, CA: Sage.

——— (1997b). Chicana lesbians: fear and loathing in the Chicano community. In *Women Images and Realities: A Multicultural Anthology*, ed. A. Kesselman, L. D. McNai, and N. Schniedewind, pp. 255–260. Mountain View, CA: Mayfield.

Part V

Conclusion

32

Mental Disorder and Its Treatment: Social and Political Implications

WILLIAM G. HERRON AND RAFAEL ART. JAVIER

At this point in time notice has definitely been given to the social and political considerations involved in the diagnosis, treatment, and prevention of mental illness. Of course, mental illness always had a variety of definitions throughout history that in varying degrees reflected the interactive influence of the individual and his or her culture, but the increasing diversity of the nation's population has provided an unprecedented focus. Mental illness has legal standing in terms of the capacity to know right from wrong, but for a detailed description the best known "official" source is the American Psychiatric Association's *DSM-IV* (1994). This contains groupings of behaviors that cause personal and social distress to the people who exhibit these symptoms as well as to those who are affected by their behaviors. *DSM-IV* also provides five ways to categorize the same behavior so as to provide what is considered a biopsychosocial assessment (Morrison 1995). These categories are mental disorders, personality disorders and mental retardation, physical conditions and disorders, psychosocial and environmental problems, and global assessment of functioning. Of these five, the first is the most used and is given to most patients who are diagnosed as mentally ill. Thus the most frequent description of mental illness at present is a symptomatic one, although

DSM-IV can be used as a multiaxial diagnostic schema. The popularity of symptomatic shorthand is reflected in the *DSM-IV* definition of mental disorder that is paraphrased by Morrison (1995): "A mental disorder is a clinically important collection of symptoms (these can be behavioral or psychological) that cause an individual distress, disability, or the increased risk of suffering pain, death, or the loss of freedom" (p. 8).

Although the description of mental illness stresses its effect on the individual with the disorder, a large number of other people are affected by the mentally ill because the cost, emotional and monetary, of dealing with the manifestations of mental illness is carried by society. The problems of an individual rarely remain solely in the realm of the individual so that mental illness has to be looked at as a social and political issue. Just as Sullivan (1964) emphasized the interpersonal field rather than the person and Winnicott (1965) stressed the concept of a relational field rather than the individual, mental illness requires the coconstruction of the individual and his or her culture, with the latter emphasizing social and political considerations. Such a view does not dismiss individuality, which must be a significant consideration, but it does highlight the simultaneous concern for what can be considered psychocultural dispositions, namely, socially shaped and shared response tendencies (LeVine 1973, Ross 1993).

The most obvious signs of mental illness, symptoms such as anxiety and depression, appear at first at the individual level where they are experienced and can be described and shown to others by the individual. At a less obvious level there are the intricate workings of a disturbed inner life, often depicted as unconscious psychodynamic processes, which are harder to articulate as well as to discern, but are nonetheless present. However, both outer and inner manifestations of mental illness have been shaped by the culture, defined here as "the particular practices and values common to a population living in a given setting" (Ross 1993, p. 21). Such an interactive view has always been contained in both psychodynamic and social learning theories, and is clearly reflected in the previously mentioned concept of psychocultural dispositions as psychological processes that color a culture at the same time that they derive in part from the culture (Whiting and Whiting 1975). Now the social and political influences have been made more apparent and require sustained consideration. This is apparent in *DSM-IV*, which does list a number of syndromes that are culturally specific. In addition, although Morrison (1995) considers *DSM-IV* to be the best candidate for a world standard of evaluation, he does caution against its lack of applicability in all cultures. Such a caution, however, does not reflect the degree of cultural sensitivity necessitated by the existence of cultural diversity in a nation such as the United States.

The designation of mental illness can be effectively thought of as resting ultimately on the culture. A self-definition has to be validated by society or the privileges (lack of responsibility, social sympathy) and punishments (lack of freedom, social disdain) of being mentally ill will not be meted out. Thus, even though a person may be mentally ill from a personal perspective, if such a view is not accepted by those who designate such a condition in society, the individual will not be socially designated as mentally ill. Conversely, if society were to designate any one of its members as mentally ill, such a designation could well prevail even if the individual were to insist that such was not the case. Some cultures have routinely used this approach to isolate dissidents as an extreme form of politicizing mental illness. All cultures have this type of designation at their disposal and many cultures use it in subtle forms in attempts to separate less desirable from more desirable members based on social norms and political considerations.

The culture as a collective product of individuals establishes categories of behaviors and standards for evaluating the actions of its members (Arvuch and Black 1991). The designation of mental illness is one of those evaluations, and it is most likely to be given to those who differ from the norms of socially acceptable, and socially agreeable, behavior. Another likely alternative for these marginalized people is that their behavior may be considered criminal and they are kept at a distance via incarceration. Limiting their economic opportunities and fostering their geographical isolation are still other possibilities. Actually, however, both criminalization and poverty are likely to result in the first alternative, mental illness, or can be products of it.

Given the increasingly diverse population of this country, the question of whether mental illness is present or absent has become increasingly problematic, as has the question of what to do about mental illness. Diversity means differences, and to the degree that those who are relatively the same feel threatened by those who are relatively different, there will be an inclination to react to the diversity by creating distance from it. In some instances this is carried out by various forms of socially stipulated segregation, or there may be an apparent embracing of the diversity through political and social programs that at first allow a "trickle of entry," but when the trickle increases its flow, attempts appear to shut it off. An example is the current backlash against affirmative action, which results in a conflict between those who consider diversity to be a cultural asset and those who see it as a distortion that weakens cultural values.

The mentally ill are members of one of those "distance groups," like the poor (Herron and Javier 1996), that then get special treatment by those who control society. This treatment can be favorable or discriminatory, with the latter being more likely, although civil rights legislation continues to provide the potential for redressing discrimination. Unfortunately, discrimination limits the opportunities of the group being discriminated against, and in turn limits the future growth and development of the society. Let us look at two key related issues in the process in regard to mental illness: designation and assistance.

DESIGNATION

The designation of mental illness has always been a confusing process. It remains so despite efforts to develop relatively objective codifications of disorders. Symptoms are often elusive, with their presence or absence open to observer interpretation as well as to the interpretation of the experiencer. Bergner (1997) has pointed out that despite the existence of the *DSMs*, an effective consensus concerning the definition of mental illness is still lacking. Nathan (1997) sees *DSM-IV* as an acceptable consensus, but the extent of disagreement with it belies that argument as does Nathan's comments on its limitations. *DSM-IV* is, however, primarily what the diagnostician has to use to designate mental illness.

Bergner (1997) considers psychopathology to be a vital social concern while noting the contextual nature of judgments regarding pathology. The social and political aspects of mental illness designation are mentioned by a number of authors who are struggling with attempts to reformulate the concept of mental illness (Wakefield 1992, Widiger 1997). Thus there is considerable theoretical and empirical support for giving renewed consideration to cultural influences in diagnosis.

Also, people in the society have very mixed reactions to mental illness. On the one hand they view it negatively, sometimes in the extreme, seeing it as frightening and unpleasantly mysterious. Their view is complicated by their inability to discriminate the various forms, types, and degrees of mental illness. As a result, calling someone "crazy" is usually a negative designation that supports a difference between the designator and the crazy person. The difference is embodied in a desire for physical and emotional distance from madness. Thus people who, for whatever reasons, do not fit in from the society's point of view may often be designated as mentally ill. Marginalized people, such as minority group members, are therefore likely to be candidates for such designation.

On the other hand there is a cultural attitude of sympathy for mental illness based on the belief that it is visited on individuals. Such diseases are considered unfortunate combinations of genetic and environmental factors that are out of the control of the afflicted person and in turn leave that person out of control in many ways. Viewed in this manner, mental illness becomes a plausible explanation or excuse for behavior that without such an etiology would make the person responsible for his or her behavior. When avoidance of responsibility is a major component of a designation as mentally ill, minority group members are often excluded from the mentally ill category and instead are blamed for their actions. For example, a minority person who demonstrates the symptoms of work phobia is more likely to be called lazy than anxious, and in turn be held responsible for tardiness or absence in contrast to a person who is not ethnically stereotyped.

For the culturally diverse, the duality of scorn and concern that represents mainstream cultural views of mental illness actually tends to have the same general effect regardless of which attitude dominates. The result is mistaken identity. Minority members are likely to be excessively designated as mentally ill when they are not or as mentally healthy when they are not (the latter may result in a more unpleasant alternative, designation as a criminal). Of course this does not signify that cultural diversity means that minorities are always at risk for distorted categorizations, but they are at higher risk than the members of the society that symbolize its political and cultural center.

Garb (1997) recently reviewed clinical judgment data in regard to race and social class bias, and concluded that it is by no means universal, certainly an encouraging finding. However, he also concluded that it does indeed exist, for example, in the high incidence of schizophrenic diagnoses of black and Hispanic patients as compared to white patients. The greater awareness of possible bias by clinicians is also encouraging, because Garb also reports a decrease in social class bias both in making diagnoses and in rating adjustment levels.

The results reported by Garb (1997) are focused on studies of clinicians integrating information and were not designed to evaluate the potentials and probabilities for social and political manipulation of diagnosis. For example, the finding that middle-class children were referred to special education programs more often than lower-class children could reflect an attitude that the lower-class group is relatively hopeless so there is no point in giving them anything extraordinary. The probability remains that the prevailing winds may often depend on which categorization in each circumstance will be most likely to maintain whatever cultural values are perceived as being threatened by the person in question. The diagnosis of mental illness within a diverse society in which there is at the same time a dominant culture will illustrate what Ross terms the "culture of conflict" (1993, p. 21). This concept describes the specific practices, norms, and institutions that are associated with conflict within a given culture.

Illness as an idea provides a way to explain behavior, and in that sense allows the integrity of social behavior to be maintained despite individual variations. However, the misuse of the designation of illness can be disruptive to social unity and development because it falsely depicts the identities of the members of a cultural group. Productive people can be removed from the probability of maintaining and enhancing the society, and unproductive people can be put in a position where they undermine the society. In essence, a healthy society depends on accurate recognition of the emotional and social health of its members. Bergner (1997) points out that both the society and its members have a significant need to make sure that the largest number of people can be competent social participants, and that failures in social capabilities, such as mental illness, are costly to everyone. People who are already marginalized and disadvantaged by virtue of their cultural and ethnic diversity are at high risk to be inaccurately recognized in terms of mental illness.

This culture reflects an awareness of that possibility and attempts to prevent such distortions, yet at the same time it continues to maintain and engender biases and stereotypes. Widiger (1997) suggests that the effect of bias in a culture is more likely to be mitigated by attempts to base cultural beliefs on objective and critical observations of empirical data. At the same time, objective criticism is mitigated by the subjectivity of interpretation that occurs in all cultures. Mainstream social attitudes are ambivalent in regard to diversity, as reflected in the current popularity of political centering. With that in mind the suggestions to be made here in regard to the designation of mental illness are attempts to utilize the positive side of the ambivalence and make good use of cultural diversity.

The spirit of this country was once embodied in the symbol of a great melting pot, although the reality was a relative democracy and sporadic equality of opportunity. The country's spirit is now embodied in multiculturalism that revolves around a core culture that continues to evolve and adapt to the shifting needs of its diverse membership. New and different ideas are as much the fuel of that culture as tradition and accrued wisdom. Diversity is the carrier of the culture, so it is vital to make good use of significant differences. This can be accomplished through the structures of the society as instruments of psychocultural processes, with the designation of mental illness as one example. The following suggestions are offered to improve the efficacy of diagnostic evaluation.

1. Assessment needs to be culturally sensitive. Past diagnostic approaches attempted panculturalism and resulted in discrimination against the culturally diverse. There is sufficient evidence to highlight the potentials for bias so that diagnosticians can have a heightened awareness of possible bias and act to avoid such distortions. New assessment procedures are available that can reflect cultural differences in regard to general mental illness constructs, such as anxiety and depression, as well as social skills and intellectual capabilities.

2. The development of culturally sensitive assessment procedures requires adherence to the pursuit of reliability and validity. A combination of scientific methodology and awareness of the subjectivity that is bound to be involved will increase the potential for effective assessment. It will be insufficient to do less or mistakes will continue to be made under a new model of apparent fairness.

3. The appraisal of emotional fitness in a multicultural context has to include adaptive ability that is referenced to the core culture that provides operational definitions of normative functioning. For example, it is useful to detect the difference between anxiety based on cultural misunderstanding and anxiety based on chronic feelings of personal vulnerability. However, to accurately understand the former and consider the degree to which it represents mental illness, it is necessary to evaluate the strengths and weaknesses of a person in terms of adaptive responsiveness to his or her anxiety. The illness is not automatically indicated by the presence of a symptom such as anxiety, nor is it eliminated from consideration by a cultural distinction. Ultimately the designation of mental illness must signify an inability to develop a positional fit with the core culture in regard to the apparent symptom manifestation. The modifier "positional" is used to leave room for people who are dissenters and try to alter the culture in some way that may well become part of a future core.

4. *Mental illness* is a term that always requires qualification but has social utility. The term represents the approximation of an objective construct that is constructed subjectively and therefore is open to personal bias and error along with social and political influences. Even with the best of intentions assessment procedures may be distorted and observers may misinterpret behavior. The influence of culture on behavior and the probability of personal bias is being increasingly recognized and the assessing professions agree that these issues must be given attention. However, such attention needs to give increased weight to a detailed appraisal of the subjectivity of the assessor.

5. The concept of mental illness reflects a social agenda within a given society. It is in many ways a "power term" that can be used to shape the people of a society and the character of that society. In that vein it is a political construct that can follow the variations of an ideology. The concept of mental illness has been insufficiently deconstructed to take into account the multiplicity of etiological, symbolic, and contextual possibilities that are involved in behavior. There are, of course, ongoing attempts at defining mental illness—and its numerous synonyms, such as psychopathology—that indeed try to provide more complete pictures of people's difficulties. Two major current examples are "harmful dysfunction" (Wakefield 1992) and "inability to engage in deliberate action" (Bergner 1997, Ossario 1985), but unanimity has not been achieved, and it may never be. The important factor is that different views of the terrain (Kaslow 1997) get attention. At present, *DSM-IV* as the prominent and official designatory system provides a pseudo-objective description of behavior of unknown etiologies that represents a social and political construction that is of limited utility given the cultural diversity of the nation's population (Herron et al. 1997). A multidimensional construct that necessitates customized evaluation and designation would be more effective, but harder to develop, not only because of its complexity but because of its effect on public policy. For example, Mechanic (1997) suggests that capacity/disability formulations of mental illness by their degree of inclusiveness make it more difficult to determine the need for treatment in terms of resource allocations for health care. However, practical difficulties in social policy implementations do not rule out the need for a flexible diagnostic system. Our point is that designation is often a social and political issue in that it requires judgments about social activity that in turn mandates clinicians' consideration of their subjective cultural views.

This list of suggestions is not meant to be exhaustive or definitive, but is designed as a beginning to provide a more accurate picture of what it means to be mentally ill. Mental illness has been, and continues to be, a relatively gross designation for a vast number of problems in living that affect all people to varying degrees and that have been codified as discrete disorders. Usually it is some aspect of the problem's context—for example, its severity— rather than the problem itself that moves the problem, and the person with the problem, into the illness category. Such a threshold approach has an evaluative appeal in establishing criteria, but it is prey to the difficulties of restrictiveness. For example, there is evidence that social disability occurs in people with depression who failed to meet the criteria for a mental illness diagnosis (Wells et al. 1996). The cultural essence is not being used to appropriately expand the concept of mental illness. Instead mental illness has been pointed in the direction of a restricted descriptive code that is periodically altered to eliminate apparently outmoded or inaccurate behavioral clusters and add newly discovered groupings. In fact, *DSM-IV* has 120 more disorders than its predecessor (Morrison 1995), but the number of disorders is not so much the issue as that the approach fails to do justice to the complexity involved. The social needs being reflected are to make illness as categorical and familiar as physical illness, and politically to maintain a medical model. There are positive aspects to doing this, such as reducing public anxiety and stigma and providing treatment access through inclusion in medical insurance coverage. However, by avoiding the complexity of the diverse society the potential for misunderstanding is enormous.

The *DSM* conception of mental illness as a number of discrete disorders implies etiologies and possible interventions, although as Mechanic (1997) notes, the disease theories have limited confirmation. The ensuing difficulties are well illustrated by the diagnosis of schizophrenia. The assessment criteria have been narrowed to reflect a group of severely disturbed people, which tends to increase the probability that if diagnosed mentally ill, minorities, based on stereotypes, are more likely to end up in this category. In addition, there is a strong current belief that the genetic basis of schizophrenia has indeed been demonstrated, which meets the social-scientific goal of having a cause for what has for so long been unknown, as well as the social-political goal of families of schizophrenics who are more comfortable with genetics than the probability of a schizophrenogenic mother. Furthermore, the disorder is frequently considered a biological disease, which is congruent with political needs to have schizophrenia as a physically based illness treatable by medication, which in turn meets the needs of psychiatrists, drug manufacturers, and an industrial complex that wants to restrict its spending on health care. Of course it is also true that prior classifications of schizophrenia as well as etiologies that relied primarily on psychodynamics or social learning lacked sufficient validation. However, in an apparent rush to objectify and develop a more scientific model, the flaws in studies supporting the model have been overlooked. The genetic hypothesis is indeed an example of selectively interpreting the evidence to support a classification of schizophrenia as primarily, if not exclusively, a genetic-biological disease. Intriguingly, this has taken place even though, in reviewing the data used to support such a view, Karon and Teixeira (1995) conclude that a genetic model is not actually warranted.

"There is no single way into schizophrenia. All of us are capable of schizophrenic symptoms. . . . Anything that makes life tougher increases the rate of schizophrenia" (pp. 93–94).

In using schizophrenia as an example we have mixed the implied (etiology, preferred treatment) with the stated (diagnostic criteria). We did that to show some of the social and political implications of classification. Furthermore, the broad designation of psychosis is moving in the direction of being equivalent to stating that a person in this category has a biological disorder, although etiologies remain unknown and probably multiple. However, it has become socially and politically expedient to view more and more types of mental illness as having biological and neurological underpinnings that, along with symptoms, can be altered by chemical means. However, this is just as unsubstantiated a view as are other views that would take a more environmental stance. We are not then arguing for a particular view of schizophrenia, or of psychosis, but we are making a point that mental illness can be conceptually structured to meet social and political needs that may not be in the best interests of those who are designated as mentally ill or of the larger society. The current classification of mental illness, as well as the direction taken by previous classifications in many of their revisions, reflects a startling lack of complexity in the face of an increasingly diverse population. At the same time, ongoing attempts to redefine the construct of mental illness often do show an awareness of social and political influences (Widiger 1997). Unfortunately, when it comes to the predominant and official designation of mental illness, it is hardly government by true representation of cultural diversity.

ASSISTANCE

Prevention

The reduction of mental illness in the society depends on prevention or intervention if the illness is already present. Prevention has always been a confusing process because of the disagreement about the causes of mental illness. Although there is at present an increased interest in the possibility of physical causes that could be remedied by medication, we have pointed out that such an interest has not validated a genetic-biological etiology. As a result, prevention has to be broad based and to emphasize what has been validated, namely, the high incidence of emotional distress in segments of the population that are disadvantaged. It is not known if mental illness is causing the disadvantage, as for example a high level of unemployment or a poor educational record, or if the disadvantage causes the mental illness. However, it is safe to assume that reducing the possibility of social discrimination in regard to basic issues such as employment, housing, and education provides a greater possibility of improving mental health.

Furthermore, it is known that the family environment has an impact on its members, even though it is not clear as to the degree the family environment is shaped by the existing pathology of its members as compared with the creation of pathology in some members by other members. Thus, if a child is diagnosed as autistic and subsequently schizophrenic, and the family appears to be dysfunctional, it is impossible to know if the dysfunction in the family is a result of the one disturbed child or if the child became disturbed as a result of already existing pathology in the family members. The limits on understanding etiologies in turn restrict prevention, but these limits do not rule out possibilities for prevention. In particular, it is clear that parent–child interactions can have an effect on the pathology of the child. For example, studies of parent–child interactions indicate that distant, harsh, or overprotective parenting increases the child's risk for psychopathology (Bornstein 1993), although the specific form of pathology remains difficult to predict from dysfunctional parenting. The prevention of family violence is likely to be most effective when there is consideration of the interaction of structural violence and the personality features of all the family members (Herron et al. 1996).

Parker (1995) notes the confusion found in advice regarding contemporary parenting designed to prevent mental illness in children. Normative prescriptions are given but accompanied by caution as to rigid interpretation of these rules as universals versus the need for individuality in parenting. The confusion, although certainly not the complexity, can be taken out of prescriptive prevention by having general guidelines that do require customized application, case by case, instance by instance. Parental ambivalence and the ambivalence of children are examples of normal phenomena that complicate child rearing and always require consideration. At the same time, the view that excesses—the extent and type of gratification and frustration—are likely to cause some type of problem for parents and children remains applicable as a preventative guideline for emotional health. Thus types of mothering such as "the Regulator," "the Facilitator," and "the Reciprocator" (Raphael-Leff 1991) are useful ways of viewing the potential impact of mother–child interaction. Such an approach is a place to start in learning about prevention. At the same time, these possible parenting styles need to be considered within a broader context of personal, social, and political issues. For example, a woman's response to the developmental task of mothering can be affected by physical health; unconscious processes; support availability; personal, economic, social, and family situations; and the responses of her children (Parker 1995). What is currently being emphasized as an additive to personal ambivalence is that the diversity of the population threatens the entrenched models of child rearing. Prevention then is hampered by tendencies to stereotype minorities in regard to pathological propensities such as domestic violence.

Diversity undoubtedly makes prevention more complicated, and from a social and political perspective raises the temptation to simplify using evidence that supports such a direction. Thus a genetic etiology of mental illness supports genetic engineering as a solution, and a social-structure causal chain supports social and political manipulations. However, the reality is more complex, with interactive etiologies being the most probable for mental illness. In that vein then the possibilities and opportunities for prevention will need to be expanded; such an idea does seem counter to the current political emphasis on the decrease of social support in favor of immediate cost savings and expediency. The danger in such an expedient approach is its potential shortsightedness because minority groups are likely to be left out of prevention programs in two significant ways. The first is that they will be shoehorned into an existing view of child rearing or various other tasks that are not appropriate to their cultural values. The result will be a bad fit that continues to pathologize minorities. In addition, these people are likely to resist the social pressure and avoid information about prevention that if they had and could use in their own fashion would be more likely to result in prevention. Mainstream prevention programs are just as unlikely to provide the breadth to accommodate diversity, and as a result will not succeed for marginalized people.

The second way that prevention may bypass a significant number of people who could use it is that prevailing cultural values may embody an impression that certain groups are sufficiently pathologized by virtue of ethnic or socioeconomic identities that they are not worth targeting for the purpose of prevention. A variation on this negative attitude is the offering of prevention programs aimed at a social ill that is linked to a high incidence of mental illness, such as poverty, but that in one or more ways are demeaning to the people who make use of them. The reduction in self-esteem can affect the potential advantages of the prevention programs and people will stop using them and discourage others from attempting these programs.

Although it remains a fact of daily life for many minorities, discrimination is not the intent of most prevention efforts. Instead, lack of knowledge and misapplication are more likely difficulties that require remedies. For example, Forehand and Kotchick (1996) stress the value of being sensitive to the context of parenting. Two parenting components, monitoring and communication, are considered significant influences in affecting deviant behavior of children and adolescents. However, most studies on these factors have used samples of white males, raising the question of the universal effectiveness of these variables. Smith and Krohn (1995) found ethnic differences in the effects of monitoring and communication. Monitoring was effective with African-American and Caucasian adolescents, whereas communication was effective for Hispanic adolescents. The possibility was raised that Hispanic cultural values place more importance on positive familial relationships. However, Forehand and associates (1997) subsequently found that parental monitoring predicted levels of adolescent deviance in both African-American and Hispanic adolescents, but communication was not a significant predictor for either ethnic group. Thus the role of diversity is difficult to discern—sometimes appearing, sometimes not. However, the most prudent course is to consider the possibility that culture can influence prevention rather than operate as though prevention methods have universal applicability.

A significant component of prevention is the prevailing attitude of the culture in regard to mental illness. Thus the continued presence of negative community views regarding mental illness and continued ethnic and racial discrimination limit prevention efforts. In particular, low socioeconomic status appears as a major factor in the formation of mental illness. For example, the significant relationship between mental illness and poverty that appeared in nineteenth-century epidemiological studies continues to appear in the most recent of such studies. The groups with the lowest socioeconomic status, defined in terms of education, income, and occupation, have the highest rates of mental illness (Basic Behavioral Science Task Force of the National Advisory Mental Health Council 1996). The BBSTF also notes that poverty cannot be demonstrated to cause schizophrenia, but is clearly related to it, and that socioeconomic and other psychosocial deficits do seem to have a causal role in depressive, substance abuse, and antisocial forms of mental illness. Because psychosocial risk factors for mental illness have a higher incidence in lower social classes, the need for lessening socioeconomic distress is very apparent. Furthermore, the negative side effects of socioeconomic disadvantages occur throughout the life span and are apparent in both financial strain and in the emotional stress that occurs in the type of jobs and work environments that are related to socioeconomic status.

Given the economic wealth of this country, it at first seems startling that more has not been accomplished in regard to the prevention of mental illness. However, the wealth has been generated on the basis of competitive enterprise in which there are always some groups that are less well off than others. The desire to make the society a level one is quite limited, and there is only a selective appeal to having the government take care of people. Thus some programs that affect vast numbers of people who represent a strong political force, such as Social Security, have a strong appeal, whereas others, such as welfare, are continually being criticized and revised with a threat toward potential elimination. It is interesting to note that the poor are nowhere near as powerful politically as are senior citizens. Thus a tendency can be detected to devote resources to the more powerful political groups.

However, along with the spirit of free enterprise and individualism that is common in this nation is a definite social concern. The increasing diversity of the country increases the need to make better use of that concern. Such use does not automatically translate into more social engineering, or into a different, more socialized form of government, because there is no substantial evidence that any form of government, democratic or socialistic or autocratic, translates well into the prevention of mental illness. The issue at the moment is to make suggestions regarding prevention that can be implemented within the existing social and political structure.

1. Although information about prevention can be confusing, general guidelines emphasize the importance of good parenting, good socioeconomic conditions, and good community support systems. The meaning of "good" is open to interpretation, particularly in the case of parenting, but helpful information has been and continues to be generated. For example, the concept of excess, whether it concerns gratification or deprivation, appears to cause problems. Again, we recognize that what is meant by "excess" is open to interpretation, but a frame of reference is available for comparison so that relative norms can be established with an awareness that such norms need periodic scrutiny and revision.

2. Conventional wisdom in particular requires continual evaluation for it indeed to be "wisdom." Cultural sensitivity is necessary in developing preventative approaches to mental illness, but that includes finding both what is subculture-bound as well as what can approach cultural universality. The test for any minority group within a given broader society is its adaptability, which can mean causing alterations in the larger society as well as in the minority group. This fit is best accomplished when there is a minimum of stress that could eventuate in mental disorders. The BBSTF (1997) has described strategies by which minority groups can avoid being marginalized to the point of significant emotional and behavioral conflict. These include being assimilated into the dominant cultural group, becoming acculturated by acquiring significant aspects of the dominant culture, developing a

biculturalism that involves sufficient proficiency in two cultures to alternate them depending on situational factors, and multiculturalism where individuals retain separate cultural identities but collaborate with various groups to bring about goals that are mutually desired. We suggested earlier in this chapter that the spirit of the country, as reflected in social and political styles, is moving in the direction of multiculturalism, which for us includes what is depicted above as both bicultural and multicultural. In regard to diversity, mental illness is more likely to be prevented if individuals can maintain the personal cultural connections that they value and acquire the skills that are basic to the dominant culture.

3. The sources of preventative support are many and vary in response to the adaptive mix of diversity with unity. The key point is that *support* is needed, and that key elements of support, such as educational and employment opportunities, mandate social attitudes of encouragement and acceptability. These attitudes generally require social programs to ensure their presence. The fact that these programs may encounter obstacles, which is at the moment happening to Affirmative Action, does not alter the basic need to increase educational and employment possibilities. Thus it is vital for the prevention of mental illness that ways to do this more effectively remain—and increase—as prominent parts of the nation's social and political agenda.

Treatment

Although the sophistication and the extent of treatment for mental illness have increased over time, the ability to alleviate serious mental illness to a significant degree is not encouraging. At the same time, a social and political sentiment has developed that discourages the widespread use of therapeutic services such as psychotherapy (Mechanic 1997). Along with this is a growing awareness of therapists' difficulties in responding effectively to culturally diverse patient populations. The last issue is probably the one most easily corrected, and the mental health disciplines appear most interested in considering ways to handle that problem. However, the response to diversity is actually connected to the other two issues—treatment of severe mental illness and the extent of treatment—in such significant ways that it will not be possible to alter it unless the other two issues are addressed. In fact, the entire question of treatment has become primarily a political-economic issue: the severely ill are treated most often by medication in line with a biological emphasis on the possible nature of their disorders and with a strong aware-ness of the suggested cost-effectiveness of such an approach. The economic push is increased by shortened inpatient stays and forced reductions in the populations of mental hospitals. The latter is supposed to be in the service of community support for patients, but frequently either the community or the patients are unwilling or unable to operate effectively. The result is that patients become problems for society by their being unable to cope effectively in whatever support system they now have or by creating an increase in the ranks of the homeless.

A great deal of money has been spent on institutional treatment of the mentally ill without dramatic improvement in their mental health. The social frustration is understandable. The appeal of community mental health services is also understandable, but this approach has not produced a marked increase in effectiveness either. That does not mean that it is an invalid theoretical conception, but certainly its implementation needs revision. Instead of effec-tiveness being demonstrated to the point where the idea of community sup-port was a reality, the action of putting the mentally ill into the community has been and continues to be implemented essentially regardless of outcome. This policy has the greatest impact on minority groups because they are the largest group of seriously mentally ill people. Furthermore, there is an under-lying, unstated philosophy to all this that represents a misplaced emphasis on individualism that is, the mentally ill are not that ill and do not need that much support. It is a "less will do more" approach that is thought to be appro-priate because more has not done enough. The latter can be granted without validating the former. In fact, less is not doing more, or even the same, for the mentally ill. Different approaches rather than more of the same may well be called for, but the need for change cannot be equated with restriction of ser-vice. The accompanying restriction of who needs service for mental illness will increase. In New York City in 1997, for example, approximately 7,100 people slept in homeless shelters each night, a 15 percent increase over a three-year period; about half of them were mentally ill (Jacobs 1997). Also, a significant amount of care is being provided by nonprofit agencies, which have a limited and variable source of funds so that if the trend continues such agencies will be insufficient supports for even a restricted political-social approach to treat-ing the severely mentally ill.

The treatment of mental illness is conceptualized as three levels: necessity, improvement, and potentiality (Herron and Adlerstein 1994, Herron, Eisenstadt et al. 1994, Herron, Javier et al. 1994). The level of necessity is basic and involves the alleviation of symptoms to the point that an individual can carry out the tasks needed to maintain his or her life, such as being able to work or care for children. This is a narrow conception of mental health in which a person may continue to experience subjective distress and to lead a relatively restricted life, but is functional. At this level there is little concern with improvement, prevention, or potential. The amount and type of care needed to accomplish the level of necessity is variable because it is related to the severity of the illness and the individual's adaptive capacities.

The level of improvement is an intermediate approach that builds on the level of necessity. Thus, once basic adaptation has been established, an attempt is made to take the next step and improve both the quality and quantity of functioning. The positive change in both emotional and behavioral aspects of life also provides support for prevention of subsequent episodes of mental illness. The level of improvement is the foundation for the extended approach in the level of potentiality that strives to help each individual achieve his or her ideal level of functioning which in turn would be helpful in maximizing the potentials of any society.

Unfortunately, social and political goals appear restricted to the level of necessity at the moment, and even at that level tend to be limited. The emphasis is on cost containment rather than mental health, which means brief treatment for most people as a favored policy. Such an approach often shortchanges the severely ill, and has a similar depriving effect on all others who have an interest in attaining levels of improvement or potentiality. In regard to the seriously ill where minority groups are overrepresented, the treatments of choice have been supportive therapies and antipsychotic medications (Garb 1997). Brevity of treatment is stressed regardless of severity, with the rationale being that other, less costly services, such as skills training or focused interest groups, will make up the difference. The accessibility of psychotherapy as a preventive or emotionally educative form of health improvement is neglected. Thus Mechanic (1997) points to the inadvisability of formulating a mental health policy based on the idea that most people have psychic pain and areas of dysfunction and therefore could benefit from psychotherapy. There is no question, of course, that when payers other than the patient are involved there will be a concern with profit so that if the funding issue is primary then the range of treatment services will be limited, just as when the patient is paying, the patient will impose a limit based on his or her use of economic resources relative to what the patient feels is being gained. The negotiation of what treatment costs has a long tradition, and the existing emphasis on managed care is another phase in the history of negotiations. Many mental health providers are not happy with the style of these current negotiations, but that is not our issue here. Instead, our concern is with the rather exclusive nature of treatment policy: brief focused strategies that are considered universally applicable. We understand that advocates of such an approach will point out that their view is not so exclusive, but there are a significant number of practitioners and consumers who see current policy as restrictive to the point of failing to adequately treat mental illness (Sank 1997). In this context consider the goals set by Shueman (1997) for service delivery modes. These include helping diverse and underserved groups, but with problem-oriented, goal-focused treatments (which we translate as brief therapies of a behavioral nature), empirically supported protocols of treatment (which are derived from research settings rather than clinical settings), and community-based resources (which are not always available and as treatment strategies are not empirically supported). Thus what sounds politically correct in its breadth is actually limited in reality.

The actuality of mental health policy is that access is being restricted in terms of treatment choices, treatment duration, and treatment providers. In a review of time-limited therapy, Miller (1996a) has illustrated a number of misconceptions; for example, there is no benefit to long-term treatment; consumers desire brief treatment; time-limited therapy must be efficient. Instead he asserts that brief therapy often compromises treatment, and because consumers are not made aware of its limitations, it has become a form of invisible rationing. This conclusion does not rule out the idea that rationing may be necessary, but it is obscured by a policy that insists on the value of brief treatment and the lack of value of lengthy or open-ended techniques. It is difficult to see how a relatively universal treatment approach is going to be effective in helping an increasingly diverse patient population. Miller concludes that "therapeutic change takes both time and effort on the part of clients, and time and skill on the part of the therapist" (1996b, p. 581). It is clear that in the current social climate the business of psychotherapy is not going to be funded extensively by parties other than patients. This is a social-political-economic decision that reflects a pragmatic value system that is at the same time cloaked in an apparent logic that says that what is being provided is of as good quality as any other approach, if not better. That logic has not been empirically demonstrated, and the complexity of mental illness coupled with the diversity of the society offers an alternative logic that what is needed is greater diversity of treatment possibilities that offer better fits to the problems of a growing multicultural society. What follows are some suggestions in that vein that also recognize that funding is an issue that certainly requires consideration. However, our belief is that mental health policy should be derived from the health needs of the population rather than from economic motives. We understand that both sets of needs are related, and because of that it may not be possible to implement aspects of an ideal policy, but that should not rule out the presence of such a policy or attempts to fund it.

1. Treatment needs to be contextual, recognizing and responding to the multicultural concerns of patients. Given that providers do not represent the same degree of diversity as clients, there is a particular need for training that emphasizes the recognition of cultural differences in the ways in which people access and can make use of therapeutic interventions. In addition, it is essential that in recognizing the subjectivity of psychotherapy, therapists are aware of possible personal biases, and that they actively work on decreasing potential negative effects of bias. For example, an apparent lack of client cooperation with the therapeutic structure needs to be considered in a cultural context rather than routinely categorized as a lack of patient motivation. Also, many people who are underserved by the mental health profession are in that position because of social barriers, such as limited funds, lack of knowledge regarding treatment, and stereotypes by therapists who have generally considered middle-class patients to be their appropriate target group. The applicability of psychotherapy to all socioeconomic groups has been demonstrated (Altman 1995, Javier and Herron 1992). Now the focus needs to be on turning that possibility into a widespread actuality.

2. The social-political concerns of treatment policies for the mentally ill need to be reformulated in such a way that the cultural diversity of patients is effectively recognized. At present a restrictive social policy of limited access and few choices of providers and treatment modalities is gaining power as the dominant approach to providing assistance for the mentally ill. Under the rubric of "medical necessity" the number and type of people who qualify for treatment reimbursement are being systematically reduced. The nation's mental health policy had been expansive, but as overall health costs have risen, outpatient mental health services in particular have fallen victim to the concept of unnecessary service. Many people who would have qualified for therapeutic assistance have now been considered not sick enough, or as overtreated based on their degree of illness. Providing treatment for anything beyond the level of necessity is being viewed as a costly and defective approach to mental health. In contrast, the value of helping people toward self-improvement and their greatest degree of self-actualization ought to be basic ingredients of mental health policy, particularly given the social and political complexity that is found in

the increasing diversity of our society. The first step then is to get beyond quick and cheap and into the unknowns of complexity, including duration, effort, and cost. The next step is to find ways to have services that are as heterogeneous as those who need them. As far as funding goes, that may well mean that providers will be paid less than in the past, and patients will pay more, and for those who cannot pay, providers will bear more of the burden unless private and public sources begin to endorse a broader policy of assistance. The central task is to develop as mentally healthy a society as is possible given the relative adequacy of the tools available to do it. Whatever the cost, it ought to be socially and politically worth it.

REFERENCES

Altman, N. (1995). *The Analyst in the Inner City*. Hillsdale, NJ: Analytic Press.

Arvuch, K., and Black, P. W. (1991). The cultural question and conflict resolution. *Peace and Change* 16:22–45.

Basic Behavioral Science Task Force of the National Advisory Mental Health Council (BBSTF) (1996). Basic behavioral science research for mental health: sociocultural and environmental processes. *American Psychologist* 51:722–731.

Bergner, R. M. (1997). What is psychopathology? And so what? *Clinical Psychology: Science and Practice* 4:235–248.

Bornstein, R. F. (1993). Parental representations and psychopathology: a critical review of the empirical literature. In *Psychoanalytic Perspectives on Psychopathology*, ed. J. M. Masling and R. F. Bornstein, pp. 1–41. Washington, DC: American Psychological Association.

Diagnostic and Statistical Manual of Mental Disorders (1994). 4th ed. Washington, DC: American Psychiatric Association.

Forehand, R., and Kotchick, B. A. (1996). Cultural diversity: a wake-up call for parental training. *Behavior Therapy* 27:187–206.

Forehand, R., Miller, K. S., Dutra, R., and Chance, M. W. (1997). Role of parenting in adolescent deviant behavior: replication across and within two ethnic groups. *Journal of Consulting and Clinical Psychology* 65:1036–1041.

Garb, H. N. (1997). Race bias, social class bias, and gender bias in clinical judgment. *Clinical Psychology: Science and Practice* 4:99–120.

Herron, W. G., and Adlerstein, L. K. (1994). The dynamics of managed mental health care. *Psychological Reports* 75:723–741.

Herron, W. G., Eisenstadt, E. N., Javier, R. A., et al. (1994). Session efforts, compatibility, and managed care in the psychotherapies. *Psychotherapy* 31:279–285.

Herron, W. G., and Javier, R. A. (1996). The psychogenesis of poverty: some psychoanalytic conceptions. *Psychoanalytic Review* 83:611–620.

Herron, W. G., Javier, R. A., McDonald-Gomez, M., and Adlerstein, L. K. (1996). Sources of family violence. In *Domestic Violence: Assessment and Treatment*, ed. R. A. Javier, W. G. Herron, and A. J. Bergman, pp. 19–34. Northvale, NJ: Jason Aronson.

Herron, W. G., Javier, R. A., Primavera, L. H., and Schultz, C. L. (1994). The cost of psychotherapy. *Professional Psychology: Research and Practice* 25:106–110.

Herron, W. G., Ramirez, S. M., Javier, R. A., and Warner, L. K. (1997). Cultural attunement and personality assessment. *Journal of Social Distress and the Homeless* 6:175–193.

Jacobs, A. (1997). Blurry world of mental illness gives way to the "incredibly normal." *The New York Times*, December 7, p. 53.

Javier, R. A., and Herron, W. G. (1992). Psychoanalysis, the Hispanic poor, and the disadvantaged: application and conceptualization. *Journal of the American Academy of Psychoanalysis* 20:455–476.

Karon, B. P., and Teixeira, M. A. (1995). Psychoanalytic therapy of schizophrenia. In *Dynamic Therapies for Psychiatric Disorders*, ed. J. P. Barber and P. Crits-Cristoph, pp. 84–130. New York: Basic Books.

Kaslow, F. (1997). Is unanimity desirable, achievable? *Clinical Psychology: Science and Practice* 4:285–287.

LeVine, R. A. (1973). *Culture, Behavior, and Personality*. Chicago: Aldine.

Mechanic, D. (1997). Psychopathology and public policy. *Clinical Psychology: Science and Practice* 4:272–275.

Miller, I. J. (1996a). Some "short-term therapy values" are a formula for invisible rationing. *Professional Psychology: Research and Practice* 27:577–582.

——— (1996b). Time-limited brief therapy has gone too far: the result is invisible rationing. *Professional Psychology: Research and Practice* 27:567–576.

Morrison, J. (1995). *DSM-IV Made Easy: The Clinician's Guide to Diagnosis*. New York: Guilford.

Nathan, P. E. (1997). In the final analysis, it's the data that count. *Clinical Psychology: Science and Practice* 4:281–288.

Ossario, P. (1985). Pathology. In *Advances in Descriptive Psychology*, vol. 4, ed. K. Davis and T. Mitchell, pp. 151–202. Greenwich, CT: JAI.

Parker, R. (1995). *Mother Love/Mother Hate: The Power of Maternal Ambivalence*. New York: Basic Books.

Raphael-Leff, J. (1991). *Psychological Processes of Childbearing*. London: Chapman and Hall.

Ross, M. H. (1993). *The Culture of Conflict*. New Haven, CT: Yale University Press.

Sank, L. I. (1997). Taking on managed care: one reviewer at a time. *Professional Psychology: Research and Practice* 28:548–554.

Shueman, S. A. (1997). Confronting health care realities: a reply to Sank (1997). *Professional Psychology: Research and Practice* 28:555–558.

Smith, C., and Krohn, M. D. (1995). Delinquency and family life among male adolescents: the role of ethnicity. *Journal of Youth and Adolescence* 24:69–93.

Sullivan, H. S. (1964). *The Fusion of Psychiatry and Social Science*. New York: Norton.

Wakefield, J. C. (1992). The concept of mental disorder: on the boundary between biological facts and social values. *American Psychologist* 47:343–388.

Wells, K. B., Sturm, R., Sherbourne, C. D., and Meredith, L. S. (1996). *Caring for Depression*. Cambridge, MA: Harvard University Press.

Whiting, B. B., and Whiting, J. W. (1975). *Children of Six Cultures: A Psycho-Cultural Analysis*. Cambridge, MA: Harvard University Press.

Widiger, T. A. (1997). The construct of mental disorder. *Clinical Psychology: Science and Practice* 4:262–266.

Winnicott, D. W. (1965). *The Maturational Processes and the Facilitating Environment*. New York: International Universities Press.

Credits

The editors gratefully acknowledge permission to reprint material from the following sources:

Chapter 2, originally titled "Cultural Influences upon Psychopathology: Clinical and Practical Implications," by Juris G. Draguns, in *Journal of Social Distress and the Homeless* 4(2). Copyright © 1995 by Human Sciences Press and used by permission.

Chapter 3, "Race, Ethnicity, and Mental Illness, " by Jeffrey S. Nevid and Rachel Goodman, in *Abnormal Psychology in a Changing World,* by J. S. Nevid, S. A. Rathus, and B. Greene. Copyright © 1997 by Prentice-Hall and used by permission.

Chapter 4, "The Feeling Edge of Culture in the American Sensitivity Shift," by Edward C. Stewart, in *Journal of Social Distress and the Homeless* 4(2). Copyright © 1995 by Human Sciences Press and used by permission.

Chapter 5, "Urban Poverty, Ethnicity, and Personality Development," by Rafael Art. Javier, William G. Herron, and Philip T. Yanos, in *Journal of Social Distress and the Homeless* 4(2). Copyright © 1995 by Human Sciences Press and used by permission.

Index